New for this Edition

Mastering Exchange Server 2003 contains three brand-new chapters:

The first, Chapter 17, "Exchange Server Reliability and Availability," is about one of the most vexing and important aspects of Exchange Server management. This chapter describes ways to make Exchange Server systems less vulnerable to hardware, software, and networking failures, covering everything from redundant hardware to disaster recovery.

Also new to this edition is Chapter 18, "Exchange Server System Security." This chapter focuses on a range of security measures, including placing Exchange servers behind firewalls so that all Exchange clients can access them; using secure networking options; controlling access to Windows and Exchange through tight, but reasonable, Windows/Exchange security options; controlling viruses and spam; and securing Exchange messages.

The last new chapter is on a hot topic: Chapter 19, "Wireless Access to Exchange Server 2003." Here you'll learn how to implement wireless access to Exchange mailboxes with options for laptops, PDAs, and smart phones, and wireless client and server software options. Special attention is directed toward Exchange Server 2003's Outlook Mobile Access for wireless clients with small screens and Exchange 2003's native support for wireless synchronization of Windows-based PDAs and phones. Together, these significantly enhance the Exchange wireless access experience.

Mastering
Microsoft Exchange Server 2003

Mastering™
Microsoft® Exchange Server 2003

Barry Gerber

SYBEX®

San Francisco   London

Associate Publisher: Joel Fugazzotto
Acquisitions Editor: Ellen Dendy
Developmental Editor: Tom Cirtin
Production Editor: Mae Lum
Technical Editor: J. Kevin Lundy
Copyeditor: Laura Ryan
Compositor: Maureen Forys, Happenstance Type-O-Rama
Graphic Illustrator: Jeff Wilson, Happenstance Type-O-Rama
Proofreaders: Amey Garber, Emily Hsuan, Laurie O'Connell, Nancy Riddiough
Indexer: Ted Laux
Book Designer: Maureen Forys, Happenstance Type-O-Rama
Cover Designer: Design Site
Cover Illustrator: Tania Kac, Design Site

An earlier version of this book was published under the title *Mastering Microsoft Exchange 2000 Server* © 2001 SYBEX Inc.

Library of Congress Card Number: 2003106721

ISBN: 0-7821-4204-4

Manufactured in the United States of America

10 9 8 7 6 5 4 3

To Jane, my wife and best friend, for reminding me in so many ways that technology should serve and not control humanity. To my children, Margot, Karl, and Georg, for showing me both how much and how little we influence others. And to everyone who is trying to make our often harsh and nasty world a better place to live in.

Acknowledgments

MICROSOFT'S EXCHANGE SERVER HAS come a long way since its first release in 1996. Keeping up with all the changes and tracking through all the beta and pre-release versions of Exchange 4.0, 5.0, 5.5, and 2000 was an adventure with all the peaks and dips of a world-class roller-coaster ride. Equally adventuresome was the production of this edition, which not only covers the new features in Exchange Server 2003, but also includes hundreds of updates and fixes to parts of the book dealing with information common to Exchange 2000 and 2003.

Without the help and support of a number of fine people, *Mastering Microsoft Exchange Server 2003* would never have happened. Words really cannot express both my indebtedness to, and respect for, the Exchange Server development teams I've worked with over the past eight years. I'll never forget the patience they showed with my seemingly endless and not always well-articulated questions, especially as product delivery deadlines approached. My Exchange Book e-mail folders for earlier editions overflow with helpful, timely, and just-in-time responses from them all: Behrooz Chitsaz, Ken Ewert, Karim Battish, August Hahn, David Johnson, Bill Kilcullen, Eric Lockard, Mark Ledsome, David Lemson, Steve Masters, Tom McCann, Ramez Naam, Jim Reitz, Todd Roberts, Rob Sanfilippo, Elaine Sharp, Rob Shurtleff, Aaron Snow, Bill Sorinsin, Paul Waszkiewicz, Jeff Wilkes, and Rusty Williams.

For this edition, Microsoft instituted a different kind of beta program: a program to help book authors get faster and more authoritative answers to their questions about Exchange 2003. The Exchange Buddy Team program wasn't a piece of software, but an effort to open continuous communications between authors and technical writers and developers at Microsoft. From my perspective, the beta was a resounding success and you, the reader, will benefit from it the most. I want to thank the members of my Buddy Team: Diane Forsyth (my main and most dedicated contact), Susan Bradley (manager of the Buddy Team program), Teresa Applegate, Christopher Budd (the fastest response gun in the West), Jyoti Kulkarni, Paul Limont, Joey Masterson, Brendan Power, David Reeb (Dell Computer), Neil Shipp, and Ifran Soomro. May the Buddy Program come gracefully out of beta and go on to many, many fruitful releases.

Finally, my heartfelt and everlasting thanks to the team of editors who kept me honest and articulate through all editions of the book. John Read at Sybex listened to my ideas for the first edition and helped shape them into the book *Mastering Microsoft Exchange Server 4*. Peter Kuhns, Neil Edde, Maureen Adams, and Tom Cirtin most ably managed editorial development on the other editions of the book. Ellen Dendy played that role for this edition and played it very well. She was always there to counsel and cajole and to help press Microsoft for both beta product and editorial help. Ellen's job was made easier by Tom Cirtin, who played a role both in editorial development and chapter-by-chapter organizational and content editing for this book. As he did on the last edition, he did these jobs with intelligence and grace under considerable pressure. This time, things were often hectic, and I didn't tell him as many times how much I appreciated his help. So let me express my deepest thanks here.

Maureen Adams, Lorraine Fry, Ben Miller, Chad Mack, Susan Berge, Cecelia Musselman, and Krista Hansing were responsible for editorial production of the Exchange 4, 5, 5.5, and 2000 books. Mae Lum and Laura Ryan took over this task for this book. Like Tom, they have made my job easier and have made me look like a far better writer than I am. I'd also like to thank proofreaders Nancy Riddiough, Laurie O'Connell, Amey Garber, and Emily Hsuan for catching the mistakes all the rest of us missed. For compositing (turning Word files into book pages) and illustrations, thanks to Maureen Forys and Jeff Wilson of Happenstance Type-O-Rama.

And last, but far from least, thanks to the technical editors who have kept me honest and on target: Eric Lockard (Exchange 4), Rob Sanfilippo (Exchange 5 and 5.5, first edition), Don Fuller (Exchange 5.5, second edition), Ed Crowley (Exchange 2000), and Kevin Lundy (this book). I appreciate the help each has given. Kevin's gentle nudges and spot-on criticisms were much appreciated and made reading technical edits a real pleasure.

Thanks to everyone for all your help. Whatever errors of fact or judgment remain are mine and mine alone.

Barry Gerber (`bg@bgerber.com`, `www.bgerber.com`)
Los Angeles, California

Contents at a Glance

Contents

Introduction

WRITING *MASTERING MICROSOFT EXCHANGE SERVER 2003* was an interesting and unique experience. After eight years with Exchange Server and four previous editions of this book, I was able to find the time to step back and assess both the organization and content of the last edition, *Mastering Microsoft Exchange 2000 Server*. Microsoft's Exchange Server 2003 is an evolutionary product. A good deal has changed, but much has stayed the same as in Exchange 2000. Rather than having to spend almost all of my time looking for and mastering the new in Exchange 2003, I was able to devote more time to reorganizing the book, fixing up what I thought were weak sections, and adding exciting new content everywhere. What you have in your hands is the best edition of *Mastering Exchange Server* that I've ever written. And, the really good news is that a great deal of the revised and new content can be applied to both Exchange 2000 and 2003.

In writing this book, I was guided by three goals:

◆ To share the excitement that I feel about both the reality and promise of electronic messaging and the Exchange 2003 client/server system

◆ To help you decide if there's a place for Exchange Server 2003 in your organization

◆ To provide information and teach you skills that you'll need to plan for and implement Exchange Server 2003 systems of any size and shape

Exchange Server 5.5 was one of the most powerful, extensible, scalable, easy-to-use, and manageable electronic-messaging backends on the market. Exchange 2000 Server retained all of 5.5's best features and added new ones. Exchange Server 2003 goes a step further, altering interfaces that didn't quite work in the 2000 flavor and adding some great new features.

Much of the change in Exchange 2000 Server related to its very tight integration with Windows 2000 Server. Exchange 5.5's directory service was the model for Windows 2000 Server's Active Directory. Active Directory is an industrial-strength directory service providing users and computers with information about and access to server and network services and resources. Information about Exchange 2000 Server recipients and services was integrated into Active Directory. All of these changes have been carried forward with well-thought-out modifications to Exchange 2003 and Windows 2003.

Additionally, unlike with Exchange 5.*x*, Exchange 2000 depended on Windows 2000's Internet Information Server for its base Simple Mail Transfer Protocol (SMTP) mail transmission services and Network News Transfer Protocol (NNTP) newsgroup services. Underlying both SMTP and NNTP was Microsoft's new virtual server technology, which supports multiple SMTP or NNTP services on a single server. Again, all of this technology was improved and carried forward to Windows 2003 and Exchange 2003.

As with Exchange 2000 Server, Exchange Server 2003 virtual servers support version 3 of the Post Office Protocol (POP3) and version 4 of the Internet Message Access Protocol (IMAP4), both available since Exchange Server 5.5. Unlike SMTP and NNTP, however, POP3 and IMAP4 are native Exchange Server services. POP3 enables nonproprietary, lightweight client access to Exchange Server messages. IMAP4 adds key features missing in the POP3 protocol, such as access to folders other than the Inbox. Any POP3 or IMAP4 client, whether running in Windows, Macintosh, any flavor of Unix, or another operating system, can access Exchange Server to send and receive messages. Furthermore, POP3 and IMAP4 clients, such as Qualcomm's Eudora, Netscape's mail client, the University of Washington's Pine, or Microsoft's Outlook Express, are easier to manage and demand fewer workstation resources than the standard Microsoft Outlook client. As a result, they can be run with less intervention by information technology staff and on lower-end workstations.

The Hypertext Transfer Protocol (HTTP), another Exchange 5.5 veteran carried over to Exchange 2000 and now to Exchange 2003, makes possible web-browser access to Exchange Server–based mailboxes, public folders, and calendars. HTTP is built on Microsoft's Internet Information Server and virtual server technology. Microsoft uses the term *Outlook Web Access* (OWA) to refer to its support for HTTP in Exchange. Like POP3 and IMAP4 clients, web browsers are both nonproprietary and lighter weight than standard Outlook clients. As a result, users and their organizations realize the same benefits that they get with POP3 or IMAP4 clients while using a client that is on virtually every desktop. HTTP support also enables controlled and selective access to Exchange Server environments by anonymous users. Finally, the Exchange Server 2003 implementation of HTTP makes it easier than it ever has been for users and developers to access messages and other items in Exchange mailboxes and public folders.

In Exchange Server 2003, HTTP plays a new role. It serves as the basis for connecting standard Outlook MAPI clients to Exchange servers over the Internet using the same Remote Procedure Call (RPC) technology that is used to connect Outlook clients to Exchange servers in LAN environments. RPC over HTTP makes WAN client/server connectivity easy and it simplifies the task of placing Exchange servers behind firewalls.

Like SMTP and NNTP, Lightweight Directory Access Protocol (LDAP) services moved from Exchange to Windows 2000/2003, with LDAP becoming a key protocol for users and managers of Active Directory. On the messaging side, LDAP supports user access to e-mail address and other information stored in Active Directory. Exchange Server users with LDAP-enabled POP3 and IMAP4 clients can find e-mail addresses in the Exchange directory from anywhere in the world. This adds an unprecedented and most welcome level of user friendliness to the POP3 and IMAP4 world.

Exchange 2000 Server's information storage technology changed drastically from Exchange 5.5, and this change was carried forward to Exchange 2003 and then significantly enhanced. Multiple mailbox and public folder store databases can be created. Databases can be larger and each database can be managed separately. Any information store database can be taken offline for cleanup, backup, and restore operations without affecting users' capability to access remaining online databases. Exchange 2003 adds recovery storage groups, which make it easier to recover an Exchange mailbox or items in an Exchange mailbox.

Exchange 2000/2003 split Exchange 5.5 and earlier sites into administrative groups and routing groups. Exchange administrators can distribute management responsibilities by delegating control over specific administrative groups to different Windows 2000/2003 security groups. Administrative groups hold servers, system policies, public folders, routing groups, and other objects. However, routing groups, which contain servers linked by high-bandwidth networks, do not have to exist in the same administrative group as the servers that they contain. In addition, servers can be moved between administrative groups and system policies, and public folders can exist in any administrative group, further extending the Exchange administrator's ability to distribute responsibility for managing specific components of Exchange 2000/2003.

Speaking of management, Windows 2000's Microsoft Management Console (MMC) technology made Windows 2000/Exchange 2000 administration easier and more intuitive. That same technology is available in Windows/Exchange 2003. Based on the familiar object-oriented tree technology of Microsoft's Windows file and directory browsers, MMC snap-ins enable focused, efficient management of everything from users and computers to Windows, Internet domains, and Exchange server and the wide array of services that it supports.

With these and an impressive array of other features, Exchange Server 2003 can help your organization move smoothly and productively into the world of advanced, enhanced electronic messaging.

What You Need to Run Exchange Server

Exchange Server 2003 is a complex product with a remarkably easy-to-use interface for administration and management. All of this complexity and parallel ease of use requires an industrial-strength computer. The minimum server computer suggested here is for testing, learning about, and evaluating the product. It's also enough for a small, noncritical installation. However, as I discuss in the book, when the server moves into critical production environments, where it will be accessed by large numbers of users, you'll need to beef up its hardware and add a number of fault-tolerant capabilities. On the client side, with the broad range of clients available for Exchange, the machines now on desktops in most organizations should be more than adequate.

At a minimum, to test, learn about, and evaluate Exchange Server, you need the following:

◆ Either Microsoft Exchange Server 2003 and any version of Windows Server 2003 or Microsoft Exchange Server 2003 Enterprise Edition and Windows Server 2003 Enterprise or Datacenter Edition.

◆ A 1GHz Pentium III- or 4-based PC with 512MB of RAM and two 9GB disk drives. This allows you to complete exercises involving a single Exchange server.

◆ A minimum of three additional computers in the class just described. This allows you to complete exercises involving multiple computers in multiple administrative groups and Windows Server 2003 domains.

◆ Tape backup hardware or at least one independent disk drive for backup.

◆ A local area network (preferably connected to the Internet).

◆ At least one 800MHz Pentium III or 4 or equivalent computer with 128MB of memory running Windows XP Professional.

How This Book Is Organized

This book comprises 20 chapters and an appendix, divided into six broad topic areas. As you proceed through the book, you'll move from basic concepts to several increasingly complex levels of hands-on implementation.

This book won't work well for practitioners of the timeworn ritual of chapter hopping. I've taken great pains to write an integrated book on Windows Server 2003 and Exchange Server 2003. Unless you already have considerable experience with these products, to get the maximum value out of this book, you need to track through the chapters in order. Readers like to send me questions by e-mail. About 25 percent of the "Why doesn't it work?" questions that I receive can be answered by "Because you didn't do what I suggested in Chapter so-and-so."

However, if you're in a hurry to get your hands dirty, start with Part II, "Installation" (Chapters 7 and 8); Part III, "The Outlook Client" (Chapters 9 and 10), and Part IV, "Basic Exchange Server 2003 Management" (Chapters 11 and 12). These chapters will help you get a Windows 2003 server, an Exchange 2003 server, and an Outlook client up and running. As long as you're not planning to put your quickie server into production immediately, there should be no harm done. Before going into production, though, I strongly suggest that you explore other parts of this book. Here's a guide to what's in each chapter.

Part I: Understanding and Planning

This part of the book focuses on concepts and features of Microsoft's Windows Server 2003 and Exchange Server 2003 client/server electronic messaging system. It is designed to provide you with the underlying knowledge that you'll need when you tackle Windows and Exchange Server 2003 installation, administration, and management later in this book.

Chapter 1, "Introducing Exchange Server 2003," presents some basic information about Exchange Server 2003 products, helping you optimize the value of these products in your organization.

Chapter 2, "Windows Server 2003 and Exchange Server 2003," looks in some detail at the similarities and differences between Windows Server 2003, Windows 2000 Server, and Windows NT Server 4. This chapter also examines the differences between Exchange Server 2003, Exchange 2000 Server, and Exchange Server 5.5, assisting you in focusing your learning efforts if you're an old hand at Windows 2000, NT 4, and Exchange 5.5.

Chapter 3, "Two Key Architectural Components of Windows Server 2003," talks about the most important aspects of Windows Server 2003, giving you a head start on the road to Windows Server 2003/Exchange 2003 competency.

Chapter 4, "Exchange Server 2003 Architecture," focuses on the organizing structures of Exchange 2003, an understanding of which is essential to successful Exchange 2003 implementation.

Chapter 5, "Designing a New Exchange 2003 System," covers Windows Server 2003 and Exchange 2003 system planning and design, facilitating your initial use of these complex products in your organization.

Chapter 6, "Upgrading to Windows Server 2003 and Exchange Server 2003," looks at the planning and design issues involved in bringing Windows 2003 and Exchange 2003 to existing Windows 2000/Exchange 2000 and Windows NT/Exchange 5.5 environments, easing the introduction of these products into your organization.

Part II: Installation

Microsoft Exchange Server 2003 runs on top of Microsoft's Windows Server 2003. This part covers the installation of both products, protecting them and their users against hardware crashes, and building a basic networking environment to support them.

Chapter 7, "Installing Windows Server 2003 as a Domain Controller," focuses on installing and configuring Windows Server 2003, setting up an uninterruptible power supply, and backing up.

Chapter 8, "Installing Exchange Server 2003," provides the details on Exchange Server 2003 installation and basic security.

This section is also important for those who need to upgrade from Windows 2000 Server and Exchange 2000 Server to the 2003 versions of these products or from NT Server 4 to Windows Server 2003 and Exchange Server 5.5 to Exchange Server 2003. Much of what is done during an upgrade is covered in these two chapters.

Part III: The Outlook Client

Exchange Server is a pretty nifty little gadget. But without clients, it's nothing more than fancy technology. Although this is a book on Exchange Server, the Outlook client merits some discussion. This section is devoted to that discussion.

Chapter 9, "Installing Outlook 2003 from a Customized Server Image," takes an administrative perspective, focusing on the Outlook 2003 client for Windows that is part of the Office 2003 Suite. This chapter covers both installation of the client on a server so that it can be installed on user workstations and then from the server onto user workstations.

Chapter 10, "A Quick Overview of Outlook 2003," describes and explains the Outlook 2003 client from the user's perspective. This includes a quick tour of Outlook's menus to get you comfortable with the extensive and impressive functionality Microsoft has built into the client.

Part IV: Basic Exchange Server 2003 Management

Attention shifts in this section to day-to-day Exchange Server operational tasks. Most of these tasks are carried out within Microsoft Management Console, which is heavily featured in Part IV.

Chapter 11, "Managing Exchange Users, Distribution Groups, and Contacts," concentrates on the Active Directory Users and Computers Microsoft Management Console snap-in and on using it to administer and manage three recipient components in the Exchange Server 2003 hierarchy: users, distribution groups, and contacts.

Chapter 12, "Managing the Exchange Server Hierarchy and Core Components," covers the management of the rest of Exchange Server's hierarchy and core components primarily by using the Exchange System Manager Microsoft Management Console snap-in.

Part V: Expanding an Exchange Server Organization

This section opens the horizons of Exchange Server to the outside world and to other Exchange servers. This is one of the most interesting and exciting parts of the Exchange 2003 experience.

The first two chapters of Part V focus on the Internet. Chapter 13, "Managing Exchange 2003 Internet Services," discusses the Internet in technical detail and provides instructions for connecting an Exchange Server system to it.

Chapter 14, "Managing Exchange 2003 Services for Internet Clients," provides a firm grounding in key Internet protocols and their management and implementation: Post Office Protocol Version 3 (POP3), Internet Message Access Protocol version 4 (IMAP4), Hypertext Transfer Protocol (HTTP), and Lightweight Directory Access Protocol (LDAP).

Chapter 15, "Installing and Managing Additional Exchange Servers," includes extensive instructions on adding Exchange 2003 servers to an Exchange organization. The focus in this chapter is on adding, administering, and managing Exchange servers at different levels in the Exchange 2003 hierarchy and Windows 2003 domain structure.

Part VI: Exchange and Outlook: The Next Level

The final section of this book deals with a series of advanced topics, discussion of which would have been premature or diverting earlier on. Chapter 16, "Advanced Exchange Server Administration and Management," covers such issues as troubleshooting, message tracking, and migrating users of foreign messaging systems to Exchange Server 2003.

Chapter 17, "Exchange Server Reliability and Availability," concentrates on the role of system redundancy and backup and recovery in stable Exchange Server systems. The chapter ends with an extensive discussion of Exchange Server disaster recovery strategies and plans and a real-world example of recovery in the face of serious disaster. Chapter 17 is new to this edition of *Mastering Microsoft Exchange Server*.

Also new to this edition is Chapter 18, "Exchange Server System Security." This chapter brings together eight years of experience battling the demons that can compromise an Exchange server system or the Windows system it rides upon. Topics in this chapter include putting Exchange servers behind firewalls, Windows and Exchange Server security best practices, securing Exchange messages, and dealing with viruses and spam.

The final new chapter in this book is Chapter 19, "Wireless Access to Exchange Server 2003," which explores the exciting new world of wireless access to Exchange mailboxes. The chapter covers wireless LAN and WAN options as well as server and client innovations in Exchange 2003 that, for the first time, make it easy to get to Exchange inboxes, calendars, and contacts without anchoring a PDA or wireless phone in a cradle.

Chapter 20, "Building, Using, and Managing Outlook Forms Designer Applications," discusses and demonstrates the use of one of the easier and more interesting application design options, the Outlook 2003 Forms Designer package, which integrates tightly with Exchange Server 2003.

Appendix: Cool Third-Party Applications for Exchange Server and Outlook Clients

This book's Appendix takes you on a thrill ride through some of the many products that exist today to enhance and extend the reach of Exchange Server. Coverage includes applications and services that:

- Make Exchange Server installation and administration easier.

- Bring faxing and document management capabilities to Exchange servers.

- Improve upon the backup software built into Windows/Exchange Server 2003.

- Provide near-line storage message archiving.

◆ Check for potential and actual internal and external security breaches.

◆ Guard Exchange servers and networks against virus attacks and spam messages.

◆ Provide messaging systems linking e-mail, telephone services, voice, and text.

◆ Improve workflow by using e-mail to connect users working on a common task.

Conventions Used in This Book

I've included many notes in this book. Generally, they are positioned below the material to which they refer. There are three kinds of notes: notes, tips, and warnings.

NOTE *Notes give you information pertinent to the procedure or topic being discussed.*

TIP *Tips indicate practical hints that might make your work easier.*

WARNING *Warnings alert you to potential problems that you might encounter while using the program.*

Remember, Exchange is designed to help your organization do what it does better, more efficiently, and with greater productivity. Have fun, be productive, and prosper!

Part 1

Understanding and Planning

In this part:

Chapter 1

Introducing Exchange Server 2003

ELECTRONIC MESSAGING HAS BECOME such a prominent aspect of our lives that it's hard to remember not having it. It is no longer a luxury for businesses, nonprofit organizations, and even individuals. E-messaging is a key component of life from selling goods and services, to disseminating information and raising funds, to communicating with family and friends. Microsoft's Exchange client/server e-messaging products have been major players in an e-messaging revolution that began in earnest in 1995. Exchange 2003 is the latest in a series of increasingly sophisticated, standards-based, industrial strength e-messaging servers. Exchange 2003 lets people work together in a variety of productivity-enhancing ways.

It is important to realize that both Windows 2003 and Exchange 2003 are evolutionary products. They are relatively modest upgrades of Windows 2000 and Exchange 2000. If you know and understand the 2000 products, you will have little difficulty adapting to most of the features of the 2003 line.

Unlike its predecessor, Exchange Server 5.5, but like Exchange 2000, Exchange Server 2003 is very tightly integrated into the Windows Server 2003 environment: You can't talk about Exchange Server 2003 without talking about Windows Server 2003. This chapter concentrates on Exchange Server 2003, but when we leave the safe confines of this introductory chapter, hardly a paragraph will go by without mention of Windows Server 2003.

Featured in this chapter:

◆ Exchange Server 2003 and the era of ubiquitous electronic messaging

◆ Why Microsoft released Windows 2003 and Exchange 2003

◆ Exchange Server 2003 applications

◆ Some Exchange Server 2003 basics

A CONFUSING ARRAY OF TERMS

Before we move on, let me clarify some of the terms that I'll be using. I'll use *Windows Server 2003* or *Windows 2003* to refer to the entire line of Windows Server 2003 products. I'll use the names of the individual Windows Server 2003 products when referring specifically to one of them—for example, *Windows Server 2003 Advanced Server.* I'll use the same conventions for Windows 2000 Server and Exchange 2000 Server and for Windows NT Server 4.

When I use the word *Exchange* or the words *Exchange system,* I'm talking about the whole Exchange Server 2003 client/server system.

Exchange Server refers to just the Exchange Server 2003 product (Server or Enterprise Edition), and an *Exchange server* is any computer running the Exchange Server 2003 product.

Got that? Okay, explain it to me.

Exchange Server 2003 and the Era of Ubiquitous Electronic Messaging

If you're currently responsible for electronic messaging in your organization, no one has to tell you about the steadily expanding use of e-messaging. You know it's happening every time you check the storage space on your disk drives or need an additional tape to complete the backup of your mail server.

Over the last 10 years, the number of e-mail addresses has grown significantly. Based on data from a July 1999 study (#19758), the technology research company International Data Corporation (IDC) estimates that in 2002 the number of e-mailboxes in the United States stood at 275 million and at well over 500 million worldwide. IDC estimates that by 2005 there will be more than 300 million mailboxes in the United States and 750 million worldwide.

Electronic messaging is more than e-mail. It involves the use of an underlying messaging infrastructure (addressing, routing, store-and-forward technologies, and so on) to build applications that are based on cooperative tasking, whether by humans or computers. Working in tandem with real-time interactive technologies, electronic messaging systems have already produced a set of wildly imaginative business, entertainment, and educational applications with high payoff potential. All of this action, of course, accelerates the demand for electronic messaging capabilities and services.

Microsoft's Exchange Server products have played and will continue to play a key role in electronic messaging. Exchange Server 2003 is one of the most powerful, extensible, scalable, easy-to-use, and manageable electronic messaging back ends currently on the market. Combined with Microsoft's excellent Outlook clients, Internet-based clients from Microsoft and other vendors, and third-party or home-grown applications, Exchange Server 2003 can help your organization move smoothly and productively into the electronic messaging future.

Why Microsoft Released Windows 2003 and Exchange 2003

If, as noted above, Windows 2003 and Exchange 2003 are relatively modest upgrades of the 2000 versions of these products, why did Microsoft release newly numbered versions? There are three reasons. First, Microsoft had to keep a promise it made to its customers. Second, the 2003 line of server products represents a new way for Microsoft to manage licensing. Third, the release of newly numbered product upgrades is a key Microsoft marketing strategy.

Prior to the release of its Windows and Exchange 2000 server products, Microsoft released service packs containing both bug fixes and product enhancements. Some customers were pleasantly surprised when a service pack showed up with a great new feature. Other customers were not happy at all to have to deal with such features and the changes they might require in both product management and end-user training. So, when Microsoft released both Windows 2003 and Exchange 2003, it promised to use service packs only to fix bugs. Enhancements would be held for release as part of a new version of the product.

Microsoft kept its promise to its customers with Windows 2003 and Exchange 2003. Now, don't get me wrong; as you'll soon see, the 2003 line includes some pretty neat new features. My favorite is Windows 2003's ability to quickly and unobtrusively make snapshot backups of files. This is a great feature just for the Windows environment, but for Exchange, it is a godsend. Though I've had to do it only a few times in my consulting life, recovering lost stuff from Exchange databases makes me really nervous. Snapshots make it much easier and more reliable.

Aside from keeping promises, the 2003 product line includes much tighter controls on product licensing. We first saw Microsoft's new approach to licensing in Office XP and Windows XP. Basically, you're required to get an authorization code for the product online, by telephone, or snail mail. The number of authorizations is limited, allowing you enough reinstalls to cover disk crashes and other circumstances, but not enough so you can put the product on every computer in the world.

My first reaction to this sort of licensing was anger. Then, when I realized that it costs Microsoft a ton of money to develop even minor enhancements to a product, the anger subsided and I understood that paying for what I use contributes to the growth and extended life of these products. As long as Microsoft charges fairly for its products, I'm happy to pay my fair share.

The last reason for the release of Windows and Exchange 2003 has to do with product marketing. Like so many vendors, Microsoft has adopted a "new model year" approach to selling many of its products. Putting a model year on a product gives it a spiffy feel when it's first released and then makes it seem obsolescent as time passes. I mean, what's more *so-yesterday* than running Exchange 2000 Server in the year 2003? I've found the model year approach cuts both ways with my clients. Some really get into it, arguing to their bosses that, like an old car, old software just won't cut it. Others resist, saying that it's all just marketing hype. Honestly, every Microsoft product update has had significant new features. Whether or not a specific organization requires those features is open to argument. One good argument for going with the latest and greatest software is that Microsoft ultimately phases out support for older products. While it will be some time before it happens, support for the NT server product line is going to disappear.

The rest of this chapter introduces you to the Exchange 2003 client/server system. We start with a quick look at several of the neat ways that you can use Exchange for e-mail and more, and then we focus on some of Exchange's key characteristics and capabilities. This is just an introduction, so don't worry if you don't understand everything completely by the end of this chapter. Everything that we discuss here is also covered in more detail later in this book.

Exchange Server 2003 Applications

I dare you not to get excited about electronic messaging and Exchange Server 2003 as you read this section. Just look at what's possible, and imagine what you could do with all this potential.

Exchange supports a range of e-mail protocols, including Microsoft's own proprietary Mail Application Program Interface (MAPI), as well as the Internet standard protocols Post Office Protocol version 3 (POP3) and the often overlooked Internet Message Access Protocol version 4 (IMAP4). But that's just the tip of the iceberg. Exchange servers can host user and organizational calendars, e-mail–enabled contact lists, to-do lists, notes, and other data. Users can access all this data using standard PC-based e-mail clients, web browsers, and even those tiny personal digital assistants (PDAs) that are all the rage today. Speaking of PDAs, I'm really jazzed about wireless access to Exchange using PDAs. The good news is that Microsoft has finally done some great things in Exchange 2003 to support wireless access.

Exchange servers are also great places to build and support custom applications. You can build simple applications using existing products such as Microsoft Word or Excel. If your application needs are more complex, you can turn to Exchange-based forms. And, if you've got the need, time, and skills, you can build applications using programming languages such as Java, Visual Basic, or C++. The .NET Framework part of Windows Server 2003 significantly enhances Exchange 2003 development options. Finally, you can use the built-in sorting and searching capabilities of Exchange public folders to build some pretty powerful applications.

E-Mail Is Only the Beginning

Together, Exchange Server 2003 and its clients perform a variety of messaging-based functions. These include e-mail, message routing, scheduling, and support for several types of custom applications. Certainly, e-mail is a key feature of any messaging system, and the Outlook Calendar is far better than previous versions of Microsoft's appointment and meeting-scheduling software. Figures 1.1 and 1.2 show the Outlook 2003 client Inbox and Calendar for Windows in action.

FIGURE 1.1

The Outlook 2003 client Inbox for Windows

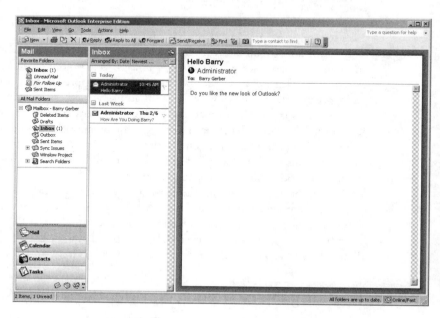

FIGURE 1.2
The Outlook 2003 client Calendar for Windows

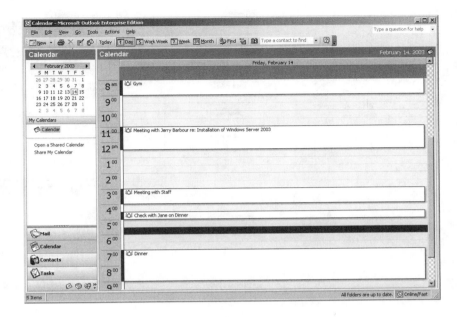

Take a look at Figures 1.3, 1.4, and 1.5 for a glimpse of the Internet-based POP3, IMAP4, and web browser clients that you can use with Exchange Server 2003.

FIGURE 1.3
Microsoft's Outlook Express POP3-compliant client accesses mail stored on an Exchange server.

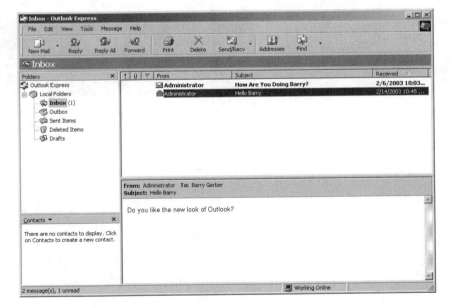

FIGURE 1.4
Microsoft's Outlook Express IMAP4 client function accesses messages and folders on an Exchange server.

FIGURE 1.5
Microsoft's Internet Explorer web browser accesses mail stored on an Exchange Server 2003.

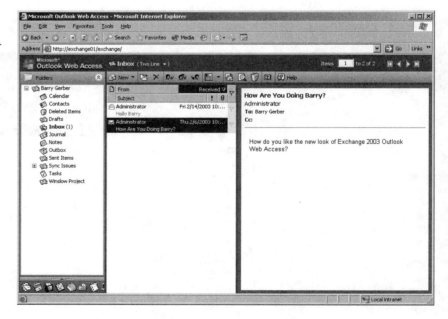

E-mail clients are exciting and sexy, but to get the most out of Exchange Server 2003, you need to throw away any preconceptions you have that messaging packages are only for e-mail and scheduling. The really exciting applications are not those that use simple e-mail or scheduling, but those that are based on the routing capabilities of messaging systems. These applications bring people and computers together for cooperative work.

So what do these hot apps look like? Let's start with the simplest and move toward the more complex.

Just a Step beyond Mail

You're probably familiar with e-mail *attachments*—those word-processing, spreadsheet, and other files that you can attach to messages. Attachments are a simple way to move files to the people who need to see them.

Sure, you could send your files on diskette or tell people where on the network they can find and download the files. But e-mail attachments let you make the files available to others with a click of their mouse buttons: Recipients just double-click on an icon, and the attachment opens in the original application that produced it. This is true, of course, only if your correspondent has access to the application or to software that lets them view documents created using the application.

Using attachments offers the added advantage of putting the files and accompanying messages right in the faces of those who need to see them. This leaves less room for excuses such as "I couldn't find/open that network folder," or "The dog ate the diskette."

As great as attachments can be, they have one real weakness: The minute an attachment leaves your Outbox, it's out of date. If you do further work on the original file, such work is not reflected in the copy that you sent to others. If someone then edits a copy of the attached file, it's totally out of sync with the original and all other copies. Getting everything synchronized again can involve tedious hours or days of manually comparing different versions and cutting and pasting them to create one master document.

Office 2003 offers two neat ways to avoid this problem. First, it lets you insert a link to a file. When the file is opened, you're really opening the linked file. If the file is changed, you see the changed file. Second, Office 2003 lets you attach a file to a message and to set a share point where an updateable version of the file is stored. When the copy attached to the user's e-mail is updated, these updates can be incorporated into the shared copy of the file. This option allows broader access to the file than a link.

The next two sections show you other ways to get around the limitations of attachments.

Off-the-Shelf Messaging-Enabled Applications

Microsoft Office enables messaging in many word-processing and spreadsheet applications. For example, when you install the Outlook client on your computer, Microsoft's Office products such as Word and Excel are enabled for electronic messaging. You can select the Routing Recipient option from the application's File ➢ Send To menu. An electronic routing slip pops up. You then add addresses to the slip from your Exchange address books or from your Outlook contacts, select the routing method that you want to use, and set other attributes for the route. Finally, you add the routing slip to the document with a click of the Add Slip button and ship it off to others using options on the File ➢ Send To menu.

As you can see in Figure 1.6, the file can be routed either sequentially or all at once to each address you selected. Routing sequentially helps eliminate problems associated with multiple users editing the same file at the same time. With applications such as Microsoft Word that keep track of each person's comments and changes, once the document has been routed, the original author can read the comments and incorporate or not incorporate them as they see fit. Figure 1.6 shows how all this works.

FIGURE 1.6

Microsoft Word 2003 includes messaging-enabled functions for sending and routing.

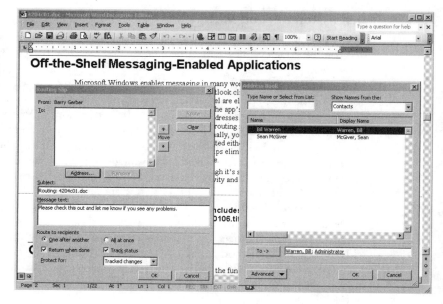

Although it's simple, application-based messaging can significantly improve user productivity and speed up a range of business processes.

Objects

Object insertion and linking further enhance the functionality of the Exchange messaging system. Take a close look at Figure 1.7. Yes, the message includes an Excel spreadsheet and chart. The person who sent the message simply selected Object from the Insert menu that appears on every Exchange message. Then they specified a file with an existing spreadsheet as the source of the object to be inserted into the message. The Outlook client then inserted the file into the message as an object.

The recipient can see the spreadsheet as a graphic image in the message, as shown in the figure. When they double-click the graphic image, Excel is launched inside the message, and Excel's menus and toolbars replace those of the message (see Figure 1.8). In essence, the message becomes Excel.

FIGURE 1.7
Object insertion makes it easy to create sophisticated messaging-enabled applications.

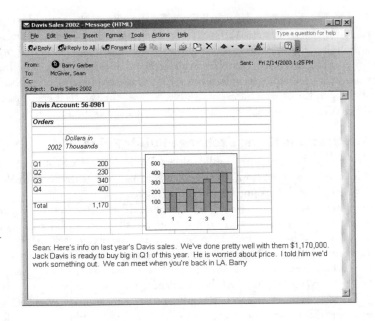

FIGURE 1.8
Double-clicking an Excel spreadsheet object in a message enables Excel menus and toolbars.

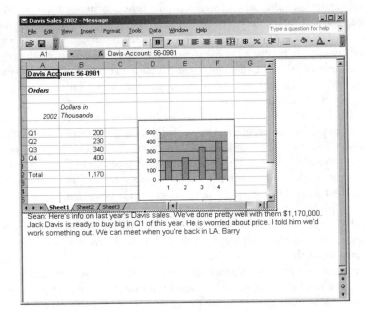

The Excel spreadsheet is fully editable. Excel must be available to a recipient for them to be able to edit the spreadsheet. Without Excel, they can only look at the spreadsheet in graphic image form, although the graphic image changes when the spreadsheet is edited in Excel.

You can also insert an object in a message that is a link to an application file. As with object insertion, your recipient sees a graphic picture of the contents of the file and can edit the file by double-clicking it. Links are a bit more flexible, because they allow users to work with files stored on a shared disk. With inserted objects, users work with a file embedded in the message itself.

Applications Using Exchange Public Folders

Exchange Server supports public folders. Public folders are for common access to messages and files. Files can be dragged from file-access interfaces, such as Explorer in Windows 98, NT 4, 2000, and 2003, and can be dropped into public folders.

You can set up sorting rules for a public folder so that items in the folder are organized by a range of attributes, such as the name of the sender or the creator of the item, or the date that the item arrived or was placed in the folder. Items in a public folder can be sorted by conversation threads. You can also put applications built on existing products such as Word or Excel or with Exchange or Outlook Forms Designer, client or server scripting, or the Exchange API set into public folders. You can use public folders to replace many of the maddening paper-based processes that abound in every organization.

For easy access to items in a public folder, you can use a *folder link*. You can send a link to a folder in a message. When someone goes to the folder and double-clicks a file you put in the folder, the file opens. Everyone who receives the message works with the same linked attachment, so everyone reads and can modify the same file. As with document routing, applications such as Microsoft Word can keep track of each person's changes to and comments on file contents. Of course, your users will have to learn to live with the fact that only one person can edit an application file at a time. Most modern end-user applications warn the user that someone else is using the file and allow the user to open a read-only copy of the file, which, of course, can't be edited. Third-party applications offer tighter document checkout control (see the Appendix, "Cool Third-Party Applications for Exchange Server and Outlook Clients").

If all this isn't already enough, Exchange is very much Internet aware. With Exchange Server 2003, you can publish all or selected public folders on the Internet, where they become accessible with a simple Internet browser. You can limit Internet access to public folders only to users who have access under Windows Server 2003's security system, or you can open public folders to anyone on the Internet. Just think about it: Internet-enabled public folders let you put information on the Internet without the fuss and bother of website design and development. Any item can be placed on the Internet by simply adding a message or other object to a public folder.

Before we leave public folder applications, I want to mention one more option: Exchange Server 2003 enables you to bring any or all of those Usenet Internet newsgroups to your public folder environment. With their Outlook clients, users then can read and reply to newsgroup items just as though they were using a standard newsgroup reader application. Exchange Server comes with all the tools that you need to do this. All you need is an Internet connection, access to a host computer that can provide you with a feed of newsgroup messages, and a set of rules about which groups to exclude. Remember, this is where the infamous alt.sex newsgroups live. But you don't have to use public newsgroups. Rather, you can create your own private newsgroups for internal communications.

Electronic Forms

Exchange Server 2003 supports Outlook Forms Designer (OFD). You can use OFD to build information-gathering forms containing a number of the bells and whistles that you're accustomed to in Windows applications. These include drop-down list boxes, check boxes, fill-in text forms, tab dialog controls, and radio buttons (see Figure 1.9).

FIGURE 1.9

Electronic forms turn messages into structured information-gathering tools.

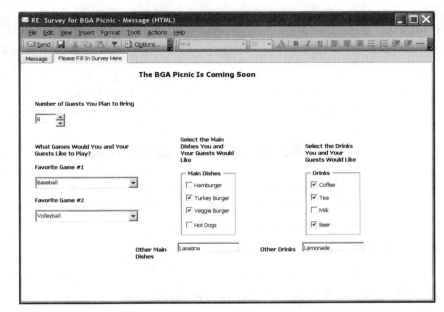

OFD, which is easy enough for nontechnical types to use, includes a variety of messaging-oriented fields and actions. For example, you can choose to include a preaddressed To field in a form so that users of the form can easily mail it off to the appropriate recipient. (The preaddressed To field for the form shown in Figure 1.9 is on the page with the tab marked Message, which is not visible in this figure.) When you've designed a form, you can make it available to all users or select users, who can access the completed form simply by selecting it while in an Outlook client.

I discuss OFD further in Chapter 20, "Building, Using, and Managing Outlook Forms Designer Applications." That chapter also includes a nice hands-on exercise using OFD.

Applications Built on APIs

If you want even more, you can go to the heart of Exchange Server and use its application programming interface (API). Exchange Server supports both the Simple and Extended versions of Microsoft's Windows-based MAPI. It also supports the X.400-oriented, platform-independent Common Mail Call (CMC) APIs, which have functions similar to those of Simple MAPI. Using Simple MAPI or CMC, you can build applications that use electronic messaging addresses behind the scenes to route data between users and programs. Extended MAPI lets you get deeper into Exchange's storage and electronic messaging address books to create virtually any messaging-enabled application that you can imagine.

These custom-built applications may involve some level of automation, such as performing regular updates of your company's price lists for trading partners or sending a weekly multimedia message from the president to employees at your organization. Building apps based on MAPI or CMC requires programming skills in languages such as Visual Basic, Java, and C++, and this is beyond the scope of this book.

Microsoft's .NET framework technology extends the Exchange application development environment. .NET is based on open standards XML Web services. It supports faster, more efficient code development as well as easier communication and sharing of data between applications written in different programming languages and running on different computing platforms. Programs using the .NET framework can run in a Microsoft Windows or Web-HTTP environment.

Some Exchange Server 2003 Basics

It's important to get a handle on some of Exchange's key characteristics and capabilities. When you do, you'll better appreciate the depth and breadth of Microsoft's efforts in developing Exchange, and you'll be better prepared for the rest of this book. In this section, we'll take a look at these topics:

◆ Exchange as a client/server system

◆ The Outlook client

◆ Exchange Server's dependence on Microsoft's Windows Server 2003

◆ Exchange Server's object orientation

◆ Exchange Server scalability

◆ Exchange Server security

◆ Exchange Server and other electronic messaging systems

◆ Third-party applications for Exchange Server

Taken together, Exchange Server 2003's attributes make it a powerful, flexible, and extensible platform, capable of meeting the needs of small and large enterprises alike.

Exchange Server 2003 as a Client/Server System

The term *client/server* has been overused and overworked. To put it simply, there are two kinds of networked applications: shared-file and client/server.

SHARED-FILE APPLICATIONS

Early networked applications were all based on *shared-file* systems. The network shell that let you load your word processor from a network server also allowed you to read from and write to files stored on a server. At the time, this was the easiest and most natural way to grow networked applications.

Microsoft's first e-mail product, Mail for PC Networks, is a shared-file application. You run Windows, OS/2, DOS, or Macintosh front ends, which send and receive messages by accessing files on a Microsoft Mail for PC Networks post office that resides on a network file server. The front end and your PC do all the work; the server is passive. Figure 1.10 shows a typical Microsoft Mail for PC Networks setup.

FIGURE 1.10

Microsoft Mail for PC Networks is a typical shared-file electronic messaging system.

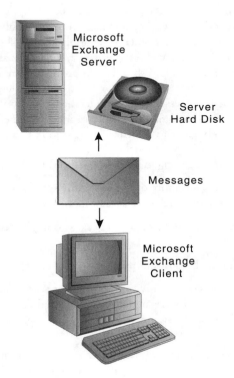

Easy as it was to develop, this architecture leads to some serious problems in today's networked computing world:

◆ Changing the underlying structure of the server file system is difficult because you have to change both the server and the client.

◆ System security is always compromised because users must have read and write permissions for the whole server file system, which includes all other users' message files. Things are so bad that in some cases a naive or malicious user can actually destroy shared-file system databases.

◆ Network traffic is high because the front end must constantly access indexes and hunt around the server's file system for user messages.

◆ Because the user workstation writes directly to shared files, the server-based files can be destroyed if workstation hardware or software stops functioning for some unexpected reason.

Shared-file applications are in decline. Sure, plenty of *legacy* (that is, out-of-date) apps will probably live on for the data-processing equivalent of eternity, but client/server systems have quickly supplanted the shared-file model. This is especially true in the world of electronic messaging.

CLIENT/SERVER APPLICATIONS

Though they have some limitations of their own, client/server applications overcome the shortcomings of shared-file apps. So, today, networked applications increasingly are based on the client/server model. The server is an active partner in client/server applications. Clients tell servers what they want done, and if security requirements are met, servers do what they are asked.

Processes running on a server find and ship data to processes running on a client. When a client process sends data, a server receives it and writes it to server-based files. Server processes can do more than simply interact with client processes. For example, they can compact data files on the server or—as they do on Exchange Server—automatically reply to incoming messages to let people know, for instance, that you're going to be out of the office for a period of time. Figure 1.11 shows how Exchange implements the client/server model.

Client/server applications are strong in all the areas in which shared-file apps are weak:

◆ Changing the underlying structure of the server file system is easier than with shared-file systems because only the server processes access the file system.

◆ System security can be much tighter, again because only the server processes access the file system.

◆ Network traffic is lighter because all the work of file access is done by the server, on the server.

◆ Because server processes are the only ones that access server data, breakdowns of user workstation hardware or software are less likely to spoil data. With appropriate transaction logging features, client/server systems can even protect against server hardware or software malfunctions.

As good as the client/server model is, it does have some general drawbacks. Client/server apps require more computing horsepower, especially on the server side. With Exchange, you should plan to start with very fast Pentium or better machines, lots of RAM, and plenty of hard disk and tape backup capacity—and expect to grow from there.

Client/server applications are more complex than shared-file apps. This is partly because of the nature of the client/server model and partly because of the tendency of client/server apps to be newer and thus filled with all kinds of great capabilities that you won't find in shared-file applications. Generally, you're safe in assuming that you'll need to devote more and more sophisticated human resources to managing a client/server application than to tending to a similar one based on shared files.

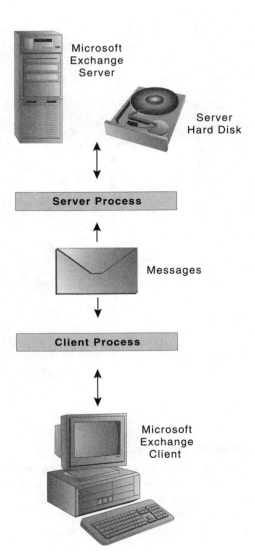

FIGURE 1.11
Microsoft Exchange is based on the client/server model.

The good news is that Microsoft has done a lot to reduce the management load and to make it easier for someone who isn't a computer scientist to administer an Exchange system. I've looked at many client/server messaging systems, and I can say without any doubt that Exchange is absolutely the easiest to administer, even in its slightly more complex 2003 implementation. Exchange Server 2003 includes a set of graphical user interfaces (GUIs) that organize the processes of management very nicely. With these interfaces, you can do everything from adding users to assessing the health of your messaging system. In Figure 1.12, I'm using the Windows Server 2003 Active Directory Users and Computers interface to modify an Exchange user's mailbox.

FIGURE 1.12

Managing an Exchange user's mailbox in the Active Directory Users and Computers interface

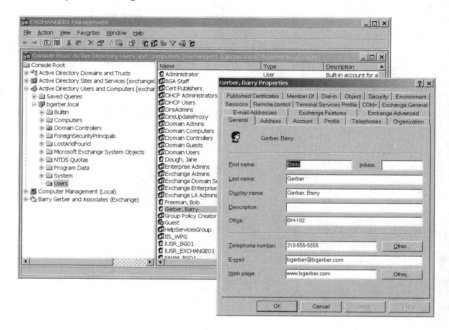

A Quick Take on the Outlook Client

As should be clear from our look at some of its applications earlier in this chapter, the Outlook client is the sexy part of Exchange. This is where the action is. Outlook is the view screen for the backroom bits and bytes of Exchange Server. Although this book is mostly about Exchange Server, you can't implement an Exchange system without the clients. So, we'll spend some time on the Outlook client in various places in this book. Meanwhile, let's discuss some client basics.

STORING AND SHARING INFORMATION

The client stores information in one of two places on Exchange Server 2003: a mailbox store or a public store. Each has a different purpose and function. Furthermore, an Outlook client can have personal folders, which reside outside the Exchange Server environment. Additionally, you can share information with others by sending it to them or placing it in public folders for them to retrieve on their own. You can drop messages, word-processing documents, other work files, and even whole applications into public folders.

Mailbox Stores and Mailboxes

Mailbox stores contain individual Exchange Server 2003 user mailboxes. Mailboxes can send and receive messages. Although you can share their contents with others, mailboxes generally hold items to which you alone have access. You access mailboxes using an Exchange client or Internet-based clients such as the POP3 and IMAP4 clients built into Microsoft's Outlook Express.

Mailboxes contain Inbox, Deleted Items, and Sent Items folders. They can also contain folders for such items as a calendar, tasks, and notes.

You can add folders to a mailbox to help you organize your messages. If you have the rights to other mailboxes, you can open them in your Exchange client as well.

Public Stores and Public Folders

Public folder stores contain, you guessed it, public folders, which hold items that you want others to see. Users whom you authorize can create public folders and then drag and drop anything that they want into them. Public folders can also be nested, and rules can be applied to them. Users can be given or denied access to specific public folders.

Public folders are key to the organization-wide implementation of Exchange. Some, all, or none of an Exchange server's public folders can be automatically replicated to other Exchange servers. This lets you post items to public folders on one Exchange server and have them quickly and painlessly appear on any combination of the Exchange servers in your system. Even without replication, users all over your organization can access public folders.

Personal Folders: Another Place for Clients to Store Information

Outlook has personal folders that reside outside the Exchange Server on local or network hard disks. Personal folders may or may not have the send and receive capabilities of mailboxes. You can create as many personal folders as you want, and a personal folder can hold as many subfolders as you want. Like the folders that you add to mailboxes, personal folders help you organize information. You can drag and drop messages between folders. Using rules (discussed in the next section), you can direct incoming mail to any of your personal folders.

ORGANIZING INFORMATION

Creating a set of mailbox, public, and private folders and then dropping messages in them is a simple way to organize information. More sophisticated approaches include the use of rules, views, and the Exchange client's message finder.

Rules   As a user, you can set up a range of *rules* to move mail from your Inbox into personal or public folders. For example, you might want to move all the messages from your boss into a folder marked "Urgent." Rules can be based on anything from the sender of a message to its contents. Depending on its type, a rule may run on the Exchange server or on the client. The Outlook client doesn't have to be running for server-based rules to execute.

Views   Exchange messages can have numerous attributes. These include the obvious, such as sender, subject, and date received, as well as less common information, including the sender's company, the last author, and the number of words. In Outlook, you can build views of messages using almost any combination of attributes and a variety of sorting schemes. Then you can apply a particular view to a folder to specially organize the messages that it contains.

The Message Finder   You can use the Outlook client message finder to search all folders or a single folder for messages from or to specific correspondents, messages with specific information in the subject field or message body or attachments, and even messages received between specific dates or of a specific size.

Exchange Server 2003's Dependence on Windows 2000 Server/ Windows Server 2003

Exchange Server 2003 runs only on Windows 2000 Server (with Service Pack 3 or higher) or Windows Server 2003. It won't run on Windows NT Server, Windows 2000 Professional, Windows XP, or any other Windows platform. When you run Exchange 2003 on Windows 2000 Server, you'll lose some Exchange 2003 functionality. I'll talk about this in Chapter 5, "Designing a New Exchange 2003 System." In this section, I'll focus on Windows 2003.

Among operating systems, Windows 2000 Server and Windows Server 2003 are the new kids on the block. As a longtime Windows NT Server user, I initially faced Windows 2000 Server with more than a little fear and foreboding. That was then. Now I am a confirmed Windows 2000 Server user and supporter. As I noted earlier in this chapter, Windows Server 2003 is an evolutionary step beyond Windows 2000 Server. I have had no difficulty adapting to Windows 2003. Its underlying architecture and management interfaces are very similar to those of Windows 2000. At this point, I'm so comfortable with Windows 2003 that my personal workstation is a Windows Server 2003–based machine, and all my servers but one are Windows 2003 servers. (The one holdout is a NetWare server that I use to ensure that Windows Server 2003 and Windows-based software work with Novell's IPX/SPX.)

What sets Windows Server 2003 apart from all other server operating systems is Microsoft Windows. Windows 2003 *is* Microsoft Windows. If you can use Windows 2000 or XP, you can get started using Windows Server 2003 in no time. You'll have to learn how to accomplish various server-related tasks, but once you figure out how to do a task, the Windows GUI greatly simplifies performing almost any task. Networking with Windows Server 2003 is pretty much a breeze if you understand a few basic concepts, and running apps on top of Windows Server 2003 is a piece of cake.

Windows Server 2003 is chock-full of features that make it an especially attractive operating system. One of these is its very usable and functional implementation of Microsoft's domain-based security system. Domains have names—mine is called bgerber.local—and can include Windows 2003, 2000, and NT 4 servers as well as a range of Windows workstations from Windows 95 through Windows XP. Although there are a number of ways to approach domain structure and security, the general rule is that the members of a domain can use any resource that they have been given permission to use in the domain—disk files, printers, and so on—no matter where these resources reside. Exchange Server 2003 depends on Windows Server 2003 domain structure and security for its security.

In Chapter 2, "Windows Server 2003 and Exchange Server 2003," Chapter 3, "Two Key Architectural Components of Windows Server 2003," and Chapter 6, "Upgrading to Windows Server 2003 and Exchange Server 2003," you'll read a lot more about Windows Server 2003 and what you need to know about it to run Exchange Server. You'll install Windows Server 2003 in Chapter 7, "Installing Windows Server 2003 as a Domain Controller."

Exchange Server 2003's Object Orientation

Like Windows Server 2003, Exchange Server 2003 is a classic example of an *object-oriented* system. Figure 1.13 shows the main tool for managing an Exchange Server 2003 organization: Exchange System Manager. Take a look at all those items on the tree on the left side of the tool, such as Barry Gerber and Associates (Exchange), Servers, EXCHANGE01, First Storage Group, and Protocols. Each of these is an *object*. Each object has attributes and can interact with other objects in specific ways. Exchange objects can hold other objects, serving as what Microsoft calls *containers*.

FIGURE 1.13

Exchange Server 2003's object orientation is evident in the Exchange System Manager tool.

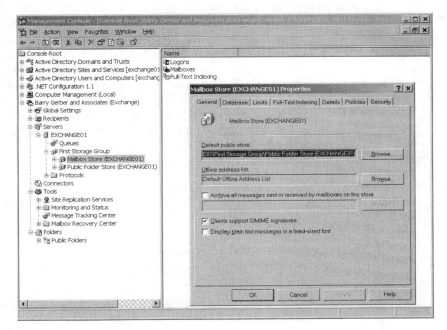

Barry Gerber and Associates is the name of my consulting business; it is the equivalent of a company name such as IBM or TRW. This top-level object is called the *organization*. The Barry Gerber and Associates organization contains all the objects below it.

The Servers container holds the individual servers in the Barry Gerber and Associates enterprise hierarchy. Right now, there's only one server in the Servers container, EXCHANGE01, but just you wait.

The First Storage Group object contains mailbox and public folder stores; remember those from earlier in this chapter?

Take a look at the dialog box on the right side of Figure 1.13. It shows the properties or attributes of the mailbox store. Objects have attributes. The attributes of a mailbox store object are puny compared to those of a Windows Server 2003/Exchange Server 2003 user: Compare this to the number of tabs on the user object back in Figure 1.12.

Object orientation makes it easy for Microsoft to distribute Exchange Server 2003's functionality and management, and it makes it easy for you to administer an Exchange Server environment. For example, based on my security clearances, I can manage any set of Windows Server 2003/Exchange Server 2003 users, from only a small group of users to all the users in my Windows Server 2003 domain.

Exchange Server 2003 Scalability

Exchange Server 2003 scales very well both vertically and horizontally. Windows Server 2003 runs on top of computers based on single and multiple Intel processors, so it's very easy to scale an Exchange server upward to more powerful hardware when increased user loads make additional computing power necessary. You can also cluster Windows Server 2003/Exchange Server 2003 so that they mirror each other in a fault-tolerant way and share the load placed on them by users. This is another way to vertically scale Exchange Server 2003 systems.

If vertical scalability isn't what you need, horizontal scaling is also a breeze with Exchange Server. You can set up a new Exchange server and quickly get its directory and public folders in sync with all or some of your other servers. You can even move mailboxes between Exchange servers with a few clicks of your left mouse button.

How do you know whether it's time to scale up or out? Microsoft has an answer for this too: You can use the load simulation tools that Microsoft provides to simulate a range of different user loads on your server hardware. By analyzing the results of your tests, you'll get some idea of the messaging loads that you can expect a server to handle in a production environment.

NOTE *Microsoft claims that Windows 2003 and Exchange 2003 have been architected in such a way to allow far more users on a single computer, so you might never have to mess with issues of server scaling, but it's good to know that you have the option.*

Exchange Server 2003 Security

Exchange Server 2003 security starts with Windows Server 2003's security system. Several different Windows Server 2003 security structure options are available; the one that's right for you depends mostly on the size and structure of your organization and the department that supports Exchange Server 2003. In all cases, the idea is to select a security model that puts the lightest burden on users and system administrators while still appropriately barring unauthorized users from messaging and other system resources (more on this in Chapter 7 and Chapter 8, "Installing Exchange Server 2003").

Windows Server 2003 also audits security. It can let you know when a user tries to add, delete, or access system resources.

The security of Exchange Server 2003 is enhanced in several ways beyond the Windows Server 2003 operating system's security. Access to Exchange Server objects such as public folders can be limited by the owner of the object. Data encryption on the server and client protects messages and other Exchange resources from eavesdropping by those with server or workstation access. Digital signatures prove the authenticity of a message. Even traffic between servers can be encrypted.

Exchange Server 2003 and Other Electronic Messaging Systems

The world of electronic messaging is far from a single-standard nirvana. A good e-messaging system must connect to and communicate with a variety of other messaging systems. Microsoft has done a nice job of providing Exchange Server 2003 with key links, called *connectors*, to other systems, including Exchange 5.5 servers. The company has also built some cross-system message-content translators into

Exchange Server 2003 that work automatically and very effectively. With these translators, you're less likely to send a message containing, say, a beautiful embedded image that can't be viewed by some or all of the message's recipients.

In the case of Microsoft's legacy messaging systems—Exchange 5.5, Microsoft Mail for PC Networks, and Microsoft Mail for AppleTalk Networks—you have an option beyond connectivity. You can choose to migrate users to Exchange. The Exchange 2003 migration facility is much improved over the one offered in Exchange 2000. Migration utilities for other messaging systems such as Lotus cc:Mail are also provided with Exchange. You can also migrate UNIX mail users. The following list describes the most prominent messaging systems in use today.

Exchange Server 5.5   Exchange Server 2003 wouldn't be much of a connectivity product if it couldn't link with its predecessor once removed, Exchange Server 5.5. It can, as you'll see in Chapter 6.

X.400   A fully standards-compatible X.400 service is built into Exchange Server. It can be used to access foreign X.400 messaging systems and to link groups of Exchange Server 2003s. The 1984 and 1988 standards for X.400 are supported.

SMTP   In league with Windows Server 2003, Exchange Server 2003 supports the Simple Message Transport Protocol (SMTP) service. Unlike the old Microsoft Mail for PC Networks SMTP gateway, this implementation is a full-fledged SMTP host system capable of relaying messages and resolving addresses, while supporting several Enhanced SMPT (ESMTP) commands. HTML, Multipurpose Internet Mail Extensions (MIME), and UUencode/UUdecode message-content standards are also supported. So, after you've moved your users from MS Mail for PCs to Exchange Server 2003, you won't hear any more of those vexing complaints about the meaningless MIME-source attachments that users get because the SMTP gateway was incapable of converting them back to their original binary format.

Microsoft Mail for PC Networks   A built-in connector makes Microsoft Mail for PC Networks 3.*x* (MS Mail 3.*x*) post offices look like Exchange Server 2003s to Outlook clients, and vice versa. If connectivity isn't enough, you can transfer MS Mail 3.*x* users to Exchange with a supplied migration tool. If all this is too much, Exchange clients can directly access MS Mail 3.*x* post offices. Thus, you can keep your MS Mail 3.*x* post offices, at least until you've got Exchange Server 2003 running the way you want and have moved everyone off the legacy mail system. If you need to migrate users from Microsoft Mail for PC Networks, see my book, *Mastering Microsoft Exchange 2000 Server* (Sybex, 2001).

Microsoft Mail for AppleTalk Networks   Connectivity for Microsoft Mail for AppleTalk Networks systems is also provided by a connector built into Exchange. When connectivity isn't enough, Mail for AppleTalk users can be migrated to Exchange Server.

cc:Mail   If Lotus cc:Mail is running in your shop, you'll be happy to hear that Exchange Server 2003 comes with tools to connect and migrate users to Exchange. Never let it be said that Microsoft doesn't care about users of IBM/Lotus products. At least there's a way to pull them into the MS camp.

Lotus Notes   Exchange Server 2003 also includes a connector for Lotus Notes. With this connector, Exchange and Notes clients can see each other's address directories and can exchange mail. Migration from Lotus Notes to Exchange 2003 is also possible.

Third-Party Applications for Exchange Server 2003

Exchange Server has been around for some time now, giving third-party application providers time to develop an exciting range of add-on products. These include sophisticated products that enhance Exchange in such areas as document management, work flow, system backup, system management, faxing, security, virus control, wireless access, and application development.

At various places in this book, I'll discuss these third-party applications. In Chapters 7 and 8, I talk about Exchange Server 2003–specific backup products. In Chapter 18, "Exchange Server System Security," I focus on apps for controlling those pesky viruses right inside Exchange Server. The Appendix contains a fairly exhaustive list of third-party apps for Exchange Server.

Summary

Microsoft Exchange Server 2003, when considered with its predecessor, Exchange 2000 Server, represents a significant upgrade over Exchange 5.5, and contains features that position it as the premier messaging package for this age of electronic messaging. If you're new to Exchange, this book will provide the background and instructions you will need to install, configure, and manage Exchange Server 2003. Even experienced Exchange 2000 and 5.5 administrators will need to digest the information in this book to become proficient with Exchange Server 2003.

For starters, Microsoft Exchange Server 2003 is closely tied to Windows 2000 Server and Windows Server 2003. It won't run on Windows NT Server. Nonetheless, it is capable of messaging with a variety of legacy systems, as well as systems from other vendors.

Outlook 2003, Exchange's *native* e-mail client, provides a large variety of features for sending, receiving, and organizing mail messages using mailboxes and user-created mailbox folders, as well as public and personal folders, and rules for automatically sorting and classifying e-mail. Furthermore, its e-mail functions are only part of the picture. Scheduling and contact management are big parts of Exchange Server 2003's features, but perhaps most impressive is its capability of dynamically linking documents that are sent as e-mail attachments. Outlook can also import documents as objects into e-mail messages from other applications, while maintaining the formatting and editing features of the original application. If all that isn't enough, you can use Exchange Server's APIs to build custom applications using a range of programming languages.

Exchange Server 2003 is the most secure Exchange release yet. It scales both vertically and horizontally to grow with the needs of your enterprise, and like Windows Server 2003, it's based on an object-oriented model.

Now that you've gotten a taste of the features and functions of Exchange Server 2003, it's time to learn about its constant companion, Windows Server 2003. Read on to learn about this subject in Chapter 2.

Chapter 2

Windows Server 2003 and Exchange Server 2003

BOTH WINDOWS 2000 SERVER and Exchange 2000 Server were major steps forward for Microsoft. As I mentioned in Chapter 1, "Introducing Exchange Server 2003," both Windows Server 2003 and Exchange Server 2003 are evolutionary products. Each is a modest, but significant, update of its 2000 version.

Active Directory and the new Windows 2000 security system alone brought Windows 2000 Server products into parity with products such as Novell's NetWare, which, along with Banyan's Vines, brought network-wide directory services to PC-based systems a number of years ago. Also new to Windows 2000 Server was the extensive use of standard Internet protocols. The Domain Name System (DNS) ceased to be an add-on seemingly fastened to the Windows NT operating system with duct tape and rubber bands. With Windows 2000, it became the basis for both internal and external host name resolution. And the Lightweight Directory Access Protocol (LDAP), first used by Microsoft in Exchange Server 5.5, became an integral part of Windows 2000's Active Directory system. With Windows 2000, the Internet's Simple Mail Transport Protocol (SMTP) and the Network News Transport Protocol (NNTP) became essential parts of the Windows operating system.

Windows Server 2003 inherited all of the above and more from Windows 2000. Windows 2003 brings improvements to Active Directory, stronger overall application security support, enhanced disk storage reliability and availability, support for Internet Protocol version 6 (IPv6), and a number of smaller changes that make Windows 2003 a better operating system.

Exchange 2000 Server also included significant improvements over Exchange Server 5.5. However, Exchange 2000 was much more an evolutionary than revolutionary product. Some of the most significant Exchange Server 5.5 features, such as Exchange directory services, a model for Active Directory, were no longer available in Exchange 2000, having been extensively updated and integrated into the Windows 2000 Server line. Furthermore, a major portion of Exchange Server 5.5 management functionality was integrated into Windows Server 2000. This was a good move because it became easier to parcel out electronic messaging management functions to different people or groups. On the negative side, Exchange Server 5.5's all-in-one-place Administrator program was replaced by a seemingly dizzying array of disparate Windows 2000 management tools, officially called *Microsoft Management Console snap-ins*.

With some improvement, the features of Exchange 2000 Server were carried forward into Exchange 2003. Exchange 2003 features enhanced security, more secure and easier to use Internet browser access to Exchange mailboxes, better protection against e-mail–borne viruses, wireless access to Exchange Server, and easier migration from Exchange 5.5 and 2000.

One of my goals in writing this book is to facilitate your entry into the new and sometimes daunting world of Windows 2003/Exchange 2003. These two are especially daunting if you are still working with NT and Exchange 5.5. As the last few paragraphs indicate, I certainly have my work cut out for me.

You might be tempted to bypass this chapter because it seems to concentrate extensively on comparisons between Windows Server 2003 and Windows NT Server 4, as well as comparisons between Exchange Server 2003 and Exchange Server 5.5. "After all," you might say, "I'm new to both Windows Server 2003 and Exchange Server 2003. What do I need with all this comparison stuff?" My advice? Read this chapter. It contains a great deal of introductory information about both Windows Server 2003 and Exchange Server 2003. The time you'll spend reading it will not only give you the lowdown on the relationship between the two products, but it also will provide a strong base for the chapters to come. Try it! You'll like it! I promise.

Featured in this chapter:

◆ Key features of Windows Server 2003

◆ Key features of Exchange Server 2003

◆ End-user support is easy

NOTE *While a good historian might continue to make distinctions between Windows 2000 and Windows 2003 or Exchange 2000 and Exchange 2003, I'm going to limit such distinctions from here on. Except when I need to make a specific reference to Windows or Exchange 2000, I'll refer to "Exchange 2003" or "Windows 2003," though the 2003 products clearly owe their very existence to the 2000 product line. However, the clearer and more important distinction between Windows NT Server 4 and Exchange Server 5.5 and their 2003 counterparts will be emphasized in this and following chapters. Some might argue that NT and Exchange 5.5 are history and should be allowed to die a peaceful death. However, I'm sure that those from the thousands of sites still running NT and Exchange 5.5 would strongly disagree.*

Key Features of Windows Server 2003

"Wait a minute!" you say. "Isn't this a book about Exchange Server 2003? Why are we starting right off talking about Windows Server 2003?" The answer is quite simple.

Windows Server 2003 and Exchange Server 2003 are so tightly integrated that we really can't talk about one without talking about the other—and Windows Server 2003 must come first. That doesn't mean that you need to be an expert in every aspect of Windows Server 2003 to implement and support Exchange Server 2003. However, you will need a solid grounding in a number of aspects of Windows Server 2003. Therefore, I'm going to spend a fair amount of time in this book covering information that Exchange Server 2003 planners, designers, administrators, and managers need to know about Windows Server 2003 to do their jobs successfully.

As you can see in Figure 2.1, on the surface, Windows Server 2003 looks a lot like Microsoft's Windows 2000 Professional or XP desktop operating systems. But that's just the surface. Under the Windows 2003 GUI is an extremely powerful operating system designed to cover everything from the end-user desktop to the very high-end mainframe-oriented server environment.

FIGURE 2.1

On the surface, Windows Server 2003 looks like Windows 2000 Professional or XP.

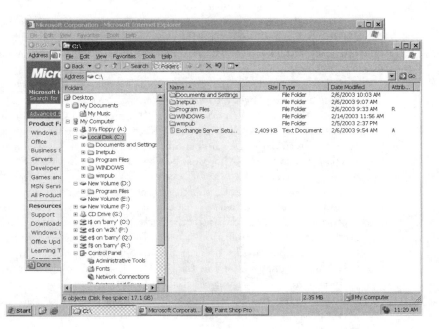

Windows Server 2003 is actually four different products. Each offers a different level of computing capacity and features. I'll talk about these in the section "The Four Flavors of Windows 2003" later in this chapter. Windows Server 2003 is a wonderfully well-thought-out amalgam of existing technologies, many of which are new to the Windows server environment or used in new ways. Some of these technologies were imported without change into Windows Server 2003. We'll take a look at the Windows 2003 product line later in this chapter. Let's begin with a discussion of the key features of Windows Server.

Active Directory, Security, and Internet Protocols

As you'll discover throughout this chapter, Windows Server 2003 is somewhat like a bride at a wedding, wearing something old, something new, something borrowed, and something blue.

First, let's examine the *old*. Some functionality in Windows Server 2003 remains unchanged from NT Server 4 and Windows 2000 Server. For example, the Control Panel still exists, albeit with fewer applets on display than NT Server 4's control panel because some functionality formerly in the Control Panel has moved elsewhere in Windows Server 2003. After you find the new homes for this functionality, you'll see that a number of other functions are performed exactly as in NT Server 4. For example, you no longer access the Open Database Connectivity (ODBC) interface through the

Control Panel. Instead, you start the applet through the Administrative Tools menu. For all this change, however, the ODBC interface itself is exactly the same in Windows 2003 as in Windows NT. In addition, you still manage the Windows Server 2003 desktop environment in pretty much the same way as with NT Server 4. More on this comes in the "What Hasn't Changed in Windows Server 2003?" section later in this chapter.

Very little in Windows Server 2003 is really *new*. What is new is the code that implements this massive operating system, and the mixture of old and borrowed functionality to create an exciting operating system with much greater capability and capacity than Windows NT Server and important improvements over Windows 2000 Server.

Microsoft *borrowed* heavily from Unix and from itself in creating Windows 2000 Server, and these changes are carried over into Windows Server 2003. From Unix came such things as the integration of the DNS into the Windows Server 2003 operating system. From the Unix world (if not exactly from Unix), Microsoft borrowed the Kerberos authentication system to beef up Windows Server security. From Banyan's Vines and Novell's NetWare—as well as one of my favorite products, Exchange Server 5.5—Microsoft borrowed the components upon which it built the very core of Windows Server 2003, Active Directory. If you know Exchange 5.5's directory service, you'll find that Windows Server 2003's Active Directory offers few surprises. Given this borrowing, you shouldn't be surprised to learn that certain queries against Active Directory are done using the LDAP protocol, which was used to query the Exchange 5.5 directory service. Also borrowed from Exchange 5.5 are sites and folder replication. Sites enable you to effectively link network segments over high- or low-bandwidth networks. Folder replication, in league with site links, lets users locally access network-based files, no matter how low the bandwidth is connecting their network to the rest of the network.

Finally comes something *blue*. I'm glad this one comes last because I have sort of a lame joke to tell here. It goes like this: As you know, Windows Server 2000/2003 are based on NT Server, and NT Server is based on OS/2 (remember that one?). OS/2 was developed jointly by Microsoft and IBM and then was taken over by IBM. Of course, IBM has long been referred to as—drum roll—*Big Blue*. Yeah, I know.

All joking aside, despite being based mostly in old and borrowed technologies, Windows Server 2003 is a very different beast than Windows NT Server. Let's take a look at some of Windows Server 2003's features. Then we'll spend a little time on what hasn't changed since Windows NT Server 4.

ACTIVE DIRECTORY AND SECURITY

I could write a whole book on Windows 2003 Active Directory and security. I'll discuss them in much more detail in Chapter 3, "Two Key Architectural Components of Windows Server 2003"; Chapter 6, "Upgrading to Windows Server 2003 and Exchange Server 2003"; Chapter 7, "Installing Windows Server 2003 as a Domain Controller"; Chapter 8, "Installing Exchange Server 2003"; Chapter 11, "Managing Exchange Users, Distribution Groups, and Contacts"; Chapter 16, "Advanced Exchange Server Administration and Management"; and Chapter 18, "Exchange Server System Security." For now, let me give you a quick overview.

Active Directory is a grand repository for information about such entities as users, domains, computers, domain controllers, shared resources (such as files and printers), and security. Active Directory lets you log into very large domains and use resources across the domain with ease. All objects in

Active Directory are protected by a security system based on Kerberos, an industry-standard secret-key encryption network authentication protocol developed at the Massachusetts Institute of Technology. (For more on Kerberos, see `http://web.mit.edu/kerberos/www`.) Windows Server 2003 controls who can see each object in Active Directory, what attributes each user can see, and what actions a user can perform on an object. The Windows 2003 permissions model is richer and more complex under the hood than NT's, but it's quite easy to manage at the user interface level. Windows 2003 group policies are also a significant improvement over NT 4's policies: For example, they enable you to set a range of policies for users and computers, determine what software can be installed on a computer, and tie the application of specific policies to Windows 2003 security groups.

Figure 2.2 shows the Properties dialog box for my Windows 2003 user account with the three major tools (Microsoft Management Console snap-ins) for Active Directory management: Active Directory Users and Computers, Active Directory Domains and Trusts, and Active Directory Sites and Services.

FIGURE 2.2

The three major tools for managing Windows Server 2003 Active Directory plus the Properties dialog box for a Windows 2003 user

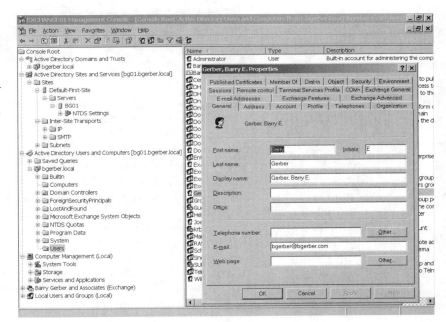

What's neat about the Windows 2003 User Properties dialog box is that it brings together functionality in the Windows NT 4 User Manager for Domains (the Account, Profile, and Terminal Services tabs, for example) and the Exchange 5.5 Administrator (the Exchange General and E-mail Addresses tabs, for example).

In fact, if you know Exchange 5.5, a lot of what you see in Active Directory should be quite familiar. The Properties dialog box in Figure 2.2 has a lot of the qualities of the Exchange 5.5 recipient mailbox Properties dialog box (see Figure 2.3).

FIGURE 2.3

Similarities exist between the Properties dialog box for a Windows 2003 user account and the Exchange 5.5 Mailbox Properties dialog box.

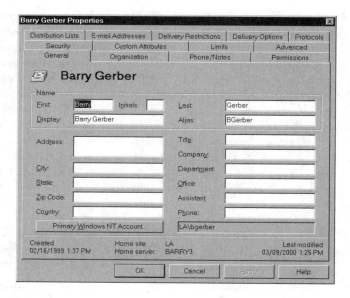

Exchange 5.5 users will also find the Active Directory Sites and Services snap-in familiar—at least the *Sites* part. Sites were used in Exchange 5.5 to integrate networks connected by slower non-LAN networking technologies into the overall Exchange environment. They ensure that continuous, high-speed connections aren't required for networks in the same organization to remain connected. Well, Microsoft has moved this sites technology from Exchange to Windows Server 2003. Microsoft implemented sites in Windows Server 2003 to make it possible to build large, single-domain Windows networks even if some segments of those networks were connected by relatively slow wide-area links. Servers can share Active Directory information and even files through site links. This is a major change in emphasis for Microsoft networking, and one that we'll revisit many times in this book.

NOTE *All of this Windows Server 2003 site stuff doesn't let Exchange Server 2003 managers off the hook. They'll still need to set up routing groups, the equivalent of Exchange 5.5 sites, and implement Exchange Server 2003 connectors between routing groups.*

Let's take a quick look at Active Directory from the user's point of view. Figure 2.4 illustrates the process of browsing available resources using Windows 2003's Add Printer and Find People tools. I can look for a networked printer using the traditional network browsing technique or I can find a printer in Active Directory. I can also search for a user in Active Directory. Double-clicking the user's name brings up a dialog box with a good deal of additional Active Directory information about the person.

FIGURE 2.4
End users can find resources and people in Active Directory.

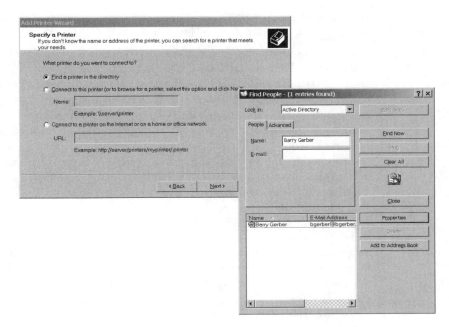

WINDOWS SERVER 2003: E-MAIL NOT INCLUDED

With one exception, e-mail services are not built into the Windows Server 2003 product line. The e-mail–related stuff that we just looked at in Active Directory doesn't exist until you install Exchange Server 2003 in a Windows 2003 domain. Unlike the Unix operating system, which comes with a working, if primitive, electronic messaging capability, Windows Server 2003 is almost mail-less without Exchange 2003. Well, maybe that's a bit of an overstatement. Although SMTP mail send and receive services do come with Windows 2003, standard Exchange mailbox services and POP3 and IMAP4 messaging servers are available only after Exchange 2003 is installed in a domain. Why does Windows 2003 have basic SMTP services? Windows 2003 uses SMTP for a good deal of its own systems-level communications.

How about third-party alternatives to Exchange Server 2003 for Windows Server 2003? There appear to be no technical barriers to third parties building their own fully functional messaging systems for Windows Server 2003 that use Windows Server 2003's basic SMTP services.

INTERNET PROTOCOLS

Windows 2000 Server introduced new functionality for the DNS and it gave a key role to the LDAP protocol. These changes remain in Windows Server 2003. Old Exchange Server 5.5 hands should know both of these intimately. Just as the concepts behind Active Directory were borrowed from Exchange 5.5, Microsoft also borrowed heavily from its implementation of LDAP in Exchange Server 5.5.

Domain Name System

NT 4 could get along quite well without DNS. You installed DNS mainly to locally support Internet name resolution—the conversion of external computer names to IP addresses, and vice versa. Although you could use DNS for local name resolution, it was usually done using NetBEUI or the Windows Internet Name Service (WINS), which resolves Microsoft NetBIOS workstation names to IP addresses.

Windows Server 2003 Active Directory can't run without DNS. As do Unix systems, Windows Server 2003 uses DNS to resolve internal as well as external computer names to IP addresses, and vice versa. Windows Server 2003 supports native NetBEUI networking, but mainly for migration from NT 4 to Windows 2003. WINS is still supported on Windows Server 2003, but only for legacy NT and other operating systems. The goal in a pure Windows Server 2003 network is for all name resolution services to be done by DNS. Put in other terms, to find the IP address of a computer on a Windows Server 2003 network, a computer should query a Windows Server 2003 running DNS.

These concepts are pretty easy to understand. However, you might scratch your head more than once trying to figure out why a Windows Server 2003 computer can't talk to an NT 4 computer on your network. The reason is very likely that you never installed NetBEUI on the Windows Server 2003. How do I know this? I've just about scratched off all the hair on the left side of my head.

A great feature of Windows Server 2003 DNS is that it can run in dynamic mode. In this mode, you can use the Dynamic Host Configuration Protocol (DHCP) to assign IP addresses to computers on your network and still have the more or less randomly assigned address correctly associated with the appropriate workstation name in the DNS.

Lightweight Directory Access Protocol

The LDAP was used in Exchange 5.5 to access information in the Exchange directory. That's also exactly what it's used for in Windows Server 2003, except that the target is Active Directory, not the no-longer-existent Exchange directory. Security willing, you can still search for e-mail addresses using an LDAP-compliant client. But, with Windows Server 2003/Exchange Server 2003, you're searching Windows Server 2003's Active Directory, not the Exchange directory. In fact, the search for Barry Gerber that I did in Figure 2.4 (shown earlier) used LDAP.

NOTE   *LDAP names use the X.500 format. The native Exchange Server address of a mailbox, for example, is in X.500 format (c = US; a = ; p = bgerber; o = LA; s = Gerber; g = Barry). Active Directory also supports Internet RFC 822 names (`bg@bgerber.com`), HTTP (Web) URL names (`http://bgerber.com`), and Microsoft UNC names (`\server1\share1`). Of course, LDAP is used only to access LDAP names. Other technologies are used to access RFC 882, HTTP, and UNC names.*

WHAT HAPPENED TO THOSE BACKUP DOMAIN CONTROLLERS?

Within a Windows NT Server 4 domain, you could have one primary and one or more secondary domain controllers. Domain controllers were the founts of network resource and security knowledge in NT 4 networks. If a primary domain controller crashed, the remaining secondary controllers held an election, and one of them became the primary domain controller. That has all changed in Windows Server 2003. All domain controllers in a Windows Server 2003 network are primary, to use an NT 4 term. Under almost all circumstances, you and Windows Server 2003 don't need to worry about failed controllers, or how and if a backup controller gets quickly and properly promoted to primary controller status. Everybody's equal.

Simple Mail Transport Protocol and Network News Transport Protocol

Two key Internet protocols that were once the exclusive province of Exchange 5.5—SMTP and NNTP—are now supported right inside Windows 2003. SMTP is used to replicate information across Windows 2003 sites. NNTP support is finally where it belongs: in the operating system. That doesn't mean that Exchange Server 2003 makes no use of these protocols, however. SMTP supports everything from Internet messaging to cross-server public folder replication in Exchange 2003, and NNTP is still supported through Exchange public folders.

Now let's look at some of the aspects of Windows Server 2003 that haven't changed all that much from Windows NT Server 4.

NOTE *One more thing before we move on: New to Windows Server 2003 is support for a fairly wide range of peripheral devices never supported by NT Server 4. Essentially, this includes pretty much the full range of devices supported by Windows XP, including support for DVD ROM and Universal Serial Bus (USB) devices. I love it; I'm running a USB video camera on one of my Windows 2003 Advanced Server computers. Like Windows 2000, Windows 2003 also supports auto-discovery and installation of new devices. This little feature has saved me hours of finding and manually installing drivers for new printers and such.*

New Features of Windows Server 2003

Among a number of other things, Windows Server 2003 includes improvements in Active Directory over and above Windows 2000 Server: easier deployment and management, increased security, and better performance and dependability. Additionally, overall security has been strengthened and support for applications that run on Windows Server 2003 has been significantly updated.

Improvements on the storage side, so important to smooth and reliable Exchange Server operations, include snapshot backups of disk volumes, system-level open file backup, and much easier Storage Area Network (SAN) management. On the networking side, Windows Server 2003 supports IPv6 for increased security and a solution to the rapid depletion of Internet Protocol (IP) addresses.

What Hasn't Changed in Windows Server 2003?

A great deal of the functionality in NT Server 4 was imported directly into Windows Server 2000 and still exists in Windows 2003. Although the code underlying this functionality might have changed somewhat, the user interface is often exactly or nearly the same.

Active Directory has brought many changes to resource management and security, but you can still access a lot of network resources in the same way that you did using NT Server 4. For example, you can still map a network drive using the familiar drive-mapping interface that you know and love from NT Server 4. Well, I should qualify that: The interface looks a little more artsy and "Webbish," but it works just like the interface in NT Server 4. In addition, you can still use the Printers applet in the Control Panel to add and manage printers.

You still manage your desktop by right-clicking it; the same holds true for the Taskbar, for you Task Manager aficionados. Aside from some Windows XP–related changes, the Windows Server 2003 desktop looks pretty much like the NT Server 4 desktop. For example, the Taskbar works just as it does in NT Server 4; it just looks like the Windows XP Taskbar and shares that Taskbar's enhanced functionality.

You can run a new-look version of the old NT 4 Explorer from the Start menu. Explorer lets you browse your computer and the network. Now you have another option, My Computer, which is also run from the Start menu. It's a little different from Explorer, but you should be pretty comfortable using it, as long as you disable Web content in folders and click the Folders button on My Computer's Standard toolbar.

As I mentioned earlier, although some functions no longer occupy a prominent place in the Windows Server 2003 Control Panel, when you find them, they function pretty much as they did in NT Server 4. For example, the ODBC applet icon is no longer available when you open the Control Panel. Where is it? It's on the Administrative Tools submenu of the Start menu and is called Data Sources (ODBC). Of course, technically, ODBC is still on the Control Panel because there's an Administrative Tools icon on the Control Panel. You just have to remember to click open Administrative Tools to see ODBC.

On the other hand, some old functions are actually easier to find. For example, although there's still a Network icon on the Control Panel, now called *Network Connections*, the same icon shows as a more easily accessed suboption of the Control Panel in Windows Server 2003. Control Panel suboptions pretty much replace the old Programs ➢ Settings option in Windows 2000. I can't tell you how much time these little enhancements have saved me. I access the Network configuration applet several times a day, and with Windows Server 2003, I no longer have to go to the Control Panel, click it open, and then double-click the Network icon to open it.

Even some things that might seem new to you really aren't. As Figure 2.2 (shown earlier) illustrates, you'll be using a number of new tools—Microsoft Management Console snap-ins, to be precise—to manage your Windows Server 2003 environment. However, while the tools are new, Microsoft Management Console (MMC), the place where you snap in and run these tools (the master window in Figure 2.2, titled EXCHANGE01 Management Console), is far from new. MMC has been used since the dawn of the NT Server 4 Option Pack to manage such NT Server add-ons as Internet Information Server.

As you can see, a lot hasn't changed between NT Server 4 and Windows Server 2003. And I've only skimmed the surface here, focusing on the kinds of functionality that are key to really basic Windows Server 2003 management. As you work with Windows Server 2003, you discover lots more under the hood that's pure NT 4 Server.

Windows Server 2003 Versus NT 4 Server

After reading about Windows Server 2003 in this section, you've probably got a fair picture of key differences and similarities between Microsoft's new server product line and its older NT 4 Server products. Let me quickly summarize these and emphasize their significance.

Active Directory and Kerberos-based security are the most important additions to the Windows Server 2003 product line. Active Directory with Kerberos security provides a new way to organize, protect, and access network resources. Large, single-domain networks are now not only possible, but highly desirable. The Active Directory tree and Windows 2003's new security model make it easy for managers to administer all or part of an organization's resources and for users to access all or part of those resources.

With Active Directory taking center stage in Windows Server 2003, you use the Active Directory Users and Computers snap-in to create new users and manage existing users. NT Server's User Manager for Domains is a thing of the past. NT Server's Server Manager has been replaced by this and other tools.

As I noted earlier, Windows Server 2003 supports native NetBEUI for migrations from NT 4 to Windows 2003. However, you shouldn't use it once migrations have been completed. If you, like I, have been cheating by running NetBEUI in nonrouted networks, you'll have to be sure to manually install NetBEUI or move to a full DNS-supported network naming environment. I recommend the DNS route.

As for the similarities between Windows Server 2003 and NT Server 4, when your first Windows Server 2003 starts up, you should find its basic user interface quite familiar, especially if you've worked with Windows 2000 or XP. Much in the basic Windows interface was borrowed from older Windows products. Also, although you might have to search a bit to find it, you'll often discover that functionality available in NT 4 Server has familiar user interfaces in Windows Server 2003.

Now let's take a look at the different products bearing the Windows 2003 name.

The Four Flavors of Windows Server 2003

Windows 2003 is packaged as four separate editions:

◆ Standard

◆ Enterprise

◆ Datacenter

◆ Web

The Enterprise and Datacenter editions of Windows Server 2003 are available in 64-bit versions, which run on Intel Itanium-based computers.

As I mentioned earlier, I'll use the term *Windows Server 2003* when I refer to the server products collectively. I'll refer to the specific edition of Windows 2003 when necessary for clarity. Let's take a look at the various flavors of Windows 2003.

STANDARD EDITION

Windows Server 2003 fully supports Active Directory and Windows 2003 security. It can run on computers with one to four processors and up to 4GB of RAM. Microsoft recommends using Windows Server 2003 to support file and print sharing, small databases, moderate throughput World Wide Web services, and the group (nonenterprise) mail services available in the standard edition of Exchange Server 2003.

ENTERPRISE EDITION

Windows Server 2003 Enterprise Edition is the middle-level product in the Windows Server 2003 line. It runs on machines with up to eight processors and up to 32GB of RAM (up to 64GB in the 64-bit version). Windows Server 2003 Enterprise Edition supports server clustering. With server clustering, you can build multi-computer redundant systems, where the cluster can continue operating even if one computer or more fails.

DATACENTER EDITION

Windows 2003 Datacenter Server is the steamroller of Windows Server 2003 products. It's the monster server for the highest-demand applications. It can run on computers with up to 64 processors and the 64-bit version supports up to 512GB of RAM. Wow! It also supports up to 8-node server clustering.

Microsoft recommends Datacenter Server for really heavy-duty database and Internet applications. It's also the place to run Exchange Server 2003 Enterprise Edition if you've got lots of users.

Microsoft also suggests that you use Datacenter Server to consolidate existing Windows NT or 2000 domains. Windows Server 2003 allows for much larger domains in terms of resources and users than either Windows NT or Windows 2000. Microsoft encourages new adopters of its Windows Server 2003 products to think in terms of big domains—really big domains—and it strongly advises that those converting from NT 4 or Windows 2000 to Windows Server 2003 should consolidate domains. In many cases, Microsoft argues, all you really need with Windows Server 2003 is one overarching domain.

WEB EDITION

The Web Edition of Windows Server 2003 is designed to support, you guessed it, Web-based applications. It's really not a home for non-Web apps. So we really don't need to spend any more time talking about it.

NOTE   *You might be wondering what happened to Windows 2003 Professional, the desktop version of Windows 2003. As of this writing, a Professional version is not expected. Rather, Windows XP Professional will serve as Microsoft's desktop product until it's time for a new desktop release. Then, who knows what the new version might be named?*

Now we're ready to take a look at Exchange Server 2003.

Exchange Server 2003 Features

Well, we're finally in Exchange Server 2003 territory. You'll find that the time we've given to Windows Server 2003 was far from wasted. Let's jump right into the similarities and differences between Exchange Server 5.5 and Exchange Server 2003. Then we'll take a look at the two products in the Exchange 2003 line: Exchange Server 2003 Standard Edition and Exchange Server 2003 Enterprise Edition.

Unlike the section on what's new in Windows Server 2003, I'm going to mix the new and the old in one section. This should cut down on some frustration, especially if you're an Exchange Server 5.5 user, because so much of what's old is hidden behind a set of new doors. If I don't open those doors in addition to showing them to you, and instead make you wait for a section on what's not changed in Exchange Server 2003, you're going to hate me by the end of the chapter!

NOTE   *As with Windows Server 2003 and Windows 2000 Server, Exchange Server 2003 relies heavily on Exchange 2000 Server. Most of what I talk about in this section came to us in Exchange 2000 Server. Again, as with my discussion of Windows Server 2003 and Windows NT Server 4, I'll use the term* Exchange Server 2003 *to cover Exchange 2000 and 2003 and Exchange 5.5. I'll make no distinction between 2000 or 2003 as the source of a feature, unless 2003 brings something new to the table when compared with Exchange 2000.*

In many ways, Exchange Server 2003 is new for what has been removed rather than for what has been added. Exchange 5.5 directory services have been replaced by Windows Server 2003 Active Directory services. Exchange Server 5.5 sites have been replaced by routing groups. These changes have led to a number of changes in the user interfaces that you use to manage Exchange Server 2003. Much of what previously was managed in Exchange Server 5.5's Administrator program is now managed either in Active Directory interfaces or in Windows Server 2003–based Microsoft Management Console snap-ins designed specifically for Exchange Server 2003.

If you're looking for really new stuff in Exchange Server 2003, you'll have to turn to things such as storage groups. So let's take a look at what's new, by this definition, in Exchange Server 2003.

Bye-Bye, Exchange Directory Services

As I noted earlier, Microsoft beefed up and extended Exchange 5.5's directory service and then turned it into Windows Server 2003's Active Directory. So, some of the things that you previously did in Exchange Server 5.5 user interfaces, you now do in an Active Directory interface. For example, you use an Active Directory user interface to enable a user's mailbox and to create what used to be called *custom recipients* (now *contacts*) and *distribution lists* (now *distribution groups*).

Figure 2.5 illustrates the process of adding a new Exchange Server 2003 distribution group to my Windows 2003 Active Directory. I'm creating this group in exactly the same place as I'd create a Windows Server 2003 security group. You should know local and global security groups from NT Server 4.

FIGURE 2.5

Creating an Exchange Server 2003 distribution group in Windows Server 2003's Active Directory

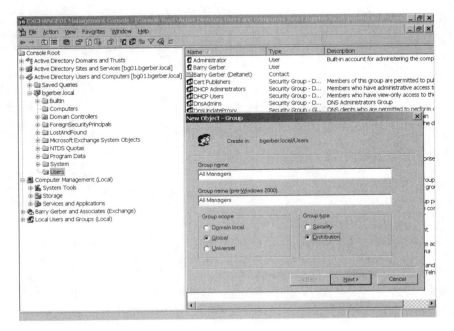

One of the major differences between a distribution group and a Windows Server 2003 security group is that one has an attribute identifying it as a distribution group and the other has an attribute identifying it as a security group. When an address list (the global address list, for example) is created and updated on an Exchange Server 2003, all eligible Active Directory groups with the distribution group attribute are included in that address list.

Figure 2.6 shows the dialog box for managing an Exchange Server 2003 distribution group. I opened it by double-clicking the All Managers row in the window just in back of the All Managers dialog box. You add e-mail addresses to the distribution group on the Members property page and then add the distribution group to other distribution groups on the Member Of property page. We'll get into the creation of Exchange Server 2003 recipients later in Chapter 11 and Chapter 12, "Managing the Exchange Server Hierarchy and Core Components." For now, I hope you're beginning to see how important it is to know how to use and manage Active Directory to manage Exchange 2003 recipient objects.

FIGURE 2.6

Managing an Exchange Server 2003 distribution group

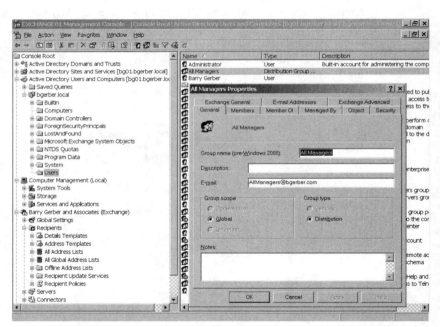

Just so you don't get the idea that all recipient management is done in the Active Directory snap-in, take a look at Figure 2.7. Here, I'm using an Exchange Server 2003 snap-in for Microsoft Management Console to view and manage the default domain addresses assigned to recipients in my Exchange 2003 system. For example, I can edit my default SMTP (Internet mail) domain address, `@bgerber.com`.

FIGURE 2.7

Managing recipient policies using an Exchange Server 2003 Microsoft Management Console snap-in

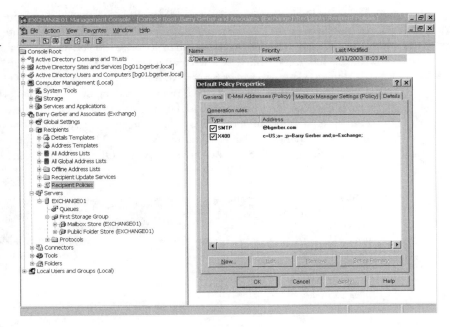

It's important to realize that, although I'm using an interface other than an Active Directory snap-in to manage these recipient objects, the objects and attributes that I'm managing still live in Active Directory. For the most part, Microsoft has very carefully isolated interfaces related to Exchange Server 2003 to assure that they show up in logical places. It makes sense to manage user mailboxes, distribution groups, and custom recipients in the Active Directory interface. It doesn't make sense to manage generic recipient attributes such as default e-mail domain names in the Active Directory Users and Computers interface.

Look at some of the other objects in the container called Recipients in the Barry Gerber and Associates (Exchange) container. Many of these should be familiar to Exchange Server 5.5 users, such as the template and address list objects.

Bye-Bye, Exchange Server Sites

Exchange Server 5.5 users will remember Exchange Server 5.5 sites as a tool both for allowing lower-bandwidth network links between servers in the same Exchange organization and for implementing distributed administrative access to groups of Exchange servers in the same organization. Say that you had an office in Los Angeles and one in New York, and the link between the two was a T1 line. With Exchange Server 5.5, it would be best to put each of the offices in its own Exchange site and connect the two sites using some sort of site connector. Site connectors didn't require continuous, high-speed connectivity to keep Exchange 5.5 directories and public folders synchronized. They communicate primarily using X.400- or SMTP-based data protocols.

Just as Exchange site connectors allowed geographically distributed Exchange 5.5 servers to participate in the same Exchange organization, Windows Server 2003 site connectors are key to building larger Windows Server 2003 domains. No longer do you have to create separate domains just because your servers are separated by low-bandwidth networks. Just link your Windows 2003 sites into a single domain using Windows Server 2003 sites.

Exchange Server 5.5 allowed for multiple redundant connectors between sites and for setting priorities between site connectors based on the bandwidth available on different connectors. Thus, you could use a T1 line for your daily site link, but specify that a DSL or even dial-up link should be used if the T1 were not available. Windows Server 2003 sites allow for similar site link prioritization options. See Figure 2.8 for a view of the Active Directory user interface for managing Windows Server 2003 sites.

FIGURE 2.8

Managing Windows
Server 2003 sites
using
the Active Directory
Sites and Services
Microsoft Management Console
snap-in

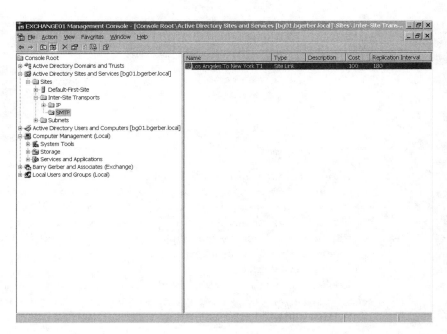

Exchange Server 2003 servers separated by lower bandwidth can still be grouped and connected to compensate for lower-bandwidth wide-area links. You don't use Windows Server 2003 sites. Instead, you use what are called *message routing groups* in Exchange Server 2003. After you're over the different naming convention, all is pretty much the same, including how you set up and use Exchange connectors. Distributed administration of groups of Exchange servers is not implemented in routing groups. Rather, Exchange 2003 administrative groups support distributed management. In Exchange 2003 message routing and distributed management have been separated, which, as many Exchange 5.5 administrators will attest, is a very good thing. Lots more on all of this will come in later chapters.

"New" User Interfaces

By way of Exchange 2000 Server, Exchange Server 2003 is chock-full of new user interfaces. Well, maybe that's a bit of an exaggeration. The interfaces aren't always all that new. Where they're located is. Borrowing an analogy from earlier in this chapter, the doors are new. What's behind them is pretty much the same. Let me talk a bit about some of the "new" interfaces that we haven't already covered.

Figure 2.9 shows the user interface for Exchange 2003 provided by the Exchange System Manager snap-in. Exchange 5.5 users will recognize a number of familiar management functions. From top to bottom, you deal here with Exchange organization-wide (global) property settings, property settings relating to Exchange 2003 recipients, server management, which includes Exchange Server 2003 storage groups and the management of a range of Internet and other protocols.

FIGURE 2.9

The Exchange System Manager Microsoft Management Console snap-in

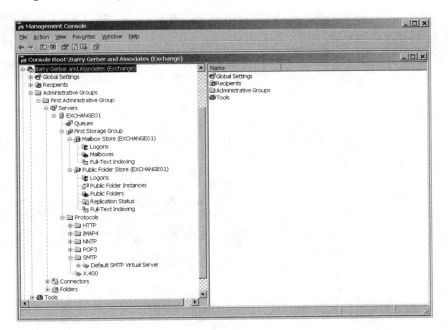

Services for both NNTP and SMTP are installed when you install Windows Server 2003. Both are required if you're going to install Exchange Server 2003. Before you install Exchange Server 2003, these two interfaces live in the Internet Information Server snap-in. After you install Exchange 2003, the interfaces move to the Exchange container shown in Figure 2.9. It took me a while to realize this and, thus, to find these interfaces after I installed Exchange Server 2003.

NOTE *As a Windows Server 2003 service, SMTP is used mostly for Windows 2003 communications; NNTP supports those neat-to-nasty Internet newsgroups. Both of these services can function just fine without Exchange Server 2003. When Exchange Server 2003 is installed, SMTP services are modified to provide Exchange 2003 mailbox users with Internet message transfer functionality, and NNTP services are enhanced to allow Exchange 2003 users to see select newsgroups in Exchange 2003 public folders. As you'll see in Chapters 13, "Managing Exchange 2003 Internet Services," and 14, "Managing Exchange 2003 Services for Internet Clients," both services are significantly enhanced when Exchange Server 2003 is installed.*

Now take a look at Figure 2.10, which shows the organization-wide System Manager user interface for Exchange Server 2003. You actually saw this interface back in Figures 2.7 and 2.9. I've just expanded it a bit here so that you can see a lot more of what's inside the container. Again, old hands at Exchange Server 5.5 will recognize a wide range of interfaces formerly found in the Exchange Server Administrator.

Notice the last container visible in Figure 2.10, the Message Tracking Center. It occupies the same level in the Microsoft Management Console hierarchy as the Barry Gerber and Associates (Exchange) organization-wide container (the highest-level container in Exchange System Manager). You'll notice that the tracking center is also visible in the Tools container within the Barry Gerber and Associates (Exchange) container. This is one of the neat capabilities of Microsoft Management Console. Not only do many containers (and their user interfaces) live within other containers, but they also can exist independently of those containers. I was able to install a separate instance of message tracking outside the Exchange Server 2003 System Manager container. This way, to get to message tracking, I don't need to drill down into the System Manager container to find it.

FIGURE 2.10

The organization-wide system manager user interface for Exchange Server 2003

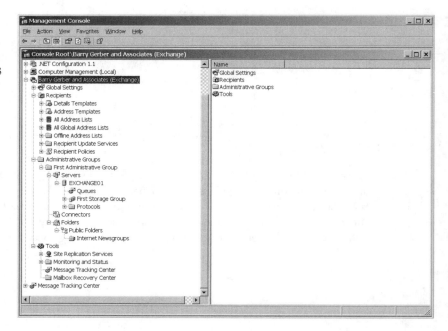

Storage Groups

As should be clear by now, from an Exchange administrator's perspective and in general, basic administration hasn't changed all that much with Exchange Server 2003. After you figure out where you have to go to do whatever you previously did in the Exchange Server Administrator program, doing it is much like doing it in Exchange Server 5.5. There are a few new features in Exchange 2003. The key new feature is storage groups.

Exchange Server 5.5 allowed for one private store and one public store per server. Exchange Server 2003 lets you create your own groups of information stores, called *storage groups* (see Figure 2.9, shown earlier). It also gives you the capability to group up to six private and public information store databases within a single storage group.

In Exchange Server 2003, private information stores are called *mailbox stores*, and public information stores answer to the name *public folder stores*. All the storage groups in an Exchange Server 2003 installation are contained in the *information store*. Storage groups enable you to organize mailboxes and public folders logically—departmentally or geographically, for example—across your organization. This helps you manage multiple mailbox and public information stores; additionally, you can back up and restore information store databases independently. This makes backups and restores faster and also allows you to back up or restore one information store database while other databases are still accessible to users. Exchange 2003 brings a new kind of storage group to the table, recovery storage groups. You can use these to restore mailbox stores so that you can recover one or more mailboxes.

File System Support and Full-Text Indexing

A couple of other features that originated in Exchange 2000 and come pretty close to qualifying as radically new are support for file system–based access to the Exchange information store and fully indexed text searches within Exchange mailboxes and public folders. There's no question that Exchange 2003's support for file system access to certain Exchange objects qualifies as really new to Exchange Server 2003. Based on your security privileges, you can march through the information store just as though it were a on a disk drive. With proper mapping, you can use a GUI-based file interface such as My Computer or command-line utilities such as DIR, looking at different mailboxes and public folders. And file system access opens a whole range of Exchange-based application development options using products ranging from Microsoft and third-party word processing programs to sophisticated applications developed in Visual Basic and C++.

Built-in full-text indexing is a great addition to Exchange Server 2003. This feature significantly speeds up searches for specific text in Exchange messages. Full-text indexing can be extended to message attachments, making it possible to search attachment content for the first time.

Upgrades

Exchange Server 2003 includes a number of upgrades from Exchange 2000 Server. Exchange 2003 brings enhanced security at several levels. Exchange 2003 is set for maximum security on installation, rather than depending on administrators to figure out all of the hoops they need to jump through to secure Exchange. Outlook Web Access (Internet browser access to Exchange mailboxes) is not only more secure, but it has a look and feel more like Outlook 2003. The Exchange 2003 anti-virus application programming interface (API) supports more virus- and spam-catching options. Wireless access to Exchange Server 2003 is greatly improved when compared to Exchange 2000 options. And, hallelujah, migration to Exchange Server 2003 from Exchange 5.5, or Exchange 2000 for that matter, has been greatly simplified.

A few features of Exchange 2000 Server were removed from Exchange Server 2003. These include real-time collaboration features, the M: drive and Key Management Services.

Real-time collaboration features such as chat, Instant Messaging, Exchange Conferencing Server, and Multimedia Messaging are gone. Some of these features will work if you upgrade from Exchange 2000 Server, but if you need these features for new installations of Exchange 2003, you'll have to install Microsoft's new real-time communications and collaboration server code-named Greenwich at the time of this writing.

The default M: drive mapping gave you file system–based access to the Exchange information store. By and large, it was more trouble than it was worth, leading to corruption of the mailbox store when file-based operations such as backup were performed. You can still access the information store through the file system, but you have to set up the drive mapping, use the special *server**sharename* that points to the information store directly, or use the *server**sharename* itself.

Key Management Services supported sending secure messages through Exchange Server. That feature is now fully supported by Windows Server 2003's public key infrastructure. So Key Management Services are no longer required.

Exchange Server 2003 versus Exchange Server 5.5

Exchange Server 2003 is an evolutionary product. Features such as directory services and sites migrated from Exchange 5.5 to the Windows 200*x* product line as Active Directory and Server sites. Exchange 2003 message routing groups serve the function of Exchange 5.5 sites.

Exchange Server 5.5 administrators will require some time to get accustomed to the fact that the functionality of the singular Exchange Server 5.5 Administrator user interface has been divided into a set of logical but quite different Microsoft Management Console snap-ins. This book is dedicated in part to opening and explicating this maze of new interfaces for both old Exchange Server 5.5 hands and those new to Exchange Server with version 2003.

Key new features of Exchange Server 2003 when compared to Exchange 5.5 are storage groups and full-text indexing. Storage groups enable you to put multiple mailbox and public folder databases on an Exchange Server 2003, and they make it easier to manage multiple mailbox and public folder databases. Full-text indexing speeds up searches through Exchange messages while adding the capability to search attachments.

Exchange Server 2003 added enhanced security, improvements to the Web interface to Exchange Server mailboxes, better anti-virus protection, and easier migration from Exchange 5.5 and 2000 to Exchange 2003. Exchange Server 2003 removed real-time collaboration to a new Microsoft server, the M: drive, and Key Management Services, replacing the latter with native Windows Server 2003 security services.

Now let's take a quick look at the Exchange Server 2003 product line.

Getting a Handle on Exchange Server 2003 Versions

Unlike the Windows 2003 product line, there are only two versions of Exchange Server 2003: Standard Edition and Enterprise Edition. Table 1.1 shows some of the similarities and differences between the two products.

TABLE 2.1: FEATURES OF EXCHANGE SERVER 2003 STANDARD AND ENTERPRISE EDITIONS

FEATURE	STANDARD EDITION	ENTERPRISE EDITION
Storage	Limited to 16GB	Unlimited
Multiple database support	No (1 storage group with 1 mailbox store and 1 public folder store)	Yes (up to 20)
Connectivity to other systems	Yes (except X.400)	Yes
Windows clustering support	No	Yes

The key differences between the Standard and Enterprise editions of Exchange Server 2003 relate to the amount of storage available and support for multiple storage groups (databases), X.400 connectivity, and Windows Server 2003 fail-safe clustering capabilities. Both products include Internet mail, and connectivity to other e-mail systems, including Lotus Notes and Microsoft Mail.

PLANNING: THERE'S REALLY NO CHOICE BUT TO DO IT

I've always been a big advocate of planning for software installations. With Windows Server 2003 and Exchange Server 2003, not planning is sure death. For example, to set up your Windows Server 2003 domain or domains without planning is to invite misery of the worst kind. To install Exchange Server 2003 before your domain model is clearly established almost assures that you'll spend double, triple, or even quadruple the time fixing things after the fact.

We'll talk about domain planning later in great detail, especially in Chapter 5, "Designing a New Exchange 2003 System," and Chapter 6, "Upgrading to Windows Server 2003 and Exchange Server 2003." Suffice it to say that Microsoft designed both Windows 2003 and Exchange 2003 with a certain organizational model in mind.

Windows Server 2003 is flexible, but there are some things that you can't change without totally reinstalling it. Your domain structure is one of these things. You can add domains to an existing domain structure, and you can even create a new and separate domain structure. But you can't delete your master domain and start over, and you can't rename your domain. Although these domains need not cement your Internet mail-addressing scheme, it's a lot easier if you can keep your Windows Server 2003 domains and Internet messaging domains in sync.

A number of the chapters in this part of the book touch on planning. Bypass them at your peril. 'Nuff said.

Exchange Server 2003 runs on Windows Server 2003 or Windows 2000 Server with Service Pack 3 or later installed. Any Windows 2000 Server that will serve as a domain controller or global catalog for Exchange Server 2003 must also have been upgraded to Service Pack 3 or later. Exchange Server 2003 Standard Edition runs on any version of Windows 2000 or 2003. Exchange Server 2003 Enterprise Edition requires Windows 2000 or 2003 Enterprise or Datacenter Edition.

End-User Support Is Easy

So, how do you feel about Exchange Server 2003 and its constant companion, Windows Server 2003? Ready to move on? Discouraged? If you're feeling a bit daunted, don't give up quite yet. For all the newness and complexity in Microsoft's new Windows and Exchange products, Exchange Server 2003 and Windows Server 2003 are conquerable. Both products offer the end user a comfortable and often better working environment than did their predecessors.

End users will hardly realize that they're using new server operating and electronic messaging systems. Logging into the network will look pretty much the same, and so will accessing file shares and printers. If they're using Outlook, POP3, or IMAP4 e-mail clients, all will appear almost exactly the same. Only users accessing Exchange Server 2003 through Outlook Web Access—that is, using their Web browser—will experience a noticeable difference. And that will be a pleasant experience, as Figure 2.11 shows.

I mean, look at that interface! It looks almost like the Outlook 2003 client. And take a close look at what I'm doing in this figure. Yes, I'm dragging a message from my Inbox and dropping it into a folder that I created a minute ago while in the Web interface. Is that cool, or what?

FIGURE 2.11

Exchange Server 2003's implementation of Outlook Web Access

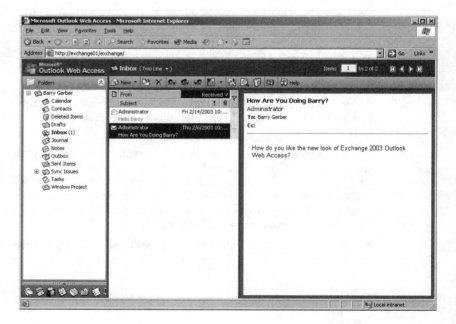

The bottom line is that you're going to have to stretch some to get your arms around Windows Server 2003 and Exchange Server 2003. The good news is that you won't have to worry much about supporting users as they access what's on these server products. And there are even a few really nice rewards for users, including the new Outlook Web Access support offered by Exchange Server 2003. Wonderful world!

In the next chapter, I'll spend a little time discussing some key information that you need to get started with Windows 2003 and Exchange 2003. Join me.

Summary

Like Exchange 2000 and Windows 2000, Exchange Server 2003 is tightly integrated with Windows Server 2003. As with other systems (Unix comes immediately to mind), with Windows Server 2003 and Exchange Server 2003, it's often difficult to tell where the operating system leaves off and the electronic messaging system begins. Integration has its price: It demands very careful planning, and after you've implemented Windows and Exchange 2003, it will keep you or those with whom you work hopping from one interface to the other to create and manage the myriad objects required to make a complex electronic messaging system work.

Windows Server 2003 is an evolutionary product featuring Active Directory, Microsoft's first system-wide user and resource directory borrowed in part from earlier implementations of Exchange, much stronger reliance on Internet standards (including DNS and LDAP), and advanced security based on Kerberos. Much of Windows 2003 hasn't changed, from the Windows GUI look and feel, to starting network drive mapping from the Explorer Tools menu. With Windows Server 2003, size does matter. Four server editions exist. The first three, in order of potential capacity and system redundancy, are Standard, Enterprise, and Datacenter. The Enterprise and Datacenter editions support either 32-bit or 64-bit CPUs. Windows Server 2003 Web Edition, the fourth Windows 2003 server, is designed to support Web-based applications.

Exchange Server 2003 is also more of an evolutionary than revolutionary product. With a good portion of Exchange 5.5's innards appropriated for use in Windows Server 2000/2003, Exchange 2000/2003 is somewhat less than it was in former incarnations. Maintenance of most recipients is done in Windows 2003 Active Directory interfaces, not Exchange 2003 interfaces. Windows 2003 provides basic SMTP and NNTP services. Exchange 2003 enhances these and incorporates them into a sophisticated electronic communications environment. Exchange 2003 sports a fair number of innovative features carried forward from Exchange 2000, including storage groups and full-text indexing. Exchange comes in two sizes, Standard and Enterprise. The former, best suited to smaller electronic messaging environments, runs on all flavors of Windows Server 2003 but Web Edition. The Enterprise edition requires Windows Server 2003 Enterprise or Datacenter Edition.

The best news regarding Microsoft's new Windows and Exchange products is for end users. Combined, the two products promise end users better access to the precious data and information stored in Windows server-based computing environments.

We're not finished with Windows 2003, not by a long shot. In Chapter 3, we'll look in more detail at Windows 2003's Active Directory and networking. Exchange Server 2003 is so dependent on these that you have to get a good handle on them before you can move on to Exchange itself.

Chapter 3

Two Key Architectural Components of Windows Server 2003

IF YOU'RE NEW TO the Windows and Exchange 200*x* product line, I suspect you're going to have a lot of what I like to call *Escher moments.* I'm sure you've seen those drawings in which a guy is walking up a set of stairs that suddenly seem to be going down. That certainly was my experience with both Windows 2000 Server and Exchange 2000 Server. I'd be reading something in the documentation or trying to fix a problem in the software itself, sure that I was on the right track, and then suddenly things veered off, leaving me without a solution and with less time to find one.

Windows and Exchange 2003 are no easier if you're coming to them anew or from NT 4. So, in this chapter, I'll cover the two biggest problems that I encountered in my early work with Windows Server 2003. These relate to the architectures of Active Directory and Windows 200*x* Server networking.

Featured in this chapter:

- ◆ What you need to know about Active Directory right now
- ◆ What you need to know about Windows Server 2003 network architecture

What You Need to Know about Active Directory Right Now

Hands down, Active Directory is the most important piece of Windows Server 2003 architecture that you need to understand. Almost everything in Windows Server 2003 revolves around Active Directory.

There's a lot to know about Active Directory. I'm not going to tell you everything that you need to know in great detail in this chapter. Rather, my goal here is to expose you to key concepts that will arm you for coming chapters and for your first experiences with Active Directory. In later chapters, I'll get into the nitty-gritty detail that you need to make your Windows Server 2003 and Exchange Server 2003 environments work.

ACTIVE DIRECTORY ISN'T THE WHOLE HOUSE

Don't let my emphasis here on Active Directory as the linchpin of Windows Server 2003 architecture lead you to believe that Active Directory is all there is. For example, Windows Server 2003's file system, NT File System 5 (NTFS 5), is a pretty impressive piece of work. Along with all the neat stuff imported from NT Server, including full integration of distributed file system technology, the file system is tightly integrated with Active Directory. In addition, NTFS 5 includes built-in disk quotas, file defragmentation, and file/subdirectory encryption.

Another key piece of Windows Server 2003 architecture is site-based routing and folder replication. Borrowed from Exchange Server 5.5, site-based routing and folder replication enable Windows Server 2003 servers to live anywhere that they need to and to communicate with other computers on a Windows Server 2003 network using whatever bandwidth technology is available and affordable. Site-based routing and folder replication are key to large, single-domain Windows Server 2003 networks.

That's not all of the new architecture, but it reinforces the idea that although Active Directory is the foundation and the framework of Windows Server 2003 architecture, it is not the entire building.

Active Directory: Five Major Architectural Components

Here's the story in a nutshell: To begin understanding Active Directory, you need to understand five of its key components: namespaces, forests, trees, domains, and objects.

- Every instance of Active Directory is a namespace.

- An Active Directory namespace encompasses one and only one forest.

- A forest consists of one or more trees.

- Trees include one or more domains.

- Each domain lives on its own server or set of servers.

How you use forests, trees, and domains depends at least in part on how your organization is structured. All the resources in an Active Directory namespace—forests, trees, domains, users, printers, files, and so on—are objects. Objects are often containers that can hold other objects. For example, a domain is a container that can hold, among other things, subdomains.

In practical terms, if you use a Microsoft Management Console Active Directory snap-in to manage a specific Active Directory, you will see all the domains and subobjects in the forest that are supported by that Active Directory, no matter which specific computer or set of computers any particular domain resides on. Figure 2.2, back in Chapter 2, "Windows Server 2003 and Exchange Server 2003," shows the major Active Directory snap-ins in action.

Let's look at each of Active Directory's components in more detail.

NAMESPACES

Like all directories, Active Directory is at heart a namespace with subnamespaces and subsub-namespaces and subsubsub...Well, you get the point. A directory namespace is the place that holds the names of objects. You look in a namespace to find an object and whatever other information you need to use an object. Namespaces are hierarchical in nature. As noted previously, the Microsoft Management Console snap-ins that we explored in Chapter 2 graphically present a variety of views of the Windows Server 2003 Active Directory namespace.

It's important to note that, in a very real sense, namespaces are concepts, not visible entities. What you see in Microsoft Management Console are the various objects that exist in the Active Directory namespace. You really don't see the namespace, per se; you see a very nice representation of Active Directory itself, which is the container for all the objects in the Active Directory namespace. Of course, all of this doesn't mean that understanding the concept of namespaces isn't important to understanding Windows Server 2003's Active Directory. *Au contraire.* Without a clear understanding of namespaces, you'll never master Active Directory. (Also, all of this doesn't mean that I and others won't slip occasionally and refer to the Active Directory namespace as though it were a real container for names.)

Let's start with an example of a namespace. The Internet Domain Name System (DNS) is a namespace. Its major function is to tie natural-language names to IP addresses because the TCP/IP protocol uses IP addresses for intercomputer communication, not the natural-language names that we're all more comfortable with.

At the top of the DNS hierarchy is a large container that holds all the top-level Internet names, including com, edu, and mil. This container is often represented by a dot. Within each of these top-level Internet subnamespaces are the subdomains or subsubnamespaces that are for a specific organization, such as microsoft or bgerber. The DNS namespace nests increasingly lower until a specific computer or cluster of computers is identified. Sometimes a specific computer will actually be included in the namespace—as in web1.bgerber.com, for example. Sometimes no computer is named, as is often the case with websites. See Figure 3.1 for a glimpse at a very small piece of the DNS namespace—my own website, `bgerber.com`.

FIGURE 3.1

A small piece of the Domain Name System hierarchy

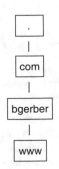

When a program such as a web browser goes hunting for a specific website, it asks an Internet domain name server for a specific domain object, such as `www.bgerber.com`. The domain name server looks up the requested name in its table. If it finds a match, it then looks up the IP address of that name, such as 216.132.83.21, and sends the IP address back to the browser. This is called *resolving* the domain name into an IP address. The web browser then uses the IP address to find and talk to the web server. The IP address belongs to the web server computer or possibly to a cluster of computers.

I should point out that www.bgerber.com is a distinguished name. I'm not saying that www.bgerber.com is distinguished in the way that a gray-haired gentleman of 60 years might be distinguished. I'm using the term in its namespace sense to indicate that www.bgerber.com identifies a unique object in the DNS namespace. An object in a directory must have a distinguished name, or it is useless.

Active Directory's namespace functions in a manner quite similar to the DNS namespace. In fact, when some names are resolved in a Windows Server 2003 network—for example, the names of internal computers running the Windows 2003 operating system—DNS is used exactly as it is used on the Internet.

Like DNS, the Active Directory namespace has a structure and specific ways of identifying objects. As noted in Chapter 2, four different naming conventions are used in Active Directory: Lightweight Directory Access Protocol (LDAP), Internet RFC 822 (DNS), Hypertext Transfer Protocol (HTTP) URLs, and Microsoft's Universal Naming Convention (UNC). Also, like DNS, clients query Active Directory for whatever lower-level identifiers are required to access a specific network resource, such as a computer, a printer, a user, a user mailbox, a security policy, a domain, and so on.

FORESTS, TREES, DOMAINS, AND OBJECTS

As mentioned earlier, Windows Server 2003 domains are contained in trees, which are contained in forests. A forest can contain one or more trees. Any given Active Directory namespace covers only one forest. In other words, a forest and a specific Active Directory namespace have contiguous boundaries.

Figure 3.2 shows an Active Directory structure based on a namespace with a forest that contains a single tree. The correct name for such a structure is a *single contiguous namespace*. Everything in my organization is a subentity of the top-level or root-level Windows Server 2003 domain, bgerber.com. The domains below bgerber.com are called *child domains*. Single contiguous namespace Active Directory structures model organizations that can be represented as a single hierarchical entity. These entities can be small, such as bgerber.com, or quite large, such as microsoft.com or us.gov. All the domains in Figure 3.2 make up the single tree in the Active Directory namespace.

ACTIVE DIRECTORY HELPS MAKE WINDOWS SERVER 2003 INDUSTRIAL STRENGTH

For the record, all the stuff in your Active Directory is represented in what is called the schema. The *stuff* is officially called *objects*. Objects represent everything from Windows 2003 user accounts to Exchange 2003 mailboxes. You can look at the schema and, if you know what you're doing, edit it.

One of the problems with Windows NT server is its somewhat limited capability to support extensive numbers of users and other resources in a domain. One NT domain allows for about 40,000 resource objects, about 20,000 of which can be users. That might seem like a lot until your organization starts growing and you've got lots of users, files, printers, and workstations to support. Then you want much more. With NT Server, the solution is to create multiple domains to handle many resources.

Active Directory supports up to 1 million objects. That's a lot! The main thing is that you no longer need to think multiple domains when structuring your Windows Server 2003 networking environment. For this and other reasons, Microsoft encourages you to think small when it comes to the number of Windows 2003 root-level domains that you create. In fact, in most cases, Microsoft's favorite number for root domains is 1. I'll talk more about this in Chapter 5, "Designing a New Exchange 2003 System"; Chapter 6, "Upgrading to Windows Server 2003 and Exchange Server 2003"; and Chapter 7, "Installing Windows Server 2003 as a Domain Controller."

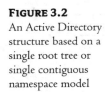

FIGURE 3.2
An Active Directory structure based on a single root tree or single contiguous namespace model

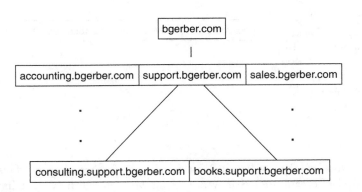

Microsoft encourages that, if at all possible, you seriously consider creating one large single tree domain such as the one in Figure 3.2. Assuming that there are no organizational reasons why you can't do this, how do you create one big, happy domain if some of your Windows Server 2003 servers are on low-bandwidth links? As I mentioned in passing in Chapter 2 and in the previous sidebar, "Active Directory Isn't the Whole House," you use the site connector and folder replication technology that Windows Server 2003 borrowed from Exchange Server 5.5.

TIP *The Active Directory naming choices that you make within your organization need have no impact on how your organization looks to the outside world. Your organization can be* `killandplunder.com` *internally and* `world-lover.com` *to the Internet. That doesn't mean that you might not want to use the same domain name internally and externally, though. In fact, that's often a very good idea. Again, planning is the key. As long as you know where you want to go both internally and externally, you'll build the right structure from the beginning. If you don't have a road map, watch out. There's nothing less fun than fixing naming decisions down the road. We'll spend more time on naming issues in Chapters 5 and 6.*

Now, let's say that you've got a more complex organizational structure and you need to preserve that structure in your Active Directory. Then you need a namespace with a forest that contains multiple trees or domains. Such namespaces are called *noncontiguous namespaces* because each tree in the forest is independent of the others. There are no unbroken lines from one tree to the other.

In Figure 3.3, you see an organization—let's call it Eat the World, Inc.—that just can't get everything into one root tree. This organization needs four root trees because Eat the World, Inc. really consists of four distinct organizational entities. Note that I've included just the top level of each root tree. Be assured, however, that each of the four trees has a full set of subtrees, just like `bgerber.com` in Figure 3.2 (shown earlier).

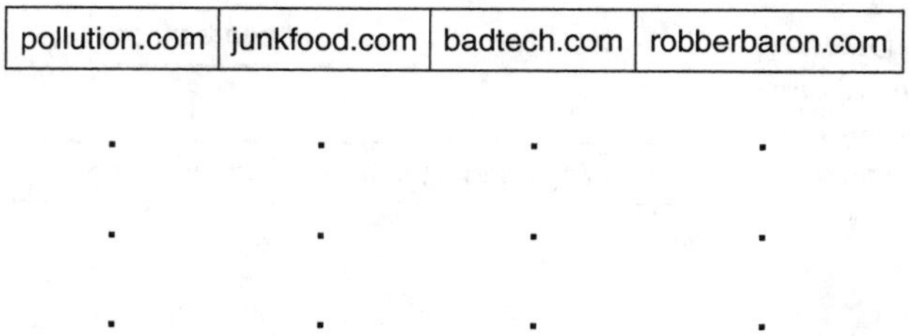

FIGURE 3.3

An Active Directory namespace based on a forest of root trees or a noncontiguous namespace model

pollution.com	junkfood.com	badtech.com	robberbaron.com

Now let's say that Eat the World, Inc. buys another company. This one, `destroyall.com`, is such a deviant organization that even the folks who run Eat the World, Inc. can't stomach it being in the same forest as their other blighted trees. Figure 3.4 shows the structure required to make this organizational decision work.

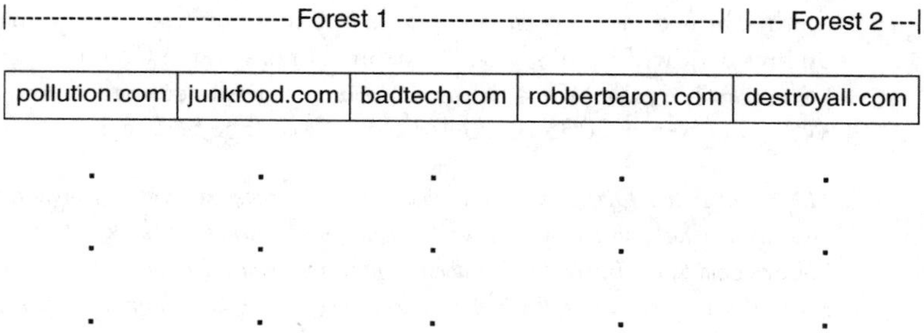

FIGURE 3.4

An Active Directory noncontiguous namespace based on two forests of root trees

|------------------------------- Forest 1 -------------------------------------| |---- Forest 2 ---|

pollution.com	junkfood.com	badtech.com	robberbaron.com	destroyall.com

The key here is to understand that both Forest 1 and Forest 2 have their own Active Directory structure and namespace—more specifically, they have their own *schema*. Each forest must be viewed independently in any Microsoft Management Console Active Directory snap-in. For example, if you open the Active Directory Users and Computers Microsoft Management Console snap-in on any computer that is a member of a domain in Forest 1, you'll be able to manage anywhere from none to all four of the domains in that forest, depending on security. If you open the same interface on a computer that is a member of the one and only domain in Forest 2, and if you have the correct security privileges, you'll be able to manage the domain `destroyall.com`.

I can just hear you. "Okay, so now I think I understand this namespace, forest, tree, and domain stuff. What's next?"

My first answer is that so much depends on Active Directory and its key components that without a good understanding of them, you're bound to make some serious mistakes. For example, if you don't get your domains and forests in order before you start planning and designing your Windows Server 2003 setup, you could face the misery of either combining domains in a forest or moving a domain from one forest to another. These are not easy tasks.

Furthermore, the domains represented by trees play a major role in Windows Server 2003 security. As with Windows NT Server 4 (and 3.51, for that matter), domains are at the heart of Windows

Server 2003 network security. A domain is a security boundary. As with NT Server, users log into domains. When a user logs into a domain, internal security willing, that user can access any resource in the domain.

Windows Server 2003 automatically sets up trust relationships between a root domain and its child domains, such as between `bgerber.com` and `accounting.bgerber.com` back in Figure 3.2. Windows Server 2003 also automatically sets up trusts between domains in a noncontiguous namespace (see Figure 3.3, shown earlier). These trusts are transitive, meaning that because all child domains in the forest have trust relationships with the root domain, they also have trusts with each other. So, you don't have to do anything to give all users access to all resources in all child domains in a root domain. Of course, you do have to do something to allow or prevent a user in one domain from accessing specific resources in another domain.

NOTE *Windows Server 2003 brings a neat new Active Directory feature to the table when compared with Windows 2000 Server. With 2003, you can set up cross-forest trusts. While this doesn't let you treat Forest A as though it were simply a domain in Forest B, it does make cross-forest authentication and, thus, resource access possible.*

Now let's talk a bit more about objects. Objects in Active Directory are the resources that you work with. In a sense, they represent the real stuff that you work with in Active Directory. Forests, trees, and domains are objects. Like all objects, Active Directory objects have attributes that define them. For example, users have first, last, and middle name attributes. Printers have paper size, ink available, and other attributes.

I won't go into detail about all the issues relating to objects. Suffice it to say that Active Directory objects are the result of a very disciplined implementation of object-oriented programming design by Microsoft. As an Active Directory user, you don't need to understand object-oriented programming. You just need to appreciate the role that objects play in making Active Directory a real-world repository for almost all the services and functionality required to run and manage a complex operating system.

Before we leave namespaces, forests, trees, domains, and objects, I should mention two other Windows Server 2003 objects: *Global Catalogs* and *organizational units.*

Every domain has a Global Catalog, which contains all the Active Directory information for its host domain. A Global Catalog also contains partial information for all the objects in other domains in the forest. This partial information is at least adequate to ensure that the object exists in the particular domain. A domain's Global Catalog allows for faster extra-domain searches, because a search for an object in another domain doesn't require time-consuming cross-domain network access and right-to-search authentication.

Organizational units are used to group objects within a domain. They're a nice way to create domainlike substructures when you want to assign different tasks or security rights to different persons or groups within a domain. Rights and privileges in an organizational unit apply only within the unit, not to the domain as a whole. Organizational units require much less overhead than domains. They help you reach Microsoft's new goal of keeping everything in one domain, if at all possible. I'll discuss these neat little tools further in Chapter 11, "Managing Exchange Users, Distribution Groups, and Contacts," and Chapter 15, "Installing and Managing Additional Exchange Servers."

Active Directory Is Real Stuff

To conclude this section, let's talk just a bit about what Active Directory is from a bits-and-bytes point of view. First, as should be quite obvious by now, Active Directory is a database. It's a grandly scaled, extensible collection of carefully architected and organized fields that represent the attributes of everything from usernames to Exchange mailboxes to security policies.

But Active Directory is something more—something without which the database would be nothing but a bucket of useless bits. Active Directory consists of the computer programs (*services*) that fill it with data and that take data from it so that a Windows Server 2003 network can operate smoothly and with high-level security.

These programs include a collection of services that come with Windows Server 2003, such as the Net Logon service, which supports pass-through authentication of logon events for computers in a domain. The Net Logon service uses information in Active Directory to perform its authentication tasks.

Active Directory–oriented services can also be developed to support applications that run on Windows Server 2003. The Exchange Routing Engine that moves messages between Exchange servers and to external messaging components is an example of such a service. The Routing Engine uses routing information stored in Active Directory to figure out where and even when to send messages.

It is even possible for end-user organizations to add their own objects to the Active Directory schema. These objects are then available to support programs that perform tasks customized to the needs of the organization. Although you've got to know a lot more than I will tell you in this book to do so, you can develop some pretty nifty messaging applications using hooks into the Exchange Server 2003 system and homegrown Active Directory objects.

So, does all this Active Directory stuff make sense? Obviously, you don't know everything about Active Directory at this point, but you should know enough to think rationally about how you can design your Windows Server 2003 environment. Hold that thought. We'll get to planning and design in Chapters 5 and 6.

What You Need to Know about Windows Server 2003 Network Architecture

As I mentioned in Chapter 2, one of the keys to understanding Windows Server 2003 networking is the much lower emphasis placed on Microsoft's older NetBEUI protocol and the WINS service. You really have to dig into the Windows Server 2003 installation process to install NetBEUI, and, if the truth be known, Microsoft would like to kill NetBEUI as a Windows Server 2003–supported networking protocol as quickly as possible. WINS is a somewhat more favored but still second-class networking citizen. It, too, is destined to die a slower but no less sure death than NetBEUI. Both protocols are there to support legacy Windows server and workstation products.

The key function of NetBEUI and WINS is to help one computer on a network find and communicate with another computer on the same network. Each Microsoft Windows computer (including each Windows 2003 computer, by the way) has what is called a *NetBIOS name*. NetBIOS names are the ones that show up in network neighborhoods in Windows Explorer.

The remainder of this section describes NetBEUI and WINS, and discusses the better option that Microsoft offers in Windows Server 2003.

Understanding NetBIOS, NetBEUI, and WINS

IBM developed the NetBIOS protocol for use in early PC networks. The protocol describes how computers on a network talk to each other. Key to this description is the concept of a NetBIOS name. Every computer on a NetBIOS network has its own unique NetBIOS name. NetBIOS was designed for early local area networks in which every network node was located on the same physical wire. NetBIOS data packets can't travel between routed networks. NetBEUI is an enhanced version of NetBIOS, also developed by IBM, which more than anything else defines the arrangement of information in a network data packet. Microsoft adopted both NetBIOS and NetBEUI for its network operating systems. Between NetBIOS and NetBEUI, NetBEUI is the current protocol of choice.

With the growing popularity of the TCP/IP protocol, which allows packets to pass from network to network over routers, Microsoft worked out a way to allow Windows computers to communicate over TCP/IP instead of NetBEUI. This required some way of resolving a NetBIOS computer name into a TCP/IP address. To answer this need, Microsoft designed the Windows Internet Naming Service (WINS, also often called *NetBIOS over TCP/IP*). WINS is essentially a namespace that links NetBIOS computer names with IP addresses.

Let's focus on NetBEUI for a bit. Those of you with massive routed NT Server networks have probably all but stamped out that cockroach NetBEUI. However, I'll bet that a lot of you still rely on the protocol—maybe even without knowing it. Historically, NetBEUI was either automatically installed or readily offered as an option when you installed one flavor or another of Windows. Even if you've installed TCP/IP and WINS, and NetBEUI is also installed, I'll bet that some communications on your network still depend on NetBEUI.

I've ceased to be surprised to find NetBEUI lurking somewhere on a network. For example, one consulting client called me in to figure out why some workstations that had just been installed couldn't get to the organization's Exchange server. I should note that these were the first workstations in the organization to be placed on a separate, routed network segment. The Exchange server supported only NetBEUI. The new workstations supported only NetBEUI. The organization hadn't changed its networking protocols to accommodate these other-side-of-the-router workstations. After we installed WINS on the network and TCP/IP on the routed workstations, all was fine.

Here's lesson one: Before you even touch a Windows Server 2003 installation CD, make sure that you know what protocols are running where on your network. If you think that the problems you had with NetBEUI in the past were a pain, wait until you see what it's like living in a world where you have to make a very conscious choice to install NetBEUI, but your mind hasn't fully absorbed the fact. It is kind of like going from driving an automatic car to driving a stick-shift car. Sometimes you almost forget the clutch and stick shift.

So what does all this have to do with your life? Well, your existing Windows 2003 domain controller and the new Windows Server 2003 that is to become a domain controller must be capable of talking to each other. This sounds simple, but the only way to really make it simple is to give up on NetBEUI and WINS, as you'll soon see.

An Alternative: Using DNS and DHCP

You can use NetBEUI to enable communication between a Windows 2003 domain controller and a stand-alone server, although you do have to remember to install it. You can also use WINS for this purpose. A third and much better option is available: the DNS and Windows 2003's Dynamic Host Configuration Protocol (DHCP).

As I mentioned previously in the "Active Directory: Five Major Architectural Components" section, the native computer naming system on Windows Server 2003 networks is DNS. That's the same DNS that served as an example of a namespace earlier in this chapter. To get started, a stand-alone Windows 2003 server that is to be promoted to a domain controller in an existing domain needs both an IP address of its own and the IP address of its DNS server. The stand-alone server needs an IP address so that it can communicate with other computers on the network, specifically upon upgrade to a domain controller, the existing domain controller. It needs a DNS server so that it can find the domain controller, connect to it, and be authenticated by it so that it can join the domain as a new domain controller.

Although you can manually set the DNS parameters discussed previously, Windows Server 2003 lets you automate the whole process using DHCP. DHCP not only can assign an IP address to the new computer, but it also can give your new computer the IP address of the DNS server that it should use. Then (and this is really neat), when your new Windows 2003 server is up and running, Windows Server 2003 DHCP can even dynamically register your new computer in the existing domain controller's DNS. This process is called *dynamic DNS*. You don't even have to make a manual entry for the computer in the DNS. Additionally, you can reserve specific IP addresses in DHCP so that you're sure that a server will get the same address each time it boots up.

Even better, like earlier Windows products, a Windows 2003 server is ready to use DHCP immediately after stand-alone server installation is completed. So, as long as DHCP is properly set up on your existing domain controller or another Windows Server 2003 on your network, you don't have to do anything to promote a stand-alone server to domain controller status except run the domain controller promotion program on it.

My goal in this chapter is not to make you an expert in adding domain controllers to Windows Server 2003 networks. We'll do that in Chapters 7 and 15, and we'll use Dynamic DNS to install a stand-alone server that will become our first Exchange server. Instead, my goal is to give you a sense of the changes in Windows Server 2003 networking compared to NT Server 4 networking.

WINDOWS 2003 SERVERS ARE DOMAIN CONTROLLER CHAMELEONS

To understand the difference between NT 4 and Windows Server 2003 servers, it's important to understand that Windows NT Server 4 servers were either stand-alone servers or primary or secondary domain controllers. You created a domain controller while installing the NT 4 operating system. A domain controller could not revert to stand-alone status, and a stand-alone server could not become a domain controller.

When you install a Windows Server 2003, you don't even have the option of making it a domain controller. Windows 2003 stand-alone servers become domain controllers after they are fully installed and running. Somewhat like a magician, you can promote a Windows Server 2003 to domain controller status anytime, and you can demote it back to stand-alone server status anytime. You can perform this metamorphosis as many times as you want or need to.

Summary

Windows Server 2003's Active Directory is central to both Windows 2003 and Exchange 2003. Active Directory is a namespace like the Internet standard Domain Name System (DNS). Active Directory is a repository for virtually all the information about users and resources (files, printers, and so on) available on a network.

Key to Active Directory creation and management are forests, trees, and domains. Forests are the top-level containers in Windows 2003 environments. A forest can contain one or more trees. Trees contain one or more domains. Domain objects in the same forest can communicate with each other automatically because transitive trust relationships are created between the domains by default. Domains in different forests require that trust relationships be specifically set up before objects within them can communicate with each other.

Windows Server 2003 networking is based on DNS. The legacy Windows NT server networking protocols, NetBEUI and WINS, are available but are totally unnecessary in Windows 2003 networks. The Windows 2003 preferred networking approach is IP supported by Dynamic DNS, which combines DHCP and DNS to deliver IP address and other information to a computer and to place the computer in the network's DNS.

That should be enough of Windows Server 2003 for a bit. Now let's move on to Exchange Server 2003 and take a look at its architecture.

Chapter 4

Exchange Server 2003 Architecture

EXCHANGE IS A CLIENT/SERVER electronic messaging system. In this chapter, we'll take a close look at the Exchange Server 2003–relevant architecture of Windows Server 2003, as well as the architectures of both the Exchange Server 2003 and client systems. We'll also see how the Exchange server and clients interact from an architectural perspective.

This is an important chapter because it exposes you to a range of Exchange terminology that you'll find useful later. It also gives you a sense of how the whole Exchange system hangs together and works. Remember that virtually all the architectural components that we discuss here are, in whole or in part, real program code running somewhere on a Windows Server 2003 or an Exchange Server 2003 or client machine.

Featured in this chapter:

◆ Key Exchange Server 2003 organizing components

◆ Exchange Server 2003 core components

◆ Optional Exchange Server 2003 components

◆ Clients for Exchange

Key Exchange Server 2003 Organizing Components

Every system, whether social, biological, or computer, needs a set of organizing components. Without these components, you'll have a devil of a time understanding or working with the system. Here's a highly simplified example using social organizations. We think of social organizations as having groups, and groups as having individual members. When we attempt to work within social organizations, it's very important to remember those groups because people often learn to behave and actually behave as group members, not as individual persons.

Like Exchange 2000 Server, Exchange Server 2003 has its own set of key organizing components. These are borrowed from Exchange Server 5.5, but a lot happened to 5.5 on the way to 2003. Let's take a look at the organizing components of Exchange Server. We'll start with Exchange Server 5.5 and then see how these components were or were not modified in Exchange Server 2003.

The key organizing components of Exchange Server 5.5 included organizations, sites, messaging servers, and message recipients (objects that can at least receive messages). In Exchange Server 5.5, those four components formed a hierarchy:

- Organizations contained sites.

- Sites contained messaging servers.

- Messaging servers contained message recipients.

An Exchange organization encompassed an Exchange Server 5.5 system that was a collection of servers in one or more sites. Think of an Exchange organization as Exchange Server 5.5's *forest*, in Windows Server 2003 parlance. Recipients in 5.5 included mailboxes, distribution lists, custom addresses (e-mail addresses outside the Exchange system), and public folders. Figure 4.1 shows the organizing components of Exchange Server 5.5.

FIGURE 4.1

Exchange Server 5.5's organizing components

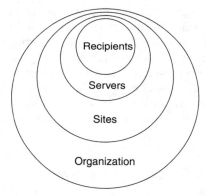

All is not quite so simple with Exchange Server 2003. All four of the organizational components are still around, but although most have retained homes in Exchange Server 2003, a few have moved at least in part to Windows Server 2003. Exchange organizations, messaging servers, and public folders (the only type of message recipients that remain organizationally in Exchange) are a part of Exchange Server 2003.

Sites are now a part of Windows Server 2003, where they function similarly to the way they did in Exchange 5.5. However, they no longer have anything to do with Exchange. In Exchange Server 2003, administrative groups and routing groups replace sites. I'll talk more about administrative groups soon; I discussed routing groups back in Chapter 2, "Windows Server 2003 and Exchange Server 2003."

The four types of recipients in Exchange 2003 are as follows:

◆ Exchange users (mailbox-enabled users and mail-enabled users)

◆ Distribution groups or mail-enabled groups (distribution lists in Exchange 5.5)

◆ Contacts (custom recipients in Exchange 5.5)

◆ Public folders

A mailbox-enabled user is a Windows 2003 user (account) with an Exchange mailbox. A mail-enabled user is a Windows 2003 user that has no Exchange mailbox, but does have an address in a foreign messaging system. See Figure 4.2 for a graphic representation of this state of affairs.

FIGURE 4.2
Exchange Server 2003's organizing components with a little help from Windows Server 2003

Exchange Server 2003

Organization

Administrative Groups

Servers

Public Folders

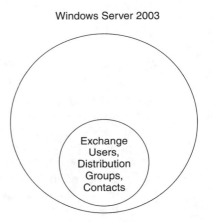

Windows Server 2003

Exchange Users, Distribution Groups, Contacts

"Wow!" you say. "That's a pretty bifurcated messaging mess." It's really not all that bad. If you're an old hand at Exchange, all you have to do is readjust your thinking about recipients. Recipients are still very important to Exchange Server 2003, no matter where they live. So, for the sake of this discussion, let's agree to treat all four kinds of recipients together. We probably shouldn't try to shoehorn them into the Exchange Server 2003 organizational hierarchy, but we can still talk about them in the same breath as the hierarchy.

You can see the hierarchy in Exchange Server 5.5's Administrator program. Figure 4.3 shows the hierarchy of one Exchange organization in the 5.5 Administrator program. GerCom is the name of the Exchange organization. LA is the name of the Exchange site. The Exchange servers are called EXCHLA01 and EXCHLA02. All recipients in a site can be viewed in the Recipients container at the bottom of the screen. You can see all four kinds of recipients in the Recipients container, mailboxes (Easton, David), distribution lists (Dead Letter Managers), custom recipients (Franklin, Marsha), and public folders (Johnson Party (Feb).

FIGURE 4.3

The Exchange Server 5.5 hierarchy as viewed through the Exchange Administrator program

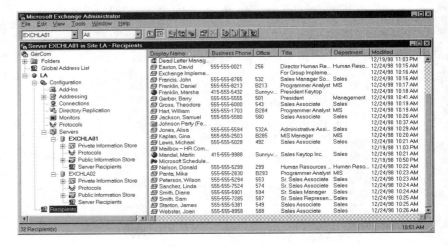

In Exchange Server 5.5, mailboxes resided on one and only one Exchange server. So, if you looked in the container labeled Server Recipients under any of the Exchange servers in Figure 4.3, you'd see the mailboxes that resided on that server. When you set up an Exchange Server 5.5 mailbox, you could designate the Exchange server where the mailbox would live. Public folders also lived on an Exchange 5.5 server, although they could be replicated to other servers. Exchange Server 5.5 distribution lists and custom recipients lived only in the Exchange directory, which could be replicated across Exchange Server 5.5 servers. Hold these thoughts: Most of this is still true with Exchange Server 2003.

Figure 4.4 shows how my Exchange 2003 environment looks in the Exchange Server 2003 System Manager snap-in for Windows Server 2003's Microsoft Management Console. My organization (Barry Gerber and Associates) includes my administrative groups (there's only one right now, First Administrative Group). My administrative group includes my Exchange servers (again, only one right now, EXCHANGE01), and my Exchange server contains a public store that includes public folders. To work on public folders, I click Public Folder Instances, right-click the folder that I want to administer, and open its properties.

"Wait," you say. "Can't I do the same thing with mailboxes in the mailbox store right above the public store?" Nope. To administer mailboxes, you must use the Active Directory Users and Computers snap-in. That's why I say that recipients other than public folders are organizationally part of Windows Server 2003.

WARNING   *If you've just installed Exchange Server 2003, your Exchange system manager snap-in won't look anything like the one in Figure 4.4. It'll look a lot more like the one in Figure 1.13 in Chapter 1, "Introducing Exchange Server 2003." You'll see a lot of the same stuff, but it won't be organized under administrative groups. You have to choose to view Administrative Groups before you can work with them. If you're accustomed to Exchange Server 5.5, where your first site was displayed automatically, you might have more trouble adjusting to this than a new Exchange Server 2003 user would. For now, don't worry. We're talking architecture here. I'll talk about displaying administrative group containers in Chapter 12, "Managing the Exchange Server Hierarchy and Core Components," and we'll create some new administrative group containers in Chapter 15, "Installing and Managing Additional Exchange Servers."*

FIGURE 4.4

The Exchange Server 2003 hierarchy as viewed through the Exchange Server System Manager snap-in for Windows Server 2003's Microsoft Management Console

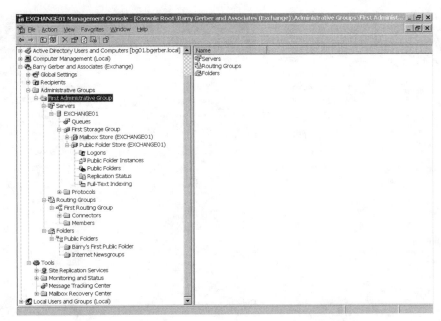

There is no container for recipients in the Exchange snap-in. "Wait," you say once again. "What about the container called Recipients that's just above Administrative Groups in Figure 4.4?" Well, that's a container for organization-wide recipient attributes such as addressing. You won't find mailboxes, distribution groups, contacts, and public folders there. Go to the public store in the Exchange system manager to administer public folders. Go to Windows 2003's Active Directory Users and Computers snap-in to administer Exchange users, distribution groups, and contacts.

TIP   *For many Exchange components, you can assign management permissions at the component level. For example, you can create administrative groups for different departments in your organization and assign different users management rights for each administrative group.*

Figure 4.5 shows what's in the Users folder in the Active Directory Users and Computers snap-in. Barry Gerber in the right pane is a user. Users are Windows Server 2003 users. They have accounts that allow them to log into domains and access resources based on their permissions. You can mailbox-enable a Windows 2003 user while or after creating the user. You manage mailboxes when you manage the users with whom they are associated. In the figure, All Managers is a distribution group; Joe Blow, about three-quarters down in the right pane, is a contact.

FIGURE 4.5
Viewing Exchange
Server 2003 recipi-
ents with the Active
Directory Users and
Computers snap-in
for Microsoft Man-
agement Console

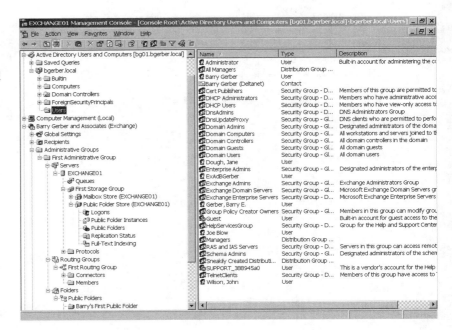

Not everything has changed with Exchange Server 2003 when compared with Exchange Server 5.5. For example, when you mailbox-enable a user, you still specify which Exchange 2003 server the user's mailbox will reside on. Public folders still reside on a single Exchange server and can be replicated to other Exchange servers. You can still see the mailboxes that reside on each server by looking in the server's mailbox store, `EXCHANGE01\First Storage Group\Mailbox Store (EXCHANGE01)` in Figure 4.4. Now, you can even see which public folders exist on a given Exchange server, `EXCHANGE01\First Storage Group\Public Folder Store (EXCHANGE01)` in Figure 4.4. Distribution groups (formerly distribution lists) and contacts (formerly custom recipients) continue to live only in a directory, but now they're in the Active Directory instead of the Exchange Server 5.5 directory.

So, in summary, Exchange Server 2003 includes four organizing components:

- ◆ Organizations
- ◆ Administrative groups
- ◆ Servers
- ◆ Recipients:
  - ◆ Exchange users
  - ◆ Distribution groups
  - ◆ Contacts
  - ◆ Public folders

Mailboxes live on Exchange 2003 servers and are managed in Active Directory. Distribution groups and contacts live on Windows 2003 servers in Active Directory and are managed using Active Directory–specific management tools. Public folders live on Exchange 2003 servers and are managed using Exchange-specific management tools.

DOES AN OBJECT LIVE ON EXCHANGE SERVER 2003, WINDOWS SERVER 2003, OR BOTH?

What follows is very important. It will help you understand the difference between objects that live only in Windows Server 2003's Active Directory and objects that live both in Active Directory and someplace else, such as Exchange Server 2003. I strongly suggest you read this very carefully.

The first thing to understand is that all objects have a presence in the Active Directory namespace. Their attributes live in Active Directory. Some objects, such as distribution groups and contacts, live only in Active Directory. Some objects also have a presence in other places. For example, mailboxes live both on Windows 2003 servers in Active Directory and on Exchange 2003 servers.

When you manage the attributes of an object, such as a mailbox, you work in Active Directory. When you change attributes, you work solely in Active Directory because the attributes are stored in Active Directory. On the other hand, when you delete a mailbox, you still work in Active Directory to request the deletion, but your work affects both Windows Server 2003 and Exchange Server 2003. The mailbox object with all its attributes is deleted from the Active Directory namespace. At the same time, the actual physical mailbox is deleted from the Exchange server.

Make sense? Good. Remembering this distinction will see you through many a dark and stormy night.

Exchange Server 2003 Core Components

We're now ready to look at some other key components of Exchange Server 2003. These are not key organizing components; rather, these components provide the core functionality of Exchange Server 2003.

Exchange Server 5.5 had four core components:

◆ Information Store

◆ Directory

◆ Message Transfer Agent

◆ System Attendant

Except for the directory, which is now Windows Server 2003's Active Directory, the other three components remain, although the Message Transfer Agent is now named the Routing Engine:

◆ Information Store

◆ Routing Engine

◆ System Attendant

Let's tackle these three core components of Exchange Server 2003.

Information Store

Although it still has the same name as in Exchange 5.5, the Exchange 2003 Information Store (IS) can do lots more than the 5.5 Information Store could. We'll talk about the neat new features in a bit. First, I need to be sure that you have a firm grounding in Exchange 2003's new IS.

Like Active Directory, the IS is a database—actually, a collection of databases—and a Windows Server 2003 program or, more correctly, *service* (see Figure 4.6). The IS is a grand container for what are called *storage groups*. Exchange Server 2003 Standard Edition—the lower-end product in the Exchange Server 2003 product line—supports one storage group per server installation. Top-of-the-line Enterprise Edition allows for up to twenty storage groups per server installation, although you're limited to about four storage groups per server unless you're using the new 64-bit Windows 2003 products.

All the storage groups in an Exchange organization constitute the organizational IS. Each storage group can contain one or more databases. Two types of databases exist: mailbox stores and public folder stores. A storage group can contain one or more mailbox and/or public folder stores. You can separately administer, back up, and restore individual databases, which allows for much better information store management and performance than were possible with Exchange Server 5.5.

To balance network loads and to reduce access costs, public folders can be replicated in whole or in part to other Exchange servers. Additionally, to lighten the load on servers with mailboxes, you can place public folders on separate Exchange servers and direct clients to those servers when they need access to public folders.

FIGURE 4.6

The Information Store is a collection of mailbox and public folder databases managed by the Information Store service.

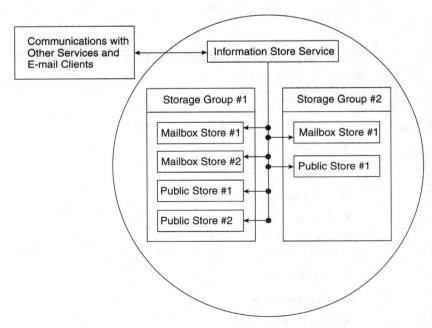

The IS service is a link between the IS databases and other components of Exchange Server. It performs a number of functions. Among other things, it receives incoming mail from and delivers outgoing mail to the Exchange Server 2003 Routing Engine and message transfer agents for other e-mail systems, notifies clients of the arrival of new mail, looks up addresses in Active Directory, and creates directory entries for public folders.

Now let's take a look at some other features of the IS. As I pointed out in a previous chapter, you can actually do Internet publishing from Exchange Server 2003 public folders. Exchange 2003 folders support the Multipurpose Internet Mail Extension (MIME) protocol. MIME lets you send messages through the Internet and preserve their content type. Put simply, you can specify that an attachment to a message is in Microsoft Word format. When you open the document, Word opens, and you can do anything with the document that you can do in Word.

Additionally, you can place actual HTML pages or Microsoft Active Server Pages (ASP) in Exchange folders. Web pages can include standard Exchange functionality such as calendars and custom Exchange applications. You can replicate these folders to other Exchange 2003 servers. Users can access these folders and pages through your Microsoft Internet Information Server, just as they would access HTML and other web-related content through the same server. Microsoft claims that web performance is better from public folders than from the file system.

Aside from the Internet, Exchange Server 2003's IS supports what Microsoft calls the *Installable File System* (IFS). IFS enables you to map Exchange Server 2003 mailbox and public stores as you would disk drives. You can then use the Windows Explorer or an instance of the command line to access these folders and their contents just as you would access file folders and their contents. With the right permissions, you can double-click messages and see them in the Exchange-compatible messaging client installed on your computer. More importantly, you can develop applications that treat mailboxes and public folders as sources and recipients of data.

The Routing Engine

The Routing Engine (RE) performs two basic routing functions. First, it routes messages between its server and other Exchange servers. Second, it routes messages between its server and Exchange connectors for foreign messaging systems. Figure 4.7 shows the RE in action. Let's look at the RE's various tasks in a bit more detail.

Recall that SMTP is the native protocol for Exchange Server 2003. You probably also remember that Windows Server 2003 comes with a basic SMTP server (service) that is enhanced when Exchange 2003 is installed. Within an Exchange 2003 routing group, the RE routes messages between its server's IS and its server's SMTP service. The SMTP service then sends the messages to the appropriate Exchange server's SMTP service. (See Exchange Server #1 in Exchange Routing Group #1 in Figure 4.7.)

When it routes messages to Exchange servers located in different Exchange Server 2003 routing groups in the same Exchange organization, the RE gets help from Exchange Server 2003 connectors, discussed in the "Exchange Connectors" section later in this chapter. In Figure 4.7, the Routing Group Connector is being used to move messages between Exchange Routing Groups 1 and 2.

FIGURE 4.7
Each Exchange server's routing engine moves messages to other LAN- and WAN-connected Exchange servers.

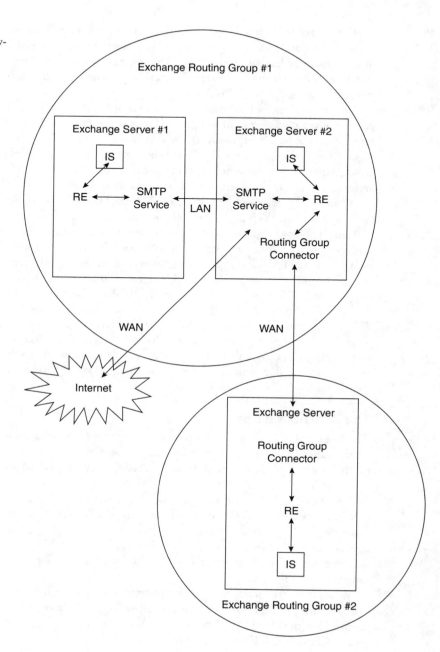

When the Exchange RE routes messages to Internet-based messaging systems, it uses the same SMTP service used to route messages internally (again, see Figure 4.7). Optionally, you can enhance the SMTP service with the Exchange SMTP Connector. Among other things, the SMTP Connector supports Internet message transfer using dial-up links. I'll discuss the SMTP Connector in Chapter 13, "Managing Exchange 2003 Internet Services."

Connectors aren't optional for communicating with foreign messaging systems other than Internet systems. For example, the RE needs help from the X.400 Connector to route messages to X.400 messaging systems.

The System Attendant

Other Exchange Server components cannot run without the System Attendant (SA); it's the first Exchange component to activate on start-up and the last to stop on shut-down. The SA performs a range of functions that are key to Exchange Server's operation. Let's take a closer look at each of these functions.

The SA helps other servers monitor network connections to its server. The System Attendant receives and replies to network link integrity messages from other Exchange servers. These servers know that something is wrong—either with the network link or the System Attendant's own server—if they fail to receive these replies.

The SA collects message-tracking data for its server. The SA logs data about sent messages, which can be used for tracking a message's status and the route that it traveled once sent. This capability is especially useful when used in conjunction with similar data gathered by the SAs on other Exchange servers.

The SA builds Windows Server 2003 routing group–based message routing tables for its server. Like any network, an Exchange Server network needs routing tables, which are used specifically for routing messages. The SA interacts with Active Directory to build tables that the RE uses to route messages to servers in its routing group.

The SA triggers the generation of foreign electronic messaging addresses for recipients on its server. The SA generates X.400 and SMTP addresses by default. When gateways are installed, the SA generates gateway-specific e-mail addresses for users. When creating addresses, the SA interacts with Active Directory.

The SA participates in certain security functions. Security in Exchange is very good. An Exchange mailbox can use both digital signatures and encryption. The SA is involved in enabling and disabling these two components of Exchange security.

Optional Exchange Server 2003 Components

You'll remember from the "Getting a Handle on Exchange Server 2003 Versions" section in Chapter 2 that there are two flavors of Exchange Server 2003: the Standard and Enterprise editions. The Standard Edition comes with all the components discussed here except the X.400 Connector. The Enterprise Edition includes all of the components discussed here.

You can at least start up Exchange Server 2003 without any of these components. That is why I call them *optional components*, not because you have to pay extra to get them. However, as you'll see, the components significantly enhance the functionality of the product, so you will very likely use a number of them. Optional components include the following:

- Microsoft Management Console snap-ins for Exchange Server 2003
- The Directory Synchronization Agent
- Event Management service
- Microsoft Search (full-text indexing) service
- Exchange Internet protocol servers:
  - Outlook Web Access Server
  - Post Office Protocol v3 (POP3) Server
  - Internet Message Access Protocol v4 (IMAP4) Server
  - Network News Transfer Protocol Server
- Exchange connectors:
  - Routing Group Connector
  - SMTP Connector
  - Active Directory Connector
  - X.400 Connector
  - Connector for Microsoft Mail
  - Schedule+ Free/Busy Connector
  - Connector for cc:Mail
  - Other legacy messaging system connectors
- Exchange gateways

All of these enhancements are described in the following sections.

Microsoft Management Console Snap-Ins for Exchange Server 2003

You saw examples of the Microsoft Management Console snap-ins for Exchange Server 2003 in action in Chapter 2 and in Figures 4.4 and 4.5 in this chapter, and you'll get to know them very well as we move along. The main point that I want to make here is that the snap-ins are *home*. They're where you go whenever you need to do almost anything with Exchange Server, from creating and managing users to linking with other Exchange servers or foreign mail systems, to monitoring the activities on your server. The snap-ins are a set of points from which you can manage anything, whether it's one Exchange server or your entire Exchange organization.

The snap-ins are home in another way, too: When you figure out which snap-in you need for a particular management task, they're easy. Soon after you start using the snap-ins, you'll feel about them the same way you feel about that comfortable old chair in the den. Really!

The Directory Synchronization Agent

The Directory Synchronization Agent (DXA) lets you create address books that include addresses from outside your Exchange system. It also enables you to send Exchange Server address information to other electronic messaging systems. It sends directory update information to and receives it from Microsoft Mail for PC Networks 3.x systems.

The DXA uses the Microsoft Mail 3.x Directory Synchronization Protocol, so any foreign, non-Microsoft electronic messaging system that is compatible with this protocol is fair game for cross-system directory synchronization.

The Event Management Service

The Event Management service supports event-driven, server-based applications developed for Exchange Server 5.5. Event-driven applications perform a set of custom actions when something happens on an Exchange server, such as when a message from a specific sender arrives.

The Microsoft Search (Full-Text Indexing) Service

Microsoft has implemented a new service called Microsoft Search that enables you to fully index text in certain BackOffice applications. This service comes with such products as SQL Server 7 or later. Exchange Server 2003 enhances this service. Full-text indexing significantly increases the speed of client searches within Exchange Server 2003 objects, such as messages.

Exchange Internet Protocol Access Components

Exchange Server 2003 comes with a set of four Internet protocol services. These let you extend the reach of Exchange users beyond Microsoft's very good, but proprietary, electronic messaging protocol MAPI. The four services are Hypertext Transmission Protocol (HTTP), which supports Outlook Web Access (OWA); Post Office Protocol (POP3); Internet Message Access Protocol (IMAP4); and Network News Transfer Protocol (NNTP):

HTTP   HTTP is the core protocol that supports web access. OWA uses the HTTP protocol to give users access to everything in their Exchange mailboxes, as well as items in public folders, using a web browser such as Microsoft Internet Explorer. On the server side, OWA is supported by Windows Server 2003's Internet Information Server.

POP3 Server   Exchange Server's POP3 server gives users with standard POP3 e-mail clients, such as Eudora or Outlook Express, limited access to their Exchange mailboxes. Users can download mail from their Exchange Inboxes, but that's all. Users have no direct access to other personal or public information stores or to their schedules. This is due to limitations in the POP3 protocol itself, not in Microsoft's implementation of the protocol.

IMAP4 Server   The Exchange IMAP4 server goes one better than POP3, adding access to folders in addition to the Exchange Inbox. With IMAP4, folders and their contents can remain on the

Exchange server, be downloaded to the computer running your IMAP4 client, or both. You can keep Exchange Server–based folders and their contents in sync with the folders on an IMAP4 client.

NNTP Server   The NNTP server lets you bring all those exciting Usenet newsgroups into your Exchange server's public folders, where your users can read and respond to them with the same e-mail clients that they use to read other public folders.

NOTE   *Wondering what happened to Exchange Server 5.5's Lightweight Directory Access Protocol (LDAP) server? It just moved uptown. As I noted in Chapter 2 and Chapter 3, "Two Key Architectural Components of Windows Server 2003," it's now a Windows Server 2003 service. Now, when a messaging client needs LDAP information, it queries Windows Server 2003's LDAP service and through that service, Windows 2003's Active Directory.*

Exchange Connectors

Exchange servers, whether the 5.5 or 2003 flavor, need to talk to each other for a variety of reasons:

- To transfer messages and other information internally between Exchange servers

- To transfer messages between Exchange servers and foreign messaging systems

- To replicate e-mail addresses and other information between Exchange servers and foreign messaging systems

As I mentioned earlier, the native communication protocol for Exchange 2003 servers is SMTP. Microsoft's Remote Procedure Call (RPC) protocol, Exchange 5.5's key interserver protocol, is supported on Exchange 2003 servers, but only to allow them to communicate "natively" with Exchange Server 5.5 systems.

The Exchange system allows for different communication methods, depending on the nature of the network connecting Exchange servers. When Exchange servers are linked by high-bandwidth, reliable, continuous networks, they can communicate with no intervening connectors. However, when Exchange servers are connected by lower-bandwidth, perhaps less reliable, and maybe even noncontinuous (dial-up, for example) networks, Exchange connectors are required. Connectors not only establish the communications protocols to be used to link Exchange servers, but they also let you monitor and even schedule connections. You can even set priorities for some connectors, forcing Exchange to pick the highest-bandwidth or lowest-cost connection when multiple connectors link the same Exchange servers to each other or link Exchange servers to foreign messaging systems.

To manage lower-bandwidth links, you first put all your servers with high-bandwidth, reliable, continuous connections into routing groups. You create one routing group per collection of well-connected servers. Then you link routing groups using Exchange connectors.

In addition to inter-Exchange server communications, Exchange servers also need to communicate with foreign messaging systems such as Internet mail systems to transfer messages. Specific Exchange connectors are available for many of these links. For other foreign messaging system links, third-party gateways must be used. I discuss gateways in the "Exchange Gateways" section later in this chapter.

So, just what is the function of an Exchange connector? Basically, it allows you to set parameters compatible with the protocol the connector supports. For example, to exchange messages, addressing, and other information with legacy Microsoft Mail or cc:Mail systems, you need to set up and configure the appropriate Exchange connector for either of these systems.

Okay, now we can talk about the Exchange connectors. There are a number of different ones, including the Routing Group Connector, the Active Directory Connector, the X.400 Connector, the SMTP Connector, the Microsoft Mail Connector, the Schedule+ Free/Busy Connector, and the cc:Mail Connector. Let's look at each of these connectors.

ROUTING GROUP CONNECTOR

The Routing Group Connector is the preferred connector for linking Exchange Server 2003 routing groups. It is quite similar to Exchange Server 5.5's Site Connector. You can also use the SMTP Connector or the X.400 Connector to link routing groups. The advantage of the Routing Group Connector is that it's easy to configure and supports multiple (redundant) links between the same two routing groups. The Routing Group Connector uses SMTP, so it preserves the native communications mode of Exchange Server 2003. The Routing Group Connector is one of the Exchange connector options shown earlier in Figure 4.7.

ACTIVE DIRECTORY CONNECTOR

This connector is new with Exchange Server 2003 and is used to link Exchange Server 2003 and Exchange Server 5.5 systems. It keeps Active Directory and Exchange Server 5.5's directory in sync. As soon as you've converted all your 5.5 servers to Exchange Server 2003, you won't need the Active Directory Connector any longer.

SMTP CONNECTOR

The Exchange Server 5.5 Internet Mail Service supported both the transfer of messages to Internet-based messaging systems and the linking of Exchange sites. In Exchange 2003, the Exchange-enhanced Windows 2003 SMTP service handles Internet messaging. The Exchange 2003 SMTP Connector isn't required for standard Internet messaging. Rather, it is used to enhance Internet messaging. For example, the SMTP Connector supports a range of options for dial-up connections to SMTP smart hosts that act as relay servers for incoming and outgoing Internet-bound messages. The SMTP Connector also supports inter-routing group connections, much as Exchange 5.5's Internet Mail Service supported intersite connections.

X.400 CONNECTOR

The X.400 Connector is used to link Exchange servers to foreign X.400 systems for user message exchange. The X.400 Connector is fully compliant with all the 1984 and 1988 X.400 transport and message content standards.

The X.400 Connector can ride on top of TCP/IP or X.25 networking services. It can also be used to link Exchange routing groups.

CONNECTOR FOR MICROSOFT MAIL

You have two post office–wide options for dealing with legacy systems running Microsoft Mail 3.*x* for PC Networks. Either you can move entire post offices and their user mailboxes to Exchange Server using migration tools that come with Exchange Server, or you can link the legacy systems to Exchange Server, providing recipients on all sides with transparent access to each other. The Connector for Microsoft Mail (CMM) supports the latter option.

The CMM creates and interacts with a shadow (emulated) Microsoft Mail post office on the Exchange server. Exchange sends and receives mail through the CMM using this shadow, which looks like an Exchange server to users on the Exchange side and looks like a Microsoft Mail 3.*x* post office to users on the MS Mail side. Microsoft Mail's EXTERNAL.EXE program, or a version of EXTERNAL.EXE that runs as an NT or Windows 2003 service, is used to transfer mail between the shadow and the real MS Mail post office. Connections can be either synchronous or asynchronous. If it can bear the traffic, you need only one MMC to link all your MS Mail post offices to the Exchange world.

Before we leave the CMM, I want to be sure that you're aware of a third option for users of legacy Microsoft Mail for PC networks systems. This one requires neither whole post-office migration nor use of the CMM. On a user-by-user basis, you can connect a user's Exchange client directly to both the user's Microsoft Mail and Exchange mailboxes. This lets the user send and receive messages from both the Microsoft Mail and Exchange systems. This option is best when you haven't got the time or other resources to migrate everyone in a Microsoft Mail post office to an Exchange server or to deal with the intricacies of the CMM.

SCHEDULE+ FREE/BUSY CONNECTOR

Microsoft Schedule+ lets Exchange and Microsoft Mail users set up meetings with each other. It uses a graphical user interface to show, in aggregate fashion, the times available to users selected for a meeting. This information is available on Exchange servers and in Microsoft Mail for PC Networks post offices. The Free/Busy Connector lets Exchange servers and Microsoft Mail post offices share schedule information.

CONNECTOR FOR CC:MAIL

The Connector for cc:Mail works a lot like the Microsoft Mail Connector. It enables Exchange Server users to continue accessing messages in their Lotus cc:Mail post office. Like the Connector for Microsoft Mail, the Connector for cc:Mail is ideally suited to keeping access to a legacy mail system alive during migration to Exchange Server.

OTHER MESSAGING SYSTEM CONNECTORS

Exchange Server 2003 comes with connectors for other foreign messaging systems. These include Lotus Notes and Novell GroupWise. These connectors function similarly to the connectors for Microsoft Mail and cc:Mail.

Exchange Gateways

Exchange Server supports internal mail and SMTP mail natively and provides connectors to other messaging systems such as X.400 or Microsoft Mail systems. To access other systems, you'll need *gateways*. Exchange Server gateways don't resemble the clunky DOS gateways used with such products as Microsoft Mail 3.*x*. Like the rest of Exchange Server, they run as processes on Windows 2003 Server. As long as gateway developers know what they're doing, gateways tend to be stable, robust, and fast.

Gateways are available for such services as IBM's PROFS and SNADS, as well as for fax, pagers, and voicemail. Microsoft produces some gateways, and third parties offer others. Keep in touch with Microsoft and the trade press for details.

Clients for Exchange

As I noted before, the real fun of Exchange is on the client side. That's where you get to see the business end of Exchange, from "simple" e-mail to complex, home-grown, messaging-enabled applications. Exchange client components include the following:

- Outlook
- Internet browser
- POP3 and IMAP4
- Schedule+
- Microsoft Outlook Forms Designer forms
- Custom client-based applications

Here's a quick look at the Exchange client components from an architectural perspective.

The Outlook Client

An Outlook client provides full access to all the client features that Exchange 2003 offers. This includes everything from folders and messages in your mailbox to items in public folders, to rules-based message management.

You receive, transmit, and access messages in the Outlook client. It's your window on your mailbox and on public folders. Earlier versions of Exchange Server came with a variety of clients, including those for Macintosh, MS DOS, and Windows 3.1. These clients worked with Exchange Server 5.5 and they will work with Exchange Server 2003.

The Outlook 2003 client ships with Microsoft Office 2003 and offers some very nice features when used with Exchange Server 2003, for example, remote client-server access and synchronization using the HTTP protocol. There are also Outlook 97, 98, 2000, and 2002 versions. Outlook nicely integrates electronic messaging, scheduling, and contact and task management with a whole bunch of other functions, including electronic journaling of every message that you read or file that you open. Take a look at Figures 1.1 and 1.2 in Chapter 1, for a refresher on Outlook's user interface.

Outlook modifies your Exchange mailbox, adding new folders for things such as your schedule, contacts, and tasks. More importantly, it uses a differently structured schedule database, so if you still have Microsoft Mail users lurking in your organization, you must decide whether you're going to use the older Microsoft Mail-based Schedule+ or Outlook for scheduling and contact/task management.

The Internet Browser Client

As I noted in Chapter 1, Exchange Server 2003 provides significantly improved support for Internet browser access to Exchange mailboxes and public folders. Using an Internet browser such as Microsoft's Internet Explorer 6 or later, you can surf the folders in your mailbox and your public folder store almost exactly as you would with a true Outlook client.

POP3 and IMAP4 Clients

Microsoft Internet Explorer 4 and later come with Outlook Express. This lighter-weight client supports both POP3 and IMAP4 server access. Except for Outlook 2003, the regular Outlook product line includes support only for POP3.

You can also find a number of POP3 and IMAP4 clients from third-party vendors. In addition to products such as Netscape's Navigator and Qualcomm's Eudora for Macs, Unix, and PCs, some of the most interesting of these clients run on handheld systems such as Palm's personal digital assistant (PDA) products and PDAs based on Microsoft's Pocket PC operating system. Armed with a POP3- or an IMAP4-capable PDA and a wireless connection, you can access, respond to, and manage your e-mail anywhere, anytime.

Schedule+ Clients

Schedule+ is a messaging-enabled application that includes scheduling, planning, and contact-management features. Version 7.5, the one that came with earlier versions of Exchange Server, was a serious update of the original version, which was labeled "version 1.0" (Microsoft has a knack for skipping version numbers). Most of the improvements lie in the way that it handles features such as schedule viewing, printing, and creating to-do lists, and less in the program's already pretty decent collaborative-scheduling function.

Microsoft Outlook Forms Designer Forms

Users and developers can create forms with the Outlook Forms Designer, a component of the Outlook client. Forms created with the designer can be used for a range of tasks, including the collection of data, and can have drop-down pick lists, multiple-choice selections, action buttons, and other useful attributes.

Forms created in the Microsoft Outlook Forms Designer can be stored on Exchange servers and made available to all or select users. With their Outlook clients, these users can send a form to specific recipients as messages, or post it in a public folder for others to access. Forms users can manually collate data collected in forms, or, with the right programming, data can be automatically extracted from forms and processed. (Look back at Figure 1.9 in Chapter 1 for a glimpse into the wonderful world of electronic forms.)

Custom Client-Based Applications

Aside from the Microsoft Outlook Forms Designer, there are a variety of ways to build client-based applications using Exchange Server's messaging capabilities:

◆ Microsoft's 95, 97, and 2000, 2002, and 2003 versions of applications (Word, Excel, and so on) include some nice collaborative tools and easy-to-use routing-slip capabilities based on Exchange messaging. Applications from other vendors also incorporate these capabilities.

◆ You can turn an Exchange message into any Object Linking and Embedding (OLE)–compliant application just by inserting an object from the app into the message.

◆ You can write programs that use Simple and Extended MAPI hooks or the X.400-oriented Common Mail Call APIs supported by Exchange Server.

◆ You can develop programs that use Exchange 2003's new file-based and Internet-based mailbox and public-folder access capabilities.

Summary

Exchange Server organizing components give hierarchical structure to your entire Exchange system. The Exchange hierarchy begins with your Exchange organization. Organizations contain administrative groups. Administrative groups contain Exchange servers. Recipients are the lowest rung of the Exchange 2003 hierarchy ladder. Four types of Exchange recipients exist: Exchange users, distribution groups, contacts, and public folders. All of these have a virtual presence in Windows 2003's Active Directory. The mailboxes of mailbox-enabled Exchange users and public folders reside physically on Exchange servers. Distribution groups and contacts are only Active Directory objects.

Core Exchange components include the Information Store, Routing Engine, and System Attendant. Each Exchange server sports one instance of each of these components. An Information Store can have one or more storage groups, depending on whether you're using the Standard or Enterprise edition of Exchange Server. Storage groups can contain one or more mailbox stores and/or one or more public folder stores. The Routing Engine moves messages between Exchange servers and between Exchange servers and the Internet. It uses SMTP services to perform these tasks. The Routing Engine also moves messages between Exchange servers and Exchange connectors. The System Attendant is responsible for a range of monitoring, security, and system maintenance tasks.

Exchange Server 2003 comes with a dizzying array of optional components, components that aren't required to start up Exchange server but that significantly enhance the Exchange environment. There are optional components for managing your Exchange organization and individual Exchange servers, keeping Exchange addresses in sync with foreign messaging system addresses, doing full-text indexing of Exchange server content, servicing a wide range of Internet protocols, and connecting Exchange servers to each other and to foreign messaging systems.

Exchange clients come in a wide variety of sizes and shapes. The Outlook client is most tightly integrated with the whole Exchange system; the Internet-based Outlook Web Access client comes in a close second. In addition, users can access messages on their Exchange servers using Internet standard POP3 or IMAP4 clients. Legacy Schedule+ calendaring information is available to Schedule+ and Outlook client users. Finally, Outlook electronic forms and custom applications can serve as clients for data stored on Exchange Server 2003.

The first four chapters of this book were designed to give you a firm grounding in Windows Server 2003 and Exchange Server 2003 architecture and concepts. With this information under your belt, you're now ready to move into the very important area of preinstallation planning, which is the topic of the next chapter. I strongly urge you not to skip Chapter 5, "Designing a New Exchange 2003 System." It not only provides you with some key information on planning, but it also discusses technical issues that are discussed nowhere else in this book.

Chapter 5

Designing a New Exchange 2003 System

WHETHER YOUR SYSTEM WILL be based on a single Exchange server in a single physical location and an Exchange 2003 administrative group or hundreds of Exchange servers spread out over multiple locations and administrative groups, you need to consider a number of design issues before implementation. This chapter presents a step-by-step planning model based loosely on a process developed by Microsoft. Tracking and retracking through these steps will help your organization decide where it wants to go with electronic messaging and how it can get there with Exchange. I can tell you from lots of experience that this process really works. Generally, I've found that I can gather any required information and generate a fairly complex first-draft plan, complete with a most convincing executive summary, in a month or so.

This chapter isn't just about design, though. It also offers practical information about Exchange Server 2003 and how it works. For example, you'll find detailed information about Exchange's network connection options: what they do and which networking topologies and protocols support them. Information such as this is central to designing and implementing an Exchange system, and it's not found anywhere else in this book.

This is a long chapter covering a great deal of information in detail. Just as you wouldn't try to implement a complex Exchange system in one day, you shouldn't try to plow through this chapter in one hour.

NOTE *Upgrading Exchange Server 5.5 systems to Windows Server 2003 and Exchange Server 2003 is covered in the next chapter. However, even if your immediate goal is an upgrade, I strongly suggest that you first carefully read this chapter.*

Featured in this chapter:

◆ Assigning accountabilities for planning, design, and management

◆ Performing a needs assessment

◆ Planning your network configuration

◆ Rolling out the plan

Taking the Large View

This discussion builds upon a 13-step process presented by Microsoft in the Exchange documentation and other Microsoft publications, but it is far from a word-for-word regurgitation. Therefore, you should blame me—not Microsoft—if you encounter any problems from following the advice I give in this chapter. (Of course, if this stuff helps in any way, you should send the fruit baskets and such to *me*.)

Here, then, are the steps that I suggest you follow in designing your Exchange Server 2003 system:

1. Assign planning, design, and management responsibilities to staff.
2. Assess user needs.
3. Study your organization's geographic profile.
4. Assess your organization's network.
5. Establish naming conventions.
6. Select a Microsoft networking domain model.
7. Define administrative group boundaries.
8. Define routing group boundaries.
9. Plan routing group links.
10. Plan servers and internal connections to them.
11. Plan connections to other systems.
12. Validate and optimize your design.
13. Roll out the plan.

These 13 steps fit nicely into four categories:

- Delegating the planning, design, and management of your Exchange 2003 system
- Analyzing user and technical needs
- The complex tasks involved in network planning
- The actual rollout of your Exchange system

Now let's discuss each of the steps in more detail. The following sections fully describe all of the tasks of designing and setting up an Exchange 2003 system and getting all the users up and running.

EXCHANGE DESIGN IS ITERATIVE, NOT LINEAR

Throughout this chapter, remember that designing an Exchange system is not a linear process, but an iterative one. You'll find yourself coming back to each of the steps to gather new information, to reinterpret information that you've already gathered, and to collect even more information based on those reinterpretations. New information will likely lead to design changes and further iterations. Even after you've fully implemented your Exchange Server 2003 system, you'll return to steps in the design process as problems arise or as your organization changes.

Within reason, the more iterations that you go through, the better your final design will be. But take care not to use iteration as a route to procrastination. Whatever you do, start running Exchange 2003—if only in a limited test environment—as soon as you can.

Assigning Accountabilities for Planning, Design, and Management

You need to ensure that two sets of specific responsibilities are assigned to staff. First, you have to assign a set of responsibilities related mostly to planning and design. Then you have to assign a second set of responsibilities that deal with ongoing management of key aspects of your Exchange Server 2003 system when it is in place.

Assign Responsibilities for Planning and Design

Microsoft has identified 14 different roles that must be filled in planning, designing, and, to some extent, implementing and operating an Exchange Server 2003 system. That doesn't mean that you need 14 staff members to fill these roles, but it does mean that you need to assign each of these roles to a staff member. If you're the only staff member, good luck!

Here's a list of the 14 roles and their related responsibilities.

Product Manager

- ◆ Sets objectives
- ◆ Manages external relationships
- ◆ Sets the budget

Program Manager

- ◆ Has overall responsibility for Microsoft Exchange network design and implementation
- ◆ Specifies Exchange messaging system functional requirements

Exchange Engineer   Determines technical configuration of all components of Exchange servers

Testing and QA Engineer   Ensures that the Exchange messaging system conforms to functional requirements and corporate standards

Operations Developer   Develops procedures, policies, and programs that monitor and control the Exchange network

Technical Consultant   Provides consulting services and problem resolution for internal business units

Training Developer   Develops training materials and documentation for end-users and technical support personnel

Rollout Planner

- ◆ Determines the most efficient way to roll out Exchange servers and accompanying Windows Servers
- ◆ Minimizes deployment costs
- ◆ Promotes efficient implementation

Migration Planner   Determines the work needed to migrate from an existing messaging system to Exchange Server 2003

Implementation Manager

- Manages the implementation of Exchange 2003 servers and associated components
- Manages the implementation of all of the plans made by all of the roles above

End-User Technical Support Technician   Provides end-user support for Exchange-related problems and questions

Messaging Transport Operations Engineer   Maintains, operates, and repairs the Exchange server environment after installation

Marketing and Consumer Relations Manager   Develops and carries out the Exchange rollout marketing program (product demonstrations, newsletters, pilot site coordination, and so on)

Financial Controller

- Monitors financial aspects of the project
- Tracks expenses against budget allocations

If you've ever implemented an information systems project, these roles are likely quite familiar to you, even if you've never thought specifically or in great detail about each of them. The key point here is that you're much more likely to successfully roll out your new Exchange Server 2003 system if you ensure that each of these 14 roles is properly filled. As we go through the planning and design process, think about these roles and how you might fill them.

Assign Responsibilities for Day-to-Day Management

When your Exchange Server 2003 system has been implemented, you need to fill five roles that support your system. Again, you might assign each of these roles to a separate person or combine them in one or two people. These five roles are listed here along with the responsibilities associated with them.

User Management   Administers at least Exchange Server 2003 aspects of Windows Server 2003 Active Directory, such as creation and management of recipients (Exchange users, distribution groups, and contacts)

Administrative Group Management   Administers select pieces of the Exchange Server 2003 environment based on organizational or security requirements

Routing Groups Management   Administers the routing groups created to allow for Exchange Server 2003 connectivity across lower-bandwidth networks

Public Folder Management   Administers Exchange Server 2003 public folder hierarchy

Application Development Management   Administers development of Exchange Server 2003–related add-on applications

This list is based on a list of three roles provided by Microsoft. I've taken some liberties with that list, separating Administrative Group and Routing Group management and adding Application Development Management.

As with the set of 14 roles illustrated in the preceding section, as we go through the planning and design process, think about these roles and how you might fill them.

Performing a Needs Assessment

A needs assessment is a two-part process. First, you must understand the current state of affairs in some detail. Then, using your knowledge about what is currently in place, you must come up with an analysis of need that focuses on both keeping the best of what is and developing new approaches where required. You should perform needs assessments in each of these categories:

- Users
- Geography
- Data networks

You'll probably find that assessing user needs will be the most difficult because you're dealing almost exclusively with people and their perceptions of their needs and those of your organization. You should focus on the fact that, in addition to being an e-mail system, Exchange is a platform for a range of collaborative applications. You also should remember that user needs and wants have significant costs in time, money, and computer and network capacity.

A geographical needs assessment focuses on what is where in buildings, cities, states, and countries. You need to know what kind of computing and networking hardware and software you have, and then you need to determine what, if any, changes must be made to ensure that everyone in your organization can participate in your Exchange system at a reasonably optimal level.

Exchange is nothing without quality network links from workstation to server and from server to server. Your network needs assessment should deal with three key issues. The first is the location and nature of your network connections, the second relates to the bandwidth on your network, and the third relates to network reliability.

Assess User Needs

Here you're interested in who needs what, when they need it, and how you'll provide it. You'll want to get a handle on the programming, software, hardware, MIS systems, systems support, and training resources that will be required to satisfy user needs.

Remember that Exchange is an electronic messaging package, not just an e-mail product. Users might need specific electronic messaging-enabled applications. Depending on what users have in mind, application development can be a real resource hog. Also remember that, in some cases, hardware and software might require new workstations, not just new servers.

Be prepared to give users a clear idea of what Exchange can do. You don't need to get technical with most users; just give them a view of Exchange from the end-user's perspective. Take another look at sections one and three of Chapter 1, "Introducing Exchange Server 2003," to see how you might organize your presentation.

Keep in mind that one of the biggest mistakes that most people make when implementing a system is to ignore or give only passing attention to this step. Knowing as much as you can about what the users require up front means that you'll have an easier time during implementation. For example, imagine that you don't know from the get-go that your organization could benefit significantly from a particular custom-programmed electronic messaging–enabled application. You go ahead and implement Exchange as an e-mail system with only the resources such an implementation requires. You get your Exchange system up, and it's perking along just fine when, maybe three months later, some user comes up with this great idea for an electronic messaging–enabled app. Boink! Suddenly you have to tell management that you need a few programmers and maybe more hardware to implement this idea that nobody thought of four or five months ago. I'll leave the rest to your imagination.

NOTE   Regardless of what you find out in your user needs assessment, add a fudge factor in favor of more hardware and support personnel. Exchange has so many capabilities that you can be sure your users will find all kinds of ways to challenge whatever resources you make available. Depending on your users and their ability to get away with unplanned demands for resources, fudging by as much as 25 percent is reasonable. You can go with less fudge if your organization is particularly cost-conscious and willing to adhere closely to plans.

Suffice it to say that a user needs assessment is the single most important part of the Exchange design process. Therefore, we'll cover it in more detail than the other 13 Exchange design steps.

QUESTIONS TO ASK

You'll want to answer a number of questions during your user needs assessment. Here are the major ones:

◆ What kinds of users (for example, managers, salespeople, clerical staff, lawyers, doctors) does my organization have, and what do they think they want from the new Exchange system?

◆ What sorts of electronic messaging services are different groups of users likely to need (for example, e-mail, calendars and scheduling, public folders, specially designed applications)?

◆ In addition to LAN access, will users need wireless LAN and/or WAN access to your Exchange system? Will this access have to be secure?

◆ Which specially designed applications can be developed by users, and which must be developed by MIS personnel?

◆ Do all users need every capability from day one, or can implementation be phased in, perhaps based on user groupings?

◆ What sorts of demands will users (or groups of users) put on your Exchange servers? Much of the information in this category can be used with Microsoft's Exchange server load simulation program to predict expected server load and project server hardware and networking requirements.

   ◆ How many mailboxes will you create per server?

   ◆ How many messages will the typical user send per day?

   ◆ How many messages will the typical user receive per day?

- How frequently will users send messages to others...

  - On their server?

  - In their routing group?

  - In each of the other routing groups in your organization?

  - Outside your organization? (Be sure to break this down by the different kinds of external connections you'll have.)

- How often will users read messages in their mailboxes?

- How often will users read messages in public folders?

- How often will users move messages to personal folders stored locally and on the network?

- How often will users move messages to public folders?

- How big will the messages be? What percentage will be 1K, 2K, 4K, 10K, 40K, 60K, 80K, 100K, 200K, and so on?

- What level of message delivery service will users want and need? This should be stated in hours or minutes between the time a message is sent and received. You'll need to specify this for both internal and external communications.

- What sorts of hardware and software resources (for example, computers, personal digital assistants, operating systems, Outlook client licenses) will different groups of users need to implement Exchange on the client side?

- What kinds of training will be required for users or groups of users?

- What sorts of MIS resources will be required to support user needs?

Study Your Organization's Geographic Profile

You need a list of all the geographical units in your organization. Here you should think not only in terms of cities, states, and countries, but also in-city and even in-building locations. Start at the top and work your way down. At this point, diagrams are important. Draw maps and building layouts.

This is the time to gather information on the workstations and servers you have in each location. You'll want to know how many run each of the different kinds of operating systems in your organization. Operating systems to watch for include these:

- Windows Server 2003

- Windows 2000 and NT Workstation and Server

- Novell NetWare 7 and earlier, and NetWare IPX/SPX workstations

- Windows 95/98/XP

- Windows 3.1*x*

- MS-DOS

- Apple Macintosh

- Unix workstations by type of operating system

- Banyan VINES servers and workstations

- Workstations used remotely

If you have hardware and software inventories for these machines, your job will be a lot easier. You can use all the information that you collect about workstations and servers to determine who's ready for Exchange and how many Outlook client licenses you'll have to buy.

As you gather information in other steps, begin to look at it in the context of your geographic profile. For example, you'll want to meld geographic information with what you find out about user needs and user groupings.

MORE ON USER WORKSTATIONS

Most user workstations are underpowered. That's a pretty strong statement, but I stand by it. I limped along for quite some time running Windows 2000 Advanced Server on a substandard 400MHz Pentium II workstation with 128MB of memory. Then I moved up to a 1GHz dual Pentium III processor and 768MB of RAM. When I ran Windows 2000 on my old, underpowered sleepwalker, it was all I could do to keep my word processor, a spreadsheet, and my e-mail software open at the same time. If I opened anything else, the machine started thrashing around so much between RAM and virtual memory that it slowed to a nearly useless crawl.

With my new system and Windows Server 2003 Enterprise Edition, I can run word-processing programs, spreadsheet programs, and Outlook together without wasting precious time to switch among them. And I still have plenty of horsepower left for all those tasks that I used to do with paper because I couldn't bring up the applications fast enough when I needed them. At will, I can now simultaneously open—and keep open—such apps as an accounting package and Microsoft Word, Excel, Project, and PowerPoint. With all that computer power, I'm also no longer reluctant to run other key programs—say, web browsers or Windows 2003 Control Panel applets—at the drop of a hat.

Here's the bottom line: I've had my new system for less than a year. By my estimates, the productivity increase that I've experienced in that time has already paid back the cost of the system's purchase.

Maybe all your users don't need a dual 1GHz Pentium system with Windows Server 2003 and 768MB of RAM. However, as you start assessing user needs, don't let the dismal state of your organization's stable of workstations stop you and your users from reaching for the stars as you think about potential applications for Exchange. You'll notice that I talk here about my Windows Server 2003 desktop system, not my Windows 95, 98, ME, or XP Home Edition system. Users don't need servers as workstations. However, I strongly urge you to consider starting with or moving to at least the Windows XP Professional Edition workstation product for desktop business computing.

Assess Your Organization's Network

In this step, you just want to know what your network looks like now. This isn't the place to get into what kinds of networking you'll need; that comes later. You need to answer four key questions here:

- What's connected to what, and how? (Okay, if you're counting, that's two questions.)
- How much bandwidth do we have on each network?
- How reliable are our networks?

WHAT'S CONNECTED TO WHAT, AND HOW?

Generally, in answering these questions, you should start at the top of your organization and work down to the domain or server level. For each link, name the

- Physical connection
- Networking topology
- Networking protocols running on the connection

For example, physical connection = local hardwire, networking topology = 100BaseT Ethernet, networking protocols = NetBEUI, TCP/IP, IPX/SPX, SNA. This information, especially when combined with the information you collected in steps 1, 2, and 3, will prove valuable as you start to plan for the Exchange connectivity that you'll need.

In looking at your organization's network, don't forget about connections to the outside world. Do you have connections to the Internet, X.400 messaging systems, or trading partners?

HOW MUCH BANDWIDTH DO YOU HAVE ON EACH NETWORK?

Although bandwidth begins with network topology (type of connection), such as 100BaseT, T1, and DSL, it doesn't stop there. You need to know how much of your network topology's theoretical bandwidth is actually available.

To assess the actual bandwidth on each of your networks, you need some help from a network monitoring tool. If your networks are Windows 2003– or NT–based, you can try using the performance monitoring tools that come with these operating systems to get a handle on traffic. For Windows NT, select Start Menu ➤ Programs ➤ Administrative Tools ➤ Performance Monitor. For Windows 2000 and 2003, select Start Menu ➤ Programs ➤ Administrative Tools ➤ Performance.

For NetWare systems, try one of the many software-based network traffic monitors out there. A lot of modern network hubs, switches, and such also come with excellent network-monitoring software. If you're flush with cash, go for a hardware-based monitor, such as Network Associates' Sniffer (www.nai.com). If cash is an issue, take a look at a software-based monitor. My favorite is CommView from TamoSoft (www.tamos.com).

What you want here is a chart that tells you, on average, how much of a network's bandwidth is available during each of the 24 hours in a day. You'll have to take several samples to get reliable data, but it's worth it. A warning light should go on in your head if you're already using more than, say, 60–70 percent of the available bandwidth on any network during daytime hours and you're not already running a heavy-duty messaging system such as Exchange. With that kind of scenario, you just might have to make some changes in the network before installing Exchange. We'll talk about those changes later; for now, be sure to collect this data on available bandwidth and incorporate it into your organizational maps.

HOW RELIABLE ARE YOUR NETWORKS?

Having a reliable network is an important issue. Increasingly in corporate America, there is strong pressure to centralize network servers. Centralization makes good economic sense. If all network servers are in one place, one set of staff can support and monitor them, ensuring 24-hours-a-day, 7-days-a-week uptime.

Of course, 24/7 server availability is useless if the networks that people use to get to the servers are unreliable. I've seen this little scenario play itself out in several organizations: They centralize the servers, the network fails, users can't get to their now mission-critical e-mail and other data, responsible IS planners are roundly criticized, and lower-level IS personnel are even more heavily criticized or fired. Grrr!

Here's the bottom line: Don't make your users work on unreliable networks. If your networks can't come close to matching the reliability of your servers, put the servers closer to their users. The little extra that it costs to manage decentralized servers is worth the access insurance that it buys. Sure, get those networks up to par, but don't risk your Exchange implementation on centralized servers before a reliable network is in place to support them.

Planning Your Network Configuration

Although it takes but a few words to say, planning your network configuration will take you on a long and winding road. In the process, you need to do the following:

1. Establish naming conventions for objects in your Exchange server hierarchy.
2. Select a Microsoft networking domain model.
3. Define administrative group boundaries.
4. Define routing group boundaries.
5. Plan routing group links.
6. Plan servers and internal connections to them.
7. Plan connections to other systems.
8. Validate and optimize your design.

You need to establish naming conventions for your Exchange organization, administrative groups, servers, and recipients. Some of these names depend on how you name Windows 2003 objects, while others have no dependency on the operating system. The Windows 2003 domain model that you choose will significantly affect how your Exchange servers interact, especially from a security standpoint.

Administrative groups replace the security groupings function of Exchange 5.5's sites. How you set their boundaries depends heavily on how you want to parcel out responsibility for Exchange server management in your organization. Routing groups replace the server-to-server communication functionality of Exchange 5.5 sites. Clear, technically appropriate routing group boundaries and links are essential to smooth wide-area exchange of messages and other information between servers in Exchange 2003 environments.

The servers where you install Exchange 2003 must have adequate capacity. Even if you plan for servers of very high capacity and even though Exchange 2003 allows lots of mailboxes on a server, you should at least consider distributing user mailboxes across multiple servers to increase performance; you also should consider setting user storage quotas to ensure adequate disk capacity over time. In addition, you should be sure that your servers are protected against low-level and catastrophic glitches by such things as fault-tolerant hardware, uninterruptible power supplies, and a reliable backup system. Finally, you should ensure that users have adequate bandwidth to access messages and other objects on your Exchange servers.

If you need to link to public messaging services such as the Internet or the X.400 system, you have to think about the Exchange connectors that support these services. If you need to access third-party messaging systems such as cc:Mail or SNADS, you have to factor connectors or gateways for these into your plans.

Finally, when key aspects of your Exchange system are in place, you need to test them to be sure that they work at all. Then you need to ensure that they work up to whatever performance and other standards you need to meet.

Okay, let's start our trip down that long and winding road.

Establish Naming Conventions

Here you set some criteria for naming the four key Exchange organizational components:

- Organization
- Administrative groups
- Servers
- Recipients

Your goal should be to establish a logical and consistent set of naming conventions that fit in well with your real-world organizational structure and culture.

NAMING THE ORGANIZATION, ADMINISTRATIVE GROUPS, AND SERVERS

Here's one easy and usually safe naming convention that you can use:

Organization The master company name, for example, Barry Gerber and Associates

Administrative Group A geographic location or a department, for example, Los Angeles or Sales

Server Generic naming, for example, EXCHANGE01

Names for organizations and administrative groups can be up to 256 characters long, but I strongly suggest that you keep names to around 32 characters, just so that you can see them in the tree of the Exchange Server 2003 System Manager. Server names are set when you install Windows Server 2003. They are limited to a maximum of 63 characters, but you should limit them to 15 characters if pre–Windows 2000/XP clients will access them.

For most names, almost any character is permitted. However, for organization, administrative groups, and server names, I strongly suggest you use only the 26 uppercase and lowercase letters of the alphabet, and the numerals 0 through 9. Don't use spaces, underscores, or any accented letters.

NAMING RECIPIENT MAILBOXES

You also need some criteria for naming mailboxes. There are four key names for each Exchange mailbox:

◆ First

◆ Last

◆ Display

◆ Alias

Mailbox administrators create and modify these names in the Windows 2003 Active Directory Users and Computers Microsoft Management Console snap-in.

The first and last names are entered when creating the user's Windows 2003 login account. The display name is created from the first and last name (as well as the middle initial or name, if present). The alias name is created from the user's Windows 2003 logon name, which is entered when the user's Windows 2003 account is created.

The first and last names and the display name are Windows 2003 objects that are also used by Exchange. The alias is an Exchange object that is used in forming some Exchange e-mail addresses, for example, the user's Internet address.

You can change the default rules for constructing mailbox names, and you can manually change these names. In Figure 5.1, you can see the first and last names as well as the display name for my Exchange 2003 mailbox. Figure 5.2 shows the alias name for my mailbox.

FIGURE 5.1
Display names are created using first and last names when a Windows 2003 user account is created.

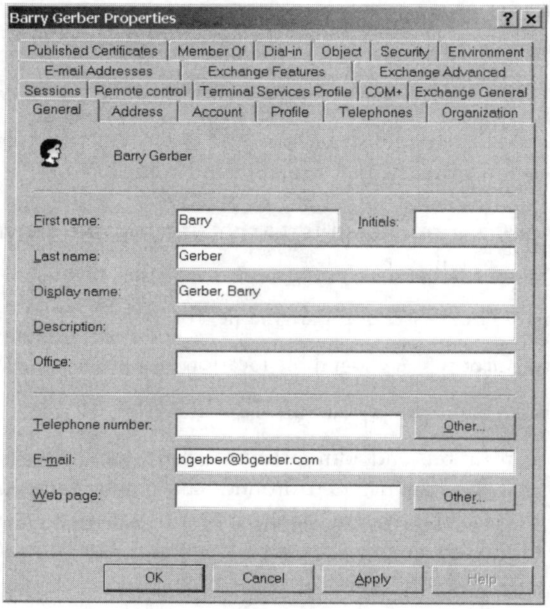

FIGURE 5.2

The alias name for an Exchange 2003 mailbox

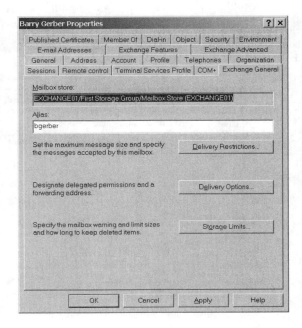

Display Names

The Outlook client global address book shows the display name for each mailbox (see Figure 5.3). You need to decide on a convention for display names. Options include: *first-name-space-last-name* (as in John Smith) or *last-name-comma-space-first-name* (as in Smith, John). The default is *first-name-space-last name*. I'll show you how to change this default in Chapter 11, "Managing Exchange Users, Distribution Groups, and Contacts."

Display names can be up to 256 characters long. Display names are only a convenience—they're not a part of the mailbox's e-mail address. However, they are the way in which Exchange users find the people they want to communicate with, so don't scrimp when setting them up. You might even want to include department names or titles in display names so that users aren't faced with ambiguous selections, as they might be if they encountered a list of 25 recipients named John Smith. You can also create custom address lists ordered by attributes of users. For example, you can create an address list that includes only users in a specific department.

Practically speaking, display name lengths should be limited only by your users' willingness to read through lots of stuff to find the mailbox they're looking for.

Full-blown arguments have sprung up around the metaphysics of display name conventions. I'll leave the decision to you, although I prefer the convention *Last_Name, First_Name* (as in Doe, Jane). It's easier for me to find Jane Doe among a list of the Does than among a list of the Janes.

FIGURE 5.3

The Exchange client global address book shows each mailbox's display name.

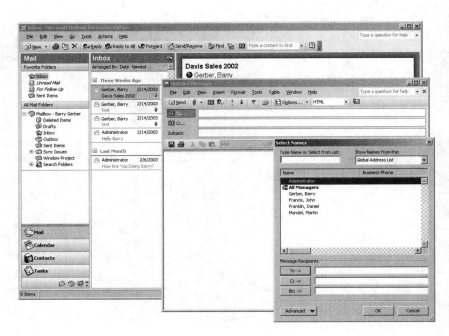

WARNING   *Something as apparently simple as changing the default order of last and first name in display names isn't all that simple with Exchange 2003. In Exchange Server 5.5, you made the change in the Exchange Administrator program. With Windows Server 2003/Exchange Server 2003, you have to edit the Active Directory Schema. Why? Display names aren't just for Exchange mailboxes anymore. They're also used whenever end users or system administrators go looking for a specific Windows 2003 user in Active Directory. That's why it's an Active Directory issue. Editing Active Directory is somewhat akin to editing the Windows registry. It's not a job for amateurs, and it's a job that may be done by someone not directly involved in day-to-day Exchange Server 2003 management. In addition, the decision to change the display name default for an Active Directory namespace is no longer simply an Exchange Server issue. It's an organization-wide issue because these changes affect more than electronic messaging.*

Alias Names

For some messaging systems, the user's mailbox is identified by an alias name, which is part of the mailbox's address. Either Exchange itself or the gateway for the foreign mail system constructs an address using the alias. For other messaging systems, the mailbox name is constructed from other information. Figure 5.4 shows the two addresses that Exchange built for me by default for the Internet and for X.400. My Internet addresses use the alias bgerber. X.400 addresses do not use the alias. Instead, they use the full first and last name attributes of the user. In addition to being available for message interchange with X.400 systems, the X.400 address is also used for internal Exchange message addressing.

FIGURE 5.4
Exchange Server uses
the mailbox alias
or the first and last
names to construct
e-mail addresses.

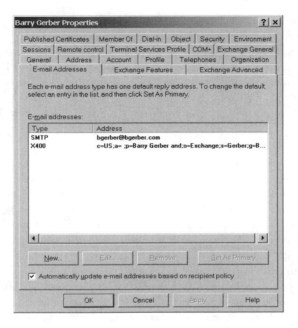

Aliases can be up to 63 characters long. That's too long, of course, because some people in foreign messaging systems will have to type in the alias as part of an electronic messaging address. Try to keep aliases short—10 characters is long enough.

For some foreign messaging system addressing schemes, Exchange must remove illegal characters and shorten the alias to meet maximum character-length requirements. For example, underscores become question marks in X.400 addresses. Do all you can to ensure that aliases are constructed using less-esoteric characters.

Alias naming conventions are a religious issue too, so you'll get no recommendations from me.

Select a Microsoft Networking Domain Model

As I noted in earlier chapters, particularly in Chapter 3, "Two Key Architectural Components of Windows Server 2003," Microsoft very much wants you to strongly consider using a single root Windows 2003 domain model for your network. You can still create child domains (subdomains) and control access to various network resources using this model.

Aside from certain security requirements, one of the main reasons for multidomain NT networks was the difficulty of building single domains that crossed lower-bandwidth links. Microsoft has outfitted Windows 2003 with such features as sites and site connectors to deal with this issue. Unless you must adhere to strong regulatory or security requirements, the single-root domain model really makes the most sense.

If it works for your organization, you can even use your Internet domain name for your Windows 2003 root domain. This simplifies Exchange server installation, although you need to be especially careful to protect any internal resources that shouldn't be accessible on the Internet. If you want to use a separate name for your Windows 2003 root domain, then do so, by all means. You can still use your Internet domain name for external Exchange messaging. I like this approach and use .local for Windows domain names, and .com, .edu, and so on for Internet domain names.

This is not the last you'll see of Windows 2003 domains in this book. Chapter 6, "Upgrading to Windows Server 2003 and Exchange Server 2003," includes a discussion of the role of domains in a Windows 2003/Exchange 2003 upgrade. Chapter 7, "Installing Windows Server 2003 as a Domain Controller," focuses on domains in the installation of new Windows 2003 servers.

Define Administrative Group Boundaries

Administrative groups play a couple of roles. First, they can be used to control administrative access to your Exchange server environment. You can set permissions on an administrative group so that only certain users can manage the servers and other objects in the group. In this way, you can parcel out responsibility for managing different sets of Exchange servers to different people. Second, you create routing groups, which we'll discuss next, inside administrative groups in what are called Routing Groups containers. When Exchange Server 2003 is installed, one administrative group is created, and within that group, one Routing Groups container is created.

The administrative group structure of your Exchange Server environment will probably depend to some extent on the structure of your organization. If you want a particular group, such as a department, to manage its own Exchange server environment, you would create an administrative group, put the department's Exchange server(s) in the administrative group, and assign permissions to manage the group to the appropriate Windows 2003 users or group.

If you want, you can create administrative groups solely for the purpose of managing message routing. In this case, administrative groups become a convenient way to group together like Exchange servers and control routing between them.

Define Routing Group Boundaries

When defining routing group boundaries, you should keep a couple of things in mind. First, Exchange routing groups and Microsoft network domains are related. Second, all the Exchange servers in a routing group should have certain networking capabilities.

REQUIRED NETWORKING CAPABILITIES

With the right security in place, the moment that an Exchange server starts running, it automatically begins communicating with other Exchange servers. Initially, these communications are mostly related to swapping messages. You can also replicate public folders across Exchange servers.

You don't have to do a thing to start inter-Exchange server communications—they just happen. The first time this happens, you'll jump for joy, especially if you're accustomed to those old-fashioned e-mail systems such as Microsoft Mail, with all their gizmo gateways, dirsync machines, and such.

You create routing groups and add Exchange servers to them to ensure that servers linked by adequate bandwidth networks communicate optimally—basically, at the highest speeds possible without any intervention on the network side other than controls built into the networking hardware and software.

You then create inter–routing group connectors to ensure the integrity and reliability of links between servers on networks with less than optimal bandwidth. For example, routing group connectors let you schedule connections where required, and some even let you build redundant links so that the failure of one link doesn't stop interserver communications.

Because users in a routing group often have some affinity for each other, you can usually expect higher user messaging and folder replication traffic between servers in one routing group than between servers in different routing groups.

All this intra–routing group/interserver network traffic requires that Exchange servers in a routing group be connected by a high-bandwidth dedicated network, but high bandwidth isn't absolute. For example, from Exchange's perspective, a 155Mbps ATM link isn't high-bandwidth if you're eating up 154.9Mbps sending continuous streams of video images. There are no hard and fast rules here, but any physical network that can provide Exchange with 512Kbps of bandwidth most of the time should be adequate. Lower bandwidths can work in cases where messaging traffic is light and public folder replication is nonexistent or kept to a bare minimum. Physical networks capable of delivering at least this kind of dedicated bandwidth include faster Frame Relay and satellite, full T1, microwave, DSL, T3, Ethernet, Token Ring, Fast Ethernet, Gigabit Ethernet, FDDI, ATM, and SONET.

CONSIDER DSL

Digital Subscriber Line (DSL) networking is finally available in many locales in the United States. DSL is a variable-bandwidth networking topology. Bandwidth ranges from as little as 64Kbps through T1. Compared with most other higher-bandwidth technologies, DSL is inexpensive: I currently pay $130 per month for a 384Kbps always-on business-oriented symmetrical DSL Internet link with multiple IP addresses. This link supports my Exchange Server connection to Internet mail as well as a lot of other Internet-based functionality, such as an FTP service, a web server, and a time-sync service. As we'll see in Chapter 15, "Installing and Managing Additional Exchange Servers," always-on links offer distinct advantages when you're connecting Exchange servers to the Internet.

Plan Routing Group Links

As I noted previously, you link routing groups by running one or more Exchange connectors on Exchange servers in each routing group. There's no need for each Exchange server in a routing group to run its own connectors; one Exchange server can serve all the inter–routing group needs of all Exchange servers in a routing group. However, if a routing group has two or more Exchange servers, it often makes sense to run routing group connectors on multiple servers. This improves performance and, if you use different network links for each connector, allows for redundant links between routing groups.

ROUTING GROUP LINK OPTIONS

You can connect routing groups either *directly* or *indirectly*. Direct connections are point-to-point connections between servers; indirect links pass through foreign electronic messaging systems. Both direct and indirect connections use SMTP messages to move user communications and public folder replication information between Exchange servers in different routing groups. With direct connections, the servers talk directly to each other. With indirect connections, the servers communicate by sending messages through a mediating messaging system. Exchange Server 2003 allows for indirect routing group connection options using either a public X.400 service or the Internet mail service.

NOTE *I use the terms connection and link to refer to two very different things. In the previous paragraph, they refer to the way servers communicate with each other, whether directly or indirectly. In other places in this book, connection and link refer to actual physical and protocol-level networking options, such as Ethernet, TCP/IP, and X.400. I tried without success to find another word to modify the terms direct and indirect.*

When connecting Exchange routing groups, you get to choose among three connector options:

◆ Routing group connector (direct link only)

◆ X.400 connector (direct or indirect link)

◆ SMTP connector (direct or indirect link)

Let's look at each of these in more detail.

The Routing Group Connector

Of all the Exchange connectors, the routing group connector is the fastest and simplest to set up and manage. In addition, of all the ways to link routing groups, the routing group connector is most similar to the automatic, built-in links between Exchange servers in the same routing group. Like built-in links, the routing group connector moves messages and folder replication information between Exchange 2003 servers using Exchange's standard SMTP messaging format. The major difference is that the routing group connector allows for scheduling connections, optionally transmitting messages with large attachments at different times than smaller messages, providing redundant links, and prioritizing multiple routing group connections based on the bandwidth available for each connection.

The routing group connector requires a continuous network. It doesn't support dial-up links, and it's best suited to Exchange inter–routing group connections with heavy user loads and public folder replication duties. If you already have a wide area network with adequate bandwidth in place, the routing group connector can be especially attractive because you don't need to add any networking infrastructure to support the connector. Of course, if you're expecting heavy cross-routing group network loads, you need high-bandwidth network connections such as those provided by topologies like T1, DSL, Ethernet, Token Ring, T3, Fast Ethernet, Gigabit Ethernet, FDDI, ATM, and SONET. When you begin considering the higher-capacity networking topologies listed here to link routing groups, you might want to go one step further and merge the routing groups to take advantage of Exchange Server's higher-performance intra–routing group communications.

The X.400 Connector

Microsoft recommends that the X.400 connector be used primarily for connecting to and exchanging messages with foreign X.400 messaging systems. Microsoft recommends the X.400 connector for direct or indirect routing group links only when an X.400 networking infrastructure is already in place.

The X.400 connector can run on top of two different networking protocols: TCP/IP and OSI TP0 (X.25). The X.400 connector can support dial-up links between Exchange servers. The X.400

connector is one alternative to Exchange 5.5's dynamic remote access connector, which doesn't exist in Exchange Server 2003.

You can schedule X.400 routing group links. This allows you to take advantage of lower off-hours connection costs. You also can schedule transmission of messages with large attachments for different hours than messages without attachments or with smaller attachments.

The X.400 connector is a bit slower than the routing group connector, both because it must translate to and from the X.400 format when that format is used for inter–routing group communications, and because there's some extra networking overhead involved in X.400 communications.

Cost considerations lead most organizations to opt for lower, sublocal area network bandwidth links to public X.400 providers. That's fine, but it means that indirect routing group links should be used mostly for low-traffic routing group connections and to provide redundant links for routing groups already connected by higher-bandwidth direct links.

The SMTP Connector

As I noted in Chapter 4, the main function of the SMTP connector is to add functionality to the SMTP service that is native to Windows Server 2003. We'll talk about SMTP services and using the SMTP connector for Internet mail in Chapter 13, "Managing Exchange 2003 Internet Services."

The SMTP connector also lets you link routing groups. You can use standard TCP/IP links or dial-up links with the SMTP connector. As with the X.400 connector, you can schedule connectivity with the SMTP service and separately schedule transmission of messages with large attachments.

NOTE *Just to be sure we've got things straight, let's go over terminology. The routing group connector allows for scheduling connections, optionally transmitting messages with large attachments at different times than smaller messages, providing redundant links, and prioritizing multiple routing group connections based on the bandwidth available for each connection. The X.400 and SMTP connectors support only scheduling and message size.*

Plan Servers and Internal Connections to Them

There's quite a bit to do in planning your servers and user links. You must decide what kinds of hardware to use for each of your Exchange servers. Then you need to think through some policies relating to storage. After that, you must figure out how to back up the servers. Then you need to make sure you've got adequate bandwidth on your local networks to keep Exchange happy; if you don't have it, you have to decide how to get it. Finally, before you go on to the next step in the Exchange design process, you must think about remote users and how you'll connect them to Exchange.

DESIGNING YOUR EXCHANGE SERVERS

The intricacies of Exchange Server design and fine-tuning could occupy a whole book; you'll have to experiment here. Fortunately, Microsoft doesn't leave you out in the cold when it comes to this experimentation. The company provides an application for testing the capacity of hardware that is a candidate to run Exchange Server 2003. It's called LoadSim. LoadSim tests your server hardware (CPU, disk drives, RAM) and network capacity by simulating messaging loads on an Exchange 2003 server. You can find it in the Exchange Server 2003 Resource Kit.

To begin your experimentation, install Windows Server 2003 and Exchange Server 2003, and then run LoadSim. Next, take out that set of user-demand numbers that you put together when you did your user needs assessment. Plug those numbers into LoadSim, and run it against a reasonable Exchange server machine—say, a 1GHz Pentium III or 4 or Xeon machine with 768MB of memory and at least two 9GB SCSI hard drives. Don't run LoadSim on your Exchange server. Instead, run it on a separate 1GHz or better Pentium-based Windows XP workstation with at least 512MB of memory. And don't try to simulate more than 200 users on one LoadSim machine. If you don't follow these guidelines, LoadSim might not be capable of generating the loads that you've asked it to, and you could be led to believe that your Exchange server hardware is adequate, when it's not.

In selecting servers for Exchange, my rule is always to go for the biggest guns that you can afford, commensurate with expected user loads. After working a while now with Windows Server 2003 and Exchange Server 2003, I have my own ideas about server sizing. My monster machine of the week would be a dual Intel Pentium III or Xeon 1GHz or greater computer with 1GB of random access memory (RAM) and a hardware RAID 5 disk capacity of at least 60GB. Such a computer should be capable of handling upwards of 1,000 average Exchange Server 2003 users, network bandwidth willing.

TIP *As Intel Itanium 64-bit processors become available, I urge you to consider them carefully. As I noted in Chapter 2, "Windows Server 2003 and Exchange Server 2003," a 64-bit processor expands some Windows 2003 capabilities, such as allowing for increased memory capacity.*

While I'm in recommendation mode, let me talk about running Exchange Server 2003 on a Windows 2003 domain controller. If you can afford the hardware, it's best to run Exchange 2003 on a Windows Server 2003 that is not also a domain controller. Unlike Exchange 5.5, which might benefit from running on an NT 4 domain controller, Exchange 2003 not only doesn't benefit from running on a domain controller, but it actually suffers as it competes with Active Directory and other CPU/disk-intensive software that runs on a Windows Server 2003 domain controller.

If you had to gulp a few times after reading my recommendations for a production Exchange 2003 server, don't worry. You can get by with less horsepower, especially if you need to support fewer users. In my experience, Windows Server 2003 alone requires more memory than NT Server 4, so don't cheap out on memory. Go for a minimum of 512MB, even in a server with a 1GHz Pentium III or 4.

If you do decide to go with less costly or less powerful hardware, I strongly suggest that you go with SCSI disk drives over Enhanced IDE drives. Enhanced IDE drives are nice, but for production Exchange Servers, I prefer SCSI drives. They're fast and tend to be more reliable than IDE drives over the long haul. For best performance, choose ultrawide SCSI drives.

NOTE *For the record, Exchange Server 2003 is compatible with Windows 2000 Server. You lose a few features that depend on Windows Server 2003 capabilities, such as the capability to quickly make volume snapshot backups. However, if you want to get started with Exchange Server 2003 quickly and your systems are Windows 2000–based, you might want to start by installing Exchange 2003 on Windows 2000 Server.*

When you're comfortable with the basic design of your servers, you need to plan for uninterruptible power supplies (UPSs). I consider a UPS to be part of a server, not an add-on. UPSs are cheap, given the peace of mind that they can bring. In spite of Windows Server 2003's and Exchange Server 2003's capability of recovering from most disastrous events, you don't want to tempt fate and risk damage to your organization's precious electronic messaging data. Get enough UPSs to serve the power needs of each server, and get a UPS that comes with software to gracefully shut down your servers if power stays off for an extended period. I'll talk more about UPSs in Chapter 7.

SERVER FAULT TOLERANCE

The more fault tolerance you can build into your Exchange server hardware, the better you and your users will sleep at night. Almost nothing is worse than losing even one user's e-mail messages. Here are a few steps that you can take to improve server fault tolerance.

◆ Look for systems with error-correcting RAM memory.

◆ On the disk side, consider multiple SCSI controllers or RAID level 5 technologies implemented in hardware.

◆ Look for computers with two or more redundant power supplies.

◆ Buy computers that let you swap out failed RAID drives and power supplies without even bringing down your system.

◆ Consider Microsoft's Windows 2003 Advanced and Datacenter Server editions, which let you set up clusters of Windows 2003/Exchange 2003 servers with the cluster being able to continue serving users even if one cluster node fails.

SETTING EXCHANGE SERVER STORAGE POLICIES

You need to start thinking now about how you'll manage user storage on each server. Storage management gives you more control over how much of what is stored on Exchange server disks, and it helps you remain within your server disk budget. You need to answer several disk management policy questions, including these:

◆ Do you want some or all of your users to store messages in personal folders on a workstation or non–Exchange networked disk drives instead of in their Exchange server–based mailboxes?

◆ For those who will use their Exchange server mailboxes, do you want to limit the amount of storage that they can use?

◆ Do you want to impose limits on the storage used by public folders?

◆ If you have public folders containing messages that lose value with time (for example, messages from Internet lists or Usenet news feeds), do you want Exchange to automatically delete messages from these folders based on message age?

◆ Will you implement Exchange Server's capability to save deleted messages for a designated period of time? This is a neat capability because users can recover messages that they accidentally deleted. However, all those "deleted" messages can take up lots of Exchange server disk space.

You can base your answers to most of these questions on the results of your user needs assessment, although you're bound to make adjustments as you pass through iterations of the design process. Also note that while it's tempting to force users to store messages in personal folders on local or non–Exchange networked disk drives to save on Exchange server disk, you then run the risk that key user messages won't get backed up. As the ever-present "they" say, "You pays your money and you takes your chances."

BACKING UP YOUR EXCHANGE SERVERS

When you know what your Exchange servers and networks will look like, you can begin thinking about backing up your servers. You need to use backup software that is especially designed for Exchange's client/server transaction-oriented architecture. Such software enables you to back up an Exchange server's information store without shutting down Exchange processes and thus closing off user access to the server. The software communicates with Exchange's information store service to ensure that the databases that it is responsible for are fully backed up. I'll talk more about the fine points of Exchange backup in Chapter 8, "Installing Exchange Server 2003" and Chapter 17, "Exchange Server Reliability and Availability."

Windows Server 2003's own backup program has add-ons to do a proper backup of Exchange servers. Windows 2003's volume snapshot capability is a great way to get a consistent image of a disk drive while applications such as Exchange are running and on-line. Other Windows Server 2003 backup vendors, such as Computer Associates' ArcServeIT (www.cai.com) and Veritas Software's Backup Exec (www.veritas.com), have released add-ons to their products that can properly back up Exchange Server 2003. They can also support Windows 2003's volume snapshot capability. These products add better backup scheduling, easier-to-use logs, multiple server backup from a single instance of the backup program, quicker and easier restore of backed up data, and disaster recovery options.

Backups can be to tape or disk or, for greater reliability, to both. Volume snapshots are best and most quickly done to disk. Do backups to tape during off-hours when backup speed is less an issue. Be sure to include both backup disk and backup tape in your hardware/software backup resources plans.

You can back up an Exchange server either locally or over the network. When you back it up over the network, you can run the backup from a Windows 2003 server or from an Exchange 2003 server. For Exchange servers with lots of disk space (5GB or more) and slow network links to potential backup servers (less than 100Mbps), I strongly suggest that you bypass the networked server backup option and do the backup locally on and from the Exchange server itself. You have to spend some money on a backup device and software for the Exchange server, but you'll get it back in available bandwidth and faster backups. Available bandwidth means that other network-dependent tasks—and there are lots of those on a Windows 2003/Exchange 2003 network—run faster. Faster backups mean shorter periods of that awful feeling you get when important data is not yet on tape.

Whether you back up over the network or locally, don't skimp on backup hardware. You're going to *add* hard disk storage to your Exchange server, not take it away. Go for high-capacity 4mm, 8mm, or DLT tape backup systems. Think about tape autoloaders, those neat gizmos that give one or more tape drives automatic access to anything from a few tapes to hundreds of them. If you choose to use disk in your backup strategy, use solid RAID-5 disk-based backup systems or, if your organization has the resources and you need their special features, consider Storage Area Networks with their sophisticated backup systems.

Don't forget those personal folders stored on user workstations. You have to decide who will be responsible for backing them up: Exchange staff, other MIS staff, or users themselves. The technology for centralized workstation backup is readily available. For example, agents for most third-party Windows Server 2003 backup products let you back up all or part of specific user workstations.

While you're at it, don't forget Windows Server 2003 backup. If you have Windows 2003 servers that don't support Exchange, you need to back them up too. You can back up a Windows 2003 server over the network, but if the servers have lots of disk space, consider the same local backup strategy for non-Exchange Windows Server 2003 that I suggested for Exchange servers. You can also consider a dedicated network just for backups. All you need is an extra gigabit Ethernet adapter in each server and in your backup computer or computers and a gigabit hub.

NETWORKING YOUR EXCHANGE USERS

When you have your server design down, you need to think about how to connect users to your Exchange servers. It's usually a no-brainer for local connections, although you want to be sure that you've got enough bandwidth to move the stuff that Exchange makes available to your users. For example, a message I put together with a very simple embedded color screen capture is 855K. The graphic looks impressive, and it let me make a point that I never could have made without it. Still, I wouldn't want my recipients to get it over a 33.3Kbps or 56Kbps connection.

If you're concerned about LAN bandwidth, you can do a couple things. First, get rid of those slower networks. Dump 4Mbps Token Ring and Arcnet networks. Yes, they are still around. If you haven't already, you might also want to consider upgrading 10BaseT networks to 100BaseT. Second, segment your LANs to reduce the number of users on any segment. In this situation, you might even put multiple network adapters in your Exchange server, one for each segment or group of segments. And do take a look at faster networking technologies such as 100Mbps Ethernet, those really neat networking switches that can replace routers and significantly improve network backbone performance, and the latest switched Fast Ethernet hubs that bring switching to workstation connectivity and are quite low in price these days. Yes, any of these options will cost your organization some bucks, but they're likely to be bucks well spent. Just as with user workstations, slow technologies don't get used, and the benefits of the applications that you're trying to run on top of them are lost.

Don't forget remote Exchange users. Many users need to keep in touch when they're away from the office, whether at home or on the road. Remote users can connect to their Exchange servers by way of direct or RPC over HTTP links through an Internet service provider (ISP) using dial-up or home-based DSL or cable connections. And don't forget the Internet-based POP3, IMAP4, and web browser–based client options that are supported by Exchange Server. With their lighter-weight demands on workstation resources, they could be just what the doctor ordered for your remote users.

We'll talk more about how to implement remote Exchange links in Chapter 14, "Managing Exchange Services for Internet Clients" and Chapter 16, "Advanced Exchange Server Administration and Management." At this point, you need to think about providing adequate bandwidth to support remote user TPC/IP connections. Unless you have just a few users who need Internet access, think at least T1 bandwidth.

Plan Connections to Other Systems

As John Donne almost said, "No organization is an island." In fact, not only is no organization an island today, but no organization can *afford* to be an island. Electronic messaging is quickly becoming the primary means of communicating and doing business. Consider connections to systems outside your organization to be necessities, not niceties.

CONNECTION OPTIONS

Exchange organizations can be connected directly to foreign X.400 systems, Internet mail systems, legacy Microsoft Mail, Lotus cc:Mail and Notes, and GroupWise systems. Legacy system links can include not just message exchange, but synchronization of Exchange and legacy address directories as well. With optional gateways from Microsoft and third-party vendors, you can connect to such systems as IBM PROFS and fax devices.

Exchange connections to foreign X.400 systems use the X.400 connector. Such connections can be either continuous and permanent or dial-up, and they can use any of the X.400 connector networking options listed previously in step 5 (Plan Routing Group Links). The SMTP connector can use a continuous and permanent or dial-up TCP/IP link to the Internet. Third-party gateways use a range of networking protocols; contact your gateway vendor for specifics. The Connector for Microsoft Mail can run on top of almost anything, including TCP/IP, IPX/SPX, NetBEUI, X.25, and voice lines. The Exchange Directory Synchronization Agent mentioned in Chapter 3 lets you keep Exchange and legacy Microsoft messaging systems in sync. It uses the same networking protocols as the Connector for Microsoft Mail.

In planning, don't underplay the importance of X.400 connections, especially if your company communicates with organizations outside the United States. The X.400 suite includes the Electronic Document Interchange (EDI) standard, which supports electronic commerce by providing secure communications when you use your messaging system to, say, purchase products and services. Yes, you can secure your Internet mail communications, but X.400 isn't dead yet.

You need only one Exchange connector to link an entire Exchange organization to a foreign messaging system. As long as inter–routing group links are in place, a single foreign messaging system connector can send and receive messages for an entire organization.

CONNECT OR MIGRATE?

Now is the time to decide whether it's better to migrate users from legacy systems to Exchange Server, or to wait and just link them to Exchange Server using various connectors, gateways, or even direct individual workstation connections in the case of Microsoft Mail. The number of users to be migrated, the kinds of messaging systems that they use, and the size of your own technical and training staff will play a big role in this decision.

If you do decide to migrate users, you should determine exactly which messaging systems you'll be migrating your users from: Microsoft Mail, Lotus cc:Mail, Lotus Notes, Novell GroupWise, IBM PROFS, Verimation Memo, DEC All-in-One, and so on. Next, you should figure out what kinds of tools, if any, exist that can help you migrate users from each messaging system to Exchange. For example, Exchange includes a nice migration application for Microsoft Mail users. When you know what kinds of migration tools are available, you must set a timetable for migration. Finally, you must determine whether, based on your timetable, you should link other messaging systems to Exchange before you've migrated all users in them to Exchange.

If you choose to migrate users to Exchange, be aware that you can create new user Windows 2003 accounts and Exchange 2003 mailboxes from text data files. If your legacy messaging system lets you output user information to a file, and if you have someone around who can write a program to ensure that all the information Exchange needs is in the file in the right format and order, you should certainly consider using this time-saving migration option. I'll talk more about migration in Chapter 16, "Advanced Exchange Server Administration and Management."

MIGRATING FROM EXCHANGE 5.5 TO EXCHANGE 2003

I must mention one other migration scenario. Technically, transitioning from Exchange 5.5 to Exchange 2003 is a migration. As with other migrations, there is planning to do, and Microsoft provides a set of useful tools to smooth your migration. That's especially nice because an Exchange 5.5 migration involves not just Exchange 2003, but Windows Server 2003 as well. We'll begin delving into this piece of the migration puzzle in the next chapter. Oh, for the days when we Exchange Server types were the ones forcing everyone else to migrate!

Validate and Optimize Your Design

Validation means ensuring that you have a system that guarantees message delivery, integrity, and security. It also means making sure that the system you designed is versatile enough to handle the range of documents, messaging formats, and applications that your organization needs. *Optimization* is a balancing act in which you try to build the fastest, most stable, and most reliable systems that you can while still meeting organizational requirements and keeping costs down.

GUARANTEED DELIVERY

Guaranteed message delivery comes with reliable Windows 2003 and Exchange 2003 servers and reliable internal and external networks. To increase the likelihood of guaranteed delivery, go for as much server fault tolerance and networking redundancy as your organization can afford. Use high-quality server and networking hardware and software inside your organization; buy outside networking services from stable, experienced, and well-established providers. Monitor the health of your networks, and be prepared to fix problems quickly. During the validation phase, send messages of all kinds through all your connections, and then check to see if they arrive intact. When problems arise, use Exchange's own message-tracking tools to catch up with wayward messages, and take advantage of Exchange's network and system-monitoring tools to discover why a message didn't get through.

Reliability is only one side of guaranteed message delivery. You also need Exchange servers that are sufficiently fast and networks that have the bandwidth to move messages quickly enough to meet maximum delivery time parameters. If you specified that all messages should be delivered to all internal users within five minutes, for example, now's the time to see if your Exchange system is capable of performing up to spec. If not, you must either increase your permissible maximum delivery times or, depending on the source of the problem, come up with speedier servers or higher-bandwidth networks.

MESSAGE INTEGRITY

Message integrity means that messages arrive in the same form as they were transmitted. Problems with message integrity can often be traced to mismatched binary message-part encoding and decoding. For example, a binary attachment to a message bound for the Internet is UUencoded by the sender, while the receiver expects MIME encoding. As you'll see later in Chapter 13, there are lots of ways to set encoding parameters in Exchange to help avoid problems such as this.

MESSAGE SECURITY

In Exchange 5 and later, RSA encryption and public keys both work within a single Exchange organization and can be enabled to work across Exchange organizations. Exchange Server 2003 uses a number of Windows 2003–based security features to significantly enhance message security. For messages destined for foreign electronic messaging systems, Exchange Server implements a set of encryption and authentication standards: NTLM encryption, TLS encryption, SASL clear-text authentication, and Secure MIME. (More on these comes in Chapter 18, "Exchange Server System Security.")

You can try to validate message security on your own or with the help of a certified electronic data processing auditor. If security is important to your organization, I strongly recommend the latter.

SYSTEM VERSATILITY

Exchange's internal message formatting, along with formatting available in X.400 and Internet mail, means that you are able to send documents of almost any type, containing virtually anything from text to last night's Letterman show. But be sure to validate that everything you need is there and works.

On the applications side, you have all the app development environments mentioned in Chapter 1. Exchange Server is a very popular product, so plenty of Exchange-based applications are already available from third-party vendors; many more are in development. Keep your eyes open for the latest "killer" Exchange apps.

OPTIMIZATION

When you've done everything to ensure guaranteed message delivery, message integrity, and security, as well as system versatility, it's time for *optimization*. You optimize your design by checking out alternatives that might help improve your Exchange system. The basic question is, can you do it better, faster, and easier? For example, you might want to consider implementing support for X.400 messaging, even though your organization has no current need for it, simply because competitors are moving toward it.

Optimization can also focus on reducing costs without compromising the quality of your system. For example, you might want to come up with lower-cost options for connecting Exchange routing groups or for realizing network redundancy.

Rolling Out the Plan

The specifics of your rollout will depend on the plans you've made. There are some basic processes you have to attend to in a rollout. Many of these processes are people-oriented processes, not technically-oriented processes. This section focuses on the former processes. *Rollout* doesn't mean dropping a whole Exchange system on your organization at once. It means making Exchange available to specific systems people and users according to a carefully thought-out schedule. You should also go through a testing phase with specific users. Rollout to your general user population needs to be geared to your assessment of user readiness, perhaps at the departmental or subdepartmental level. Rollout also must be deeply rooted in the capacity of systems and user support staff to handle the many issues that arise during implementation of a major new software product. And, in all of this, don't forget that without MIS commitment and support, it's highly unlikely that you'll be able to smoothly pull off a successful Exchange rollout.

Start in the Right Place   You might start your rollout in MIS—maybe just with yourself, if you're part of MIS. Next, you might move on to samples of users based on the groupings that you uncovered in your user needs assessment or an assessment of user readiness for the change you are about to drop on them. Remember, you've been working with Exchange and its clients for a while. MIS support and users might have had little exposure to it. They will see the change you are bringing as much more world-shaking than you. Then move steadily onward until all users are up and running in Exchange. The key is to get Exchange out to all users as fast as possible without crashing your organization. (Here I'm referring to your *real* organization, not your Exchange organization.)

Don't Forget Design During Rollout   Remember that rollout is an integral part of the Exchange design process. As you step through your implementation plans, be ready to change your design. If something doesn't work, change it now. Don't let things pile up to the point that change becomes virtually impossible. How you schedule your rollout relative to user need and readiness as well as MIS support capacity will determine how able you are to keep up with change orders.

Pay Close Attention to Users   Whether you're in a test or production rollout phase, be sure to keep your big shot and plain old users in the loop. Get them committed to Exchange. Let them know if and when they're going to see a new e-mail client. Show them the client, just so they can see how really easy it is to use to get basic work done. Explain to them how they can use the client you plan to provide both to do what they're already doing and to get other tasks done.

This is where user training comes in. You probably already know this, but user training is both essential and a major drain on resources. Spend lots of time planning user training. Think very carefully about the amount of time and dollars you're willing to devote to user training. Training is a very specialized activity. If you don't have enough training resources in-house, consider outsourcing user training. Know that some users will get it right away and some will come back again and again seeking answers to questions that were answered both in group training and one-on-one by user support personnel. Finally, remember that your Exchange rollout can be a great success technically, but if no one comes to the show, it will be considered a failure by your bosses or your clients and their bosses.

Stay Close to MIS Staff   Keep MIS staff involved and informed as well. An Exchange installation and implementation is a big deal for an MIS department. I bet that over time just about everyone in MIS will get involved with Exchange. MIS staff should understand and welcome Exchange, not see it as a threat to their jobs. Train MIS personnel as data-processing colleagues rather than just end users. You don't have to tell everyone in MIS everything there is to know about Exchange—they can buy this book for that purpose (hint, hint). But be sure to talk to them about both server and client basics from a more technical perspective.

Summary

Designing a new Exchange system is neither easy nor fast. You must complete several steps and then track back to ensure that you've taken each step's impact on other steps into account. Moving through this iterative process while covering each of the steps in painstaking detail ensures that your Exchange system will function pretty much as expected from the get-go and that costly redesign is kept to a minimum.

One of the most important steps in the design process is the allocation of responsibility for very specific stages of the design and implementation process. This should be the first step in the design process. It ensures that the right people with the right skills and knowledge are in place and that they are clearly in charge of and must account for their particular piece of the design puzzle.

Needs assessments are another key to effective Exchange system design. You must perform assessments of user need, the geographic distribution of your organization and its computing and networking resources, and your data network. Needs assessments focus on not only what is required as new, but also on what of the old can be preserved.

Exchange Server 2003 is a network-dependent, network-intensive system. You need to establish a consistent set of conventions for naming your Exchange organization, administrative groups, servers, and recipients. You must choose a Windows 2003 networking model that fits well with your organization's geographical distribution and business structures. You must define the boundaries of Exchange administrative groups, the administrative units into which you break your Exchange organization. As with domain models, geographic distribution and business structures might be key to setting these boundaries. If required, you must define boundaries for Exchange routing groups and determine how your routing groups will communicate across wide area networks.

Next, you must design your Exchange servers, paying attention to performance, storage capacity, reliability, backup, and networking users to your servers. When you've designed your Exchange server environment, you must deal with connecting your servers to other messaging systems, both public and private. Here you must select from among available Exchange connectors and gateways. As your Exchange network becomes a reality, you must ensure, through exhaustive testing, that everything works as planned and up to whatever performance, reliability, and other standards you must adhere to.

Finally, you need to develop a plan for rolling out your Exchange system when everything is ready and has been tested. You shouldn't expect everything to be perfect on first rollout. However, if you've adhered to the design steps laid out in this chapter, your rollout experience should be a fairly pleasant one.

In the next chapter, I'll talk about upgrading from NT 4 Server to Windows Server 2003, and from Exchange Server 5.5 to Exchange Server 2003. Even if you don't need to do an upgrade, I encourage you to read the next chapter. Thinking through the upgrade process will help you better understand the inner workings of Windows Server 2003 and Exchange Server 2003.

Chapter 6

Upgrading to Windows Server 2003 and Exchange Server 2003

"WELCOME TO HELL!" That's the first title that I wanted to use for this chapter. Upgrading operating systems and key applications is always scary, very scary. The thought of upgrading both Windows and Exchange is enough to stop even the strongest heart for at least a few beats. Here's the good news: If you've already upgraded to Windows 2000 and Exchange 2000, your job will be relatively easy. If your organization is among that large group still running Windows NT and Exchange 5.5, upgrading to 2003 will be less traumatic than it was for those who upgraded to Windows 2000 and Exchange 2000 early on, but you'll still need to do a few unexpected tasks.

The good news is that Microsoft has done something to simplify your task whatever your Exchange upgrade or installation needs. After much complaining from us users, Microsoft did something to make upgrading or freshly installing Exchange servers much easier by implementing Exchange Deployment Tools (EDT) for Exchange 2003. Basically, EDT is a set of interactive checklists that guide you through each step of an Exchange 2003 upgrade or installation. EDT checklists include everything from upgrading Exchange 5.5 to Exchange 2003, to installing a brand new Exchange 2003 system. And you can't escape EDT. When you insert the Exchange 2003 CD, the first screen you see offers a bunch of informational resources and an opportunity to run EDT. That's it! If you want to install Exchange 2003, you have to choose the tools.

TIP *You can always run* `SETUP.EXE` *in the* `\SETUP\I386` *directory on the Exchange 2003 CD if you want to bypass EDT. Keep in mind, however, that* `SETUP.EXE` *is for real Exchange experts who have manually completed the pre-*`SETUP.EXE` *steps that EDT will automatically guide you through.*

Much of what I explain in this chapter can be done through EDT. So, I suggest you read what I have to say and then start up EDT and select your upgrade scenario. Sometimes you'll find that EDT assumes you've made certain planning and implementation decisions, such as selecting a model for your upgrade. Also, you may find yourself doing something recommended by EDT that you don't understand or are concerned about running. The pearls of wisdom in this chapter help put EDT in perspective.

As we go through this chapter, I'll call your attention to the deployment tools when it's time to use them. If you forget about the tools, don't worry, you'll be reminded about them when you insert the Exchange 2003 CD.

Even though I've done it a number of times now, I still tremble a little when I have to do a Windows or an Exchange upgrade. So, I'm going to try to help you avoid some of the anxiety I feel about upgrading. Even so, you might need help from others, especially on the NT upgrade side. Take a look at *Mastering Windows Server 2003,* by Mark Minasi, Christa Anderson, Michele Beveridge, C.A. Callahan, and Lisa Justice (Sybex, 2003). Also, be sure to read the Exchange Server 2003 docs on upgrades. They do a pretty good job of laying out your options for both NT 4/Windows 2000 and Exchange 5.5 Server/Exchange Server 2000 upgrades. The main problem with them is their organization and the lack of integration between the two. In this chapter, I give you a more synergistic view of Windows and Exchange upgrades than the one provided in the Exchange docs.

Much of what I talk about here depends on your knowledge of topics covered in the first five chapters. If you've skipped to here because you just couldn't wait to get into the knotty issues related to upgrading, you're soon going to be even more anxious than I was when I first confronted the subject. If you haven't already done so, go back and at least look carefully at Chapter 2, "Windows Server 2003 and Exchange Server 2003"; Chapter 3, "Two Key Architectural Components of Windows Server 2003"; Chapter 4, "Exchange Server 2003 Architecture," and Chapter 5, "Designing a New Exchange 2003 System."

MIGRATING FOR THE EASIEST UPGRADE

By using the Exchange Migration Wizard, you can avoid a lot of the time, effort, and problems related to upgrading an Exchange server, especially an Exchange 5.5 server, to Exchange 2003. There are two requirements and one caveat.

◆ You must be willing to change the name of your Exchange organization, placing it in a new Windows 2003 forest and domain.

◆ You must set up a new domain controller and Exchange 2003 server. Both of them can be on the same computer if resources are scarce. See Chapter 7 and Chapter 8.

◆ This method works best with Exchange servers with a small number of smaller mailboxes and public folders, though it can work with any size server.

The Exchange Migration Wizard (All Programs ➢ Microsoft Exchange ➢ Migration Wizard) creates Windows 2003 users with all of the Exchange parameters and then replicates mailboxes from the old to the new server. You can move public folders by copying them into a mailbox, running the Wizard, and then copying them from the replicated mailbox into the Exchange All Public Folders folder. When you're done migrating, you restart Exchange services on the new server, set users to connect to the new Exchange server, and you're finished. Using a 300 MHz Pentium Exchange 5.5 source server and a 2.4GHz Xeon Exchange 2003 target server, I got a mailbox transfer rate of about 2.4MB per minute. That's pretty slow if your source server has very large mailboxes or a lot of larger mailboxes. But without having to jump through all the hoops that I'm going to talk about in this chapter.

For more on the Exchange Migration Wizard, see the section "Migrating Foreign Messaging System Users to Exchange" in Chapter 16, "Advanced Exchange Server Administration and Management." Don't be put off by the word "foreign." The Wizard considers any messaging system other than Exchange 2003 to be foreign.

Also, I strongly recommend that you read Chapter 7, "Installing Windows Server 2003 as a Domain Controller," and Chapter 8, "Installing Exchange Server 2003," before starting an upgrade. There's lots of information there that you'll find quite useful both before and after you complete an upgrade. For example, in this chapter, I lightly cover some of the processes and tasks required in an upgrade because they are discussed in more detail in Chapters 7 and 8.

Featured in this chapter:

◆ Upgrading from Windows 2000 Server to Windows Server 2003

◆ Upgrading from Exchange 2000 Server to Exchange Server 2003

◆ Upgrading Windows NT Server 4 to Windows Server 2003: processes and techniques

◆ Upgrading Exchange Server 5.5 to Exchange Server 2003: processes and techniques

◆ Windows NT4–to–2003 and Exchange 5.5–to–2003 upgrades: putting it all together

Upgrading from Windows 2000 Server to Windows Server 2003

WARNING *This section is about upgrading from Windows 2000 to Windows 2003. You can't use the information in this section to upgrade from NT 4 to Windows 2003. If you need help with an NT 4–to–Windows 2003 upgrade, see the sections, "Upgrading Windows NT Server 4 to Windows Server 2003: Processes and Techniques" and "Windows NT 4–to–2003 and Exchange 5.5–to–2003 Upgrades: Putting It All Together," later in this chapter.*

Because I assume you have experience with Windows 2000, I'm going to move pretty quickly through this section. I'm not going to explain each step in a Windows 2000 to Windows 2003 upgrade in great detail. If you need more info on some of this stuff, take a look at the section "Upgrading From Windows NT Server 4 to Windows Server 2003" later in this chapter and Chapter 7.

To upgrade from Windows 2000 to Windows 2003, you have to do the following:

◆ Check the hardware and software on the servers you plan to upgrade from Windows 2000 to Windows 2003.

◆ Ensure that Windows 2000 servers to be upgraded are running at least Service Pack 3.

◆ Upgrade the Windows 2000 forest schema in Active Directory.

◆ Upgrade each Windows 2000 domain in which you plan to upgrade Windows 2000 servers to Windows 2003.

◆ Install Windows 2003 on each Windows 2000 server to be upgraded.

Let's look at each of these tasks. Remember to check documentation on the Windows Server 2003 CD for the latest on upgrades. This documentation also contains detailed information that you might find useful in planning and carrying out an upgrade to Windows 2003.

Checking Hardware and Software on Windows 2000 Servers to Be Upgraded to Windows 2003

You need to be sure that the hardware and software on each Windows 2000 server that you plan to upgrade is Windows Server 2003–ready. When you install Windows Server 2003, you'll be told about any incompatibilities between Windows 2003 and your existing hardware and software. That's nice, but just a bit too late. The last thing that you want to do is to get everything ready for an upgrade and then find out that your server's hardware or software isn't up to snuff for Windows Server 2003.

Fortunately, Microsoft has an answer. The Windows Server 2003 installation disk comes with compatibility analysis software. This software checks a computer that is a candidate for upgrade to assure that its hardware and software will work with Windows 2003. When you insert the Windows Server 2003 CD ROM, the main menu includes an option for checking system compatibility. In addition to an automatic compatibility check, you can choose to go to a website where you can manually check hardware and software compatibility.

You can run the analyzer any time before you do an upgrade. The tool checks your hardware and software and gives you a list like the one in Figure 6.1.

Problematic hardware and software are listed with icons indicating the severity of the incompatibility. The yellow triangle with an exclamation mark in it indicates products that are incompatible in their existing form; remove these at your discretion. A red circle with an X in it indicates hardware or software that absolutely must be removed before Windows 2000 is upgraded to 2003. As you can see in Figure 6.1, you can get detailed information on any particular item listed in the Readiness Analyzer by clicking Details.

FIGURE 6.1

List of incompatible hardware and software provided by Microsoft's Windows 2003 Readiness Analyzer

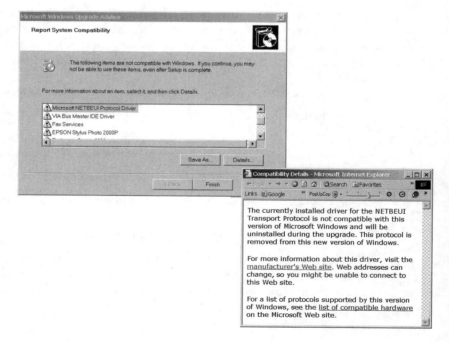

TIP *If you don't have a Windows Server 2003 installation CD, you can get the compatibility checking software off Microsoft's website. Do a search for "windows compatibility" at* www.microsoft.com.

In addition to checking hardware and software compatibility, you need to make sure that hardware on servers to be upgraded is adequate to handle the load that Windows Server 2003 will put on them. If necessary, consider adding memory or disk space, or even upgrading to new server hardware before upgrading to Windows 2003. The good news is that, though Windows 2003 increases the data stored in Active Directory, such increases are quite modest compared to upgrading NT 4 to Windows 2003. So, if a Windows 2000 server you plan to upgrade is working well, it should be fine after you upgrade it to Windows 2003.

If you think you need to upgrade, take a look at my hardware suggestions in the previous chapter. Also, check out the Active Directory Sizer tool available for download from Microsoft. Search Windows Server 2003 downloads for "active directory sizer." This tool helps you estimate the hardware capacity that you'll need to deploy Active Directory in your organization. The Sizer tool's estimates are based on your organization's profile, domain information, and site topology. You must gather the information and enter it manually into the Sizer, but I think you'll find the time and effort well spent.

Ensuring that Windows 2000 Servers to Be Upgraded Are Running at Least Service Pack 3

I could have included this one in the last section. However, it is so important that you install Service Pack 3 or higher on any Windows 2000 server you plan to upgrade to Windows 2003 that I decided to make this a separate section. At one point or another, Microsoft says Service Pack 2 is enough. Play it safe, upgrade to Service Pack 3. Of course, do be sure to check the Windows Server 2003 CD for indications that you need an even later service pack.

EXCHANGE SERVER 2003 AND WINDOWS 2000 SERVER

As I noted in Chapter 1, "Introducing Exchange Server 2003," you can run Exchange Server 2003 on a Windows 2000 server. You will need to prepare your Windows 2000 server according to the documentation that comes with Exchange 2003, including assuring that at least Service Pack 3 is installed on your Windows 2000 server. And, remember, features supported only in Windows 2003 won't be available. These include

- Enhanced clustering support
- Mount point support with clusters
- Database snapshot
- RPC over HTTP client server support
- IPSec support for front-end/back-end clusters
- Virtual memory allocation control

Upgrading the Windows 2000 Forest Schema in Active Directory

As I noted in Chapter 3, Windows 2000 introduced forests and trees to organize the way we think about networks. Forests are independent networking entities that can have trees and always have at least one domain. Information about a forest is stored in what is called "the forest schema." The schema is stored in Active Directory. Windows 2003 retains forests and trees, but it expands their capabilities, for example making interaction between forests easier. So, it is necessary to update a Windows 2000 forest schema to upgrade Windows 2000 servers to Windows 2003.

You have to perform this update only once in a forest. Here's how to do it.

1. Find the server that is the schema master. This is usually the first Windows 2000 server you installed. Use the Active Directory Schema plug-in for Microsoft Management Console to find the schema master. Right-click the plug-in and select Operations Master. If you don't see the Active Directory Schema plug-in on any server including the one you're pretty sure is the schema master, install the Windows 2000 Administration Tools from the Windows 2000 CD.

2. Disconnect the schema master server from the network.

3. Fully back up the schema master server, including its system state. If the schema master update fails, you will be able to restore the schema master from your backup. Now is also the time to fully back up the Windows 2000 infrastructure masters for domains where you will be performing updates from Windows 2000 to Windows 2003. See the next section for information on finding infrastructure masters. Don't wait until the next section to back up infrastructure masters. By then it might be too late to back them up as they could already have all or part of a corrupt new schema on them.

4. On the schema master, with Windows 2000 running, run the program ADPREP from the \i386 folder on the Windows 2003 CD. Select Start ➢ Run and enter **\i386\ADPREP / ForestPrep**. To do this task, you must be a member of the Enterprise Admins group and the Schema Admins group or you need to have been delegated the appropriate authority by those who control rights in your network. When ADPREP finishes, it will indicate whether the schema update was successful or not.

5. Even if ADPREP says all is well, ensure that the forest update worked. No error messages should have shown up during the update. Run DCDIAG.EXE from the \supporttools folder on the Windows 2003 CD. There should be no messages in the Windows Event Viewer System Log. If all of this is true, reconnect the schema master to the network and go on to the next section.

6. If you encountered errors and fixes were suggested, perform the fixes. If significant errors occurred that can't be fixed, restore the schema master from the backup and figure out what you need to do to run ADPREP /ForestPrep successfully.

Upgrading Each Windows 2000 Domain in Which You Plan to Upgrade Windows 2000 Servers to Windows 2003

You'll need to run ADPREP again, but this time on what is called the "infrastructure master" and with the switch /DomainPrep. You have to do this only once for each domain. Here's how to update Active Directory information for a domain.

1. Find the server that is the infrastructure master. This is likely the first Windows 2000 server you installed in a domain. Right-click on the Active Directory Users and Computers Microsoft Man-

agement Console plug-in and select Operations Masters. The server named on the Infrastructure tab is the one you're looking for.

2. If the infrastructure master is a different server from the schema master, wait for the schema changes to replicate to the infrastructure master. This takes around 15 minutes if the two computers are in the same site and as much as a half-day if the computers are at different sites connected by slower network technology. If replication hasn't finished, when you try to run ADPREP, you'll get an error message telling you to wait for replication to finish.

3. On the infrastructure master, run ADPREP /DomainPrep. This task requires membership in the Domain Admins or Enterprise Admins group or that you have been delegated appropriate rights. When the update is finished, the program will indicate that it ran successfully.

4. Even if ADPREP says the update was successful, ensure that the domain update went well. There should have been no error messages during the update. Run DCDIAG.EXE and check to see that there are no errors in the System Log. If all is well, you're ready to upgrade to Windows 2003. Be sure to wait 15 minutes for the changes you just made to replicate to other domain controllers; half a day for controllers in other sites connected by slower networking technologies.

5. If you encountered errors, try to fix them according to any information provided in the error messages. If things are a real mess, restore the infrastructure from the backup you did in the last section.

Installing Windows 2003 on Each Windows 2000 Server to Be Upgraded

This is the easy part. Start with your domain controllers, schema and infrastructure masters first, and then you can upgrade your stand-alone servers. Just insert the Windows 2003 CD and follow the on-screen instructions to do the upgrade.

Upgrading from Exchange 2000 Server to Exchange Server 2003

WARNING   *This section is about upgrading from Exchange 2000 to Exchange 2003. You can't use the information in this section to upgrade from Exchange 5.5 to Exchange 2003. If you need help with an Exchange 5.5–to–Exchange 2003 upgrade, see the sections "Upgrading Exchange Server 5.5 to Exchange Server 2003" and "Windows NT4–to–2003 and Exchange 5.5–to–2003 Upgrades: Putting It All Together" later in this chapter.*

As with the section on Windows 2000 to Windows 2003 upgrades, I assume you have some familiarity with Exchange 2000. So, I will not discuss every upgrade step in exhaustive detail. If you need more information, check out Chapter 8 and the "Upgrading Exchange Server 5.5 to Exchange Server 2003" section later in this chapter.

Upgrading from Exchange 2000 Server to Exchange Server 2003 is very easy. You can do a simple in-place upgrade of each server. Upgrades are made easier by the fact that Exchange Server 2003 can coexist with Exchange 2000 Server and, when running in Exchange mixed mode, with Exchange 5.5 servers. This gives you time to carefully and correctly upgrade your Exchange servers.

WARNING   *Remember, you must perform the Windows 2000 upgrades in the previous section before you can upgrade Exchange 2000 to Exchange 2003.*

I suggest you use the Exchange Deployment Tools (EDT) that I discussed at the beginning of this chapter to do your Exchange 2000–to–2003 upgrade. They make the job easier. As you might remember, you just have to insert the Exchange 2003 CD, select Exchange Deployment Tools, find the scenario for your Exchange 2000 to Exchange 2003 upgrade, and track through the interactive checklist that EDT provides.

EDT will run you through some tests. For more on the tests, see the list at the beginning of the section "Upgrading Exchange Server 5.5 to Exchange Server 2003" later in this chapter.

Next you'll find more detail on some of the tasks you will perform using EDT. I've included this information to put specific tasks in perspective and so you can get a better handle on why you're performing the tasks. These include:

◆ Preparing the forest for installation of Exchange 2003

◆ Preparing the domain for installation of Exchange 2003

◆ Upgrading to Exchange 2003

Preparing the Forest for Installation of Exchange 2003

As you had to update the forest schema to ready it for Windows 2003 installation, you also have to update the schema for Exchange 2003 installation. To run an Exchange 2003 forest update, you must be logged into an account that belongs to the Enterprise Admins and Schema Admins groups. Generally, you should follow the directions in the section "Upgrading the Windows 2000 Forest Schema in Active Directory" earlier in this chapter.

Run the command `\SETUP\I386\SETUP` on the Exchange 2003 CD. You can run ForestPrep on any domain controller in the domain where the Active Directory schema resides.

Once SETUP starts and you've waded through the opening screens, make sure the Action on the Component Selection screen is set to ForestPrep. If you don't see ForestPrep, you probably misspelled ForestPrep when you issued the `SETUP` command. Get out of the Component Selection window and rerun the `SETUP` command.

While running ForestPrep, you might be asked to specify the Windows 2003 group that should have rights to install Exchange. You can specify an administrators group such as Enterprise or Domain Admins or you can specify a group you created. See the section "Component Management Security" in Chapter 8 for more on creating a group to act as the master Exchange installation group.

When ForestPrep has finished running, you're ready for the next step. If ForestPrep fails for any reason, check the reason and try to fix any problems. Then rerun SETUP.

Preparing the Domain for Installation of Exchange 2003

If you've been tracking through the 2000-to-2003 upgrade process, you've probably already figured out that you have to next prepare the domain where you're going to upgrade one or more Exchange 2000 servers. That's correct, but it's not all you have to do. You have to run DomainPrep once for

◆ Root domains

◆ All domains where you plan to install Exchange Server 2003

◆ All domains that will contain mailbox-enabled objects, for example, users and groups

You can run DomainPrep on any server in your target domain. If you have a simple single domain setup, you need to run DomainPrep only once.

The account under which you run DomainPrep must belong to the Windows 2003 Domain Admins group. Run \SETUP\I386\SETUP from the Windows 2003 CD. If DomainPrep fails, check errors, fix any problems, and rerun SETUP with the ForestPrep switch.

Upgrading to Exchange 2003

As with Windows 2000–to–Windows 2003 upgrades, you're now rolling downhill. Just insert the Exchange 2003 CD and follow the on-screen prompts to upgrade from Exchange 2000 to Exchange 2003.

For the record, the Exchange 2003 installation program installs and enables two Windows 2003 features required for it to work. These are .NET Framework and ASP.NET service.

Upgrading from Windows NT Server 4 to Windows Server 2003: Processes and Techniques

If you're like me, you just can't wait to do your first NT 4 upgrade and you're even more excited about doing an Exchange 5.5 upgrade. However, I must ask you to be patient. Upgrading is a complex multi-step process. Even if you've done upgrades from NT 4 and Exchange 5.5 to Windows 2000 and Exchange 2000, there are some new and important issues that you must understand. Unless you want to spend more time in hell than is necessary, I strongly suggest that you read through the rest of this chapter before touching a keyboard or inserting a CD. Most of what you'll find in this and the next section is key information regarding processes and techniques for performing NT 4 and Exchange 5.5 upgrades. Not until the section "Windows NT4–to–2003 and Exchange 5.5–to–2003 Upgrades: Putting It All Together" will we put all the information together so that an upgrade becomes practical.

When upgrading from NT Server 4 to Windows Server 2003, you need to do the following:

◆ Specify how you will translate your NT Server 4 domain structure into a Windows Server 2003 domain structure.

◆ Select appropriate Windows Server 2003 versions.

◆ Specify the strategy that you will use to upgrade your NT 4 servers.

WARNING   *While you can upgrade an NT 4 server to Windows 2003, you can't simply upgrade an Exchange 5.5 server to Exchange 2003, even if you have upgraded the server to Windows 2003. Let that sink in a bit. It's not that you can do such an upgrade with great difficulty. You can't do it at all! So, be sure to read the section on Exchange 5.5–to–2003 upgrades before jumping off and upgrading the NT 4 server or servers on which you have Exchange 5.5 installed.*

TIP   *You'll notice that I don't mention NT 3.51 here. There's a very good reason for that. NT 3.51 does not work in a Windows 2003 environment. What should you do? Upgrade 3.51 servers to NT Server 4, replace them with Windows 2003 servers, or shut them down forever.*

Specifying a Windows Server 2003 Domain Structure

Before you can decide on a Windows 2003 domain model, you need to understand your existing domain structure well. Then you can focus on selecting a Windows 2003 domain structure. Let me start by refreshing your memory on NT Server 4 domains and trust relationships. After that, I'll describe the process of documenting your domain structure and its components.

NT SERVER 4 DOMAINS

Microsoft NT Server 4 networks are built around *domains.* An NT Server 4 network can have one or many domains, each of which is a logically separate entity. A resource in a Microsoft network can belong to one and only one domain.

Generally, domain users log in to domains, not the individual machines in a domain. Domains can make life easier both for users and for system managers. Users don't have to remember more than one password to access any resource in the domain to which they have been granted rights (unless it is protected by a special password). System managers can centrally create and administer user accounts for the domain.

Domains also make interserver communications easy. If servers live in the same domain, each has to log in to the domain only once to communicate with all other servers in the domain—unless, of course, a special password is required for specific communications.

Domains require *domain controllers,* which is where

◆ NT administrators

    ◆ Create and manage accounts for domain users

    ◆ Set access rights for domain resources

◆ The NT Server 4 operating system

    ◆ Stores user account information for the domain

    ◆ Stores resource access rights for the domain

    ◆ Authenticates domain users

    ◆ Enforces access rights for domain resources

NT SERVER 4 CROSS-DOMAIN TRUSTS

When one NT Server 4 domain (called the *trusting* domain) trusts another (the *trusted* domain), it accepts the other domain's authentication of a user or server. The user or server doesn't have to log in to the trusting domain to access its resources; one login to a trusted domain is enough to access resources in a trusting domain to which an account has been granted access.

Figure 6.2 shows how cross-domain trust relationships make it easier for users and servers to access resources across an NT Server 4 network. The users and servers in domain B (the trusted domain) can access resources in domain A (the trusting domain) without using additional passwords. Note that the figure's arrowhead points *to* the trusted domain and *away* from the trusting domain.

NT Server 4 trusts are not only good for users; they're just what the doctor ordered for busy system administrators as well. Trusts expand the reach of administrators in creating and maintaining user accounts. After setting up a trust relationship between domains, an administrator in one domain can create a user account and an administrator in the other domain can grant access to one, a few, or all resources in the resource domain.

Trust relationships have all kinds of implications for the way users and system managers operate day to day. For example, with the right kind of trust relationship and security rights, an administrator can manage an Exchange 5.5 organization not on a domain-by-domain basis, but from a multidomain or network-wide perspective.

Also, NT Server 4 trust relationships are key to cross-domain interaction between Exchange 5.5 servers. With the appropriate trust relationships and rights in place, Exchange 5.5 servers in different domains can interact to exchange messages and to cross-replicate directories and public folders.

FIGURE 6.2

NT Server 4 trust relationships open a network to users.

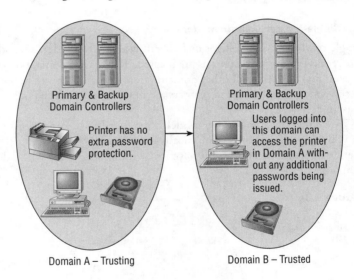

Primary & Backup Domain Controllers

Printer has no extra password protection.

Primary & Backup Domain Controllers

Users logged into this domain can access the printer in Domain A without any additional passwords being issued.

Domain A – Trusting   Domain B – Trusted

NOTE   *A good deal of NT Server 4 networking found its way into Windows Server 2003 networking. Domains remain and function pretty much as they did in NT Server 4, at least from a security perspective. Cross-domain trusts are still with us, although as I noted in Chapter 3, trusts are automatically created between parent and child domains.*

DOCUMENTING YOUR EXISTING DOMAIN STRUCTURE

With a little bit of background about NT Server 4 domains and trusts under your belt, you're now ready to tackle the first step in an upgrade from NT Server 4 to Windows Server 2003, specifying exactly what type of NT Server 4 domain model you have. NT Server 4 domains fall into the following categories:

◆ Single-domain model

- ◆ Single-master domain model
- ◆ Multiple-master domain model
- ◆ Complete trust domain model

The following discussion of NT Server 4 domain models should help clarify these domain models.

The Single-Domain Model

Single-domain systems have no need for trust relationships because there is only one isolated domain. (See Figure 6.3 for a graphical depiction of a network with a single domain.) The NT Server 4 single-domain model is used when there is no business or technical need for more than one Windows organizing or security locus.

The Single-Master Domain Model

Single-master domain systems include one administrative domain and one or more resource domains where servers and workstations are located. The master domain handles all security tasks. It is a trusted domain, while all other domains are trusting. Users are in the master domain; resources such as servers, workstations, and printers are in the resource domain. (See Figure 6.4 for a diagram of a master-domain system.)

The single-master domain model is deployed in organizations that need to segment resources (say, by department or geographically) and that have a centralized MIS department. Each department or geographical unit can have its own domain, while MIS administers from the master domain.

FIGURE 6.3
A network based on the single-domain model

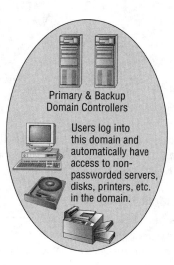

Primary & Backup
Domain Controllers

Users log into this domain and automatically have access to non-passworded servers, disks, printers, etc. in the domain.

FIGURE 6.4

A network based on the master-domain model

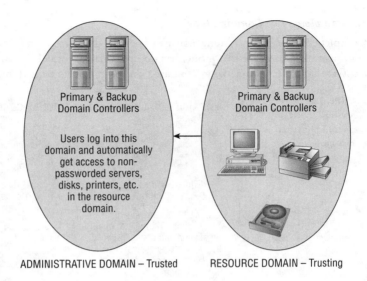

Primary & Backup
Domain Controllers

Primary & Backup
Domain Controllers

Users log into this
domain and automatically
get access to non-
passworded servers,
disks, printers, etc.
in the resource
domain.

ADMINISTRATIVE DOMAIN – Trusted   RESOURCE DOMAIN – Trusting

The Multiple-Master Domain Model

Multiple-master domain systems have two or more master domains and two or more resource domains. Each master domain is responsible for some portion of users based on a logical segmenting factor, such as the first letter of the user's last name, or the geographical breakdown of the company. Each resource domain trusts all the master domains. Figure 6.5 depicts the multiple-master domain model. Here the master domains trust each other and are trusted by both of the resource domains. This is not required, however; each master domain can be trusted by one or a set of resource domains. In the figure, for example, Administrative Domain 1 could be trusted only by Resource Domain 1, while Administrative Domain 2 could be trusted by both resource domains.

Often two-way trusts are implemented between the master domains. That way, system administrators with appropriate rights are able to create new users, and so on, in any master domain as needed.

The multiple-master domain model is implemented in larger organizations that need to segment both resources and MIS administration. Resource domains are often based on departmental divisions.

Multiple-master domains also allow MIS administration to divide the task of managing domains into smaller units. This tends to reduce the likelihood of error and lets large multinational organizations spread the management tasks across geographical and sociopolitical boundaries.

The Complete Trust Domain Model

Complete trust domain systems consist of several domains; each domain handles its own security administration. Because this model has no master domains, all domains must be both trusted and trusting. Figure 6.6 shows a system based on the complete trust domain model.

FIGURE 6.5

A network based on the multiple-master domain model

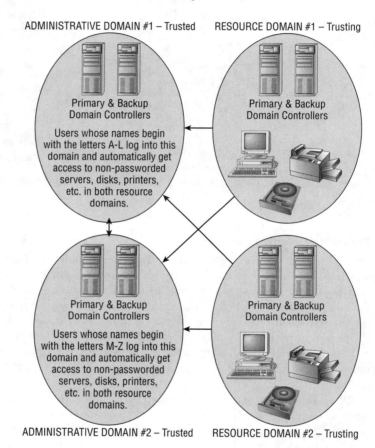

Complete trust domain systems are implemented when an organization lacks central MIS administration and is segmented in some way, such as by department. Each department becomes a domain, and control of the domain is in the hands of the department, but more centralized management and cross-domain resource use are still possible. Complete trusts are also useful in multinational corporate environments. A domain can be created for each country in the corporate organizational structure.

FIGURE 6.6
A network based on
the complete trust
domain model

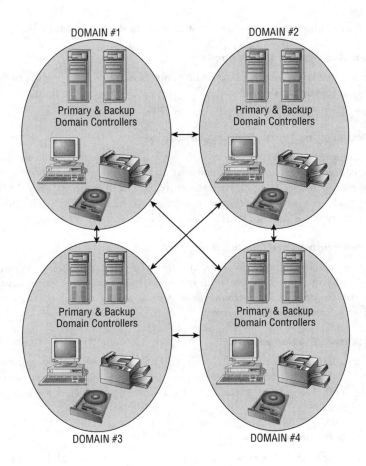

DOCUMENTING YOUR NT SERVER 4 DOMAIN COMPONENTS

You must document the following components in your existing NT Server 4 domains:

- ◆ Domain controllers
- ◆ Types of domains
- ◆ Trust relationships
- ◆ Namespace(s)
- ◆ Servers

The following discussion explains what to document and why.

Documenting Domain Controllers

You must know where your domain controllers are, which are primary domain controllers (PDCs), and which are backup domain controllers (BDCs). As you upgrade an NT domain to Windows 2003, you must first upgrade the PDC in the domain.

Documenting Types of Domain Structures

Whether you plan to retain or alter your existing domain structure during the upgrade process, you must know which of your domains are account domains and which are resource domains. If you want to retain your existing domain structure, you need to know what you're retaining. If you want to upgrade to a different domain structure, you need to know what you have so that you can match it to the types of domain structures available in Windows Server 2003.

Documenting Trust Relationships

Trust relationships are preserved during an upgrade from NT to Windows 2003 networking. If only so that you know what you're dragging over to your new environment, you must know what's what with trust relationships. If you revise your domain structure during an upgrade, you must know how trust relationships might change.

Documenting Namespaces

Carefully document both your NT and DNS domain naming structures. Though you can rename Windows 2003 domains after they're created, you might want to get naming straight before upgrading. You also need to watch out for duplicate names, which are not permitted in Windows 2003 networks.

Documenting Servers

Knowing your NT servers is an important key to a successful Windows 2003 networking upgrade. Which servers are functioning as DHCP, WINS, or DNS servers? Which are application servers, such as Exchange servers, SQL servers, or Internet proxy servers? Don't forget other operating systems. Do you have NetWare or Unix servers? Do you have any NT 3.51 servers?

You need to be especially careful about your DNS servers. As I noted in Chapters 2 and 3, DNS is *the* preferred way for servers and workstations to resolve computer names to IP addresses. Windows Server 2003 supports WINS, but Microsoft wants you to get rid of it as soon as possible after an upgrade.

You also need to decide which computers will run DNS. If DNS ran on a separate server from your NT domain controllers, you'll probably want to take Microsoft's advice and run it on your Windows 2003 domain controllers. DNS is an integral part of the Windows Server 2003 operating system. Generally, you don't want to degrade the performance of your Windows 2003 domain controllers by requiring that they cross your networks to get DNS information.

Do you have Exchange 5.5 servers that are running on NT Server 4 domain controllers? If so, for easier implementation and for performance reasons, you might want to consider running Exchange Server 2003 on Windows 2003 servers that are not domain controllers.

If you have NetWare servers, do you want to synchronize Novell's Novell Directory Services with Active Directory? How will your Windows 2003 and Unix servers interact with regard to DNS and file and printer sharing? As I noted earlier in this chapter, NT 3.51 servers must be upgraded to NT Server 4, if they are to continue to exist in a Windows 2003 structure.

WARNING   *While you're at it, you should actually count the number of instances of each of the four components discussed in this section. It's one thing to say, "I have trust relationships or application servers or WINS servers." It's quite another thing to say, "I have 25 trust relationships, 6 DNS servers, or 6 Exchange 5.5 servers, or 50 Exchange 5.5 servers." Counting gives you a concrete indication of the work ahead of you, in terms of both planning and implementation. It helps you estimate the load that an upgrade will put on your staff or any consultants whom you might bring in.*

WINDOWS 2003 FUNCTIONAL LEVELS

Before moving on to Windows 2003 domain structures, let's talk about Windows Server 2003 functional levels. When you create a new Windows Server 2003 domain by installing Windows 2003 from scratch or by upgrading an NT Server 4 server, the domain is set to the functional level Windows 2000 mixed.

At the Windows 2000 mixed level, Windows 2003 domain controllers can communicate with NT 4 domain controllers in the same or other domains. Cross-domain trusts work like they do in NT 4 domain networks. Windows 2003 domain controllers emulate NT 4 domain controllers when interacting with NT 4 domain controllers. Additionally, NT 4 domain controller emulation allows for free replication of user and other information between Windows 2000, Windows 2003, and NT 4 domain controllers.

You must leave a Windows 2003 domain at the Windows 2000 mixed functional level until your last NT 4 server domain controller is gone. Then you need to switch the domain to the Windows Server 2003 level.

Once at the Windows Server 2003 level, Windows 2003 domains soar. They can support up to one million objects per domain, as opposed to 40,000 in mixed mode. They can also support multiple Active Directory masters, several new kinds of security groups, nested groups, full cross-domain administration, and Kerberos-only authentication. Additionally, as you might remember, in the section "NT Server 4 Cross-Domain Trusts" earlier in this chapter, Windows Server 2003 automatically sets up trusts between parent and child domains. This happens only after you switch a domain to the Windows Server 2003 level.

For now, just in case you stumble on the fatal level-switching dialog box, note that once you've made the switch, there's no going back except by starting all over again. Once a Windows 2003 domain is at the Windows Server 2003 level, NT 4 servers can't interact with Windows 2003 servers. So, don't click that button until you're absolutely ready. For your edification, Figure 6.7 shows the level-switching dialog box. At this point, you should think of this figure like you think of the skull and crossbones on poison bottles. It's your warning about a bad place that you don't want to go, until you fully understand what you're doing.

FIGURE 6.7

Avoid the level change dialog box until all NT Server 4 domain controllers have been upgraded to Windows Server 2003.

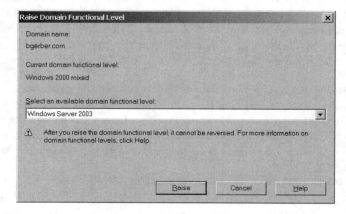

HOW WINDOWS 2003 AND NT 4 DOMAINS GET AND STAY IN SYNC

When you upgrade an NT 4 domain controller to a Windows 2003 domain controller, Active Directory is automatically populated with user and other information from the NT domain controller. While a Windows 2003 domain is at the Windows 2000 mixed level, NT 4 and Windows 2003 domain controllers are capable of automatically cross-replicating user and other resource information.

When a domain is running in mixed mode, you should always make changes, such as adding a new user, on the Windows 2003/Active Directory side. Then you can be assured that users receive attributes that are unique to Active Directory, while relevant user information is replicated to NT 4 domain controllers.

CHOOSING A WINDOWS SERVER 2003 DOMAIN STRUCTURE

Let's look at upgrade scenarios as they might be implemented, given one or another NT server domain structure. If you need a refresher on Windows 2003 domain structuring, take a look at Chapter 3.

NOTE *As you're selecting a domain model, you should also be thinking about your Active Directory namespace. How will you name the domain or domains that you create? Will you use existing names or create new ones? How will you realize your plans in hardware? What type of hardware do you need in terms of horsepower, disk space, and RAM? See the sections in the previous chapter that focus on these issues.*

Upgrading the NT Single-Domain Model

A single-domain model can readily be upgraded to a Windows 2003 system with an Active Directory that has a single contiguous namespace. The single NT domain becomes the root domain in Active Directory. The neat thing is that, unlike with your NT domain, when the upgrade is complete, you can use Windows 2003 organizational units to organize user accounts and resources, and then hand off responsibility for administering specific organizational units to others. For more on organizational units, see the sidebar "Global Catalogs and Organizational Units" in Chapter 3.

Upgrading the Single-Master Domain Model

With a single-master-domain model, you upgrade the administrative domain to become the root domain in a single contiguous namespace Active Directory and add the resource domains as child domains. Take a look at Figure 3.2 in Chapter 3 for a graphic refresher on this approach.

If your organizational and networking structure allows, you can even consolidate the child domains into the root domain after you've fully upgraded the domain and switched to native mode. Then you can use organizational units to play the role that resource domains played in your NT server network. You can even reorganize your resources within your new organizational units. This is the real power of Windows Server 2003.

Upgrading the Multiple-Master Domain Model

No matter how you might want your Windows 2003 domain structure to look in the end, a multiple-master domain network should first be upgraded to a noncontiguous Active Directory namespace. This means that each master domain becomes a root domain in Active Directory. See Figure 3.3 in Chapter 3 for an example of a noncontiguous namespace.

After upgrading your multiple-master domain and switching it to native mode, you should very seriously consider converting it to a single-domain structure. As I noted in Chapters 2 and 3, Microsoft has gone out of its way to make it easier for you to build large-scale, single-root domain (contiguous namespace) networks. For example, Windows Server 2003 sites let you effectively connect segments of your network linked by lower-bandwidth networking topologies, and Windows Server 2003 supports enough user accounts and other objects to keep most organizations happy for many years to come. You can use Windows Server 2003 organizational units to retain whatever organizational, security, or administrative separation you need while simplifying your entire network and making managing it much, much easier.

Upgrading the Complete Trust Domain Model

The complete trust domain model can be upgraded in a variety of ways, depending on your needs. You can take the same approach as with the multiple-master domain model, starting with a multiple-root domain, noncontiguous namespace. Then you can consolidate all into a single-root domain, contiguous namespace after you've completed the upgrade and switched to native mode.

You can also make one domain the root domain and the other domains child domains. This can be the end of your domain structuring, or you can then do as you might with a single-master domain model, consolidating the child domains into the root domain and possibly re-creating child domain functionality with organizational units.

If organizational, economic, political, or legal/regulatory needs dictate, you can retain the multiple-master structure in Windows 2003 by locating each domain in a separate forest. (See Figure 3.4 in Chapter 3 for an example of a multiforest Windows 2000 network.) This is the most extreme approach, and can lead to greater administrative costs. However, if ya gotta do it, ya gotta do it.

STRUCTURAL DOMAINS

If you're upgrading a multiple-master or complete trust domain, you might want to consider using what Microsoft calls a *structural domain*. A structural domain has no users or other resources. It is the root directory within which you create child domains as you upgrade each of your NT domains. Using a structural domain lets you establish a single-root tree, contiguous namespace while making no particular NT 4 domain the root domain. It also helps simplify and make Active Directory replication more efficient. Structural domains are often simply named "." (dot, in Internet parlance).

WINDOWS 2003 SITES AND ORGANIZATIONAL UNITS

When you've selected a Windows 2003 domain model, you're ready to think about two subcomponents of Windows 2003 domains: sites and organizational units.

Windows 2003 sites group together computers on the same LAN. Site boundaries can cross Windows 2003 domains, trees, and even forests. Sites are used by Active Directory in authentication and replication. Windows 2003 site connectors let you connect sites without concern for the lower-bandwidth network links between them.

Active Directory throttles down replication to sites, to account for lower bandwidth connections. During authentication, Active Directory directs each workstation to domain controllers that are in the same site as the workstation. All of this nicely supports lower-bandwidth intersite links.

Two types of intersite transports are available in Windows 2003:

◆ Point-to-point low-speed synchronous (continuous) links based on Microsoft's remote procedure call (RPC) protocol connections

◆ SMTP messaging-based links

If a Windows 2003 domain crosses two or more sites, you can use only a point-to-point synchronous RPC-based link to connect the sites. You can use SMTP messaging-based links for communications between two or more domains, each of which is located in a different site.

From a planning perspective, you must determine whether you need sites. If you do, you need to review existing bandwidth and plan for more, if necessary.

We've already discussed organizational units (OUs) to some extent in Chapter 3 and in the preceding section, "Choosing a Windows Server 2003 Domain Structure." I just want to remind you here that you need to consider how you'll use OUs to organize users and other resources, and to delegate management responsibilities.

Selecting from Among Windows Server 2003 Versions

Now that you know what your Windows Server 2003 domain structure will look like, it's time to decide on the Windows Server 2003 version or versions you need.

As I noted in Chapter 2, there are three editions of Windows Server 2003 that can serve as platforms for Exchange Server 2003: Standard, Enterprise, and Datacenter. These are listed in order of increasing capability to handle server loads and the number of servers that can be clustered. (See Chapter 2 for more on load-handling capacity and clustering.)

Chapter 2 also discussed the two versions of Exchange Server: Standard Edition and Enterprise Edition. (Check out Chapter 2 for the differences between these two products.)

You can install Exchange Server 2003 Standard Edition on any version of Windows Server 2003. Exchange Server 2003 Enterprise Edition requires either Windows Server 2003 Enterprise or Datacenter Edition.

Checking the Readiness of Your NT Server 4 System

You need to be sure that the hardware and software on each NT 4 server that you plan to upgrade is Windows Server 2003–ready. When you install Windows Server 2003, you'll be told about any incompatibilities between Windows 2003 and your existing hardware and software. That's nice, but just a bit too late. The last thing that you want to do is to get everything ready for an upgrade and then find out that your server's hardware or software isn't up to snuff for Windows Server 2003.

You can use the compatibility analysis software that comes on Windows 2003 installation CDs to check your software and ensure that an NT 4 server is ready for upgrade to Windows 2003. For more on this tool, see the section titled "Checking Hardware and Software on Windows 2000 Servers to Be Upgraded to Windows 2003" earlier in this chapter.

A Windows 2003 Upgrade Strategy

When you've completed all the tasks described in the preceding section, you must specify a Windows 2003 upgrade strategy. Here are some suggestions:

- Schedule upgrades at the least intrusive times.

- Ensure that every existing NT 4 domain has at least one BDC. That way, if an upgrade fails, you'll always be able to fall back to the BDC to keep the domain running.

- Synchronize all BDCs with the PDC.

- Take one BDC off line to act as a backup in case your upgrade fails, and to be sure that it isn't corrupted during the upgrade.

- Back up each NT 4 server to tape just before upgrading it. Test each backup.

- Upgrade the PDC in any NT domain first.

- Upgrade BDCs as soon as possible.

- For upgrades of multiple-master or complete trust domains, consider the following. Create a new root domain before upgrading. Do this on a new computer, and add a Windows 2003 domain controller or two. Then upgrade the NT 4 PDC to act as a Windows 2003 domain controller for a new child domain.

- Upgrade other servers and workstations as time permits, but as quickly as possible. Existing workstations and non-domain-controller servers needn't be updated immediately. Only after you've installed Windows 2003 will servers and workstations be capable of taking full advantage of Active Directory services.

I'll expand on these items later in this chapter.

WARNING   *Again I must remind you not to upgrade NT 4 servers that support Exchange 5.5. It's not worth upgrading these servers because, as I noted earlier, you can't upgrade Exchange 5.5 on them to Exchange 2003. You must take another approach to Exchange upgrade. I'll discuss that approach later in this chapter.*

Active Directory Migration Tool

Microsoft has designed a pretty neat tool, called Active Directory Migration Tool (ADMT), to help you move smoothly from NT 4 to Windows 2003. You can use ADMT to migrate users, groups, computers, and some Exchange information from NT 4 server environments to Active Directory. You can also use ADMT to ensure that correct file permissions are set on your new Windows 2003 systems. In addition, you can use ADMT to issue reports that help you uncover potential problems in the migration and see how well your migration is going. You can even roll back a piece of your migration, if you discover problems.

If that's not enough to whet your appetite, ADMT features a nice wizard that makes the migration process even easier.

ADMT is a Microsoft Management Console snap-in on the Windows Server 2003 CD in the directory `\I386\ADMT`. To install the tool, right-click on the file `ADMIGRATION.MSI` and select Install. We'll spend more time with ADMT in the next section, "Upgrading from Exchange Server 5.5 to Exchange Server 2003."

TIP   *Once installed, run Active Directory Migration Tool as follows: Start ➤ Administrative Tools ➤ Active Directory Migration Tool. To select a particular migration option in Active Directory Migration Tool, left-click Active Directory Migration Tool in the Microsoft Management Console.*

WARNING   *Don't confuse ADMT with the Exchange Migration Wizard discussed in the sidebar "Migrating for the Easiest Upgrade" at the beginning of this chapter. The Wizard lets you migrate users and their mailboxes from, among other things, an Exchange 5.5 or 2000 server to an Exchange 2003 server. ADMT migrates users, groups, computers, and so on from NT 4 to Windows 2003's Active Directory. Mailboxes are not moved. ADMT is only part of the migration process that I discuss in this chapter. The Migration Wizard does a complete migration in certain kinds of Exchange 5.5 or 2000 environments.*

Remember, if you upgrade an NT 4 domain controller or install a new Windows 2003 domain controller in an existing NT 4 domain, you don't need ADMT. Both processes automatically import NT data into the Windows 2003 Active Directory.

At this point, you're almost ready to undertake an upgrade to Windows Server 2003. However, you first need to consider exactly how your Windows Server 2003 upgrade relates to upgrades that you will do from Exchange 5.5 to Exchange 2003. So, don't do anything yet. Read the rest of this chapter first. In the next section, I'll talk even more about the NT 4–to–Windows 2003 upgrade process and provide more detail on Windows 2003 upgrade strategies.

Upgrading from Exchange Server 5.5 to Exchange Server 2003: Processes and Techniques

Upgrading to Exchange Server 2003 is fairly straightforward after you've done your Windows Server 2003 upgrade. Exchange 2003 adds a fair amount of functionality to a Windows 2003 server, but the most important additions (at least, from an upgrade perspective) are those made to Active Directory. Your major tasks when upgrading from Exchange 5.5 revolve around ensuring that Active Directory is correctly populated with Exchange 5.5 directory objects.

Before we look at various NT 4–to–Windows 2003 and Exchange 5.5–to–2003 upgrade scenarios, I need to talk about the Exchange 2003 Active Directory Connector.

WARNING   *I've been hammering on this topic throughout this chapter, but I'll say it again: you cannot upgrade an existing Exchange 5.5 server to Exchange 2003. This sort of "in-place" upgrade was possible with Exchange 2000 Server. It can't be done with Exchange Server 2003. Instead, you must link an Exchange 5.5 server to an Exchange 2003 server. Then you must move objects and their attributes from Exchange 5.5's directory to Active Directory.*

Preparing Active Directory for Exchange Server 2003

Unlike Exchange 5.5, Exchange Server 2003 does not have a directory of its own. As I noted in Chapters 2 and 3, Microsoft "stole" the Exchange 5.5 directory, improved it, and turned it into Windows Server 2003's Active Directory.

Exchange Server 2003 uses Active Directory pretty much as Exchange 5.5 used its own directory service. When Exchange Server 2003 is installed on a Windows 2003 server, a number of Exchange-specific objects and attributes are added to the Active Directory schema. If you're doing a new installation of both Windows and Exchange 2003, you really don't need to worry about anything beyond ensuring that the new schema objects get installed.

However, if you're doing an upgrade, you must make sure that your Exchange 5.5 directory objects and attributes get moved into the new Active Directory Exchange–specific objects and attributes. In Microsoft's terminology, you must *populate Active Directory*. Active Directory is populated when both NT 4's user account information and Exchange 5.5's recipient-related directory information reside in Active Directory.

As you'll see in a bit, the Exchange upgrade process is pretty simple when you can upgrade your entire network to Windows Server 2003 and Exchange Server 2003 in a very short time—like in one night. Upgrades become more complex when your network is so large that upgrading will take several days, weeks, or even months. At that point, you must plan very carefully to ensure that NT 4 and Windows 2003 servers as well as Exchange 5.5 and 2003 servers can coexist. That means, more than anything else, that key Windows 2003 domains remain at the Windows 2000 mixed functional level and that you use the Exchange 2003 tool designed to keep Exchange 5.5/2003 information in sync, Active Directory Connector.

USING ACTIVE DIRECTORY CONNECTOR

We really can't go any further until I talk about one of the primary tools for synchronizing Exchange 5.5 and 2003 information, the Active Directory Connector (ADC). Before you can install Exchange 2003, you must install and run the ADC that comes with Exchange 2003. ADC lets you replicate Exchange-relevant recipient and other configuration information between Exchange 5.5 and 2003 servers.

You must manually install the ADC. After the ADC is installed, you should make changes on the Exchange 2003 side and let those changes replicate to the Exchange 5.5 side. This ensures that Active Directory receives all the rich Exchange 2003 information it needs and that Exchange 5.5 servers get what they need.

ADC runs on Windows 2003 servers. You must run it on a Windows 2003 domain controller before Exchange 2003 has been installed. You can run ADC just to do a one-time move of Exchange 5.5 directory information to Active Directory. You can also use ADC to keep Exchange 5.5 directory information in sync with Exchange 2003 (Active Directory) on an ongoing basis, until you eliminate all Exchange 5.5 servers from your network.

The good news with ADC is that, as an Exchange 5.5 administrator, you should have little trouble understanding, installing, or running it. ADC is very similar to Exchange 5.5's directory synchronization connector for Microsoft Mail–type systems. The main difference is that you need to set up what are called *connection agreements*. Connection agreements support synchronization of user and configuration information between Exchange Server 5.5's directory service and Active Directory.

One of the most important lessons that you should carry away from this section is that Exchange Server 2003 installation isn't always straightforward and that it's a bit more complex than you might be used to. You don't upgrade from Exchange 5.5 to Exchange 2003 simply by running the installation program from the Exchange 2003 CD-ROM disk. You have to get your Exchange 5.5 directory and your Windows 2003 Active Directory in sync before you install Exchange Server 2003. That's where the ADC comes in.

Windows NT 4–to–2003 and Exchange 5.5–to–2003 Upgrades: Putting It All Together

We're finally ready to look at some upgrade scenarios. First we'll explore a simple upgrade from NT4 to Windows 2003 and Exchange 5.5 to Exchange 2003. I'll show you how to use tools provided by Microsoft to make your Exchange upgrade easier and more reliable. Even so, I expect that you're not going to find even this simple upgrade scenario all that simple. Reading the following section thoroughly and then planning and testing will help. However, as you'll see below, there are lots of details to attend to and you need to assure that you're at your sharpest mentally. I have never found Windows and Exchange upgrades to be easy, fun, or really simple.

After the section on simple upgrades, I'll talk about more complicated Windows NT and Exchange 5.5 upgrades. Much of what I have to say about simple upgrades applies to complex upgrades. The major differences are related to the kind of NT domain structure you're upgrading: Multi-domain networks require a different approach to setting up your Windows 2003 domain structure and getting NT user and other information into Active Directory. Everything I said in the above paragraph about the painfulness of the simple upgrade process applies here. So, I will say no more.

A Simple NT 4–to–Windows 2003/Exchange 5.5–to–2003 Upgrade for Starters

Even if your upgrade scenario doesn't involve the sort of simple upgrade described here, I very strongly encourage you to read this section because it will give you a sense of the issues that you need to deal with, no matter what your upgrade scenario. Upgrades from Exchange 5.5 to 2003 aren't always as intuitive as you might expect. A little grounding in the upgrade process based on a simple example will prepare you for both the intuitive and the nonintuitive aspects of an upgrade.

Let's look at the simplest possible upgrade first. Imagine that you have an NT 4 server functioning as the PDC in a small network in which the only other NT servers are a BDC and an Exchange 5.5 server. First we'll do the NT 4 upgrade and then the Exchange 5.5 upgrade.

TIP *If you have difficulty with some of the concepts and terms in this section, be sure you've read the earlier chapters, earlier parts of this chapter on NT 4–to–Windows 2003 upgrades, and, if necessary, jump over to Chapter 7 for more on Windows 2003 installation.*

UPGRADING NT 4 SERVER TO WINDOWS 2003

We're going to do an in-place upgrade of our NT 4 PDC to Windows 2003. That's pretty simple. Let's look in detail at the steps in an NT 4–to–Windows 2003 upgrade.

Why upgrade the NT 4 PDC first? Because an NT–to–Windows 2003 domain upgrade requires that you upgrade your PDC before you upgrade any other domain servers or member servers in the domain.

For starters, be sure you have considered all of the information in Chapters 1 through 5. These chapters help you understand what is going to happen when you upgrade to a Windows 2003 domain controller and how your Windows 2003 domain controller will fit into your NT 4/Windows 2003 environment.

Once you're sure you understand what's going to happen, make sure that your NT 4 PDC is running Service Pack 5 or later. Unless you have good reason not to, I suggest you install SP 6a.

Next, back up the domain controller. Because you have a BDC, the backup you make of the PDC is extra money in the bank. If your upgrade fails, you can turn first to the BDC and then to the backup of the PDC, if necessary.

After backing up your NT domain controller, check the compatibility of your NT server with Windows 2003 by running the software I discussed earlier in this chapter, in the section "Checking the Readiness of your NT Server 4 System."

Next, make sure you have enough disk space for the upgrade. An NT 4–to–Windows 2003 upgrade is a real disk hog. In addition to temporary disk space requirements, Active Directory can take as much as ten times the amount of disk space as NT 4 equivalent system information storage databases. If your NT domain controller is short on C: volume disk space, either upgrade to a larger drive (not fun) or consider using a new computer, making it a BDC while installing NT 4, promoting it to PDC, and then installing Windows Server 2003 on it. To do this, you have to leave this section and move on to later sections where I discuss more complex NT–to–Windows 2003 upgrade processes.

While you're looking at disks, your NT domain controller should have at least one NTFS partition. Ideally, all partitions should be formatted as NTFS. If you need to reformat partitions to NTFS, check the Windows NT 4 documentation or the documentation that comes on the Windows 2003 CD. Also, if you have mirrored or striped disk sets, you have get rid of them. See the Windows docs on the Windows 2003 CD for more information.

That's it. Now you're ready to start the Exchange 5.5–to–Exchange 2003 upgrade process. As you'll see in a minute, this isn't as simple as performing an in-place upgrade on your NT 4 PDC.

UPGRADING EXCHANGE 5.5 TO EXCHANGE 2003

Whoopee! We're finally ready to do an Exchange 5.5–to–Exchange 2003 upgrade. An upgrade to Exchange involves a number of tasks, none of which can be skipped. You can perform all of these tasks with the Exchange Deployment Tools (EDT) that I discussed at the beginning of this chapter. You are offered an opportunity to use them when you insert the Exchange 2003 CD.

Perform these tasks in the following order when guided by EDT:

1. Install Windows 2003 and any required service packs on the server that will become your Exchange 2003 server. Unless otherwise noted, perform the remaining steps on this server.

2. Install and enable (or ensure installation and activation of) specific services on your Windows 2003 server: Exchange Internet Information Server, Simple Mail Transport Protocol (SMTP) Server, Network News Transfer Protocol (NNTP) Server, ASP.NET, and .NET Framework.

3. Run DSScopeScan (this program focuses on the Exchange 5.5 directory and assures that it is ready for upgrade).

4. Install the Windows 2003 support tools (they're on the Windows installation CD).

5. Run DCDiag, which tests network connectivity and DNS name resolution.

6. Run NetDiag, which tests Domain Name System (DNS) functionality and other network functionality.

7. Review log files from DCDiag and NetDiag, and the ExDeploy.log file, which summarizes errors in the DCDiag and NetDiag log files. Correct any errors.

8. Run ForestPrep to prepare your Windows forest for Exchange 2003.

9. Run DomainPrep to prepare your Windows domain for Exchange 2003.

10. Run OrgPrepCheck to ensure that Exchange schema extensions installed by ForestPrep and DomainPrep are OK and that certain security and domain controller permissions are properly set.

11. Review the ExDeploy.log file for errors generated by OrgPrepCheck and correct any errors.

12. Install Active Directory Connector on your Windows 2003 domain controller using the Exchange 2003 CD.

13. Run the Active Directory Connector Tools on your domain controller and preliminarily set up connection agreements.

14. Wait for objects to replicate to Active Directory from the Exchange directory.

15. Run SetupPrep, which ensures that DNS is functioning; checks the version of Exchange running on each server; and verifies that public folder security conversions were correctly done.

16. Review the OrgNameCheck.log file and the ExDeploy.log file for any errors and correct the errors.

17. Install Exchange 2003.

18. Check the installation by running

    ◆ ADCConfigCheck, which ensures that Exchange 5.5 directory configuration objects were properly replicated from the Exchange 5.5 directory to Active Directory

    ◆ ConfigDSInteg, which detects problems in Active Directory after Active Directory Connector has been running

◆ RecipientDSInteg, which checks each recipient object—user, group, contact, or public folder—to detect problems in Active Directory after Active Directory Connector has been running

◆ PrivFoldCheck, which ensures that the directory and the private information store are synchronized

As I noted at the start of this section, you can literally complete all of the tasks in this list using the great interactive checklists provided by Exchange Deployment Tools. Next you'll find a more detailed discussion of two of the items in the list and one that isn't. This is both so you can better understand what's going on within EDT and so you can perform them outside of EDT if you wish. Just be sure to check off the item in the checklist even if you complete it outside of EDT.

Installing and Enabling Windows 2003 Services Required by Exchange 2003

You can't install Exchange 2003 unless the following Windows 2003 services are enabled.

◆ World Wide Web

◆ SMTP

◆ NNTP

◆ ASP.NET

◆ .NET Framework

To enable these services, use the Control Panel Add or Remove Programs applet (choose Start ➤ Control Panel ➤ Add or Remove Programs, and then click Add/Remove Windows Components).

To enable ASP.NET, click Application Server in the Components list and then click Details. Check ASP.NET in the Subcomponents of Application Server list. If, for some reason, this or any other service has already been installed, it will be checked.

For World Wide Web, SMTP, and NNTP services, click Internet Information Services in the Subcomponents of Application Server list and click Details. You'll see the three services listed in the Subcomponents of Internet Information Services (IIS) list. Check the three services. Click next and the services will be set up.

Make sure that the World Wide Web, SMTP, and NNTP services are running (choose All Programs ➤ Administrative Tools ➤ Services).

To enable ASP.NET support for .NET Framework, you need to do one more thing. Open the Internet Information Services Manager (choose Start ➤ All Programs ➤ Administrative Tools ➤ Internet Information Services Manager). Double-click your server, then double-click Web Service Extensions, click Active Server Pages, and finally click Allow.

Preparing the Windows 2003 Forest and Domain Where Exchange 2003 Will Be Installed

If you don't have full security privileges for the Windows 2003 Active Directory and domain where Exchange Server 2003 will be installed during the upgrade, you need a little help from your friends before you can do the upgrade. You have to ask whoever is responsible for Active Directory or domain maintenance to run the Exchange Server 2003 setup program with two special switches at a command prompt. Let's take a quick look at these two special switches: *ForestPrep* and *DomainPrep*.

When the Exchange setup program is executed with the ForestPrep switch, it adds the Exchange Server 2003 objects to the Active Directory schema when you installed Active Directory Connector. When setup is executed with the DomainPrep switch, it identifies a recipient update server for the domain (in this case, your about-to-be Exchange 2003 server) and adds permissions within the domain required by Exchange 2003. Each of these programs need to be run only once in a given forest or domain, respectively.

For more on the two Exchange 2003 setup program switches and the process of running setup with the switches, see Chapter 8.

NOTE   *The capability to run the Exchange Server 2003 setup program with the ForestPrep and DomainPrep switches allows organizations to distribute responsibility for managing a Windows 2003/Exchange 2003 environment among different IS staff groups. The group that manages Active Directory runs ForestPrep. The group that manages a particular domain runs DomainPrep. The Exchange group installs Exchange Server 2003 without needing security access to run either ForestPrep or DomainPrep.*

Installing and Running Active Directory Connector

Active Directory Connector imports Exchange 5.5 objects into Active Directory. Here's how to install and run ADC on your Windows 2003 domain controller.

You install Active Directory Connector from the Exchange 2003 CD. It's located in the folder \ADC. To install it, run \ADC\I386\SETUP.EXE.

Of course, before ADC can import Exchange 5.5 objects into Active Directory, it has to make a place for them. To do this, ADC extends the Active Directory schema. This extension doesn't cover all possible Exchange objects. More will be added when you prepare your Windows 2003 forest and domain or domains for Exchange.

Once ADC is installed, you need to set up connection agreements between your Exchange 5.5 server and your Windows 2003 domain controller. This is quite simple and is managed by a wizard.

Moving Mailboxes and Public Folders from the Exchange 5.5 Server to the Windows 2003 Server

This is not included in the EDT check list. When you're comfortable that your Exchange installation went well, you're ready to bring mailboxes and public folders over to your new Exchange 2003 server. Old Exchange 5.5 hands know how easy it is to move mailboxes and folders between Exchange 5.5 servers. Well, it's just as easy to move them between Exchange 5.5 and Exchange 2003.

For more on moving mailboxes, see the section "Moving a Mailbox from One Exchange Server to Another" in Chapter 15, "Installing and Managing Additional Exchange Servers." Even though Chapter 15 deals with Exchange 2003 servers, everything works the same if one of the servers is an Exchange 5.5 server.

"Move" isn't exactly the correct term for how you get Exchange 5.5 public folders over to your Exchange 2003 server. You do this by replicating Exchange 5.5 public folders to your Exchange 2003 server. See the sections "Working with Public Folders" and "Managing Public Folders" in Chapter 15.

Okay, we've covered a "simple" Windows NT 4–to–Windows 2003/Exchange 5.5–to–Exchange 2003 upgrade. If such an upgrade works for you, consider yourself lucky and done. If your NT 4/Exchange 5.5 system is more complex, read on and discover the joys of more complex upgrades.

More Complex Upgrades from Windows NT 4–to–2003 and Exchange 5.5–to–2003

If your NT 4 domain structure consists of more than a couple of domain controllers and an Exchange server, the simple upgrade strategy outlined earlier isn't going to work for you. For example, if you have a ton of NT 4 domains, simply upgrading all of your domain controllers might not be the best answer. The simple upgrade in the previous section also won't work for complex Exchange 5.5 systems. So, it's time to explore some other upgrade strategies.

In my experience, the biggest problem with complex upgrades is on the Windows side, not the Exchange side. You have to get all those users and such into Active Directory. So, let's begin by looking at some strategies for populating Active Directory when you have complex NT 4 domain structures.

STRATEGIES FOR POPULATING ACTIVE DIRECTORY

Populating Active Directory with NT and Exchange 5.5 information is the hairiest part of any Windows 2003/Exchange 2003 upgrade. Microsoft has identified five strategies that you might use to populate Active Directory. These strategies are based mostly on assumptions about the size and breadth of your Windows network, on the NT domain structure that you're coming from, and on the Windows 2003 domain structure that you're planning to implement.

For all the fire and brimstone that might be thrown from the volcano, Microsoft's five Active Directory population strategies are designed to accomplish nothing more than importing or replicating NT 4 information and Exchange 5.5's directory information into Active Directory.

Remember that none of these strategies includes installing or upgrading to Exchange Server 2003. That comes right after you've completed all of the steps in any of the five strategies. Let's look at Microsoft's five strategies in a little detail.

Active Directory Population Strategy #1

The first two Active Directory population strategies are accomplished using a single Windows Server 2003 domain. In the first strategy, you create a Windows Server 2003 domain by upgrading an NT domain controller to a Windows Server 2003 domain controller. In the second strategy, you create a Windows Server 2003 domain by installing Windows Server 2003 from scratch. Here's the first strategy (see Figure 6.8):

1. Upgrade an NT 4 domain controller to Windows Server 2003.
2. Synchronize Exchange 5.5 with the new Windows 2003 Active Directory using Active Directory Connector.

FIGURE 6.8
Active Directory
population
strategy #1

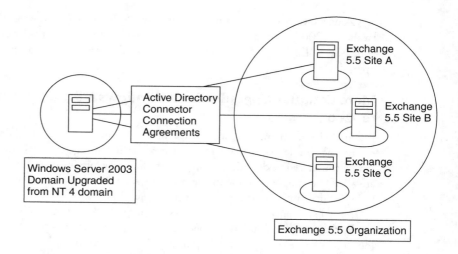

This is a pretty simple strategy and it should sound pretty familiar. It's pretty much like the one we used in the simple upgrade scenario. I put it here for contrast with the other strategies. In this strategy, you upgrade an NT 4 server to Windows Server 2003. Then you set up Active Directory Connection agreements to bring over Exchange-specific information from one or more Exchange 5.5 servers. When the information you need has been pulled over, you're ready to upgrade your Exchange 5.5 server or servers.

Active Directory Population Strategy #2

In this strategy, you create a Windows 2003 domain without having to upgrade any NT servers. Active Directory population is accomplished manually after your new Windows Server 2003 is installed:

1. Install Windows Server 2003 from scratch, creating a new Windows Server 2003 domain. Don't join the NT 4 domain from which you are planning migration to the Windows 2003 environment.

2. Use the ADMT to clone NT 4 accounts into Active Directory on the new Windows Server 2003.

3. Synchronize Exchange 5.5 with the new Windows 2003 Active Directory using the Active Directory Connector.

Figure 6.9 shows the second Active Directory population strategy in graphic form. The numbers in Figure 6.9 correspond to the numbers in this list. This numbering scheme is used in the rest of the figures showing Active Directory population strategies.

You'll remember ADMT from the section "Active Directory Migration Tool" earlier in this chapter. This tool allows you to pull NT Server information from one or more NT servers and then bring it into Active Directory.

After you've completed the three steps in this strategy, you can upgrade Exchange 5.5 or install Exchange 2003 immediately. You can also upgrade other NT servers and the domains that they occupy when you're ready.

FIGURE 6.9
Active Directory
population
strategy #2

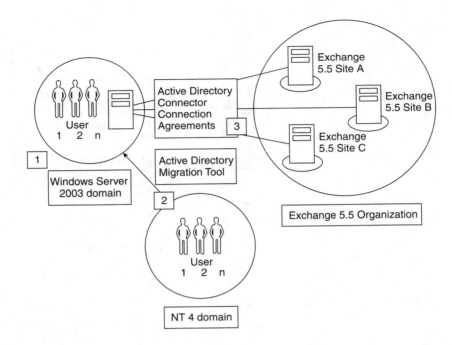

Active Directory Population Strategy #3

The first two Active Directory population strategies used a single Windows 2003 domain. The next two strategies use two domains. A new domain is created from scratch to hold either Exchange 5.5 or NT 4 information. A second domain in the same forest is created either from scratch or as a result of an NT 4 upgrade. This domain holds whatever information, Exchange 5.5 or NT 4, isn't in the first domain. Because the two domains are in the same forest, they're in the same Active Directory. You then merge the Exchange 5.5 and NT 4 information for each user in the Active Directory to create a fully functioning user. Here's the third Active Directory population strategy:

1. Install Windows Server 2003 from scratch, creating a new Windows Server 2003 domain.
2. Synchronize Exchange 5.5 with Active Directory on the new Windows 2003 server using Active Directory Connector, thereby creating disabled user objects that contain Exchange information.
3. Upgrade each NT 4 user account domain as time allows.
4. As you upgrade an NT domain and its users, use the Active Directory Account Cleanup Wizard to merge the Active Directory Connector–created accounts with upgraded accounts.

Figure 6.10 shows the third Active Directory population strategy. This strategy adds a new player to the game, the Active Directory Account Cleanup Wizard (ADACUW). The ADACUW comes with Exchange Server 2003. You'll find it on the Windows 2003 Start Menu under Programs ➤ Microsoft Exchange.

FIGURE 6.10
Active Directory
population
strategy #3

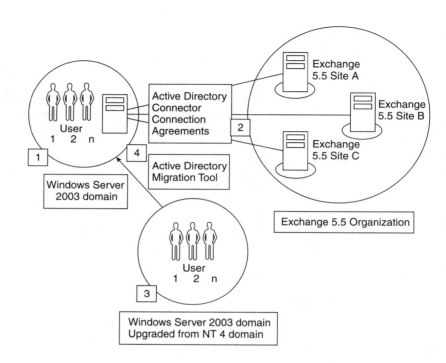

The ADACUW is designed to bring together Exchange 5.5 and NT 4 information about a user that has found its way to Active Directory. Here's how it accomplishes this task: All information about an NT 4 user is stored using a unique security identifier (SID). Each user's SID is an index that represents the user. When information is synchronized into Active Directory, wherever it comes from, the NT 4 SID is preserved. So, when Exchange 5.5 information for a user comes into Active Directory by way of Active Directory Connector, the user's NT 4 SID is stored along with the Exchange 5.5 information. When NT 4 information for the same user comes into Active Directory by way of an upgrade or ADMT, the user's SID is stored with the information.

The ADACUW goes through Active Directory, matching NT 4 information with Exchange 5.5 information. It uses each user's SID to make the match. When a match is made, ADACUW firmly links NT 4 and Exchange 5.5 information for a user in Active Directory.

So, in this strategy, you first use Active Directory Connector to bring Exchange 5.5 information into Active Directory on a newly installed Windows 2003 server. Then, after you upgrade each NT domain to a Windows Server 2003 domain, which brings NT 4 information into Active Directory, you use ADACUW to merge the two kinds of information in Active Directory.

Until you upgrade an NT 4 domain, the Exchange 5.5 information lies in a dormant or disabled object. With the upgrade, an enabled user object is created for each user in the upgraded NT 4 domain. ADACUW merges the disabled and enabled objects, creating fully functional Active Directory users.

Active Directory Population Strategy #4

This strategy is similar to the third strategy, but you don't create the second domain by upgrading an NT 4 domain controller. Instead you use ADMT to clone accounts from the NT 4 domain into a transition domain:

1. Install Windows Server 2003 from scratch, creating a new Windows Server 2003 domain.

2. Synchronize Exchange 5.5 with Active Directory on the new Windows 2003 server using Active Directory Connector, thereby creating disabled user objects that contain Exchange information.

3. Create a transition Windows Server 2003 domain, and use the ADMT to clone Windows NT user accounts into Active Directory in the transition domain.

4. Use the ADACUW to merge the Active Directory Connector–created accounts with cloned accounts.

See Figure 6.11 for a graphic view of the fourth directory population strategy. Here's how it works: In this strategy, you create two domains in the same forest by installing Windows Server 2003 from scratch on two different computers. Then you use the Active Directory Connector to create disabled Exchange 5.5 user information in the first domain. You also use the ADMT to clone NT 4 users into the second (transition) domain. Because the two domains are in the same forest (Active Directory), you can then run the ADACUW to merge Exchange 5.5 and NT 4 information.

Active Directory Population Strategy #5

This is the last strategy for populating Active Directory. Like the first two strategies, this one uses a single Windows Server 2003 domain:

1. Install Windows Server 2003 from scratch, creating a new Windows Server 2003 domain.

2. Synchronize Exchange 5.5 with Active Directory on the new Windows 2003 server using ADC, thereby creating disabled user objects that contain Exchange information.

3. Enable the user objects created from Exchange 5.5 information in Active Directory by ADC.

4. Use the ADMT to match user objects in the new Windows 2003 domain's Active Directory to existing NT 4 accounts.

Figure 6.12 shows the fifth Active Directory population strategy. In this strategy, you enable the user objects created from your Exchange 5.5 environment by the Active Directory Connector. Because user objects have been enabled, NT 4 information is merged with Exchange 5.5 information in Active Directory through the use of the ADMT.

You enable a disabled user object through the Active Directory Users and Computers snap-in for the Microsoft Management Console. Find the user in the Users subcontainer; right-click the user, and select Enable Account. That's it. (You can also enable user objects by updating the Active Directory schema, but that is something you don't want to get into unless you really know what you're doing.)

FIGURE 6.11
Active Directory
population
strategy #4

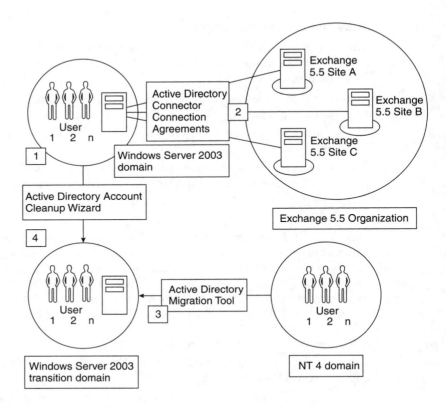

Do You Need a Group Management Domain?

Before we finish with Active Directory population strategies, we should talk about one other issue. Exchange 5.5 distribution lists can be used to send messages to a group of recipients. They can also be used to control access to Exchange resources such as public folders. If you use distribution lists for this latter function, you might have a bit of a problem in Exchange Server 2003.

With Exchange Server 2003, you can control access to Exchange resources only by using Windows 2003 universal security groups. When you run the Active Directory Connector with a connection agreement between an Exchange 5.5 server and a Windows 2003 domain at the Windows Server 2003 functional level, Exchange 5.5 distribution lists serving an access control function in Exchange 5.5 become universal security groups in Windows 2003. As such, you can use these groups for Exchange Server 2003 access control.

Unfortunately, universal security groups are available only when a Windows 2003 domain is running at the Windows Server 2003 functional level. So, if you're all switched to this level, all is well. If you're not, you have to run what Microsoft calls a *group management domain.* A group management domain is a Windows Server 2003 domain running at the Windows Server 2003 functional level.

FIGURE 6.12
Active Directory
population
strategy #5

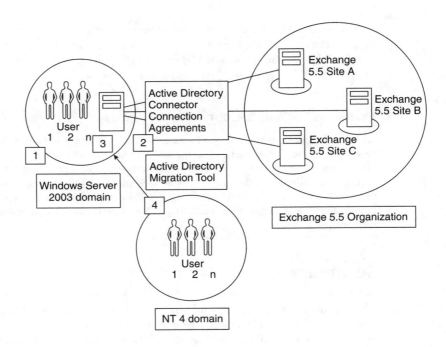

Remember that you need a group management domain only if you want to continue using distribution list–like management of access to Exchange resources. You could also use Windows 2003 local or global domain groups. Note, however, that using local or global groups for this function requires more time and effort, and might require more involvement by Windows 2003 networking managers outside your group of Exchange managers.

If you opt for a group management domain, you need to set up a Windows Server 2003 domain and switch it to the Windows Server 2003 functional level. Before you upgrade any Exchange 5.5 servers, you also need to set up one or more Active Directory Connector connection agreements between your new Windows 2003 group management domain and NT 4 domains containing the Exchange 5.5 servers. Yes, Active Directory Connector can run in a Windows Server 2003 domain at the Windows Server 2003 functional level.

If you decide to use the fourth Active Directory population strategy and you can switch the transition server domain to the Windows Server 2003 functional level, you're in luck. You can use the transition domain as your group management domain.

EXCHANGE SERVER 5.5 UPGRADE STRATEGIES FOR MORE COMPLEX EXCHANGE 5.5 ENVIRONMENTS

Upgrading Exchange 5.5 servers to Exchange 2003 is pretty much done as it is with the simple upgrade I discussed earlier. Basically, you install Windows 2003 (or upgrade to it, if it's not supporting Exchange 5.5). Then you go through the Exchange 2003 server installation/upgrade process as per my discussion of a simple upgrade.

With more complex Exchange environments, you might want to consider consolidating two or more Exchange 5.5 servers on a single Exchange 2003 server. You'll need quality server hardware, good CPU horsepower, more RAM memory, and solid, higher-speed disk drives, but like Windows 2003, Exchange 2003 is designed to support lots of users. So, go for it.

EXCHANGE 5.5/2003 COEXISTENCE

Active Directory Connector allows Exchange 5.5 servers and Exchange 2003 servers to coexist. In most cases, coexistence is required only long enough to upgrade all Exchange 5.5 servers to 2003 status. However, I have worked in situations where coexistence was a long-term thing. For example, your Exchange 5.5 organization might include some sites that lack adequate technical or financial resources to permit an upgrade to Windows 2003 and Exchange 2003. The nice thing about the upgrade paths that Microsoft has architected for Exchange is that everything will work pretty well, whether short- or long-term coexistence is necessary.

Summary

Whew! That really was hell. Just kidding. (I think.) In this chapter, we focused on upgrade issues. First we looked at upgrades from Windows 2000 to Windows 2003 and from Exchange 2000 to Exchange 2003. These upgrades are pretty much no-brainers, though you do have to be sure that forest and domain data in Active Directory for both Windows 2003 and Exchange 2003 are properly upgraded.

Next, we took a long, hard look at the upgrade process from NT Server 4 to Windows Server 2003. Then we walked the upgrade path from Exchange Server 5.5 to Exchange Server 2003. We discovered that Exchange 2003 upgrades are intimately linked to Windows 2003 upgrades. We also discovered that, except for the fact that you can't do an in-place Exchange 5.5–to–2003 upgrade, upgrades from NT 4 to Windows 2003 are more difficult than Exchange 5.5–to–2003 upgrades.

Upgrades from NT 4 to Windows 2003 begin with a clear mapping between your current NT 4 domain structure and your future Windows 2003 domain structure. There is nothing to stop you from mapping any of the four NT 4 domain models to a nearly parallel Windows 2003 domain model. However, the preferred approach is to create a single Windows 2003 domain that incorporates all your NT 4 domains. Windows 2003 includes features that make this process easier such as sites and organizational units.

Also, when upgrading from NT 4 to Windows 2003, you must select from among the three flavors of Windows Server 2003: Standard, Enterprise, and Datacenter Edition. And you must select carefully, remembering to keep the power of Windows 2003 Server editions in line with the Exchange Server 2003 you'll be using. You must also ensure that your server's hardware is adequate to support the Windows 2003 software that you'll be installing and that all the software on the server is compatible with Windows 2003. In addition, you must create an upgrade plan that takes into account the specifics of your NT Server 4 environment, the Windows 2003 domain model that you're shooting for, and the process of getting from NT 4 to Windows 2003 without risking a large amount of downtime.

As with Windows 2000–to–Windows 2003 upgrades, you need to upgrade your forest and the domain in which you're installing Windows 2003. And, unlike a Windows 2000–to–Windows 2003 upgrade, depending on how you upgrade to Windows 2003, you might have to replicate NT 4 account and other security information into Active Directory.

You must complete a number of tasks to upgrade Exchange 5.5 environments to Exchange 2003. Fortunately, Microsoft developed and provides a set of mandatory Exchange Deployment Tools that walk you through the upgrade process. You must run all of the tools or you won't be able to install Exchange 2003. Steps in an Exchange upgrade include an assessment of your network and servers, preparation of your Windows 2003 forest and domain or domains for an Exchange 2003 installation, and installation of Active Directory Connector to import Exchange 5.5 directory information into Windows 2003's Active Directory.

Now we're ready to move on to the hands-on part of this book. We'll begin by installing and using Windows Server 2003 and Exchange Server 2003. Even though Chapters 7 and 8 don't include specific upgrade information, you should read both chapters carefully. Why? See the introduction to Part II, "Installation."

Part 2

Installation

Chapter 7

Installing Windows Server 2003 as a Domain Controller

THIS IS A DUAL-PURPOSE chapter. First, it's designed to help you install Windows Server 2003 as a domain controller that fully supports network login, access to various resources, DHCP, and DNS. Second, this chapter is designed to help you install a stand-alone Windows Server 2003. It assumes that you will install a Windows 2003 domain controller first and then, in conjunction with reading Chapter 8, "Installing Exchange Server 2003," install a stand-alone server on which you will install and run Exchange Server 2003. I have constructed this chapter so that you know when I'm talking about installing a domain controller and when I'm talking about installing a stand-alone server. I use warning notes to call your attention to critical points at which you take one path if installing a domain controller and another path if installing a stand-alone server.

NOTE *This is ultimately a book about Exchange Server 2003. So, it's not possible for me to cover everything about Windows Server 2003 in great detail. For more, check out* Mastering Windows Server 2003, *by Mark Minasi, Christa Anderson, Michele Beveridge, C.A. Callahan, and Lisa Justice (Sybex, 2003).*

In this chapter, I presume that you'll be installing Windows Server 2003 on a computer with nothing on it that you want to preserve. For example, I assume that you don't need to upgrade an NT 4 or Windows 2000 server to Windows Server 2003 and preserve the software that you've installed under the existing operating system. If you need to upgrade an NT 4 server, see Chapter 6, "Upgrading to Windows Server 2003 and Exchange Server 2003."

Windows Server 2003 installation is a multi-step process. These steps are listed at the start of this chapter, and we'll look at each of these steps in detail.

WARNING *Things are likely to change by the time you read this book. The Internet and the high-speed, high-pressure marketing and software delivery channels that it has fostered make unending, unpredictable, and incredibly quick software modification not only possible, but also economically necessary for vendors. Before you install Windows Server 2003, check the Web to be sure that a new service pack isn't available for the product or that you don't have to do something new and special when installing Windows Server 2003, if you plan to install Exchange Server 2003. The best websites are* www.microsoft.com/windows2003 *(or, as time passes,* www.microsoft.com/windows*) and* www.microsoft.com/exchange *for updates. You can also update Windows 2003 directly over the Internet. Just select the Windows Update option on the Start menu. The system can even check for new updates and let you know when an update is available. This is a really neat capability.*

Have you ever gone on the Alice in Wonderland ride at Disneyland? It starts by taking you down a rabbit hole, with Alice saying, "Here we goooooooooooooooooooo." That extended "go" fades away toward the end, adding to the ride's excitement and sense of entering the unknown. Like Alice, we're about to embark on a wild and exciting adventure. I promise to do all I can to make our hands-on trip through Windows and Exchange 2003 interesting, productive, and fun—but a little less bumpy, arbitrary, and confusing than Alice's sojourn through Wonderland. Let's go.

Featured in this chapter:

◆ Setting up server hardware

◆ Installing Windows Server 2003 software

◆ Configuring your first Windows 2003 server

◆ Using Microsoft Management Console

◆ A quick look at Active Directory

◆ Configuring DHCP and Dynamic DNS

◆ Configuring unallocated disk space

◆ Installing an uninterruptible power supply

◆ Setting up a Windows Server 2003 backup

Setting Up Server Hardware

Setting up the hardware is a pretty straightforward process. First, you pick a server platform and outfit it with various components. Then you test its memory, disk drives, and other hardware to ensure that everything is working well.

From a hardware perspective, Windows Server 2003 is much easier to install than NT 4. Running on a modern plug-and-play PCI bus–based computer, with PCI adapters and its own Windows XP–like plug-and-play capabilities, Server 2003 automatically recognizes and installs hardware drivers. In such an environment, you rarely have to manually configure video, SCSI, modem, or other adapters. That alone is almost worth the price of admission to Windows Server 2003.

WARNING Throughout this chapter and in Chapter 8, I assume that the first Windows Server 2003 that you will install will be a domain controller. I also assume that you will not run Exchange Server 2003 on this computer. When we get to Chapter 8, we'll install Exchange on another Windows 2003 server, a stand-alone Windows Server 2003 that isn't a domain controller. If you're hard-pressed for hardware, for testing purposes, you can try installing Exchange on a Windows 2003 domain controller. However, I join Microsoft in strongly recommending against doing this in a production environment, no matter how powerful you might think your computing hardware is. In this chapter, you'll learn how to install Windows 2003 as both a domain controller and a stand-alone server. I'll use a warning note like this one at the beginning of sections of this chapter where you should do things differently depending on whether you're installing a domain controller or a stand-alone server.

WHAT TO BUY

Microsoft publishes a hardware compatibility list for its Windows products. The HCL names the components that work with Windows Server 2003 and other Windows-based operating systems. You can find this list on the Web at `www.microsoft.com/hwdq/hcl/`. Before you buy anything, consult this guide.

One crucial bit of advice: Don't be cheap! Lots of vendors sell components such as SIMMs, DIMMs, disk drives, motherboards, and CPUs at unbelievably low prices. Don't bite. Trust me on this one: I've been through the mill with cheap, flaky components. Windows Server 2003 all by itself can beat the living daylights out of a computer. Add Exchange Server 2003, and you'll pay back in your own sweat and time every penny and then some that you saved by buying cheap. Buy from stable, long-lived vendors at reasonable but not fairy-tale prices. RAM for a Windows Server 2003 should always be ECC-type. Quality components cost a little more but are well worth the money.

'Nuff said.

Getting Server Components in Order

In Chapter 5, "Designing a New Exchange 2003 System," I wrote of my computer of choice for running Exchange Server 2003: 1GHz Pentium III or 4 or Xeon machine with 768MB of memory and at least two 9GB SCSI hard drives. That's pretty much my recommendation for an Exchange-less Windows 2003 domain controller in a serious networked computing environment. Ideally, I'd like to see you use a dual-processor machine with 1GB of RAM memory and at least 60GB of RAID 5 disk storage for your domain controller.

If you're just going to test Windows 2003 and promise not to put your test configuration into production, you can use a somewhat lesser hunk of hardware than the one that I tout. I'd recommend, at minimum, a 800MHz Pentium PC with 512MB of RAM and a 40GB or so IDE or SCSI hard disk. I suggest that you outfit your system with a high-resolution VGA display adapter, at least a 17-inch monitor, a 24-speed or faster CD-ROM drive, two or more serial ports, two or more USB ports, a mouse, and one or more network adapters.

Regarding the serial and USB ports, you need one serial or USB port to interface your Windows Server 2003 to an uninterruptible power supply (UPS). This assumes that you are not using a UPS that communicates with servers using the TCP/IP protocol, which is the method of choice for connecting very large, very high-capacity UPSs to the servers they protect. You also might want to use a serial port for a mouse. If you plan to provide Microsoft's Remote dial-up access to your Windows Server 2003 users, use a PS/2 mouse port to free a serial port for dial-up. If you need a lot of dial-up ports, look at multiport boards from companies such as Digi International (`www.dgii.com`).

Testing Key Components

The networking services provided by a Windows 2003 server are critical applications. You should also consider fault-tolerant hardware, as discussed in Chapter 5. But even before you consider this option, you should be sure that everything in your server is working properly. You'll want to test five key components as soon as your server is in-house:

◆ Memory

◆ Hard disks

- ◆ CD-ROM drives
- ◆ SCSI controllers
- ◆ Network adapters

Good memory and disk tests are time-consuming. Testing out the high-end computer that I recommend could take a week or more. Don't let that deter you, though. You want to be sure that you've got a solid platform under your organization—if for no other reason than that you'll sleep better at night.

During Windows Server 2003 installation, the system is automatically configured for a variety of hardware options, so you should be sure that all your hardware is working during the installation process. For this reason, you'll want to test your CD-ROM drive, SCSI controllers, and network adapters before installing Windows Server 2003. Test all these together to be sure that no IRQ, I/O address, or DMA conflicts occur, although this should be less of a problem if your computer and adapters support plug-and-play hardware.

It should go without saying, but I'll say it anyway: Don't consider your testing phase finished until all components pass the tests you set out for them. Now let's start testing:

Testing memory   Because the quick boot-up memory test on Intel-based PCs cannot find most memory problems, use Smith Micro Software's CheckIt (`www.smithmicro.com/checkit/`) or PC-Doctor's PC-Doctor for DOS (`www.pc-doctor.com`) to test memory. You should run either of these programs from DOS with no memory manager present, and run the complete suite of tests in slow rather than quick mode.

Testing hard disks   There are two kinds of software-based hard disk testers: those that write one pattern all over the disk and then read to see whether the pattern was written correctly (MS-DOS's SCANDISK is such a tester), and those that write a range of patterns and test to see whether each was properly written. You'll want a multipattern tester because it is more likely to find the bit-based problems on a disk. SpinRite from Gibson Research (`http://grc.com/default.htm`) is a good multipattern tester that can find and declare off-limits any bad areas on the disk that the manufacturer didn't catch.

Testing CD-ROM drives   I test my CD-ROM drives in DOS using MSCDEX.EXE and the DOS driver for the drive. If I can do a directory (DIR) on a CD-ROM in the drive that I'm testing and copy a file or two from the CD-ROM, I assume that it's working well enough to move on to Windows 2003 installation.

Testing SCSI controllers   If you tested your hard drives as suggested previously, you've also tested their controllers, at least in isolation from other adapters. Just be sure to run your tests again with active CD-ROM drives and network cards to ensure that no adapter conflicts are lurking in the background just waiting to mess up your Windows Server 2003 installation.

TIP   *If you've got enough hardware, you might want to run your RAM and disk tests simultaneously. This will cut down on testing time somewhat.*

Testing network adapters   I never install a machine that will be networked without making sure that it can attach in MS-DOS mode to a server. I use Microsoft's NDIS drivers. Make sure to connect your LAN-side adapter to your network before you begin installing Windows 2003.

If you're going to connect your server both to your LAN and directly to the Internet without an intervening firewall, I strongly suggest that you install only the LAN-side network adapter before installing Windows 2003. That way, there's no chance that the adapter might be accidentally activated by Windows Plug-and-Play hardware system when you first boot up after installing Windows 2003. This could expose your server to the Internet and its seemingly endless threats to computer security. While I'm strongly urging you to do things, let me almost insist that you put your server behind a firewall. I'll talk more about how you do this in Chapter 18, "Exchange Server System Security."

WARNING   Use solid, top-name brand server-quality adapters. I've seen a lot of workstation-quality adapters from second-level name-brand vendors such as LinkSys and D-Link permanently or temporarily go south at the worst times. You're better off with cards from vendors such as 3Com. I like the 3C905CX-TX adapters. I've experienced breakdowns with these cards, but far less frequently than with the others. And don't think you need good adapters only for Internet connections. Windows 2003 servers need LAN access too, and Exchange 2003 can't function at all without access to domain controllers, which should be on the LAN side.

Installing Windows Server 2003 Software

As with setting up hardware, installing Windows Server 2003 is fairly straightforward. If you've read Part I, "Understanding and Planning," you should encounter no surprises. We'll go through all the steps that you take to get Windows Server 2003 up and running.

I'd love to show you all the screens that you'll see during installation. However, because no operating system is yet in place, there's no way to capture these screens. Rest assured that each step discussed here parallels a screen that you'll see during installation. Later in this chapter—after we've got Windows Server 2003 installed—I'll show you enough setup screens to make up for the early deficit.

TIP   My first encounter with the Windows Server 2003 documentation was pretty scary. I nearly panicked when I saw nothing about choosing whether a new server was to be a domain controller or a stand-alone server. After all, this was a major and irrevocable decision point in the installation of an NT 4 server. My discomfort subsided when I realized that Windows 2003 servers become domain controllers after, not during, initial installation. So, relax and track through the initial installation process with me. After that, we'll turn our newly installed server into a domain controller.

Starting the Installation

Now I'm going to discuss how to install Windows Server 2003 Enterprise Edition. If you're installing this product or the Datacenter Edition, your experience will be pretty much the same as what I show you here. To make things a bit easier, I'll refer to the product that we're installing as *Windows Server 2003*.

Windows Server 2003 comes on a CD-ROM. Insert the CD in the CD-ROM drive, and boot your computer. The Windows 2003 Setup program will start automatically.

The first notable thing you'll see is a blue screen with "Windows Setup" displayed in white letters at the top of the screen. At the bottom of the screen, you are offered an opportunity to load drivers that aren't on the Windows 2003 CD. If you need such drivers, insert the disk containing them and press F6. After the drivers are loaded from the disk, you'll see the message "Setup is loading files," along with text in parentheses indicating which file is being loaded. Windows 2003 is loading files into RAM memory at this point. These files support the installation of Windows 2003 itself, as well as a variety of disk drives, CD-ROM drives, SCSI and RAID devices, video adapters, file systems, and so on. Windows 2003 will use these drivers during the setup phase. All this takes some time, from 1 to 5 minutes, so be patient.

Next you have the option of installing Windows 2003 or exiting the Setup program. Press Enter to continue with the installation. The following screen lets you set up Windows 2003, repair an existing Windows 2003 installation, or quit Setup. Press Enter to select the first option to begin installation. When the licensing dialog box pops up, page down through the licensing agreement and press F8 to agree to the conditions of the license. F8 doesn't show up on the screen until you've paged all the way down to the end of the license.

Preparing Disk Partitions

Next, Setup shows you the unpartitioned space on the hard disk drives that it detected and asks how you want to set up your partitions and where you want to install Windows Server 2003. If you've worked with NT 4 or DOS disk partitions, what follows should be pretty familiar. You can choose to set up partitions of any size, up to the capacity of a disk drive. I recommend setting up a minimum 10GB partition for the Windows Server 2003 operating system.

For now, you need to worry about only the primary partition that Windows Server 2003 will be installed on. You can take care of other partitions later using Windows 2003's Disk Management application. I'll talk more about this application in the section "Configuring Unallocated Disk Space" later in this chapter.

Choose to install in the default partition or to create a new partition. If you select the first option, installation will begin immediately. If you pick the second option, you'll see a new screen that lets you select the size of the partition and create it.

Now comes the $64,000 question: Do you want to format the partition as a file allocation table (FAT) or Windows 2003 NT File System (NTFS) partition? And you have two options each for FAT and NTFS: quick or full formatting. Quick formatting is faster, but not as thorough as full formatting. Quick formatting sets up the file system, but does not check the integrity of each sector on the disk. Full formatting sets up the file system and identifies and marks bad sectors so they aren't used during installation or thereafter. I always use full formatting, and all of my Windows Server 2003 operating system partitions are formatted as NTFS. NTFS is far more fault-tolerant and secure than FAT. Furthermore, Active Directory runs only on NTFS. In addition, unlike in the past, when FAT file access was faster than NTFS file access, performance is now comparable between the two file systems. My own opinions notwithstanding, choose the format that you want and press the Enter key. Setup displays a little gauge showing formatting progress. Formatting takes quite a bit of time. Depending on the size of the partition you're formatting and the speed of your CPU, disk drives, and RAM, you're looking at 10 to 15 minutes.

Next, Setup begins copying files from the CD-ROM to the partition that you designated. Like formatting, this can take a while. After copying the files, Setup tells you that it has finished this phase of installation and lets you reboot your computer or reboots it for you.

Setup's Installation Wizard

Upon reboot, you'll see a screen that shows the progress of the setup process and an estimate of the time remaining to complete setup. Don't worry if the time-to-completion information sits at a particular number of minutes for longer than a minute. This is only an estimate and is subject to the vagaries of CPU power, amount of RAM memory, and disk drive performance. If the squares at the bottom right of the screen light up in rotation, all should be okay. You can also watch for disk drive action to ensure that nothing has gone amiss.

At some point in this process, hardware device detection and driver installation begins. As you watch the little progress gauge at the bottom left of the screen turn greener and greener, you're participating in one of the little miracles of the twenty-first century. Windows 2003's device detection code finds all relevant hardware devices—keyboards, mouse devices, display adapters, network adapters, USB-connected devices, and so on—and installs drivers for them from the vast array of files cached on the CD. If the right driver isn't present, you're given the chance to load it from alternative media. If you don't have the driver, installation can sometimes continue. Just follow Windows 2003's lead.

When device installation has completed, Setup brings up a wizard to guide you through the next phase of Windows Server 2003 installation. The wizard looks a lot like the installation wizards that come with a range of products designed for the Windows operating system. It leads you through the selection of a number of important options for installation, the installation of Windows 2003 networking, and a bunch of other housekeeping chores.

The sections that follow guide you through the various phases of Windows Server 2003 installation. They're keyed to the title of each installation wizard screen; click Next on the wizard to move on to the next phase of installation.

REGIONAL AND LANGUAGE OPTIONS

The next step in the installation process involves selecting appropriate regional settings. These include the standards, formats, locale settings, and text-input language settings (Windows 2003 can handle multiple languages). These settings support various number, currency, time, date, and keyboard layouts.

Generally, the default settings work fine if you're in the United States or if you're using a CD with a localized version of Windows 2003.

PERSONALIZING YOUR ORGANIZATION

If you've ever installed a Windows product before, you've filled in this screen. Enter your name (or whatever name your organization wants in the name field). Enter whatever is appropriate in the Organization field, or leave it blank. Here you're just entering identifying information. This information is often used in installing other software, such as Microsoft Office. It has nothing to do with how your computer or domain will be named.

YOUR PRODUCT KEY

Next, the wizard requests the Product Key for your installation of Windows 2003. This is a long alphanumeric code that comes with your Windows 2003 CD. You can't install the product without a valid key.

LICENSING MODES

Select the licensing type that you've paid for, per server or per seat, and enter any required values. Heed the wizard's warning to use the License Manager in the Administrative Tools program group to set the number of client licenses purchased after your Windows Server 2003 is up and running. If you don't, users and other systems won't be able to connect to the server.

COMPUTER NAME AND ADMINISTRATOR PASSWORD

The wizard next asks you to name your Windows 2003 server and suggests a name. If you like the name, fine. If not, change it. If you'll be running Exchange 2003 on this server, the name should follow the Exchange Server naming scheme that you developed based on discussions in Chapter 5. If this server won't be running Exchange, use whatever naming scheme you've chosen for non-Exchange servers.

I'm naming my first server BG01. Following my own advice, this server won't run Exchange 2003; it'll be a domain controller running Active Directory, DHCP, and DNS. That's more than enough for one server.

The name can be up to 63 characters long. If this computer will interact with non–Windows 2000/ 2003 clients, the name should be 15 characters or less in length.

You're also asked for a password for the Administrator account on this server. Enter the password and confirm the password by reentering it. Passwords can be up to 14 characters long. Use a password that isn't easy to crack. Mix uppercase and lowercase letters and numbers.

DATE AND TIME SETTINGS

Use this page of the wizard to enter date, time, and time zone settings.

NETWORK SETTINGS

Windows Server 2003 is nothing without networking. Next, the Setup program installs some networking software and checks to see if you have one or more supported network adapters in your computer. A supported adapter is one that was found during device recognition and for which a driver was installed during device recognition. If Setup finds no supported network adapters, it moves on to the next steps in the installation process. You can install network adapters and drivers any time after installation has completed.

NOTE *I assume in this section that you followed the advice I gave earlier in this chapter and installed only your LAN adapter. And that you will install a WAN adapter, if you need one, after installing Windows 2003.*

If the network adapter you installed was recognized as supported during the device detection phase, the installation wizard opens again and takes you into the network installation portion of the Setup process. You're asked if you want typical or custom settings.

◆ Select the custom settings option if you're installing the first domain controller in your domain.

◆ Select the typical settings option if you've already set up a domain controller and Dynamic DNS, as I recommend later in this chapter, and are installing a stand-alone server for Exchange 2003.

Custom settings let you put in IP address, DNS, and other information. You have to do this for at least the first DHCP server on your network. Typical settings assume that a DHCP server is already on your network and that you want the server you're installing to use the DHCP server to get IP address, DNS, and other information.

If you select typical settings, click Next and you are taken to the Workgroup or Domain page of the Windows Server 2003 installation wizard. For information on how to use this page, go to the next section, "Workgroup or Domain Computer."

After you choose custom settings and click Next, the wizard shows you the Networking Components page. You can use this page to install additional networking components such as the NetBEUI or IPX/SPX networking protocols. If you need to install other networking components, click Install. You can also use this page to modify settings for existing components.

Unless you have a good reason for doing otherwise, leave all settings but Internet Protocol (TCP/IP) at their default levels. Click Internet Protocol (TCP/IP) and choose Properties. You can use the Internet Protocols (TCP/IP) Properties dialog box that pops up to set an IP address, address mask, gateway router, and DNS servers for your new server.

For the LAN adapter, assign an IP address. You can use any address range, but it's best to use addresses reserved for internal use, such as the 192.168.0.x range, say 192.168.0.102. The networking mask for this address range is 255.255.255.0. Enter this computer's IP address in the DNS field. We're building a Windows 2003 network that uses DNS to identify other Windows servers. So, you don't need to install WINS if you're not installing into a larger network where WINS is already being used. If you're doing that and this server is to be a domain controller, then you should install WINS server on this server. If you don't want to install WINS on your domain controller or this is to be a stand-alone server supporting Exchange 2003, point this computer to your WINS servers. To set WINS addresses, click Advanced on the Internet Protocols (TCP/IP) Properties dialog box.

WORKGROUP OR DOMAIN COMPUTER

Next, the Setup Wizard shows you a page where you can specify the domain status of your new server. If you're installing the first domain controller in your domain, ensure that the first option (No, This Computer Is Not on a Network…) is selected. After installation, you'll convert this computer to a domain controller. You can leave the workgroup name as is; you'll be able to change it later.

If you're installing a stand-alone server, select the option Yes, Make This Computer a Member of the Following Domain. Then, enter the pre–Windows 2003 name of your domain. My domain is called BGERBER. When you click Next, the Join Computer to Domain dialog box pops up and requests a username and password. Enter the name of an account that belongs to the Domain Admins group (for example, Administrator) and that account's password. There will be a little pause while your new server uses DHCP to obtain an IP address from your domain controller and then requests that it be allowed to join the domain. When all this is done, your new server will have been assigned the IP address that you reserved for it and will be a full-fledged member of the domain. You should find its name in the Computers container of the Active Directory Computers and Users snap-in in your Microsoft Management Console.

After you finish with this step, the Setup program copies more files from the Windows 2003 CD and performs a variety of installation and setup tasks. During this process, Setup shows you how much longer it estimates it will take to complete its work.

Installation, and Up and Running at Last

At this point, Setup copies the files needed for your installation from the CD-ROM to your server's hard disk. Then it installs the Start menu for your server, registers installed components, saves settings, and removes temporary files created during the install. Finally, Setup lets you know that the installation was successful and invites you to click Finish. The server reboots and, lo and behold, your Windows 2003 server is up and running. Press the familiar Ctrl+Alt+Delete keys, and log in as Administrator.

After a bit of churning, you'll see the Windows 2003 Manage Your Server Wizard. We'll be using the wizard in a bit, but first you can go ahead and do some manual cleanup. You can fiddle with your display adapter's video resolution, if necessary, and do any other housekeeping chores that you want. To modify display adapter resolution, right-click the desktop and choose Properties ➢ Settings. If you have to reboot, the Manage Your Server Wizard will open on startup.

At last, you get your reward. It might seem anticlimactic, however. All that work and what do you get? The Microsoft Windows XP desktop, that's what! Heck, you've probably seen that a hundred times. No bells? No whistles? No dancing bears? Nothing—just plain-vanilla Windows XP front-ending one of the most powerful, multitasking, multithreaded operating systems in the world. Enjoy!

WARNING You have to activate your installation of Windows Server 2003. If you don't, after 15 days you won't be able to use it. Activation registers with Microsoft the Product Code you entered when you installed Windows 2003. You're allowed to install the product a limited number of times. When you exceed the limit, you have to either buy another license (product code) or explain to Microsoft why you should be able to install more copies. It's easy to activate Windows 2003. Just click the Activation icon on the right side of the Taskbar, which is located by default on the bottom of your screen. You can activate Windows 2003 over the Internet or by telephone.

Configuring Your First Windows 2003 Server

Back in the days of Windows 2000, configuring your first Windows 2000 server was quite a chore. You had to go through a number of steps beginning with the installation of Active Directory, DNS, and DHCP. You also had to make a number of unnecessary choices, such as whether you were installing the first server in a new Windows forest or domain.

WARNING *If your server needs a second network adapter that connects to the Internet or another WAN, right now is the time to install it, before you start the configuration process. Just to make the point more strongly, now is really, really the time to install the second adapter in your first server. If you're not sure about some of the terms I use in this Warning, first read through all of this section. You need to shut the server down, install the card, and turn it back on. If the adapter is recognized when the server comes back on, it will be installed and you can then configure it. If the adapter isn't recognized, provide the driver for it when asked. To configure your new adapter, select Start ➢ Control Panel ➢ Network Connections ➢ New Connection Wizard. Move through the wizard, supplying IP address, network mask, and other information as requested. Enter the address of the Default Gateway to the WAN and the appropriate DNS addresses. DNS addresses should point to DNS servers that can resolve names into external IP addresses. If you have such servers on your network, enter their addresses in the DNS server fields. If you have no such servers, then you need to enter the DNS addresses provided by your Internet service provider.*

Windows Server 2003 is much smarter than Windows 2000 Server. You can choose to do a pretty much fully automatic typical first computer installation. Let's do one. Be sure the Windows 2003 CD is inserted.

As I noted earlier, when Windows 2003 reboots after installation is complete, the Manage Your Server Wizard opens. Figure 7.1 shows the wizard. To begin configuring your first Windows 2003 server, click the green button with the arrow on it next to Add or Remove a Role.

FIGURE 7.1

The Windows Server 2003 Manage Your Server Wizard

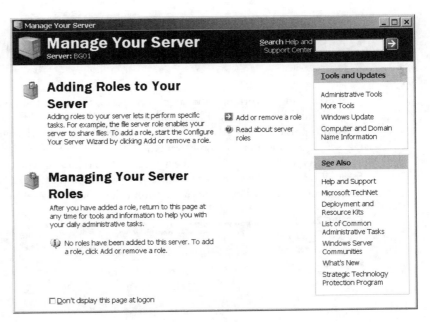

This opens the Configure Your Server Wizard and displays the Preliminary Steps page shown in Figure 7.2. Read the page and at least ensure that your LAN network adapter is working. Open a command prompt (Start ➢ Command Prompt) and ping the IP address(es) of the network adapter(s) in your Windows 2003 computer; for example, enter the command **ping 192.168.0.102** and press Enter. If you get four replies, all is well. If you get four "request timed out" responses, your network adapter isn't working. If the first test works and there are any other computers on your network, try to ping them. A response from one of these indicates that your network hub or switch and cabling are working.

FIGURE 7.2
The Windows Server 2003 Configure Your Server Wizard's Preliminary Steps page

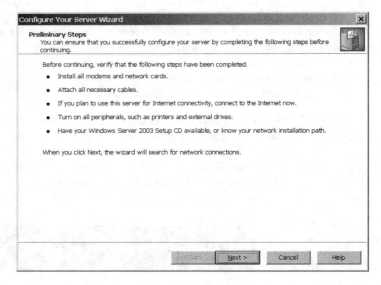

If everything is working, you can click Next on the wizard. If your network adapter or network infrastructure isn't working, I'll leave it to you to diagnose and fix any problems.

At this point, the wizard evaluates your server and its network environment (see Figure 7.3). This takes a bit of time, but when the evaluation is finished, the wizard offers you a set of intelligent options. As shown in Figure 7.4, the wizard offers a typical and pretty much automatic configuration for a Windows 2003 domain controller. The wizard also offers to help you do a custom configuration of your server. Choose the first option if it's not already selected and click Next.

FIGURE 7.3
The Configure Your Server Wizard evaluates your computer.

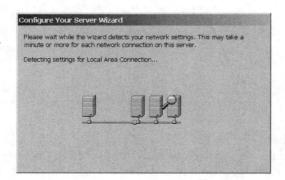

FIGURE 7.4

Selecting a typical configuration for a first server using the Configure Your Server Wizard

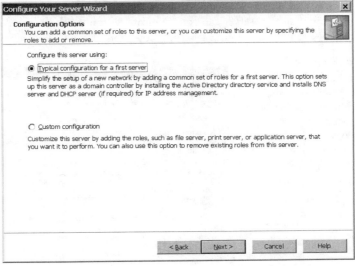

On the next wizard page, you name your internal or Active Directory Windows 2003 domain (see Figure 7.5). Active Directory domain names use standard Internet naming standards. Take the wizard's suggestion that you affix the suffix .local to your domain name to isolate your Active Directory domain name from your Internet domain name.

FIGURE 7.5

Naming your internal Windows 2003 domain using the Active Directory Domain Name page of the Windows Server 2003 Configure Your Server Wizard

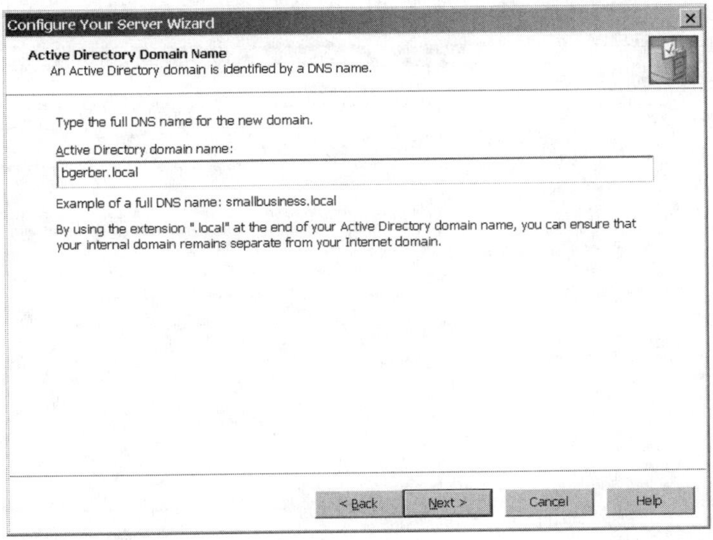

In addition to an Internet-formatted Active Directory domain name, you need a NetBIOS domain name so that your server can communicate with non–Windows 2000/2003 servers such as Windows NT 4. Unless you have strong objections, accept the name offered (see Figure 7.6).

FIGURE 7.6

Selecting a NetBIOS domain name using the NetBIOS Name page of the Windows Server 2003 Configure Your Server Wizard

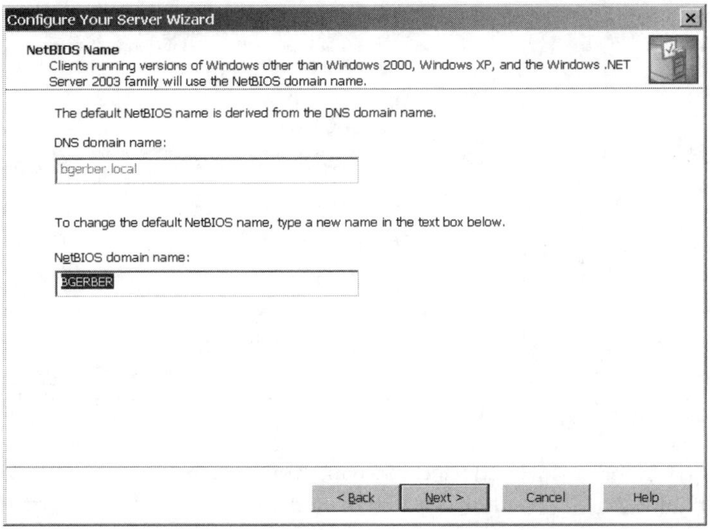

The next wizard page is wonderful. It sets up DNS query forwarding (see Figure 7.7).

FIGURE 7.7

Setting up a DNS server that Windows 2003 DNS can use to resolve names that it can't resolve in its own database.

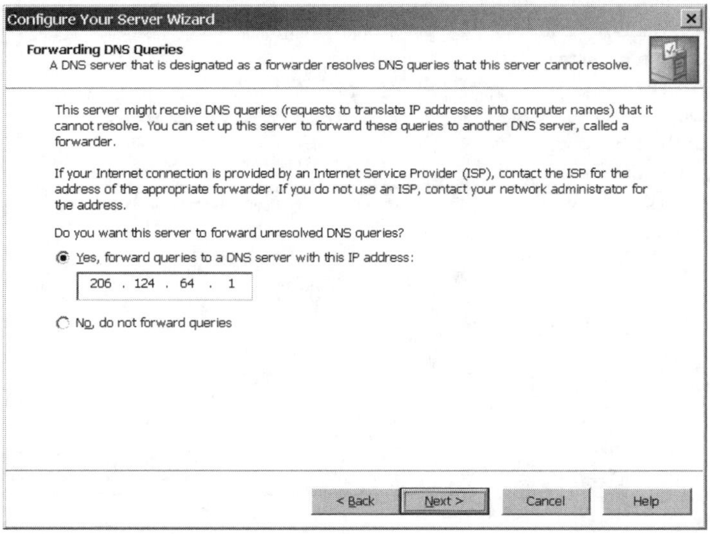

Here's why DNS query forwarding is so important. Remember that DNS services resolve computer names (for example, mail.bgerber.com) into the IP address of the computer (for example, 200.123.1.23). This allows computers to communicate with each other. First and foremost, Windows 2003's DNS serves your internal network. Assuming that NetBIOS and WINS are not installed, local computers use the Windows 2003 DNS to find each other. This applies not just to a computer finding, say, an internal web server, but to one Windows 2003 server finding another server for Windows 2003–based interaction. So your Windows 2003 DNS servers have to be able to resolve internal name resolution requests. But computers on your network need to be able to resolve the names of Internet-based computers. "Oh," you say, "I'll just set up each computer with both internal DNS and external DNS servers." If you set up a computer with a bunch of DNS servers, the computer will query only the first one on the list that is available. It keeps looking until it finds an available DNS server. However, it won't move on to an alternative server if the first available server can't resolve the name.

So, you must point internal users to an internal DNS server, but that server must also be able to resolve external names. Enter DNS query forwarding. If your internal DNS server can't resolve a name in its own database, it forwards the request to other servers you specify, gets resolution information from one of those servers, and passes it back to the local computer looking for the information. Voila!

Back in Figure 7.7, I'm setting up the DNS service that is being installed on my new Windows 2003 server so that it forwards a request to an Internet-based DNS server when it can't resolve a name.

Why is this wizard page so neat? With Windows 2000, you had to figure out query forwarding by yourself and then set it up or turn on the spit because your servers and user workstations couldn't find anything outside your internal Windows network.

TIP   *The Configure Your Server Wizard lets you set up only one DNS query server ("forwarder"). After the wizard is finished running and your computer reboots, you can add as many additional forwarders as you like. To do so, choose Start ➢ All Programs ➢ Administrative Tools ➢ DNS. Once the DNS manager opens, right-click the DNS server and select Properties. Then use the Forwarders page on the DNS server's Properties dialog box to add additional forwarders.*

Next, as you can see in Figure 7.8, the Configure Your Server Wizard shows you what it's going to do. If you're happy with what's going to happen, click Next. If you want to make changes, click Back until you get to the correct wizard page.

While configuration is in process, you're notified that your server will reboot after the Configure Your Server Wizard is finished. As Figure 7.9 shows, you're also advised to close all open programs.

The wizard also lets you know that it's working and that your computer probably hasn't locked up with the window shown in Figure 7.10.

FIGURE 7.8
The Configure Your Server Wizard shows a summary of the actions it will take.

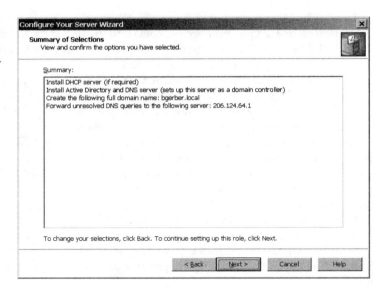

FIGURE 7.9
The Configure Your Server Wizard warns that it will reboot the computer when it is done and that any open programs should be closed.

FIGURE 7.10
The Configure Your Server Wizard displays a window to indicate that it is still running.

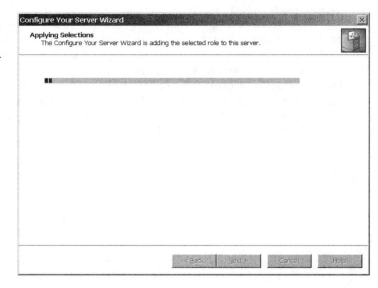

The little blue squares in the long, thin, gray rectangle move in marquee fashion. While the wizard is configuring Active Directory, you'll see the dialog box in Figure 7.11.

FIGURE 7.11
The Configure Your Server Wizard shows its progress in configuring Active Directory.

Your server then reboots. When it is back up and you've logged in, the wizard shows its progress in completing various configuration tasks and then tells you it is done (see Figures 7.12 and 7.13).

FIGURE 7.12
After your server reboots, the Configure Your Server Wizard shows its progress completing various tasks.

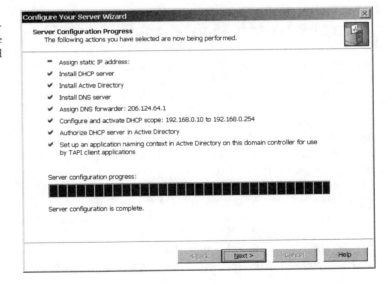

FIGURE 7.13
When it has completed its tasks, the Configure Your Server Wizard displays this window.

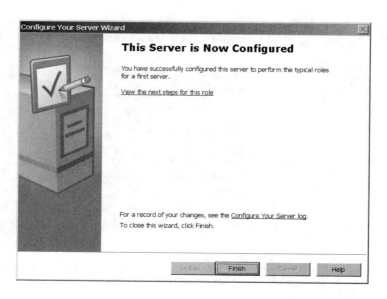

Using Microsoft Management Console

WARNING *If this server is a domain controller, complete this section. If this server is a stand-alone server on which you'll install Exchange Server 2003, read through this section, but don't try to do the hands-on setup work. We'll set up Microsoft Management Console for your Exchange server in the next chapter.*

You've just installed some pretty neat software. To view the fruits of your labor, you need to use some of the tools that Microsoft provides with Windows Server 2003. You can find most of these tools by choosing Start ➤ All Programs ➤ Administrative Tools (see Figure 7.14). The items on the menu pretty much speak for themselves. You'll get to know a number of them in a bit more detail before the end of this chapter.

If you've had any experience with NT 4, the Administrative Tools menu should look somewhat familiar. You're probably wondering where things such as User Manager for Domains and Server Manager have gone, but DHCP, DNS, Event Viewer, and Licensing ("Licensing Manager" in NT) should be old friends. The Services applet has moved from the Control Panel to the Administrative Tools menu.

The Administrative Tools menu is one way to get to many of the tools that you need to manage your Windows 2003 servers. But it's not the only way and, for many tasks, not the easiest.

Unless you've got a real aversion to it, you're going to want to start using Microsoft Management Console (MMC). MMC is a container into which you can add a wide range of management snap-ins. If you've managed Internet Information Server 4 or Microsoft Transaction Server in an NT 4 environment, you already know MMC—at least, in an earlier incarnation. Figure 7.15 shows IIS 4/ Microsoft Transaction Server's MMC. Figure 7.16 shows Windows Server 2003's MMC. No snap-ins have been installed in the Windows 2003 MMC. We'll do that soon.

FIGURE 7.14
Windows
Server 2003's
Administrative
Tools menu

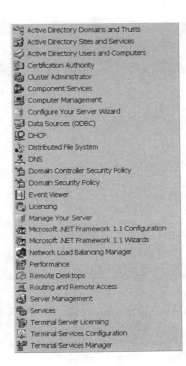

FIGURE 7.15
Microsoft Management Console for Internet Information Server 4 and Microsoft Transaction Server

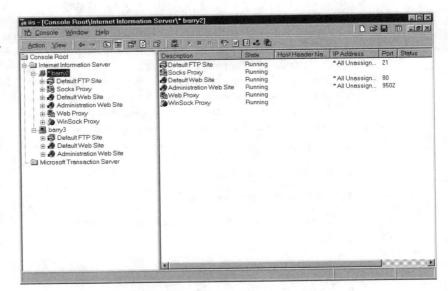

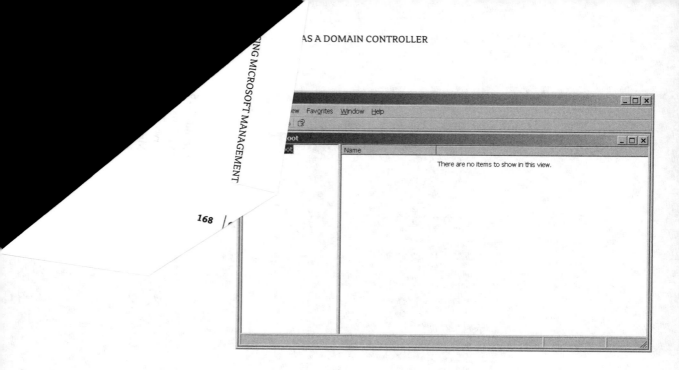

Let's focus on the Windows 2003 MMC shown in Figure 7.16. Each MMC can hold many instances of a snap-in, although this makes sense only if each snap-in of the same kind is for a different entity in your Windows Server 2003 world (for example, a separate snap-in for managing each of two remote Windows 2003 servers). You can have as many MMCs as you want, and you can mix and match MMCs to your heart's content. You save each MMC under a different name, and you can open one or more MMCs any time. You might want to use different MMCs to manage Active Directory, your local computer, and Exchange 2003, for example.

To open a new console, select Start ➢ Run; type **MMC** in the Open field, and click OK. To add a snap-in to MMC, just choose File ➢ Add/Remove Snap-in. (Windows 2000 users take note: It's File now, not Console.) This opens the Add/Remove Snap-in dialog box shown in Figure 7.17. Click Add to open the Add Standalone Snap-in dialog box (see Figure 7.18).

To add a new snap-in, select it in the Add Standalone Snap-in dialog box, and click Add. When you're done, close the Add Standalone Snap-in dialog box, and click OK on the Add/Remove Snap-in dialog box. Go ahead and add the following snap-ins:

- Active Directory Domains and Trusts

- Active Directory Sites and Services

- Active Directory Users and Computers

- Computer Management (for your local computer)

- DHCP

- DNS

- Event Viewer (for your local computer)

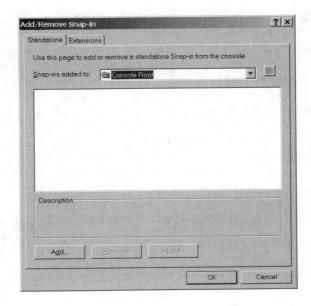

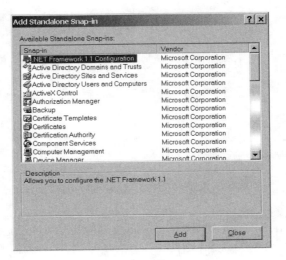

What's this *local computer* stuff? If you're a fugitive from NT 4, you remember that both Server
Manager and Event Viewer let you partially manage activities on computers other than your own.
You did this within the Server Manager or Event Viewer for your local computer. Windows
Server 2003 offers the same capability and more, but by using an instance of Computer Manager

for each computer that you want to manage. Here you set up a snap-in only for the server you just installed, your *local server*. But, if they exist and you need to manage them, you could also have set up Computer Management snap-ins for other servers and managed those servers from the same instance of MMC. As you'll see, this snap-in does lots more than NT's Server Manager, but it's Windows 2003's way of providing remote computer management similar to what you had with NT 4.

The same goes for Event Viewer. The instance of the Event Viewer snap-in that you just installed lets you view the event logs on your local server. You can also install instances of the Event Viewer snap-in for other servers that you need to manage and to which you have access.

Now size the two MMC windows so that they look like the MMC shown in Figure 7.19. Save this particular instance of MMC by selecting File ➢ Save As. Then, when you need it, just choose Start ➢ All Programs ➢ Administrative Tools and the name under which you saved this MMC.

FIGURE 7.19

An instance of MMC ready for use

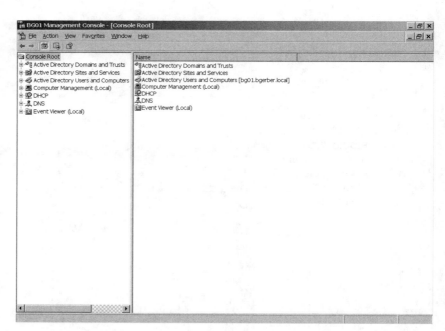

Okay, we're ready to use MMC to do some preliminary exploring and a bit of serious work. Let's start by looking at Active Directory.

TIP *You really didn't have to add DHCP, DNS, and Event Viewer to your MMC. They're already there, under Computer Management. Check it out. I had you install these three to make your introduction to MMC easier and to show you that you can load some important sublevel snap-ins at the root of your MMC so you can get to them quickly.*

A Quick Look at Active Directory

WARNING   *If this server is a domain controller, read this section and complete the hands-on part. If this server is a stand-alone server, read through this section, but don't do the hands-on part. Remember my discussions in Chapters 5 and 6 on the division of responsibility for Windows 2003 and Exchange 2003 management? If your organization won't let you touch Active Directory, then much of this section will either be hands-off or have to happen on a test server. I do encourage you to go the test-server route. Even if you'll never touch Active Directory in the real world, you need to understand it and how it works to do an effective job as an Exchange 2003 system manager.*

I've talked much about Active Directory in this book. Given its central role, I can think of no better place to start our exploration of Windows Server 2003. For now, we'll concentrate on users and computers, so let's open the tree for Active Directory Users and Computers. Figure 7.20 shows the domain container (mine is bgerber.local) and its five default subcontainers. The Builtin container holds security groups created during installation. Any computers in your domain are placed in the Computers container—that is, any computers except for domain controllers. These live in the Domain Controllers container. Because there is one and only one computer in your new domain and it is a domain controller, you should see nothing in the Computers container and just your new computer in the Domain Controllers container.

FIGURE 7.20

The Active Directory Users and Computers domain container and default subcontainers

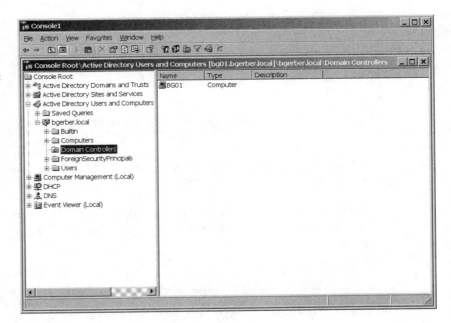

The ForeignSecurityPrincipals container holds security information for domains other than the current domain. These can be domains in the same forest or in another forest. Because you currently have only one domain, you shouldn't see anything in this container.

You will come to know and love the Users container. This is where you create Windows users and security groups. And after Exchange is installed, this is where you mail- and mailbox-enable Windows users and create Exchange contacts and distribution groups. This is the Windows Server 2003 equivalent of NT 4's User Manager for Domains. Figure 7.21 shows the Users container on my newly installed server. NT Server 4 users should have no difficulty identifying many of the users and groups in the container.

FIGURE 7.21

The Active Directory Users and Computer Users container

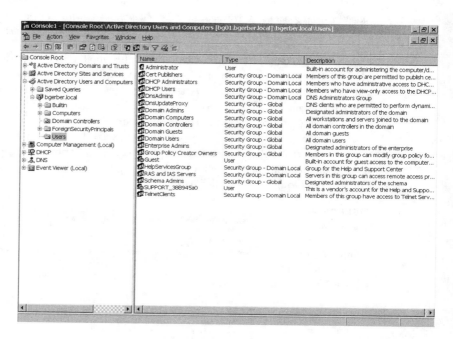

Here's how to create a new user. Right-click the Users container. Then select New ➢ User from the pop-up menu (see Figure 7.22).

NOTE *Instead of right-clicking on objects in your MMC to view and select from your options, you can use the Action menu. See Figure 7.22 for the location of the Action menu. Just select an object and open the Action menu to see your options.*

On the New Object - User Wizard, shown in Figure 7.23, fill in the First Name, Initials, and Last Name fields. The Full Name field is automatically filled in and shows the name in FIRST_NAME MIDDLE_INITIAL LAST_NAME order. I edited the field so that the Full Name is shown as LAST_NAME, FIRST_NAME MIDDLE INITIAL. Next, enter the user logon name. The pre–Windows 2000 (NT) logon name is filled in automatically (you can edit it, if you need to).

FIGURE 7.22

Creating a new user: step 1

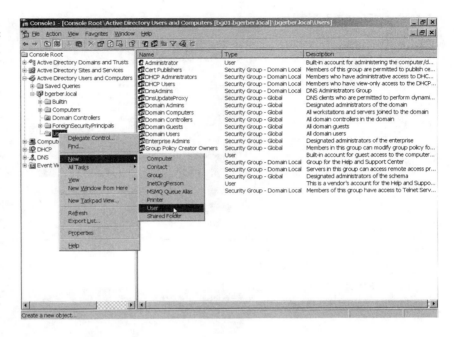

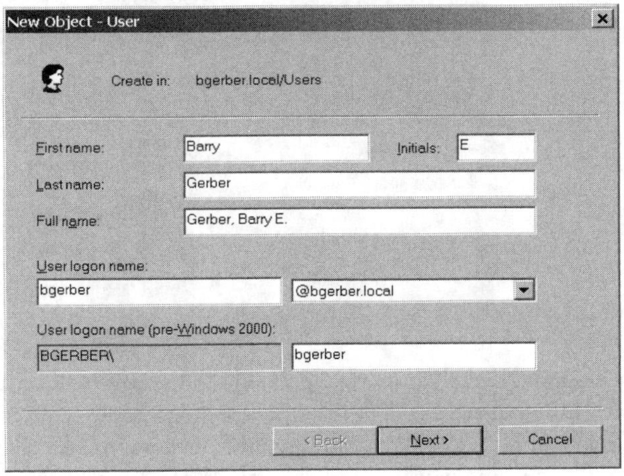

FIGURE 7.23

Creating a new user: step 2

Click Next, and enter a password and select any special options relating to the password (see Figure 7.24). Finally, review the information presented in the dialog box in Figure 7.25, and click Finish. Your new user shows up at the end of the list in the right pane of MMC. To get the list in correct alphabetical order, you might have to click the gray column header labeled Name in the pane at the right.

FIGURE 7.24
Creating a new user:
step 3

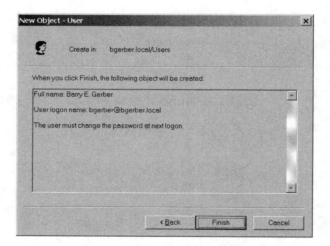

FIGURE 7.24
Creating a new user:
step 3

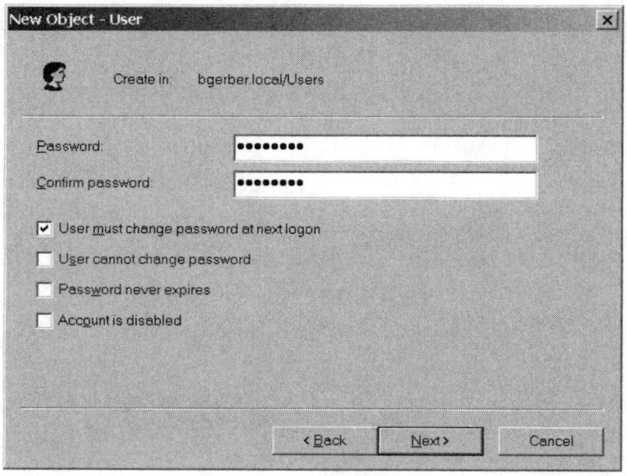

FIGURE 7.25
Creating a new user:
step 4

The new user account that you just created for yourself will be able to log into your domain and function with minimal rights. Windows Server 2003 comes equipped with some of the very best security features around. We'll talk about some of them in later chapters. Suffice it to say that you'll need to spend some time working out the details of your security system and implementing it.

Don't give your account any more rights than you would give a standard user. That way, you'll be able to test to see whether a particular setup, such as Outlook client access to Exchange Server 2003, works for a typical user. When you need to do administrator-like tasks, log in as Administrator or as a user with just enough rights to complete a specific task. You can also use the Run As feature of Windows 2003 to run an application as a user with adequate rights to run the application. For example, to run a saved MMC as an Administrator when you're logged in to a different Windows 2003 account, find and right-click Start ➤ All Programs ➤ Administrative Tools and then the name of the saved MMC. Then select Run As from the pop-up menu. Enter the username, password, and Windows domain on the Run As Another User dialog box, and click OK to start the MMC.

Configuring DHCP and Dynamic DNS

This section covers three tasks relating to DHCP and DNS:

◆ Configuring DHCP to automatically assign IP addresses to computers on your network

◆ Ensuring that Dynamic DNS is enabled

◆ Configuring DHCP to automatically assign fixed IP addresses to computers on your network

Configuring DHCP to Automatically Assign IP Addresses to Computers on Your Network

WARNING   *If this server is a stand-alone server, read through this section, but don't do the hands-on part. If the server is a domain controller, read this section and complete the hands-on part.*

Windows 2003 networking is based on the TCP/IP protocol. Every workstation or server in your Windows 2003 network requires at least one IP address. You can manually assign these addresses, or you can use the Dynamic Host Configuration Protocol (DHCP) to automatically assign the addresses. Addresses are leased to a computer for a given period of time (usually several days). When the lease is up, the computer needs to release its IP address and request another from a DHCP server.. Unless you reserve an address for a specific computer, the computer might get a different IP address.

Open the DHCP tree in your MMC and select the DHCP container for your computer (see Figure 7.26). As you can see, the Configure Your Server Wizard has already done quite a bit for you. If you worked with DHCP in Windows 2000, you remember that you had to do quite a bit of configuring to get to the point where the Windows 2003 Configure Your Server Wizard leaves you by default. For example, unlike with the Windows 2000 DHCP setup wizard, your Windows 2003 DHCP server was authorized by default. A DHCP server that isn't authorized can't hand out IP addresses. You can tell that your DHCP server is authorized by the little up-pointing green arrow on the server icon. To unauthorize the server, which you might want to do if you're experiencing security problems, just right-click the server and select Unauthorize from the menu that pops up.

Now, let's look at each of the subcontainers in the DHCP container. Notice the Scope container. A scope is a range of addresses for DHCP to lease out. Scopes can also contain information about routers, DNS servers, and other things. One DHCP server can support many scopes. By default, the Configure Your Server Wizard activates your first scope. You can deactivate it by right-clicking on the scope and selecting Deactivate from the menu that pops up. Don't deactivate the scope unless you have good reason to do so or DHCP clients won't be able to obtain addresses—unless, of course, there are other scopes to do the job.

FIGURE 7.26
The DHCP container for Windows Server 2003

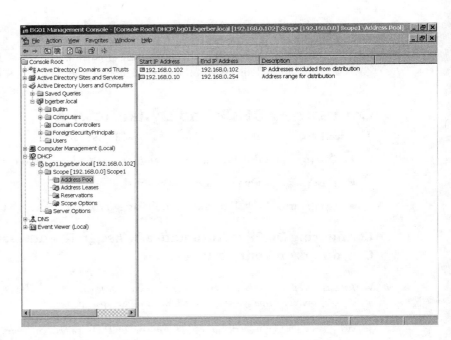

You can configure some key scope settings by right-clicking the Scope container and selecting Properties. Then use the Scope Properties dialog box shown in Figure 7.27 to set such things as the length of address leases. We'll get back to this dialog box and its other two pages in a bit.

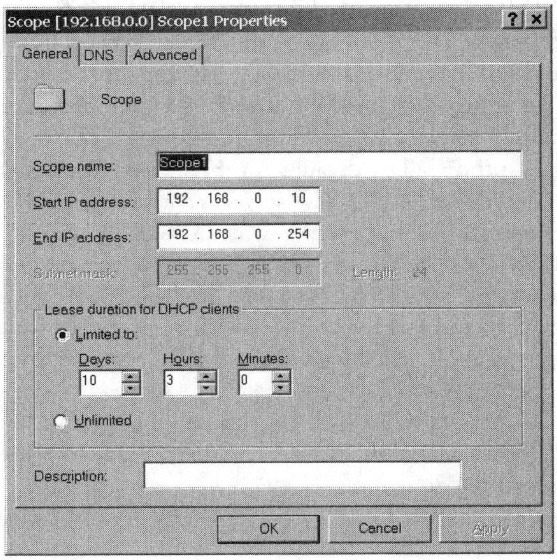

FIGURE 7.27
Configure key scope settings using the Scope Properties dialog box.

Within the Scope container, the Address Pool container holds address ranges, from which your server's DHCP service picks the addresses it leases to its clients. You can see that the Configure Your Server Wizard set the range 192.168.0.10 through 192.168.0.254 for the DHCP service.

You can prevent DHCP from leasing specific addresses. In fact, as you can see earlier in Figure 7.26, the Configure Your Server Wizard excluded the address of my Windows 2003 server, 192.168.0.102, from the addresses that can be leased. To exclude additional addresses, right-click the Address Pool container and select New Exclusion Range. In Figure 7.28, I'm excluding the addresses 192.168.0.230 through 192.168.0.254 from the addresses DHCP can lease. Figure 7.29 shows the new exclusion range in the Address Pool container.

FIGURE 7.28

Excluding addresses from a DHCP address pool

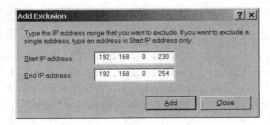

FIGURE 7.29

A new exclusion range for a DHCP address pool

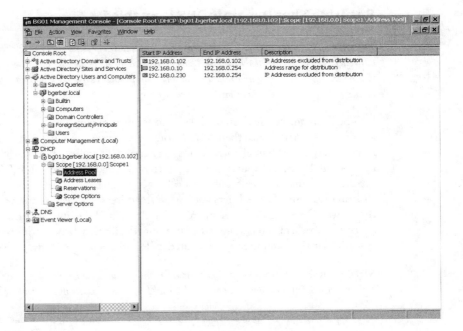

The Address Leases container (see Figure 7.26, shown earlier) shows information on currently leased IP addresses. You can modify leases here. If this is your first DHCP-enabled Windows 2003 domain controller, there should be no addresses in this container. Once DHCP starts handing out addresses, you'll see them here.

You reserve specific IP addresses for specific computers in the Reservations container (see Figure 7.26, shown earlier). We'll get back to this container soon. Hang on.

The Scope Options container (see Figure 7.26, shown earlier) contains information for the scope. This information is handed out to DHCP clients along with their IP address leases and includes such things as the IP addresses of DNS servers, gateway routers, and time servers. So, just as you don't have to manually enter IP addresses on each client computer when you use DHCP, you also don't have to enter DNS server and other information on each client. You can delete any option by right-clicking it and selecting Delete. You can add options by right-clicking the Scope Options container and selecting Configure Options.

You use the Server Options container (see Figure 7.26, shown earlier) to set scope options that can apply to any scope on your server. It works just like the Scope Options container. By default, the Configure Your Server Wizard creates an option in the Server Options container specifying that your new server is a DNS server. This option is included in the Scope Options container by default. You can delete this option in either the Server or the Scope Options container and you can create new Server or Scope Options to your heart's content.

Ensuring That Dynamic DNS Is Enabled

WARNING   *If this server is a stand-alone server, you can skip this section. If this server is at least your first domain controller, read and complete the hands-on part of this section. If you don't complete this task, your Exchange 2003 server will not become a part of your DNS domain and will thus not be available to users trying to open their mailboxes or to other servers trying to send mail to your Exchange server.*

The Domain Name System (DNS) contains the names of computers, called hosts, and the IP addresses associated with them. Traditionally, you make manual entries into DNS for each computer in your network. Manual entry is not only time-consuming, but it also doesn't work when you're using DHCP. If a computer can get a different IP address from DHCP every time its address lease expires, your manual DNS entry is no longer correct.

Enter Dynamic DNS. It lets you assign IP addresses to servers and workstations using DHCP, and then have DNS entries for them created and updated dynamically in your DNS namespace. Even if a server or workstation is assigned a different IP address when its address lease expires, Dynamic DNS ensures that the computer and its current IP address get properly placed in your DNS system.

NOTE   *Dynamic DNS is based on a standard promulgated by the Internet Engineering Task Force. The standard can be found in Request for Comment (RFC) 2136, "Dynamic Updates in the Domain Name System (DNS Updates)."*

It's easy to check to see that Dynamic DNS is enabled. Go ahead and right-click your DHCP server. My DHCP server is the container just under the DHCP master container. It's labeled "bg01.bgerber.local" in Figure 7.29, shown earlier. Then select Properties to open the Properties dialog box for your DHCP server and tab over to the DNS page (see Figure 7.30). Remember I promised we'd revisit this dialog box. As you can see in Figure 7.30, the Configure Your Server Wizard enabled Dynamic DNS and set some parameters that you can leave alone for now, unless you have a good reason for changing them. For the curious, DNS A records link host (computer) names with their IP addresses, and PTR (pointer) records are used to support various DNS-based actions such as what are called "reverse lookups" where an IP address is resolved to a domain name, rather than a domain name being resolved to an IP address.

FIGURE 7.30

Ensuring that Dynamic DNS is enabled

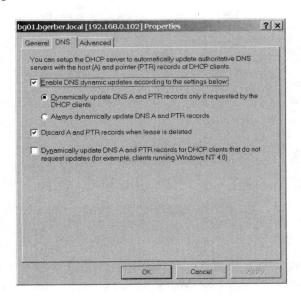

With Dynamic DNS enabled, the next time a new computer with its DNS client enabled logs into your new network, not only will it get all the information that DHCP has to offer, but it also will automatically be registered in the DNS. By default, all newly installed modern Microsoft Windows clients are configured to use DHCP, so you don't have to do a thing after installation to enable DHCP. Amazing! All this used to require such manual drudgery.

NOTE *You can configure Dynamic DNS to work with pre–Windows 2000 clients such as NT or Windows 95/ 98 clients. Just select Always Dynamically Update DNS A and PTR Records instead of the default shown earlier in Figure 7.30.*

For the record, the Configure Your Server Wizard set up DNS. As you can see in Figure 7.31, the wizard created the domain bgerber.local along with a Windows 2003 domain (msdcs.bgerber.local). See how tightly Windows 2003 networking is linked to DNS? In addition, BG01, my new server, was added to the zone bgerber.local and was linked with the IP address 192.168.0.102. At this point on BG01, I could open a command prompt, type **ping bg01** or **ping bg01.bgerber.com**, and get a response. And I didn't have to do a thing.

FIGURE 7.31
DNS, set up by the
Configure Your
Server Wizard, is up
and running on a
Windows 2003
server.

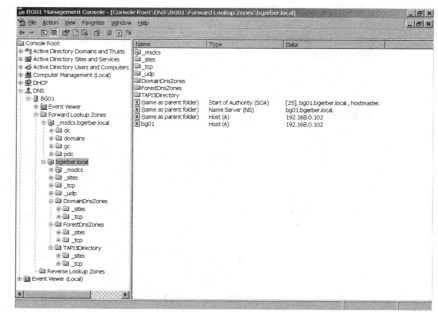

Configuring DHCP to Automatically Assign Fixed IP Addresses to Computers on Your Network

NOTE   If this server is a stand-alone server, you can skip this section. If this server is your first domain controller, read and complete the hands-on part of this section. If you don't complete this task, based on the way we're going to do things in this book, your Exchange 2003 server will not become a part of your DNS domain and will thus not be available to users trying to open their mailboxes, or to other servers trying to send mail to your Exchange server.

In Chapter 8, you'll install a Windows 2003 stand-alone server and then install Exchange Server 2003 on it. Before installing Windows 2003 on your soon-to-be Exchange server, you must set up your domain so that the new server can easily enter your network. You can do that right here using a special capability of DHCP called *address reservation*.

Address reservation allows DHCP to automatically allocate the same IP address to a server or workstation each time the computer's address lease expires. That way, your Exchange server will always have the same IP address. And, everything is done on the DHCP server side. You don't have to touch your soon-to-be Exchange 2003 server, which is, of course, a DHCP client in this case.

Address reservations are important especially when outside servers need to find your Exchange server's address. It takes a few minutes to a few days for a new DNS entry to propagate across the Internet. So, if your Exchange server's IP address changed every day, servers trying to send mail to the server could be out of touch for an unacceptable period of time.

You could assign a hard IP address to your new server. However, that would mean you have to go through hell and high water any time you needed to change that address. With a DHCP address reservation, all you have to do is remove the reservation and run a program called IPCONFIG.EXE on the server with the lease to release the old address. At that point, you've reclaimed the address and can use it for any other purpose.

Okay, let's get going. I assume here that you have access to the Administrator account for your domain controller. If you don't, someone else will have to do the following. Go to your domain controller. As you might remember, my domain controller is called BG01. Log in as Administrator.

Here's how to set up a DHCP reservation. Start up your Microsoft Management Console (MMC), and click open the DHCP container until it looks like the one in Figure 7.32. Now, do what the right pane of the Reservations subcontainer says: Select New Reservation from the Action menu.

This brings up the New Reservation dialog box shown in Figure 7.33. Give the reservation a name, and enter the IP address that you want to assign to your new server.

FIGURE 7.32

Ready to create a new DHCP IP address reservation using the Microsoft Management Console DHCP snap-in

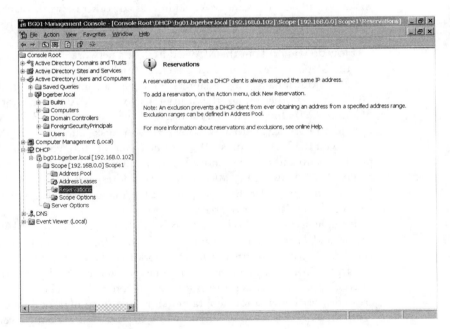

FIGURE 7.33
Creating a new
DHCP IP address
reservation

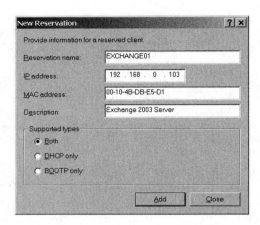

Next type in the Media Access Control (MAC) address of the network adapter to which you want to assign the address. The MAC address is a unique address that's burned into each network adapter when it is manufactured. An international standard ensures that no network adapter, no matter who makes it, will have the same MAC address as any other network adapter. That's how DHCP knows which machine to give the reserved address to when contacted by a bevy of IP address–hungry computers.

How do you find out the MAC address of a network adapter? Good question. For some adapters, the MAC address is actually on a little sticker on the adapter or on the box that the adapter came in. Additionally, most adapters come with a configuration utility that can be run under MS DOS. Among other things, the utility tells you the MAC address of the adapter. For example, 3Com's 3C90x line of adapters comes with a program called 3C90XCFG.EXE. When you boot up under DOS (say, with a Windows 98 boot disk) and run 3C90XCFG.EXE, the first screen shows you the MAC address. If, by some chance, before you install Windows 2003 on the computer, it is up and running under Windows 2003 (or NT 4), you can open a command prompt and type **IPCONFIG -ALL | MORE**. The MAC address is listed as the physical address, usually on the first screen right under the description of the adapter itself. Copy the address exactly as you see it. You don't have to enter the dashes.

It might seem like a heck of a lot of work to find an adapter's MAC address. Actually, it's quite simple, and when you see how automatic fixed address assignment simplifies network management, you'll agree that it's worth a little extra work to obtain the address.

Next, if you want, you can enter some text in the New Reservation box's Description field. Leave Supported Types set to Both. When you're done, click Add. When the address has been created, your Reservations container should look something like the one in Figure 7.34. The DNS servers information that you set by the Configure Your Server Wizard is inherited by the reservation (see the right pane in Figure 7.34). If you add new options information, it will also be inherited by the server.

FIGURE 7.34

The newly created IP address reservation, complete with inherited DNS server information

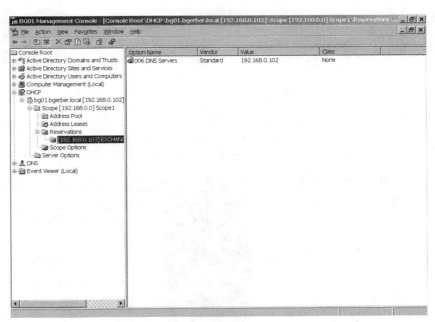

That's it. Your DHCP server is configured to provide your Exchange server a fixed IP address when you install it in the next chapter. And, remember, because Dynamic DNS is enabled, your server will also be automatically registered in your domain DNS. That's about as easy as it gets.

GETTING THE MOST FROM DHCP

You can use DHCP address reservations for any computer that is part of your network. This includes most domain controllers. The only computers on your network that must absolutely have fixed addresses assigned to their network adapters when Windows Server 2003 is installed are domain controllers that serve as DHCP servers. For safety, you should be sure that there are at least two DHCP servers on any network segment. You don't want your network to be without an IP address server if your one and only DHCP server fails. When you set up additional DHCP servers, remember that, except for reserved addresses, the specific IP addresses in each server's address pool(s) must be unique.

If you wish, you can set up a new DHCP scope for external Internet addresses. This will let you automatically assign addresses to computers connected to a WAN. Again, don't use DHCP and reservations for servers that provide DHCP services. Be sure to set a reservation for each address so that IP addresses aren't leased to just any computer that hits your DHCP server. Reserve each external IP address, even if you're not ready to use it. Use a bogus MAC address, if you don't have the MAC addresses of the network adapters you plan to use for external connections. The MAC address should be 12 characters long and can consist of the letters A–F and/or the numerals 0–9. For safety, use bogus MAC addresses beginning with "99." It will be a long time, if ever, before MAC addresses that begin with "99" show up. To see the current assignment of MAC address prefixes to network adapter manufacturers, check out `http://standards.ieee.org/regauth/oui/oui.txt`.

Configuring Unallocated Disk Space

Now let's get to some tasks that directly impact your server. If you installed more than one hard disk drive in your server, or if the volume that you installed Windows Server 2003 on is smaller than the disk drive on which the boot partition resides, you need to set up and format remaining unallocated disk space.

We'll use the Disk Manager to do this task. It's located in the Computer Management (Local) snap-in of the MMC that you created earlier. Open the snap-in's tree, and select the Disk Management folder. If you have one or more disk drives that haven't been initialized, in a moment or two you'll see the Initialize and Convert Disk Wizard, shown in Figure 7.35.

FIGURE 7.35

The Initialize and Convert Disk Wizard

This wizard performs a couple of simple tasks. First, it initializes a disk by writing a unique identifier on whatever new physical disks you select. A disk's unique identifier is used to store information about it in the Windows 2003 registry. After the identifier is written, the wizard will upgrade the basic disk to a dynamic disk, if you desire.

You can do a number of things with dynamic disks, including mirroring, setting up various levels of Redundant Array of Independent Disk (RAID) storage, spanning across multiple physical drives, or striping a volume across multiple drives for better performance. You can also expand single-disk volumes and volumes that cross multiple volumes without rebooting your server. Add to this the capability to set up a Computer Management snap-in for servers other than your local one, and you've got a tremendous amount of control over storage on your Windows 2003 network.

WARNING   Although software implementation of the redundant storage solutions discussed previously works just fine, you should strongly consider implementing these solutions in hardware. Hardware implementations include smart disk controllers that do work that must be done by software run on your server's CPU. Software-based redundant storage solutions can significantly affect performance by placing a heavy load on a computer's CPU.

Back to the wizard. Click Next, and you're offered the opportunity to select the physical disks which you want to initialize (see Figure 7.36). Because I have only one new physical disk in my new server, the wizard offers me only the opportunity to initialize it.

FIGURE 7.36

Selecting a physical disk drive to be initialized

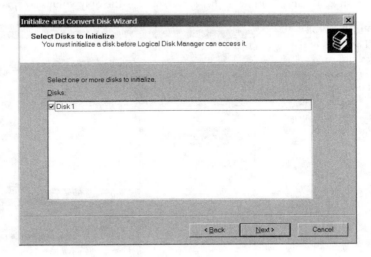

When you click Next, the disk is quickly initialized, and the disk becomes a basic disk. Then the Initialize and Convert Disk Wizard offers to upgrade your disk to a dynamic disk (see Figure 7.37). Your new disk or disks should already be selected for upgrade to dynamic disk status. Accept this default unless you have a good reason to do otherwise. Click Next once more, and then click Finish on the final page to begin the upgrade.

FIGURE 7.37

Selecting a physical disk drive to be upgraded to dynamic disk status

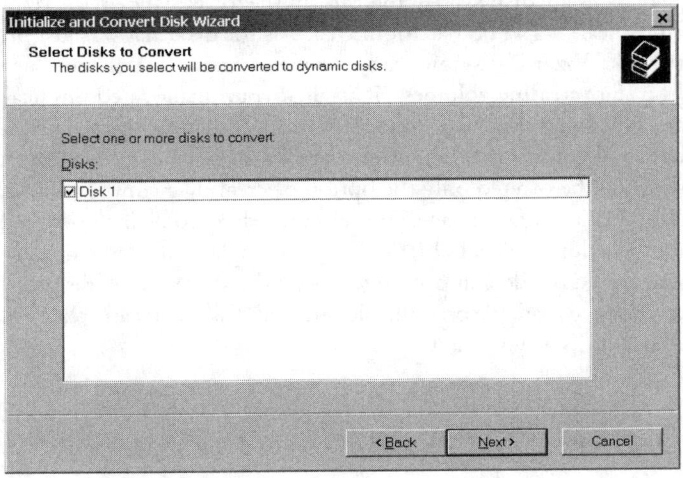

When the wizard is finished, your server's disk configuration shows up in the right pane of the MMC. Figure 7.38 shows my disk setup after processing by the wizard. In the top pane on the right side is a list of my current volumes. The boot volume created during Windows Server 2003 installation is the only volume on my server, so it is the only volume displayed.

FIGURE 7.38

The status of physical disks and volumes as shown in the Disk Management subfolder of the Computer Management snap-in

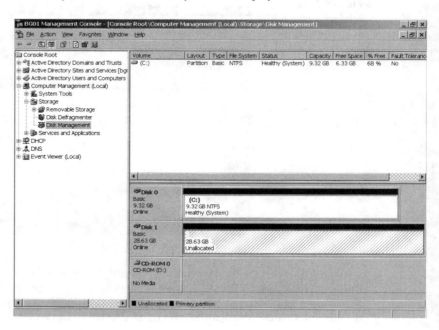

My disks are displayed graphically in the lower pane on the right side. There you see my first disk with its healthy NTFS partition. Disk 1 is the disk that was just processed by the Initialize and Convert Disk Wizard. It's now ready for me to create one or more new volumes on it.

To start creating volumes, right-click your unallocated physical disk space and select New Volume. This starts the New Volume Wizard, shown in Figure 7.39. Click Next on the wizard to select the type of volume that you want to create (see Figure 7.40). Assuming that you've installed but one disk, you'll be offered only the option of creating a simple volume.

On the next wizard page, you select the disks to be included in a volume and set the size that you want the volume to be. In Figure 7.41, my single unallocated disk has been automatically selected, and I've accepted the default option to use all the space on the disk for the new volume. If you have unallocated space available on multiple physical disks, you can create volumes that span as many or as few of those disks as you want.

FIGURE 7.39
Starting up the New
Volume Wizard

FIGURE 7.40
Accepting the cre-
ation of a simple vol-
ume using the New
Volume Wizard

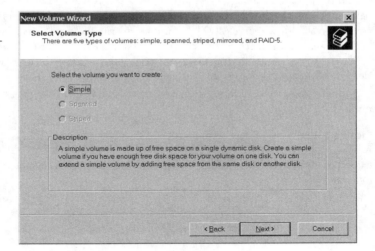

FIGURE 7.41
Accepting default values for the disk to be included in a new volume and the size of the volume using the New Volume Wizard

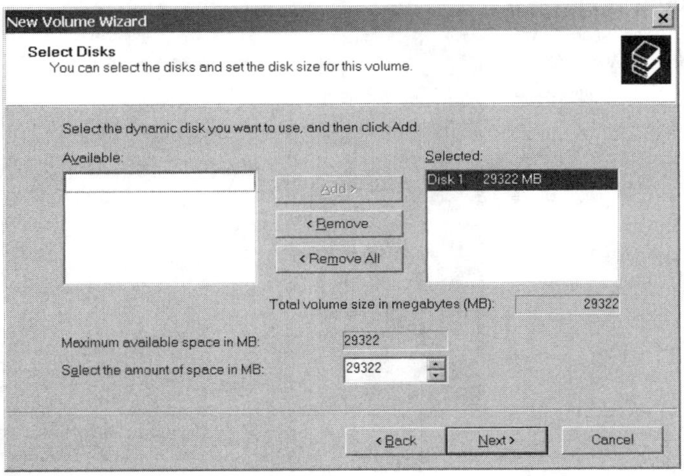

On the next wizard page shown in Figure 7.42, you assign a drive letter or mount point for your new volume. Drive letters are old stuff. Mount points, borrowed from the Unix operating system, are new to Windows Server 2003. Mount points finally let you create volumes unlimited by the number of available drive letters. I've chosen to assign a drive letter to my new volume.

You select formatting parameters for your volume using the next wizard page (see Figure 7.43). I've chosen to format my new volume with the NTFS file system, I've accepted the default allocation unit size, and I've labeled my volume LocalDisk E. You can't go wrong for now following my lead.

FIGURE 7.42
Assigning a drive letter or mount point for a new volume using the New Volume Wizard

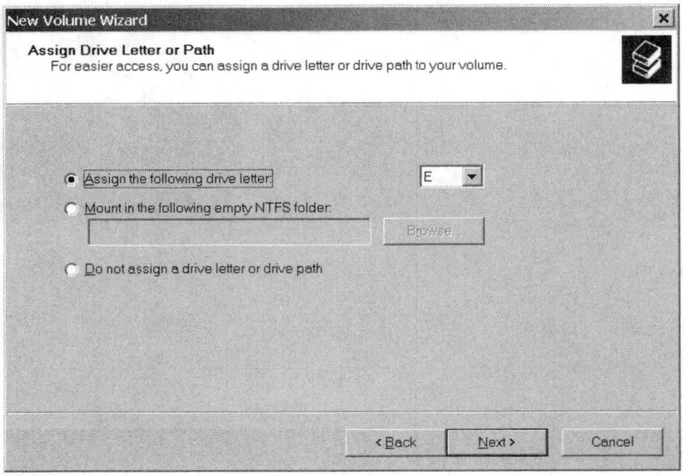

FIGURE 7.43

Selecting formatting parameters for a new volume using the New Volume Wizard

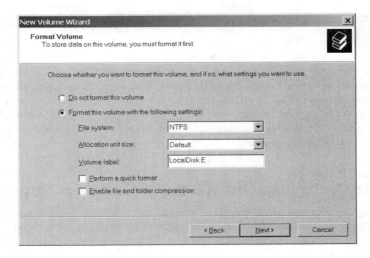

Finally, the wizard shows you what it's about to do. Click Finish, and the wizard begins formatting your new volume. This takes some time. When it has finished its work, if the wizard tells you that your computer needs to be rebooted, do so.

Now the right pane of \Computer Management (Local)\Storage\Disk Management in your MMC should look something like the one in Figure 7.44. Your new volume has been created and is in a healthy state. What else could you ask for?

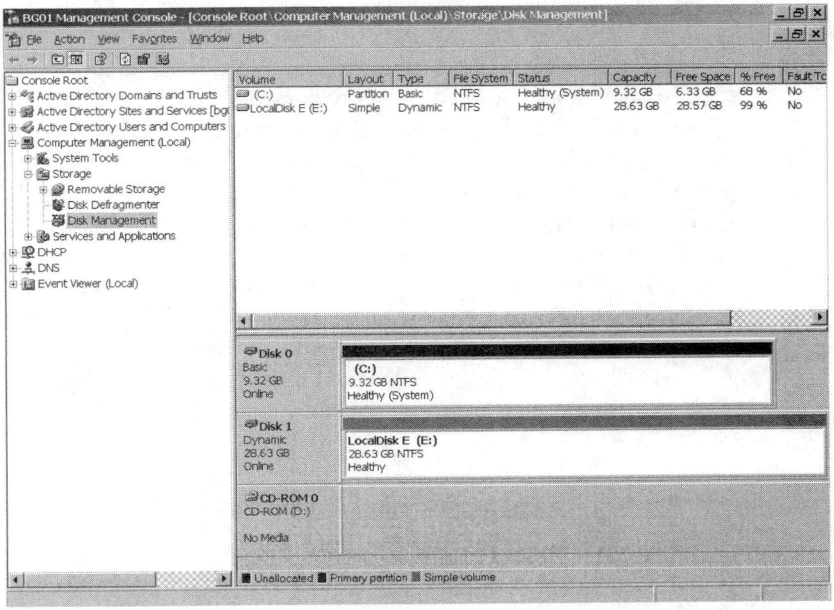

FIGURE 7.44

A newly created volume as shown in the Disk Management subfolder of the Computer Management snap-in

DON'T FORGET SHUTDOWN

Like all good operating systems, Windows Server 2003 must be shut down; you should never just turn off Windows Server 2003. Windows Server 2003 buffers a lot of data to RAM before writing it to disk. Although the writes from RAM are done quickly, on a busy server there's always data waiting in the buffers. A graceful shutdown ensures that this data is all written out to disk. To shut down a server, click the Start menu icon and select Shut Down. You can select from four options: Log Off, Shut Down, Restart, or Stand By. The latter option is for computers with energy-saving capabilities. If you pick Shut Down and the computer doesn't shut itself down, don't turn off the computer until you see a message telling you that it's okay to turn off the computer.

Installing an Uninterruptible Power Supply

An uninterruptible power supply (UPS) takes power from the wall socket and feeds it to a battery to keep it charged. The UPS continuously feeds power from its battery to your computer through internal power-conversion circuitry. When power from the wall socket fails, the UPS battery continues to supply power to your computer, letting it run until wall-socket power returns or the battery is exhausted and, if so configured, shutting down the computer before UPS battery power is exhausted.

UPSs can interface to your server through an RS-232 serial or Universal Serial Bus (USB) or a network connection. Newer USB or network UPS links offer an attractive alternative to finicky RS-232 connections.

As I noted in Chapter 5, a UPS should be considered part of your Windows Server 2003 installation. Let's install one right away.

The UPS Itself

Buy a UPS with "online" circuitry; these tend to be the best and most responsive in power outages. This also should be one that can be controlled by a Windows 2003 server, so it should be equipped with a USB or an RS-232 port that you connect by a cable to one of the server's USB or serial ports. If you're going to use RS-232, get the cable from the UPS's vendor, if at all possible; then you won't have to mess with that old devil known as RS-232 interfacing. Larger capacity UPSs come with Ethernet ports. You connect the UPS to your network for both management and graceful shutdown of servers.

Windows Server 2003's built-in UPS software listens to the UPS and can shut down the server gracefully, just as if you'd done it manually. Get a UPS that can detect and signal both a wall-socket power failure and a low battery. With low-battery information available, Windows Server 2003 doesn't have to begin a shutdown immediately on power failure. If AC power returns before the low-battery signal, no shutdown needs to occur at all.

WARNING   *Be sure to put each of your Windows 2003 servers on its own UPS. Most UPSs usually have one USB or serial port and can thus automatically shut down only a single server. If you need a UPS for multiple servers, take a look at the ones that include Ethernet ports and Simple Network Monitoring Protocol (SNMP)–related software.*

Configuring UPS Support

To configure UPS support in Windows Server 2003, select Start ➢ Control Panel ➢ Power Options. This opens the Power Options Properties dialog box. The first three pages on this dialog box are for managing your computer's use of power. The fourth page, shown on the left side of Figure 7.45, is for UPS management.

FIGURE 7.45

Selecting an interface and default settings for a UPS

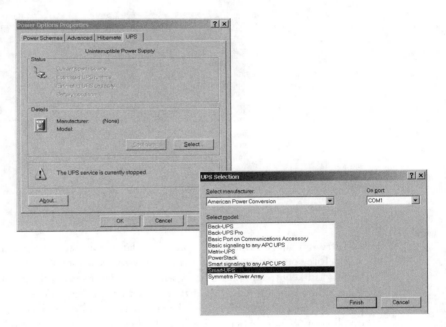

American Power Conversion (APC) created custom user interfaces and default settings for its UPS product line. These were in the initial Windows 2003 release. Other manufacturers are sure to follow with their own interfaces. For now, owners of UPSs from other manufacturers can use a generic interface and set of defaults.

To select a UPS to configure, click Select on the Power Options Properties dialog box to open the UPS Selection dialog box. In Figure 7.45, I've chosen to set up an APC Smart-UPS model. To select the generic interface and defaults, select Generic from the Select Manufacturer drop-down list on the UPS Selection dialog box. Click Finish on the UPS Selection dialog box when you're done choosing a UPS model.

Next, click Configure on the Power Options Properties dialog box to open the UPS Configuration dialog box (see the right side of Figure 7.46). Unless you have reason to do otherwise, accept the defaults for notifications.

FIGURE 7.46
Configuring a UPS

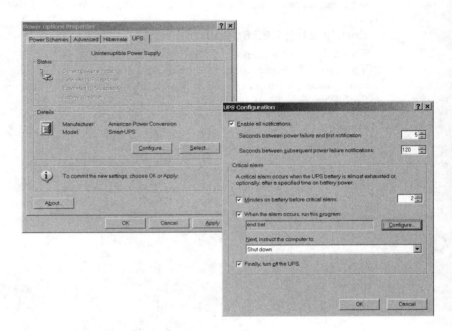

I strongly suggest that you set a critical alarm and specify a file to run when the critical alarm fires and before your server is shut down. Be sure to allow lots of time for a smooth shutdown before the battery is likely to run out. The two-minute default setting for Minutes on Battery Before Critical Alarm should be fine. You want to be sure that the server doesn't crash due to the lack of battery power before all buffered data has been written to your server's databases. You'll want to put a UPS on all your Windows Server 2003, including the ones that run Exchange 2003.

Back in Figure 7.46, I've told Windows Server 2003 to execute a batch file, END.BAT, before shutting down. This particular file closes one of my applications and then deletes some temporary files generated by the application.

That's it. Press OK to exit the two dialog boxes shown in Figure 7.46, and your UPS is configured.

TIP   *Of course, you need to test your UPS regularly. Do the tests during off-hours, and warn users that you'll be taking the system down. Testing is simple: Just cut power to the UPS and make sure that everything goes as expected. Be sure to let the test go far enough for the battery power to run out and the UPS service to shut down the server. When testing, you should shut down key Windows 2003 services, especially Exchange 2003 services. If the UPS fails, you don't want to run the risk of destroying key Windows 2003 services—supported databases.*

TIP   Some UPSs come with special software for Windows Server 2003. This software replaces the UPS software that comes with Windows Server 2003, providing such enhanced features as scheduled periodic testing of the UPS and monitoring of power quantity and quality over time. This software doesn't add much to the cost of a UPS, and it's well worth having.

Setting Up a Windows Server 2003 Backup

As I mentioned in Chapter 5, a variety of products are available for backing up Windows Server 2003. Additionally, Windows 2003 comes with its own backup software, which is quite functional for local server backup if you're not using a tape autoloader. It's important to get some sort of backup going immediately on your Windows Server 2003, so let's get Windows Server 2003's own Backup Utility up and running right now.

Hardware

Okay, let me say it right at the start: Don't use anything other than 4mm, 8mm, or DLT SCSI-compatible tape drives. Forget those awful third-party minicartridge thingies that take forever to back up a byte of information to low-capacity tape cartridges. And don't mess with those fancy units that use gigantic but relatively low-capacity (and high-priced) 3M cartridges. Stick with the proven, working, relatively inexpensive 4mm, 8mm, or DLT tape technologies. Whatever technology you decide on, go for more rather than less capacity. You'll need it sooner, rather than later.

If you have a larger computing environment, take a serious look at tape systems with autoloaders that allow you to put many tapes online at the same time. These save you from having to manually insert tapes into a drive when it's time to change to a new tape either because the tape change cycle dictates or because you've filled the tape sooner than expected. All this ensures that data gets backed up when it should, not the next morning after you and all your users have arrived at the office.

Installing a SCSI tape backup unit is easy. Just install an appropriate SCSI adapter and plug in the drive, being sure that your SCSI chain is properly terminated. You can use the same SCSI controller that you use for your disk drives, although you'll get better backup throughput if you use a separate controller for the tape drive, or at least a separate channel on the controller. Also be sure to use the shortest SCSI cables you can: When a SCSI cable chain (including the cable inside your computer that supports internal disk drives) gets too long, you'll start experiencing some pretty crazy data glitches on your disks and tape drives.

NOTE   Windows Server 2003 comes with device drivers for a wide range of tape drives. The correct driver should be installed automatically the first time you boot with your new tape drive installed. If you need to provide a driver that Windows 2003 doesn't have, you are offered the opportunity after new tape hardware has been discovered.

TIP   In addition to tape, consider backing up to disk. You can back up to a disk drive on your server. Of course, that disk should be separate from the disk or disks you're backing up or you'll be up a long creek without a paddle should anything happen to the disk that holds both your backup and the stuff you backed up. You might also consider storage area networks (SANs), which are generally disk arrays connected to your server through a computer network. Be careful that your SAN of choice is supported by Windows 2003, especially for Windows 2003's new volume shadow snapshot capability.

Setting Up a Basic Backup

Our real interest in backups comes with Exchange Server 2003. However, we're not ready to tackle Exchange backup right now. Nevertheless, you should have a backup in place immediately. So, right now I'll take you through a simple backup scenario using Windows Server 2003's Backup Utility. In the next chapter, I'll show you how to back up Exchange Server.

We're going to schedule our backup, so we need to be sure that Windows 2003's Task Scheduler is running. In your MMC, go to `\Computer Management (Local)\Services and Applications\Services`. Find Task Scheduler. If it's not set to start automatically, double-click the service, set startup type to Automatic, and click Start. When the service starts, click OK.

To open the Windows Server 2003 Backup Utility, select Start ➢ All Programs ➢ Accessories ➢ System Tools ➢ Backup. This opens the Backup or Restore Wizard, shown in Figure 7.47.

FIGURE 7.47

The Windows Server 2003 Backup or Restore Wizard's welcome screen

We're going to use the wizard to set up a backup in just a bit. Let me talk about manual backups and restores first. To go to manual mode, click Advanced Mode on the first Wizard page. This turns the Wizard window into a manual backup/restore interface. You use the Backup, Restore, and Schedule Jobs pages to perform various tasks. You can also create a disk to be used for automated system recovery (ASR) by selecting Tools ➢ ASR Wizard. This diskette is the equivalent of the pre–Windows 2003 emergency repair disk with the added capability to kick off an automatic recovery of your computer. You should create an ASR disk and update it whenever you change the hardware or software on your system. You should also heed Backup Utility's warnings to try everything else to get your computer running again before using the ASR diskette.

OK, now let's set up a backup using the Backup or Restore Wizard. Click Next for the Backup or Restore page shown in Figure 7.48. As you can see, you can choose to back up or restore from a previous backup. Select Back Up Files and Settings and click Next.

FIGURE 7.48
Using the Backup or
Restore Wizard's
Backup or Restore
page to select a back-
up job

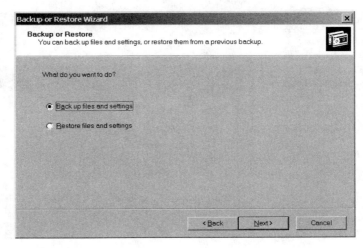

The next wizard page (shown in Figure 7.49) asks if you want to back up everything on your computer or just selected disks and files. Ensure that Let Me Choose What to Backup is selected, then click Next.

FIGURE 7.49
Using the Backup or
Restore Wizard's
What to Back Up
page to choose a
backup of selected
items on a computer

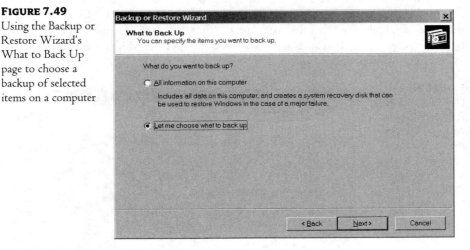

On the following page, Items to Back Up, shown in Figure 7.50, be sure that the drive that supports your Windows 2003 system (the C: drive in my case) and System State are selected. The System State is a collection of information on your computer including registry settings. When you capture the System State, you are in a position to recover from a major crash or a critical problem introduced by the addition of a piece of software or hardware. You should back up a server's System State as frequently as you back up other items on the server.

FIGURE 7.50
Using the Backup or Restore Wizard's Items to Back Up page to choose a backup of selected items on a computer

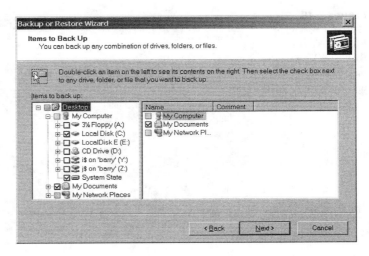

On the next wizard page, the Backup Type, Destination, and Name page (see Figure 7.51), be sure that the correct backup media type is selected. My server does not have a tape drive, so I'm offered only the option to back up to disk. I'm backing up to the second disk drive in the computer, drive E:. The name for the backup is BG01 Backup Normal. Having made the choice to use drive E: for backup, I really shouldn't install any software on the drive or use it for file storage and back it up. If the drive fails, I'll have neither the programs and files that were on it nor the backups that were written to it. If you use a tape drive, you are offered backup opportunities appropriate to tape drives, as well as an option to back up to disk.

FIGURE 7.51
Using the Backup or Restore Wizard's Backup Type, Destination, and Name page to select where the backup will be stored and how it will be named

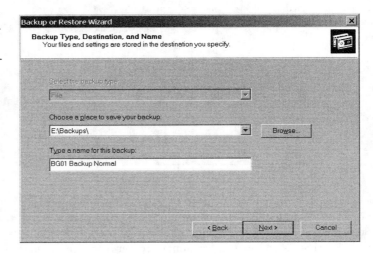

Click Next, and you'll see a page like the one in Figure 7.52. This page summarizes the backup as it stands at this point.

FIGURE 7.52

The Backup or Restore Wizard presents its backup plan and offers an opportunity to set advanced options.

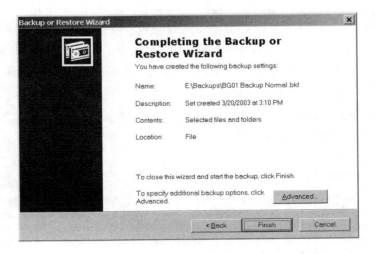

But you don't have to stop here. By clicking the Advanced button, you can set up some more interesting and valuable options. Go ahead, click Advanced to bring up the first of the advanced options wizard pages, the Type of Backup page (see Figure 7.53). Here you choose the type of backup that you want. This includes the way that you want files to be backed up and whether you want to back up files that have been migrated to near-line (remote storage) media. This second option is necessary now that Windows Server 2003 can move less-used files from disk to other media such as tape and bring them back if someone tries to use them.

FIGURE 7.53

Using the Backup or Restore Wizard's advanced options to select the type of backup to be performed

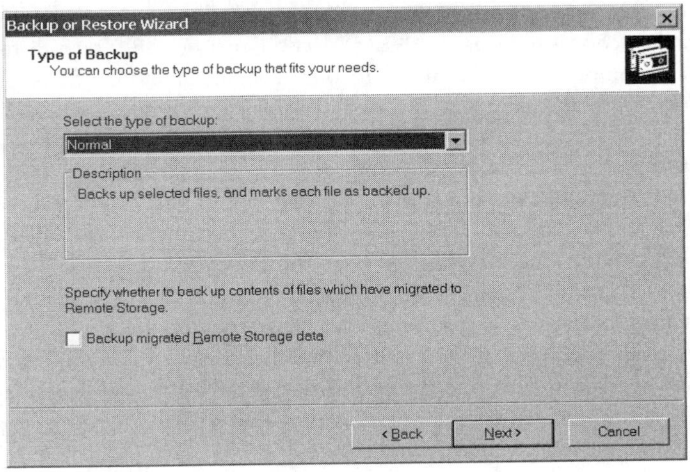

You have five options for the way that you want files backed up:

Normal backup   Backs up all files that have been selected and marks them as having been backed up (clears or turns off what is called the *archive bit* for each file). When a file is changed or a new file is created, its archive bit is set to indicate that it is a candidate for backup.

Copy backup   Backs up all selected files, but doesn't clear the archive bit.

Incremental backup   Backs up all files with their archive bit set and clears the archive bit.

Differential backup   Backs up all files with their archive bit set and does not clear the archive bit.

Daily backup   Backs up all selected files that have been modified on the day of the backup, but doesn't clear the archive bit.

SETTING UP A REAL BACKUP STRATEGY

There's no need to back up every file every night. In spite of what I set up in this little demonstration of the Windows 2003 Backup Utility (daily full backups), the usual practice is to back up an entire disk once a week (normal backup) and then to perform either a differential or incremental backup every other day of the week. Differential backups grow larger every day because you're backing up everything that changed on all previous days, plus whatever changed on the day of the backup. Incremental backups are smaller because you back up only what changed on the day of the backup. Differential backups are easier to restore because you need to restore only from the last normal backup and the last differential backup to fully restore a disk drive. With incremental backups, you must restore the last normal backup and all incremental backups done since the normal backup. Take your pick, depending on the issues raised previously and the capacity of your tape backup hardware. I'll leave it to you to decide whether you can benefit from copy and daily backups.

You use the next wizard page, How to Back Up, shown in Figure 7.54, to specify whether data should be verified after backup, whether hardware compression is to be used, and whether volume shadow copy is to be used. Always select the first option. You are offered the second option, Use Hardware Compression, If Available, if you're backing up to tape. Select this option if you're sure that you'll always have the same kind of drive available to read the compressed data. Use volume shadow copy unless you have a strong reason not to. Volume shadow copy gives you a consistent snapshot-like backup of an entire disk volume at a given point in time. You can restore this backup to a computer and it will function just as it was when the backup was done. Do note, however, that third-party applications must support volume shadow copy for it to work on their open files. Remember, volume shadow copy is the default. Checking the box turns it off.

The Backup Options page shown in Figure 7.55 lets you choose whether to append to your backup medium or overwrite it. I've chosen to overwrite the disk file I'm backing up to. I could also set up another job that does a differential backup every day for the rest of the week and I might choose to append that backup to the same disk file. All of this applies to tape backups too. You can also use this wizard page to restrict access to the backup medium only to the person setting up the backup or to someone logged in as Administrator.

FIGURE 7.54

Using the Backup or Restore Wizard's advanced options to determine whether data verification, hardware compression, and volume shadow copy should be used

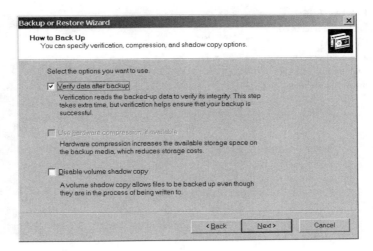

FIGURE 7.55

Using the Backup or Restore Wizard's advanced options to specify whether the backup medium can be overwritten and who can access the medium

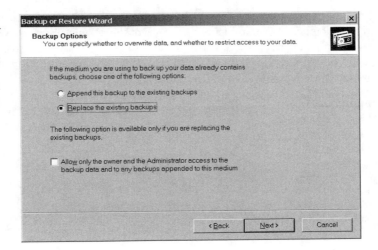

The final advanced options page, When to Back Up, enables you to run your backup immediately or schedule it to run one or more times (see Figure 7.56). Leave the default setting of Now to run the backup immediately. Select Later to schedule your backup. Enter a job name and click Set Schedule.

FIGURE 7.56
Using the Backup or Restore Wizard's advanced options to back up immediately or on a schedule

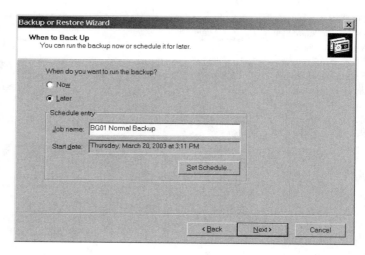

At one or more points as you complete the Backup or Restore Wizard, you are asked to specify an account under which your scheduled backup will run. You do this with the Set Account Information dialog box shown in Figure 7.57. Accept the default, or enter a Windows 2003 account to run the backup under. This account should at least belong to the Backup Operators security group in the \Active Directory Users and Computers\Built-in container. Don't forget to enter a password for whatever account you choose.

FIGURE 7.57
Using the Backup or Restore Wizard's advanced options to enter a Windows 2003 account and password to run the backup under

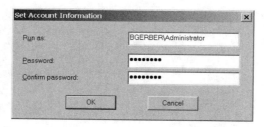

The Schedule Job dialog box comes up next (see Figure 7.58). It enables you to do some pretty fancy scheduling. I've selected to run my normal backup every day at 11:30 P.M. Click Advanced to open the Advanced Schedule Options dialog box shown in Figure 7.59. Here you can set an end date for your backup job and choose to do the backup more than once in a given time period (day, week, month). This is useful if you want to capture several images of a volume or specific files each day. It is especially useful for taking regular volume shadow copy snapshots each day. These might be snapshots of the Windows 2003 side of your server or, later, the Exchange 2003–side. Think how great it will be to get accurate hourly or even half-hourly snapshots of the volumes on an Exchange server, including mailbox and public stores. Wow!

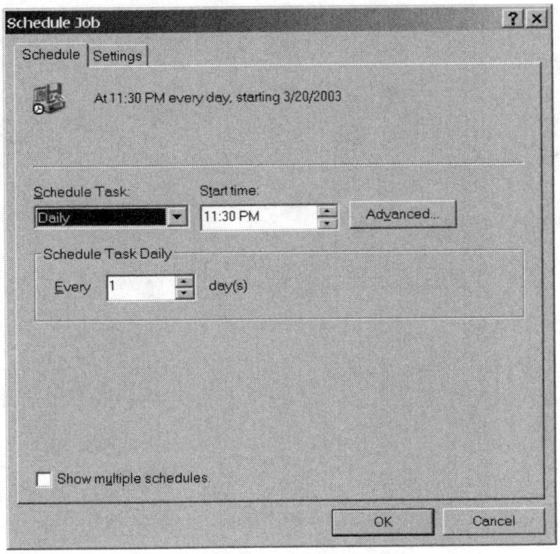

FIGURE 7.58
Using the Backup or
Restore Wizard's
advanced options to
refine the parameters
for a scheduled a
backup

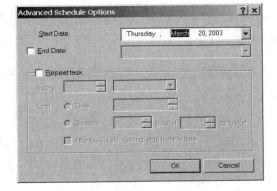

FIGURE 7.59
The Backup or Re-
store Wizard's ad-
vanced options can
be set to run a back-
up job more than
once a day.

Figure 7.60 shows the Settings page of the Schedule Job dialog box. See Figure 7.58 (shown earlier) for the Schedule page of this dialog box. You use the Settings page to force the Windows Task
Scheduler to stop a job if it runs for a period longer than normal. You must judge what is normal.
For most jobs, 72 hours is far too long. You can also use the Settings page to specify that the job
should start or stop, depending whether the computer is busy with other tasks or not. Finally, you can
set various power management–related parameters.

FIGURE 7.60
The Backup or Restore Wizard's advanced options can be set to control how a scheduled backup job runs.

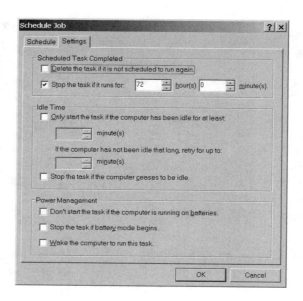

When you've finished with the Schedule Job dialog box, click OK to close it. This returns you to the Backup or Restore Wizard's When to Back Up page. Note in Figure 7.61 that the scheduled backup time is now 11:30 P.M., the time I selected for the backup earlier in Figure 7.58, not the time before I scheduled the backup as shown previously in Figure 7.56.

FIGURE 7.61
A backup has now been scheduled using the Backup or Restore Wizard's advanced options.

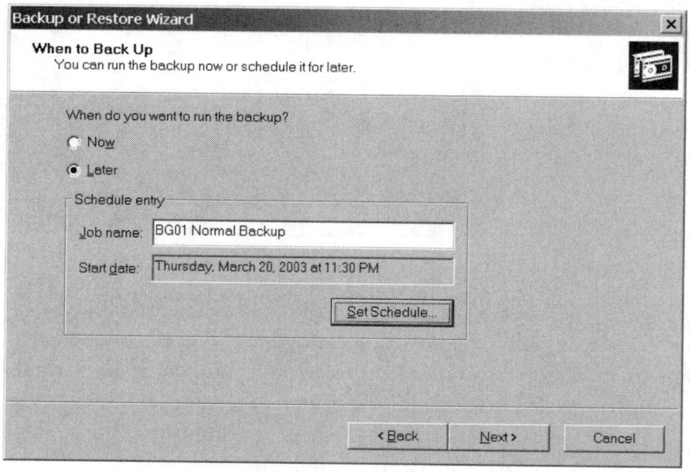

Click Next on the Backup or Restore Wizard's When to Back Up page and you'll see a page similar the one shown in Figure 7.62. This summary page tells you everything you need to know about your scheduled backup. If you don't like what you see, click Back to fix things or click Finish to schedule the backup and exit the Backup or Restore Wizard.

FIGURE 7.62

The Backup or Restore Wizard shows summary information about the backup and allows you to finish setting up the backup or go back and make changes.

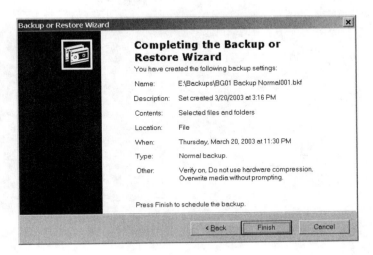

Before we move on, I want talk a bit about the integration of backup job scheduling into Windows 2003 task scheduling. Backup job scheduling is done using interfaces integrated into the Windows 2003 Backup Utility. However, the Windows Task Scheduler actually manages and runs backup jobs and any other jobs scheduled in other applications or directly in the Task Scheduler. If you look at a job in the task scheduler, you'll see many of the same interfaces you saw in the Backup Utility. Just open a backup job or any other task. To do so, select Start ➤ Windows Explorer and expand the Control Panel. Look in the Scheduled Tasks folder (see Figure 7.63) and you'll find your scheduled backup jobs. Double-click a job and, as Figure 7.64 shows, you'll see a dialog box with the same pages you used when scheduling a backup job.

You can check out and manage your backups on the Schedule Job page of the Backup Utility window. Remember, you open this dialog box by clicking Advanced Mode in the Backup or Restore Wizard welcome screen (see Figure 7.47, shown earlier). In Figure 7.65, you can see the jobs that I've scheduled. A blue letter "N" indicates a normal job. Differential jobs are marked with a green letter "D."

FIGURE 7.63
The Scheduled
Tasks folder in
Windows Explorer
shows scheduled
backup jobs.

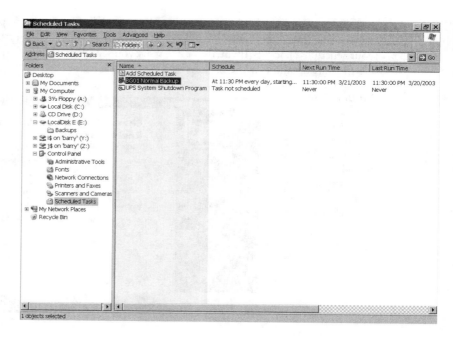

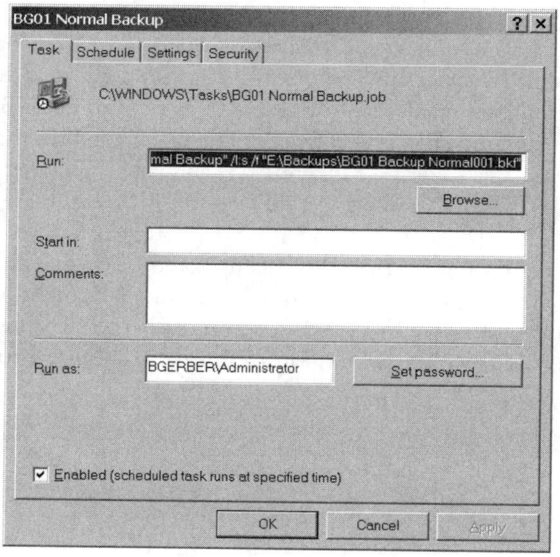

FIGURE 7.64
The dialog box for a
scheduled backup
job includes schedul-
ing pages like the
ones used in the
Windows 2003
Backup Utility.

FIGURE 7.65

Managing scheduled backups in the Schedule Jobs page of the Backup Utility window

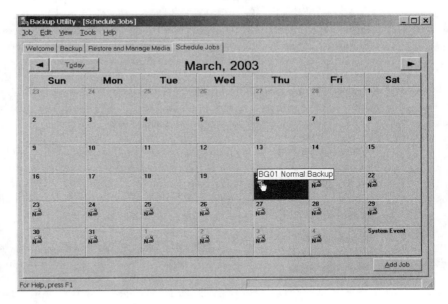

That handlike cursor that you see on the 20th of the month in the calendar functions just like the hand in Microsoft's Internet Explorer web browser. Hover over a particular backup, and you see its name, as in Figure 7.65. If you click the backup you're hovering over, you get a dialog box that lets you manage the backup (see Figure 7.66). This is better by several magnitudes than backup scheduling with NT 4's Backup program.

FIGURE 7.66

Managing scheduled backups in the Scheduled Job Options dialog box

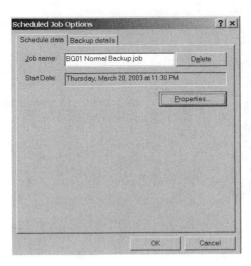

You can do a number of other tasks using the Advanced Mode dialog box. For example, to look at the log for a job, select Tools ➢ Report and then select the log you're interested in from the list. Figure 7.67 displays the log for the completed backup that we set up earlier. Notice that backups to local disk are pretty fast. It took seven minutes to back up 1GB.

Use the Restore Wizard to restore some data from your backup. After our little trip through the Backup Wizard, you should find it pretty easy to use. You've probably heard this before, but I'll say it anyway: Be sure to do test restores frequently. A perfectly executed backup scheme isn't worth anything if you can't restore what you've backed up.

NOTE   *Consider third-party backup solutions for Windows Server 2003. These offer a range of options not available in Windows 2003's Backup Utility. They can, for example, back up system state and registry data on remote computers. See the Appendix, "Cool Third-Party Applications for Exchange Server and Outlook Clients" for information on some very nice third-party backup products for Exchange Server 2003 that also have much to offer when used to back up Windows Server 2003.*

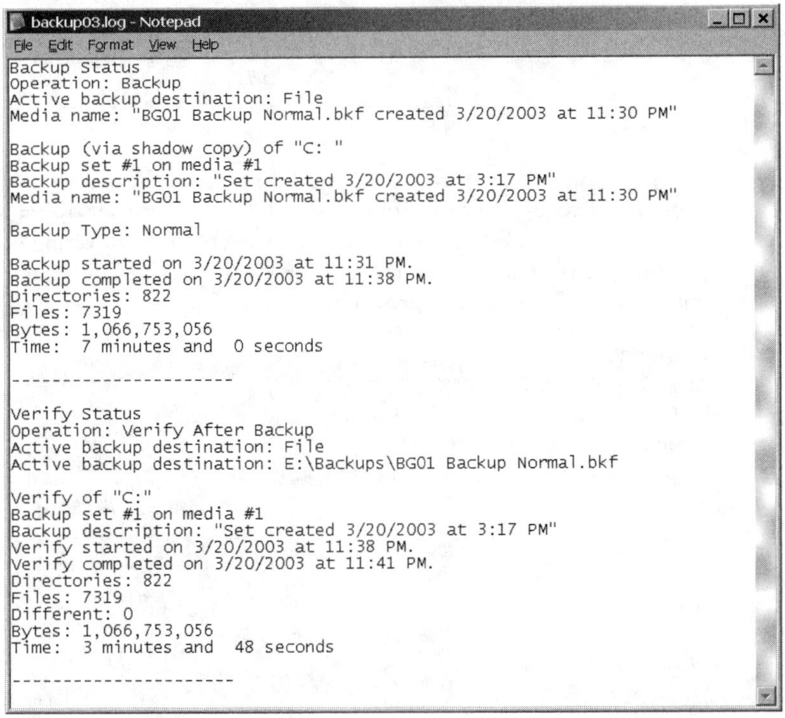

FIGURE 7.67

The log for a completed backup job

Summary

This chapter covered the installation of both Windows 2003 domain controllers and Windows 2003 stand-alone servers. Domain controllers make Windows 2003 networks happen. Stand-alone servers are the workhorses of your network, hosting applications such as Exchange Server 2003.

Before installing the Windows Server 2003 operating system on any computer, you need to ensure that your hardware ducks are in a row. Your server hardware should have adequate capacity to support the Windows 2003 and application functionality that you require. You also should exhaustively test your hardware to ensure that it is functioning properly.

The actual installation of Windows Server 2003 software is fairly easy. This is especially true if you've prepared well by tracking through the planning steps described in Chapter 5. If you're familiar with NT Server 4, you need to adjust your thinking a bit to deal with such things as Active Directory forests and trees, as well as the fact that domain controllers come into being after, not during, installation.

After your Windows Server 2003 is installed, you can turn to managing it. Microsoft Management Console (MMC) is the home for a range of snap-in Windows 2003 management tools. For example, you use the Active Directory Users and Computers MMC snap-in to create and manage users.

Dynamic DNS is central to Windows 2003 networking. Working in tandem with DHCP, it enables you to install new servers and workstations without having to worry about assigning IP addresses or other TCP/IP-related parameters to the new computer during installation. Both Dynamic DNS and DHCP are managed within MMC.

When you install Windows Server 2003, a disk partition is created to hold the operating system. You partition any remaining disk space using the Computer Management MMC snap-in (Disk Management container) and disk management wizards, which size, create, and format partitions. You can also use functionality provided in the Disk Management folder to set up a range of software-based fault-tolerant disk options such as RAID 5.

After your Windows Server 2003 is up and running, it's time to ensure its reliability and stability. You must install and configure an uninterruptible power supply and set up backups. Both of these tasks can be accomplished using software built into Windows 2003 or enhanced software from various third-party vendors.

With Windows Server 2003 in place, we can now move on to installing Exchange Server 2003 itself. Here we go oooooooooooooooooooooooo (fade toward the end). You didn't think our trip to Wonderland was over, did you?

Chapter 8

Installing Exchange Server 2003

THIS WILL BE A fun chapter. After all the theory, concepts, and planning and installation of Windows Server 2003, we're actually going to get an Exchange server up and running. Installing an Exchange server is a four-step process:

1. Install Windows Server 2003 in stand-alone mode.
2. Prepare to install Exchange Server 2003.
3. Actually install Exchange.
4. Do some key housekeeping chores when installation is complete.

After you've completed these tasks, you're ready to create an Exchange mailbox and set up a backup of your Exchange server. We'll take on these two tasks here as well. Let's get to work.

Featured in this chapter:

◆ Installing a Windows 2003 stand-alone server

◆ Getting ready to install Exchange Server 2003

◆ Running the Exchange Server 2003 Setup program

◆ Post-installation activities

◆ Mailbox-enabling a Windows 2003 user

◆ Backing up Exchange Server 2003

Installing a Windows 2003 Stand-Alone Server

Before you install Windows Server 2003, you need to verify that you've got the right hardware and that it's functioning properly. Then you need to be sure which version of Windows 2003 you're going to install and where you're going to install it.

Verifying Server Hardware

Unless you're running a really basic test machine, I assume that you've got that 1GHz Pentium III or 4 or Xeon machine with 768MB of memory and at least two 9GB SCSI hard drives that I recommended back in Chapter 5, "Designing a New Exchange Server 2003." If you're setting up a heavy-duty Exchange system, you should seriously consider upping memory to 1GB, adding a second processor, and using RAID 5 disk storage, again as recommended in Chapter 5. You should also have installed a UPS and a 4mm, 8mm, or DLT SCSI tape backup device or disk storage that you can dedicate to backups. Be sure to test your hardware, as suggested in Chapter 7, "Installing Windows Server 2003 as a Domain Controller."

ADDING A SECOND NETWORK ADAPTER FOR INTERNET MAIL

If your Exchange server is going to connect to the Internet to support Internet mail functions, you should install a second network adapter. You can wait to install a second adapter until after you've installed Windows 2003 and Exchange 2003. This adapter should be set up with Internet IP address information as provided by your Internet service provider or your organization's Internet support personnel. You can do this manually by creating a network connection for the adapter: choose All Programs ➢ Control Panel ➢ Network Connections and then either ➢ New Connection Wizard or ➢ [Connection_Name] if a connection is created automatically when the new adapter is discovered by Windows 2003. If you created a DHCP reservation for your second adapter as discussed in Chapter 7, then the appropriate address should be automatically assigned to the adapter.

What to Install Where

In what follows, I assume that you're installing Exchange 2003 on a stand-alone server—that is, a server that is not a Windows 2003 domain controller. That means I assume that, at the very least, two things are true:

- You have already installed Windows Server 2003 on a computer and have promoted the server to domain controller status, as per Chapter 7.

- You will install another copy of Windows Server 2003 on another computer without promoting this server to domain controller status, also as per Chapter 7.

The first server is your domain controller. You'll install Exchange Server 2003 on the second computer. I strongly recommend against installing Exchange 2003 on a domain controller to avoid performance problems when you attempt to run Exchange 2003 on a Windows 2003 domain controller. So, I won't discuss doing that here in detail. If you absolutely must do this, just promote your second server to domain controller status and proceed from there. In this chapter, I will mention anything special that you need to do if you do choose the domain controller route.

If you're going to install Exchange Server 2003 Standard Edition, you should install Windows Server 2003. If you need Exchange Server 2003 Enterprise Edition, you must install Windows 2003 Advanced Server or Windows 2003 Datacenter Server.

Installing Windows Server 2003

It is time to install Windows Server 2003 on your soon-to-be Exchange server. I carefully constructed Chapter 7 so that you could use it to install a domain controller or a stand-alone server. So, please do use it to install the stand-alone server that will become your Exchange 2003 server. Let me re-emphasize several points here that are also made in Chapter 7 regarding installing Windows Server 2003 on a computer that will support Exchange Server 2003:

- See the section "Enabling Windows 2003 Services Required by Exchange 2003" in Chapter 6, "Upgrading to Windows Server 2003 and Exchange Server 2003." Here you'll find specifics on enabling the following services, which must be in place before you begin installing Exchange 2003.
  - World Wide Web
  - SMTP
  - NNTP
  - ASP.NET
  - .NET Framework
- Be sure that you have set up DHCP and Dynamic DNS on your domain controller, as specified in Chapter 7, or will supply IP addresses manually, or are using a DHCP/DNS system separate from the little Windows 2003/Exchange 2003 environment we're setting up here.
- Set your new server to join your Windows Server 2003 domain when asked during installation whether you want to join a domain or a workgroup.
- Don't promote your server to a domain controller.
- When you're all done installing your new server, make sure that it is capable of joining your domain. Using the Microsoft Management Console (MMC) that you created in Chapter 7, you should see your server in `\Active Directory Users and Computers\Computers` and in the DNS container for your domain.

Okay, now go ahead and install Windows Server 2003. When you're finished, I'll meet you in the next section.

Getting Ready to Install Exchange Server 2003

Yay! Your Windows 2003 stand-alone server is installed. Now you're ready to begin preparing to install Exchange 2003. You have to do the following:

- Ensure that all aspects of security are properly set up.
- Gather some information.

Security Issues

You need to consider three security issues. These relate to the following:

◆ Ensuring that you've enabled security appropriately for the Windows Server 2003 domain model that you're working under

◆ Logging in to your Exchange server under an appropriate account

◆ Setting privileges relating to who can administer a specific Exchange 2003 component

DOMAIN SECURITY

If you're installing Exchange Server in a single contiguous namespace domain (also called a *single-root tree domain*) as defined in Chapter 3, "Two Key Architectural Components of Windows Server 2003," you won't have to take any special steps before installation. If your Exchange Server will operate in a noncontiguous namespace domain (*forest of root trees domain*), as defined in Chapter 3, you might have to set up the required cross-domain trusts. In your first time through this chapter, you should be working in a single contiguous namespace domain, and you shouldn't have to worry about cross-domain trusts. Later in this book, you'll get into installing multiple Exchange servers in multiple domains. Then you'll need to think about cross-domain trusts.

INSTALLATION SECURITY

To install Exchange Server 2003, you must be logged in to an account that is a member of the following Windows 2003 security groups:

◆ Domain Admins

◆ Enterprise Admins

◆ Schema Admins

The Administrator account for your domain that's created when you install Windows Server 2003 on your domain controller belongs to all these groups. If you have access to this account, use it to install Exchange 2003.

*TIP   Throughout this chapter, I talk about logging in to your domain on a particular server using the domain administrator account, Administrator. I also talk about logging directly into a particular server using the server's local Administrator account. Here's how to do both of these: To log in to your domain on a particular server, such as your Exchange server, using the domain Administrator account, first press Ctrl+Alt+Del and then click Options in the Log On to Windows dialog box. Select your domain from the drop-down list. Then enter the account name **Administrator** and its password, and click OK. To log in directly to your Exchange server, select its name from the drop-down list, type the username **Administrator** and its password, and click OK. Note that you cannot log in locally to a server that is a domain controller. The option to do this simply is not presented.*

If your organization divides responsibility for Active Directory and Exchange Server between two groups, you can still install Exchange 2003. However, before you can install Exchange, you have to ask the Active Directory folks—the ones with access to an account that is a member of all three of the previous groups—to run the Exchange Server 2003 setup program with a couple of switches at a command prompt.

The setup program is on the Exchange Server 2003 CD-ROM in the directory `\setup\i386`. The switches are called *ForestPrep* and *DomainPrep*. The full commands are `\SETUP\I386\SETUP.EXE / ForestPrep` and `\SETUP\I386\SETUP.EXE /DomainPrep`. I'll refer to running the setup program with one of these switches simply as ForestPrep or DomainPrep.

ForestPrep should be run before DomainPrep. Run ForestPrep on a domain controller logged in as a domain administrator. Run DomainPrep on the computer where you plan to install Exchange Server 2003 logged in to the domain as a domain administrator.

ForestPrep extends the Active Directory schema, adding Exchange Server 2003–relevant objects. DomainPrep identifies an Exchange Server 2003 that will act as the recipient update server for the domain, and it adds permissions within the domain required by Exchange 2003. A recipient update server uses Active Directory information from Windows Server 2003 accounts with mailboxes to keep Exchange 2003 e-mail addresses and address lists up to date.

After ForestPrep and DomainPrep have been run, you can install Exchange 2003 using an account that belongs to the Domain Admins and Enterprise Admins groups.

WARNING *When you install Exchange Server 2003 under the domain Administrator account, ForestPrep and DomainPrep run as part of the installation. You don't need to run them before running the Exchange 2003 installation itself.*

COMPONENT MANAGEMENT SECURITY

You can set extensive security permissions for most Windows Server 2003 objects. Exchange Server 2003 objects are no different. On installation, the account installing Exchange 2003 gets full access to Exchange objects. You can play with rights on objects to control who can access and manage different Exchange objects. In this way, you can remove permissions installed by default and give select Exchange permissions to other accounts or security groups. For example, if you create multiple Exchange administrative groups (see Chapter 4, "Exchange Server 2003 Architecture"), you can assign different accounts rights to manage different Exchange objects.

Whatever you decide to do with component security in the future, it's a good idea to set up a Windows 2003 group that has specific rights to administer one or more Exchange servers and their components. Then, when you need to give someone these rights, all you have to do is add them to the Exchange administration group.

If you expect to be the one and only Exchange administrator, and if you can operate using the domain controller's Administrator account, then you probably can get by without an Exchange administration group. Even in such a case, however, I strongly recommend that you explore the use of an Exchange administration group. If nothing else, you'll learn quite a bit about Windows 2003 and Exchange 2003 security in the process.

NOTE *In various sections of this book, this being one, you might not be able to accomplish some of the tasks that I ask you to perform because you don't have the required Windows Server 2003 permissions. This often happens in organizations in which operating system management is the responsibility of one group while management of a specific application, such as Exchange, is the responsibility of another. In such a case, you can ask whoever manages the operating system either to grant you the rights you need or to do the task for you.*

To perform the following tasks, you should be logged in to your domain on your domain controller under an account with Administrator privileges.

We'll create the Exchange administration group in a bit. First, however, we need to create a Windows 2003 user account that will be added to the group. I don't want you to use the account that you created for yourself in the last chapter because we're saving that one to test a typical Exchange user's experience. So, create a new account with the name ExAd, followed by your first initial and last name. (My account will be named ExAdBGerber.) For specific instructions on creating a new account, see Chapter 7. Hint: Right-click the container \Active Directory Users and Computers\Users, and select New ➢ User.

Okay, now you can create your Exchange administration group. Call it Exchange Admins. Use the MMC that you set up in Chapter 7. Right-click the container \Active Directory Users and Computers\Users, and select New ➢ Group. This brings up the New Object - Group dialog box shown in Figure 8.1. Type in the Group Name. The pre–Windows 2003 group name is filled in automatically. Make sure that Global is selected for Group Scope and that Security is selected for Group Type. Click OK.

TIP *To open an MMC that you've saved, select Start Menu ➢ All Programs ➢ Administrative Tools ➢* name_ of_MMC, *where* name_of_MMC *is the name that you used to save the MMC.*

FIGURE 8.1
Setting up a global security group for Exchange Server administration

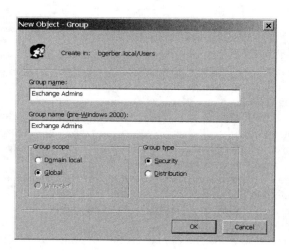

Now, find your new group in the right pane of the Users container, and double-click it. Add a description, as I have in Figure 8.2. Finally, tab over to the Members property page (see Figure 8.3), add the user that you just created to your new group, and click OK. You can type part of the name, *exad* for example, and then click Check Names or click Advanced to do a more complete search for an object to become a member of the group.

FIGURE 8.2
Adding a description for the Exchange Server Administrative group

FIGURE 8.3
Adding a Windows Server 2003 account to the Exchange Admins global security group

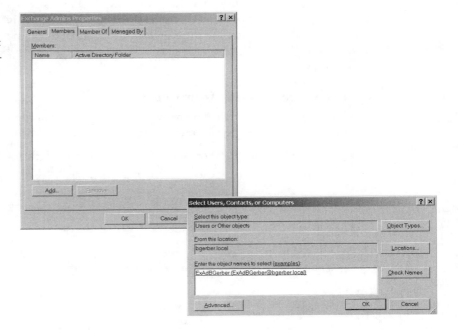

After Exchange Server 2003 has been installed, you can grant your group the proper permissions. I'll cover that process later in this chapter in the section "Granting Permission for the Exchange Administration Group to Manage Exchange Server."

WARNING   *If you installed Exchange on a stand-alone Windows 2003 server, you can move on to the next section because the hands-on tasks that immediately follow won't even work. If you installed Exchange on a Windows 2003 domain controller, you must read and do the hands-on tasks immediately following, or what follows in the next section won't work for you.*

If you installed Exchange Server 2003 on a domain controller, you must give log on locally permissions to the ExAd Windows 2003 account that you created just a bit ago. If you don't do that, this user will be able to administer Exchange only from another workstation or server and only after the Exchange management tools have been installed on that workstation or server. For now, I want you to administer Exchange on your Exchange server, so let's give your ExAd account log on locally permissions.

Select Start ➢ All Programs ➢ Administrative Tools ➢ Domain Controller Security Policy. Open the Security Settings container, then open the Local Policies container, and finally click the User Rights Assignment container. In the right pane, double-click Allow Log On Locally, then click Add User or Group on the Local Security Policy Setting dialog box. Add the user that you just created, and press OK until you've exited the dialog boxes that you opened. Finally, to implement the policy that you just added, at a command prompt (Start ➢ All Programs ➢ Accessories ➢ Command Prompt), type `secedit /refreshpolicy machine_policy /enforce`. When this program is finished running, close the command prompt. You're done granting your new user permission to log on locally and you've had a little look at Windows Server 2003's policy-based approach to security.

Gathering Installation Information

The Exchange Server 2003 Setup program will give you a number of options. To respond to these options, you need some specific information, including the following:

◆ The product identification number for your copy of Exchange Server 2003

◆ A list of the Exchange Server components that you want to install

◆ The path where Exchange Server is to be installed

◆ The name that you want to give your Exchange organization

◆ The Windows Server 2003 account to be granted Exchange administrative rights

Let's look at each of these in a bit more detail.

PRODUCT IDENTIFICATION NUMBER

You are asked to enter a product identification number. This is on the Exchange Server 2003 CD-ROM case.

WHAT WILL BE INSTALLED?

As with most programs installed in Microsoft Windows environments, you can choose which Exchange Server 2003 components you want to install. Options include:

- Microsoft Exchange [install]
- Microsoft Exchange Messaging and Collaboration Services [install]
  - Microsoft Exchange Connector for Lotus Notes
  - Microsoft Exchange Connector for Novell GroupWise
  - Microsoft Exchange Calendar Connector
- Microsoft Exchange System Management Tools [install]
  - Microsoft Exchange 5.5 Administrator

Check out Chapter 4 for more on these components. I suggest that you install components marked *[install]* in this list. These are the basic components required to run and manage Exchange server. The good news is that you can install additional components anytime.

THE INSTALLATION PATH

The Setup program defaults to the path C:\EXCHSRVR. Unless there's some reason that you don't want to use this path (for example, to install Exchange Server on another drive), accept the default. To improve performance, we will place Exchange 2003 databases on other drives. However, there is no reason that Exchange executables and basic Exchange data files cannot be installed on the C: or system drive, at least for a very modest Exchange system.

EXCHANGE ORGANIZATION NAME

The Exchange organization name is the top item in the Exchange organizing hierarchy. You should have decided on a name back in Chapter 5.

WINDOWS SERVER 2003 ACCOUNT TO BE GRANTED EXCHANGE ADMINISTRATIVE RIGHTS

As with the recipient update server, if you're installing Exchange as Administrator or its equivalent, you won't need this information. The installation program will assume that you want the account that you're installing under to receive Exchange administrative rights. On the other hand, if someone has to run ForestPrep for you, that person will be asked for an account name when running the program.

Running the Exchange Server 2003 Setup Program

At last! Insert the Exchange Server 2003 CD-ROM into your CD-ROM drive. The Exchange Server 2003 Setup program should open (see Figure 8.4). If the application doesn't open, run SETUP.EXE from the root directory of the CD-ROM.

FIGURE 8.4

The Exchange Server 2003 Setup application

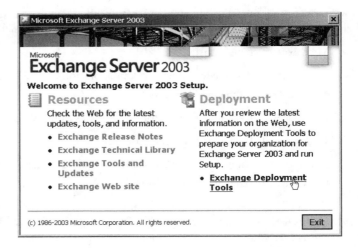

As I noted in Chapter 6, Exchange Server 2003 now includes a great set of tools to guide you through a variety of Exchange installation scenarios. The tools are called the Exchange Deployment Tools (EDT). As you can see in Figure 8.4, the only option you have if you want to install Exchange 2003 is to use the Deployment Tools.

If you've had experience with past versions of Exchange, you'll notice in Figure 8.4 that you can't run the real Exchange Setup program, \SETUP\I386\SETUP.EXE, using the Exchange 2003 setup application. This is all by very careful design. People have had so much trouble upgrading and installing Exchange that Microsoft decided to hide the real setup program and almost force you to use EDT.

Installing a new Exchange 2003 server on top of a new Windows 2003 server is fairly straightforward. You can't miss whether you use EDT or just run \SETUP\I386\SETUP.EXE.

If you use EDT, you can find more information about what's going on in some of the steps you're going through in Chapter 6, in the section "Upgrading Exchange 5.5 to Exchange 2003." If you've decided to use EDT, and I strongly recommend that you do so especially if you're new to Exchange, when you're finished with your installation, you can just slide over to the next section of this chapter, "Post-Installation Activities." Well, before you run EDT, you might want to read through the rest of this section so you better understand the steps EDT guides you through.

The rest of this section is about installing Exchange Server 2003 using the basic installation application that you run by double-clicking \SETUP\I386\SETUP.EXE on the Exchange CD-ROM. This opens the Microsoft Exchange Installation Wizard. Click Next and indicate your agreement with the End-User Licensing Agreement. On the next wizard page, enter the product identification number and click Next for the Component Selection page (see Figure 8.5). As with most software, you have three basic installation options: minimum, typical, and custom. Accept the default option, Typical, to install the components that I mentioned in the previous section.

FIGURE 8.5

Selecting Exchange 2003 features to be installed using the Microsoft Exchange Installation Wizard's Component Selection page

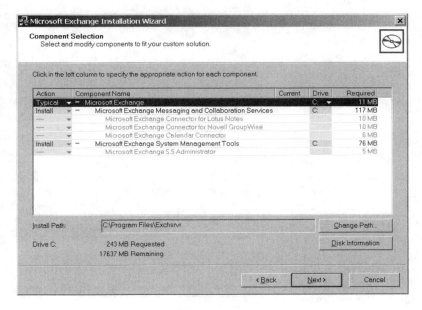

You also pick the drive or drives on which to install Exchange 2003 on this wizard page. As you can see, I've chosen to install Exchange on my C: drive. This will install the Exchange mailbox and public stores on the C: drive. These databases can grow quite large and you really want to ultimately place the databases on other physical drives. I'll show you how to move the databases in Chapter 12, "Managing the Exchange Server Hierarchy and Core Components."

Next, as you can see in Figure 8.6, you're asked whether you want to create a new Exchange Organization or join an existing Exchange Server 5.5 Organization. Pick the second option if you have a 5.5 system and want to begin your migration to Exchange 2003 by setting up an Exchange 2003 server in the 5.5 system. See Chapter 6 for more on upgrade/migration issues related to moving from version 5.5 to 2003. We're installing a new Exchange 2003 system here, so be sure that the first option is selected.

On the following Wizard page, you're asked to name your new Exchange 2003 organization. Enter a name, as I have in Figure 8.7.

On the next wizard page, you're asked to agree to Exchange Server 2003's per-seat-only licensing (see Figure 8.8). If you don't agree, it's all over. So, unless you've decided to abandon the product, be sure that the first option is selected, and click Next for the Installation Summary page (see Figure 8.9). This page shows you which Exchange features will be installed. If all is well, click Next; if not, back up to the Component Selection page and alter your selection.

FIGURE 8.6

Choosing to create a new Exchange 2003 organization using the Microsoft Exchange Installation Wizard's Installation Type page

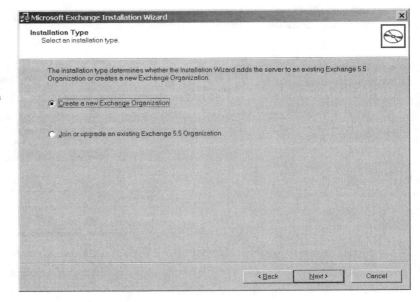

FIGURE 8.7

Entering a name for a new Exchange 2003 organization using the Microsoft Exchange Installation Wizard's Organization Name page

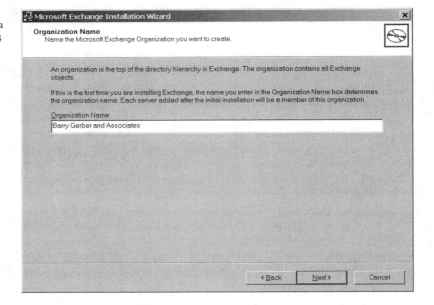

FIGURE 8.8
Accepting Exchange 2003's per-seat licensing policy using the Microsoft Exchange Installation Wizard's Licensing Agreement page

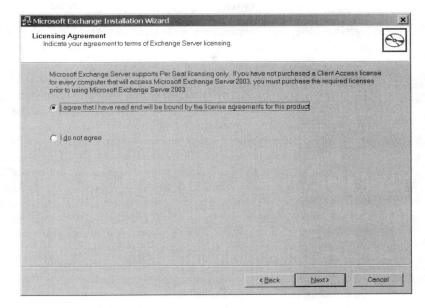

FIGURE 8.9
Reviewing the Exchange 2003 features to be installed using the Microsoft Exchange Installation Wizard's Installation Summary page

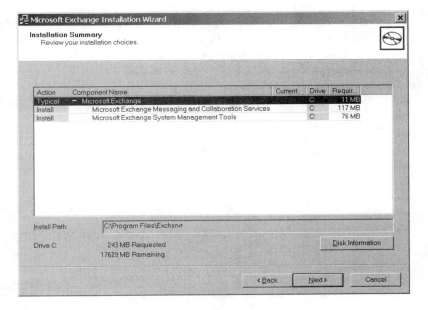

At this point, installation starts. If you're installing Exchange Server 2003 with the correct permissions, both ForestPrep and DomainPrep run silently as part of the installation process. ForestPrep needs no input, so it just runs when its time comes. This is coffee-break time in the extreme. Things can be so slow that, after watching the Active Directory schema update progress meters for a while, you might have difficulty distinguishing between the frozen image in Figure 8.10 and the real-world meters on your screen.

Because you're creating a new organization, DomainPrep assumes quite logically that you want your new Exchange server to act as the recipient update server, and it needs no input from you to set up Exchange-related permissions.

When ForestPrep and DomainPrep are done, the wizard goes on to install lots of files on your server. Then it does some registry tricks and starts up the Exchange 2003 services.

When all is done, the final wizard page congratulates you on the successful installation of Exchange 2003 and asks you to click Finish to close the wizard. After the wizard closes, exit the Exchange Server 2003 Setup program, and you're done. Well, it would be more appropriate to say that *you're* done, but your server isn't. It'll grind away for a while, setting everything up. The server spends a good deal of its time futzing around with the information store. Just let it do its thing.

If you want to watch what's going on, right-click the Windows 2003 Taskbar (the one with the Start Menu button) and select Task Manager from the pop-up menu. Tab over to the Processes page, and click CPU. That sorts the tasks running on your computer by the percentage of CPU being used. Notice that STORE.EXE is a busy little beaver. That's the Exchange information store process. When System Idle Process consumes a steady 98 or so percent of CPU capacity, the Exchange services have finished their post-installation tasks. Now you have some post-installation stuff to take care of yourself.

WARNING   *Don't expect messaging outside your local network to work when Exchange Server 2003 has finished installing. We won't actually activate Internet messaging until Chapter 13, "Managing Exchange 2003 Internet Services." For now, you want to get Exchange installed, experiment with the Outlook messaging client, and learn how to administer a basic Exchange Server 2003 system.*

FIGURE 8.10

Monitoring Exchange 2003 installation using the Microsoft Exchange Installation Wizard's Component Progress page

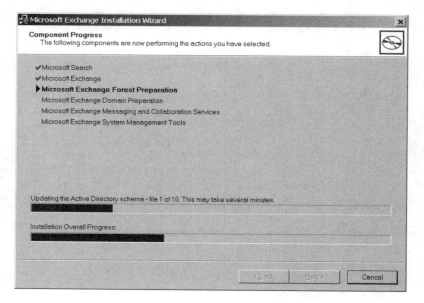

Post-Installation Activities

You need to complete a series of tasks immediately after installation:

◆ Check out Exchange server's Windows program group.

◆ Ensure that all required Exchange Server processes are up and running.

◆ Ensure that Exchange communications are working properly (by using the MMC to do a little administrative work).

◆ Set permissions for the Exchange Server administration group.

It's best to do these tasks while logged in to your domain on your Exchange server as a domain administrator. You can do all but the last task logged directly into your Exchange server as Administrator. (See the note earlier in this chapter in the section "Installation Security" if you need help with these two types of logons.)

Exchange Server 2003's Windows Program Group

Select Start ➤ All Programs ➤ Microsoft Exchange to view the programs installed with Exchange Server 2003 (see Figure 8.11).

Additional resources include web-based documentation and tools.

FIGURE 8.11
Viewing programs in the Microsoft Exchange program group

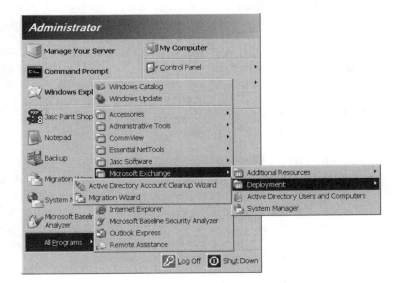

You can find out more about the Active Directory Account Cleanup Wizard in Chapter 6. This wizard is used in certain Exchange 5.5–to–Exchange 2003 upgrade scenarios.

The Migration Wizard helps you transition from other messaging systems to Exchange Server 2003. It works with a wide range of systems, including earlier versions of Exchange Server, Microsoft Mail, Lotus cc:Mail and Notes, and Novell GroupWise. Active Directory Users and Computers is in this program group to make it easy for you to run the application used to set up user mailboxes, distribution groups, and contacts.

System Manager is a stand-alone version of the snap-in that you use to manage much of your Exchange Server 2003 environment. You'll see a lot more of this application throughout this book.

Verifying That Exchange Server Services Are Running

Now you need to make sure that all Exchange Server services are running. If they're not, you'll have to do some troubleshooting. Before you can check out the Exchange services, you need to set up an MMC on your Exchange server.

SETTING UP A MICROSOFT MANAGEMENT CONSOLE ON YOUR EXCHANGE SERVER

You can use the instructions in Chapter 7 to set up your MMC. The MMC should include at least the following snap-ins:

◆ Active Directory Users and Computers

◆ Computer Management

◆ Event Viewer

Before you create your MMC, be sure that you understand the following information.

When creating your MMC, you should be logged in to your Exchange server as domain Administrator or as a user with domain administrator rights. If you're not permitted to do this, then you have to log in to the Exchange server itself as server Administrator. If you have to do the latter, you will be able to usefully add only the snap-ins for Computer Management and Event Viewer. You can add but not use the Active Directory Users and Computers snap-in.

Now, go back to Chapter 7 and set up the MMC following the instructions in the section "Using Microsoft Management Console." If you're permitted to log in as domain Administrator, do so and add the Active Directory Users and Computers snap-in as well as the Computer Management and Event Viewer snap-ins. If you're not permitted to log in as domain Administrator, log in to your Exchange server as Administrator and install the Computer Management and Event Viewer snap-ins. Then join me in the next section.

ARE THE SERVICES RUNNING?

Using the MMC that you just created for your Exchange server, click the Services container in `\Computer Management (Local)\Services and Applications`. The right pane of your Services container should look something like the one in Figure 8.12. I've scrolled up the right pane so that you can see the Exchange-specific services. For more on these services, see Chapter 4. Be sure that the Exchange services in your Services container are in the same state as the ones in Figure 8.12. If they are, your Exchange services are correctly up and running.

TIP   *Windows 2000 users might be somewhat taken aback by the new look of the Services applet. To view the applet in its more traditional form, click the Standard tab at the bottom of the MMC window. However, before you do that, take a look at what the extended view adds. You can actually read the description of each service without having to size the MMC to something approaching the dimensions of the side of a barn.*

FIGURE 8.12

The Services container with Exchange Server 2003 services displayed

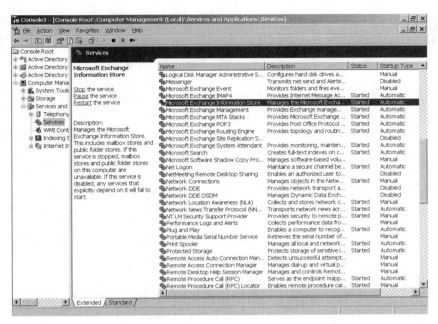

TROUBLESHOOTING PROBLEMS WITH SERVICES

If some or all of the Exchange Server processes that should be running aren't, first take a look at the Windows Server 2003 Application Event Log using the Event Viewer. In your MMC, click on the Application container in `\Computer Management (Local)\System Tools\Event Viewer`. Look for events related to Exchange Server marked with an icon showing a white *X* on a red background—these indicate serious problems such as failure to start a service. Click on the event to open the Event Properties dialog box that shows details of the event. If you find a problem that you think you can handle, try to fix it; otherwise, check with Microsoft regarding the event.

TIP You might not have to contact Microsoft directly if you have a problem that is represented in the Event Viewer. Windows Server 2003 includes a neat new feature. If you see an Internet URL in the Event Properties dialog box, you can click it to try to get some additional help through the Internet.

You can also try shutting down the server and rebooting it. If that doesn't fix things, try to start non-running Exchange processes manually. To do this, double-click on a service in the Services container (see Figure 8.12, shown earlier), and then click the Start button on the Properties dialog box that opens. Your Windows 2003 server will chug away for a bit, and then the service should start up—along with any other services that this service depends on.

Setting Up Microsoft Management Console for Exchange Server 2003

At this point, you need to set up the MMC on your Exchange server for Exchange Server 2003 management. You need to do this for two reasons. First, you want to be sure that your Exchange server's various components are capable of communicating with client processes. Second, to set permissions for the Exchange Server administration group (Exchange Admins) that you created a while back, you need the Exchange System Manager snap-in that you're about to add to MMC. If you need to, check out Chapter 7 for a review of MMC and adding snap-ins.

To ensure that you can do some of the tasks in the next sections, be sure that you're logged in to your domain on your Exchange server as Administrator. You can also add the snap-in while logged directly into your Exchange server as Administrator, but you won't be able to do many of the tasks in the next section.

To add the Exchange System Manager snap-in, select Add/Remove Snap-in from the MMC's File menu. Click Add on the Stand-alone page of the Add/Remove Snap-in dialog box. You'll see two Exchange-oriented snap-ins. We are going to work with just one of these; in later chapters, we'll talk about the other snap-in. Select the Exchange System snap-in from the Add Stand-alone Snap-in dialog box, and click Add.

Be sure that the option Any Writable Domain Controller is selected on the Change Domain Controller dialog box. Here you're selecting the domain controller to which any additions, deletions, or edits you make to your Exchange environment will be written. You might select a specific controller as opposed to any writable domain controller for a variety of reasons. For example, you might want to write to a controller that runs on a massively fault-tolerant computer to ensure that changes you make are very reliably entered into your domain's Active Directory. Or, you might want to pick a controller that is on the same local area network as the Exchange server you're managing. For now, any writable domain controller is a good choice. When you're done with the Change Domain Controller dialog box, click OK.

The snap-in should now show up in the Add/Remove Snap-in dialog box. Close the Add Stand-alone Snap-in dialog box by clicking Close, and then click OK in the Add/Remove Snap-in dialog box. At this point, your MMC should look something like the one in Figure 8.13.

The snap-in shows the Exchange organization created during Exchange 2003 installation. As you'll remember, during installation I named my organization Barry Gerber and Associates.

The Exchange System snap-in is the same as the System Manager on the Start ➢ All Programs ➢ Microsoft Exchange menu (see Figure 8.12, shown earlier). That's why I call the snap-in Exchange System Manager.

You've seen the Exchange System Manager in earlier chapters. Now you'll actually start using it. Just to get a feel for how it works, open the Exchange System Manager and then open the Servers container so that your MMC looks like the one in Figure 8.14. Exchange Server 5.5 users will be happy to see a somewhat familiar environment.

FIGURE 8.13
Microsoft Management Console with the Exchange System Manager snap-in installed

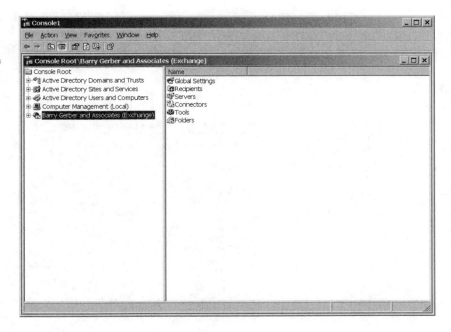

FIGURE 8.14
The Exchange System Manager snap-in open to reveal some of its subcontainers

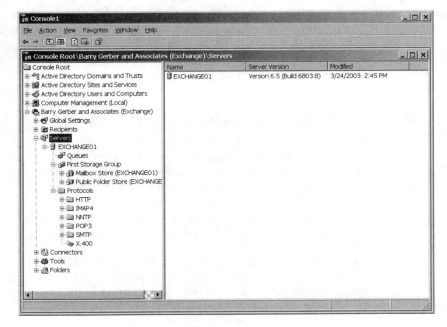

Just for fun, right-click your Exchange server (EXCHANGE01, in my case), and select Properties to open the Exchange Server Properties dialog box shown in Figure 8.15. Again, Exchange 5.5 users should find at least some of what they see on this dialog box familiar. I'll talk a lot more about what you see here in later chapters. For now, I just want to familiarize you with the Exchange System Manager snap-in. Go ahead and muck about a bit in the snap-in. Just be careful not to add or delete anything at this point, and be sure to close the Properties dialog box. I'll be waiting right here when you're done.

FIGURE 8.15

Right-click on an Exchange server in Exchange System Manager and select Properties to open the server's Properties dialog box.

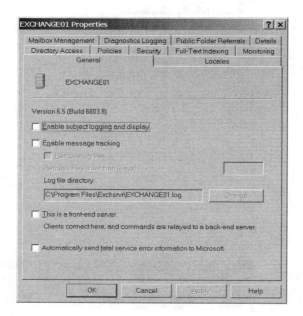

RUNNING EXCHANGE SYSTEM MANAGER REMOTELY

As long as you have the right security permissions, you can run Exchange System Manager and other Exchange-specific applications from any networked Windows 2000 workstation or server. You can also run the System Manager on any Windows 2003 server or Windows XP workstation. This is convenient because you won't have to keep running to an Exchange server to administer it. Remember, you do have to be logged in to the appropriate domain and have the correct permissions to run the System Manager.

You must install the Exchange System Management Tools on a computer in the Exchange server's domain or in a domain trusted by the server's domain. To install Exchange System Manager, run the Exchange Server 2003 Setup program on the computer from which you want to run Exchange System Manager. Select the Custom installation option, and select only the Microsoft Exchange System Management Tools for installation. When Exchange System Manager is installed, snap it into an MMC, and you're off and running. If you wanted to do the tasks in the next section on your domain controller, you would have to install the management tools on the domain controller.

Granting Permission for the Exchange Administration Group to Manage Exchange Server

Now you're ready to give members of your Exchange administration group, Exchange Admins, permissions to administer Exchange. You should be logged in to your domain on your Exchange server as Administrator. Assuming that you're still in Exchange System Manager in your MMC, right-click the Manager's root container and select Delegate Control. (My root container is called Barry Gerber and Associates [Exchange] in Figures 8.13 and 8.14, shown earlier.) This brings up the Exchange Administration Delegation Wizard.

Click Next to see the Users or Groups page of the wizard, shown in Figure 8.16. Click Add on the Users or Groups page to open the Delegate Control dialog box (see right side of Figure 8.16). Click the Browse button to find and select your Exchange Admins group. The Role field's drop-down list gives you a choice of three roles:

- Exchange View Only Administrator

- Exchange Administrator

- Exchange Full Administrator

As its name implies, View Only Administrator permits no editing of Exchange parameters. Exchange Administrator allows for viewing and editing of most Exchange parameters. Excluded are things such as the capability to change permissions. Exchange Full Administrator has complete control over the Exchange Server 2003 environment.

FIGURE 8.16

Granting the Exchange Admins group permissions to administer an Exchange Server 2003 organization

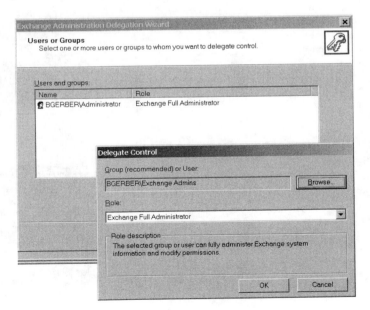

Select Exchange Full Administrator from the drop-down list, and click OK. Then click Next and then Finish on the last page of the Exchange Administration Delegation Wizard.

After the Wizard closes, you'll see a dialog box like the one in Figure 8.17, warning you that the users or groups to which you've delegated Exchange administrative privileges must also be members of the computer's local Administrators group. To do this, add the Local Users and Groups snap-in to your MMC and use it to add Exchange Admins to your Exchange server's local Administrators group (see Figure 8.18). If you've installed Exchange on a domain controller, there is no local administrators group. In this situation, Exchange Admins will still be able to do some Exchange management tasks. This alone is a good reason for not installing Exchange on a domain controller.

FIGURE 8.17
A warning to place newly created Exchange administrative users or groups in the Exchange server's local Administrators group

FIGURE 8.18
Adding the Exchange Admins group to the Exchange server's local Administrators group

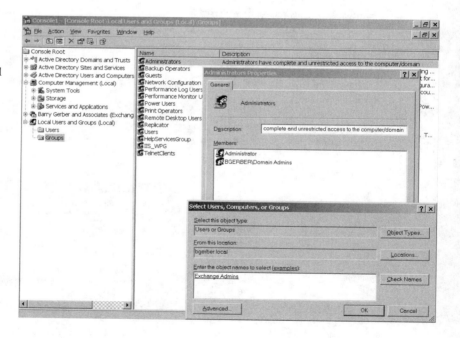

The permissions that you've delegated to Exchange Admins cascade down through all of the sub-containers under the Exchange System Manager root container for your Exchange Organization. This means that Exchange Admins have management rights in all the existing subcontainers and any new subcontainers you create.

Now, and don't forget to do this step, you must delegate certain permissions to your Exchange Admins group in the User subcontainer of the Active Directory Users and Computers container. Right-click the Users container and select Delegate Control. A wizard pops up. Use the Users or Groups wizard page to add Exchange Admins. Then on the next wizard page, Tasks to Delegate, select Create, Delete, and Manage User Accounts and finish out the wizard. If you do not do this, you won't be able to add mailboxes for users when you complete certain tasks later in this chapter.

You can go a step further and grant one or more other groups permissions in the certain subcontainers of the Exchange System Manager root container. In this way, you can assign rights to manage pieces of your Exchange Organization to different individuals or groups. This is especially useful when you begin creating Exchange administrative group subcontainers that contain pieces of your Exchange organizational hierarchy you want others to be able to manage. See Chapter 4 for more on administrative groups.

TIP *If you want to see the permissions that you've granted to the Exchange Admins group, right-click your Exchange server in the Exchange System Manager and select Properties. Tab over to the Security page and click the Exchange Admins group. The Permissions field shows the rights you've granted to Exchange Admins.*

NOTE *Remember, we've gone through all of this delegation of control stuff to allow a group and its members to administer various Exchange server-related functions. The domain Administrator account with the rights it has out of the Windows 2003 box can do all this without you granting it anything special. We created this group for security reasons, so that an Exchange administrator doesn't need to have total control of a Windows 2003 domain or forest.*

Now for the moment of truth: Log out of your Exchange server, and log back in to your domain on your Exchange server as the special Exchange Administrator account you created. (My account was named ExAdBGerber.) When you're logged in, set up an MMC with the following snap-ins:

◆ Active Directory Users and Computers

◆ Computer Management

◆ Exchange System Manager

If you've set up everything as I advised, including adding your ExAd account to the Exchange Admins account, you should be able to open Exchange System Manager without any error messages. You should also be able to add and then delete a new storage group by right-clicking your Exchange server container in the Exchange System Manager's Servers container. In Figure 8.19, I'm adding the new storage group. To delete the new storage group, right-click it and select Delete from the pop-up menu.

FIGURE 8.19
Adding a new storage group to an Exchange server using a Windows Server 2003 account that was added to a Windows Server 2003 security group and delegated authority to manage an Exchange Server 2003 organization

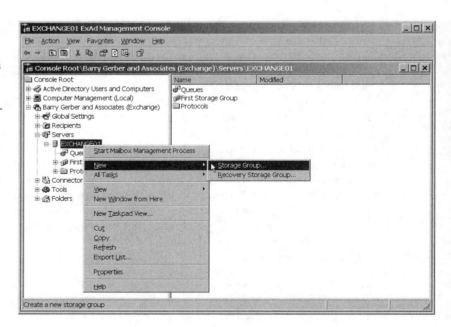

Mailbox-Enabling a Windows 2003 User

The next two chapters of this book deal with the Microsoft Outlook e-mail client. To use the client, you need an Exchange 2003 mailbox—or more correctly, you need to mailbox-enable your Windows 2003 user account. This is the account that you created back in Chapter 7. Mine is called bgerber.

To start, log in to your domain on your domain controller using your ExAd account. You can also use the domain Administrator account if you wish. Open your MMC, find your account in the \Active Directory Users and Computers\Users container, and right-click it. Then select Exchange Tasks from the pop-up menu.

This brings up the Exchange Task Wizard. Click Next to move to the Available Tasks page, shown in Figure 8.20. Be sure that Create Mailbox is selected, and click Next. The Create Mailbox page offers default options for the mailbox's alias and the Exchange server and mailbox store on the server where the mailbox will be created (see Figure 8.21). Accept the defaults. In later chapters, we'll play with other available options.

FIGURE 8.20
Choosing to create a new mailbox using the Exchange Task Wizard

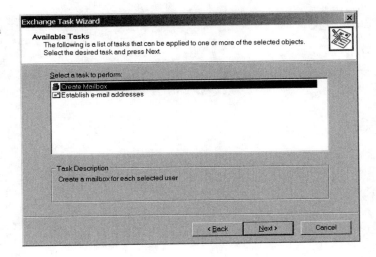

FIGURE 8.21
Accepting default options for a mailbox using the Exchange Task Wizard

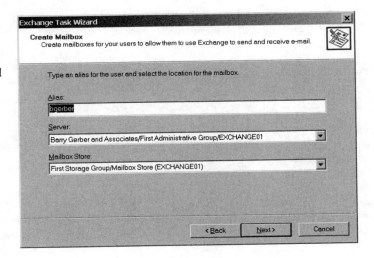

Click Next, and the Task in Progress page shows Exchange Server 2003's progress in creating the new mailbox. When the task has completed (see Figure 8.22), click Finish.

FIGURE 8.22
The Exchange Task Wizard has completed creation of a new mailbox.

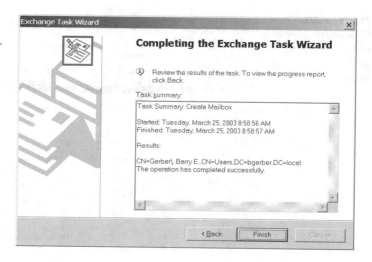

Next, right-click your account in `\Active Directory Users and Computer\Users` and select Properties from the pop-up menu. As Figure 8.23 shows, during creation of the new mailbox, several new Exchange-based pages were added to the Properties dialog box for the account. We'll delve into these new pages in great detail in later chapters.

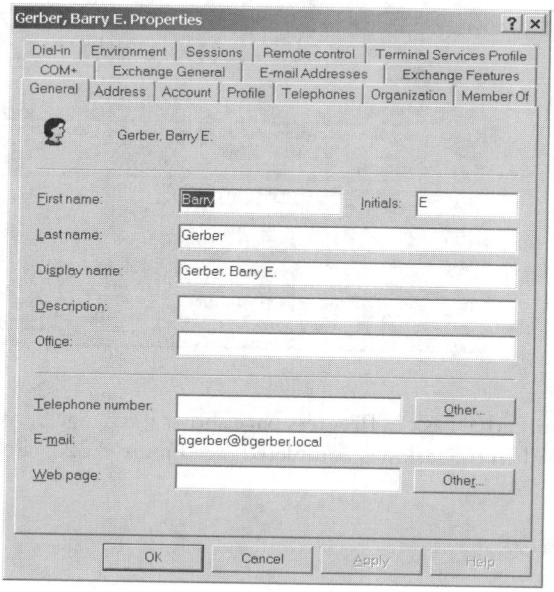

FIGURE 8.23
Several new Exchange-based property pages were added to the User Properties dialog box during mailbox creation.

By the way, notice the e-mail address I've been assigned, `bgerber@bgerber.local`. My real e-mail address will be `bgerber@bgerber.com`. Right now, Exchange doesn't know anything about that address. I'll show you how to change that in Chapter 13.

That's it. Your Exchange server is installed and ready to use. Now you need to set up a backup regimen for the server.

Backing Up Exchange Server 2003

Now, let's set up a backup for our Exchange Server 2003. We're going to use the Windows Server 2003 Backup application. When you install Exchange Server 2003, Exchange-based application program interfaces (APIs) are installed for backup. Windows Server 2003 Backup takes advantage of these APIs to let you access and properly back up your Exchange 2003 server.

I'm going to move through this pretty fast because I already discussed the Backup application in Chapter 7. To perform the backup:

1. Log in to your domain on your Exchange server as Administrator or to the server itself as Administrator.

2. Select Start ➢ All Programs ➢ Accessories ➢ System Tools ➢ Backup to run the Backup application. This brings up the Backup or Restore Wizard.

3. Click to the next wizard page called What to Back Up (see Figure 8.24).

4. Select Let Me Choose What to Back Up, and click Next.

5. On the Items to Back Up wizard page, select the Microsoft Information Store, as I have in Figure 8.25. You should also select the C: drive and System State under My Computer.

FIGURE 8.24

Telling the Windows Server 2003 Backup program to back up selected items using the Backup or Restore Wizard

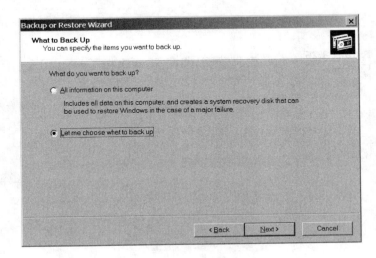

6. Click Next, and use the Backup Type, Destination, and Name page to set the correct parameters (see Figure 8.26). I'm backing up to disk. If you're backing up to tape, you'll see a page appropriate for tape backup.

7. To back up immediately, click Next on the Completing the Backup or Restore Wizard page (see Figure 8.27). You can also click Advanced to, among other things, schedule your backup. (Check out Chapter 7 for details on scheduling a backup and other advanced options.) I suggest you do a normal (full) backup of your Exchange server every time you back it up. It's much easier to restore a normal Exchange backup than an incremental or differential one.

FIGURE 8.25

Selecting Exchange components to be backed up by the Windows Server 2003 Backup program using the Backup or Restore Wizard

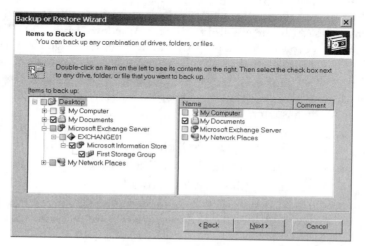

FIGURE 8.26

Confirming backup type, location, and name to be used by the Windows Server 2003 Backup program using the Backup or Restore Wizard

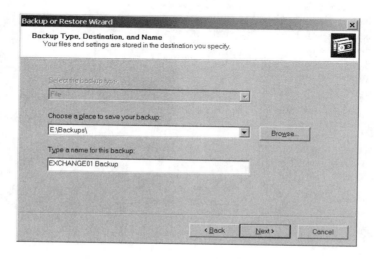

FIGURE 8.27

Using the Backup or Restore Wizard's Completing the Backup or Restore page to finish and start a backup, or to select advanced options, including backup job scheduling

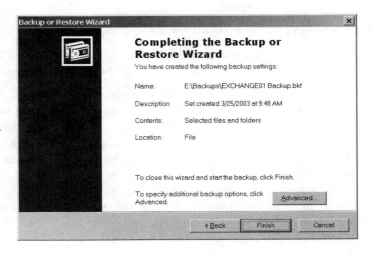

To see the logs for your backups, select Reports from the Backup program's Tools menu. Be sure to test your backups regularly to ensure that you can restore from them.

Any vendor can splice into the application-programming interface that Windows Server 2003 Backup uses when it does an online backup of the Exchange information store. A number of vendors have done just that, including Computer Associates (ARCserveIT; `www.cai.com`), LEGATO Systems (Legato NetWorker for Windows NT; `www.legato.com`), and Veritas Software (Backup Exec; `www.veritas.com`).

Third-party backup solutions add value beyond Windows Server 2003's own built-in backup program. For example, they can do the following:

◆ Let you easily and efficiently back up multiple servers and even other workstations on the network, including registry and system state information

◆ Support online Exchange Server backup as well as online backup of other application services such as Oracle or Microsoft SQL Server

◆ Make scheduling and monitoring the whole backup process very easy

◆ Send you e-mail containing information about the most recent backup

Summary

You must take care of a number of preliminaries before actually installing Exchange Server 2003. You need to set up and test your server hardware, including disk drives and tape backup system. Then you must install the correct version of Windows Server 2003 on a stand-alone server and ensure that it is capable of joining its domain.

After you have installed Windows 2003, you need to do some tasks before installing Exchange 2003:

◆ Ensure that security matters have been taken into account, including setting up any cross-domain trusts and establishing a security group to manage your soon-to-be Exchange server.

◆ Gather information that you will need when installing your Exchange server, including where on your server's disk drives you want to install Exchange, the Exchange components that you want to install, and the name that you want to use for your Exchange organization.

After all the preparation, Exchange server installation is a piece of cake. An installation wizard guides you through the process. The only thing that you might find a bit daunting is the long waits while certain steps in the process take place, such as Active Directory schema updating.

After Exchange Server 2003 is installed, you must check to ensure that Exchange services are running and that you can communicate with your server. To do this, you need to create a MMC and add basic plug-ins as well as the Exchange System Manager. With the System Manager installed, you can grant your Exchange security group permissions to manage your Exchange server and begin managing the server. One of your first Exchange management steps should be to add a new mailbox. Finally, you should be sure to set up backup for your Exchange server.

Now that you have a mailbox, it's time to use it. In the next couple of chapters, I'll introduce you to Microsoft's Outlook e-mail client. First I'll show you how to set up Outlook so that users can install it preconfigured from a centralized server. Then I'll spend some time helping you get familiar with Outlook from an end user's perspective.

Part 3

The Outlook Client

In this part:

Chapter 9

Installing Outlook 2003 from a Customized Server Image

EXCHANGE SERVER IS A PRETTY nifty little gadget. But without clients, it's nothing more than fancy technology. Although this is a book on Exchange Server, we need to spend a little time talking about the Outlook client. This and the next chapter are devoted to that discussion.

Exchange Server has been around for more than eight years. In that time, Microsoft has generated a slew of new and increasingly improved Exchange clients:

- Original DOS and Windows 3.x, 95, and NT clients that came with Exchange Server 4 and 5

- Exchange client for Macintosh

- Windows 95 and NT Outlook clients that came with Office 97

- Windows 95 and NT Outlook clients that came with Exchange Server 5.5

- Outlook 98 client

- Outlook 2000, 2002 (XP), and 2003 clients

- Outlook Web Access (web browser–based client)

In addition to these Exchange clients, which provide access to the full range of Exchange Server capabilities, Exchange Server also supports POP3 and IMAP4 clients from Microsoft and other vendors. I'll focus here on the current native Exchange Server client, Outlook 2003, and reserve discussion of the Outlook Web Access, POP3, and IMAP4 clients for Chapter 14, "Managing Exchange 2003 Services for Internet Clients."

TIP *Most of what I say about Outlook 2003 applies to Outlook 2000 and 2002. Both of these clients, as well as most of the older ones, can access an Exchange 2003 server. However, the methods for distributing Outlook from a central server that we look at in this chapter apply only to the Outlook 200x product line.*

In this chapter, we'll take an administrative perspective as we focus on the Outlook 2003 client for Windows that is part of the Office 2003 suite. First we'll tackle customizing Outlook 2003 for installation from a network server to user workstations. Then we'll install Outlook 2003 on an individual workstation using our custom server-based setup. If you need to install any of the older Exchange Server clients, check out the docs that come with the client that you need to install.

In the next chapter, we'll take a look at the Outlook 2003 client for Windows from the user's perspective. We'll take a quick tour of Outlook's menus to get comfortable with the impressive functionality that Microsoft has built into the client.

WARNING   *Office 2003 runs only on Windows 2000 or Window XP workstations. You can also run it on Windows 2000 and 2003 servers. Additionally, Office 2003 includes a load of applications from the familiar Word, Excel, and Outlook to new stuff such as OneNote and highly integrated SharePoint services. You can install one or more of these applications. If you're just interested in Outlook, you can use the directions I provide in this chapter to install only that piece of the Office 2003 suite.*

NOTE   *"Wait," you say, "setting up server-based installations isn't my thing. I want to get started using Outlook 2003 right away." If that's you, go ahead and install Office 2003 or just Outlook 2003 directly on your workstation. Pop in the Office 2003 CD-ROM, and follow the online installation instructions. You might want to take a look at the last section in this chapter, "Installing the Outlook 2003 Client on a Workstation," before you begin installation. When you're done, flip to Chapter 10, "A Quick Overview of Outlook 2003," for a look at Outlook 2003 in action.*

Featured in this chapter:

◆   Customizing Outlook 2003 for installation on user workstations

◆   Installing the Outlook 2003 client on a workstation

Customizing Outlook 2003 for Installation on User Workstations

If you've ever attempted to customize the installation of older Office products for Windows and you're still certifiably *sane*, you'll really appreciate the custom installation wizard for Office 2003 products such as Outlook 2003. Installations of pre–Office 2000 components used the infamous Acme Setup program. Bad old Acme required endless lines of text instructions to copy program files, set Windows registry entries, and do whatever else was required to get Office programs on a user's computer.

Office 2003 Windows installer technology places all the default data required to install each Office 2003 product in a relational database with the extension `.msi`, for Microsoft Installer. Data to uniquely customize an Office 2003 installation—data you create that overrides or adds to default settings—is stored in relational databases with the extension `.mst`, for Microsoft Transform. Not only are data in these files used to set up basic and custom installations, but they're also used to update and repair existing installations. You can even install apps or parts of apps so that they aren't actually placed on a user's hard disk until they are used for the first time.

All things considered, we IS types are the winners here. Customizing installations is easier and, to a fair extent, Office 2003 reduces day-to-day maintenance because it is self-healing in a variety of ways.

TIP *For more on Windows installer technology, take a look at* Microsoft Office 2003 Resource Kit *(Microsoft Press, 2003).*

In this chapter, we're going to focus on building the MST databases required to deliver customized versions of Outlook 2003 to a user's desktop. Then we'll manually run a customized installation of Office 2003 on a workstation. I'll leave it to you to deal with automatic delivery of the software to the user hard disks. There are several ways to accomplish this end:

◆ Automating the execution of the customized installation program through a batch file or an NT or Windows 2003 logon script

◆ Automating the customized installation using Microsoft's Systems Management Server (SMS) or other systems management tools such as LANDesk Software's LANDesk Management Suite (`www.landesksoftware.com`)

◆ Burning and running a CD-ROM or DVD that executes the customized installation program

The following approaches won't work with the method I'm discussing here, but they will also get Outlook installed on user workstations:

◆ Use Windows 2003's own Remote Installation Services (RIS) to install desktop operating-system software including Office 2003 or Outlook 2003. You can script an RIS installation, or you can install a hard disk image as with Norton Ghost.

◆ Use Norton Ghost (`www.symantec.com`) to create a hard-disk image of a model end-user drive with everything from the operating system to Outlook and other applications preinstalled, then automatically write the image to each new hard disk.

◆ Use WinINSTALL (`www.veritas.com`) to create an image of Office 2003 or Outlook 2003 and install it on user workstations.

◆ Use InstallShield Professional (`www.install.com`) to do a scripted installation of Office 2003 or Outlook 2003 and install it on user workstations.

Check the Office 2003 Resource Kit for more on these options.

Installing Office 2003 on an Administrative Installation Point

Before you can customize an Office 2003 installation, you first must install a copy of Office 2003 on a server. This copy of Office 2003 is installed on what is officially called an *administrative installation point.*

WARNING *You can complete the tasks in this and the next section only if you have an Office 2003 product ID obtained through a Microsoft Volume Licensing Agreement (VLA). If you don't have a VLA product ID, don't waste your time. The installation that I discuss in this chapter won't work.*

CREATING AN ADMINISTRATIVE INSTALLATION POINT

An administrative installation point is a shared folder on a Windows NT, 2000, or 2003 server or a Windows 2000 Professional or XP workstation. You can put an administrative installation point on your Exchange server for testing, but I suggest that you use another server in production mode. Office 2003 installations can eat up a lot of server resources, resources better dedicated to running Exchange Server.

In spite of my warnings to the contrary, for this chapter and the next one *only*, I'm going to install my administrative installation point on the Exchange server we set up in Chapter 8, "Installing Exchange Server 2003." So, I'll refer to the Windows 2003 operating system and its tools here.

You need about 500MB of free disk space to install Office 2003 on an installation point. So, don't move on to the next paragraph until you've located a disk drive with sufficient space.

We'll use Windows 2003's Windows Explorer (Start ➤ Windows Explorer) to set up our shared folder. First, click the location where you want your shared folder. Then, with your mouse pointer in Explorer's right pane, right-click and select New ➤ Folder. Name the folder Office or anything else you like.

To share your new folder, right-click it and select Sharing and Security from the pop-up menu. On the Sharing tab of the properties page, click Share This Folder and optionally enter something in the Description field. Next, click the Permissions button on the Properties dialog box. In the Permissions dialog box, ensure that the group Everyone has only Read permissions. Then add the Windows 2003 group Domain Admins (or whatever user or group will install software in this folder) and give it Full Control permissions (see Figure 9.1).

That's it! Now you can install Office 2003 on the administrative installation point.

FIGURE 9.1

Setting up a share for an administrative installation point

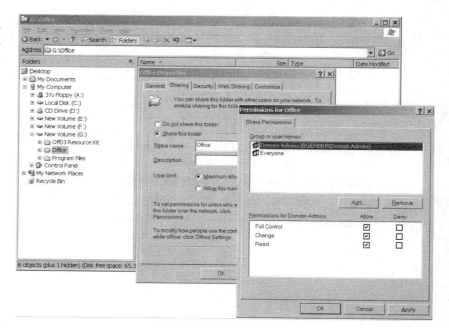

INSTALLING OFFICE 2003 ON AN ADMINISTRATIVE INSTALLATION POINT

Before we begin our installation, I need to make three points:

♦ I want to be sure you understand that we are not installing Office 2003 on this computer so that we can use it for word processing, e-mail, spreadsheets, and so on. We're installing it so that we can customize it and make it available for installation on the workstations of others.

♦ Although we will install all of Office 2003, if you purchase a separate copy of Outlook 2003, you can install it just as we are here.

♦ You must purchase a workstation license for each workstation on which one or more Office 2003 components will be installed. Check with Microsoft or a reseller for information on licensing plans and prices.

To install Office 2003 on an administrative installation point, follow these steps:

1. Put the CD-ROM labeled Office 2003 into the CD-ROM drive on the server where you want to do the installation.

2. Open a command prompt (Start ➢ Command Prompt).

3. At the command prompt, change to your CD-ROM's root directory, and type **setup.exe /a pro11.msi**. (At the time of this writing, Office 2003 was still in beta testing. The `.msi` file was named `pro11.msi` in the beta version. It might have a different name in the release version of Office 2003. The filename in Office 2000 was `data1.msi`.)

The file `pro11.msi` is the MSI database that comes with Office 2003. When you type the previous command, you're telling `setup.exe` to use this file for all the default Office 2003 application settings.

The installation wizard for Office 2003 starts up in administrative mode (see Figure 9.2). Enter the default organization name for all installations from this administrative installation point. This can be the same as or different from your Exchange Server organization name. Select the install location and enter the Product Key that you received with your copy of Office 2003 Enterprise Edition.

Click Next, read and agree to the license terms, and then click Install. Installation begins. When it is finished, you're ready to move on to the next section.

Customizing Outlook 2003

Before you can customize the installation of Office 2003 that you just placed on your new administrative installation point, you must install the Office 2003 Custom Installation Wizard. The wizard comes with the Office 2003 Resource Kit that I mentioned earlier in this chapter. To install the wizard and a whole bunch of other neat tools and docs, put the Office 2003 Resource Kit CD-ROM into your CD-ROM drive and track through the auto-run Resource Kit installation program.

GETTING STARTED WITH THE CUSTOM INSTALLATION WIZARD

When installation is finished, run the Custom Installation Wizard by choosing Start ➢ All Programs ➢ Microsoft Office ➢ Microsoft Office Tools ➢ Microsoft Office 2003 Resource Kit Tools ➢ Custom Installation Wizard. Whew! The wizard opens to the panel shown in Figure 9.3.

The wizard has lots of panels to guide you through customization of Office 2003. Let's take a look at key panels, especially as they relate to Outlook 2003. I assume that you can handle any panels that I don't discuss here without any input from me. If you have any questions, check out the Office 2003 Resource Kit or Microsoft's website (www.microsoft.com).

FIGURE 9.2

The installer for Office 2003 in administrative mode

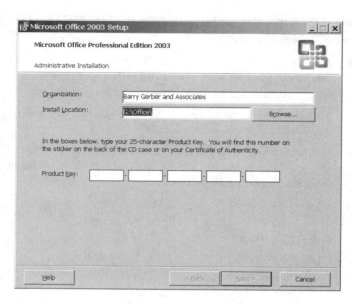

FIGURE 9.3

The first panel of the Microsoft Office 2003 Custom Installation Wizard

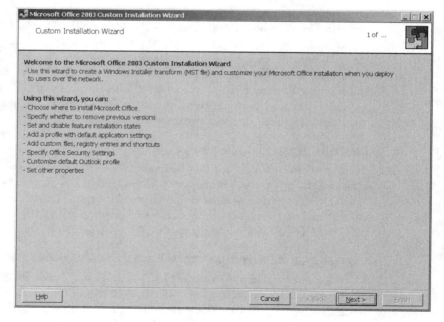

WARNING   You might not see all the Wizard panels that I discuss next. Whether a panel is displayed or not depends on the options you choose in previous panels. Also, if a panel is not displayed, subsequent panels might not have the same number as the ones I use. A quick check of the figures that accompany the following text should quickly orient you to a specific panel even if its number is different.

In the second panel of the wizard, you select the MSI file that holds the default settings for your Office 2003 installations. In Figure 9.4, I'm pointing the Custom Installation Wizard to the file `pro11.msi` on the administrative installation point where I just installed Office 2003.

FIGURE 9.4

Setting the default configuration file to be used during Office 2003 customization

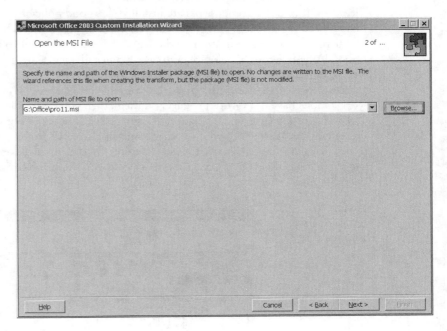

In the third panel, accept the default option Do Not Open an Existing MST File. Because you haven't yet customized the configuration for this administrative installation point, there are no MST files to open. You want to create a new MST file. If you were coming back to modify a custom configuration, you would select Open an Existing MST File and do your modifications using it as your starting point.

Use the fourth panel of the wizard to specify the name of the new MST file that you want to use for this customization session. You can accept the rather long default name or use a shorter one such as `CUSTOM01.MST`.

On the fifth wizard panel, you set the default directory to be used when Office 2003 applications are installed, for example, `D:\Program Files\Microsoft Office` or `<Program Files>\Microsoft Office`. `<Program Files>` tells the installer to put Office 2003 components into the first directory named Program Files that it encounters on a user's workstation. If users are likely to have multiple Program Files directories, and if you care which one Office 2003 apps are installed in, use the full path, including the hard disk drive letter, to force installation on a particular drive.

On the fifth wizard panel, you can also change the name of the organization for this custom installation. If you don't change the organization name, the one that you entered when you installed Office 2003 on your administrative installation point will be used. This is the place where you can specify organization names such as Accounting or Los Angeles Office.

The sixth wizard panel lets you choose which legacy Office applications should be removed when the new Office 2003 components are installed. It's good policy to remove all the old Office stuff before installing the latest and greatest Office apps. To do so, select Remove the Following Versions of Microsoft Office Applications and uncheck any that you want to keep. If you accept the default option Default Setup Behavior, the Office 2003 installer will ask the person doing the installation on a workstation if it should remove old Office applications if they exist on that workstation. If you want to do a silent installation with no queries from the installer and no input from a human, and if your workstations have old Office products on them, then you don't want the default here.

Panel 7 of the Custom Installation Wizard is full of neat options (see Figure 9.5). This is where you tell the installation program whether to install various Office 2003 features, and where and when to install them. You can choose to install features on users' hard disks or on network drives, or to run them from the CD-ROM. You also can decide if you want installation of all or some features to be deferred until a user first tries to run them.

FIGURE 9.5

Setting feature installation states

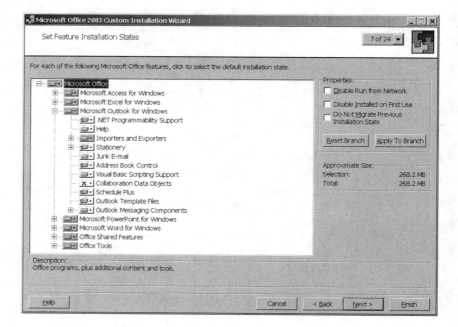

In Figure 9.6, you can see the various feature installation state options that you can choose from in panel 7. The Not Available option tells the installer not to install the feature at all. Any of these state options can be applied at any level in the feature list, including at the top level. If you choose the Not Available option for an entire Office 2003 application, that application won't be installed.

FIGURE 9.6

Feature installation state options

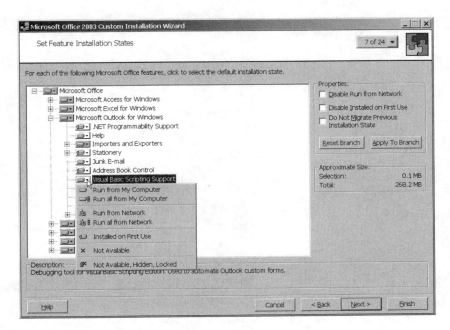

On the eighth panel of the Wizard, as shown in Figure 9.7, if you wish, you can enter product key information and accept the terms of the license for Office 2003. The product key will then be used when installing Office 2003 on workstations from the installation point. All of this makes the installation go more smoothly, especially if end users will be installing Office 2003 on their own workstations. You must, of course, have a product key that supports the number of installations you need. Contact Microsoft to purchase an appropriate product key. For the record, the product key shown in Figure 9.7 is not valid. Just want to keep us all honest.

CUSTOMIZING OUTLOOK 2003 WITH AN OPS FILE

The ninth wizard panel shown in Figure 9.8 is an important one. To understand this panel's function, you must understand how Office 2003 application installations are customized.

FIGURE 9.7
Entering product key information and accepting licensing terms for Office 2003 to make installation from an installation point quicker and easier

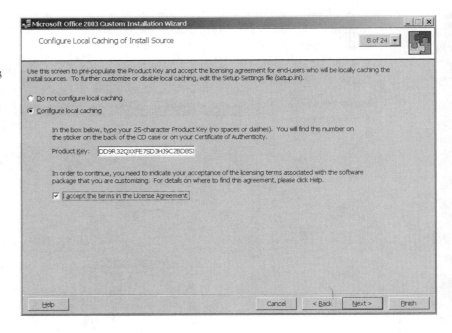

FIGURE 9.8
Selecting an Office application settings profile, which will be used to customize an Office 2003 installation

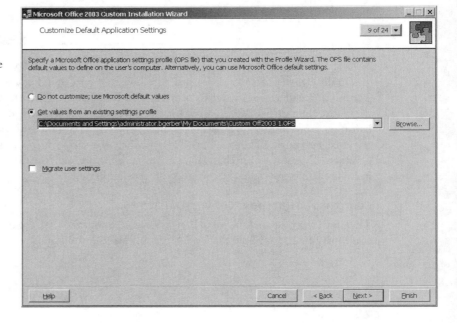

As you'll see in a bit, many important Outlook settings can be modified right in the Custom Installation Wizard. But there are other options that you can customize only using what is called an *Office 2003 profile*. Just to prevent a little confusion, these profiles have nothing to do with either Microsoft operating-system profiles, which simplify and control user access to Windows resources or Outlook profiles, which mostly point to the locations of various Exchange databases and local files used by Outlook. I discuss Outlook profiles later in this chapter when I talk about panel 17 of the Custom Installation Wizard. I'll also discuss Outlook profiles in the next chapter.

You customize all the major Office 2003 applications with a single profile file. To create a profile, you first install and run each Office 2003 application that you want to customize, changing its custom configuration settings to suit your needs. Then you run the Office 2003 Resource Kit's Office Profile Wizard on the same computer. This wizard processes your custom settings and creates an Office application settings profile file with the extension `.ops`. This file is then used by the installer to customize the settings for Office 2003 applications when they are installed on a user's workstation.

WARNING   *Oops! If you plan to use a customized OPS file, the file must exist in the directory you specify before you can use it here. If the file isn't there, you can click Next until the cows come home. Every time you do, you'll see a dialog box warning you that the specified OPS file doesn't exist. So, create your OPS file before getting into the Office 2003 Custom Installation Wizard.*

Let's walk quickly through this process, as it might be implemented for Outlook 2003. Let's say that, to reduce network traffic, you want to change the frequency with which Outlook checks the Exchange Server for new e-mail. You'd run Outlook on a workstation, bring up the Options menu, and change the mail-check frequency. Then you'd close Outlook and run the Profile Wizard to convert the custom configuration for that instance of Outlook 2003 into the OPS file format. Finally, you'd use the Profile Wizard to save the converted configuration into an OPS file, which then can be used to customize all installations of Outlook 2003.

The only pain in all this is that you have to install Outlook and other Office 2003 applications that you're interested in to generate a custom OPS profile. On the other hand, this is heaven compared to the hoops that you had to jump through to create and edit profiles for earlier Office products.

TIP   *The first time I ran the Profile Wizard, I forgot to note where the wizard stored the OPS file it had created. I spent a fair amount of time looking for the file and quietly cursing. The Profile Wizard shows the path where it saves each OPS file. Be sure to write down the path. The wizard saves OPS files in your personal folder. For Windows 2003, that's* `C:\Documents and Settings\`*WINDOWS2003_USERNAME*`\My Documents`, *where* WINDOWS2003_USERNAME *is the Windows Server 2003 account that you were logged in under when you ran the Profile Wizard. For NT, the OPS file is saved in* `C:\WINNT\ Profiles\`*<NT_USERNAME>*`\Personal`. *If you were logged in to your Windows 2003 domain at the time you created the OPS file, and if you also have logged in to the workstation on which you created the OPS file, the pre–Windows 2003 domain name will be appended to* WINDOWS2003_USERNAME. *So, if you logged in as Administrator to a domain called* `mydomain.local`, *the directory would be* `administrator.mydomain.local`.

Now back to the ninth Custom Installation Wizard panel. You use this panel, shown earlier in Figure 9.8, to specify whether you want to use default configuration profiles for the various Office 2003 applications or use a custom OPS file that you've created.

In Figure 9.8, I've chosen to use a custom OPS file that I created. Note that there is room here for only one OPS file. As I pointed out earlier, for a given installation, all the custom profile settings for Office 2003 applications that can be optimized using an OPS file must reside in one and only one OPS file. This file is incorporated right into the MST database file. This means that, unlike with older Office customization processes, you don't need to keep track of the location of separate profile files.

If you put a check mark in the Migrate User Settings box on panel 9 of the Custom Installation Wizard, the installer will retain each user's Office 97, 2000, or XP settings where they exist. This option is automatically disabled when you select Get Values from an Existing Settings Profile. That's because you'll likely want to leave the settings in your new OPS file in place and not replace them with older settings.

TIP You can control which applications and registry settings the Profile Wizard includes in an OPS file. To do so, edit the file `OPW11ADM.INI`*. This file can usually be found in* `\PROGRAM FILES\ORKTOOLS\TOOLS\PROFILE WIZARD`*. The INI file name I provide here is based on the Office 2003 Resource Kit Beta available at the time of this writing. It might have a different name by the time you see the Resource Kit.*

MORE OUTLOOK CUSTOMIZATION OPTIONS

Figure 9.9 shows the tenth panel in the Office 2003 Custom Installation Wizard. This panel is truly amazing. You can use panel 10 to set up a truckload of defaults for each of the Office 2003 applications. There's so much here, that I'm going to leave it to you to peruse panel 10 and set up what you need.

FIGURE 9.9
Viewing some of the options for changing default settings for an Office 2003 installation from an administrative installation point

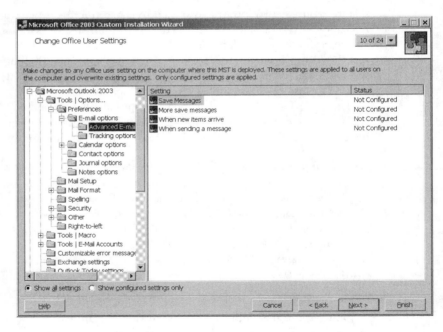

Let me show you one example. To set up a particular default, locate and click the folder it's stored in. Then double-click the item itself. Figure 9.10 shows the interface for setting up a bunch of defaults for what happens when a message is sent. To get to this interface, I double-clicked When Sending a Message in the right pane of Figure 9.9. In Figure 9.10, I've unchecked Delete Meeting

Request from Inbox When Responding. I hate it when I can't find evidence of a meeting being requested because the original request is deleted from my Inbox. And, I should note, this is not a trivial concern. Once I investigated a potential Exchange security violation relating to a meeting request. It sure would have been helpful to have the request as received by invitees to the meeting. For more about this investigation, see Chapter 18, "Exchange Server System Security."

FIGURE 9.10

Deselecting the deletion of Outlook meeting requests for an Office 2003 installation from an administrative installation point

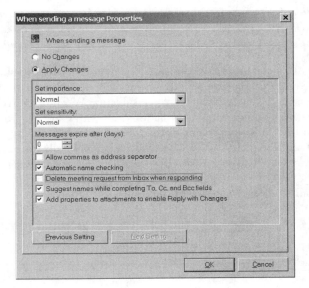

CONTINUING ON WITH THE CUSTOM INSTALLATION WIZARD

The next wizard panel, number 11, lets you request that non–Office 2003 files be added to or removed from a workstation while the regular Office 2003 application files are installed on the workstation. You could use this to install special templates or sample data files used in your organization, such as Word or Excel files. You use the next panel, panel 12, to add or remove registry entries during the Office 2003 installation. You might use this to modify a standard Office 2003 registry entry.

The thirteenth of the Custom Installation Wizard's panels lets you specify which Office 2003 program icon shortcuts are displayed on the user's workstation. In panel 14, you can create a list of all servers that have a share with a copy of the administrative installation point and its contents. Users can then install from any of these installation points. One of these alternative servers is used when the original installation server is not available and a workstation needs to repair itself, access Office 2003 files set to run from a server, or install new software set for installation on first use.

Use wizard panel 15 to customize Office 2003 security settings. Here you can add digital certificates to a list of trusted software publishers. You can also set security levels, from low to medium to high, for the running of macros. You can establish different settings for each Office 2003 product. By default, these settings aren't configured. You should set at least a medium level, unless virus software that deals with macros is running on servers and workstations. You can also use the fifteenth wizard panel to set an Office 2003–wide security level for potentially unsafe Active-X controls. I suggest setting this option to prompt the user before running an unsafe control.

TIP *You can modify Outlook security even further using the Outlook Administrator Pack that comes with the Office 2003 Resource Kit. The pack includes a template that you can set up in an Exchange 2003 public folder. You can then use that public folder to increase or reduce security settings such as how e-mail attachments are dealt with. Outlook checks the public folder each time a user logs on to the Exchange server. Modified security settings are applied to the user's Outlook-Exchange sessions until you use the template to change the settings. Some users find the default Outlook security limits exasperating. The Outlook Administrator Pack helps you alleviate some of that exasperation.*

On panel 16, you can specify other installations or programs that should run with the installation of Office 2003 on a workstation. You have a wide range of options as to when the programs should be run.

The seventeenth Office 2003 Custom Installation Wizard panel is just for Outlook. This is where you set the manner in which the installation deals with Outlook profiles, which are stored in text-based PRF files. Outlook profiles point the user to an Exchange Server, set the mailbox to be accessed, and specify additional files, such as a local mailbox and locally stored personal folders. As you can see in Figure 9.11, you have four basic options. You can use whatever profile exists on the user's workstation at the time of installation. If you don't need to make changes to profiles, this should work just fine, especially for newer versions of Outlook.

FIGURE 9.11
Choosing how Outlook profiles will be handled during installation of Office 2003 from an administrative installation point

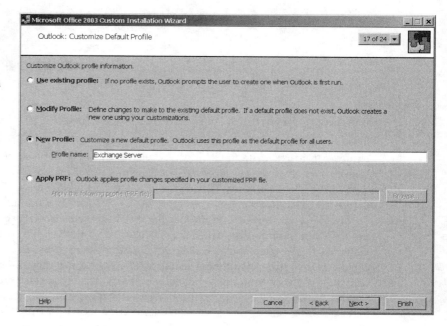

If a user's existing default profile, the one used when Outlook runs, is pretty much okay except for some modifications, the second option on panel 17 lets you specify changes to be applied to the profile. If you select this option, you'll see a set of customized Wizard pages you can use to specify the changes you want. If there is no profile on the user's computer, the user will be prompted to create a profile. Be careful here. You don't want users who don't know what they're doing to create profiles.

To create a new profile, choose the third option. As with the second option, the wizard will display a set of customized pages for creating a new profile. If a user already has profiles on their computer, they are not deleted. The new profile is simply added to the existing profiles and becomes the default profile.

The fourth option on panel 17 is to use an existing PRF file. If the file was created for Outlook 2003, it can include both MAPI and Internet mail options. If the file was created for Outlook 2002 and earlier, you can only use the part that applies to MAPI mail options.

As Figure 9.11 indicates, I'm going to create a new profile for this Office 2003 installation. Figure 9.12 shows wizard panel 18. I've chosen to configure an Exchange Server connection.

FIGURE 9.12

Entering Exchange Server information to be used when Office 2003 is installed from an administrative installation point

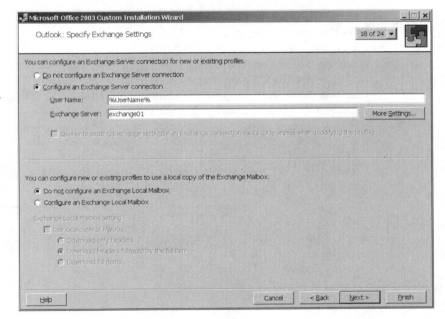

The wizard automatically enters *%USERNAME%* in the User Name field (see Figure 9.12). In the NT, 2000/2003, and XP operating systems, *USERNAME* is a system environment variable that contains a user's NT/2000/2003 username, which is what you type in before your password to log in to your NT/2000/2003 account on a workstation. By default, the username is also the name of each user's mailbox.

So, if I'm installing Office 2003 on my workstation and I'm logged in to my domain as bgerber, then the variable *USERNAME* on my workstation is set to *bgerber*. And, *bgerber* is inserted in the Outlook profile created for me while Office 2003 is installed on my workstation. This is a very simple way to set up a profile so that it opens the correct user mailbox.

Why the percent signs in *%USERNAME%*? When an environment variable is used as a variable in a program, it is prefixed and suffixed with a percent sign.

As shown earlier in Figure 9.12, I entered the name of my Exchange server, *exchange01*, in the Exchange Server field on the eighteenth wizard page. "Wait!" I can hear you saying, "Does that mean I have to create a whole Office 2003 installation for every Exchange server I set up in an Exchange organization?" The good news is that the answer is no. The even better news is that any Exchange server in an organization can redirect Outlook to the correct server for the specified mailbox. Not only that, but the server name is changed in the user's Outlook profile the first time Outlook is redirected.

As you can see back in Figure 9.12, you can also specify whether a local mailbox should be created on the user's workstation. Local mailboxes and mailboxes on Exchange servers can synchronize with each other. This is especially useful when a user's workstation is not connected to the Exchange server, either by design with a laptop or by chance as with a network outage.

Figure 9.13 shows wizard panel 19. You use this page to add other e-mail-related services (called "accounts" on the panel) to an Outlook profile. You select the accounts to be installed with Outlook from the Add Account dialog box shown in Figure 9.13. You can add POP3 and/or IMAP Internet mail access. Old Outlook hands will cheer the addition of IMAP to Outlook 2003. I'll talk much more about POP3 and IMAP in Chapter 14. HTTP supports the connection of Outlook 2003 clients to an Exchange 2003 server over the Internet using the HTTP protocol. This feature is new to Exchange 2003 and is discussed in Chapter 16, "Advanced Exchange Server Administration and Management." Personal folders live outside of Exchange mailboxes on local or networked drives. Outlook Address Books hold Outlook Contacts. They are stored in Exchange mailboxes. Personal Address Books perform a similar function, but are stored locally.

FIGURE 9.13

Selecting additional e-mail accounts to be installed when Office 2003 is installed from an administrative installation point

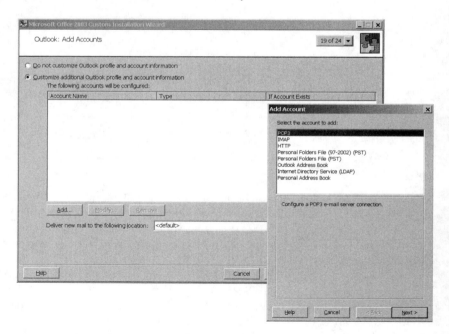

The Microsoft LDAP Directory service is neat. As you'll learn in Chapter 14, the Lightweight Directory Access Protocol (LDAP) is a way to access information about e-mail addresses and such from servers anywhere on the Internet. Windows Server 2003 supports LDAP for lookup of Exchange Server 2003 recipients, but this service is more about LDAP on other Internet-based servers. A bunch of these servers just sit out there collecting names, e-mail addresses, and so on. When you search for an e-mail address by a person's name, your Outlook client firsts looks locally at your contacts and at addresses on your Exchange servers. If it doesn't find the name there, it goes out to one of the big LDAP servers in the sky. Amazingly, it often finds the name that you're looking for. Unless your corporate policy runs contrary to this sort of stuff, do include the LDAP service in your Outlook installations.

WARNING   *If you select a mail service, be sure to configure it by clicking it in the Add Account dialog box and clicking Next in the same dialog box (see Figure 9.13, shown earlier). If you don't, your users will be asked all kinds of confusing questions about parameters for any unconfigured mail services when they start up Outlook 2003 for the first time. Of course, if you have knowledgeable users or plan to provide training or cheat-sheets, you can ignore this warning.*

You use wizard panel 20, shown in Figure 9.14, to export your Outlook profile settings to a PRF file. You can then edit this file using a standard text editor and apply it using option four on wizard panel 17 (see Figure 9.11, shown earlier).

If, during the installation of Office 2003, you need to force a conversion of an older Outlook Personal Address Book to an Outlook Address Book, you can do so on the twenty-first wizard panel, shown in Figure 9.15. You can also use panel 21 to modify defaults for the editor used in Outlook (Microsoft Word or Outlook's built-in editor) and for mail format settings (HTML, rich text, and plain text).

FIGURE 9.14

Choosing to export Outlook settings to a profile settings file

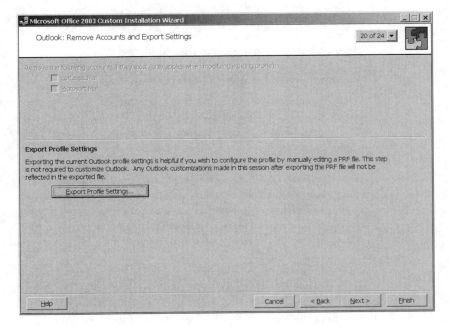

FIGURE 9.15
Selecting address book upgrade and default editor and e-mail format settings for installation of Office 2003 from an administrative installation point

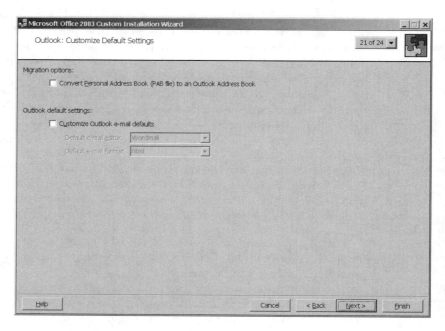

You use panel 22, shown next in Figure 9.16, to set up offline folder synchronization. If you requested that a local mailbox be created on an earlier wizard panel, then you can set up some of the parameters for synchronization here. I cover Exchange folder synchronization in the next chapter. So I'll simply call your attention to this option here.

FINISHING WITH THE CUSTOM INSTALLATION WIZARD

Wizard panel 23 is used to modify setup parameters. At least from an Outlook perspective, you shouldn't need to do anything on this panel. Panel 24 is the final panel. Click Finish to save your MST file to the root of your administrative installation point. After the MST file has been created, you'll see the informational dialog box shown in Figure 9.17. Exit that dialog box and you're done.

Notice in Figure 9.17 the suggested arguments for running a customized installation from a command line using SETUP.EXE in the root of my administrative installation point, G:\OFFICE. You could ask your users to enter such a command at a command prompt or by using the Run option on the Start menu. I can hear you saying, "No way! I'm not sure how often I'd get that line of gibberish straight and I'm sure not going to ask my end users to deal with that chunk of gobbledygook." Rest easy, there are other options.

You can set up a batch file to automate the installation or you can use a file called SETUP.INI. When a user runs SETUP.EXE by opening or double-clicking it, SETUP.INI, which must be located in the root of your administrative installation point, can provide a range of functionality, including command-line arguments for SETUP.EXE. I trust that you can create a Windows batch file. So, I'll concentrate here on SETUP.INI.

If you can't find a copy of SETUP.INI in your administrative installation point root folder, there should be one in a subfolder. Try \OFFICE\FILES\SETUP. Copy this file to your administrative installation point root. Remember that mine is G:\OFFICE.

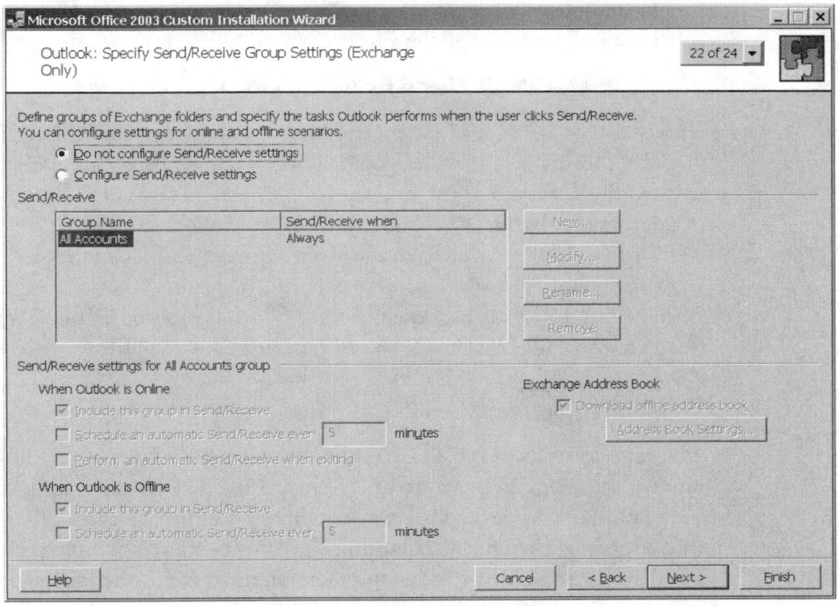

FIGURE 9.16
Setting up Exchange
Server offline folder
synchronization for
installation of
Office 2003 from
an administrative
installation point

FIGURE 9.17
A final dialog box
indicates that the
creation of an MST
file for a custom
installation of
Office 2003 has
been completed
and offers
information on
use of the file.

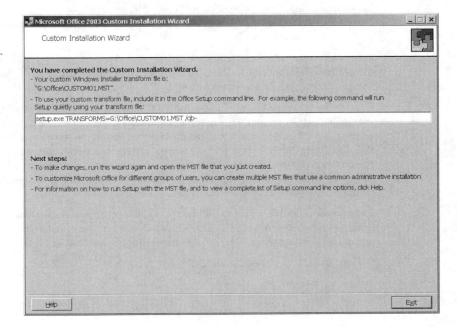

Double-click SETUP.INI to open it in Window's Notepad app. Add a line like the one that follows to the [MST] section of the file:

```
MST1=\EXCHANGE01\OFFICE\custom01.mst
```

This tells the SETUP.EXE program to use the database CUSTOM01.MST located on my Exchange server EXCHANGE01 in the share OFFICE when it installs Office 2003 from this administrative installation point. Remember, I shared the folder G:\OFFICE as OFFICE earlier in this chapter. Oh yes, if there is a comment character (a semicolon) in front of [MST] in SETUP.INI, be sure to remove it, or your MST file won't be included in the installation and all your work will be for naught. Guess whose work went for naught for quite some time until he figured that one out?

You can do lots more to enhance the installation of Office 2003. For example, you can add the following to the [DISPLAY] section your SETUP.INI file:

```
Display=None
Completion Notice=Yes
```

The first line tells SETUP.EXE to run without displaying anything unless for some unusual reason user input is required. The second line allows SETUP.EXE to speak up just once, when it has completed the installation of Office 2003. These two lines result in a quiet installation that informs a user that all went well or poorly when the installation completes. Setting Completion Notice to No results in a totally silent installation. Be sure to remove the semicolons in front of Display and Completion Notice.

WATCH THOSE *SETUP.EXE* COMMAND-LINE ARGUMENTS

Let's say you can't or don't want to use SETUP.INI and a simple entry that eliminates drive letters and the complications they bring such as MST1=\EXCHANGE01\OFFICE\custom01.mst. The following information and cautions should save you some grief as you design your batch file.

First, some information: Look again at the command line suggested earlier in Figure 9.16. TRANSFORMS= G:\OFFICE\CUSTOM01.MST points SETUP.EXE to your MST file. /gb- works something like Display= None and Completion Notice=Yes.

Now for the cautions: You might be tempted to create a batch file on the administrative installation point that includes the command in Figure 9.17 and have users run it to install Office 2003. If this command is run on the workstation where you installed Office 2003 on the administrative installation point, all will be fine. G: directs the workstation to the correct path for the installation point. However, if this command is run on any other workstation, it won't work, unless the net use command is run before SETUP.EXE in the same batch file to map the drive letter G to the share containing the administrative installation point, which is \EXCHANGE01\OFFICE in my case.

The next command in the batch file after the net use command should be G: to ensure that the workstation is on the right drive to run SETUP.EXE. If you do map the drive before running SETUP.EXE, remember to unmap the drive letter after SETUP.EXE runs using the net use /delete option. Here's an example:

```
net use J: \EXCHANGE01\OFFICE

J:

setup.exe TRANSFORMS=J:\Office\custom01.MST /gb-

net use J: /delete
```

If you're not sure about the syntax for the net use command, just type **net use /?** at the command prompt.

Installing the Outlook 2003 Client on a Workstation

First, let me offer a bit of advice on where to install Outlook. Remember, from this point forward and all through Chapter 10, you're trying to replicate an end user's experience with Outlook. So, install the product in a typical end-user environment. Install Outlook on a Windows 2000 Professional or XP Professional workstation, not on a Windows 2003 domain controller, a Windows 2003 stand-alone server, or an Exchange 2003 server. To install on the latter three systems, you'll need to mess too much with user permissions and will deviate too much from a standard user's experience.

USERS NEED SPECIAL PERMISSIONS TO INSTALL OFFICE 2003 ON WINDOWS 2000 OR XP WORKSTATIONS

You must grant permission to an ordinary user to install Office 2003 on a Windows XP workstation. You do this by making the user a member of the workstation's Administrators group. To do so, follow these steps:

1. Select Start ➢ Control Panel ➢ User Accounts.

2. Tab over to the Advanced page of the User Accounts dialog box and click Advanced.

3. In the Local Users and Groups window that opens, click Groups.

4. Double-click the Administrators group and click Add.

5. Be sure your domain is displayed in the From This Location field in the Select Users and Groups dialog box. Select the user.

You can accomplish the same end slightly differently by creating a Windows security group, adding users who need to install software on their computers to the group, and adding the group, not a specific user, to the Administrators group. The difference here is that anyone who belongs to the group has Administrators rights to every computer where the group has been granted permissions. This can be good or bad, depending on who should have what amount of control on which workstation.

Okay, now let's start installing Outlook. From your workstation, log in to your Windows 2003 domain using the personal account that you created back in Chapter 7, "Installing Windows 2003 Server as a Domain Controller." My account is named bgerber. From a workstation that doesn't have Office 2003 installed on it, open Windows 2000's or XP's My Computer. Find and open Network Neighborhood inside My Computer. Then find the server with your Office 2003 administrative installation point, and click the installation point, in my case, \EXCHANGE01\OFFICE. Find SETUP.EXE and double-click it.

The setup wizard starts, gives you a few installation options, and begins installation. When the installation is done, your computer will reboot, your system settings will be updated, and Office 2003 installation will run to completion.

At this point, Office 2003 is in place, and Outlook 2003 and any of the other Office 2003 components that you installed should run like a charm with little or no intervention on your part. We'll actually run Outlook 2003 for the first time in the next chapter.

That's it for workstation installation. Not much, huh? That's because of all the work you did preparing everything with the Custom Installation Wizard.

Updating a Custom Installation

Suppose you need to change installations on workstations where Office 2003 has already been installed from an administrative installation point? No problem. Microsoft provides a version of the Office 2003 Custom Installation Wizard that lets you revise existing workstation installations. It's called the Office 2003 Custom Maintenance Wizard. The wizard, which is also part of the Office 2003 Resource Kit, features most of the panels from the Custom Installation Wizard. These are the panels where post–Office 2003 workstation installation revisions make sense.

The Custom Maintenance Wizard creates a file that contains modification information. The file has a `.cmw` extension. To install revisions on workstations, you must first copy the file `MAINTWIZ.EXE` to the root of your administrative installation point. Then, on each workstation that is to be updated, you run `MAINTWIZ.EXE` with an appropriately modified version of the command-line argument suggested on the final panel of the Custom Maintenance Wizard. You can do this in a batch file that is called from a login script, or you can ask the user to click on the batch file to run it.

Summary

Installing Office 2003 (or only Outlook 2003) on a server for others to install is a fairly complex process. First you need to install the product on an administrative installation point on a server. Then you customize your Office 2003 programs using the Office 2003 Custom Installation Wizard that comes in the Microsoft Office 2003 Resource Kit. The Custom Installation Wizard allows for a fair amount of customization, including setting a default Exchange server and a variable that specifies a unique user account for first and subsequent logins to Exchange server.

You might not be able to do all the customization that you need with the Custom Installation Wizard. You can further customize your Office 2003 installation by creating an Office 2003 profile and then converting that profile into an OPS file. You create the profile by accessing a copy of Outlook 2003 (or any other Office 2003 application) on a workstation. After you've modified such attributes as the frequency Outlook 2003 checks for e-mail messages, you use the Office 2003 Resource Kit's Office Profile Wizard to create the OPS file.

When the Custom Installation Wizard finishes, it creates an MST file in the root folder of your administrative installation point. This file contains all of the customization parameters you set using the wizard.

After you've customized the copy of Outlook or all of Office 2003 on your administrative installation point, installation on any workstation can be a piece of cake. You can set up a special `SETUP.INI` file that provides command-line arguments to Office 2003's `SETUP.EXE`. In this case, all users need to do to install Office 2003 as you've configured it is double-click `SETUP.EXE` in the root folder of your administrative installation point. You can also set up a batch file that runs `SETUP.EXE` with command-line arguments. In this case, users need click only on the batch file to install Office 2003 as you've configured it.

Now we're ready to explore Outlook 2003. If you will, please join me in the next chapter.

Chapter 10

A Quick Overview of Outlook 2003

BECAUSE THE FOCUS OF this book is on Exchange Server 2003, I really don't have a lot of space for the client side of things. My goal here is to provide you with enough information to use Outlook 2003 in your explorations of Exchange Server 2003 from this point forward. For lots more on Outlook, see *Mastering Microsoft Office 2003 for Business Professionals,* by Gini Courter and Annette Marquis (Sybex, 2003).

In spite of the limited text that we can devote to Outlook 2003, we're still going to cover quite a bit of territory in this chapter. We'll set up a new Outlook 2003 client, send and receive a message, continue the exploration of Outlook profiles that we began in the last chapter, create a new public folder, and take a quick tour of some Outlook 2003 menus. That's quite a handful, so let's get started.

Featured in this chapter:

- ◆ Starting up and modifying a newly installed client

- ◆ Sending and receiving a message with an Outlook 2003 client

- ◆ Outlook profiles continued

- ◆ Creating a new public folder

- ◆ Using Outlook 2003's e-mail menus

BEFORE WE BEGIN...

As you go through this chapter, remember that this is exactly the experience that an end user will have when starting and using Outlook 2003 for the first time. Thinking like a nontechnical user will help you come up with ideas for special instructions or other help that you might want to give your users. As will become more obvious as you move through the rest of this chapter, it's much easier on your users if you do some of the preliminary setup work that I discussed in the last chapter.

I'm assuming that you'll use the Windows 2003 account that you created for yourself. If you expect to have new users who will log in to their Windows 2003 accounts for the first time to set up and use their Outlook clients, you need to provide each user with whatever password information they need to log in. This will depend on the options that you select when creating each account.As of this writing, only a later beta version of Outlook 2003 was available. So things may look different in the release version of the product.

Starting Up and Modifying a Newly Installed Client

In the last chapter, you installed Outlook 2003 on an administrative installation point and then installed a customized copy of Outlook 2003 on a workstation from the installation point. Now you're ready to use Outlook.

Log in to your Windows 2003 domain using the personal account that you created back in Chapter 7, "Installing Windows Server 2003 as a Domain Controller." Mine is bgerber. When you're logged in, to start Outlook 2003, find the desktop icon labeled Microsoft Outlook and double-click it. The Outlook 2003 client should open right up in your Exchange mailbox if you did the following:

◆ Mailbox-enabled your personal Windows 2003 user account back in Chapter 8, "Installing Exchange Server 2003"

◆ Installed the Outlook client on a workstation while logged in as yourself, as per my instructions at the end of Chapter 9, "Installing Outlook 2003 from a Customized Server Image"

◆ Are now logged in to your Windows 2003 domain on your workstation using the personal account that you created in Chapter 7

◆ Modified your Outlook client as I suggested in Chapter 9

If things don't seem to be working as advertised, welcome to the club. It took me several iterations of the installation customization steps in Chapter 9 to get Outlook to behave as I expected it to.

This is Square One. (Square One? Don't ask; you'll understand in a bit.) Check to make sure that your custom MST file is indeed in the shared directory that is your administrative installation point. If it's not there, then either you saved it somewhere else while running the Custom Installation Wizard or the wizard never saved it. If the file is missing, you can look for it with Windows Explorer or just rerun the wizard and create a new MST file. Be sure to save the file in your administrative installation point.

If your MST file is there, rerun the wizard, open the MST file, and check to make sure that all the custom settings you set up are there. If anything is missing, add it back and save the changed MST file.

When you're sure about your MST file, run SETUP.EXE from your administrative installation point, and choose to remove Office 2003 from your workstation. After everything is removed, run SETUP.EXE again and reinstall Office 2003. If all is well, Outlook 2003 should act as indicated. If not—you guessed it—back to Square One. All I can say is, given the time that it takes to uninstall, reboot, and reinstall Office 2003, you'll find that patience is a real virtue as you work the kinks out of your custom installation.

Okay, your Outlook 2003 client is finally up and running. If you haven't handled activation some other way, you'll be asked if you want to activate Office 2003 via the Internet or by phone. Make your choice and move on.

By default, Outlook 2003 stores incoming mail in a personal folder, if one is available, rather than in your Exchange mailbox. If you requested installation of a personal folder in Chapter 9 or you manually installed Outlook, you should see something like the image in Figure 10.1. You might also see a small floating bar for voice and handwriting input. I'm not hot about the idea of delivering mail into local personal folders. Though you save server disk space and assure users that they can use Outlook when they can't connect to their Exchange server and must work offline, the risk of losing mail is too high. In a bit, I'll show you a much safer way to deal with offline access.

If you need to set up Outlook so that incoming mail is stored in your Exchange mailbox:

1. Select Tools ➤ E-mail Accounts from Outlook 2003's main window. This opens the E-mail Accounts Wizard.

2. Click View or Change Existing E-mail Accounts on the wizard's main page.

3. On the next wizard page, select your Exchange mailbox from the drop-down list labeled Deliver New E-mail to the Following Location and click Finish.

4. Click OK on the dialog box that follows; exit from Outlook and reopen it. Notice that your mailbox is now the first object in the All Mail Folders folder.

FIGURE 10.1

The Outlook 2003 client immediately after installation

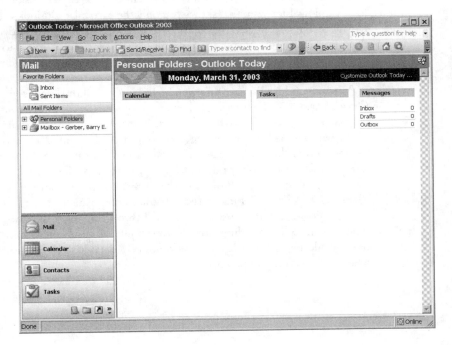

If you want to get rid of the Personal Folders object:

1. Close Outlook, then right-click the Outlook icon on your desktop and select Properties.
2. Click Show Profiles. Select your Outlook profile and click Properties.
3. Click Data Files, select Personal Folders on the Outlook Data Files dialog box, and click Remove.
4. OK your way out of the dialog boxes and reopen Outlook. You should now see only your Exchange mailbox in the All Mail Folders folder.

Finally, here's how to assure that your Exchange mailbox is replicated on your computer so that you can access your e-mail if you're unable to connect to your Exchange server:

1. Select Tools ➢ E-mail Accounts from the Outlook main window.
2. Select View or Change Existing E-mail Accounts and click Next.
3. On the E-mail Accounts wizard page, click Change and ensure that Use Local Copy of Mailbox is checked.
4. Navigate out of the dialog boxes you just opened. Your Exchange mailbox will be replicated on your computer.

If you've used versions of Outlook prior to the 2003 flavor, you might find the current user interface a bit confusing. For example, if you click open your Exchange mailbox, all you see are folders relating to mail. Your calendar, contacts, tasks, and so on aren't in the tree. As you can see in Figure 10.1, shown earlier, one way to get to these folders is by clicking the large icons in the bottom left pane of the Outlook window. However, that shows you only the particular Outlook folder. If you want to see a folder tree more reminiscent of earlier Outlook products, click the large Folder List icon in the bottom left of the Outlook window. If you don't see this icon, click the small folder icon way down at the bottom left of the Outlook window. Now you should see something like the folder list from earlier versions of Outlook.

With the folder list showing, you really don't need the large icons on the bottom left side of the Outlook window. To get rid of them, move your mouse pointer over the little dots just above the large icons and hold down the left mouse button. Then, drag the sizing bar down toward the bottom of the window. While you're dragging, notice that the number of large icons you can see depends on the location of the sizing bar and that, when a large icon disappears, a smaller version appears on the left side of the Outlook window at the very bottom of the screen.

I need for you to set Outlook so that it displays the Advanced toolbar. To do so, select View ➢ Toolbars ➢ Advanced. Finally, turn off the reading pane by choosing View ➢ Reading Pane ➢ Off.

I'm going to use the setup in Figure 10.2 throughout the rest of this chapter. I'm comfortable with it and, as an Exchange administrator, you should be quite comfortable with it too. If you think your users would fare better with the Outlook 2003 default setup or another setup, be my guest and use whatever interface you prefer.

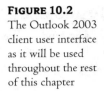

FIGURE 10.2
The Outlook 2003 client user interface as it will be used throughout the rest of this chapter

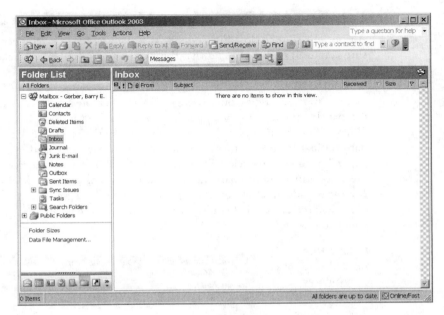

Now you should be able to see all seven of the client's default column titles. These include the following:

Envelope with arrow   Sort by header status

Exclamation mark   Message importance

Sheet of paper   Type of message

Paperclip   Message attachments

From   Who sent the message

Subject   What the sender says the message is about

Received   The date and time that the message was received by the Exchange Server

Size   Size of message in bytes

Flag   Status of messages marked for follow-up

Outlook remembers the window size that you've set when you exit. Every time you run the client, the window will be set to that size. In the setup that we've chosen to use, Outlook is divided into two resizable panes. The left pane, Folder List, shows mailboxes and public and personal folders in a hierarchical arrangement (see Figure 10.2, shown earlier). The right pane, the message items pane, displays the messages contained in the folder that has been selected in the folder list.

Sending and Receiving a Message with an Outlook 2003 Client

Alright, it's time to do a little e-mail. We're going to do a very, very basic send and receive. I'm sure you're an e-mail wiz and that this is going to seem really Mickey Mouse, but humor me. There's some meat here and, if nothing else, you can use this little exercise to get familiar with Outlook 2003.

Let's start by sending ourselves a message. Click the New Mail Message button on the Standard toolbar. It's the icon in the upper-left corner of the Outlook window that says, you guessed it, "New." This opens a New Message window like the one in Figure 10.3. If you don't see the Standard toolbar for managing messages in the New Message window (the one with the Send button, paperclip, and so on), select Standard from the Toolbar submenu on the message's View menu. If the text-formatting toolbar (the one that lets you alter the look of text) isn't visible in the New Message window, select Formatting from the Toolbar submenu on the message's View menu. Your client will remember that you've turned on these toolbars and will present them on every new message window.

FIGURE 10.3

An Outlook client's New Message window

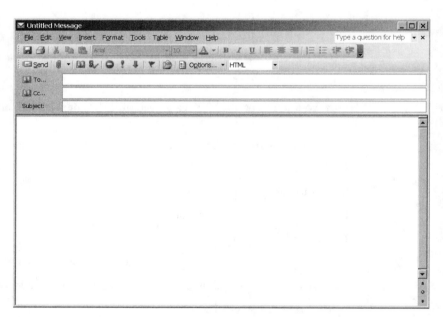

If you didn't know that you were in an Outlook client, you just might think you were running a word-processing application. The top of the screen includes drop-down menus and a number of icons that you've probably seen in your Windows-based word processor. These enable you to produce very rich messages that can include text in different fonts, sizes, formats, and colors, as well as variously formatted paragraphs and lists.

The New Message window starts to look more "e-messagy" just below the Standard toolbar. This is where you enter the address of the recipient(s) of your message. Click To; this brings up the Outlook Address Book (Select Names) dialog box (see Figure 10.4).

FIGURE 10.4

The Outlook address book

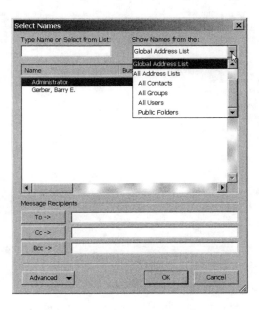

Notice in Figure 10.4 that I've clicked open the drop-down list of address lists and selected the Global Address List. It holds addresses for all unhidden recipients in your Exchange organization. We'll talk about hidden and unhidden recipients in Chapter 12, "Managing the Exchange Server Hierarchy and Core Components." The All Address Lists container and its subcontainers let you quickly find a type of address. You'll usually want to store your own addresses, such as personal Internet mail addresses, in an Outlook Contacts List. If your Outlook Contacts folder doesn't show up in the Outlook Address Book, here's what to do:

1. Right-click your Contacts folder in the Outlook folder tree and select Properties.
2. Tab over to the Outlook Address Book page of the Contacts Properties dialog box and select Show This Folder as an E-mail Address Book. Click OK and you're done.

To send a message to yourself, follow these steps:

1. Click your name in the Global Address List.
2. In the Select Names dialog box, click To, and then OK. This returns you to your message (see Figure 10.5).
3. Now move to the Subject field, using either your mouse or the Tab key. Type in some text for a subject title.

FIGURE 10.5

Composing a new
Outlook message

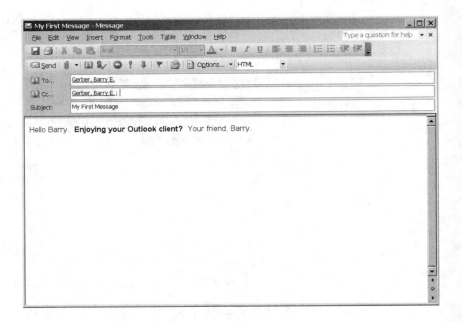

4. Next, move to the Message field and type in a message.

5. Now place the text cursor in the Cc (carbon copy) field of your message. Type the first letter of your first or last name. Outlook should fill in your whole name. Press the Tab key to accept the name and to have Outlook insert your address automatically.

6. Now click the Send button on the Standard toolbar. In a second or two, the message should show up in your Inbox.

TIP   *Not sure what an Outlook icon button is for? Just put your mouse pointer on the icon and wait a second for a tiny information box to show up.*

MICROSOFT SHAREPOINT SERVER MAKES COLLABORATION MUCH EASIER

Outlook 2003 features a great new way to deal with attachments that you send to multiple recipients. You can choose to send the attachment as a Regular attachment. With this option, each recipient gets their own copy of the attachment. Or you can send the attachment as a Shared attachment. In this case, each recipient gets a copy of the attachment, but there is also a shared copy of the attachment that can be automatically updated as recipients make changes in their copies. All of this isn't implemented in Exchange Server. You must purchase and install Microsoft's SharePoint server products to implement this feature in Outlook 2003 and other Windows 2003 products.

Let's take a look at your newly received message. Double-click anywhere on the message line in the Inbox window (see Figure 10.6) to open it. Figure 10.7 shows the open message.

FIGURE 10.6

The new message shows up in the Outlook 2003 client's Inbox.

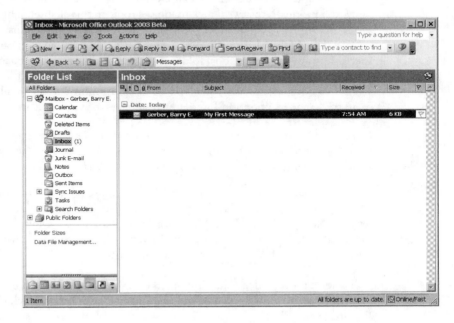

FIGURE 10.7

A received Exchange message

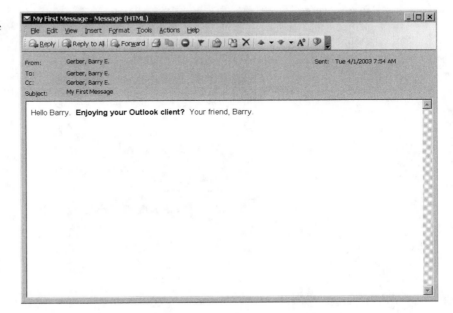

Outlook Profiles Continued

Back in Chapter 9, we customized an Outlook profile using the Office 2003 Custom Installation Wizard. I promised that we'd pick up on the topic in this chapter. This time, instead of dealing with Outlook profiles in the abstract, we take a hands-on look at them using our Outlook 2003 client.

You'll remember that profiles determine what e-mail system you can access and provide you with special features such as personal folders and special address books. Each Outlook 2003 user can have one or many personal Outlook profiles. You can set up different Outlook profiles so that each allows access to a different Exchange mailbox, or to one or more Internet mail services, or to a combination of an Exchange mailbox and Internet mail services, or you name it.

NOTE   It's important to understand that you don't need to complete this exercise to use the Outlook client. We are doing it just to get comfortable with profiles. At the very least, I strongly recommend that you read through this section because I guarantee you're going to have to deal with profiles sometime and you might as well start now.

Be sure that Outlook 2003 is closed. Then choose Start ➢ Control Panel and double-click the Mail icon in the Control Panel. This opens the Mail Setup–Outlook dialog box, which you use to set up e-mail accounts and non-Exchange Server–based storage options and profiles. Click Show Profiles on this dialog box. This opens the Mail profiles dialog box shown in Figure 10.8. Your default profile is displayed. We'll talk about default profiles in a bit.

To add a profile, click Add. This opens the New Profile dialog box (see Figure 10.9). Type a name for your new profile. I'm naming my new profile BarryGerber. Click OK and the E-mail Accounts Wizard opens (see Figure 10.10). Let's step through the wizard's various pages.

FIGURE 10.8

The Outlook Mail profiles dialog box

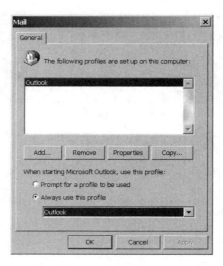

FIGURE 10.9
Selecting a name for
an Outlook profile

FIGURE 10.10
The Outlook E-mail
Accounts Wizard

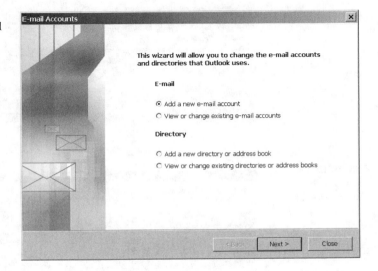

Accept the default setting on the wizard and click Next. You use the next page of the wizard shown in Figure 10.11 to select an e-mail server type that you want to access through your new profile. To select multiple e-mail systems for a profile, you have to run the wizard multiple times. Right now, select Microsoft Exchange Server and click Next. I'll cover POP3 and IMAP servers in Chapter 14, "Managing Exchange 2003 Services for Internet Clients."

In the next panel of the wizard, you indicate the Exchange server and mailbox that you want to use (see Figure 10.12). I've created a new mailbox called bgerber2 for this profile. You can enter either the mailbox name or the display name for the mailbox in the User Name field. To ensure that the mailbox exists, click Check Name. If the mailbox is there, the wizard will show the fully qualified domain name of your Exchange server in the Microsoft Exchange Server field and the display name of the mailbox in the User Name field. Text in both fields will be underlined as in Figure 10.13.

FIGURE 10.11
Selecting an e-mail server type using the Outlook E-mail Accounts Wizard

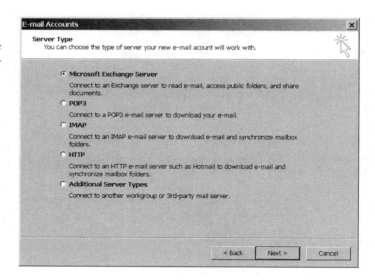

FIGURE 10.12
Specifying the Exchange server and mailbox for a new profile

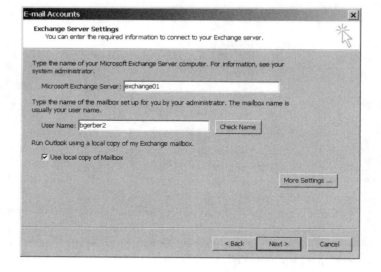

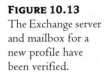

FIGURE 10.13
The Exchange server
and mailbox for a
new profile have
been verified.

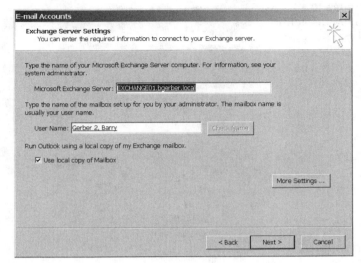

I've already talked about the option Use Local Copy of Mailbox shown in Figures 10.12 and 10.13, but let me expand a bit. If this option is checked, the profile will support synchronizing your Exchange Server–based folders for e-mail, contacts, to-do lists, and so on to a local file on your computer's hard disk. Then, when you're not connected to the network, you can still access your Outlook messages, contacts, and so on. A check mark in this box also enables you to compose e-mail messages while you're not connected to the network. When you reconnect, the messages that you've composed are sent. This is especially useful for laptop computers that you carry home or on trips. I love this capability.

The More Settings button on the Exchange Server Settings wizard page opens a dialog box that you can use to set such parameters as how Outlook connects to Exchange Server, additional mailboxes to open, encryption and other security options, and dial-up mail settings. Figure 10.14 shows this dialog box. Let's look at some of its pages in a bit more detail.

You can use the General tab of the Microsoft Exchange Server properties dialog box to indicate if you want your Outlook 2003 client to automatically detect whether it can connect to your Exchange server or default to an offline or network-based connectivity mode. You also can set the timeout period after which Outlook will assume that it can't connect to your Exchange server and will open in offline mode.

On the Advanced tab, you can open additional mailboxes so that you can access them in Outlook at the same time as your own mailbox. You can also use the Advanced property page to modify the Use Local Copy of Mailbox setting and manage the file that holds the folders that are included in the local copy of your mailbox. For example, you can compress the file to save room on the hard drive that holds the local copy of your mailbox.

You use the Security tab to turn on e-mail encryption and choose the kind of network security that you'll use. You can also require that you be prompted for your username and password, even if you're opening Outlook while logged in to Windows with the same security credentials.

FIGURE 10.14

The Microsoft Exchange Server properties dialog box

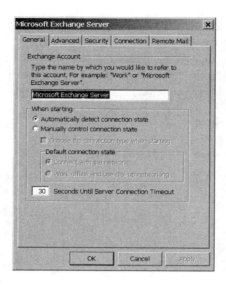

Using the Connection tab of the Microsoft Exchange Server properties dialog box, you can specify parameters to be used when you dial up directly to an Exchange server from Outlook, as opposed to logging in to your Windows domain account through a dial-up connection.

You can use the Remote Mail tab to designate how Outlook will act when it contacts your Exchange server through a direct dial-up connection that you've set up on the Connection property page. For example, you can download only message headers (sender, subject, date, time, and so on) and then choose which messages to download in their entirety. I'll leave it to you to follow through on direct dial-up connections and remote mail settings.

OK, now let's go back to the Outlook E-mail Accounts Wizard. The last wizard panel tells you that you've supplied sufficient information to set up your account in your new profile. Click Finish to complete setup and leave the wizard. The Mail dialog box now reopens showing your original and new profiles (see Figure 10.15). You can select which profile to use when Outlook starts up by clicking Prompt for a Profile to be Used, or you can change the default profile that is used when Outlook opens with the Always Use This Profile drop-down list. To open the Mail dialog box anytime, close Outlook, choose Start ➤ Control Panel, and double-click the Mail icon in the Control Panel. Then click Show Profiles on the Mail Setup–Outlook dialog box that opens.

Creating a New Public Folder

For upcoming chapters, we're going to need a public folder or two, so I'll show you how to create one now. Exchange public folders can be created by mailbox-enabled users in their e-mail clients. They can also be created by an Exchange administrator using the Exchange System Manager. I'll show you how to do that later; for now, we'll create a public folder using the Outlook 2003 client.

FIGURE 10.15
The Mail dialog box showing a newly created profile

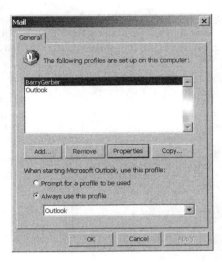

Open your Outlook client and make sure that the folder list is displayed. Next, double-click Public Folders in the folder list, or click the plus icon just in front of Public Folders. Do the same for the All Public Folders subfolder. Your client window should look something like the one in Figure 10.16. (Notice that the little plus sign becomes a minus sign when a folder is expanded to show the folders within it.)

FIGURE 10.16
The top-level folder for public folders and two default subfolders

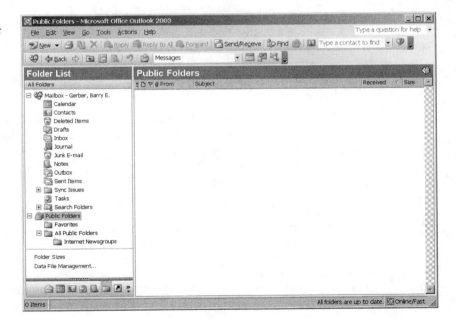

You've opened the top-level folder for public folders, which contains two subfolders: Favorites and All Public Folders. The All Public Folders folder has one subfolder: Internet Newsgroups. If your Exchange organization has a large number of public folders, you can drag the ones that you use a lot to your Favorites subfolder. This makes them easier to find. Folders in the Favorites folder are also the only ones that are available when you work offline without a connection to your Exchange server.

To create new public folders in the folder All Public Folders, follow these steps:

1. Right-click All Public Folders, and then select New Folder from the menu that pops up. This brings up the Create New Folder dialog box (see Figure 10.17).

FIGURE 10.17

Naming a new folder

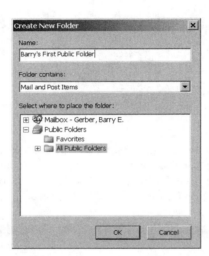

2. Enter a name for the folder; I've given mine the somewhat unimaginative name Barry's First Public Folder.

   Note that the folder will hold e-mail and posted items. E-mail items are messages. Posted items contain a subject and text. You can post an item in a folder designed to hold posts without having to deal with messaging attributes such as whom the item is sent to. To post an item, click the down arrow near the New icon on the main Outlook window and select Post in This Folder from the drop-down menu.

   When you're done creating your folder, click OK.

If you're told that you don't have sufficient permissions to create the folder, you need to give yourself those permissions in the Exchange System Manager.

NOTE *Have you noticed that public folder Internet Newsgroups? It was created when I installed Exchange Server back in Chapter 8. It holds Usenet (Internet-based) and local newsgroups and their messages. I'll talk more about newsgroups in Chapter 14.*

The new public folder now shows up under the All Public Folders hierarchy (see Figure 10.18). If you can't see the full name of your new folder, make the Folder List pane a little wider.

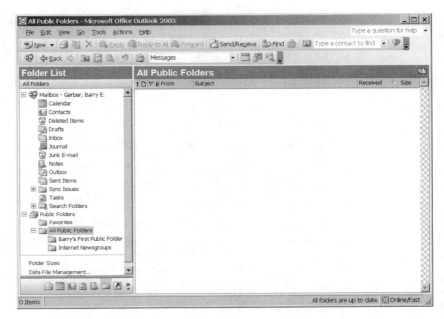

Now right-click your new folder and select Properties from the pop-up menu. This brings up the Properties dialog box for the folder, shown in Figure 10.19.

FIGURE 10.19
The Outlook client's
Properties dialog
box for a public
folder

We're not going to spend a lot of time with this dialog box. Among other things, mailbox owners use public folder Properties dialog boxes to do the following:

◆ Add a description for other mailbox owners who access the folder

◆ Make the folder available on the Internet

◆ Set up a default view of the folder, including grouping by such things as the subject or who an item is from

◆ Set up some administrative rules on folder characteristics, access, and such

◆ Manage some neat electronic forms, which I'll talk about in Chapter 20, "Building, Using, and Managing Outlook Forms Designer Applications"

◆ Set permissions for using the folder

Go ahead and look around in the Properties dialog box. When you're done, click Cancel, unless you've made some changes. If you have, then click OK to save your changes.

NOTE   *You create and manage private folders inside mailboxes in the same way that you create and manage public folders in the Public Folders hierarchy. 'Nuff said.*

Using Outlook 2003's E-mail Menus

To conclude this chapter, we'll take a quick tour of the e-mail menus for the main window of an Outlook 2003 client. These menus apply to Outlook's Deleted Items, Drafts, Inbox, and Outbox folders.

My goal here is merely to highlight the capabilities of Outlook as an e-mail client, not to teach you how to use all the options on the Outlook e-mail menus. To save time, I'll skip obvious items that you should know about from using other Windows applications, such as the File menu's Page Setup, Print Preview, and Print options, or the Edit menu's Cut, Copy, and Paste options. And I won't discuss the menus for new and received messages here, partly because some of what's in them was covered when we looked at message menus earlier in this chapter, and partly because I don't want to turn this into a full-blown tutorial on Outlook clients.

NOTE   *Menus for non-e-mail folders created by Outlook in a mailbox (Calendar, Contacts, Tasks, and so on) have a lot in common with their e-mail brethren. However, they also have their own special options. For example, the Calendar folder's File menu includes an option to save your calendar as a web page for viewing by others. I'll leave to you the joy of discovering all the neat non-e-mail folder options.*

The File Menu

The Outlook 2003 File menu is shown in Figure 10.20. The File menu is like most File menus with a few twists. You can use it to open files and other people's Outlook folders that are stored on your Exchange server. The File menu is also the place to go when you want to work with your Exchange folders, manage data files, export data from and import it into Outlook, archive data in your Outlook folders, and manage your connection to your Exchange server.

FIGURE 10.20
The File menu of an
Outlook client's
main window

If you see a little double arrow pointing down at the bottom of the menu, it means that all the selections on the menu aren't being displayed. To display all selections, wait a second or two, or move your mouse pointer over the double arrow at the bottom of the menu and click it. The menu will bloom open, and you'll see all of the menu's options. You can also customize menus so that you always see the entire menu. On the Outlook main window, select Tools ➢ Customize. On the Customize dialog box, check Always Show Full Menus.

NEW

The New submenu on the Outlook 2003 File menu holds a whole bunch of exciting options. Here you can start a new message or enter a new item for Outlook's Calendar, Contact Manager, Task List, Journal, or Notes Folder. You can also select forms or templates to use in messages, or you can even create a new folder.

A number of functions on the New submenu can also be initiated by clicking a button or a down-pointing arrow next to a button (for example, the New Mail Message button on the main Toolbar), or by right-clicking an object and selecting an option (for example, to create a new subfolder).

OPEN

The File menu Open option in most applications is pretty boring, but this is not the case with Outlook 2003. Of course, you can open (display) messages in a folder by highlighting them and selecting the Selected Items option on the Open submenu. But what's really interesting is the option that lets you open certain folders in another user's mailbox. Assuming that you've been given rights to do so, you can open one or more of the following folders in another user's mailbox: Inbox, Calendar, Contacts, Journal, Notes, or Tasks. I often use this option to make calendar folders for scheduling rooms and other resources available to Exchange Server users.

TIP *To allow someone to access one of your folders, right-click the folder and select Properties from the pop-up menu. Select the Permissions property page, click Add, and select the user's name from the Outlook Address Book.*

You can also open an Outlook data file. This is a personal folder stored not inside your Exchange server, but on your computer's hard disk or a network drive.

CLOSE ALL ITEMS

If you have a number of messages open, click Close All Items to close all of them.

SAVE AS

This works pretty much like Save As for files. However, it lets you save an item in a folder as a text file; as an Outlook message file, in HTML format; or as an Outlook template. If the item in a folder is an application file, such as a Word document, you can save it to disk as an application file.

SAVE ATTACHMENTS

If a message contains attachments such as spreadsheet files, you can use the Save Attachments submenu to select the attachments that you want and save them to disk.

FOLDER

Use the Folder submenu to create subfolders; to copy, move, delete, rename, or check the properties of the selected folder; or to add a public folder to the Favorites folder. (See Figure 10.16, shown earlier, and related text for more on the Favorites folder.) The Folders submenu is also the place to go if you want to copy the design of one folder to another folder. Folder designs include such things as the attributes of messages that are displayed in the columns of a folder and specifications for the way messages are sorted in a folder.

DATA FILE MANAGEMENT

The Data File Management menu option lets you create new private folders and remove existing private folders. You can also set encryption parameters and a password for the file that holds your private folder.

IMPORT AND EXPORT

Use the Import and Export options to input data into Outlook 2003 from a range of applications such as cc:Mail, Eudora or Netscape mail, ACT!, ECCO, Schedule+, or Sidekick. You can also import data in standard VCARD format (for Outlook 2003 Contacts), or standard iCalendar or vCalendar format (for Outlook 2003 Calendar). Items in a folder can be exported in a variety of file formats, including comma-delimited and Access and Excel format. Import and Export operates on the currently selected folder.

ARCHIVE

You can save Exchange server storage space by moving Outlook folder contents to a Personal Folders archive file. Use the Archive option to customize the archiving process to your heart's content.

EXCHANGE CONNECTION

This is a neat new option with Outlook 2003. You can select the speed (bandwidth) of your workstation's link to the Exchange server. You can choose fast, slow, or automatic detection. Outlook adapts to this setting, for example, getting only message headers, rather than downloading whole messages. When you open a new message, then it is downloaded.

WORK OFFLINE

Select this option to toggle working offline with the local copy of your Exchange mailbox on and off.

EXIT

Select Exit to leave Outlook and log off your Exchange server.

The Edit Menu

The Outlook client's Edit menu is shown in Figure 10.21. You use this menu to move and copy folders, mark messages as read or unread, and set up categories that you can use to classify messages.

FIGURE 10.21
The Edit menu of
the Outlook client's
main window

OFFICE CLIPBOARD

The Office Clipboard is a multi-clipboard version of the single page Windows Clipboard. It supports up to 24 clipboards (buffers). You can do some pretty fancy cutting and pasting with such a large number of buffers.

MOVE TO FOLDER AND COPY TO FOLDER

You can use these menu options to copy or move an item or a set of items from the currently selected folder to another folder. You can also move items by highlighting them, right-clicking them, and selecting Move to Folder from the menu that pops up. In addition, you can simply drag highlighted items from one folder to another to move them. If you hold down the Ctrl key while dragging, the items are copied to the second folder instead of being moved to it.

MARK AS READ, MARK AS UNREAD, AND MARK ALL AS READ

When a message has not been read, its subject line as seen in a folder appears in bold type. When a message has been read, its subject line is in plain type. Select the messages for which you want to change the read status, and then click either of the first two options on the menu as appropriate. Choosing Mark All as Read marks all messages in the open folder as having been read, regardless of which lines are selected.

CATEGORIES

You can place messages in one or more categories. Categories are used like keywords when you search for messages. To categorize one or more messages, select the messages that you want to categorize in the message items pane, and click Categories on the Edit menu. Then, in the Categories dialog box that pops up, check off the categories that you want to use for the message. You can add new categories by clicking Master Category List in the Categories dialog box.

The View Menu

The Outlook client's View menu is shown in Figure 10.22. This is where you can set up a custom view of your mailbox. You can also choose to preview messages in two different formats when you select them, and turn toolbars and the informational status bar on or off.

FIGURE 10.22
The View menu of the Outlook client's main window

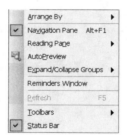

ARRANGE BY

The Arrange By submenu lets you view the messages in a folder in a range of interesting ways. Among other things, Arrange By submenu options let you see only the last seven days of messages or to sort messages by conversation topic or sender. As you'll see in a bit, you can create your own views that are then available under the Arrange By submenu.

The Arrange By submenu also lets you customize your view of the currently selected folder by adding columns (such as Message Size) to the view, or by sorting and grouping by one or more columns (such as Sender or Message Importance). And, if that weren't enough, you can format the columns that are displayed in a folder and design your own custom views.

NAVIGATION PANE

This View menu option lets you toggle the navigation pane on and off. This is the pane on the left side of the main Outlook window that shows the folder tree in the Outlook setup I've encouraged you to use. You can see the navigation pane in a number of the figures in this chapter. In Figure 10.2, shown earlier, it's the pane that holds the folder list.

READING PANE

The reading pane is a window pane that shows the content of a selected message. It can be turned on and off, and it can be located on the right side or the bottom of the message items pane (the large pane on right side of the main Outlook window with the list of messages; refer back to Figure 10.2). Use the reading pane so that you don't have to open the message to see what's in it. Go to the Reading Pane submenu to select the location of the reading pane or to turn the pane on or off.

AUTOPREVIEW

The View menu's AutoPreview option shows you each message and the first several lines of each message. AutoPreview differs from the reading pane in that AutoPreview shows you all messages in the message items pane (message header followed by content), while the reading pane shows you the message header in the message items pane and the message's content in the reading pane.

EXPAND/COLLAPSE GROUPS

If you've set up group-by-options capabilities for the columns in a folder, you can use this submenu to expand or collapse the grouped views. As with hierarchies in Outlook 2003's Folder List, groupings that can be expanded are shown with a little plus sign to their left. Expanded groupings have a minus sign in front of them. You can click the pluses and minuses to open and close groupings instead of using the Expand/Collapse Groups option.

REMINDERS WINDOW

The Reminders window is a little pop-up that opens when the time for an appointment or other scheduled event arrives. It opens automatically when it is time for an event. You can also look at the window by selecting Reminders Window from the View menu.

TOOLBARS

Use the Toolbars submenu to turn Outlook's Standard, Advanced, Task, and Web toolbars on or off. The Standard toolbar is just below the menu bar on the Outlook client. The Task pane is a window pane that opens on the right side of the main Outlook window. It may contain the Office Clipboard, or Outlook Help, or any other Outlook feature that runs in the Task pane. You can close the Task pane by clicking the X in the pane or by toggling the pane off using the Toolbars ➤ Task Pane option. You'll only see the Task Pane option in the Toolbars submenu when the Task Pane is open. Don't confuse the Task pane with the Task folder where you set up tasks and monitor your progress in completing them.

You can also customize toolbars by adding or removing commands from them and setting a variety of formatting options for them. To do this, select View ➤ Toolbars ➤ Customize.

STATUS BAR

The status bar is at the bottom of the Outlook client's main window. It provides information about the contents of whatever folder is displayed in the window. Back in Figure 10.6, the status bar reads "1 Item" and "All folders are up to date." The status bar in the figure also shows that Outlook is connected to an Exchange server (Online) and that the connection is a high-speed one (Fast).Use the Status Bar option to toggle the status bar on and off.

The Go Menu

This is a pretty straightforward menu. It allows you to go to the different folders in your mailbox, Calendar, Contacts, Deleted Items, Inbox, Tasks, and so on. The menu is simple enough that I'm not going to spend any more time on it here.

The Tools Menu

The Outlook client's Tools menu is shown in Figure 10.23. You can use the Tools menu to initiate mail transmission and reception for your Exchange and other mailboxes, and to synchronize your Exchange mailbox and selected public folders with a copy of your mailbox and public folders stored on your computer. The Tools menu is also the place to find and organize messages in folders and set up rules for the automatic handling of incoming and outgoing messages. Finally, the Tools menu lets you empty your Deleted Items folder, work with forms, set up Outlook's new speech capabilities, modify Exchange and other e-mail services, set a wide range of options, and customize toolbars and menus.

FIGURE 10.23
The Tools menu of the Outlook client's main window

SEND/RECEIVE

First, send and receive does just what it says: It sends any messages in your Outbox and picks up any new messages on your Exchange server that haven't automatically come into your Inbox. Send/Receive also includes options to send and receive items for any other mail services (POP3, for example).

The Send/Receive submenu also has menu items for synchronizing your Exchange mailbox with the local copy of your mailbox. You can synchronize when connected remotely or when connected directly to the network, as you might do with a laptop. If you're connected remotely by modem and your connection isn't too expensive, you can fire off a synchronization nightly or even set synchronization to happen every few minutes. If you're using a laptop on the road, when you return to the office with your folders full of new items, you can update your online Exchange environment by synchronizing it with the local copy of your Exchange Server mailbox. If any messages are waiting to be sent in your Outbox, they're sent out through your server, and any messages waiting for you on the server are copied to folders stored in the local copy of your Exchange mailbox. You can synchronize with one copy of your local mailbox on one workstation or a local copy of your mailbox on each of two or more workstations.

I already showed you how to set up a local copy of your mailbox earlier in this chapter. The only other thing I want to show you here is how you select the folders in your Exchange mailbox that you want synchronized with the local copy of your mailbox.

1. In the main Outlook window, select Tools ➢ Send/Receive ➢ Send/Receive Settings ➢ Define Send/Receive Groups.

2. Click Edit on the Send/Receive Groups dialog box that opens (Figure 10.24), being sure that All Accounts is selected.

FIGURE 10.24
The Send/Receive
Groups dialog box

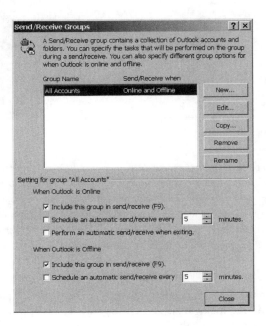

3. Finally, select the Exchange Server folders that you want to synchronize with your local mailbox copy from the tree on the Send/Receive Settings–All Accounts dialog box (Figure 10.25).

NOTE *Most of the folders in your Exchange mailbox are automatically set for synchronization when you set up your local mailbox copy. You'll find this option most useful for synchronizing folders that you create in your mailbox and for folders not automatically set for synchronization such as the Notes folder.*

FIGURE 10.25
Using the Send/
Receive Settings dia-
log box to select Ex-
change Server folders
to be synchronized
with a local mailbox

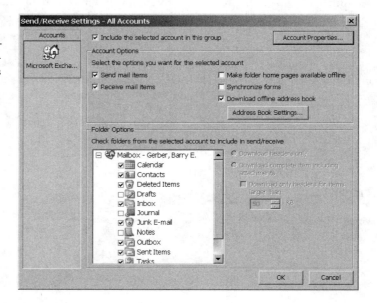

TIP *When setting up people to use an Outlook client at home, I often ask them to bring their workstation to the office. I connect the workstation to the network and then set up and perform a synchronization of all their folders to a local copy of their mailbox. For users with big mailboxes, this method is especially nice because those users don't have to run the first and most time-consuming synchronization when connected at home at 56.6Kbps or even at higher DSL speeds. And don't forget those public folders. Any public folder that you drag into the Favorites folder under Public Folders will be copied during synchronization if you've selected the folder for synchronization.*

FIND

The Find option on the Tools menu lets you open a Quick Search pane on your Outlook main window or an Advanced Find dialog box. The Quick Search pane appears above the message items pane.
You can search in the currently selected folder or in a range of other folders. Type in the pane what
you want to find, click Find Now, and Outlook shows you the messages it has found.

The Advanced Find dialog box is an impressive GUI that lets you specify multiple find criteria,
including those in the Find command. Advanced Find adds such filters as whom the message was sent
to, times such as sent time or received time, items with or without attachments, and so on. You can
even select any combination of folders for your search. You name it and Outlook 2003's advanced
Find feature has it.

ADDRESS BOOK

Select the Address Book menu item to see and work with the Address Book. Because you can easily access the Address Book when composing a message (by clicking the To, Cc, or Bcc button), you're most likely to select it from here when you want to add an item to your Personal Address Book. (You can also bring up the Address Book by pressing Ctrl+Shift+B or by clicking the Address Book icon in your Outlook client's main window.)

ORGANIZE

You can organize any folder in a variety of ways by selecting the Organize option on the Tools menu while the folder is selected. Like Find, Organize uses a pane on the Outlook 2003 GUI. You can create rules to move messages from the currently selected folder to other folders, set Outlook to display messages in the folder from different senders in different colors, and change the current view that is used with the folder.

RULES AND ALERTS

When installed, Exchange Server and Outlook 2003 can perform a wide range of functions with mail that comes into your Inbox—for example, putting the mail into another folder, forwarding a message to another address, or performing a custom action that deals with the message. All these tasks can be based on various properties of the messages, from the sender to the occurrence of specific text in the subject line or body of the message. You set up rules using the Rules Wizard.

Alerts can come from a variety of sources. For example, Microsoft's SharePoint Server can alert you that there have been changes in the documents managed through it. You can set an alert to let you know that one or more documents have changed.

OUT OF OFFICE ASSISTANT

The Out of Office Assistant is another neat GUI-based agent that you can use to send an auto-reply message telling people that you're out of the office—and letting them know what the consequences might be (for example, that you won't be getting to your mail until a specific date). The Out of Office Assistant generates only one message to a specific message originator during the time you're away from the office. If the original message is sent to an Exchange Server distribution group, the Out of Office Assistant generates out-of-office messages for the list's members, provided that the option has been selected on the Exchange Advanced property page of the distribution group. You can also set up rules for handling messages that come in while you're out of the office.

MAILBOX CLEANUP

Using the Mailbox Cleanup dialog box, you can see how large the folders in your mailbox are and find items based on message age and size. You can then delete all or selected found items. The Empty "Deleted Items" Folder and message archiving options are also available in the Mailbox Cleanup dialog box. The dialog box even includes a way to deal with different versions of the same message.

EMPTY "DELETED ITEMS" FOLDER

This one's obvious. The key here is that nothing is permanently deleted until it is removed from the Deleted Items folder. The Empty "Deleted Items" Folder option clears the Deleted Items folder of all deleted messages. With Exchange Server 2003, even that might not be the end of deleted items because you can set up Exchange server so that items that are deleted from an Outlook user's Deleted Items folder remain on the Exchange server for a set period of time. I'll talk more in a later chapter about setting up Exchange Server to hold on to deleted items.

RECOVER DELETED ITEMS

These are the deleted items stored on an Exchange server for a specific period that I just talked about. To recover deleted items, follow these steps:

1. Click the Deleted Items folder and select Recover Deleted Items from the Tools menu.
2. You'll be offered a list of items that can be recovered. Select the ones that you want, and click the little envelope on the Recover Deleted Items window.

Be sure to note the date or time of the item that you're recovering, because the item is silently recovered to your Deleted Items folder. If that folder is full of yet-to-be-deleted items, you might have a difficult time finding the recovered item if you don't know its date. This works best, of course, if your Deleted Items folder is sorted by the default received date.

FORMS

I talked a bit about electronic forms back in Chapter 1, "Introducing Exchange Server 2003" (see Figure 1.10 and related text). I'll go into much more detail about them in Chapter 20. You use the Forms submenu to select existing forms and to create new ones.

MACRO

Using Visual Basic for Applications, you can create macros to do various tasks in your Outlook 2003 client. You create and execute macros from the Macro submenu.

SPEECH

You use the Speech option on the Tools menu to set up Outlook (Office 2003) for speech recognition.

E-MAIL ACCOUNTS

You use the E-mail Accounts option to add, modify, or delete e-mail accounts. I covered this option earlier in this chapter. If you can't perform a particular task when selecting E-Mail Accounts from this menu, it's because Outlook is open. To perform these tasks, close Outlook and open the Mail Setup - Outlook dialog box by clicking the Mail icon in the Control Panel. Then click E-Mail Accounts.

CUSTOMIZE

This option lets you customize toolbars and menus.

OPTIONS

The Options item is where you can override many of Outlook's default settings. It's also the place to give permission to other recipients to send messages on behalf of yourself as well as myriad other neat functions.

The Actions Menu

The Outlook client's Actions menu is shown in Figure 10.26. You use the Actions menu to compose, reply to, or forward a message; set up follow-up parameters for messages; and block junk mail.

FIGURE 10.26

The Actions menu of the Outlook client's main window

NEW MAIL MESSAGE

Select New Mail Message to compose a message in a new message window. Clicking the New Mail Message icon in the main Outlook window or pressing Ctrl+N has the same effect.

NEW MAIL MESSAGE USING

You can create messages with a variety of look-and-feel options. These range from plain old text messages to messages that use one of the cool-looking pieces of electronic stationery that come with Outlook 2003 and messages based on Microsoft Access databases, Excel spreadsheets, or Word documents. This latter capability is really great. It lets you create e-mail–enabled applications with a few clicks of a mouse.

FOLLOW UP

The Follow Up option lets you flag Outlook items for followup and set dates and times when you want to be reminded to do followup.

JUNK E-MAIL

Outlook 2003 can deal with junk and pornographic messages. You manage this feature here.

REPLY AND REPLY TO ALL

Use the Reply or Reply to All options to answer a selected or open received message. You can reply either just to the person who sent the message (Reply) or to all its recipients (Reply to All). When working with an open received message, you'll find it far easier to use the message's own Reply and Reply to All icons, which appear on the message's toolbar (see Figure 10.7, shown earlier). You can also use these keyboard alternatives: Ctrl+R for Reply to Sender, or Ctrl+Shift+R for Reply to All.

FORWARD

The Forward option sends a copy of a received message to one or more other recipients; Ctrl+F is the keyboard alternative. As with replies, it's easier to use the Forward icon on the toolbar of an open received message (see Figure 10.7, shown earlier).

Summary

Outlook 2003 is a pretty user-friendly electronic-messaging client with lots of bells and whistles, such as calendaring capabilities, contacts, and a notepad. When Outlook 2003 is installed properly on a server, as in Chapter 9, a user can easily install Outlook on a workstation and begin using it without having to respond to a single installation query.

Creating, composing, and reading Outlook messages are very straightforward tasks. The Outlook address book, which includes Exchange mailboxes, distribution groups, contacts, and public folders, simplifies the e-mail addressing process. As with managing messages, basic public folder creation and management is an easy task, most of which can be done right in the Outlook client.

Among other things, Outlook profiles allow a single user to access a range of mail accounts with ease. Each user may have one or more Outlook profiles. When creating an Outlook profile, you can choose to access messaging services such as Exchange Server and Internet mail servers. You can also include personal folders and specific kinds of address books in a profile. By selecting a profile when Outlook 2003 starts, you choose which set of messaging services and other features will be available during your Outlook session.

The Outlook 2003 menu structure is complex, but it's easy to use when you're clear on what certain menu items do. Exchange Server 2003 brings several significant enhancements to the Outlook 2003 menu structure. One of these enables an Outlook user to recover items that were accidentally deleted.

This concludes the part of this book dedicated to the Outlook 2003 client. Now we're ready to get into Exchange Server 2003 management. We'll start small in the next part, focusing on the Exchange server that you created in Chapter 8. Then, later in the book, we'll move on to larger, multi-server, multidomain Exchange 2003 environments.

Part 4

Basic Exchange Server 2003 Management

In this part:
- Chapter 11: Managing Exchange Users, Distribution Groups, and Contacts
- Chapter 12: Managing the Exchange Server Hierarchy and Core Components

Chapter 11

Managing Exchange Users, Distribution Groups, and Contacts

So you have Exchange Server up and running, and you have the Outlook clients under your belt. Although you used Microsoft Management Console (MMC) a little back in Chapter 8, "Installing Exchange Server 2003," you now need to get comfortable with it, some of its snap-ins, and how these are used to administer and manage Exchange Server 2003. In this chapter, we'll focus on the Active Directory Users and Computers (ADUC) MMC snap-in and on using it to administer and manage three recipient components in the Exchange Server 2003 hierarchy: users, distribution groups, and contacts.

This chapter and the next one walk you through lots of menus, dialog boxes, and pages for setting properties of one kind or another. I think you'll find it useful to track through everything once and set some specific Exchange Server parameters when appropriate. When you need to come back to a particular section, it should be relatively easy to find. Just remember that this chapter deals with the management of all Exchange recipients except public folders, while Chapter 12, "Managing the Exchange Server Hierarchy and Core Components," covers objects in the Exchange hierarchy, including the four core Exchange components and public folders.

Featured in this chapter:

♦ An overview of the Active Directory Users and Computers snap-in

♦ Preliminary settings

♦ Managing Exchange recipients

WARNING   *Throughout this chapter, you need to be logged on to your network as a user with adequate permissions to perform a particular task. I'll be logged in as a domain administrator so that I can show you every aspect of recipient management. If you can do that, great. If not, then you need to work with someone who can so that you can complete tasks such as creating users and their mailboxes. You should also try out the ExAdFirst_Initial_Last_Name account that you created back in Chapter 8. You'll find that it has considerable control over the Exchange environment because it belongs to the Exchange Admins group to which you delegated Exchange organizational control in Chapter 8.*

An Overview of the Active Directory Users and Computers Snap-In

You use the ADUC snap-in to create new Exchange Server 2003 mailboxes, distribution groups, and contacts. The ADUC snap-in lives in MMC. Before we tackle ADUC, let's spend a little time talking about MMC itself.

Microsoft Management Console

MMC is a generic container that can hold one or many specialized management applications (snap-ins) for a wide range of programs that run on Windows 2003 servers. MMC centralizes system management in a single interface.

In designing MMC and its snap-ins, Microsoft sought to create a more object-oriented environment. In addition to pre–Windows 2000 drop-down menus, MMC snap-ins include menus that pop open when an object is right-clicked. For example, with Exchange 5.5, you create a new mailbox by selecting New Mailbox from the Exchange Administrator program's File drop-down menu (see Figure 11.1).

FIGURE 11.1

Using Exchange Server 5.5's Administrator program to create a mailbox

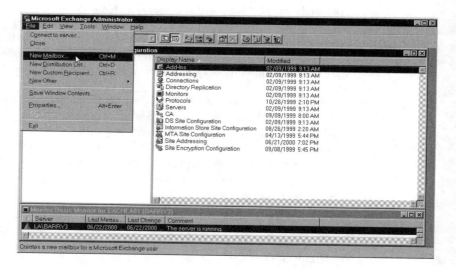

With Exchange 2003, however, you don't create new mailboxes: You mailbox-enable a Windows 2003 user account. We'll get into this in the section "Managing Exchange Users" later in this chapter. You have the option to mailbox-enable a user account while creating the account. But, let's say that you didn't, for some reason. There are two ways to start mailbox-enabling a user account. You can select the user account and then select Exchange Tasks from the Active Directory Users and Computers snap-in Action menu (see Figure 11.2), or you can right-click the user and select Exchange Tasks (see Figure 11.3). The Exchange Tasks Wizard helps you do such tasks as mailbox-enabling a user account or mailbox-disabling a user account.

FIGURE 11.2
Using the Action menu on the Active Directory Users and Computers snap-in to begin mailbox-enabling a user account

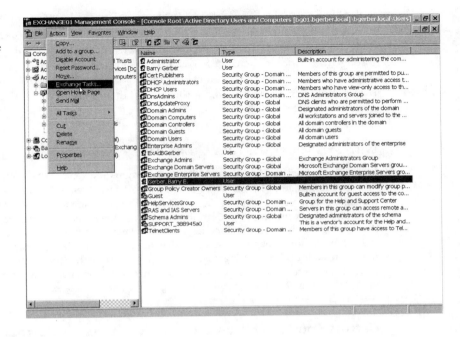

FIGURE 11.3
Right-clicking a user in the Active Directory Users and Computers snap-in to start creating a new mailbox

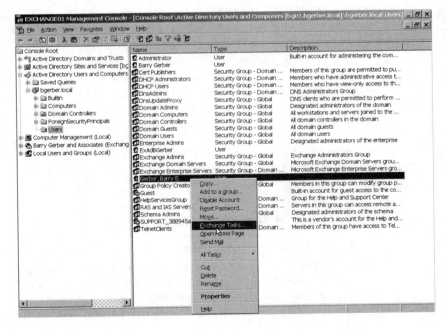

In addition to this seemingly minor change related to MMC snap-in design, Microsoft has renamed and even redesigned some of Exchange Server's key components. So, before you can even look on the Action menu or right-click an object, you're going to have to find the object. As we move through the world of Exchange Server 2003 management, I'll try to alert you to the changes between 5.5 and 2003, and point you quickly to the object that you need to complete a specific task. I'll use the right-click method throughout this book, but you can always turn to the Action menu if you're more comfortable with it.

WHY DO I HAVE TO USE THAT *+@#!% MMC?

It appears that not everyone loves MMC. Focus groups and general user comments have not always been favorable to this new Microsoft tool. So what else is new? I really like MMC because it lets me put all my management tools in one place. Sure, many key snap-ins are available as stand-alone programs in the same place that your saved MMCs reside (Start ➤ All Programs ➤ Administrative Tools). But I really don't like ripping through a bunch of menus every time I need to administer or manage a server component. As the number of programs administered and managed through MMC grows, this one program/one management app madness is only going to get worse. I don't even do the Start menu dance to get to my main MMC. I put a shortcut to it on my desktop, and now I'm one double-click away from all my beloved tools. In this book, MMC rules. MMC haters will have to go elsewhere for solace.

Getting Comfortable with the Active Directory Users and Computers Snap-In

You used ADUC for some simple tasks back in Chapter 7, "Installing Windows Server 2003 as a Domain Controller," and Chapter 8. However, that was a closely guided experience. Now I want to give you a grounding in the snap-in so that you can work with it more creatively. In the process, I'll also be exposing you to some of the standard features of all MMC snap-ins. As my discussion of ADUC proceeds, track along on Figure 11.3 (shown earlier) and on the MMC that you created back in Chapter 8.

First, notice that each snap-in that you add to an MMC occupies one row in the Console Root. In the left pane in Figure 11.3, the snap-ins are as follows:

◆ Active Directory Domains and Trusts

◆ Active Directory Sites and Services

◆ Active Directory Users and Computers

◆ Computer Management (Local)

◆ Barry Gerber and Associates (Exchange)

◆ Local Users and Groups (Local)

You can open any snap-in or its subcontainers by double-clicking it or by clicking the plus sign just to the left of the snap-in or subcontainer. Back in Figure 11.3, Active Directory Users and Computers is open to show some of its subcontainers.

All Active Directory–oriented snap-ins use the Windows 2003 domain for internal organization. In Figure 11.3, Active Directory Users and Computers is open for the domain bgerber.local. You can see the first two characters of the domain name in the figure after "Active Directory Users and Computers." The title at the top of the window, however, reveals all. Within a domain are subcontainers that hold various components relevant to the function of the snap-in. The subcontainers within an ADUC snap-in include, but are not limited to, these:

◆ Builtin

◆ Computers

◆ Domain Controllers

◆ ForeignSecurityPrincipals

◆ Users

The Builtin container holds local Windows 2003 groups essential to the operation of the domain. These include groups such as Administrators, Backup Operators, and Users. Non-domain-controller computers are held in the Computers container, while domain controllers find a home in the Domain Controllers container. Security information relating to other domains is held in the ForeignSecurity-Principals container.

With the exception of groups in the Builtin container, system- and user-created groups and user accounts live in the Users container, at least in simple systems. Technically, users and groups can live in any container in ADUC. You'll probably want to leave default users and groups in the Users container and create new users and groups in that container. However, if your system is complex, you might want to create organizational unit containers to better organize your users and groups and to allow you to distribute administrative responsibility. To create an organizational unit, right-click your domain in ADUC and select New ➢ Organizational Unit.

It could probably go without saying, but I'm going to say it anyway: The right pane always shows what's in the selected container in the left pane. Back in Figure 11.3, the Users container has been selected, and the users and groups in the container are displayed in the right pane.

TIP *The columns in the right pane of any container show attributes of the objects in the container. Some containers show only a few of the many attributes available for a container; the Users container is one. To show more or fewer columns, select the container and select Add/Remove Columns from the snap-in's View menu. This brings up a dialog box that you can use to add columns to the right pane or to remove them.*

As I noted previously, you initiate tasks relating to a specific object in a container either by selecting the task from the Action menu or by right-clicking the object and selecting the task from the pop-up menu. As its name implies, the Action menu is the place you go for just about everything. Even the Refresh command, to update whatever is in the right and left panes, is in the Action menu, not in its familiar pre–Windows 2000 location in the View menu. As you'll see in a bit, the View menu is important, but not for something as mundane as refreshing your view of a window.

The Favorites menu, in the upper-left portion of Figure 11.3 (shown earlier), works just like Favorites in Microsoft's Internet Explorer and Outlook. You use the Add To Favorites item on the Favorites menu to select a specific container for inclusion on the Favorites menu. With Internet Explorer, the Favorites option is a shortcut to often-used Web URLs. With MMC snap-ins, the option is a shortcut to often-used containers. In Figure 11.4, I've added the Exchange System Manager and the Active Directory Users and Computers Users container to my Favorites menu.

FIGURE 11.4

The Exchange System Manager and the Active Directory Users and Computers Users container

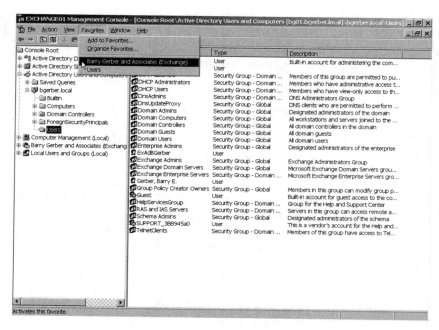

TIP   *If you want to find computers, users, or groups in ADUC containers, you can do a query. Queries can be saved in the Saved Queries container, shown in Figure 11.4. To do a query, just right-click Saved Queries and select New Query.*

Preliminary Settings

Now that you have some ADUC snap-in basics under your belt, you're almost ready to use the snap-in. Before you start, however, you need to set a parameter for ADUC and ensure that you're happy with a couple of formats used when e-mail addresses are created for new users.

Turning On Advanced Features

The Active Directory Users and Computers container is like a chameleon. In its default mode, you see the containers shown back in Figure 11.3. When you turn on what are called Advanced Features, the chameleon figuratively turns a very different color. You not only see additional containers within a domain container, but you see a lot of additional attributes for many objects. These additional containers and attributes allow you to do a range of neat tasks that are otherwise unavailable in the default mode.

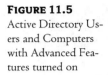

FIGURE 11.5

Active Directory Users and Computers with Advanced Features turned on

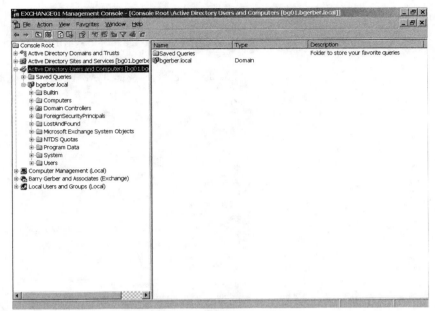

Okay, let's turn on Advanced Features. This is a no-brainer. On your MMC, while in any container in ADUC, select View ➢ Advanced Features. As Figure 11.5 shows, five new containers become visible:

- ◆ LostAndFound

- ◆ Microsoft Exchange System Objects

- ◆ NTDS Quotas

- ◆ Program Data

- ◆ System

LostAndFound is a place where objects that have become detached from their home container are placed. Microsoft Exchange System Objects holds system-created Exchange Server–related public folders and users. NTDS quotas are limits on the number of Active Directory objects a security principal (user, computer, application, and so on) can create. These quotas are stored in the NTDS Quotas container and are designed to prevent disk space problems at the Active Directory level. Program Data holds data for various applications, such as Microsoft's own applications. System is where a range of Windows 2003 system objects are represented, from default domain policy to IP security, to policies. Now, don't get too excited about these three containers; you really can't do much within them other than find something in them or move them somewhere else.

The real power of the Advanced Features setting is in the attributes of objects that it exposes. Here's an example: Figure 11.6 shows the dialog box for my Windows 2003 user account with Advanced Features turned off. Figure 11.7 shows the same dialog box with Advanced Features activated.

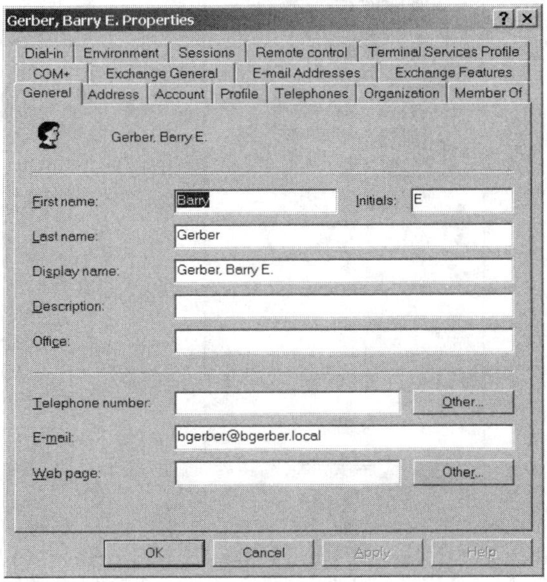

FIGURE 11.6

The dialog box for a Windows 2003 user account without Advanced Features

FIGURE 11.7

The dialog box for a Windows 2003 user account with Advanced Features

Figure 11.6 might be daunting enough with its 16 tabs. Add Advanced Features, and you've got another 4 tabs, for a total of 20. Yipes!

Not to worry. We'll talk about the Exchange-related tabs in both figures in some detail before this chapter comes to an end. For now, just appreciate that without Advanced Features, you won't see the Published Certificates, Object, Security, and Exchange Advanced tabs.

Now that you've turned on ADUC Advanced Features, I'd like to be sure that your MMC opens with Advanced Features activated. To do this, close your MMC. When you're asked whether you want to save your MMC console settings, click Yes. Now, as long as you don't turn off Advanced Features and resave your settings, every time you open your MMC console, Advanced Features will be turned on.

WARNING *Mark this page in your copy of this book. As you move into later chapters, I'll ask you to do something that requires Advanced Features without necessarily telling you that it's an advanced feature. If this ever happens, hopefully you will remember this page and come back here. How do I know this? A good deal of the e-mail that I have received from readers in the past regarding doing one task or another in Exchange Server 5.5 and Exchange 2000 Server was due to their forgetting to do the equivalent of setting Advanced Features in the Exchange 5.5 Administrator program or the Exchange 2000 System Manager. For Exchange 5.5 aficionados, it was Tools ➤ Options ➤ Permissions ➤ Show Permissions page for all objects. For Exchange 2000 buffs, 2003 is no different from 2000.*

Default E-Mail Address Formats

There are two defaults for e-mail addresses that you should consider now. The first has to do with the format of display names, as these were defined in Chapter 5, "Designing a New Exchange 2003 System." The second default has to do with the format of e-mail addresses, such as @bgerber.com. You may change either of these at any time. However, it is best to get things straight now, so take a moment to peruse the next two sections.

SETTING THE DEFAULT FORMAT FOR DISPLAY NAMES

The display name is the one that a user sees when looking for an e-mail address in the Outlook address book or for a user in Active Directory. With Exchange Server 5.5, setting the default format for a user's display name (Martha E. Jones vs. Jones, Martha E., for example) was a very simple task. You chose Options from the Tools menu, and then selected the format or set up a custom format.

With Exchange 5.5 and NT 4, e-mail and user display names were essentially two different things stored in two different places. With Exchange 2003 and Windows 2003, e-mail display names and operating-system display names are the same thing. The display name is created when the user's Windows 2003 account is created. You can change a display name in ADUC, but the default format for the display name must be set in the Active Directory schema.

Messing with Active Directory's schema is akin to messing with a server or workstation's registry, but it's a thousand times more dangerous because you can affect a whole Windows 2003 forest, not just one computer. That said, I'm going to show you how to change the default display name format (*first_name*[space]*middle_initial*[period][space]*last_name*) to *last_name*[comma][space]*first_name*[space] *middle_initial*[period] by editing Active Directory. Be careful! Of course, if you're happy with the default, you can just follow along here without doing anything for a lesson in the fun and games of Active Directory editing.

First, you must install a program called ADSI Edit (for Active Directory Service Interfaces Edit) on your Windows 2003 domain controller. You use this program to change the default display name format. ADSI Edit is one of a number of support tools that you install from your Windows Server 2003 CD-ROM. To install the support tools, on the CD, find and double-click the file `\support\tools\ setup.exe` or find `\support\tools\suptools.msi`, right-click the file, and select Install from the pop-up menu. In either case, follow the simple directions for installation.

When the support tools are installed, you're ready to use ADSI Edit. Add ADSI Edit to your domain controller's MMC. In a second or so, you should see a window like the one in Figure 11.8. If you don't see this window, follow these steps:

1. You need to connect to your domain. Right-click the ADSI Edit container and select Connect To.

2. In the top field of the Connection Setting dialog box that opens, type your domain name; my domain is bgerber.local.

3. Select Configuration in the Well Known Naming Context field and select your domain controller under Select or Type a Domain or Server. Click OK.

Now, click open the Configuration Container and its subcontainers until your ADSI Edit window looks like the one in Figure 11.9. Select the correct language container. CN=409 is for English. Find the object user-Display in the right pane, and double-click it (see Figure 11.10). Select and double-click createDialog from the Attribute list in the Properties dialog box for user-Display, as in Figure 11.10. This opens the String Attribute Editor dialog box for createDialog. Enter %**<sn>**, %**<givenName>** %**<initials>**. in the Value field of this dialog box. This entry will cause the surname (last name) to appear first, followed by a comma, the given Name (first name), a space, the initials (middle initial or initials), and a period. Click OK and then click OK again to close the Properties dialog box for user-Display.

FIGURE 11.8
ADSI Edit as it appears when it starts up

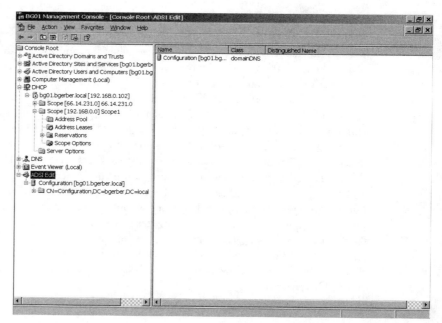

FIGURE 11.9

Accessing the appropriate ADSI Edit language subcontainer

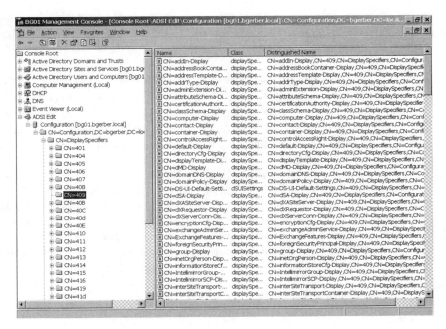

FIGURE 11.10

Editing the Active Directory schema to change the format of the Windows 2003/ Exchange 2003 display name

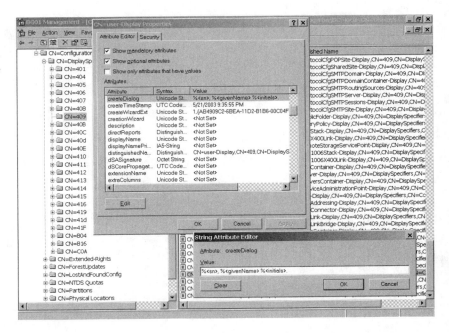

For the record, ADSI Edit gives you access to your Active Directory's schema by way of the Lightweight Directory Access Protocol (LDAP). LDAP has come a long way since its first implementation in Exchange Server 5.5.

SETTING THE DEFAULT FORMAT FOR ORGANIZATIONAL E-MAIL ADDRESSES

When you installed your Exchange server (assuming that you followed the directions in Chapter 8), two addressing defaults were created for your Exchange organization: one for SMTP (Internet) and one for X.400. These addressing defaults are contained within what is called the *default recipient policy*. The SMTP addressing default is appended to each Exchange user's alias name to create the user's full SMTP address.

This is very important: The default is based on the name of your Windows 2003 domain. You'll remember that I named my domain bgerber.local. So, currently the default for my Exchange organization is @bgerber.local. My Internet e-mail address is `bgerber@bgerber.local`. To confirm this, check out Figure 11.11, which shows the E-Mail Addresses property page of the Properties dialog box for user Gerber, Barry E. Open your own user account in `Active Directory Users and Computer\Users`. If you followed my lead earlier, your Internet e-mail address should be `something@something.local`.

FIGURE 11.11

A user's Exchange e-mail address, as shown in the user's Properties dialog box

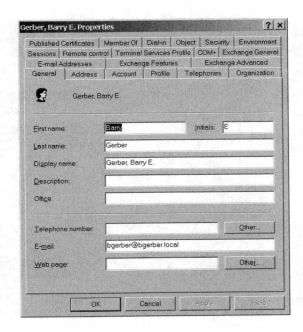

"That's no good," you say, "I want my address to be, say, `bgerber@bgerber.com`." What to do? No big deal. To change addressing defaults, open your Exchange System Manager until it looks like the one in Figure 11.12. Find and click Recipient Policies. Keep tracking on Figure 11.12. Locate the Default Policy object in the right pane, and double-click it. Tab over to the E-Mail Addresses property page on the Default Policy Properties dialog box. Click SMTP, and the SMTP Address Properties dialog box opens. Simply change the address to whatever you need. I changed mine to `@bgerber.com`. Click OK to close the SMTP Address Properties dialog box and then OK again to close the Default Policy Properties dialog box. Next a dialog box will pop up telling you that the change was done and asking if you want to apply the change to existing e-mail addresses. Click OK and you've changed every existing SMTP e-mail address and set things so that future SMTP e-mail addresses will conform to your new default.

FIGURE 11.12

The Default Policy Properties dialog box is used to change the addressing default for an Exchange organization.

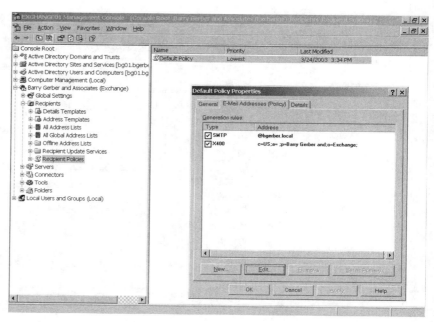

Your changes might not happen immediately. To force updates to existing addresses, click the Recipient Update Services container (see Figure 11.12). You'll see two objects in the right pane of this container. The first is for your domain and the second is for your Exchange organization. Right-click each, select Rebuild, and click Yes on the dialog box that pops up. This will update your addresses. Open your account in `Active Directory Users and Computers\Users`. You should now see your new SMTP e-mail address.

NOTE *Your Windows 2003 domain still has the name you gave it when you installed Windows Server 2003. Tab over to the Account page on the Properties dialog box for your Windows account. Your account still has its original address; mine is `bgerber@bgerber.local`. All you've changed is the format of the SMTP e-mail address used for Internet mail; mine is `bgerber@bgerber.com`. This is neat and proves conclusively that you don't have to have the same name for your internal Windows domain and your Internet e-mail domain.*

In addition to changing the addressing default for an organization, you can add policies for specific types of Exchange recipients. As you begin to develop a multiserver Exchange hierarchy, you can develop additional recipient policies for specific types of Exchange recipients that apply to specific Exchange servers. This lets you create different addressing defaults for different servers.

Addressing defaults are not limited to the SMTP and X.400. When you install a new Exchange connector or gateway (say, for cc:Mail or MS Mail), Exchange generates addressing defaults for the new messaging system.

We're done with the preliminaries. Now we're ready to begin working with Exchange recipients.

Managing Exchange Recipients

If you're familiar with Exchange Server 5.5, a lot of what follows should make sense. However, because Windows 2003 and Exchange 2003 take an object-oriented approach to system management, you often have to start and complete a specific task in a different way in Exchange 2003.

In this section, we'll focus on managing three of the four Exchange recipient types:

◆ Users who may be either *mailbox-enabled* or *mail-enabled*

◆ Distribution groups, also called *mail-enabled groups*

◆ Contacts

In the next chapter, we'll work with public folders. Why not deal with public folders in this chapter? As I've mentioned before, you work with mailboxes, distribution groups, and contacts in `Active Directory Users and Computers\Users`, while you work with public folders in Exchange System Manager. We deal in great detail with Exchange System Manager in the next chapter, and I'm waiting until we get there to get into public folder management.

Now let's move on to managing each type of Exchange recipient. As we look at Exchange users, distribution groups, and contacts, we'll first focus on creating one of these objects and then on the details of further managing it. You've already created a mailbox, so the creation section will be relatively brief.

At the end of this section, I show you how to search for Exchange recipients. As your Exchange organization grows, I guarantee that you'll find this capability more and more useful.

Managing Exchange Users

As I noted in the previous section, there are two types of Exchange users: mailbox-enabled users and mail-enabled users. A mailbox-enabled user has a mailbox in your Exchange system and can send and receive messages from that mailbox. A mail-enabled user has no mailbox in your Exchange system. Rather, a mail-enabled user has an e-mail address outside your Exchange system. A mail-enabled user can log on to your Windows 2003 network and act as any other Windows 2003 user. However, such a user must send and receive messages in another messaging system. When a mailbox-enabled user sends a message to a mail-enabled user, Exchange sends the message to the mail-enabled user's external e-mail address.

Mail-enabled users are new to Exchange. They make it easy to deal with Windows 2003 users who want to use an external e-mail account.

Don't confuse mail-enabled users with contacts (custom recipients in Exchange 5.5). Contacts point to addresses that are external to your Exchange system, just like mail-enabled users. However, that's all they do. There is no Windows 2003 user connected with a contact.

To start, I'll show you how to create and manage a new mailbox-enabled user. After that, I'll show you how to create and manage a mail-enabled user.

NOTE *You'll notice that here I use the term* user *rather than* user account. *An Exchange user is a Windows 2003 user account that has been either mailbox- or mail-enabled.*

Creating and Managing Mailbox-Enabled Users

This is a pretty complex section. Creating a mailbox-enabled user is a piece of cake, but managing one isn't so easy. Because a mailbox-enabled user is both a Windows 2003 and an Exchange 2003 user, the management interface for such a user is full of mind-boggling and sometimes diverting detail. You'll spend a good deal of time in this section doing hands-on tasks, but you'll also devote considerable effort to understanding the dizzying array of management options available for mailbox-enabled users.

In this section, we first create a mailbox-enabled user. Then we take a look at all of the management options available for each user on the user Properties dialog box.

CREATING A MAILBOX-ENABLED USER

Let's create a mailbox-enabled user for Jane Dough, a securities consultant for a major multinational conglomerate. Because Jane doesn't exist as a user, we'll first have to create her user account to mailbox-enable that account.

To start, right-click the Users container and select New ➤ User from the pop-up menu. The New Object - User dialog box opens (see Figure 11.13). Fill in at least your user's first and last names. Each field that you're filling in contains a *property* or, more specifically, an *attribute* of the user. The user's full name is automatically created. Notice in Figure 11.13 that the system uses the *last_name, first_name middle_initial.* format for display names that I created in the section "Setting the Default Format for Display Names" earlier in this chapter. Finally, enter a user login name. The pre–Windows 2000 name is automatically created.

FIGURE 11.13
Using the New
Object–User
dialog box to
create a new
user account

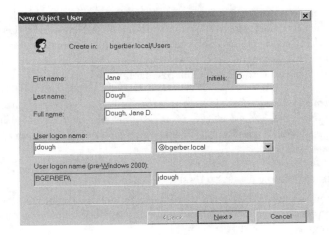

Click Next and enter a password for the user. Click Next again and view and accept the creation of an Exchange mailbox (see Figure 11.14). This is where you choose whether or not to mailbox-enable this user. Note that you can change the default mailbox alias and select the server and mailbox store on which the mailbox will be created. Click Next, and then Finish on the last page of the New Object - User dialog box.

FIGURE 11.14
Mailbox-enabling a
new user

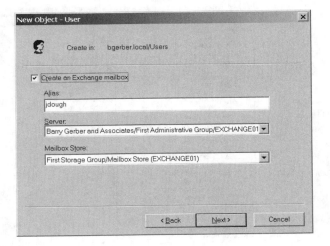

Find your new user in the Users container, and double-click it (see Figure 11.15). This opens the Properties dialog box for your new user. If the dialog box doesn't show the new user's e-mail address yet, close the dialog box and wait a few minutes for the Recipient Update servers to create the address.

You don't have to create a new user account and mailbox-enable the user at the same time. You can deselect the Create an Exchange Mailbox option on the New Object–User dialog box (see Figure 11.14, shown earlier), create the user account, and then mailbox-enable the user later. To mailbox-enable an existing user account, right-click the account in the Users container and select Exchange Tasks. A wizard will then guide you through the mailbox-enabling process.

TIP   When a user account has been mailbox-enabled, how do you get rid of the mailbox? Just open the Exchange Task Wizard (right-click the user and select Exchange Tasks from the menu that pops up) and select Delete Mailbox. To delete a user account, whether it's mailbox-enabled or not, select it and either press the Delete key or right-click it and select Delete from the menu that pops up.

MANAGING MAILBOX-ENABLED USERS

Okay, now let's take a tour of the user Properties dialog box shown previously in Figure 11.15. Before we begin that tour, I need to talk a bit about the property pages on the dialog box that are relevant to Exchange and those that are not.

Exchange-relevant means that a property page contains e-mail-specific attributes—attributes that provide information about a user that other users can view, or attributes that are necessary to the proper functioning of the electronic-messaging environment.

FIGURE 11.15

The Properties dialog box for a new user

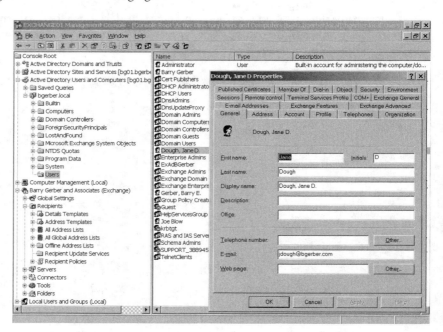

E-mail-specific attributes are attributes relating directly to a mailbox-enabled user's mailbox. These include limits on what can be stored in the mailbox, who can access it, and such. E-mail-specific property pages in Figure 11.15 include these:

◆ Exchange General

- ◆ E-mail Addresses

- ◆ Exchange Features

- ◆ Exchange Advanced

Attributes that provide information about a user that other users can view are attributes that an Outlook user can view. Figure 11.16 shows the Properties dialog box for user Jane Dough that opens when you click on her name in the Address Book that is part of the Outlook client. (See Chapter 10, "A Quick Overview of Outlook 2003," for a refresher on the Address Book.)

The General tab, which you can see in detail, and the other four tabs, which you can't, include a great deal of the information that is administered and managed on various property pages of the user Properties dialog box, shown earlier in Figure 11.15. Information carries over to the Outlook Address Book properties dialog box (Figure 11.16) from the following property pages on the user Properties dialog box (Figure 11.15):

- ◆ General

- ◆ Address

- ◆ Telephones

- ◆ Organization

- ◆ Member Of

So, as an Exchange Server 2003 manager, you should focus on 9 of the 20 property pages on the user Properties dialog box. Does that mean that you don't have to worry about the other 11 pages? No such luck. Although these pages focus heavily on Windows 2003 account attributes, you need to understand some of them so that you can either use them when necessary or ask a Windows Server 2003 administrator to set up certain attributes for you. These pages, which have attributes that are *necessary to the proper functioning of the electronic messaging environment,* include

- ◆ Account

- ◆ Profile

- ◆ Published Certificates

- ◆ Security

- ◆ Environment

All right! Now, let's look at the 9 Exchange-specific property pages and the 5 property pages that cover attributes necessary to the proper functioning of the Exchange environment that appear on the user Properties dialog box. We'll look at each property page in the order specified here. After I discuss the 14 Exchange-specific property pages, I'll quickly discuss the remaining 6 property pages on the user Properties dialog box.

FIGURE 11.16

Viewing user attributes in the Outlook Address Book

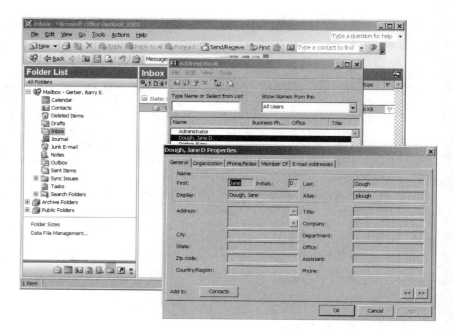

NOTE *There are other ways to manage the mailboxes of mailbox-enabled users other than with individual user property pages. I'll talk about these in Chapter 12. For now, suffice it to say that these include setting storage parameters for an entire mailbox store and using Exchange Server's Mailbox Manager.*

E-Mail-Specific Property Pages

Exchange 5.5 administrators will find most of the mailbox management user interfaces that they are accustomed to in the four e-mail-specific property pages. A number of property pages were displayed on Exchange 5.5's mailbox dialog box. To avoid property page mania, Exchange 2003 adds only four e-mail-specific property pages to the user Properties dialog box. Two of these pages, Exchange General and Exchange Advanced, contain buttons that open seven additional property pages. Let's take a look at the four e-mail-specific property pages on the Windows 2003 user Properties dialog box:

E-Mail Addresses   The E-Mail Addresses property page shows a mailbox's addresses for different types of messaging systems (see Figure 11.11, shown earlier). As I noted in the earlier section "Setting the Default Format for Organizational E-Mail Addresses," two addressing defaults are created by default when you install Exchange Server 2003: SMTP and X.400. These addressing defaults are then used to generate specific addresses for each recipient.

Using the E-Mail Addresses property page, you can add a new address or manually change or even remove an existing address. For example, I sometimes give certain users a second SMTP address that includes their specific department. Adding, modifying, or removing addresses manually is fun, but not for those new to Exchange 2003, both because it's a little dangerous to play with addresses and because it's sometimes not enough to just add, change, or remove the address. You might also have to do some things in other areas within Exchange and maybe even in external systems. I'll talk about all this stuff in Chapter 16, "Advanced Exchange Server Administration and Management."

You can also use the E-Mail Addresses property page to set an address of a particular type as the primary address. The primary address is the one that appears in the From field of a message. It is also the return address for replies to the message. You need two addresses of the same type to change the primary address. In the case of my second SMTP address example, I leave the system-generated address as the primary address.

Exchange Features   You use the Exchange Features property page, shown in Figure 11.17, to enable and disable client-oriented features such as wireless and Internet-based access to your Exchange server. We'll look at this page again in Chapter 14, "Managing Exchange 2003 Services for Internet Clients" and Chapter 19, "Wireless Access to Exchange Server 2003."

Exchange General   Now, click over to the Exchange General property page. The store holding the mailbox is shown in the Mailbox Store field (see the left side of Figure 11.18). You can't change the mailbox store here; you have to move a mailbox to change its store. We'll get into moving mailboxes later in this book.

The alias for the user's mailbox is shown immediately after the name of the mailbox store. You can change the alias here, but that won't change the aliases used in Exchange addresses that have already been generated for this mailbox. The change will affect any addresses added in the future.

FIGURE 11.17

Using the Exchange Features property page to enable and disable various client access services

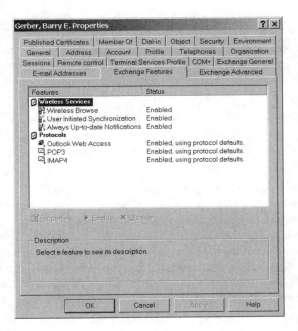

FIGURE 11.18

The Exchange General property page and its Delivery Restrictions property page that is opened by clicking the Delivery Restrictions button

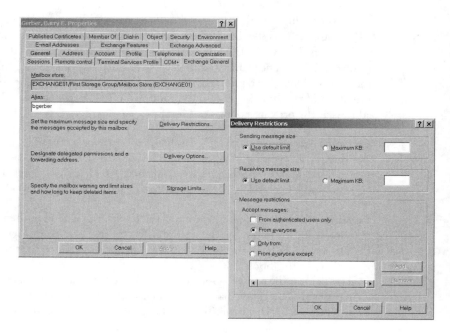

Delivery Restrictions, Delivery Options, and Storage Limits   The three buttons on the Exchange General property page open subproperty pages for further setting properties. These pages enable you to set a range of attributes relating to messages and permissions:

Delivery Restrictions   Sending and receiving messages takes network bandwidth. You can control bandwidth usage by setting limits on the size of messages that a user can send and receive. As you can see on the right side of Figure 11.18, shown earlier, you can choose to use the default limit for sent and received messages, or set a specific limit for the mailbox. I'll talk about setting default size options in the next chapter.

In addition to setting message size limits, you can restrict the senders a mailbox can receive messages from. The default, as you can see in Figure 11.18, is to accept messages from everyone. Alternatively, you can choose to allow the mailbox to receive messages from a specific list of senders or from all senders but a specific list. You must choose the senders from among users, groups, and computers in your Active Directory. So, you can't use message restriction options to control messages from outside your Exchange organization unless you enter a specific address as a contact in your Active Directory and then select that address. I'll talk more about restricting messages to and from external mail systems in Chapter 13, "Managing Exchange 2003 Internet Services."

Delivery Options   Figure 11.19 shows the Delivery Options subproperty page of the Exchange General property page. This one's pretty neat. You can grant another user permission to send messages on behalf of this mailbox. The From field in Send on Behalf messages identifies both the person sending the message and the individual on whose behalf the message was sent. Can you imagine going through and setting Send on Behalf options for each user? Whew! But don't worry: Users can do it for themselves using their Exchange clients.

FIGURE 11.19

Using the Delivery Options property page to give other recipients special rights to a mailbox, set a forwarding address, and limit the number of recipients a mailbox can send messages to at one time

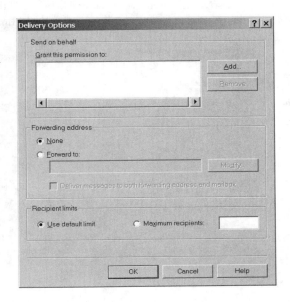

The Forwarding Address option is quite neat too. With Exchange 5.5, users had to set up forwarding in their Outlook clients. They can still do this, but Exchange 200x administrators now have the option of setting the forwarding address, which, if nothing else, means that forwarding from Exchange environments should be more accurate.

As with message restrictions in the last section, you can forward to an address only in your Active Directory. So, you have to enter a contact for external addresses. Even so, this little addition alone is almost worth the price of admission to Exchange Server 2003.

Some organizations have their mass mailers. These are people who write a message and then send it to everyone that they can find on their corporate address list, either by picking everyone's name or by using one or more distribution lists. The Recipient Limits option on the Delivery Options property page lets you limit the number of recipients that a mailbox user can send a message to. In computing this limit, a distribution group is not equal to one recipient. Instead, it is equal to all the recipients on the list. This is a nice way to cut down on all that internal spamming on your system. The default is a whopping 5,000 recipients. I'll show you how to change the default in the next chapter.

Storage Limits   Use the Storage Limits subproperty page of the Exchange General property page to either accept the store's default maximum-size limits (you'll learn how to set the default in the next chapter) or set specific maximum limits for the mailbox. As shown in Figure 11.20, you can use any or all of three options when setting limits. The mailbox user gets a warning when the first limit is reached and then on a specific schedule thereafter until storage drops below the limit. I'll show you how to set the default warning message schedule in the next chapter.

When the second limit is reached, the mailbox can no longer send mail. It can still receive mail, however, because you might not want those who send messages getting a bunch of bounced message notifications just because a mailbox user is a resource hog. The third limit prevents reception as well as sending of messages. This option is useful when a user will be out of the office for an extended period and you don't want that person's mailbox to fill up with gobs of unanswered messages.

FIGURE 11.20

Using the Storage Limits property page to limit the amount of disk space available to a mailbox and determine how deleted but retained items are handled

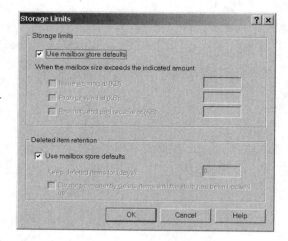

Exchange 5.5 brought a great new concept to Microsoft messaging: deleted item retention. Essentially, when a user deletes messages from the Deleted Items folder, the messages no longer show up in the folder but are retained in the Exchange server message store for a specific time. Using an Outlook 2000 or 2003 client, a user can retrieve "deleted" messages not yet deleted from the store. I'll show you how to set default deleted-item retention parameters in the next chapter. You can use the Storage Limits property page to set retention parameters for a specific mailbox. You can set the number of days that deleted items are kept on the mailbox's Exchange server before they are automatically and finally deleted, or you can specify that items should not be deleted until the store in which they are located has been backed up.

Exchange Advanced Properties Page

The Exchange Advanced properties page brings together a number of Exchange 2003 attributes that you might need to modify (see Figure 11.21). Exchange 5.5 refugees will be happy to see that they can manage many of their favorite Exchange attributes using this page. Let's look at these attributes in the order that they appear on the page.

Simple Display Name   The Simple Display Name field is especially useful in certain multilingual Exchange environments. Exchange clients and the Exchange System Manager show the simple display name when the full display name can't be properly shown. For example, if a full display name is stored in a double-byte character set such as Chinese Traditional or Korean, and if a particular copy of the client or the Exchange System Manager isn't set to display the character set, the simple display name is shown in place of the full display name.

FIGURE 11.21

The Exchange Advanced property page

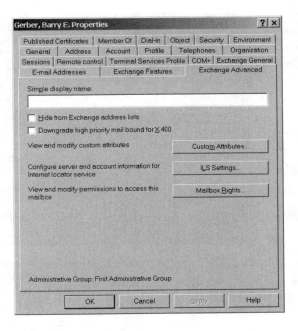

Hide from Exchange Address Lists   Select Hide from Exchange Address Lists to prevent a mailbox from showing up in the various address lists supported by Exchange. Generally, you want to hide a mailbox from the Address Book to protect a particular mailbox's privacy or when it is used by custom-programmed applications rather than by human users.

Downgrade High-Priority Mail Bound for X.400   Check this box to prevent the mailbox from sending X.400 mail at high priority. If the mailbox user attempts to send a message destined for an X.400 system at high priority, the Exchange Server downgrades the priority to Normal. You use this option to ensure that messages to X.400 mail systems conform with the older 1984 X.400 standard.

Custom Attributes, ILS Settings, and Mailbox Rights   Now let's focus on the subproperty pages on the Exchange Advanced properties page that you view by clicking the button bearing their names.

    Custom Attributes   You use the Custom Attributes property page, shown in Figure 11.22, to fill in custom information for a mailbox. For example, you can use one of the custom fields to hold the Employee ID for the user of the mailbox. You would, of course, use the same custom field for the same item for each user's mailbox. You can rename the attributes, but it requires digging deeply into Active Directory. I talk a little about how you go about digging in Chapter 16.

FIGURE 11.22

Setting custom attributes for a mailbox

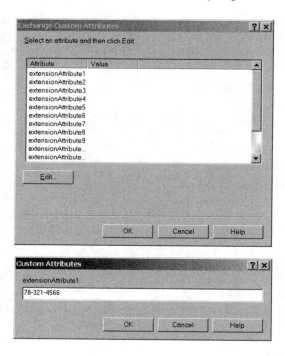

ILS Settings Microsoft's Internet Locator Service (ILS) is designed to make it easier for users to find each other so that they can hold electronic discussions or conferences. You enter information about the mailbox user's ILS server and account on the dialog box that pops up when you click ILS Settings. ILS runs as a Windows 2003 service.

Mailbox Rights You use the Mailbox Rights property page to establish or change permissions for the mailbox. Figure 11.23 shows the default mailbox access permissions granted to the user for whom the mailbox is created. SELF is an Active Directory–wide group—that is, it is not limited to any specific domain in Active Directory. SELF has a range of rights, including Exchange-specific rights. When a user is created, that user is added to the group. Members of the group SELF get the default mailbox permissions shown in Figure 11.23 by virtue of belonging to the group. These permissions apply only to the user's mailbox, not to all mailboxes.

WARNING *The following is intended to be instructional only. Don't change any permissions unless you're very sure you know what you're doing.*

The permissions listed in the Permissions For SELF box are fairly self-explanatory. However, to be sure that we're all on the same page, Table 11.1 is a list of the permissions and a brief explanation of their functions.

FIGURE 11.23

Using the Mailbox Rights property page to view and modify permissions on the mailbox

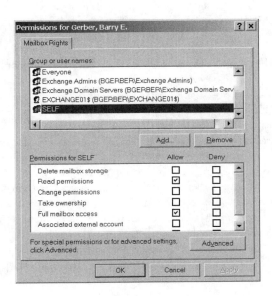

TABLE 11.1: PERMISSIONS

PERMISSION	DESCRIPTION
Delete mailbox storage	If allowed, the user or group may delete the mailbox itself.
Read permissions	The user or group can read the permissions granted to the mailbox.
Change permissions	The user or group can change mailbox permissions.
Take ownership	The user or group can take ownership of the mailbox.
Full mailbox access	The user or group can access the mailbox and all its contents, including all subfolders.
Associated external account	The account, which is a Windows Server 2003 account outside the Windows 2003 forest where your Exchange system resides, may access the mailbox.
Special permissions (not visible in Figure 11.23)	Special permissions are the mechanism by which the object SELF is granted Read and Full Mailbox Access permissions.

TIP   *If you see only the group SELF on the Mailbox Rights property page, that's because the user's mailbox has yet to be created. Yeah, I know, Exchange said it was creating the mailbox, but it lied. The mailbox isn't created until the first message is sent to the user. So, to see all the groups that have permissions on the mailbox, just send a message to the user and then close and reopen the Mailbox Rights property page. Alternatively, if you sent yourself a message back in Chapter 10, look at the Mailbox Rights property page for your mailbox.*

Scroll through the Name field at the top of the Mailbox Rights property page, and find and select the group Exchange Admins. Notice that the group has permissions that allow it to fully administer the mailbox, but not to access the messages in it. Those permissions were inherited from the permissions set on the Exchange organizational container (mine is Barry Gerber and Associates) when you delegated control to Exchange Admins back in Chapter 8.

You probably won't need to grant others permissions to a mailbox very often. As I noted in Chapter 10, users can grant others access to all or part of their mailboxes right inside Outlook. So, why might you want to give others permissions to a mailbox? One reason would be to create a shared mailbox. Maybe you want people to send help desk–type messages to a mailbox and then have several staff members access the mailbox to read the messages and resolve problems. Or a specific department might want to collaborate using a common mailbox. You could do these sorts of tasks using a secure public folder, but a mailbox might work better in some cases.

So, to give other users permissions to access a mailbox, click Add on the Mailbox Rights property page. Then use the Select Users, Computers, or Groups dialog box to pick the users or groups allowed access to the mailbox (see Figure 11.24).

FIGURE 11.24

To give others permissions to a mailbox, select them from the Select Users, Computers, or Groups dialog box.

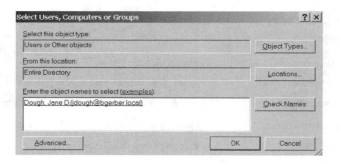

The Advanced button on a Mailbox Rights property page allows you to give additional permissions to an object. Click Advanced and then double-click the object you want to view or manage. As Figure 11.25 shows, you can actually change the user or group to whom the permissions are granted, and you can choose how the permissions are to be applied. If an object has inherited permissions that were set higher up in the Exchange hierarchy, the Change button and the Apply Onto field are grayed out and therefore unchangeable. Check this out by clicking Advanced on the Permissions property page and then double-clicking Exchange Admins. See Figure 11.23 (shown previously) for the location of the Advanced button.

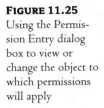

FIGURE 11.25
Using the Permission Entry dialog box to view or change the object to which permissions will apply

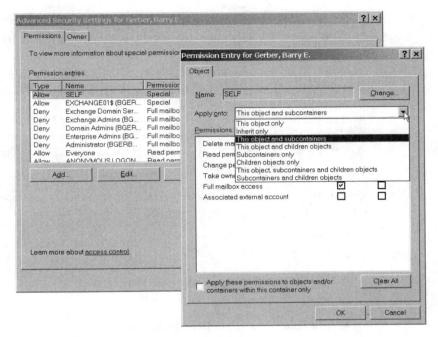

Property Pages That Provide Information Useful to Users

Now let's turn to the property pages that aren't e-mail-specific and that include information end users will encounter in one place or another as they move through your Exchange and Windows 2003 system. I think that Exchange managers are more attuned than Windows 2003 administrators to users and to both how they perceive this information and how they might use it. Additionally, Exchange administrators managed this information in Exchange 5.5. Therefore, I believe that Exchange managers should administer this information or at least be intimately involved in its administration. Let's take a brief walk through these property pages.

General   As you can see back in Figure 11.15, you use the General property page to set basic attributes for a user. Leaving out the attributes that I discussed in the previous section, "Creating a Mailbox-Enabled User," the General properties page includes the following attributes:

Description   A brief description of the user.

Office   Some way of identifying the user's office, such as the office number.

Telephone number   The telephone number that you want other users to see in the Outlook Address Book. Click Other to add more telephone numbers for the user. These other numbers are not available to other users through the Outlook Address Book. You could make them available through custom applications that access Active Directory.

E-mail   The user's SMTP address, automatically displayed in this field.

Web page   The user's web page. The Other button works as it does for the telephone number.

TIP   When creating a new account and mailbox, you don't have to fill in every last lovin' field on every property page. Only the First and Last names and login name fields on the General property page must be filled in.

Address   The Address properties page is designed to hold the user's mailing address. These attributes were part of the Exchange 5.5 directory. They are now standard Windows 2003 attributes. As I mentioned previously, I still believe that Exchange 2003 managers should be heavily involved in supporting this property page.

Telephones   As you might expect, you manage a user's telephone numbers on the Telephones property page. The page has room for five phone numbers. The defaults are these:

◆ Home

◆ Pager

◆ Mobile

◆ Fax

◆ IP Phone (an Internet IP address–based phone)

You can change the defaults.

The Telephones property page also includes a text box for notes. Exchange 5.5 managers will be happy to see that this pretty much keeps intact the content of the Phone/Notes property page of the Exchange 5.5 mailbox Properties dialog box.

Organization   You use the Organization property page to record information about the user's status in your organization's hierarchy. See Jane Dough's Organization property page on the left side of Figure 11.26. Here you can set the following user information:

◆ Title

◆ Department

◆ Company

◆ Manager

FIGURE 11.26
Using the Organization property page to show a user's place in an organization's corporate hierarchy

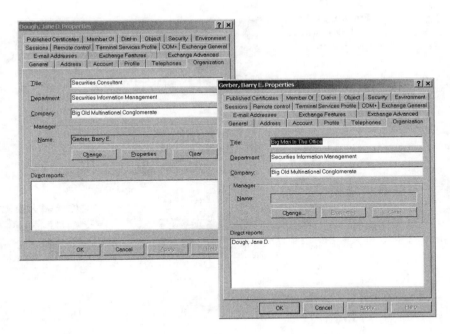

You can also view the names of the individuals who directly report to the user. Jane Dough has no direct reports. However, she does have a manager: me. If you look at my Organization property page on the right side of Figure 11.26, you'll see that she is listed in the Direct Reports box. That's because I've set myself as her manager on her Organization property page.

This is a big improvement over Exchange 5.5's Organization property page. With 5.5, you had to jump through too many hoops to produce essentially the same information that you see here. Of course, neither 5.5 nor 2003 works if you have one of those dysfunctional organizations where people are expected to serve multiple masters. That's a joke, sort of.

Member Of The Member Of property page is used to add users to groups. You can add users to security groups or to distribution groups. You don't have any distribution groups yet, so you can't do it now; in Figure 11.27, however, I'm adding my mailbox to a distribution group that I sneakily created while you were otherwise occupied. I just tabbed over to the Member Of property page, clicked Add, typed in **sneakily** in the Enter Object Names To Select field, and clicked Check Names. Exchange System Administrator found the group Sneakily Created Distribution Group and replaced *sneakily* with the group's full name. Then I clicked OK and I immediately became a member of the distribution group. We'll get into creating distribution groups later in this chapter in the section "Managing Distribution Groups."

FIGURE 11.27
Adding a user to a distribution group

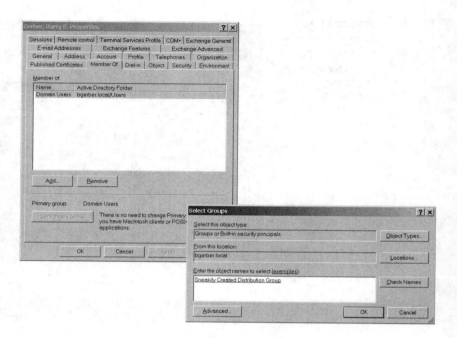

Property Pages Essential to the Proper Functioning of Exchange

A number of property pages contain an attribute here or there that you need to be aware of when managing mailbox-enabled users. I discuss these next:

Account A good deal of the contents of the Account property page appeared in NT 4's User Manager for domains. Much of advanced security functionality, such as the kind of encryption used for the password, is also managed on the Account property page. As should be obvious in Figure 11.28, much of what's on this page relates to Windows 2003 security. The page is important for Exchange 2003 managers mainly because it is where the user logon name is managed.

FIGURE 11.28

The Account property page is used to manage a range of Windows 2003 security options.

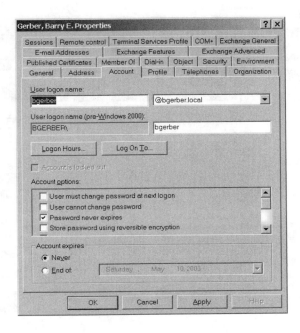

Profile   The Profile property page is another page imported pretty much intact from NT 4's User Manager. As an Exchange manager, your main interest in this page is likely to be in the script that is run when a user logs in to your Windows 2003 network. Some programs, such as the third-party application Profile Maker, need to run when the user first logs in. Profile Maker ensures that a user's Exchange profile (see Chapter 10) is properly created and remains as the Exchange administrator wants it to be. It is especially useful for roaming users. You can run a program such as Profile Maker in the logon script. (See the Appendix, "Cool Third-Party Applications for Exchange Server and Outlook Clients," for more on Profile Maker.)

NOTE   *Oh yes, just for the record, the* Profile *in Profile Maker has nothing to do with the name of this property page, which is about Windows 2003 profiles.*

Published Certificates   You can view the security certificates that have been assigned to the user on the Published Certificates property page. If and when you get into Exchange Advanced Security, you'll see the certificates for this service on this property page.

Security   You should treat the Security property page as you would the registry on your server or Active Directory. Make changes with great care. You can see in Figure 11.29 that a number of groups have permissions on this mailbox. Most of those permissions were inherited from upper-level containers. Some were granted specifically for the user when the user was created.

FIGURE 11.29
The Security property page is used to modify permissions on the user object as a whole.

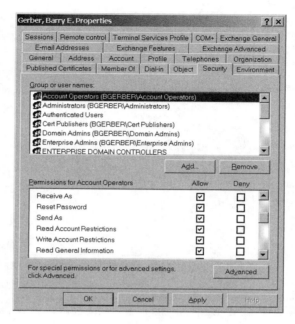

I won't go into great detail here, but I do want to talk about a couple of permissions, Receive As and Send As:

Receive As   Allows the user or group granted the right for a mailbox to open the mailbox inside an Outlook client. The user or group member operates out of their own mailbox. That person can read messages in any mailbox to which Receive As permission has been granted, but this user can not send messages. To open an additional mailbox in Outlook 2003, select Tools ➢ E-Mail Accounts, click View Or Change Existing E-Mail Accounts, and then click Next. Then be sure Microsoft Exchange Server is selected and click Change. On the next page, click More Settings and tab over to the Advanced page on the dialog box that opens. Click Add in the Mailbox area to select a mailbox to open in addition to your own. See Chapter 10 for more information.

Send As   Allows the user or group granted the right for a mailbox to send messages from other mailboxes to which the user or group has rights so it appears that the messages came from the Send As mailbox. This right can be useful when, for example, you want an administrative assistant to send messages from their own mailbox that appear to have come from a corporate mailbox (such as President at Barry Gerber and Associates). The right is exercised inside the Outlook 2003 mailbox of the user by using the From field, which is exposed by clicking the down arrow next to the Options field on a message and selecting From. (You can also select the Blind cc field here.) Once you choose this option, the From field will show on all new messages until you deselect it. Send As rights should be granted with care. They can be dangerous in the wrong hands, such as when a disgruntled employee sends out a nasty message that appears to have come from some innocent person's mailbox.

You might be wondering why Send As and Receive As permissions are granted on the Security property page and not on the Exchange Advanced/Mailbox Rights property page. Exchange 2003 was designed to better protect user mailboxes from the prying eyes of rogue Exchange administrators than Exchange 5.5 did. As I noted back in the section "Mailbox Rights," Exchange administrators (for example, members of the Exchange Admins group that we created back in Chapter 8) aren't given access to user messages. And, although Exchange administrators can administer mailbox rights, they can not administer the Security property page that contains Receive As and Send As permissions. Only a user with permissions to change objects in the Active Directory Users and Computers Users container can modify attributes on the Security property page. There's nothing to stop someone from giving such permissions to the group Exchange Admins. The key point is that someone other than a member of that group must grant the permissions. I'll go into all of this in Chapter 18, "Exchange Server System Security."

WARNING *The Send on Behalf Of option, which can be set by a user in an Outlook client or by an administrator on the Delivery Options property page, is quite different from the Send As option, which you can set on the Security property page for a user. Send on Behalf Of lets a user send a message for another user while also identifying the actual sending user. Send As lets the user of one mailbox send a message as though it came from another mailbox, without any hint that the other mailbox didn't send the message itself. If you worry about users sending embarrassing messages that look like they came from another user, then Send on Behalf Of is a far safer option than Send As. If both options are granted to a user, Send As will override Send on Behalf Of.*

Environment   The Environment property page includes a number of attributes relating to Windows 2003 startup. The only one of these that you might find useful has to do with starting a program when a user logs in. You can specify the program on this page. As I pointed out earlier in the section "Profile," you can also start a program in the user's logon script.

Property Pages Peripherally Related to Proper Functioning of Exchange

We've covered all but six of the property pages on the user Properties dialog box. This remaining group of pages has little to do directly with Exchange server. I'll cover them quickly:

Dial-In   You set parameters here for the user's dial-in to Windows 2003's remotely, including enabling or disabling dial-in, and whether the user is called back at a specific phone number for security purposes.

Object   This page contains information about the user as an object. This includes the object's name and class, the dates it was created and modified, and its initial and current update sequence number, which tell you how many times the object was updated.

Terminal Services Profile   This is where you set a home directory to be used when the user logs in through a Windows 2003 terminal server session and give permission to actually log in to the terminal server.

COM+   This page is of special use to application developers. An Exchange-related application might use this page, but most Exchange administrators will want to leave its administration to developers and Windows administrators.

Remote Control   You set the capability for another to remotely view and control the user's terminal server session here. This works only under Terminal Services.

Sessions   This is another terminal server–oriented property page where you set session termination and reconnection parameters.

Creating and Managing Mail-Enabled Users

As you'll remember, a mail-enabled user is a Window 2003 user with an external e-mail address, a user without an Exchange mailbox. Exchange routes messages sent by a mailbox-enabled user to the mail-enabled user's external e-mail address.

Mail-enabled users are a lot like mailbox-enabled users. So, I'm going to move quickly through this section, pointing out only differences between the two types of Windows 2003 users.

CREATING A MAIL-ENABLED USER

To create a mail-enabled user, create a user just as you did in the section "Creating a Mailbox-Enabled User" earlier in this chapter, but don't accept the creation of an Exchange mailbox. Then, when the user has been created, right-click the user and select Exchange Tasks. This opens the Exchange Task Wizard. Click over to the Available Tasks page, shown in Figure 11.30, and select Establish E-Mail Addresses. Then click Next to move to the next wizard page, Establish E-Mail Addresses.

You use the Establish E-Mail Addresses page of the Exchange Task Wizard, shown in Figure 11.31, to add an e-mail address for your mail-enabled user. You're offered an alias for the user, an opportunity to enter the user's e-mail address and select an Exchange administrative group where the user will be managed. To enter the e-mail address, click Modify.

FIGURE 11.30
Choosing to mail-enable a user using the Exchange Task Wizard

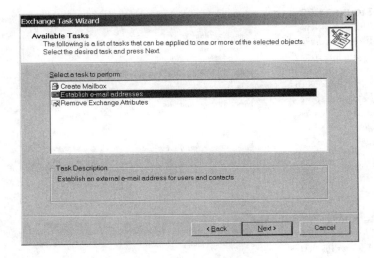

FIGURE 11.31
Using the Exchange Task Wizard to manage the alias, external e-mail address, and administrative group attributes of a new mail-enabled user

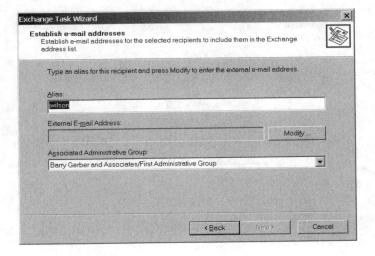

This opens the New E-Mail Address dialog box, shown in Figure 11.32. Select the type of address that you're going to enter (I'm selecting SMTP Address). Click OK to open the properties dialog box for the type of address you want to create. In my case, the Internet Address Properties dialog box opens (see Figure 11.33).

Enter the address for your mail-enabled user. You can use the Advanced property page, shown in Figure 11.34, to override default settings that you made on your Exchange server regarding Internet mail. We'll get into all this stuff in Chapter 13.

FIGURE 11.32
Using the New
E-mail Address
dialog box to
specify the kind of
e-mail address to
be created for a
mail-enabled user

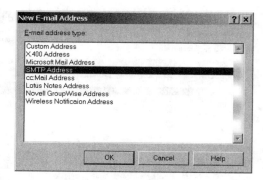

FIGURE 11.33
Using the Internet
Address Properties
dialog box General
property page to en-
ter the e-mail address
for a mail-enabled
user with an SMTP
address

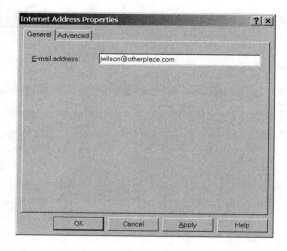

FIGURE 11.34

Using the Internet Address Properties dialog box Advanced property page to override Exchange server Internet mail defaults for a mail-enabled user

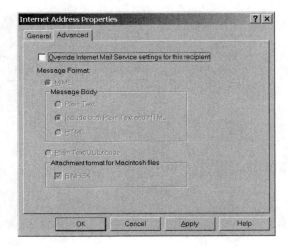

When you've finished working with the address, click Next and then click Finish on the final wizard page. That's it. You've created your first mail-enabled user. Now let's move on to the management of mail-enabled users.

TIP   At some point, you might need to mail-disable a user. To do so, open the Exchange Task Wizard and select Delete E-Mail Addresses. To delete a user account, whether it's mail-enabled or not, select it and either press the Delete key or right-click it and select Delete from the menu that pops up.

MANAGING MAIL-ENABLED USERS

In the container `Active Directory Users and Computers\Users`, find and double-click the mail-enabled user that you just created. Figure 11.35 shows the Properties dialog box for my new user, John Wilson. Because Wilson is a Windows 2003 user, all of his property pages but the e-mail-specific pages are exactly the same as they are for a mailbox-enabled user. Even the e-mail-specific pages are quite similar to those for a mailbox-enabled user. So, this is going to be a very quick trip.

FIGURE 11.35

The Exchange General property page for a mail-enabled user

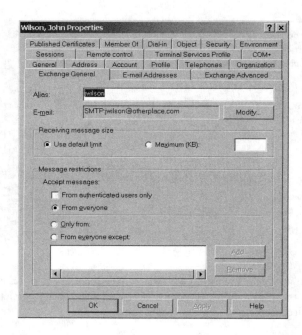

The Exchange General property page for mail-enabled users is a combination of the Exchange General page for mailbox-enabled users and the Delivery Restrictions subproperty page of the Exchange General property page for mailbox-enabled users. Wow! That's a mouthful, but it actually makes sense. For a refresher, take a look at Figure 11.35 and the section "Managing Mailbox-Enabled Users," especially Figure 11.18, earlier in this chapter.

The Exchange Advanced property page, shown in Figure 11.36, contains one field that needs some explaining, Use MAPI Rich Text Format. If this option is selected for an Exchange mail–enabled user, messages sent to the user by mailbox-enabled users can contain such attributes as color, bold, and italic text. By default, mailbox-enabled users send messages to mail-enabled users in plain text. Of course, the mail-enabled user's messaging system or e-mail client must support messages with MAPI attributes for all this to work. We'll encounter this field again when dealing with Exchange contacts later in this chapter. That's because both mail-enabled users and contacts have external e-mail addresses that might or might not support MAPI attributes.

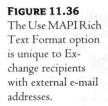

FIGURE 11.36
The Use MAPI Rich Text Format option is unique to Exchange recipients with external e-mail addresses.

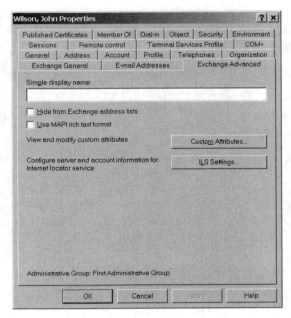

TIP *Many e-mail clients, including Outlook, can send messages in HTML format. HTML is a better format choice than MAPI rich text. You don't have to do anything to enable HTML message formatting on your server; that's done on the user's e-mail client. So, unless you know your mail-enabled user can benefit from MAPI rich-text formatted messages, leave this item unchecked.*

Creating and Managing Distribution Groups

Distribution groups, also known as mail-enabled groups, are used to group together all four types of Exchange recipients: users, contacts, public folders, and even other distribution groups. They are the equivalent of Exchange 5.5's distribution lists.

New to the distribution group family with Exchange 2003 are query-based distribution groups. I'll talk about them at the end of this section.

CREATING A DISTRIBUTION GROUP

To create a new distribution group, right-click the Users container in Active Directory Users and Computers, and then select New ➤ Group. The New Object - Group dialog box pops up, as shown in Figure 11.37.

Figure 11.37 shows you how the dialog box looks immediately upon opening. This dialog box is used to create both security and distribution groups. You can create three kinds of groups: domain local, global, and universal. You can create a universal security group only after you've set your domain to native mode. (See Chapter 6, "Upgrading to Windows Server 2003 and Exchange Server 2003," for more on mixed- and native-mode domains.) That's why Universal is grayed out in Figure 11.37, where the default group type is Security.

FIGURE 11.37
Using the New Object - Group dialog box to create a new distribution group

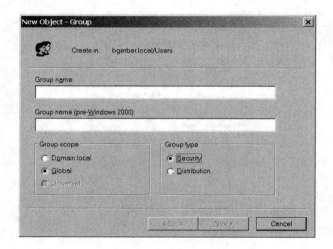

Universal groups, new to Windows 2003, make more sense than the local domain and global groups of NT 4, which are carried over to Windows 2003 for the sake of compatibility. Local groups hold users and global groups. Global groups exist simply to hold users and be included in local groups. It's kind of strange. A universal group can hold users or other groups. That's so much less complex. NT 4 domain controllers are incapable of dealing with the deep nesting of universal groups. That's why they're not available in mixed mode for security groups.

Okay, now select Distribution as the group type and name your group. I chose Managers for the name of my group. Things should look pretty much as they do in Figure 11.38. Notice that distribution groups can be universal.

FIGURE 11.38
Naming a new distribution group and specifying its scope

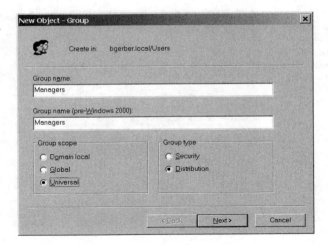

In the next dialog box, you're offered the opportunity to create an e-mail address for your distribution group (see Figure 11.39). Select Create an Exchange E-Mail Address and click Next. The last dialog box shows you what is about to happen. Click Finish to create your new distribution group.

FIGURE 11.39
Accepting creation
of an e-mail address
and the location for
the address

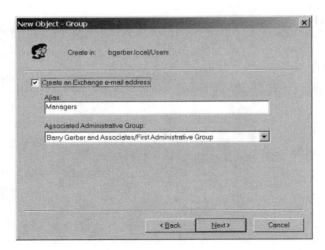

MANAGING DISTRIBUTION GROUPS

In the section on managing mailbox-enabled users, you had a fair amount of exposure to the format of a range of property pages. Because we were looking at the user Properties dialog box, we explored pages of varying relevance to the functioning of Exchange Server 2003. In this section, we're going to move pretty quickly through the distribution group Properties dialog box, both because there are far fewer pages and because you've seen some of the pages already. If I skip a page, the page has the same format and function as the same page on the mailbox-enabled user Properties dialog box.

ANY WINDOWS 2003 GROUP CAN BE MAIL-ENABLED OR MAIL-DISABLED

You can mail-enable any group, including a security group. As with a distribution group, when you create a security group, you're asked whether you want to give it an e-mail address. To e-mail-enable a group, right-click it and select Exchange Tasks from the pop-up menu. Using the Exchange Task Wizard that pops up, select Establish an E-Mail Address, and complete the wizard.

To mail-disable a group, use the Delete E-Mail Addresses option on the Exchange Task Wizard. To delete a distribution group, select it and press the Delete key, or right-click it and select Delete from the pop-up menu.

General

To open the Properties dialog box for your new distribution group, find and double-click it in the Users container. The General property page shows naming, descriptive, e-mail, and group attributes. It also provides a field for notes. As you can see in Figure 11.40, if you have the right permissions (remember, I'm a domain administrator), you can change the group's pre–Windows 2003 name, description, and e-mail address.

FIGURE 11.40

FIGURE 11.40
Using the General property page to view and edit the basic attributes of a distribution group

Members

You use the Members property page to add recipients to a distribution group. In Figure 11.41, I'm adding our friend Jane Dough to the Managers list. I know, she wasn't a manager back in the section where I talked about the user property page, Organization, but now she is. Hey, what can I say? She's a really good worker and is rising quickly through the organizational hierarchy.

Distribution groups can contain public folders, the only recipient that we are not covering in this chapter. However, they're a hot topic for the next chapter. To add a public folder to a distribution group, right-click the group and select Add Exchange Public Folders from the pop-up menu. This brings up a dialog box that you can use to pick the folders that you want to include in the list.

FIGURE 11.41

Using the Members property page to add a user to a distribution group

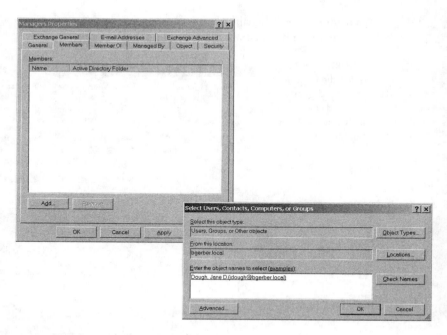

Member Of

The Member Of property page shows you the security and distribution groups to which your distribution group belongs. If you have adequate rights, you can add your distribution group to other distribution groups right here. You don't have to open the other group and use its Members property page.

Managed By

The manager of a distribution group can add and remove group members right inside their Outlook client. In Figure 11.42, using the Managed By property page, I've made Jane Dough the manager of the Managers distribution list. I did this by clicking Change and selecting the manager using the Select Users, Contacts, Computers, or Groups dialog box that popped up. The office, address, and phone information that I entered for Jane Dough automatically fills the fields on the property page. I entered only her phone number here, so that's all that shows.

The Properties button is neat. Click it, and the Properties dialog box for the manager opens. In this case, Jane Dough's user Properties dialog box opens.

Exchange General

The Exchange General property page looks a lot like a combination of several user and Exchange mailbox pages that we looked at back in the section "Managing Mailbox-Enabled Users." However, rather than flipping back and forth to previous sections of this chapter, take a look at Figure 11.43.

FIGURE 11.42

Using the Managed By property page to give a user permission to manage a distribution group from an Outlook client

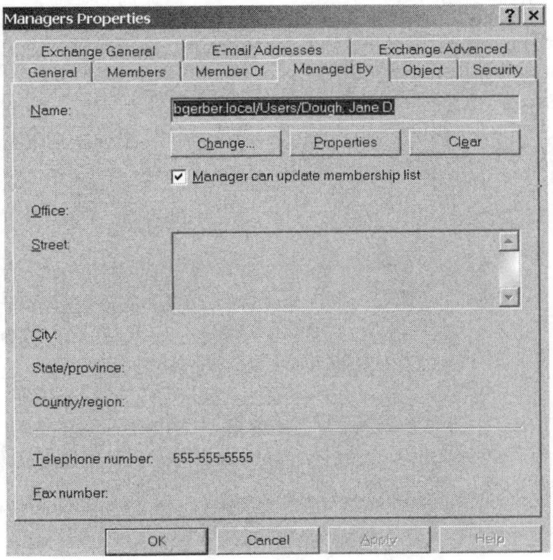

FIGURE 11.43

Using the Exchange General property page to manage a distribution group's alias, display name, outgoing message size limits, and message restrictions

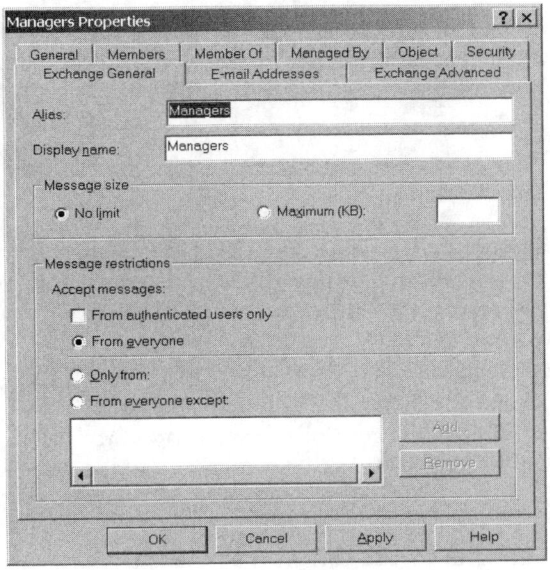

Unlike mailboxes, distribution lists don't have different size limits for incoming and outgoing messages. That's because distribution groups almost always receive messages. The limits that you set are for outgoing messages only. You saw everything else on this page in the section "Managing

Mailbox-Enabled Users," earlier in this chapter, so I'll leave it to you to give meaning to the rest of this property page.

Exchange Advanced

As you can see in Figure 11.44, distribution groups have much thinner Exchange Advanced property pages than mailboxes. However, there are a number of attributes on this page that you haven't seen before. So, let's dive in. I'll talk only about fields that I haven't already discussed in this chapter.

FIGURE 11.44

Using the Exchange Advanced property page to manage a distribution group's visibility, out-of-office messaging, reporting responsibilities, and custom attributes

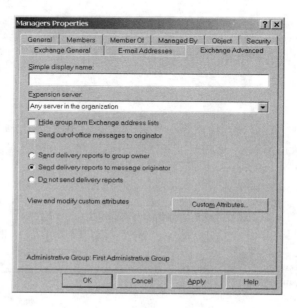

Distribution groups must be *expanded*—that is, the members of the group must be identified and an efficient route to each group member must be determined. Expansion is done on an Exchange server in the organization; if a distribution group is large (with thousands of users), you might want to specify an expansion server for it that is less busy. For smaller lists, you don't have to change the Any Server in the Organization default.

You can set a number of additional options on the Advanced property page. You can hide a group from address lists, control how out-of-office messages are sent for a distribution group, specify to whom reports will be sent, and enter information relating to a group's custom attributes:

Hide group from Exchange address lists   This one is pretty obvious.

Send out-of-office messages to originator   An out-of-office message goes to the sender of a message to the distribution group if even one member of the group has set up an out-of-office message.

Send delivery reports to group owner   This sends notification to the owner of the distribution group when a message sent to the list could not be delivered.

Send delivery reports to message originator   This sends notification to the sender of a message when a message sent to the group could not be delivered. In most cases, this is the preferred default.

Do not send delivery reports   You can select only one of the previous two options or this option. If you want no delivery reports when a message to the group isn't delivered, select this one.

Custom Attributes   Clicking Custom Attributes opens the same Exchange Custom Attributes dialog box, shown earlier in Figure 11.22. The same attributes apply to mailboxes, distribution groups, and contacts. So, if you've staked out an attribute to represent a specific variable for mailboxes such as employee number, you can't use it for something else for distribution groups or contacts.

QUERY-BASED DISTRIBUTION GROUPS

Query-based distribution groups (QBDGs) are new to Exchange 2003. In a way, QBDGs make the Managed By property page for distribution groups almost obsolete. QBDGs are essentially virtual distribution groups. You set the parameters for including an Exchange recipient object in a QBDG. For example, you can specify that the group include all mailboxes and/or contacts and/or distribution groups and/or public folders, and so on. Then as you add or remove recipient objects of the type you specified from your Windows domain, your Exchange server dynamically adds or removes them from the QBDG. You can even create a QBDG with custom settings that let you specify very fine-grained criteria for inclusion in the list.

Once created, QBDGs are displayed in address lists just like distribution groups. QBDGs are represented in the `Active Directory Users and Computers\Users` container. They have Properties dialog boxes that you should be quite comfortable with by now, and they even have e-mail addresses just like distribution groups. Like distribution groups, they can be manually managed—however, the real beauty of QBDGs is that they shouldn't generally have to be.

To create a QBDG, right-click the `Active Directory Users and Computers\Users` container and select New Query-Based Distribution Group. Then use the New Object - Query-Based Distribution Group dialog box that pops up to set up your QBDG. With distribution groups under your belt, you should have no trouble working with query-based distribution groups.

HIDING DISTRIBUTION GROUP MEMBERS FROM EXCHANGE ADDRESS LISTS

The Exchange 5.5 Advanced property page included an option for hiding the members of a group from the Exchange address book. This is a nice feature if you want users to see a distribution group in Exchange 2003 address lists but don't want them to see the membership of the group. So, how do you do it in Exchange 2003? Run the Exchange Task Wizard (right-click on the group and select Exchange Tasks) and select Hide Membership.

Creating and Managing Contacts

Contacts are essentially aliases for recipients in foreign messaging systems. Their equivalent in Exchange 5.5 is the custom recipient. Contacts are helpful when a lot of people in your organization need to communicate with users of external messaging systems. If a couple of users need such communication, you don't have to create an Exchange contact. Each user can set up a contact in their Outlook Address Book.

NOTE *You might be wondering how contacts differ from mail-enabled users. Both have external e-mail addresses. Neither has an Exchange mailbox. However, mail-enabled users have Windows 2003 accounts and can log in to your Windows network; contacts can't.*

CREATING A CONTACT

To create a contact, right-click the `Active Directory Users and Computers\Users` container and select New ➢ Contact from the menu that pops up.

As with mailboxes and distribution groups, you use a dialog box, the New Object - Contact dialog box, to create a new contact. Figure 11.45 shows the first property page of the dialog box. When you fill in the user's first name, middle initials, and last name, the full name is automatically generated. Of course, you may edit the full name. You manually enter the display name.

FIGURE 11.45
Using the New Object - Contact dialog box to enter the naming attributes of a new contact

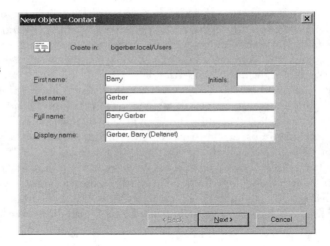

Because I'm creating a contact for my e-mail address at one of my Internet service providers, Deltanet, I'm careful to note that in the display name. This way, users are less likely to pick the wrong address when sending messages to me. Of course, you usually wouldn't create a contact for an Exchange mailbox–enabled user like me.

The next dialog box property page is exactly the same as the Establish E-Mail Addresses page of the Exchange Task Wizard, shown earlier in Figure 11.31. Check out that figure and the accompanying text for details on entering an e-mail address for your new contact.

When you're done entering the contact's address, click OK. You'll see the address that you entered in the E-Mail field of the New Object–Contact dialog box. Click Next, and the next dialog box tells you what it's going to do. Click Finish, and your new contact is created.

TIP *To delete a contact, select it and either press Delete or right-click it and select Delete from the pop-up menu.*

MANAGING CONTACTS

A contact is very much like a mail-enabled user from a management perspective. Based on my discussion of mail-enabled user property pages in the section "Managing Mail-Enabled Users" earlier in this chapter, you should find the contact property pages familiar.

Finding Exchange Recipients

Now that you know how to create and manage Exchange users, distribution groups, and contacts, I bet you'll be swimming in Exchange recipients before long. That means that your `Active Directory Users and Computers\Users` container is going to fill up to the point that finding a particular user or set of users is a royal pain. Enter Windows 2003's fantastic Find dialog box, enhanced by your installation of Exchange Server. You can use this dialog box to search the Users container or any container in Active Directory Users and Computers. To open the Find dialog box, select Find from the Action menu. This opens the Find Users, Contacts, and Groups dialog box, shown in Figure 11.46.

In Figure 11.46, I'm searching in the Users container for any object that begins with *Barry*. Three objects were found: my mailbox-enabled user object (type: User), another mailbox-enabled user I created for fun (type: User), and my contact object (type: Contact). You can double-click any found object and open its Properties dialog box.

FIGURE 11.46

Using the Find Users, Contacts, and Groups dialog box to search for objects that begin with specific text

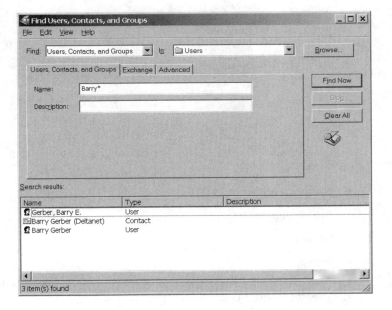

You can select other types of objects to be found by using the Find drop-down list in the upper-left corner of the dialog box. Other choices include computers, printers, Windows 2003 organizational units, and Exchange recipients. Each selection on the drop-down list has its own set of property pages.

The Find Exchange Recipients option is shown in Figure 11.47. It has three Exchange-oriented property pages. The Storage property page lets you further qualify your search by looking for recipients on a particular Exchange server and in a particular mailbox store on the server. Figure 11.48 shows how you can use the Advanced property page in the Find Exchange Recipients dialog box to further qualify your search by looking for specific values for specific user attributes. These are not just Exchange attributes, but all available Windows 2003 user attributes.

FIGURE 11.47

Using the Find dialog box to refine a search to include or exclude specific Exchange recipient objects

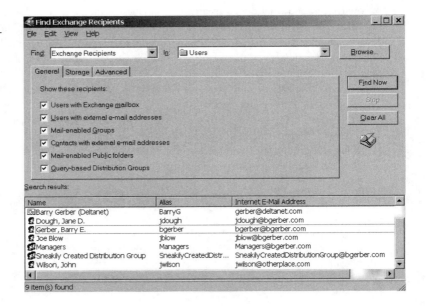

Now, look back at Figure 11.46. The Exchange tab lets you confine your search to one or more of the following:

◆ Mailbox-enabled users

◆ Mail-enabled users

◆ Groups

◆ Contacts

The Advanced property page works like the one on the Exchange Recipients Advanced property page, shown in Figure 11.48.

Pretty neat, huh? The Find dialog box is a real improvement over Exchange 5.5's Find Recipients dialog box.

FIGURE 11.48
Using the Find dialog box to refine a search to include or exclude specific user attributes

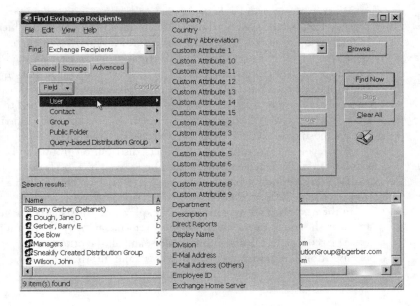

Summary

You've just completed the basic course on management of Exchange users, distribution groups, and contacts. In Chapter 16, I'll cover some advanced techniques for managing these recipients. Meanwhile, here's a quick summary of this chapter.

Before you start managing Exchange Server recipients, you should do three things. First, you need to become familiar with both MMC and the Active Directory Users and Computers (ADUC) snap-in for MMC. Second, you should ensure that the formats used for Windows 2003/Exchange 2003 user display names are set as you want them to be. Third, you need to make certain that the addressing defaults for your Exchange organization are as you want them to be.

Three types of Exchange Server recipients are managed with ADUC. These are users, distribution groups, and contacts.

Two types of users exist: mailbox-enabled users and mail-enabled users. Mailbox-enabled users are Windows 2003 users with Exchange mailboxes. Mail-enabled users are Windows 2003 users without mailboxes, but with e-mail addresses in messaging systems outside of your Exchange system.

Distribution groups are collections of Exchange recipients. A copy of a message addressed to a distribution group goes to each member of the group.

Contacts are non–Windows 2003 users with e-mail addresses that are located in external messaging systems. The main difference between mail-enabled users and contacts is that mail-enabled users have Windows 2003 accounts, while contacts do not. Contacts are totally external to both your Windows 2003 and Exchange 2003 environments.

When you create an Exchange user, distribution group, or contact, you name it, set any required security parameters, specify where it is to reside in your Exchange hierarchy, and set available messaging attributes such as alias and e-mail address. Managing an Exchange user, distribution group, or contact is largely a matter of finding the right property page on the Properties dialog box for the object and manipulating the attributes on the page. Users, distribution groups, and contacts have similar property pages. Generally, you use these property pages to set display names, aliases, and e-mail addresses, as well as to restrict what can be received from whom and to limit the size of incoming and outgoing messages. When modifying restrictions and limits for individual recipients, you're essentially choosing to override Exchange server–based defaults.

When you start creating Exchange users, distribution groups, and contacts, it gets increasingly difficult to find these recipients in Active Directory. The Find feature of ADUC makes this task much easier. You can find Exchange recipients based on their type and on a wide range of Windows 2003 and Exchange 2003 attributes.

In the next chapter, we continue our exploration of basic Exchange Server management. We'll focus on the management of Exchange Server's hierarchy and core components. This includes the last of the Exchange recipients, public folders, and all the other aspects of the hierarchy, including the organization, administrative groups, servers, and information stores.

Chapter 12

Managing the Exchange Server Hierarchy and Core Components

AFTER COMPLETING THE LAST chapter, you should have a firm grounding in the use of the Active Directory Users and Computers snap-in to manage Exchange users, distribution groups, and contacts. Now I want to show you how to use the Exchange 2003 System Manager to administer the Exchange Server hierarchy and core components. As in the last chapter, I focus mainly on the basics here, saving advanced administration and management for later chapters.

Featured in this chapter:

◆   The Exchange Server 2003 hierarchy

◆   Exchange core components

NOTE   *As you've probably already discovered, some types of property pages are very similar, no matter where you encounter them. The Security page is a good example. From this point on, if we've already covered the subject matter of a particular property page, I'll skip it without comment. I'll still let you know when we're bypassing material that we'll cover in later chapters, though. Therefore, if I don't say anything at all about a specific property page or property, I'm assuming that you already know how to deal with it. Check back to earlier discussions for specifics.*

The Exchange Server Hierarchy

You'll remember from Chapter 4, "Exchange Server 2003 Architecture," that the Exchange Server 2003 hierarchy includes the following components:

◆   The organization

◆   Administrative groups

◆   Servers

◆   Recipients

In the last chapter, we talked a good deal about three kinds of recipients: Exchange users, distribution groups, and contacts. Here we'll focus on the organization, administrative groups, and servers. We'll also cover the last of the four recipient types: public folders.

Open your Microsoft Management Console (MMC) and then open the main subcontainers in Exchange System Manager so that it looks like the one in Figure 12.1.

FIGURE 12.1

Exchange System Manager, ready to administer and manage the Exchange hierarchy

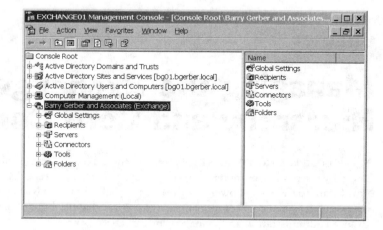

"Wait," I can hear you saying, *"this* is the Exchange hierarchy? Where are administrative groups?" Good eyes. You have to turn on the display of administrative groups. Right-click your Exchange organization—my organization is called Barry Gerber and Associates (Exchange)—and select Properties from the pop-up menu. This brings up the organization Properties dialog box, shown in Figure 12.2. Select Display Administrative Groups. Click OK to close the dialog box. Exit your MMC and open it again.

FIGURE 12.2

Using the organization Properties dialog box to display administrative groups

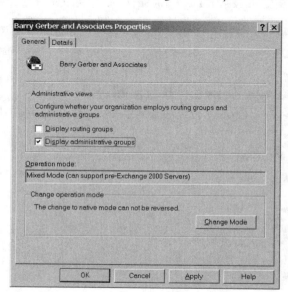

WARNING   *If you have or expect to have Exchange 5.5 servers in your Exchange organization, don't click Change Mode on the organization Properties dialog box shown in Figure 12.2. Native Exchange mode is a nice place to be, but not until all your Exchange servers are running Exchange Server 2003 or at least Exchange 2003 and Exchange 2000.*

WARNING   *Setting an Exchange organization to native mode is not the same as setting a Windows 2003 domain to native mode. The two are totally unrelated. As I mentioned in Chapter 6, "Upgrading to Windows Server 2003 and Exchange Server 2003," you set a domain to native mode when you no longer need to support NT 4 servers, when all your servers are running Windows Server 2003. You set an organization to native mode when you no longer need to support Exchange 5.5 servers.*

Your System Manager should now look like the one in Figure 12.3. As we move along, refer back to this figure if you need help in finding a particular object in the Exchange hierarchy.

FIGURE 12.3
Exchange System Manager, with administrative groups displayed

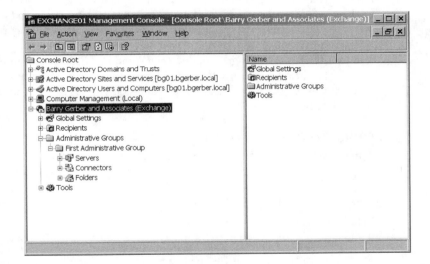

Managing the Organization

As it was in Exchange 5.5, the organization is the topmost rung on the Exchange 2003 hierarchy. More than anything else, it is a holding tank for other Exchange objects. We'll talk specifically about these objects in this and later chapters. There isn't a heck of a lot that you need to do in relation to your organization; the Properties dialog box in Figure 12.2 is almost all you have. The Details tab of the dialog box shows when the organization was created and when changes were last made, and it allows for free-form text notes.

Two interesting options appear on the menu that pops up when you right-click your organization: Delegate Control and Export List. There are other fun options and we'll get to them later.

Delegate Control opens the Exchange Administration Delegation Wizard. You used this wizard back in Chapter 8, "Installing Exchange Server 2003," to give the group Exchange Admins permission to manage your Exchange organization. We'll talk about it again when we get into administrative groups in the next section.

The Export List option appears on most MMC pages. Selecting it enables you to save a list of objects in a container to a tab- or comma-delimited file. All the attributes of the object that are visible in the container are saved to the file. As I noted in the last chapter, you expose hidden attributes in a container by selecting Choose Columns from a snap-in's View menu. Exporting object attributes can be useful when you need to modify Active Directory data or use Active Directory data in an external application, such as a database. We'll get into all of this in Chapter 16, "Advanced Exchange Server Administration and Management." For now, that's it for managing your Exchange organization.

Managing Administrative Groups

Administrative groups are containers for Exchange servers, connectors, public folder trees, policies, and routing groups. A group can hold one or more of these Exchange objects. Upon installation of your first Exchange 2003 server, a default administrative group is created, called First Administrative Group. It includes containers for servers, connectors, and public folders (see Figure 12.3, shown earlier).

You use administrative groups to isolate a specific set of Exchange objects so that management responsibilities can be assigned to different Windows 2003 groups or users. You use system policies within administrative groups. System policies make it easy to apply a set of attributes to multiple objects, such as a set of Exchange servers. Let's look more closely at administrative group models and system policies.

ADMINISTRATIVE GROUP MODELS

Three basic administrative group models exist:

◆ Decentralized

◆ Centralized

◆ Mixed

As the names of these models imply, administrative groups enable you to build an Exchange management infrastructure that fits the hierarchical or geographic structure of your organization. Let's look at each model in more detail.

Decentralized

You use the decentralized administrative group model when you want to parcel out full responsibility for administering different segments of your Exchange system to different groups. For example, you might want to give one group full responsibility for your Exchange system in the United States, and another group full responsibility for your European Exchange system.

To do this, you create two administrative groups, one for the United States and one for Europe. Then you put all the Exchange objects (servers, public folders, policies, routing groups, and so on) for each geographical region in the appropriate administrative group. Finally, you delegate control for each administrative group to the appropriate groups or users for each geographical area. Delegating control is done just as you did it in Chapter 8, when you delegated control of your Exchange organization to the group Exchange Admins. To begin, right-click the appropriate administrative group and select Delegate Control from the pop-up menu. Then give the appropriate users or groups the appropriate control over each administrative group.

This model has political advantages in some organizations. It also works well where high-bandwidth network connections aren't available between geographically distributed offices.

This model will likely seem familiar to Exchange 5.5 administrators. It is the way Exchange 5.5 sites were used.

Centralized

In a centralized administrative group structure, you use one or very few administrative groups. You use the groups more to distribute the workload among a centralized staff than to distribute responsibility among organizationally decentralized staff, as you would with decentralized administrative groups.

This model is especially effective for small to medium organizations. It also works in large organizations, though it works best when high-bandwidth connections exist between distributed offices.

Mixed

A mixed-mode administrative group environment includes either a centralized or a decentralized model, plus administrative groups for specific Exchange objects that you don't want managed by the centralized or decentralized managers. For example, you might want to consolidate control of Exchange policies in one group while leaving all the rest of Exchange management to a decentralized set of Exchange managers at your organization's branch offices.

To do this, you create an administrative group for each of your branch offices, leaving out policy objects. Then you delegate control for each decentralized administrative group to the appropriate Windows 2003 groups or users. Next you create an administrative group for policy management, add a policy container, and delegate control to the users or groups that you want to manage Exchange policies.

Right now you have one Exchange server and a very simple Windows 2003/Exchange 2003 environment, so there isn't a lot you can do with Exchange administrative groups. However, as you add Exchange servers to your Exchange organization in Chapter 15, "Installing and Managing Additional Exchange Servers," you'll be able to make very good use of administrative groups. For now, we'll use our single administrative group to organize our Exchange hierarchy.

USING WINDOWS 2003 ORGANIZATIONAL UNITS TO DISTRIBUTE RESPONSIBILITY FOR USERS, GROUPS, CONTACTS, AND COMPUTER OBJECTS

You can also distribute responsibility for administering Active Directory user, group, contact, and computer objects among different users or groups in your organization. To do this, you create one or more Windows 2003 organizational units in Active Directory using the Active Directory Users and Computers snap-in (right-click the domain container and select New Organizational Unit from the pop-up menu). Your organizational units can parallel your administrative groups in focus and membership, or they can have an entirely different focus and membership. When your organizational units are in place, you can move pre-existing users, groups, contacts, or computers into the appropriate organizational unit and delegate control for each unit to the appropriate groups or users. You can also create new users, groups, contacts, or computers in any organizational unit.

EXCHANGE SYSTEM POLICIES

Exchange policies are a quick way to assign properties to groups of Exchange objects. These are generally the same properties that you can assign to individual objects using a Properties dialog box. You create policies and then apply them to the appropriate objects.

Two basic types of Exchange policies exist:

◆ Recipient

◆ System

As you'll remember from the last chapter, recipient policies relate to how e-mail addresses are generated for one or more types of Exchange recipients. Recipient policies are managed in the Recipients container of your Exchange organization. System policies are managed in administrative groups. Administrative groups must be displayed before you can use system policies.

Three types of system policies exist:

◆ Server

◆ Mailbox store

◆ Public store

I'll discuss each of these in the next sections.

SERVERS

Servers constitute the third level of the Exchange 2003 hierarchy. Their major function is to hold mailbox and public stores that make up one of Exchange's core components, the Information Store.

In Figure 12.4, I've expanded my administrative group to show key containers for my one and only server, EXCHANGE01. The server supports a range of protocols as well as a storage group that includes a mailbox store and a public store. We'll get into storage groups later in this chapter, in the section "The Information Store."

Server Properties

Let's start by looking at the properties of Exchange servers that we can manipulate. Right-click your server—mine is named EXCHANGE01—and select Properties from the pop-up menu. This opens the server Properties dialog box, shown in Figure 12.5.

Because they should be familiar to you, I'll skip the Details and Security pages. We'll deal with server policies later in this chapter, in the section "Creating and Managing Server Policies," and we'll cover full-text indexing in the section "The Information Store," also later in this chapter. Let's look at the remaining property pages of this dialog box.

FIGURE 12.4
Exchange System Manager, with the Servers container expanded

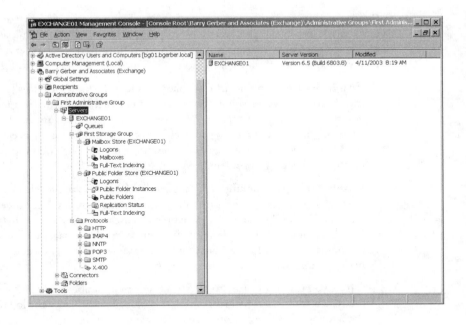

FIGURE 12.5
The server Properties dialog box with its General property page exposed

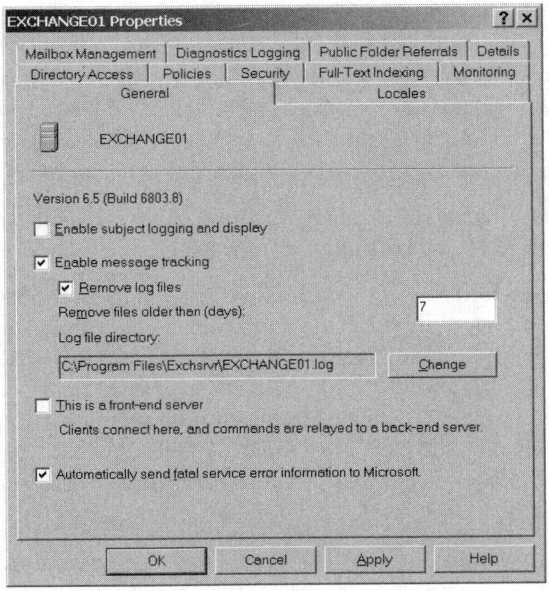

General   You use the General property page, shown previously in Figure 12.5, to enable and disable message subject logging and message tracking, to set log file deletion parameters, to specify whether the server is a front- or back-end server for certain Internet-based services, and to indicate whether you want to automatically send serious error messages to Microsoft. I'll discuss each of these next.

Enable Subject Logging and Display   When tracking messages (see the next subsection), you can choose to have the subject line of each message included in the tracking log and displayed when you're tracking the message. It can be helpful when tracking messages to see the subject. However, some might consider viewing subject lines to be an invasion of privacy. Also, storing the subject of each message takes disk space. Depending on how long you keep your tracking logs, this could create a disk storage problem.

Enable Message Tracking   If the Enable Message Tracking check box is selected, a daily log file is kept on all messages that the Information Store handles. Exchange Server's Message Tracking Center (which I'll talk about in Chapter 16) uses these log files to help you figure out what might have happened to wayward messages. You can track messages to foreign messaging systems up to the point of successful delivery by your Exchange server. You can't track what happened to such messages inside the foreign messaging system.

Often, you use this feature to satisfy a user's request about what happened to a message. I suggest that you enable message tracking right now and start building the log files. If you want to play with the Message Tracking Center after something is in the log files, open the Tools container in Exchange System Manager, click Message Tracking Center, and have at it.

Remove Log Files   You can't track messages if the log for the day they were sent has been deleted. So, you must time log file deletion with this in mind. For now, it's pretty safe to accept the default that message-tracking log files more than seven days old should be deleted. If you back up your server regularly using the backup cycle that I suggested in Chapter 7, "Installing Windows Server 2003 as a Domain Controller," and Chapter 8, seven days should be fine. You'll always be able to restore recent log files from your backup if you need them.

By the way, deleting log files (in fact, performing most scheduled activities) is the job of the System Attendant service. You'll remember that the SA is one of the core components of Exchange Server.

This Is a Front-End Server   With Exchange 5.5, the Information Store (IS) took care of both mailbox and public folder databases and Internet client access protocols such as Post Office Protocol v3 (POP3), Internet Message Access Protocol v4 (IMAPv4), Network News Transfer Protocol (NNTP), and Outlook Web Access (OWA). The IS also managed Microsoft's non-Internet-oriented Messaging Application Programming Interface (MAPI) client access protocol. The IS managed MAPI communications directly and communicated with Internet Information Server (IIS) to accomplish its Internet protocol access tasks.

With Exchange 2003, the IS continues to handle MAPI access. However, the Internet client access protocols are managed by IIS. A front-end Exchange server handles communication between IIS and back-end Exchange server information stores. A front-end server still has at least a basic IS. You can create mailboxes in it or not, as you want.

This new front-end/back-end server technology is a very good idea because it reduces the load on Exchange servers by moving management of Internet access protocols to IIS. It also makes it very easy for a user to access a single front-end server to get to an Exchange mailbox or, when the protocol supports it, a public folder using a POP3, IMAP4, NNTP, or the OWA client.

For now, don't check This Is a Front-End Server. In Chapter 14, "Managing Exchange 2003 Services for Internet Clients," I'll talk more about Internet clients and front- and back-end servers.

Automatically Send Fatal Service Error Information to Microsoft   This is a new feature with Exchange 2003. If something serious goes wrong with one of the services on your Exchange server and this box is checked, information about the failure will be transmitted over the Internet to Microsoft. Generally it's a good idea to select this option. The more information Microsoft has on fatal errors, the more likely it is to fix them in future service packs. Of course, if your server is not connected directly to the Internet or if you'd prefer not to send this information to Microsoft, you don't have to enable this feature.

Locales   Let's move to the Locales property page on your Exchange server's properties dialog box. Users of Outlook clients can select a locale-specific format for the display of such things as currency, time, and date. The options that they can choose from are set on the server Locales properties page (see Figure 12.6). To add country-specific locale information, click Add and select the locales from the Add Locale dialog box. Remove locales with the Remove button.

FIGURE 12.6

Using the Locales property page to add country-specific currency, time, and date display options to a server

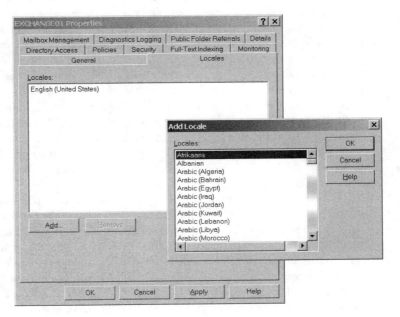

Directory Access You use the Directory Access property page to view the characteristics of your Windows domain controllers. You can see which controllers support the Windows global catalog, which controller supports domain configuration and which LDAP protocol port a domain controller uses for domain controller and general catalog communications. This information is useful for Exchange administrators and developers who might not have access to Active Directory information though Active Directory plug-ins.

Policies This is a very basic property page. You don't set up policies on this page. Rather you can view system and recipient policies that apply to your Exchange server. We'll get into policy creation later in this chapter.

Full-Text Indexing Like the Policies page, you don't set up full-text indexing of messages on the Full-Text Indexing page. Instead you use the page to set the amount of your server's CPU resources full-text indexing should use: minimum, low, high, or maximum. You'll need to experiment with these options to find out which is best for your hardware configuration and full-text indexing needs. For now, accept the default (low) setting.

Monitoring Server monitors are really impressive. They watch over Exchange servers, their resources, and the services running on them. One server monitor can operate on one or more of the servers in an Exchange organization. You can set up multiple monitors on a server.

Monitors have both warning and critical state criteria. You can set up notifications to trigger when warning or critical states are reached. You can set up monitoring so that you're notified by e-mail when a warning or critical state threshold is reached on one or more of your servers. You can also set up monitoring so that a script executes when there's a problem. A script can be any executable program file or batch file. Scripts can send console messages to you or a group of Exchange administrators, or they can communicate by another method, such as a pager. Scripts are especially valuable when your Exchange system is in a state in which it can't send e-mail.

Server monitors are important. You should get comfortable with them right away.

Exchange comes with a default monitor called Default Microsoft Exchange Services, as shown in Figure 12.7. The monitor checks the status of a range of key Exchange services. Notice the Critical State column on the Monitoring property page. That's not the current state of the Exchange services; it's the state at which the monitor goes critical. That is, the monitor goes into a critical state when one or more services are not running (stopped).

To check the status of your monitors, open the monitor by double-clicking it on the Monitoring property page, as I have done in Figure 12.7. This opens a dialog box for the monitor that shows the services being monitored. See the Default Microsoft Exchange Services dialog box. Note on the dialog box that all the services being monitored are running fine. You can also view the status of your server and its monitors in the Status subcontainer of the Tools container, shown in the lower-left corner of the figure.

Let's create a new monitor. Close the Default Microsoft Exchange Services dialog box, if it's open. Then click Add on the Monitoring property page. The Add Resource dialog box, shown in Figure 12.8, includes a list of resources that you can monitor. Each monitor can monitor one of these resource sets. There can be only one of each resource monitor on a server per specific resource. For example, there can be only one SMTP queue growth monitor, but there can be (really *must* be) a free disk space monitor for each disk drive.

FIGURE 12.7
Viewing the default server monitor that comes with Exchange Server 2003

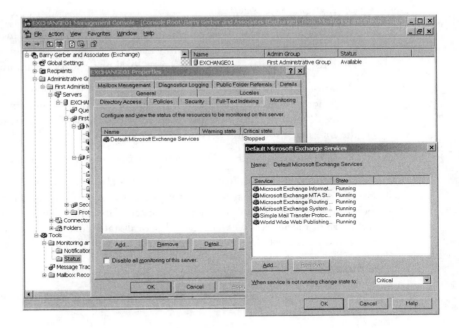

FIGURE 12.8
Using the Add Resource dialog box to select the type of monitor to be created

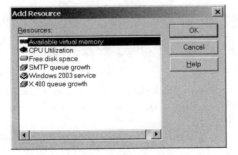

Here's a quick overview of the resource monitors available:

Available Virtual Memory   This is the disk-based paging memory used by Windows 2003 services and programs to gain memory beyond the physical RAM memory in a computer. You don't want virtual memory to run too low, say, below 25 percent.

CPU Utilization   As a rule of thumb, CPU utilization above 90 percent for a sustained period (10 minutes) indicates either a problem on your server or inadequate capacity to run the installed services.

Free Disk Space   I like to have at least 1GB available on all of my Exchange server disks.

SMTP Queue Growth   Remember from Chapter 4 that SMTP is the communication protocol of Exchange server-to-server communications. Interserver e-mail messages and other information, such as public folder replication information, pass through SMTP queues. If queues continue to grow for 20 minutes, you usually have a local or network communication problem.

Windows 2003 Service   This innocent item lets you monitor as many Exchange and non-Exchange services as you want. It's a good idea to monitor non-Exchange services that Exchange Server depends on. For example, users can not access their mailboxes with a web browser unless the Internet Information Server's World Wide Web Publishing Service is up and running.

X.400 Queue Growth   This one works the same way as the SMTP queue growth monitor.

Okay, back to the monitor we're creating: It's always a good idea to monitor available disk space, so let's set up a free disk space monitor. Select the disk space option from the Add Resource dialog box, and click OK. This opens the Disk Space Thresholds dialog box, shown in Figure 12.9. Select a drive to be monitored, set warning and critical-state remaining-space thresholds, and click OK. You need to do a separate free disk space monitor for each disk on your server that you want to monitor.

FIGURE 12.9

Using the Disk Space Thresholds dialog box to configure a free disk space monitor

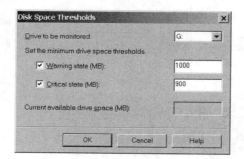

As I mentioned previously, you check the status of a server in the Status subcontainer of the Tools container. In Figure 12.10, you can see the general status of the server in the right pane of the MMC snap-in. The server is in fine shape—or, as Exchange puts it, it is *available*. By double-clicking the server, I open the EXCHANGE01 Properties dialog box (also shown in Figure 12.10), which looks pretty much like the Monitoring property page in Figure 12.7, shown earlier, except for the addition of the free disk space monitor.

Double-clicking a monitor opens its dialog box. In Figure 12.10, I've opened the Disk Space Thresholds dialog box that not only shows me what thresholds I've set and allows me to change them, but also shows the amount of disk space remaining on my G: drive. This is where you'd go to check out a problem on your server.

"Ah," you say, "but how do I know there is a problem on my server?" Funny you should ask. There are two answers to that question. The first is that you regularly do exactly what we just did. You look at your servers and their monitors. The second is that you use monitoring notifications that let you know what's going on without your having to check things out manually.

FIGURE 12.10
Viewing a server's
monitoring status

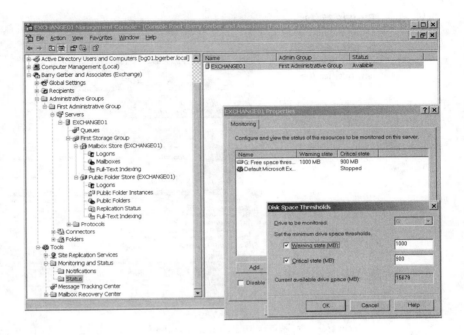

You set up e-mail and other monitoring notifications in the Notifications subcontainer (see Figure 12.10, lower-left corner, for its location). It's important to remember that what you're doing here is setting up a notification, not a monitor. A notification uses the monitors that have been created on the Monitoring page of a server. It can also generate notifications about the status of Exchange connectors such as an Exchange SMTP connector. Exchange connectors are automatically monitored by the system. A notification doesn't create any new monitors.

Setting Up E-Mail Notifications To create an e-mail notification, right-click the Notifications subcontainer and select New ➢ E-mail Notification from the pop-up menu. Use the resultant Properties dialog box to set up the notification (see Figure 12.11).

The monitoring server is the server where the notification you're setting up runs. It's called a *monitoring server* because it watches the status of all the monitors on all the servers that the notification includes. We have only one server right now, so we'll run our notification on that server. However, you really don't want to run a notification on the server that it is going to be watching. If something goes wrong with the server, it might not be capable of running the notification. It's best to set up a cross-server notification plan so that a server runs notifications for one or more other servers, not itself.

FIGURE 12.11

Using the notification Properties dialog box to create a new notification

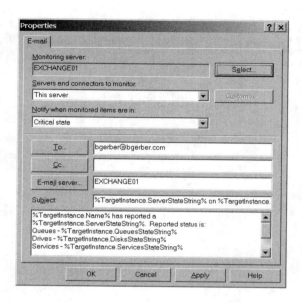

You use the Servers and Connectors to Monitor field to select the monitors that the notification will watch. Your options include these:

◆ This server

◆ All servers

◆ Any server in the routing group

◆ All connectors

◆ Any connector in the routing group

◆ Custom list of servers

◆ Custom list of connectors

As I noted previously, connectors are monitored by default. In other words, you don't have to set up connector monitors; Exchange just starts monitoring connectors upon creation. We'll return to connector monitoring and notifications when we get into Internet messaging in Chapter 13, "Managing Exchange 2003 Internet Services," and we'll cover installing, managing, and connecting additional Exchange servers in Chapter 15.

Use the Customize button, shown earlier in Figure 12.11, to set up a custom list of servers or connectors. Notice that you can set up a notification for servers or connectors, not for both.

The next field, Notify When Monitored Items Are In, lets you select the state when an e-mail notification is triggered. Your choices are critical state and warning state, and they relate to the way you've set state thresholds on your monitor.

Select the user or distribution group to which notifications will be sent using the To and Cc fields. Specify the Exchange server to be used to send the messages using the E-Mail Server field.

The Subject and message content fields contain variables and constants that form the subject line and body of the notification message to be sent. You can modify these two fields, although you should make any modifications with care to ensure that the message clearly indicates the reason for the notification.

When you're done with your notification, click OK. Then be sure that the notification appears in the right pane of your MMC.

Setting Up Scripted Notifications   A scripted notification runs a program or batch file when a specific state occurs on one or more servers. For example, you can run a program that notifies your pager of a problem, or, more simply, you can set up a batch file that notifies a user or group about a problem by sending a Windows 2003 console message. A console message shows up on the desktop of whatever user or group it is sent to. Console messages are generated with the command **net send**. For example, I could include the following line in a batch file and then select the batch file as the script to be run by a notification:

```
Net send /bgerber EXCHANGE01 has reached a critical state. Please check it out.
```

To set up a scripted notification, right-click the Notifications container and select New ➤ Script Notification. The dialog box for a new scripted notification is pretty much like the one for an e-mail notification. Basically, script-oriented fields replace e-mail-oriented fields. There's a field for the path to the script and the script filename, as well as a field for any command-line arguments to be included when the script file is run.

TIP   There is another way to monitor Exchange services and take limited but effective action, depending on the status of a service. It involves setting specific recovery actions to be taken by a server when a service becomes unavailable. Actions include attempting to restart a service or to reboot the server that a service runs on. You can even set a series of increasingly more drastic actions for a service that's in trouble. I discuss this option for monitoring services in Chapter 14, in the section "Exchange 2003 Virtual Servers Are Not Just for SMTP."

I'll leave it to you to come up with other neat ideas for implementing script-based notifications.

TIP   You can also use Windows 2003 performance logs and alerts to monitor your Exchange server. Hundreds of Exchange-related counters are available, ranging from message queue size growth to number of messages submitted by users per minute to authentication failures for the Internet mail protocols POP3 and IMAP4. In addition, there are lots of counters for the Windows 2003 side of your server. These include everything from CPU usage to disk access times to network logon errors. For more on all this, see the books Mastering Windows Server 2003, *by Mark Minasi, Christa Anderson, Michele Beveridge, C.A. Callahan, and Lisa Justice (Sybex, 2003), and* Microsoft Windows Server 2003 Administrator's Companion, *by Charlie Russel and Sharon Crawford (Microsoft Press, 2003).*

Mailbox Management   If you see this property page, you've been messing around out of school. Mailbox management is neat. However, you have to turn it on and you don't turn it on in this page.

When you turn on mailbox management, you see this property page. I sneakily turned on mailbox management when you weren't looking. I'll talk about mailbox management later in this chapter.

Diagnostics Logging Exchange Server writes diagnostic information to Windows 2003's Application event log. You should keep an eye on the Application and System Event logs to be sure that Exchange's services are up and functioning properly. Also watch the Security log to be sure that none of the services on your Exchange server are having trouble accessing Exchange resources. You'll find these logs in the MMC snap-in under `Computer Management (Local)\System Tools\Event Viewer`.

Some Exchange server logging is enabled by default. You use the Diagnostics Logging property page to specify additional items to log and the depth of logging to be done for each. Most of the time, you enable more extensive diagnostics logging when you think you've got a problem. In many cases, technical support folks at Microsoft or another group will tell you what they want logged and then ask you to turn it on. However, it's still worth knowing how to use the Diagnostics Logging page, so let's try it.

When you first select the Diagnostics Logging property page, it looks pretty sparse. All you see are the name of the server, a tree listing several cryptic names that you might correctly assume represent Exchange Server objects, and, at the bottom, some unselected logging-level options.

You can set diagnostic logging options for most services at the root level, except for the Information Store, MSExchangeIS. Double-clicking MSExchangeIS (or clicking the plus sign in front of MSExchangeIS) opens a list of system, public folder, and mailbox information store services (see Figure 12.12).

FIGURE 12.12

Using the Diagnostics Logging property page to set additional Exchange Server logging options

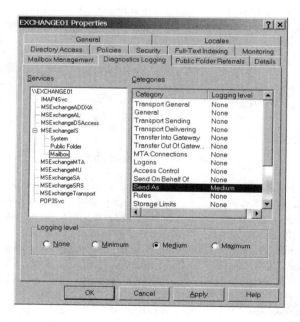

When you click a service in the Services pane, the right pane shows the specific items within the service that can be logged. Figure 12.12 shows some of the diagnostic items for the MSExchangeIS (Information Store) service.

You can set a logging option for any item in the right pane by clicking the item and then selecting an option in the Logging Level area at the bottom of the property page. (In Figure 12.12, I've chosen a medium level of logging for the use of the Send As permission that I discussed in the previous chapter.) As you'll remember from the previous chapter, Send As is a scary thing. If anyone is using it, you want to know. That's why I like to log its use.

To set the same logging level for a group of items, just use the standard Microsoft Windows selection options: Ctrl+mouse clicks for noncontiguous items, and Shift+mouse begin- and end-clicks for contiguous items.

WARNING *Generally, you should use diagnostics logging with care and as a short-term debugging tool. Extensive diagnostics logging fills the Application log with so much stuff that you have a difficult time finding other important logged events. Also, diagnostics logging can eat disk space faster than you can say "Exchange Server," especially when you set logging levels to Maximum. If the disk happens to be the one where your Exchange server's databases or logs reside, Exchange Server might not have enough disk space to run, and it will shut itself down. You can view the log and limit the amount of space allocated to the Application log or any other log using the Event Viewer application (Start ➤ All Programs ➤ Administrative Tools ➤ Event Viewer).*

Public Folder Referrals Public Folder Referrals is the last page in an Exchange server's Properties dialog box (see Figure 12.6, shown earlier). Public folder referral functionality facilitates access to public folders by e-mail clients in remote Exchange routing groups. You use the Public Folder Referrals property page to specify whether to use the Exchange connectors in a routing group on your server or connectors on another server to perform public folder referrals. All of this will be clearer and of infinitely more value when we get to multiserver Exchange organizations in Chapter 15.

Creating and Managing Server Policies

Before we start, let me reiterate a point that I made earlier: Exchange policies are designed to make it easy for you to apply a set of properties to a group of objects—recipients, servers, mailbox stores, and public stores—without having to open the dialog box for each object (100 servers, for example). What we're about to do might seem kind of meaningless right now because we have only one server. However, it's important that you understand Exchange policies, and now is a good time for that to happen. We'll return to Exchange policies in Chapter 15, when you begin adding servers to your Exchange organization.

To create a new server policy, right-click your administrative group (it should be called First Administrative Group) and select New ➤ System Policy Container from the pop-up menu. Then locate the System Policies subcontainer that was just created in your Administrative Groups container, right-click it, and select New ➤ Server Policy. This opens the New Policy dialog box, shown in Figure 12.13. You can create server policies only for the General property page of the server dialog box. So, I've chosen that page and clicked OK.

FIGURE 12.13

Using the New Policy dialog box to create a policy for the General property page

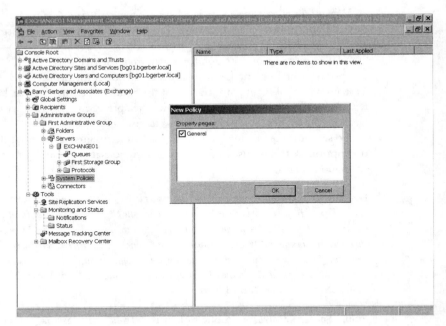

This opens the Properties dialog box that you use to create a new server policy. Give your policy a name using the General property page. I've creatively called mine Server Policy #1.

Next tab over to the General (Policy) property page (see Figure 12.14). Compare Figure 12.14 with Figure 12.5: They are essentially the same, but the property page for server policies does not include the front-end server option. This option needs to be set with some refinement. The key difference between these two property pages is that when I use the General property page for a server (see Figure 12.5), I'm able to set properties for only that server while, when I use the General property page for server policies (see Figure 12.14), I can change properties for as many servers as I want.

Fill in the dialog box and click OK. When you're done, your MMC should look something like the one in Figure 12.15.

To add servers to your policy, as in Figure 12.15, right-click the policy and select Add Server from the pop-up menu. Just for fun, add your one and only Exchange server. If you had more servers, of course, you could add all or some of them to this policy. You can create as many policies as you need to ensure that all your servers have the appropriate policy applied to them.

When you're done, you should see your server in the container for the policy that you just created. It's a subcontainer of the System Policies container. Double-click your server, and you'll see the server Properties dialog box, shown in Figure 12.16. However, properties controlled by the policy are grayed out because they can't be altered. While your server Properties dialog box is open, tab over to the Policies property page. Miracle of all miracles, your new policy shows in the Policies field (see Figure 12.17).

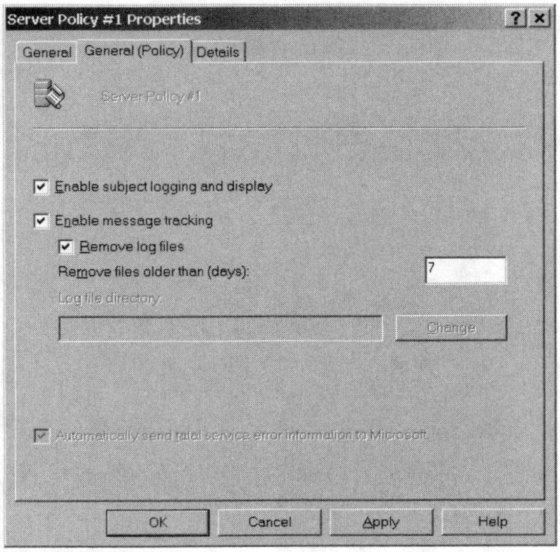

FIGURE 12.14

Using the server policy Properties dialog box to specify how specific properties should be handled under a new policy

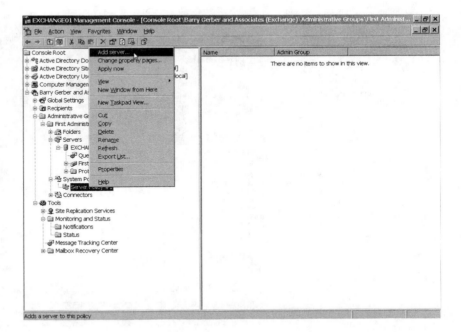

FIGURE 12.15

Choosing to add a server to a policy

FIGURE 12.16
The server Properties dialog box after a server policy has been applied to a server

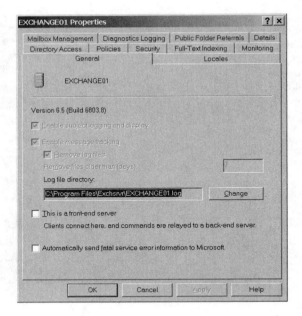

FIGURE 12.17
The Policies property page shows a newly added server policy.

Creating and Managing Public Folders

Okay, we're ready to tackle the last of the four recipient types, public folders. When we've completed our look at public folders, we'll also have completed our look at basic management of the Exchange hierarchy.

CREATING A PUBLIC FOLDER

Back in Chapter 10, "A Quick Overview of Outlook 2003," we created a public folder using the Outlook client. I named my public folder Barry's First Public Folder. You can see it in the Public Folders container on the left side of Figure 12.18.

FIGURE 12.18

Viewing a public folder created in Outlook, and creating a new public folder in Exchange System Manager

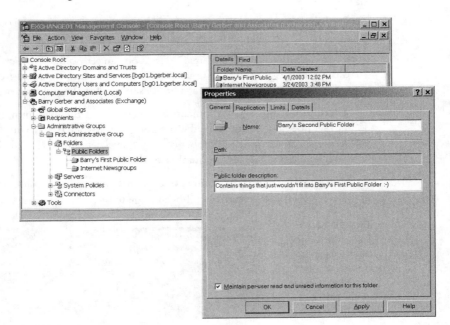

In Exchange 5.5, you could create a folder only using an e-mail client. You couldn't create one in the Administrator program. Exchange 2003 lets you create public folders in Exchange System Manager as an Exchange administrator. That's what I'm doing on the right side of Figure 12.18. I right-clicked the Public Folders container and selected New ➤ Public Folder from the pop-up menu to bring up the new public folder Properties dialog box. Let's take a look at the key property pages on this dialog box.

General

You use the General property page, shown in Figure 12.18, to name your folder and enter a description of the folder. The Path field shows where the folder is located in the Public Folder hierarchy after it has been created. If Maintain Per-User Read and Unread Information for This Folder is selected, each user will see items in the folder that they have read in nonbolded text. If this option is not selected, all items show in bolded text for all users whether they have been read or not.

Replication

This is a very important property page because it is used to manage replication of folders between this server and other Exchange servers. Replication enables you to put copies of the same folder on multiple Exchange servers. It is very useful either for local load balancing or to limit wide area network traffic and improve performance by placing copies of folders in routing groups at geographically distant sites.

Important as replication is, we're not ready for it. We'll tackle it in Chapter 15 after we have some servers to replicate to.

Limits

You've seen limits property pages before. This one is interesting, as you can see in Figure 12.19. Let's look at each of the three types of limits on this page.

Storage Limits   Similar to mailboxes, you can set points at which warnings are sent and posting to the folder is prohibited. You can also set a maximum posted-item size. If you want, you can choose to use the default storage limits settings for the public store where the folder resides.

Deletion Setting   As with mailboxes, you can set the maximum number of days that a deleted item will be kept for recovery before being totally deleted. If you deselect Use Public Store Defaults, you can enter a number of days that deleted items should be retained. If you don't want items retained at all, set the number of days to 0.

Age Limits   This is the number of days that an item in the folder lives before being deleted. This is a very useful tool for controlling storage usage.

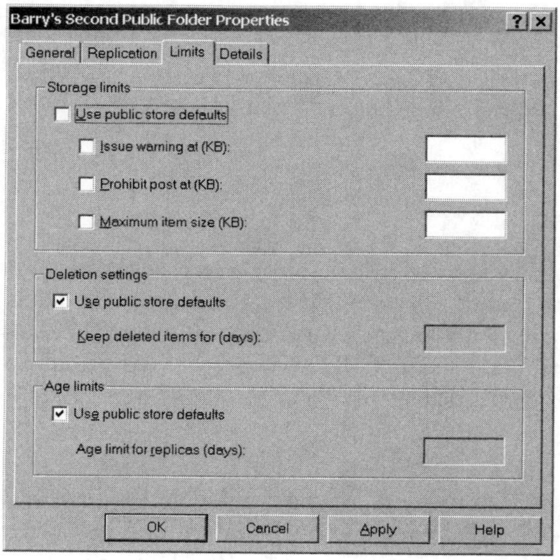

FIGURE 12.19

Using the Limits property page to set storage, deletion, and aging limits for a public folder

When you're finished creating your public folder, click OK and admire your handiwork in the Public Folders container. See Figure 12.20 for my admirable handiwork. Notice that I created my folder in the `Folders\Public Folders` container, not in the Public Folder Store. The Public Folder Store holds created folders. You create new public folders in the `Folders\Public Folders` container. Seems simple, but if I had a dollar for every time I wrongly went to the Public Folder Store to create a new public folder, well, I'd at least be on the beach in Hawaii right now.

FIGURE 12.20

A new public folder takes its place in the Public Folders container.

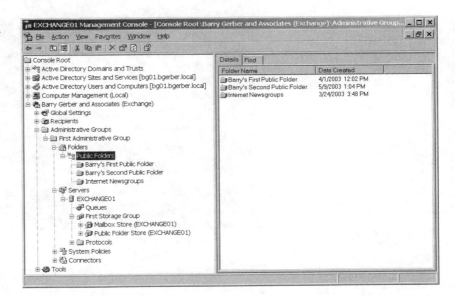

WARNING *By default, the Windows group Everyone has rights to create folders in the Public Folders container. This right extends to both top-level folders (folders within and, thus, just below the Public Folders container) and subfolders within top-level folders. If you want to alter this right, right-click the Public Folders container and select Properties. Use the Security tab in the Public Folders Properties dialog box to add or remove users and groups or their rights in the Public Folders container. Even if you don't want to change the default, I strongly recommend that you take a look at the Security tab. Many of the permissions on it are specific to public folders and, therefore, are quite different from the permissions for other types of Exchange recipients.*

MANAGING PUBLIC FOLDERS

You set a number of public folder management parameters while creating your public folder in the previous section. A good deal of public folder management has to do with replication and limits. However, there is more to public folder life than replication and limits. Let's take a look at some of the public folder management options available to you.

You need to open the Properties dialog box for your new folder. To do this, right-click your folder and select Properties from the pop-up menu. Figure 12.21 shows the Properties dialog box for my new folder; you've seen most of these pages before. We need to talk at least a bit about the General, Exchange General, Exchange Advanced, Permissions, and Member Of property pages.

FIGURE 12.21

The public folder Properties dialog box, with the General property page showing

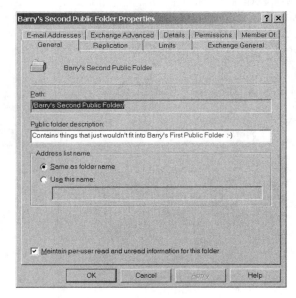

General

The only thing on this page that wasn't on the General property page of the dialog box that you used to create the folder (see Figure 12.18, shown earlier) is the Address List Name field. Before I explain this field, I need to fill you in a bit on e-mail-enabled public folders.

Public folders created in the Public Folders tree—that is, inside the Public Folders container—are automatically e-mail-enabled. This means that they are assigned e-mail addresses. That is why the dialog box in Figure 12.21 has an E-mail Addresses property page. E-mail-enabled public folders can receive and even send messages. You send a message from a public folder by having send-on-behalf-of or send-as permissions on the folder and using the From field in an Outlook message. (I discussed these permissions in Chapter 11, "Managing Exchange Users, Distribution Groups, and Contacts.")

NOTE *As you'll see later in this chapter, not all public folders are automatically e-mail-enabled. You can actually create additional public folder trees that are parallel to the Public Folders tree. Folders created in these trees are not automatically e-mail-enabled.*

Okay, back to the Address List Name field in Figure 12.21: You can use this field to have Exchange display a different name for the folder in Exchange's address lists than the name you gave the folder when you created it. That's it for the Address List Name field.

Exchange General

This page is very much like the Exchange General property page for a mailbox. It has buttons for opening property pages for delivery restrictions (size of incoming and outgoing messages, and where messages will be received from) and delivery options (delegate send-on-behalf-of permissions and set a forwarding address). These pages look and behave just like the same pages for a mailbox (see Figures 11.18 and 11.19 in Chapter 11).

Exchange Advanced

The Exchange Advanced property page is similar to the same page for a mailbox (see Figure 11.21 in Chapter 11). You can use it to set a simple display name and to unhide and hide a public folder from Exchange address lists. By default, a new public folder is hidden from address lists. You must deselect Hide from Exchange Address Lists to expose it to the address lists.

The Exchange Advanced property page contains a Custom Attributes button. Click it to enter custom information for this recipient (see Figure 11.22 in Chapter 11).

Permissions

The Permissions property page for a public folder includes a range of security options. As you can see in Figure 12.22, these options cover client permissions, directory rights, and administrative rights. I'll cover each of these next.

Client Permissions   The right side of Figure 12.22 shows the Client Permissions dialog box. You use this dialog box to assign specific folder access rights to Exchange users and distribution groups, who can then work with a public folder using their Outlook clients. For emphasis, let me restate what I just said in a somewhat different form: You grant public folder access permissions to Exchange recipients, not to Windows 2003 users and groups. Once access to a public folder is granted, Exchange recipients access the folder in their Outlook client while connected to their mailbox.

FIGURE 12.22

A public folder's Permissions property page and its Client Permissions dialog box

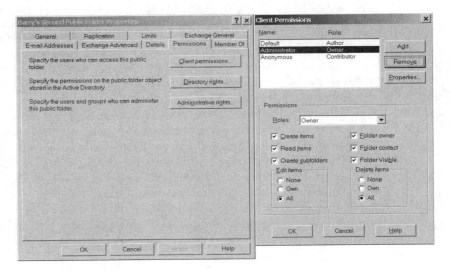

For a graphic reinforcement of this point, click Add in the Client Permissions dialog box to start adding a new user or group that will have access to this public folder. This action opens a dialog box that looks very much like the Outlook Address Book that you use to select recipients to send a message to, not the dialog box that you use to select Windows 2003 users and groups (see Figure 12.23). 'Nuff said. Click Cancel to get out of the Add Users dialog box.

FIGURE 12.23

The dialog box used to select new users or groups that will be granted permissions on a public folder in Exchange System Administrator looks like the Outlook Address Book.

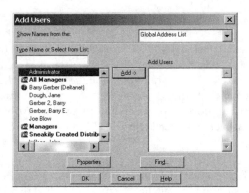

Now look back at Figure 12.22. Because I created the public folder in Exchange System Manager while logged in as the domain administrator, Administrator is given the role of Owner. As Figure 12.22 shows, the owner of a public folder has complete control over the folder.

If a user has the correct permissions on a public folder, that user can change access permissions on the folder for other users. Permissions on a public folder can be modified in two places. They can be modified from within the Outlook client using the Permissions property page for a public folder (see Figure 12.24). Permissions can also be modified using the Client Permissions dialog box that is available in Exchange System Manager (see Figure 12.22, shown earlier). Which of these you use depends on your security rights. If you are an Exchange user with no extraordinary permissions who is an owner of a public folder, you manage permissions for the folder in Outlook using the Permissions property page for a public folder, shown in Figure 12.24. If you're a user with Exchange administrative rights—for example, if you're a member of the group Exchange Admins that we created back in Chapter 8—you can change permissions on any public folder using the Client Permissions dialog box shown back in Figure 12.22.

There is a group named Default that includes all Exchange recipients not separately added to the Name list box. When the folder is created, this group is automatically given the default role of Author. As Figure 12.25 shows, Authors don't own the folder and can't create subfolders. Also note that Authors can edit and delete only their own folder items.

Microsoft has come up with several interesting roles—including Owner, Publishing Editor, Editor, Publishing Author, Author, Nonediting Author, Reviewer, Contributor, and Custom—each with a different combination of client permissions. I'll leave it to you to check out the specific permissions assigned to each of these roles. I'll also leave it to you to explore your options regarding public folder access permissions. Generally, the default settings work fine for most folders.

NOTE *Wondering about that Anonymous user in Figures 12.22, 12.24, and 12.25? You set access rights to a public folder for users who don't have Exchange mailboxes through the Anonymous user. When such users access a public folder, for example, with an Internet browser, the rights granted to the Anonymous user control what they can do with the folder.*

FIGURE 12.24
The Permissions property page for a public folder, as seen from within the Outlook client

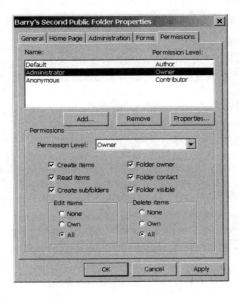

FIGURE 12.25
The permissions granted to the role Author in the Exchange System Manager Client Permissions dialog box

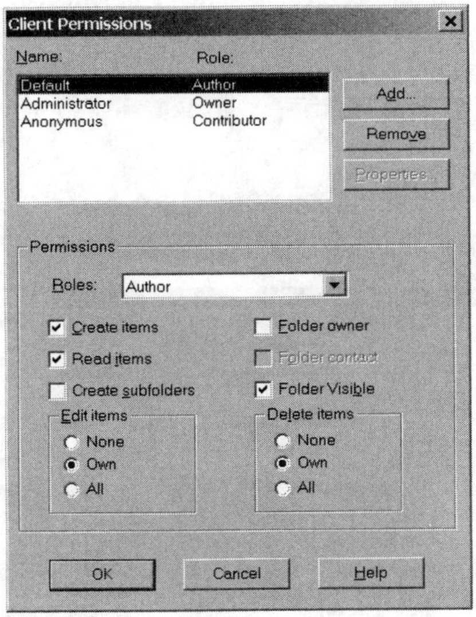

Directory Rights   Okay, back to Figure 12.22: Users and groups with appropriate permissions at the directory rights level can change the properties of a public folder object in Active Directory. The Directory Rights property page that pops up when you click Directory Rights is the same as the Security property page for other Exchange recipients (see Figure 11.29 in Chapter 11 and its related text). That's why public folders don't have a Security property page.

Administrative Rights   Administrative rights are permissions to manage a public folder using Exchange System Manager. Click Administrative Rights to open the Administrative Rights property page. As you can see in Figure 12.26, permissions include rights to modify the public folder access control list and the public folder administrative access control list. These rights include permission to use the Directory Rights property page and the Administrative Rights property page, the very page that I'm talking about right now. Permissions also include the right to set deleted-item retention time and space quotas for the public folder. You had the option of exercising both of these rights on the Limits page when you created your public folder earlier in this chapter.

Note in Figure 12.26 that our old friend, the group Exchange Admins, has full administrative rights to this folder. That's because we delegated full Exchange administrative control to the group at the Exchange organizational level back in Chapter 8 and because the rights granted at the organizational level were inherited by this public folder object.

Let me conclude this section by pointing out that administrative rights are granted to Windows 2003 users and groups, not to Exchange 2003 users and distribution groups.

Member Of

I don't need to say a lot about the Member Of property page in the public folder Properties dialog box in Figure 12.22. I just want to point out that public folders, just like other Exchange recipients, can belong to security and distribution groups. When you send a message to a distribution group that includes a public folder, the message appears in the folder.

FIGURE 12.26
Using the Administrative Rights property page to set public folder administrative permissions for others

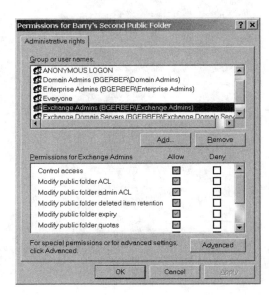

Exchange Core Components

We're now ready to take on Exchange 2003's three core components:

◆ Information Store

◆ Routing Engine

◆ System Attendant

The Information Store holds mailboxes and public folders. I'll give these thorough coverage in the following sections. The Routing Engine helps move messages from one Exchange server to another and out to foreign messaging systems. The System Attendant performs a range of housekeeping tasks that keep Exchange running smoothly and efficiently. We'll cover the minimal control that you have over the System Attendant in this chapter.

For more information about the function of these components and how they fit into the Exchange system, check out Chapter 4, "Exchange Server 2003 Architecture." Okay, let's take a look at each of Exchange's core components.

The Information Store

The Information Store on an Exchange server is composed of storage groups. The Information Store has no physical being in Exchange System Manager other than in its storage groups. That's why there is no Information Store container in Figure 12.27, which shows the one and only storage group that is the Information Store on my Exchange server EXCHANGE01.

FIGURE 12.27

The Exchange Information Store is composed of storage groups.

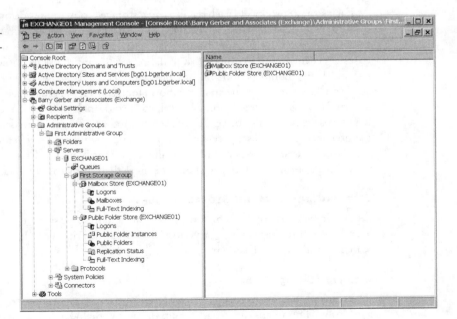

A storage group is supported by an instance of Microsoft's Extensible Storage Engine (ESE). A storage group can contain one or more databases. Databases, also called *stores*, can contain either mailboxes or public folders, but not both. Figure 12.27 shows the mailbox store and public store in my server's storage group. Each database is made up of two files, an EDB file and an STM file. These are not shown in Figure 12.27. The EDB file holds rich-text messages like the ones generated by Outlook and message header information (From, To, Cc, Time Sent, Subject, and so on). The STM (for "streaming") file contains Internet content in pure Multipurpose Internet Mail Extensions (MIME) format. MIME supports everything from rich-text-like formatted text with bolding and color to multimedia audio and video content. A message with MIME content is divided into header information, which goes to the EDB file, and other content, which is stored in the STM file. The ESE seamlessly stores content into and delivers content from the EDB and STM files as needed.

A storage group has a set of transaction log files. Data destined for a particular database is quickly and dirtily written to a log file. Then, as time allows, the data is transferred into the database file. Transfer to the database file is significantly slower than the write to the transaction log file because a number of issues such as data indexing must be attended to. Log files are designed to speedily move data from RAM memory to disk, both to ensure against hardware failure and to improve performance in the early stages of committing data to disk.

Exchange Server 2003 Standard Edition supports one storage group per server. This storage group can contain two databases: one mailbox store and one public folder store. You can also create one recovery storage group for restoring mailboxes and public folders that you have backed up. Exchange Server 2003 Enterprise Edition supports up to 20 storage groups and up to six databases per storage group, depending on whether your hardware is 32- or 64-bit.

Each storage group and each database in a storage group can reside on the same or different physical disk drives. With Exchange Server 2003 Standard Edition, the maximum size of a database is limited to 16GB. There is no limit on database size with Enterprise Server. However, practically speaking, databases larger than 200GB don't work well. So, you'll want to use multiple storage groups and databases to handle large numbers of mailboxes, not one gigantic database. If your needs exceed the capacity of a single server, of course, you can create more storage groups and databases on other Exchange servers. By keeping database size at a reasonable level, you avoid single points of failure, you can distribute database load across multiple disk drives or even servers, and you can maintain databases separately. Independent maintenance of databases—restoring one database while the others remain online and continue to function, for example—is one of the really important bonuses of Exchange 2003.

With all of this in mind, you should be more than ready to get into Information Store management.

CREATING AND MANAGING STORAGE GROUPS

As should be pretty obvious by now, you create and manage storage groups in Exchange System Manager. So, be sure that you've got your MMC open and that your Exchange System Manager looks something like the one shown earlier in Figure 12.27.

Creating a Storage Group

To create a new storage group on your Exchange server, right-click the server and select New ➤ Storage Group. This opens the storage group Properties dialog box (see Figure 12.28). Here's a quick take on your options on this dialog box.

Name   The name of your new storage group.

Transaction Log Location   The disk drive and path where the group's transaction logs should be stored. When mailbox or public folder stores are created in a storage group, their databases are stored here. You can change the suggested location anytime after the store is created.

System Path Location   The disk drive and path where the group's temporary and recovered files will reside. You can change this location as well.

TIP   *After you create a storage group, you can use the transaction log and system path location options to move the logs and system files to a new directory on a disk drive or to a new disk drive.*

Log File Prefix   The default prefix assigned to each log file. This is a view-only field visible after group is created.

Zero Out Deleted Database Pages   Checking this box improves security, but it does cost some in server performance.

Enable Circular Logging   When circular logging is disabled for a storage group, a new log file is opened every time the 5MB limit for a log file is reached. When circular logging is enabled, log files are overwritten when the 5MB limit is reached. This saves disk space, but you can't recover changes to databases in a storage group after the last backup because the required log files are no longer available. I suggest that you leave circular logging disabled and rely on Windows 2003's backup program or an Exchange-aware third-party backup program to take care of pruning transaction logs. After backing up a storage group using a full or incremental backup, Exchange-aware backup programs delete transaction log files if all the data in them has been transferred to the database.

When you're finished with the storage group Properties dialog box, click OK.

FIGURE 12.28
Using the storage group Properties dialog box to create a new storage group

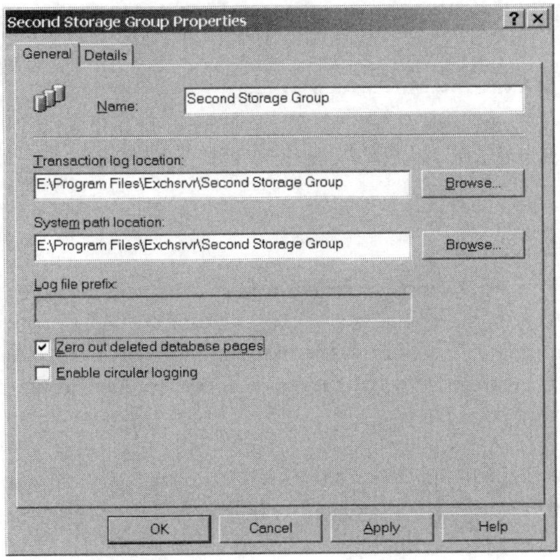

Managing Storage Groups

Your new storage group should show up in the left pane of your MMC (see the left side of Figure 12.29). Right-click the new storage group and select Properties to open the Properties dialog box for the group (see the right side of Figure 12.29). Notice that you still have control over file placement, zeroing of database pages, and circular logging. That's pretty much the extent of your ability to manage storage groups.

FIGURE 12.29

A new storage group and its Properties dialog box

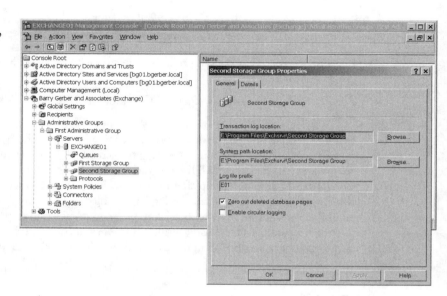

CREATING AND MANAGING MAILBOX STORES

Storage groups are really shells for mailbox and public folder stores. Stores are the really fun part of the Information Store. So, we'll get right to creating and managing stores. We'll start with mailbox stores.

Creating a Mailbox Store

We could create a new mailbox store in our first storage group, but, just for fun, let's put it in the storage group that we just created. Right-click your new storage group, and select New ➤ Mailbox Store from the pop-up menu. This opens the mailbox store Properties dialog box, shown in Figure 12.30. Right now, we need to look at the General, Database, and Limits property pages. We'll look at the Full-Text Indexing page later.

General   Most of the properties on the General property page require a fair amount of explanation, so we're going to spend a little more time here than we usually do on General pages.

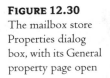

FIGURE 12.30

The mailbox store
Properties dialog
box, with its General
property page open

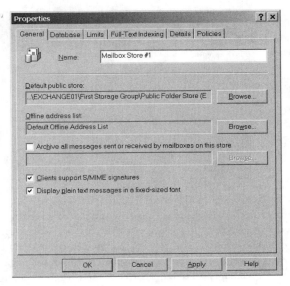

Use the Name field to specify a name for your mailbox store. This is the name that will appear in Exchange System Manager. Naming conventions for mailbox stores depend on how you plan to use them. You might want to create different stores for different user groups. You could create one store for clerical personnel, another for salespeople, and another for top management. You could name each store for the group that it supports. Then you could set the attributes of each store differently. For example, you might set different storage limits on each store, or you might use different security measures for digital signatures. On the other hand, you might decide to use mailbox stores to distribute loads across your organization. You could still set different attributes for different stores, but you would probably use generic names for the stores, as I have in Figure 12.30. The choice is yours.

You're probably staring at the Default Public Store field on the General property page in disbelief. I know I did when I first saw it. I mean, why does a mailbox store need a default public store? The answer is simpler than you might imagine. Every mailbox store needs to be associated with the default public store on an Exchange server. The default public store on my Exchange server is named Public Folder Store (EXCHANGE01) in Figure 12.27, shown earlier. There is one default public store on a server, and that store is created when Exchange is installed. A mailbox store can be associated with the default public store on its own server or on any Exchange server in the organization. The public folder store associated with a mailbox store is the public folder store that users of mailboxes in the mailbox store see when using an Outlook or IMAP4 client.

Figure 12.31 helps make all this clearer. If more Exchange servers existed in my Exchange organization, their default public folder stores would also show up in the Select Public Store dialog box. By the way, I opened the Select Public Store dialog box by clicking the Browse button next to the Default Public Store field in the General property page.

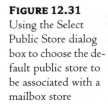

FIGURE 12.31
Using the Select
Public Store dialog
box to choose the de-
fault public store to
be associated with a
mailbox store

Back to Figure 12.30: An offline address list is a list of Exchange recipients that is used to select message recipients when a user runs Outlook while disconnected from their Exchange server. Offline address lists are most useful when a user is incapable of connecting to an Exchange server, such as when in flight on an airplane. Offline address lists reside in the organizational Recipients container in Exchange System Manager. A default list is created when Exchange is installed, and it shows all unhidden Exchange recipients. You can create a new address list and use it here. We'll get into address lists in Chapter 16. For now, just accept the default.

If you've been bugged by people in high places in your organization for a way to check on Exchange messages sent and received by users, Exchange 2003 has a nice but just a little bit scary solution. It's all in that innocent Archive All Messages Sent or Received by Mailboxes on This Store field. Click the check box and then click Browse to select any Exchange user, distribution group, contact, or public folder where you want all messages archived to. If you pick a mailbox-enabled user or distribution group, copies of all messages show up in the user's or users' Inbox. If you select a mail-enabled user or contact, copies of the messages are sent to the mail-enabled user's or the contact's external e-mail address. If you select a public folder, copies of the messages are placed in the public folder.

There are two drawbacks to this capability. First, someone needs to carefully consider the privacy issues related to archiving. Second, you must consider disk space issues. A message is actually stored only once in a mailbox store, no matter how many recipients it has. Each recipient gets a pointer to the single instance of the message. The message is deleted when the last pointer is deleted. So, if you don't clear your archives, you'll be keeping a copy of every message ever sent or received by a mailbox in the mailbox store forever. Also, if you archive to mailboxes or public folders on a different mailbox store, there will be one copy of the message in the original store and one in the archive store.

Secure Multipurpose Internet Mail Extensions (S/MIME) signatures provide a secure way of sending e-mail over the Internet. We'll talk more about S/MIME signatures in Chapter 18, "Exchange Server System Security." Select the check box if the e-mail client used in your organization supports S/MIME. Outlook 98 or later supports this protocol.

Plain-text messages are messages that don't include the rich formatting attributes of messages sent through e-mail clients such as Outlook. Typically, they are received from the Internet. If the Display Plain Text Messages in a Fixed-Sized Font option is selected, e-mail clients will be instructed to use a nonproportional screen type font. This ensures that lists and diagrams display properly without the user having to change the display font of a message.

Database   Compared to the General property page, the Database page is fairly simple, as you can see in Figure 12.32. To start, you select the disk drive and path to use for both the Exchange database (.EDB file) and the Exchange streaming database (.STM file). If, for better hard-disk performance, you want your database log files and your two database files to reside on different drives, here's where you do it. Remembering where I proposed placing my database log files back in Figure 12.29, the way things are set in Figure 12.32, my database log and database files will be on the same drive. Before I finish, I'd better change the location of the database files.

FIGURE 12.32

Using the Database property page to set file location, maintenance, and other properties for a new mailbox store

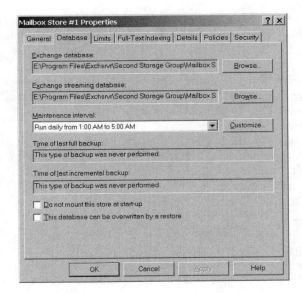

TIP   You can use the database location options shown in Figure 12.32 to move a mailbox store to a new directory on a disk drive or to a new disk drive.

Mailbox store maintenance is an automatic process that includes checking to see whether mailboxes have exceeded their storage limits and managing deleted messages. You set parameters for these maintenance processes on the Limits property page, which I'll discuss in the next section. You set the schedule under which these processes are executed in the Maintenance Interval field. It's best to let your server perform maintenance during off hours. You can select a schedule from the drop-down list or create a customized maintenance schedule by clicking Customize.

The two backup fields are a nice addition to Exchange 2003. They tell you when the last full and incremental backup of your Exchange server happened. This information is especially useful when

Exchange managers are not responsible for backup of their own servers. At least an Exchange manager so situated can check to see if and when either or both kinds of backup occurred.

A store is offline if it isn't mounted. A dismounted store is not available to its users. Typically, you dismount a store when you want to do manual maintenance on it, such as restore a database. You can dismount a store by right-clicking it and selecting Dismount. Why would you want a mailbox store to remain dismounted after Exchange starts up? Perhaps because you're still working on fixing a problem with the store, or perhaps to control when a particular store is available to users. Use the Do Not Mount This Store at Start-up box as needed.

Select This Database Can Be Overwritten by a Restore only when you've exhausted all other means of recovering a damaged database. If you recover a database from a backup, you'll lose all messages that entered the database since the backup.

TIP   You could use Exchange 5.5's Optimizer program to move databases to different directories and drives on your Exchange server. Exchange 2003 has no Optimizer program. To move databases, first use the first two fields on the Database property page (see Figure 12.32, shown earlier) to change the directory where you want the Exchange database or Exchange streaming database to be stored. After you've made these changes, you must dismount the storage group's databases and then manually move the databases to the new directory and mount the databases. You can use this same technique with storage groups and public folder stores.

Limits   Among other things, you use the Limits property page, shown in Figure 12.33, to set the default storage and deleted-item retention limits for your mailbox store. These defaults are applied to a mailbox in the store unless you specifically set alternative limits for it. See Chapter 11 (Figure 11.20 and related text) for more on setting alternative limits for a mailbox and on the limit options in Figure 12.33. Unless you plan to set storage limits for each mailbox or you have infinite storage, be sure not to leave the storage limits fields blank. Are the numbers I entered for storage limits in Figure 12.33 reasonable? They're probably too low. You have to work out limits for yourself based on available storage, legitimate e-mail storage needs, organizational politics, and a bit of guessing.

You set the schedule for checking to see whether any mailboxes have exceeded their storage limits on the Database property page that I discussed in the last section. You set the schedule for sending warning messages using the Warning Message Interval field on the Limits property page. Any mailboxes that have exceeded their storage limits receive an appropriate message.

Note that, in addition to setting a default value for deleted item retention—Keep Deleted Items for (Days)—you can set a retention period for deleted mailboxes. No matter what deleted items and mailbox retention schedule you set, you can also instruct Exchange to not permanently delete items or mailboxes until they have been backed up (the Do Not Permanently Delete Mailboxes and Items Until the Store Has Been Backed Up box). This is a nice option that you'd be wise to check no matter what schedule you've set, but especially if you've set retention times of zero days. This way, you're sure that deleted items and mailboxes are protected by a backup. Checking this option also protects you against the unlikely situation in which your backups fail for a number of days greater than the retention periods that you've set.

When you're done setting up your new mailbox store, click OK on the mailbox store Properties dialog box. You should now be able to see and open your new mailbox store, as I have done in Figure 12.34.

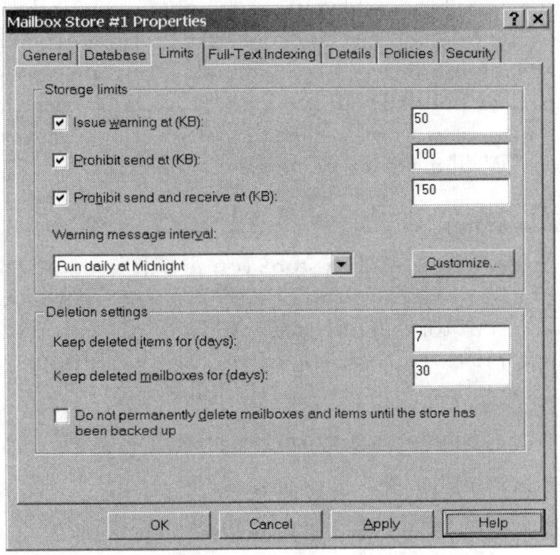

FIGURE 12.33
Using the Limits property page to set storage and deleted items parameters for a mailbox store

FIGURE 12.34
Viewing a newly created mailbox store

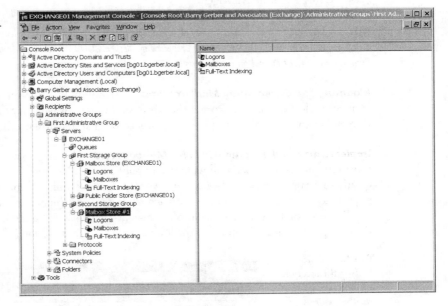

Now create a new mailbox-enabled Exchange user following the instructions in Chapter 11. When you get to the point where you can set parameters for the creation of a new mailbox, open the drop-down list for the Mailbox Store field. You should see not only the default mailbox store created when Exchange was installed, but also your new store. Just as I promised in Chapter 11, this is how you create a mailbox in a mailbox store other than the default store. Anyway, create the user's mailbox in your new mailbox store. We'll make use of this user soon.

Managing Mailbox Stores

Because you've created a new mailbox store, you already know a heck of lot about mailbox store management. The properties that you set while creating your new mailbox store can be altered by opening the Properties dialog box for the store, just as we did in the previous section. As we move through this section, when appropriate, I'll show you how to use the remaining property pages on the mailbox store Properties dialog box. We'll look at the following:

◆ Mounting and dismounting a mailbox store

◆ Implementing full-text indexing on a mailbox store

◆ Monitoring mailbox logons and resource use

◆ Setting policies for a mailbox store

◆ Using Mailbox Manager

NOTE *This section deals with a variety of ways you can manage mailbox stores using a mailbox store's property pages. In the next section, we'll explore the use of Exchange Server 2003's Mailbox Manager, which nicely supplements the management options offered on the property pages.*

Mounting and Dismounting Mailbox Stores To mount or dismount a mailbox store, right-click the store and select Dismount Store if the store is mounted, or Mount Store if the store is dismounted. Remember that you dismount stores mostly to do maintenance on them.

Implementing Full-Text Indexing on a Mailbox Store Exchange Server 2003 comes with a really neat capability: full-text indexing of mailbox and public stores. Yes, every word in a store can be indexed to greatly speed up user searches for specific words or phrases. Full-text indexing comes at a price in storage requirements and demands on server capacity, but it is something that you'll almost always want to turn on. To turn it on for your new mailbox store, right-click the store and select Create Full-Text Index. Use the dialog box that pops up to set the location for the index catalog (see Figure 12.35).

FIGURE 12.35

Setting the location of the catalog for a mailbox store's full-text index

You now have to populate your new index with information. But, first send a message to that new user you created in the store. This initializes the user's mailbox. If you don't do this, you won't be able to create an index. You can do this with an Outlook client or with the Web-based Outlook Web Access client. If you don't see the new user when you attempt to place the user in the To field of your message, go to the Recipient Update Services container under Recipients in Exchange System Manager, right-click the recipient update service for your domain, and select Update Now. Wait a bit and you should be able to find the new user and place the user in the To field. Once the message has been sent, check the subcontainer Mailboxes in your new mailbox store. You should see the new user's mailbox, and the mailbox should have one item in it.

Now, right-click your mailbox store and select Start Full Population from the pop-up menu (see Figure 12.36). The Start Incremental Population option enables you to manually start an update of your index anytime. When your index is initially populated, you can fully rebuild the index manually anytime by selecting the Start Full Population option.

FIGURE 12.36

Starting full population of a mailbox store's full-text index

Manual population and updating of a full-text index might be some people's idea of fun, but for me it's a royal pain. You can schedule automatic updates of your index using the Properties dialog box for your mailbox store. Open the dialog box and tab over to the Full-Text Indexing property page. Figure 12.37 shows this page.

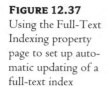

FIGURE 12.37
Using the Full-Text Indexing property page to set up automatic updating of a full-text index

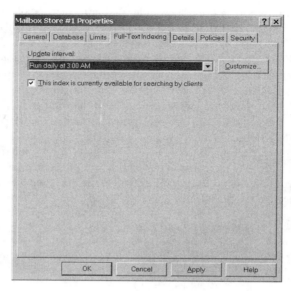

The update interval is the frequency at which text in new items in the mailbox store is added to the index and text from deleted items is removed from the index. Options on the drop-down list include these:

◆ Never run

◆ Run daily at 10:00 P.M.

◆ Run daily at 1:00 A.M.

◆ Run daily at 3:00 A.M.

◆ Run every hour

◆ Always run

You can also set a customized schedule by clicking Customize. Notice that Microsoft is trying to encourage you to run indexing during off hours. That's because it takes up lots of CPU cycles and disk accesses.

Be sure that you select the option This Index Is Currently Available for Searching by Clients. When might you disable indexed access to your mailbox store? Well, for sure when you're manually rebuilding your index.

You need to do one more thing before you're done setting up your index. Open the Properties dialog box for your server, and tab over to the Full-Text Indexing property page. You can use the drop-down list on this page to select how much of the resources on your server you want to devote to indexing. Options include minimum, low, high, and maximum amounts. The fewer resources used, the more resources will be available to other tasks, but the slower indexing will be.

To see the results of your handiwork, click the Full-Text Indexing subcontainer of your new mailbox store. Your MMC should look something like the one in Figure 12.38. If it doesn't look like any indexing has happened, select Refresh from the Action menu. If it still doesn't look like anything happened, manually start another full population. After a bit, select Refresh again. That should do it. Of course, there should be messages in your mailbox store to index or none of this will be much fun.

FIGURE 12.38

Checking full-text indexing progress in the Full-Text Indexing container

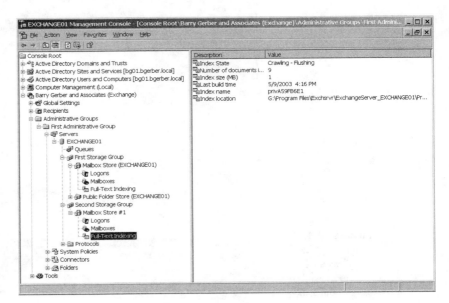

> **WARNING** *Full-text indices can get really big. Don't waste tape or disk backup space by backing them up. If you lose all or part of a mailbox store, after you restore what you need from a backup, you can just recreate the index. If you lose the index, just re-index the store. This applies to full-text indices for public folder stores, which I will talk about soon.*

Monitoring Mailbox Logon and Resource Usage If you need to know when particular users last logged in to their mailboxes or last accessed the Exchange system and with which client, look in the Logons container shown in Figure 12.39. Joe User is the mail-enabled user that I created at the end of the earlier section "Creating a Mailbox Store." The other two users support SMTP and system services for the mailbox store. Our friend Joe used an HTTP client. It was, in fact, the Outlook Web Access client supported by Exchange 2003.

Want to know how many messages a user has in a mailbox or how much storage a mailbox is taking up? Look in the Mailboxes container (see Figure 12.40). Now, what you see in Figure 12.40 isn't very interesting, but imagine you need to find out why your backup tape is running out before the completion of even one backup of your Exchange information stores. Just click the Size (KB) column to sort mailboxes in descending order by size and you'll find the culprits at the bottom of the list.

FIGURE 12.39
Monitoring user logins to mailboxes in a mailbox store in the Logons container

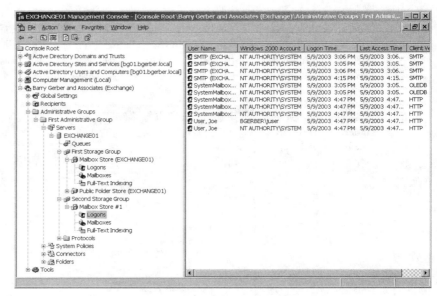

FIGURE 12.40
Monitoring the use of mailbox resources in mailbox store in the Mailboxes container

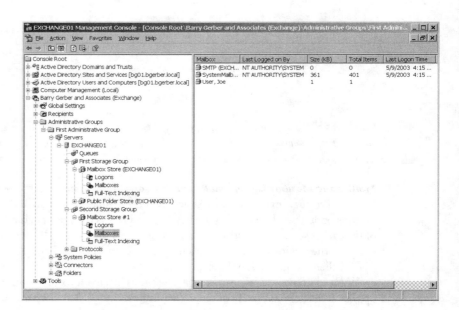

I've met some Exchange 5.5 administrators who would give their left arm to be able to save the contents of the 5.5 Administrator's Logons container to a file. Why? They wanted to process the file to determine which users hadn't logged in to their mailboxes since a certain date. Then they wanted to check if it was okay to delete the mailboxes of such users. Well, all you 5.5 refugees can save the contents of the Logons container just as you can save the contents of any MMC container. Just right-click the container and select Export List from the pop-up menu, then just follow the online instructions to create a tab- or comma-delimited file with one row for each user that includes the data for all the columns visible in the container. For more about the Export List option, see the section "Managing the Organization," earlier in this chapter.

Setting Policies for a Mailbox Store   You'll remember that Exchange policies apply properties to groups of objects. We set up a policy for a server in the section "Creating and Managing Server Policies," earlier in this chapter. Now we're going to set up a mailbox store policy.

In Exchange System Manager, find and right-click the System Policies container that you created earlier in this chapter. Select New ➢ Mailbox Store Policy from the pop-up menu. This opens the New Policy dialog box, shown in Figure 12.41. From the dialog box, select the property pages that you want the policy to apply to, and click OK.

FIGURE 12.41

Selecting property pages to be included in a mailbox store system policy

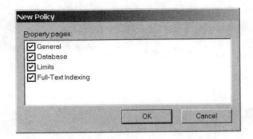

The Properties dialog box for the policy opens (see Figure 12.42). You can now bop around the various property pages and set the properties as you wish. You can set all properties that make sense when you remember that this policy will apply to a group of mailbox stores. For example, you can set a generic maintenance interval on the Database (Policy) page, but you can't set the database paths, set startup mount status, or determine whether restores overwrite the databases. That makes sense because you really have to set these policies on a store-by-store basis.

Set properties for the policy the same way as you set them for your new mailbox store. When you're finished selecting properties for your policy, click OK to create the policy.

To add a mailbox store to the policy, follow the instructions in the section "Creating and Managing Server Policies," earlier in this chapter. You'll be offered the standard dialog box for finding and adding Active Directory objects. Search for "mailbox" and you should see two mailbox stores that you can add to the policy: the default mailbox store and the mailbox store that you just created. For fun, add the default mailbox store to the policy. Then open the Properties dialog box for the store. Look at the various property pages (see Figure 12.43). Note how much is grayed out, meaning not only that you can't change the properties, but also that the properties were set simply because you added the store to the policy. Now, imagine that you had 10 or 20 Exchange servers, each with multiple mailbox stores. Even if you had to set up two or three policies to cover all the mailbox stores, the job of setting and maintaining properties for the stores would be so much simpler with policies than without them.

FIGURE 12.42
Setting properties for a mailbox store system policy

FIGURE 12.43
The Properties dialog box for mailbox store after the store has been added to a policy

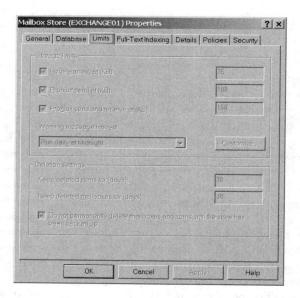

Now, tab over to the Policies property page for your default mailbox store. You should see the policies that you just added the mailbox store to. Also check the subcontainer for the policy that you just created in the System Policies container. Because it was added to this policy, your new mailbox should be in the subcontainer. Check out the previous section "Creating and Managing Server Policies" if any of this is a bit murky.

Using Mailbox Manager   One way to control the amount of storage used by a mailbox is to simply limit the number of bytes all users or a specific user has for storage. Storage limits are a good and viable approach to storage conservation. However, what if you don't want to use limits, or if you decide to use limits, but still want your users' mailboxes to occupy as little of their allotted storage as possible? That's where the Exchange Mailbox Manager comes in.

Mailbox Manager can find items in Exchange mailboxes that exceed age and size limits. It can then do anything from reporting on this situation to removing items that exceed these limits. Note that I use the term *items* and not *messages*. Exchange mailboxes contain not only messages, but also calendar, task, journal, contacts, and notes objects. Hence the term *items* to refer to all of the types of objects that can live in an Exchange mailbox. Having explained my use of the term *items,* I must now call your attention to the fact that the official Microsoft term for what I'm calling *items* is, as you'll see very soon, *message classes. Message classes* seems a bit confusing to me when you're talking about things that are not specifically messages—contacts, for example—but who am I to argue with the powers that be?

Okay, let's get to using Mailbox Manager. First, Mailbox Manager isn't enabled by default. You enable it for each recipient policy. I briefly discussed recipient policies in the last chapter, when I talked about the default SMTP and X.400 addressing scheme or schemes used in an Exchange organization. Recipient policies reside in the Recipient Policies container. At this point, you should have one recipient policy: the default policy. Right-click this policy and select Change Property Pages, as shown in Figure 12.44. Use the dialog box that pops up to select Mail Box Manager Settings and click OK.

FIGURE 12.44

Selecting Change Property Pages to activate the Mailbox Manager property page for a system policy

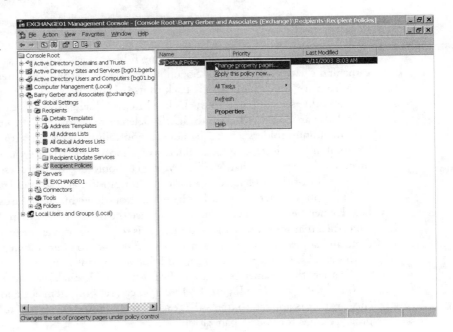

Now double-click your default recipient policy and tab over to the Mailbox Manager Settings (Policy) properties page. This is where you set the rules for Mailbox Manager. As you can see in Figure 12.45, you can choose the action you want Mailbox Manager to perform when it starts processing mailboxes. Actions range from the innocuous generation of a report on mailbox usage figures through immediate deletion of messages from selected mailbox folders.

FIGURE 12.45

Activating the Mailbox Manager property page for a system policy

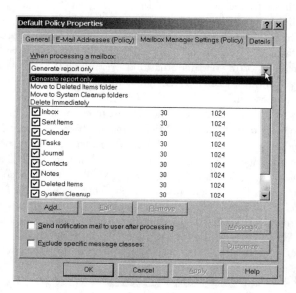

When items are placed in system cleanup folders, they go in replicas of the folders from which they came in the user's own mailbox. So, unlike items moved to Deleted Items, it is possible to recover an item from system cleanup folders back to its original folder. Additionally, moving items to system cleanup folders, as opposed to the Deleted Items folder, assures that items moved without the user's knowledge aren't deleted when the user's Deleted Items folder is automatically or manually emptied. System cleanup folders give users more responsibility for cleaning up their mailboxes.

Speaking of selected mailbox folders, you choose those folders immediately below the drop-down menu used to specify what Mailbox Manager should do when processing mailboxes. Figure 12.45 shows most of the folders you can select. Only All Other Mail Folders is hidden from view. This option applies the action you select from the drop-down menu to the user-generated folders in a mailbox. Remember, system cleanup folders place the onus of mailbox management on users. If you're concerned that some users might not take this responsibility seriously, you can create a policy just for them and apply a set of mailbox management settings to their system folders. See the note at the end of this section for more on creating additional recipient policies.

To select the parameters for a specific folder, double-click the folder to open the Folder Retention Settings dialog box (see Figure 12.46). You can set both item age and size limits. The action you chose earlier is applied to items that exceed these limits. I'll leave it to you to come up with appropriate settings for your organization.

FIGURE 12.46

Selecting age and size limits to be used by Mailbox Manager for items in a specific mailbox folder

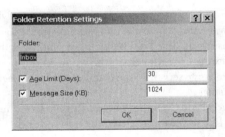

Let's go back to Figure 12.45. If you select Send Notification Mail to User After Processing, be sure to edit the message to be sent by clicking Message. The default message is "The Microsoft Exchange Server Mailbox Manager has performed an automatic cleanup of your mailbox." Now, this is fine if you've informed your users about all this stuff and you've set the Mailbox Manager to do an actual cleanup. However, if you're just doing reporting and that message goes out to your users, I guarantee you're going to get some pretty anxious e-mails and phone calls. Most of them will be of the form "What in the heck did it delete?" How do I know this? Let's just say, from experience, and leave it at that.

The last option on the Mailbox Manager Settings (Policy) property page allows you to exclude specific message classes from the mailbox management process. Here you can designate item types that you don't want Mailbox Manager to process, for example, contacts or calendar items.

When you're finished setting up your Mailbox Manager, click OK to close the dialog box. Now you're ready to set a schedule for Mailbox Manager. Mailbox Manager runs on each Exchange server and processes only the mailboxes on that server. Mailbox Manager does nothing until you schedule it to run and start it up, which you do on an Exchange server. So, open the Properties dialog box for your Exchange server and tab over to the Mailbox Management page, shown in Figure 12.47.

FIGURE 12.47

Setting schedule, reporting, and administrator options for Mailbox Manager at the server level

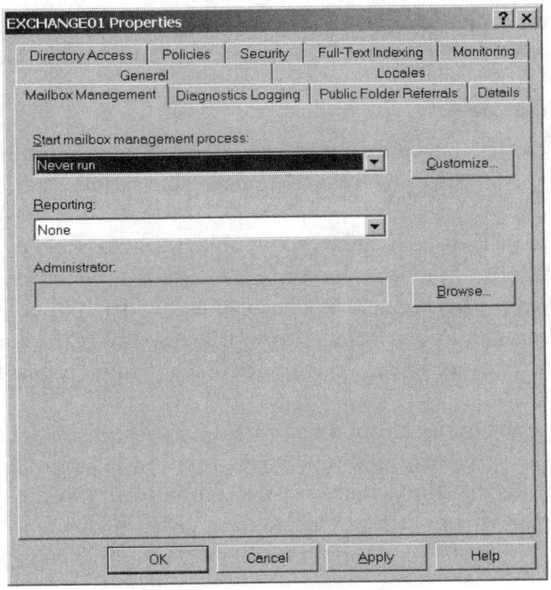

As Figure 12.47 shows, in addition to setting a schedule for your Mailbox Manager, you can select the type of reporting you want and you can set an Administrator to receive reports. In addition to Never Run, scheduling options include Run Saturday at Midnight, Run Sunday at Midnight, and Use Custom Schedule. Running once a week on the weekend during off hours is generally adequate for most installations of Exchange server. Large installations can benefit from more frequent custom-scheduled mailbox maintenance.

Reporting options include None, Send Summary Report to Administrator, and Send Detail[ed] Report to Administrator. I like to start out setting the option for the action to be performed by Mailbox Manager (see Figure 12.45, shown earlier) to Generate Report Only and reporting options to Send Summary Report to Administrator. A summary report shows you the number of mailboxes processed, the number of messages that would be moved or deleted, and the total size of those messages. Once you get a feeling for their sheer size, you can run a detailed report for each mailbox. Detailed reports include "would be moved or deleted" information for each mailbox for each folder you select for processing. You can use that information to decide how to tackle the mailbox cleanup task. If you have a few offending users, you might ask them to clean up their mailboxes on their own, without any intervention by Mailbox Manager. If you decide to go with Mailbox Manager, you can use the reports you get to refine the age and size limits for specific folders.

Mailbox Manager runs as a part of the System Attendant service on your Exchange server. You start Mailbox Manager by right-clicking the icon for your Exchange server and selecting Start Mailbox Management Process. You can stop the service at any time by right-clicking the icon for your Exchange server and selecting Stop Mailbox Management Process.

NOTE   *Recipient policies are set for your Exchange organization as a whole. You can create recipient policies that apply to specific groups of mailboxes. I'll show you how to do that in Chapter 16.*

CREATING AND MANAGING PUBLIC STORES

Public stores are a lot like mailbox stores, so I'm going to discuss some issues very quickly and skip others that I covered in the section "Creating and Managing Mailbox Stores," earlier in this chapter.

Creating a Public Store

Before you can create a new public store, you need to understand how public stores and what are called *public folder trees* relate to each other. You absolutely will not be able to use public stores without this understanding.

Each public store is directly linked to a public folder tree. The default public folder tree on an Exchange server, Public Folders, is linked to the default public store, Public Folder Store (SERVER_NAME) on the server. In Figure 12.48, you can see my default public folder tree, Public Folders, and the default public store, Public Folder Store (EXCHANGE01). A public store can link to only one public folder tree, and vice versa. You can not link any more public folder trees to the default public folder store.

The default public folder tree and store are unique: They are the only tree-store combination that is MAPI-enabled. If you create additional tree-store combinations on a server, they can not be MAPI-enabled. This means that the default tree-store combination is the only one that can be accessed by MAPI-aware e-mail clients such as Outlook and IMAP4 clients.

FIGURE 12.48

Viewing an Exchange server's default public folder tree and default public store

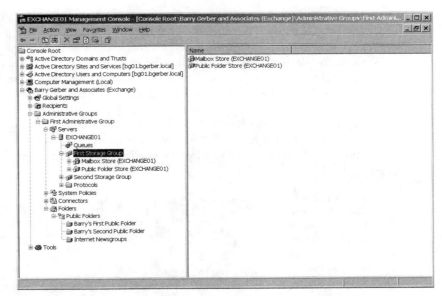

When you look at public folders in Outlook, you're looking at the default tree/store combination associated with the mailbox store containing your mailbox. Think back to the section "Creating a Mailbox Store," when you had to associate a mailbox store with the default public store on an Exchange server. That's how you told Exchange which public folders (tree-store combination) to present when a client such as Outlook opened a mailbox in your new mailbox store.

If clients such as Outlook can see only the default tree-store combination on an Exchange server, of what use are additional tree-store combinations? Good question. The answer is simple. You can access additional tree-store combinations using any of the following clients:

- A client that can access a Windows file system that has been enhanced using Exchange 2003's Installable File System (IFS)

- An enhanced Internet-standard Web-Distributed Authoring and Versioning (WebDav) client

- An Internet-standard Network News Transfer Protocol (NNTP) client

IFS is a very special kind of share on an Exchange 2003 server that points to the mailbox and public stores on the Exchange server. You can map a drive to the share or use it directly. I'll show you some ways to use IFS later in this section.

WebDav clients are implemented in web browsers. Microsoft has enhanced the WebDav Internet draft standard to allow it to work seamlessly with Exchange Server 2003. WebDav is at the heart of Outlook Web Access, which lets you access your Exchange mailbox and public folders with an Internet browser.

Finally, additional tree-store combinations can be made available through a Windows 2003/Exchange 2003 NNTP server, which can be accessed with a Network News Transfer Protocol client such as the one in Microsoft's Outlook Express.

Okay, let's create a public store. Before you can do so, however, you must create a public folder tree to associate it with. To create a new public folder tree, find and right-click the Folders container for your administrative group, then select New ➤ Public Folder Tree from the pop-up menu. The public folder tree Properties dialog box opens. Enter a name for the tree. I'm going to call mine Demo Public Folder Tree. When you're done, click OK. You should now see your tree in the Folders container.

Now you can go ahead and create your public store. Right-click either your default storage group or the storage group that you created earlier in this chapter. Then select New ➤ Public Store from the pop-up menu to open the public store Properties dialog box, shown on the left side of Figure 12.49. Name your new public store in the General property page. Next, click Browse next to the Associated Public Folder Tree field and select the public folder tree that you just created, as I'm doing on the right side of Figure 12.49.

FIGURE 12.49

The public store Properties dialog box, with its General property page and Select a Public Folder Tree dialog box open

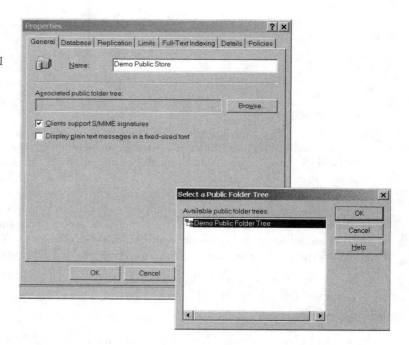

The Database property page looks and works exactly like the same page on the mailbox store Properties dialog box. We'll talk about the Replication page in Chapter 15, when we have at least one more server to replicate public folders to. The Limits page has a Deleted Items field, but it doesn't have a Retention field for mailboxes, for obvious reasons. Public stores don't hold mailboxes. The Limits page also has an additional field, Age Limits for All Folders in This Store. Use this field to set a default number of days before an item in any public folder in the store is deleted. You can override the default using the Limits page for any public folder, as you saw in the earlier section "Creating a Public Folder." The Full-Text Indexing and other pages look and work just as they do for mailbox stores.

When you're done creating your public store, click OK on the public store Properties dialog box. Your MMC should look something like the one in Figure 12.50.

Now, you should create a public folder in your new tree-store. We'll use the folder later. Call the folder Test. To create the folder, follow the directions in the earlier section "Creating a Public Folder."

FIGURE 12.50

A new public store, its subcontainers, and its associated public folder tree

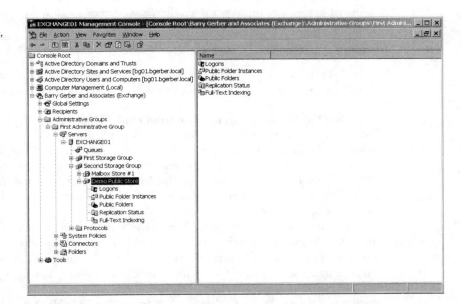

Managing Public Stores

Based on your experience with it when creating a public store, you should have no trouble using the public store Properties dialog box to manage your new public store. I won't discuss the dialog box any further here; instead, I'm going to discuss three aspects of public store management in this section:

◆ Using public store management containers

◆ Mail-enabling public folders in a nondefault public folder tree

◆ Providing access to public folders in a nondefault public folder tree

Using Public Store Management Containers   As you saw back in Figure 12.50, a public folder store has a range of subcontainers, just like a mailbox store. As with mailbox stores, these subcontainers are used for managing the store. Many of the subcontainers are used in the same way that they're used for mailbox stores:

Logons   Works just like the Logons subcontainer for mailbox stores.

Public Folder Instances   Shows information for all public folder instances in a public store. This includes not only the folders in the Public Folders subcontainer, but also folders that have been replicated to this server from other Exchange servers.

Public Folders   Shows resource usage and other information for all public folders in the store, in a manner similar to the Mailboxes subcontainer for mailbox stores. These are folders that originated in the store or, to put it another way, that are local to the store.

Replication Status   Shows progress when replicating folders across Exchange servers. I'll cover this subcontainer in Chapter 15.

Full-Text Indexing   Works just like the same subcontainer for mailboxes. In fact, you set up full-text indexing for public stores exactly as you set it up for mailbox stores.

Mail-Enabling Public Folders in a Nondefault Public Folder Tree   As I noted in the earlier section "Managing Public Folders," when you create a public folder in the default public folder store, it is automatically mail-enabled. It can send and receive messages. Public folders created in other public stores can send and receive e-mail messages too, but you have to mail-enable them before this is possible. Let's mail-enable the folder Test that I asked you to create at the end of the earlier section "Creating a Public Store." To mail-enable a public folder, right-click it and select All Tasks ➤ Mail Enable from the pop-up menu.

After a few seconds, select Refresh from the Action menu and open the Properties dialog box for the folder. Miracle of miracles, the folder now has an E-Mail Addresses property page and a set of e-mail address to boot. Open your Outlook client and notice that the folder is in the Address Book. You can send messages to it. Don't close your Outlook client; we're going to use it in the next section.

Providing Access to Public Folders in a Nondefault Public Folder Tree   Just to prove that nondefault public folder trees are unavailable to Outlook clients, look at the public folder hierarchy in your client. You see the default public folder tree, Public Folders. However, you don't see the new tree that you just created.

As I mentioned earlier, you can access nondefault public folder trees using three types of clients:

◆   Windows 2003 file system enhanced by Exchange 2003's Installable File System (IFS)

◆   Web-Distributed Authoring and Versioning (WebDav)

◆   Network News Transfer Protocol (NNTP)

Let's focus on IFS here. Back in the old days, when you installed Exchange 2000 Server, the M: drive was automatically mapped to the Exchange IFS. A lot of problems arose from that sweet little mapping. Many of them had to do with what happened to mailboxes and so on when the M: drive was backed up. So, with Exchange 2003, there is no automatic mapping to the IFS. You have to manually map a drive letter to the IFS. You don't set the mapping as you would with other drives. You actually have to edit the registry. Here's how to do it.

Open the Windows 2003 registry editor by entering **regedit** in the input field that becomes available when you choose Start ➤ Run. This opens the registry editor program. Find the registry key `HKEY_LOCAL_MACHINE\SYSTEM\CurrentControlSet\Services\EXIFS\Parameters` (see Figure 12.51).

Right-click the Parameters container and select New ➤ String Value. A new item appears in the Parameters container. Name the string value **DriveLetter** (all one word), then double-click it. In the Value Data field, enter the drive letter you want to be assigned to your IFS. Click OK and you're done. Restart the Exchange services and open Windows Explorer and you should see a new drive letter.

FIGURE 12.51

You must edit the Windows Server 2003 registry to map a drive letter to the Exchange Installable File System

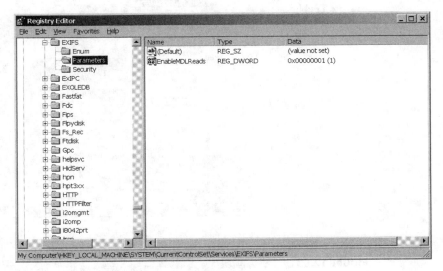

In Figure 12.52, you can see that I made the necessary registry changes to map the P: drive to the IFS on my Exchange server. The folder MBX contains all the mailboxes in all the mailbox stores on my server. I'll leave it to your imagination to come up with neat ideas for using the MBX folder, but be aware that access to individual mailboxes is initially limited to only the primary account associated with the mailbox. That is, Administrator can access the Administrator mailbox, bgerber can access bgerber's mailbox, and so on. The folder PUBLIC FOLDERS includes all public folders on my server. And, of course, the folder DEMO PUBLIC FOLDER TREE is the public folder tree that I created earlier in the section "Creating a Public Store."

Like any other disk-based directory (folder), you can share one or more of the folders or subfolders on the drive mapped to the IFS. You control access to such shares like you control access to any Windows 2003 share: through the Windows 2003 security system, not the Exchange 2003 system.

Back in Figure 12.52, I'm right-clicking the folder that represents my new public folder tree, and I'm selecting Sharing and Security from the pop-up menu. In Figure 12.53, I've chosen to share my new folder tree. Among other things, I can set the name that users will see when using the share, and I can control access to the tree by clicking Permissions. Notice the Web Sharing tab. Yes, like all disk-based directories, you can also share this folder through your Internet Information Server for access with a web browser such as Microsoft's Internet Explorer. Pretty neat.

FIGURE 12.52
Viewing the IFS, which has been mapped to the P: drive on an Exchange server, and choosing to share a public folder tree on the P: drive

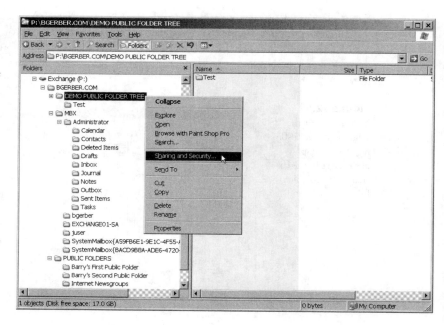

FIGURE 12.53
Sharing a public folder tree

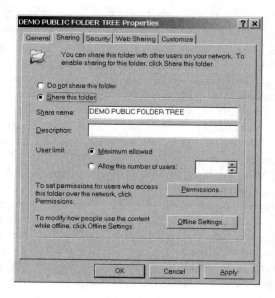

When you've shared your public folder tree, users can access it using a standard Windows file browser such as Windows Explorer, My Computer, or My Network Places—assuming, of course, that they have permissions to do so. In Figure 12.54, I'm using Windows 2003's My Network Places to view the contents of the folder Test. That's the folder that I asked you to create in your new public folder tree back in the section "Creating a Public Store."

FIGURE 12.54

Using Windows 2003's My Network Places to view the contents of a public folder in a public folder tree, and preparing to create a new item in the folder

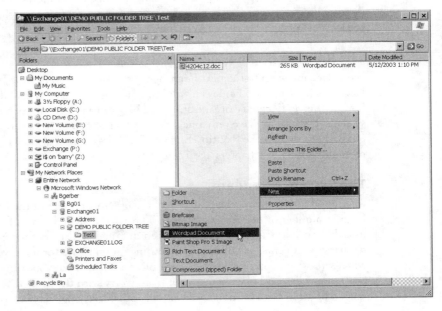

You can map the public folder tree share or any folders in it to a drive letter. To map the tree, you have to drill down into the local computer or network hierarchy and find it on your Exchange server. You can map folders within the tree either at the extra-computer level, shown in Figure 12.54, or by drilling down and finding the folder on the server.

Because nondefault public folder trees don't support MAPI content, you can't post Exchange messages in them. However, you can send messages to them if they're mail-enabled, and you can drag and drop Exchange items such as messages from an Outlook client into them. You can also drag and drop any file that you want into them, as I did with that Word document you see on the right side of Figure 12.54. Finally, you can right-click the folder and choose to begin creating a new file using whatever applications are supported on your computer. In Figure 12.54, I'm about to create a new WordPad document in the folder Test.

WARNING *Be careful when you share a public folder or a public folder tree. Initially, the Windows 2003 group Everyone, which includes all Windows 2003 user accounts, has a lot of control over the folder. The group can read and add items to the folder, including subfolders. Thankfully, the group Everyone does not have delete rights by default, but you might not want it to have all of the rights granted by default. You can change Everyone's rights in the Security tab, shown earlier in Figure 12.53.*

Before we leave public stores and public folder trees, take a moment to think about what's going on here. By every method, from e-mail to drag-and-drop, you can store anything in Exchange 2003 public stores and access it in a variety of ways through public folder trees. The stores are essentially mountable file systems protected by Exchange Server 2003's powerful online backup and offline restore capabilities, and they are supported by such services as full-text indexing. Remember how Exchange 5.5 was the developmental model for major Windows Server 2003 components such as Active Directory, organizational units, and routing sites? Could Exchange Server 2003 be the model for the next generation of the Windows server operating system?

The Routing Engine

Now, let's move on to the next Exchange core component after the Information Store, the Routing Engine. The Routing Engine is involved in moving messages in and out of an Exchange Server 2003, both within an Exchange organization and between an Exchange organization and foreign messaging systems. Because we have only one server that's not connected to any foreign messaging system, it's too early to discuss the Routing Engine. We'll devote lots of time to the management of Exchange message routing in Chapters 13, 15, and 16.

The System Attendant

As I noted in Chapter 4, the System Attendant (SA), the last of the Exchange core components, performs a number of housekeeping tasks. The SA is assigned some of its tasks when Exchange is installed, such as triggering the generation of e-mail addresses for foreign messaging systems for Exchange recipients, or building interrouting group tables for its server. You turn on other SA tasks when setting up a particular Exchange object, such as when you turn on message tracking for a mailbox store. The good news is that your main worry with the SA is that its service remains up and running. The service can be monitored like any other Exchange service, so even that worry is manageable.

Summary

This chapter dealt with two key elements of Exchange Server 2003: the Exchange Server 2003 hierarchy and Exchange Server 2003 core components.

The Exchange Server 2003 hierarchy consists of the Exchange organization, administrative groups, servers, and recipients. Exchange organizations are largely containers that hold all the objects that make up an Exchange system. We dealt with a number of these objects in Chapter 11 and this chapter, and we'll continue to deal with them in later chapters. However, when it comes to directly managing your Exchange organization, there is little that you can or need to do. One of the most important organizational management tasks is delegation of control over your organization to Windows 2003 users and groups. That's how you parcel out responsibility for managing the wide range of objects in your Exchange organization.

Exchange administrative groups are key organizing and security control objects. They enable you to bring together Exchange servers, system policies, connectors, and folders in such a way that you can delegate management responsibilities to Windows 2003 users and groups at a more refined level than the Exchange organization. A default administrative group is created when Exchange is installed. You must enable display of the group. As you add new Exchange servers, they can be part of an existing administrative group, or you can create new groups for them.

You create system policies for servers, mailbox stores, and public stores within the System Policies folder in an administrative group. Essentially, system policies are templates that enable you to automatically fill in the property pages for a group of objects, thus customizing the object to behave as you want. This saves time when you need to configure a number of servers, mailbox stores, or public stores at the same time. It also enables you to ensure that objects are configured appropriately. When a policy has been created, you add objects, such as servers, to the policy, and thus apply the policy to the objects.

More than anything else, Exchange servers are home to Exchange storage groups. Servers are so vital to the operation of an Exchange system that monitoring them and ensuring that they are up and running should be considered a task of major importance. You can create a wide range of server monitors and manually or automatically (through e-mail or scripted notifications) keep tabs on them.

We dealt with all the Exchange recipients but public folders in the last chapter and we covered public folders in this chapter. If they have permissions, users can create public folders in their Outlook clients. Exchange managers can also create public folders in Exchange System Manager. Rights to public folders can be controlled either from Exchange System Manager or by folder owners in their Outlook clients. You can set storage, deleted-item retention, and automatic item-deletion properties for public folders.

Exchange Server 2003 core components include the Information Store, the Routing Engine, and the System Attendant. The Information Store consists of storage groups. Storage groups contain mailbox and public folder stores. Mailbox stores contain user mailboxes. Public folder stores hold public folders. Public folders are organized in public folder trees. Management of both mailbox and public folder stores is quite similar. As with individual mailboxes and public folders, you can control storage limits and deleted-item retention. You can also control automatic deletion of items from public folders. When you set these parameters at the store level, they become the defaults for newly created mailboxes and public folders.

Public folder stores and their related public folder trees are an interesting pair of items. Only the public folder store and the public folder tree created when Exchange is installed on a server are fully MAPI-enabled and capable of being seen by Outlook and IMAP clients. Any tree-store combinations that you create can not be accessed through these clients. They can be accessed only through the Windows Server 2003 file system, an enhanced web browser, or an Internet news (NNTP) client. All kinds of public folders can be replicated to other Exchange servers. We'll talk more about this in Chapter 15.

The Routing Engine is an important component of Exchange Server 2003. We'll spend considerable time on message routing in later chapters. The System Attendant is a silent but key participant in an Exchange system. It does a range of housekeeping chores and requires no management other than ensuring that it is functioning properly.

Now you're ready for one of the most interesting and exciting pieces of Exchange Server 2003 architecture: Internet messaging. In Chapter 13, we'll add and manage an e-mail link to the Internet. In Chapter 14, we'll set up support on our server for a number of Internet protocols.

Part 5

Expanding an Exchange Server Organization

Chapter 13

Managing Exchange 2003 Internet Services

So FAR, YOU'VE BEEN working within some pretty narrow confines: one Exchange 2003 server on a network that is isolated from all others, whether private or public. Now comes the really fun part of the Exchange 2003 experience: connecting to the world outside your one and only server.

In this and the next chapter, we'll focus on the Internet. In today's networked world, among all the foreign messaging-system options available, you'll most likely have to implement Internet messaging support. The Internet is the most widely used conduit for the exchange of e-mail messages between a wide range of messaging systems. The Internet is based on a set of standards for the content of messages and for moving messages between messaging servers and between messaging servers and clients.

In this chapter, we look at the inner workings of Internet messaging. We'll focus heavily on the Transmission Control Protocol/Internet Protocol (TCP/IP), the Domain Name System (DNS) service, and the Simple Mail Transfer Protocol (SMTP), and we'll explore how these support worldwide Internet messaging. We'll also spend some quality time with the Windows 2003/Exchange 2003 SMTP Virtual Server, the engine that moves Internet messages into and out of your Exchange organization, and the Exchange 2003 SMTP Connector that enhances SMTP Virtual Server functionality. Finally, we'll look at some of the things you need to do to ensure that your Internet connection stays up and running.

Featured in this chapter:

◆ How Internet messaging works

◆ Internet messaging: getting and staying connected

How Internet Messaging Works

Internet messaging depends on TCP/IP, DNS, and SMTP. Without any one of these, Internet messaging can't work.

As it does inside Windows 2003 LANs, the TCP/IP protocol supports communication between computers connected to the Internet. It provides a way of both packaging data and moving it reliably between computers, and it provides an addressing scheme so that one computer can precisely specify the computer to which it needs to send data. TCP/IP serves not only Internet messaging, but also a number of other Internet protocols. We'll talk about these in a bit.

DNS is a client/server service. A computer that needs to communicate with another computer to send an Internet message, for example, uses DNS to figure out the Internet address of the receiving computer. DNS translates English-language domain-based addresses such as `barrywin2k.bgerber.com` into number-based addresses that computers can use.

SMTP, another client/server protocol, defines a range of messaging standards. These include message content and specific protocols for computers to use when sending or receiving Internet messages to other servers. It is at the heart of both Exchange Server 2003's internal interserver routing system and its services for Internet messaging. SMTP also plays a major role in POP3 and IMAP4 client/server communications by relaying messages that are sent by POP3 and IMAP4 clients to recipients on the Internet.

This section focuses on Internet messaging from a conceptual and descriptive perspective. In the section "Internet Messaging: Getting and Staying Connected" later in this chapter, I'll talk very specifically about how you set up TCP/IP, DNS, and SMTP.

WHERE TO GO FOR MORE ON TCP/IP, DNS, AND SMTP

Throughout this section, I'm going to assiduously avoid interesting, though diverting, treatises on TCP/IP, DNS, and SMTP. Instead, I'll present enough practical information so that you can set up and operate your Exchange Internet messaging system. For lots more on these topics, see *Mastering Windows Server 2003*, by Mark Minasi, Christa Anderson, Michele Beveridge, C.A. Callahan, and Lisa Justice (Sybex, 2003). Also take a look at the Windows Server 2003 and Exchange Server 2003 documentation. Other sources of DNS information include the documentation that comes with your DNS software (if you're not using Windows Server 2003's DNS), and the books *sendmail, 3rd ed.*, by Bryan Costales with Eric Allman (O'Reilly & Associates, 2002), and *DNS and BIND, 4th ed.*, by Paul Albitz and Cricket Liu (O'Reilly & Associates, 2001).

TCP/IP: The Backbone of Internet Networking

TCP/IP is the information superhighway's data packaging and cargo service. Programs based on the protocol assemble data into standardized packets and ship the packets from computer to computer. It supports the smooth movement of data across bridges and routers from subnetwork to subnetwork. And, all of this happens more or less at the speed of light.

TCP/IP's Transmission Control Protocol describes how data packets are to be organized and reliably delivered from one computer to another. The Internet Protocol (IP) defines how Internet addresses are formed (the familiar *xxx.xxx.xxx.xxx* format) and specifies that every computer on the public Internet must have a unique address.

TCP/IP is not just for Internet messaging. It also supports such Internet services as ping, File Transfer Protocol (FTP), whois, finger, and the Web's Hypertext Transfer Protocol (HTTP). Essentially, almost anytime that a packet needs to move across the Internet, TCP/IP does the work. The User Datagram Protocol (UDP) carries most of the other traffic on the Internet not carried by TCP/IP, for example, much of the high data-rate audio and video traffic transmitted.

TCP/IP is implemented in software on networking hardware. TCP/IP software prepares and drops packets into network adapter, bridge, and router hardware environments. This hardware, supported by more software, moves the packets to their next destination and finally to their target destination. The next time you browse over to your favorite website, think about all this and marvel at the speed and accuracy with which everything happens. You have TCP/IP to thank for a great deal of this experience.

NOTE   *There are two types of IP addresses: public and private. Public IP addresses are the ones that you use when connecting to the Internet. You must obtain these addresses from a valid supplier of public addresses, such as an Internet service provider (ISP). There can be only one instance of a public IP address on the entire worldwide Internet network. Private addresses are addresses in a certain range that are never exposed to the Internet. They are defined in the Internet Task Force's RFC 1918 and range from 192.168.0.0 to 192.168.255.255. Private addresses are used on internal networks. If you have Internet connections, you must hide private addresses behind routers or network address translation (NAT) devices that allow many computers with private IP addresses to reach the Internet through one public IP address. Many modern network routers and firewalls include NAT capabilities. Check out RFC 3022 for more on NAT.*

Let me offer a few last words on TCP/IP standards and security. First, we're running out of public IP addresses. A new IP standard has been promulgated. It is officially called "IP Version 6" (IPv6) and is often referred to as "IP Next Generation" (IPng). Without getting too technical, among other important things, IPv6 supports more addresses and interoperability with earlier IP standards. Implementation of IPv6 has been slow, because of required hardware changes, but it is coming and, in fact, must come if the Internet is to continue growing.

As for IP security, there are standards for securing IP traffic. Known as IPSEC, these standards are implemented in Windows 2003. Again, without getting technical, just let me say that you should approach IPSEC with caution; there's a lot to understand and do before turning it on.

DNS and SMTP: The Dynamic Duo of Internet Messaging

When you address a message, for example, to `bg@bgerber.com`, how does that message get from your computer to *bg* at `bgerber.com`? Everything starts with a service called an *SMTP host*. SMTP hosts are responsible for sending and receiving Internet mail.

Let's take a basic example assuming that you're using a simple POP3 e-mail client such as the one available in Outlook Express. When you send your message, the POP3 client contacts the SMTP host that you've specified as the SMTP (outgoing mail) server in your e-mail client. I'll go into detail on how the POP3 client finds the SMTP server later in this section. If the SMTP server hasn't been barred from relaying messages for you, it takes the message and puts it into its send queue.

Before it can relay your message, the SMTP host must translate the e-mail address `bg@bgerber.com` from human-friendly to computer-friendly. To start this translation process, the SMTP host parses the address into two parts:

◆   The e-mail domain name (`bgerber.com`)

◆   The addressee or mailbox (*bg*, short for *Barry Gerber*)

Next, the sending SMTP host needs to find the IP address of an SMTP host that serves the domain specified in the e-mail address (the *receiving SMTP host*). To do this, it queries a DNS server (called a *name server*) in the receiving domain for the IP address of the receiving SMTP host. You'll remember from Chapter 7, "Installing Windows Server 2003 as a Domain Controller," that DNS servers contain, among other things, the names and matching IP addresses of computers in one or more domains.

I'll get into the process involved in finding the IP address of an SMTP host in just a bit. For now, accept that the DNS finds the match.

When the IP address of a receiving SMTP host in the domain bgerber.com, for example, has been found, the sending SMTP host uses the address to contact the receiving host. When contact has been made, the sending SMTP host tells the receiving SMTP host that it has a message for the addressee *bg*. The receiving SMTP host checks to see whether the addressee exists; if it does, the host accepts the message. With the message now inside the local messaging system, local services take over and deliver the message to the proper mailbox.

Now let's look more closely at the role of DNS in all of this. The Domain Name System is an interesting combination of centralization and decentralization. A specific DNS server doesn't have to know about all the domain names and matching IP addresses in the world. It can query other DNSs for matches.

A query starts with a group of servers managed by an organization called *InterNIC*. These servers contain the name servers for all the registered .com, .net, .org, and .edu domains that exist and referrals to servers that support other domains such as .mil. When you apply for a domain name, you must supply the names of at least two name server computers for your domain. These can be part of your domain or external to it, as long as they are the place to go to get authoritative information about the computers and services in your domain.

You can find the name server information for any domain at www.internic.net. Find and click the whois hotlink, and enter the name of the domain. Here's the current name server information for my domain bgerber.com from InterNIC:

```
Whois Server Version 1.3

Domain names in the .com and .net domains can now be registered
with many different competing registrars. Go to http://www.internic.net
for detailed information.

    Domain Name: BGERBER.COM
    Registrar: NETWORK SOLUTIONS, INC.
    Whois Server: whois.networksolutions.com
    Referral URL: http://www.networksolutions.com
    Name Server: BIGGUY.GTE.NET
    Name Server: OTHERGUY.GTE.NET
    Status: ACTIVE
    Updated Date: 10-feb-2003
    Creation Date: 08-mar-1999
    Expiration Date: 08-mar-2010

>>> Last update of whois database: Thu, 15 May 2003 06:01:43 EDT <<<
```

Notice that the name servers for bgerber.com are operated by the ISP that supplies my Internet connectivity, Verizon (formerly GTE). I plan to take on management of DNS services for my domain soon, now that Windows Server 2003 provides such excellent and well-integrated DNS support. Perhaps by the time you read this, you'll find that the Verizon name servers have been replaced by two `bgerber.com` name servers.

NOTE *DNS servers are born knowing that they should go to the InterNIC servers to get a list of name servers for a particular domain. You don't have to tell them; they just do it. So, as long as your DNS is set up properly, as in Chapter 7, and your server is connected to the Internet, your DNS will automatically hit InterNIC's name servers.*

As soon as the sending SMTP host has secured a list of name servers for the receiving domain from the InterNIC servers, it asks one of the name servers for the name of the SMTP host for the domain. The name of the SMTP host is contained in what is called an *MX record.* (*MX* stands for *mail exchanger.*) A mail exchanger server is an SMTP host for the domain. I'm sure I don't have to say it, but I will: The *exchange* in *mail exchanger* has nothing to do with Exchange server. It's a concept and reality in the Internet messaging arena.

Here's a sample MX record:

```
bgerber.com. IN MX 10 exchange01.bgerber.com.
```

For our purposes right now, this MX record has two key parts:

◆ `bgerber.com` specifies the domain name used in addressing e-mail (`bg@bgerber.com`).

◆ `exchange01.bgerber.com` is the name of the SMTP host for `bgerber.com`.

You'll learn more about MX records later in this chapter in the section "Setting Up and Managing DNS," when you actually set up your DNS service for Internet messaging.

"Wait!" you exclaim. "The sending SMTP host still doesn't have an IP address to send the message to." You're right. Now it must query the receiving domain's DNS one more time for the IP address of the SMTP host (the mail exchanger server), `exchange01.bgerber.com` in my case. As you might imagine, this requires another DNS record, an Address or *A* record that exposes the IP address of the receiving SMTP host for `bgerber.com exchange01.bgerber.com`. Here's an example of this record:

```
exchange01.bgerber.com. IN A 66.14.231.120
```

In this A record, the following is true:

◆ `exchange01.bgerber.com` is the name of the SMTP host.

◆ `66.14.231.120` is the IP address of the SMTP host.

I'll talk more about A records later in this chapter in the section "Setting Up and Managing DNS."

Okay, now let's pull it all together. Figure 13.1 shows how TCP/IP, DNS, and SMTP all work together to enable Internet messaging.

TIP *InterNIC is not just a place for servers to go to find a domain's name servers. It's also a great place to find out about getting a domain name. Go to* `www.internic.net` *for more information and a list of authorized domain-name registrars, companies that can sell you a valid domain name.*

FIGURE 13.1
TCP/IP, DNS, and SMTP, the lynchpins of Internet messaging

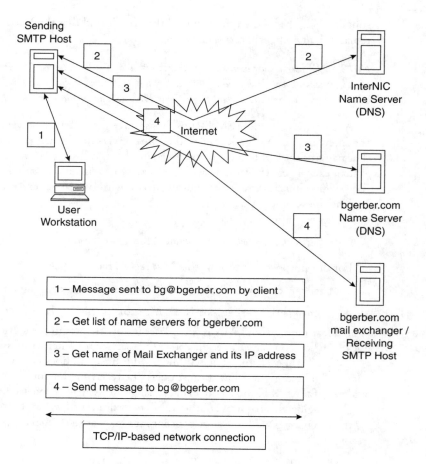

1 – Message sent to bg@bgerber.com by client

2 – Get list of name servers for bgerber.com

3 – Get name of Mail Exchanger and its IP address

4 – Send message to bg@bgerber.com

TCP/IP-based network connection

Internet Messaging: Getting and Staying Connected

Now that you have a basic grounding in TCP/IP, DNS, and SMTP, you're ready to connect your Exchange organization to the Internet and manage that connection. You perform both tasks by setting up and managing your good friends TCP/IP, DNS, and SMTP for and on your Exchange server. Let's get started. TCP/IP is our first victim.

Setting Up and Managing TCP/IP

As an Exchange Server 2003 administrator responsible for Internet messaging, your task is to ensure that those of your Exchange servers that will support Internet messaging are assigned valid public Internet addresses. Additionally, of course, you need to ensure that the correct hardware (a modem or one or more network adapters) is installed in your server and that your server is physically connected to the Internet.

"Did you say 'modem'?" Yes, modem. There are two kinds of TCP/IP connections: continuous and noncontinuous. A continuous TCP/IP connection is always on. Continuous TCP/IP connections ride on top of networking topologies such as Ethernet, Asynchronous Transfer Mode (ATM), Frame Relay, and Digital Subscriber Line (DSL). Noncontinuous connections require a connection before they become active. Asynchronous dial-up, serial port–based connections, are the most prevalent type of noncontinuous connections.

The SMTP mail system runs most naturally on continuous networks. When an SMTP host needs to contact another SMTP host to send it a message, the receiving SMTP host must be available to receive the message within a particular time window. As you'll see in a bit, SMTP host contacts aren't predictable. They happen when a message is available and then at specific intervals thereafter until a timeout period has been reached, typically two to three days. When the timeout period has been reached, the SMTP host returns the message to the sender as undeliverable. All this means that you can't just connect your modem-based SMTP host to the Internet at a particular time and expect to receive messages from all SMTP hosts that happen to have messages for you.

SMTP can still work with noncontinuous networks. However, things must be set up so that a continuously connected SMTP host sends and receives messages for a noncontinuously connected SMTP host. Let's call the continuously connected SMTP host a *smart host*. Then the noncontinuously connected host can contact the smart host on a regular basis to pick up new messages and send outgoing messages that have queued up since the last contact. Usually you go to your ISP for smart hosting. You can also use this approach within your own organization for connections by smaller remote offices.

TIP *The use of smart hosts isn't limited to noncontinuous TCP/IP connections. Your Exchange server can use smart hosts even if it is continuously connected to the Internet. For example, you might choose to isolate all or part of your Exchange server environment from direct Internet access by installing only one of your Exchange servers as a smart host and having other Exchange servers send and receive messages through that smart host.*

In Windows 2003 environments, dial-up noncontinuous TCP/IP links are built on the Remote Access Service (RAS). If you need to operate an internal smart host for other internal SMTP hosts to dial in to, you also use RAS on the continuously connected host.

If you're going to use RAS for a noncontinuous Internet link, don't forget to set up RAS with dial-out capabilities. Also, remember to create a RAS phone book entry for the ISP to which you'll be connecting. For more on RAS, check out the Windows Server 2003 books referenced in the sidebar "Where to Go for More on TCP/IP, DNS, and SMTP" at the beginning of this chapter.

I strongly suggest that you try really hard to use a continuous connection for your SMTP host or hosts. Back in Chapter 5, "Designing a New Exchange 2003 System," I touted the wonders of modern continuous connect technologies for linking to the Internet. I spoke especially fondly of DSL technology. It's fast (up to T1 speeds), reliable, and inexpensive (I pay less than $130 for 384Kbps of business-level, multi–IP address DSL bandwidth). Setting up a continuous-connection link to the Internet is easier, and, with a good provider, continuous links are less prone to problems than noncontinuous links. Higher-speed continuous links buy you quick and easy access to other Internet services such as web browsing, chat, and FTP. I strongly suggest that you go for a continuous link, unless you're really cost-constrained.

If the default network adapter in your Exchange server uses private IP addresses, as defined in the earlier section "TCP/IP: The Backbone of Internet Networking," then you need a second network adapter to link your Exchange server to the Internet. The adapter must have a valid public Internet address. See Chapter 7 and the references in the sidebar "Where to Go for More on TCP/IP, DNS, and SMTP" at the beginning of this chapter, for more on setting up TCP/IP on a network adapter in Windows Server 2003. You can also use one of the NAT devices I discussed earlier in this chapter. A NAT device can send and receive packets for a valid Internet address and transmit them to a back-end computer that has only a LAN address.

Setting Up and Managing DNS

More than anything else, DNS is a repository for information about computers on your network. You set up DNS when you installed your Windows Server 2003 domain controller back in Chapter 7. In this section, you'll learn how to create specific DNS entries (records) to support Internet messaging on your Exchange server.

WARNING   *Please don't skip the following paragraph. If you do, you could wind up doing a lot of unnecessary and fruitless work.*

If the DNS servers on your own Windows 2003 network are registered with InterNIC as *the* DNSs to be contacted for name resolution information about your public Internet domain (as opposed to your internal Windows 2003 domain), then you do the following on your DNS servers. If your DNS servers are not so registered, then the following *must* be done in its DNS servers by your ISP or whatever entity is registered with InterNIC to provide information about your public domain. The information I am about to discuss will do no good if it is not available to external SMTP hosts trying to contact your Exchange server. If the information sits inside local DNS servers that have not been registered with InterNIC, your Exchange server will not be able to receive e-mail from the Internet.

CREATING KEY DNS RECORDS FOR EXCHANGE

You or your ISP need to create two DNS records. These are the Address and Mail Exchanger records that I discussed briefly in the earlier section "DNS and SMTP: The Dynamic Duo of Internet Messaging."

Creating an Address Record

As you know from earlier in this chapter, address or A records link the name of a computer to an IP address. In setting up an Exchange server, the A record associates the name of the Exchange server that serves as an SMTP host with its IP address. My server is called `exchange01.bgerber.com`, and its IP address on the Internet side is 66.14.231.120. Although I haven't set up the SMTP host on my Exchange server yet (that comes in the later section "Setting Up and Managing SMTP"), my Exchange server will soon become the SMTP host for my Exchange organization. The A record should look like this:

```
exchange01.bgerber.com. IN A 66.14.231.120
```

IN means that this is an Internet record.

WARNING *The period after "com" in* `exchange01.bgerber.com.` *is required, as are all the periods in the DNS records listed in this chapter.*

If this is the name and address that you gave your Exchange server back when you installed Windows 2003, you don't even have to make this DNS entry. The entry should already have been made when DNS was installed. If not, here's how to create the Address record in your Windows 2003 DNS. Remember, if your DNS servers aren't registered with InterNIC, the A record *must* be created in the DNS servers of the entity registered with InterNIC as the place to find information about your public domain.

If you need to create an entry for your server in your local DNS, find and right-click your domain in the DNS snap-in in your Microsoft Management Console, and select New ➢ Host. Fill in the New Host dialog box, shown on the right side of Figure 13.2. The PTR record is a reverse lookup record that lets a DNS client query the DNS server not for the IP address associated with a particular host, but for the host associated with a particular IP address. PTR records are created in the Reverse Lookup Zones container shown on the left side of Figure 13.2. See Mark Minasi's book on Windows 2003 or the DNS book referenced in the sidebar "Where to Go for More on TCP/IP, DNS, and SMTP" at the beginning of this chapter for more information.

Remembering that I called my original DNS zone bgerber.local, you might be wondering where that bgerber.com zone in my DNS came from. I created the zone. I did that by right-clicking the Forward Lookup Zones container and selecting New Zone.

TIP *You can associate any computer name that you want with any IP address. I could have named my Exchange server* `mickeymouse.bgerber.com` *if I wanted to. As long as the name is used consistently, the specific name that you choose doesn't matter.*

FIGURE 13.2

Using the New Host dialog box to add a new Address record to DNS

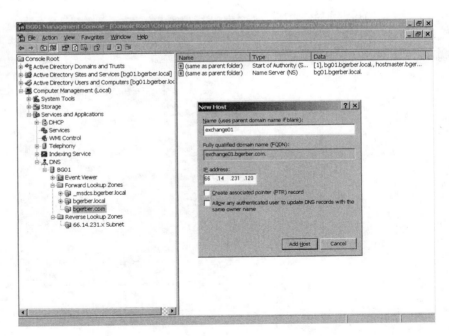

Creating a Mail Exchanger Record

Now, if your DNS and not your ISP's DNS will publicly support access to your Exchange SMTP e-mail system, you need to set up an MX record to provide DNS with the name of a computer that functions as an SMTP host for your Exchange organization. As I noted in the previous section on DNS, the MX record for my domain `bgerber.com` looks like this:

```
bgerber.com. IN MX 10 exchange01.bgerber.com.
```

This record says that mail bound for the domain named `bgerber.com` should be sent to the DNS-defined SMTP host `exchange01.bgerber.com`. The number *10* is a preference value. If there are multiple MX records for mail delivery to a given domain, an external SMTP host will first attempt a delivery to the internal receiving host with the lowest preference value.

To add an MX record, follow the instructions in the previous section for creating an Address record, but select New Mail Exchanger (MX) from the menu that pops up when you right-click your domain. In Figure 13.3, I've already filled in the Properties dialog box for my new MX record. Because my SMTP host will support the parent domain, `bgerber.com`, I've left the Host or Child Domain field blank.

There's one neat thing that you can do with MX records: You can set up domain aliases. For example, if people in the Barry Gerber and Associates consulting department want to use the domain name `consulting.bgerber.com` on their business cards (instead of the simple `bgerber.com`), I can add an MX record to direct mail sent to `consulting.bgerber.com` to `exchange01.bgerber.com`. The record would look like this:

```
consulting.bgerber.com. IN MX 10 exchange01.bgerber.com.
```

FIGURE 13.3

Using the New Resource Record dialog box to add a new Mail Exchanger record to DNS

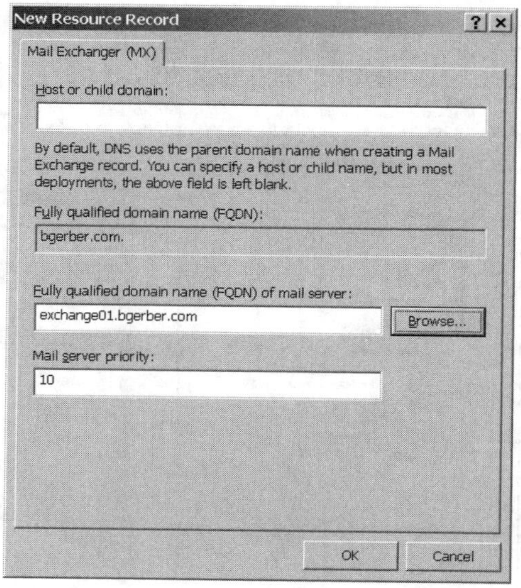

This record says that mail bound for `consulting.bgerber.com` should be sent to `exchange01` at `bgerber.com`.

To create an MX record like this using the interface shown earlier in Figure 13.3, you'd enter **consulting** in the Host or Child Domain field.

Of course, if you're going to use addresses such as `JoeJones@consulting.bgerber.com`, you need to be sure to add that SMTP address to Joe Jones' list of SMTP addresses, as per my instructions in Chapter 11, "Managing Exchange Users, Distribution Groups, and Contacts."

Again, remember that you create this record in your Windows DNS only if your DNS servers are registered with InterNIC to provide information about your public domain. If not, the entity that is registered to provide this information must create the MX record in its DNS servers.

WE GET LETTERS

You might have noticed that my e-mail address is included in the Acknowledgments section at the front of this book. Since the publication of the first edition of *Mastering Microsoft Exchange Server*, I've received hundreds of e-mail messages from readers. Most of those messages are about Internet access, and most of the Internet access questions are about using SMTP mail. The rest are predominately about Outlook Web Access—getting to an Exchange mailbox with a web browser. I'll talk about OWA in the next chapter. Right now, if only to save a few million future electrons, I'll talk about one key SMTP messaging issue raised by readers. I'll also sprinkle other questions and responses throughout the rest of this book, as appropriate.

Here goes: If your SMTP host is going to send and receive messages through a smart host using a noncontinuous connection, special care is required in setting up DNS records. The DNS entries must be for that host, not for your Exchange server. For example, if your SMTP connector is going to pick up and send messages through a proxy SMTP server (SMTP smart host) operated by your ISP, the DNS entries must be for the smart host. Your ISP will make the DNS entries for you in its DNS. All you need locally is a DNS or hosts file entry for the IP address and the name of your ISP's SMTP host. I'll show you how to set up a noncontinuous SMTP link later, in the section "Installing and Managing the Exchange SMTP Connector."

Setting Up and Managing SMTP

SMTP in an Exchange Server 2003 environment is not one pack of services all neatly managed under one user interface roof. To set up and manage SMTP services for your Exchange organization, you have to focus on one and maybe two different sets of services:

- Windows 2003 SMTP services

- Exchange 2003 SMTP Connector services

SMTP services are installed when you install Microsoft's Internet Information Server (IIS) on a Windows 2003 computer. You did this back in Chapter 7, when you installed Windows 2003. You work with SMTP services through what is called an *SMTP virtual server* (SMTPVS). SMTP virtual servers are SMTP hosts.

One SMTP virtual server is installed by default when you install IIS. This is usually enough to cover the messaging requirements of most organizations. However, if you need more SMTP virtual servers, you can create as many as you like. You would add SMTP virtual servers, for example, if you needed to provide different users with different levels of security or to send messages of markedly different sizes through different SMTP virtual servers.

When you install Exchange Server 2003, Exchange hijacks the SMTPVS and makes it its own. This fact is most obvious in the way that you manage SMTP virtual servers before and after you install Exchange 2003 on a Windows Server 2003. Before Exchange 2003 is installed, you manage SMTP virtual servers through the IIS interface. After Exchange is installed, you manage SMTP virtual servers through the Exchange System Manager.

Under the covers, the most significant change that comes with installation of Exchange 2003 is that users of the standard Outlook client can send and receive Internet messages without enabling an Internet messaging client such as a POP3 client. Your Exchange server communicates with SMTP hosts to send and retrieve messages for Exchange mailbox-enabled users. These users view and compose messages to or from Internet correspondents using Outlook in exactly the same way as they do for messages to or from Exchange mailbox-enabled users. When an Outlook client connects to an Exchange server, as I described in Chapter 10, "A Quick Overview of Outlook 2003," the client sends all its messages to and receives all its messages from the Exchange server, whether those messages are to or from internal Exchange server users or to or from external Internet mail users. The Exchange server becomes the only point of contact that a user needs to access the electronic messaging world.

In taking over the Windows 2003 SMTPVS world, Exchange changes the directories that the SMTPVS uses to manage message traffic. When you install IIS, a set of directories is created for the default SMTPVS under IIS's Inetpub directory in a directory called `mailroot`. When you install Exchange 2003, another set of directories is created for SMTPVS use. The Exchange installation program places these directories in the directory structure used by Exchange: `\Exchsrvr\Mailroot\ vsi 1\Mailroot`. Subdirectories of `mailroot` include these:

`Badmail`   Holds messages that can neither be sent nor returned to their senders.

`Pickup`   Holds outgoing messages created as text files in standard RFC 822 format; Exchange moves properly formatted messages in this directory to the Queue directory.

`Queue`   Holds messages for delivery, whether to other SMTP servers (outgoing) or to the Exchange mailbox store structure (incoming).

Exchange hijacks the SMTPVS in another way. Upon installation, an Exchange server is ready to use the SMTPVS to move messages between itself and other Exchange servers in its routing group.

As you can see, the SMTPVS is at the heart of Exchange Internet messaging. The Exchange 2003 SMTP Connector (SMTPC) is important, too, although its role is to supplement the functionality of the SMTPVS.

The SMTPC links your Exchange Server 2003 environment to the Windows 2003 virtual server environment, allowing you to select the SMTPVS that will support its activity. The SMTPC also enhances your SMTPVS in several ways, adding such features as enhanced security and connectivity. If you don't need these enhanced services, the SMTPVS will perform all the SMTP host functions for your Exchange server environment.

Now let's look at the SMTPVS and SMTPC in detail.

NOTE *If you want to run your Exchange-based SMTP host in dial-up (noncontinuous) mode, I'll have to ask you to be patient for a little while. I need to explain how both the SMTPVS and SMTPC work. I promise that we'll get to dial-up options before the end of this chapter.*

MANAGING SMTP VIRTUAL SERVERS

An SMTPVS behaves like the generic SMTP host that I described in the section "DNS and SMTP: The Dynamic Duo of Internet Messaging" earlier in this chapter. The SMTPVS

◆ Can be used with a connection to the Internet or to your organization's own TCP/IP LAN or WAN.

◆ Operates in continuous connect mode.

◆ Can operate in noncontinuous connect mode only with the assistance of the SMTPC.

◆ Attempts to send outgoing messages at user-settable intervals.

◆ Keeps trying to send a message until a preset timeout period is reached, returning the message to the sender when the timeout period has been reached.

You manage the SMTPVS with a nice graphical user interface. The interface, which we'll look at in just a bit, gives you considerable control over your Internet messaging environment. It lets you do the following:

◆ Limit the number of simultaneous server connections

◆ Log server activity

◆ Set up a range of security controls

◆ Control absolute message size as well as message traffic per connection

◆ Specify how undeliverable messages are to be handled

◆ Set message delivery timing and timeout options

To open the SMTPVS management user interface, find your Exchange server in Exchange System Manager and click it until you see the container labeled Default SMTP Virtual Server. See the left side of Figure 13.4 for help in locating the virtual server. If you don't like the name given to your virtual server when IIS was installed, you can change the name by right-clicking the server and selecting Rename. To open the Properties dialog box for your virtual server, right-click the virtual server and select Properties from the pop-up menu. The dialog box is shown on the right side of Figure 13.4.

TIP *If you ever have a reason to do so, you can start, stop, or pause your SMTPVS by right-clicking it and selecting the appropriate option from the pop-up menu. You can also accomplish these tasks by using the start, stop, and pause buttons, shown at the top of Figure 13.4, just below where it says "Window."*

As you can see in Figure 13.4, the virtual server Properties dialog box has four property pages: General, Access, Messages, and Delivery. Let's look at each of these in order.

FIGURE 13.4
Exchange System
Manager with the
default SMTPVS
exposed and the
SMTPVS Proper-
ties dialog box
opened

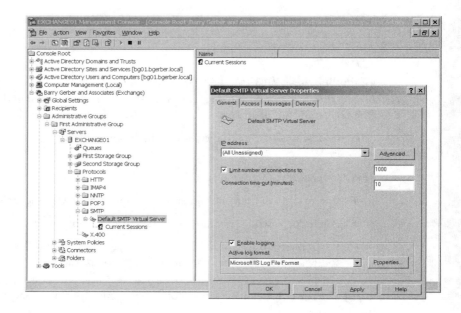

General

You use the IP Address field on the General property page to specify which IP address or addresses your SMTPVS will listen on. This refers to the IP addresses assigned to network adapters installed in your Exchange server. If you have one adapter in your server, that is your only IP address option other than All Unassigned, which in this case, selects your one adapter anyway. If you have two or even more adapters in your server, you can pick any one address or you can pick All Unassigned to have your server listen on all network adapters. If you have servers on your internal network that will send notification messages using your SMTPVS—a server running a tape/file backup application, for example—then you want to be sure that the SMTPVS listens on your Exchange server's internal network adapter. If your SMTPVS also must listen on its external (Internet) adapter, then you have to pick the All Unassigned option.

In a simple Exchange environment, your Exchange server is likely to have two adapters. One adapter is set up to support connectivity to the server by workstations and servers on your internal networks, and the other adapter is set up to support your Exchange server's connection to DNS servers and SMTP hosts on the Internet. The main purpose for the internal network adapter is to support user access to the Exchange server. It could also be used to give users access to the SMTPVS on your Exchange server, allowing them to use clients other than MAPI-based Outlook clients such as Outlook 2003. Here's a good rule of thumb: Unless you have good reason, don't allow internal users with direct access to an Exchange server to send messages from any client but a MAPI-based Outlook client.

That little button labeled Advanced on the General property page is a humdinger. You can do some really neat stuff with it. Let's check it out. Click Advanced to open the Advanced dialog box, shown in Figure 13.5. You can use this dialog box to change the TCP port on which other computers contact the SMTPVS, and you can set filters to prevent specific external users from sending messages to the SMTPVS.

FIGURE 13.5

Using the Advanced dialog box to change the SMTPVS TCP port and to set filters to reject messages from specific e-mail addresses

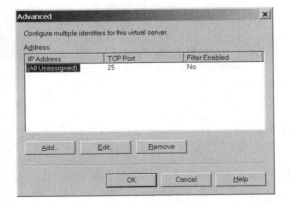

TCP port 25 is the default port for SMTP services. When other computers try to contact your SMTP host, they normally do it on port 25. If you change the port number, they won't be able to contact the host. So why would you change the port number? The answer: usually for security purposes. As long as SMTP-oriented client or server applications know that they should contact the SMTP host through the new port number, the host is considerably safer from hackers than a host using port 25. For now, leave the port number as it is.

If you ever do need to change the port, select the appropriate row in the Address field in the Advanced dialog box, and click Edit (see Figure 13.5, shown earlier). This opens the Identification dialog box, shown in Figure 13.6. Just change the TCP port number and click OK.

FIGURE 13.6

Use the Identification dialog box to change the SMT-PVS TCP port and apply filters

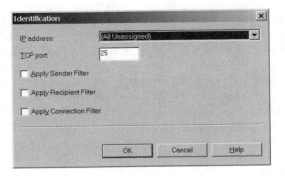

"So, what's all this filters stuff?" you say, eyeing Figures 13.5 and 13.6. Filters prevent the flow of messages into your SMTPVS. More than anything else, they are designed to be used to control Internet SPAM messaging.

You can apply filters to the following types of messages into the SMTPVS:

◆ From specific senders and domains

◆ Intended for specific recipients on the Exchange server

◆ From a list of domains provided by a third-party spam-blocking provider

Because I consider anti-spamming techniques to be a part of Exchange server security functionality, I'll talk in more detail about filters in Chapter 18, "Exchange Server System Security." If you need anti-spamming help right away, trot over there for more on filtering.

The next field in the SMTPVS Properties dialog box (back in Figure 13.4) lets you control how many connections your SMTVS will accept. One SMTP host can open multiple connections to another SMTP host. So, it's not just a matter of how many hosts might try to connect to your SMTPVS at once, but how many connections each might open. There's no hard-and-fast rule on settings here. You might want to start with a setting of 1,000. Then monitor your SMTPVS using Windows 2003's Performance Monitor. Reduce the number of connections if the SMTPVS seems to be struggling to meet demand or if your server's processor or disk drives are getting overworked. Up the number if message delivery drags and other components of your system aren't significantly taxed.

The Connection Timeout field in the SMTPVS Properties dialog box allows you to set the number of minutes after which an inactive client is disconnected from the SMTPVS. I wouldn't suggest going below the default setting of 10 minutes.

Select Enable Logging to record SMTPVS sessions. These log files record the details of the interaction between your SMTPVS and other SMTP hosts. You can select the type of log that you'll use. Unless you are sure that you have an application that allows you to read a file in any other format, select Microsoft IIS Log File Format from the drop-down list labeled Active Log Format. You can read files in IIS log file format as text files or through IIS. By default, SMTPVS log files are stored in the directory `\WINNT\SYSTEM32\LOGFILES\SMTPVS`x, where x identifies each existing SMTP virtual server (for example, log files for the default SMTPVS are stored in the directory `\WINNT\SYSTEM32\LOGFILES\SMTPVS1`). See the Exchange 2003 documentation for file formats, file-naming conventions, and additional information. Click the Properties button to specify how frequently a new log file is created (such as every day), how many log files can accumulate before older ones are deleted, and where the log files are stored. Log files can get big, so be sure that you have lots of disk space to hold them and that you don't allow too many to accumulate before older files are automatically deleted.

NOTE *The logs you enable here are not the same as the logs you enable for an Exchange server, as discussed in Chapter 12, "Managing the Exchange Server Hierarchy and Core Components." The logs you enable for a server include details regarding who sent what to whom and when. Those logs are used for Exchange server message tracking. The logs discussed in this chapter are more for tracking the communication process between your SMTPVS and other SMTP hosts.*

Access

As you can see on the left side of Figure 13.7, the Access property page focuses on the limits that you can place on intranet or Internet access to this SMTPVS. At times you might find yourself using Access property page features to control access by other SMTP hosts. However, you're more likely to use these features to control access by external users of POP3 or IMAP4 e-mail clients who want to relay SPAM messages out to the Internet through your SMTPVS. You need to control use of your

SMTPVS by these folks both to limit the load on the SMTPVS and to prevent e-mail spoofing. E-mail spoofing is the transmission of an e-mail message in such a way that it appears to have been sent by someone in your e-mail domain when that someone is actually not a member of the domain. Also, if your SMTPVS gets to be known on the Internet as a source of spam, you might find that some SMTP hosts will no longer accept messages from your SMTPVS.

FIGURE 13.7

The Access property page of the SMTPVS Properties dialog box, with the Authentication dialog box open

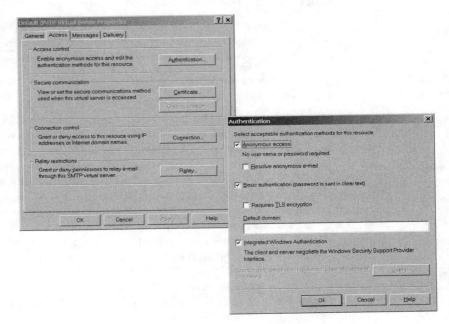

You can control authentication, communication security, access based on IP address, and use of the SMTPVS by others to relay outgoing messages. Access control is both an important and often confusing area. Let's take a close look at your options on the Access page.

Authentication   Click Authentication to open the Authentication dialog box, shown on the right side of Figure 13.7. Three authentication methods are available:

Anonymous access   Other computers may access this SMTPVS without providing a username or password.

> **Resolve anonymous e-mail**   Senders of anonymous e-mail are spammers. They do everything they can to hide their identity. If Resolve Anonymous E-mail is checked, the SMTPVS attempts to figure out the real source of anonymous messages. If it is successful, this information is added to the message, which is then sent on to the recipient.

Basic authentication   Other computers may access this SMTPVS, sending their passwords without encryption.

Requires TLS encryption   Transport-layer security encrypts usernames, passwords, and message content as TCP/IP packets containing them pass over the Internet; if selected, clients that don't support TLS will not be able to connect to the SMTPVS. You must generate a key certificate if you're going to use TLS (see the next section, "Secure Communication"). TSL will replace the Secure Sockets Layer (SSL) protocol as soon as the TSL protocol makes it through the Internet Task Force's arduous review and approval cycle.

Default domain   When basic authentication is selected, text entered in the Default Domain field specifies the Windows domain used to match client-submitted usernames and passwords; clients in a trusted domain can submit usernames as `domain_name\username`.

Integrated Windows authentication   Standard Microsoft Windows–encrypted usernames and passwords are accepted; message content is not encrypted.

By default, all three authentication methods are selected. This means that a client can access the SMTPVS using any one of the methods. For standard SMTP host functionality, anonymous access is required. Remember that any SMTP host in the world could potentially contact your SMTPVS with a message. By default, SMTP hosts do not use any authentication method. On the other hand, if your SMTPVS is going to operate only in a tightly controlled environment where contact is limited to a few password-protected SMTP hosts, you'll want to turn off anonymous access and select basic authentication or integrated Windows authentication, as appropriate.

If you want to control access to your SMTPVS outgoing message-relaying functionality, this isn't really the place to do it, unless you're going to dedicate this SMTPVS to relaying outgoing Internet-bound messages. Later in this section, I'll discuss a better way to control relay access.

Secure Communication   As I mentioned in the previous section, if you're going to support TLS secure communications, you need a security certificate. You also need to specify that a secure channel should be opened using the certificate.

Security certificates can serve two purposes. They authenticate the certificate owner, and they provide a public key for encryption of data transmitted between computers operated by the certificate owner and other computers.

If your web browser has ever initiated download of software from a certificate-bearing website, such as Microsoft's site, you've seen the authentication function of security certificates in action. I'm talking about that little dialog box that pops up stating that what you're about to download and install on your computer is indeed coming from the source shown on the dialog box.

Public key encryption involves the use of public and private keys to scramble (encrypt) and unscramble (decrypt) communications. As I noted previously, the public key comes with the certificate. A server and its client may have and use pre-existing private keys, or private keys may be generated during a communication session.

Certificate creation and management is based in IIS. If someone has already secured a certificate for your IIS, you can use it for TLS communications. In the alternative, you can create a new certificate.

WHERE DO I GET A CERTIFICATE?

You secure certificates from certificate authorities (CAs). Windows 2003 has its own CA, which is used to issue internal certificates and which you must set up on a Windows Server 2003. This CA is used for Exchange internal messaging security. We'll talk about it in Chapter 18.

For communications with the outside world, you want a certificate from a neutral third-party CA. One of the better known CAs is VeriSign, at www.verisign.com. At the time of this writing, VeriSign certificates ranged in price from around $350 to $900 per server, depending mostly on the services included and whether 40- or 128-bit encryption is used. You can also get a 14-day free trial certificate from VeriSign.

Here's how to create a new certificate or use an existing certificate. When you click Certificate on the SMTPVS Properties dialog box (see the left side of Figure 13.7, shown earlier), the Web Server Certificate Wizard opens. On the second page of the wizard, the Server Certificate page, you can choose to create a new certificate, assign an existing certificate to your SMTPVS, import a certificate from a file, or copy or move a certificate from another server. Select the appropriate option.

Using an existing certificate is very easy. Select the certificate that you want to use from the list on the next wizard page, and follow the online instructions. That's it. Now move to the last paragraph in this section.

If you choose to create a new certificate, you are asked on the next wizard page if you want to prepare a certificate request to be sent later or to send the request immediately. Basically, the wizard prepares a text file whose contents are used by a certificate authority when it generates your certificate. The prepare-now-send-later option lets you interact with both Windows and non-Windows certificate authorities. The Send Request Immediately option is for certificates generated by a local Windows-based certificate authority. It is available only if you have a Windows 2000– or 2003–based certificate authority running on your network. Even if you have such an authority on your network, you don't want to use it to generate a new certificate for your SMTPVS, for the reasons noted in the previous sidebar "Where Do I Get a Certificate?" The bottom line is this: Be sure to select *prepare the request now, but send it later.*

The next wizard page asks for a name for the certificate, the bit length of the encryption key, and lets you request the option to select a cryptographic service provider. The certificate name is used to identify your certificate in the IIS user interface. Use a descriptive name such as Exchange Default SMTPVS. You're offered a choice of encryption bit key lengths between 512 and 16,384. High-bit keys increase security, but they can significantly slow encryption and decryption. Unless you have a good reason to do otherwise, select 1024-bit key length. Cryptographic service providers are software, not organizations. Windows 2003 comes with two such providers: Microsoft DH SChannel Cryptographic Provider and Microsoft RSA SChannel Cryptographic Provider. Other providers can be added. If you're not sure what to choose, don't check the box that lets you choose a provider.

If you asked to choose a cryptographic provider, you use the next wizard page to make your choice. If you didn't, you input a name for your organization and an organizational unit on the next wizard page. Here you're striving for a unique identifier. Generally, using your corporate name and a departmental identifier works fine. For example, I might use Barry Gerber and Associates as my organization name, and Exchange Messaging as my organizational unit name.

On the next wizard page, you enter your organization's common name, a fully qualified domain name for the Exchange server running the SMTPVS. Use the server's DNS name. For example, I would use `exchange01.bgerber.com`.

The next wizard page is a bit tricky. All it wants is your country/region, state/province, and city/locality. You select the country/region from a drop-down list, so that's no problem. However, you must type directly into the other two fields, even though they are ostensibly drop-down lists. (Actually, the lists are filled as you enter certificate requests.) Type the full name of your state or province. Abbreviations are not acceptable to certificate authorities. Therefore, it's *California*, not *CA*, and *Los Angeles*, not *LA*.

You enter the name of a file in which the certificate request with all the stuff you've entered should be saved. Unless you want to change the location of the certificate request file, accept the default. Whatever you do, be sure to note the location of the file and its name.

That's about it. The next wizard page summarizes your earlier choices. Click Next and click Finish on the final wizard page.

Now, to get your certificate, you go to the website of a certificate authority (see the previous side-bar "Where Do I Get a Certificate?") and follow the directions on the website. At some point, you are asked to paste the certificate request that you just created into a field on your web browser. Just open the certificate request file in Notepad, select its entire contents, copy the selected text, and paste the copied text into the field on your browser.

After you've completed the certificate request process at the certificate authority, you'll receive your certificate in an e-mail message. Copy the certificate and save it to a new file on the same directory on Exchange server as you saved the certificate request. You don't have to save the certificate here, but it helps to standardize the location of certificate requests and the certificates themselves.

To install the certificate, restart the IIS Certificate Wizard. It will remember that you have a request pending and asks you if you want to install the certificate. Reply in the affirmative, and follow the onscreen directions. That's it. You now have a certificate to support your SMTPVS's TLS-based security functionality.

Remember that your certificate supports both authentication and encrypted (secure channel) communications. If you want to use the latter functionality, you must tell your SMTPVS to use a secure channel for communications. To do so, direct your attention back to Figure 13.7, click Communication, and select Require Secure Channel. If the option is available, you can also choose to use 128-bit encryption. That's it. You're done with installing and activating your security certificate.

For more on certificates, including references, see Chapter 18.

Connection Control   For security purposes, you can limit the computers that can connect to your SMTPVS. Limits may be based on the following:

◆   The IP address of a single computer

◆   The subnet IP address of a group of computers

◆   A DNS domain name

As I mentioned earlier in this chapter, under most circumstances, you wouldn't want to limit access to your SMTPVS because doing so means that any SMTP host on the Internet wouldn't be able to send e-mail to your messaging domain. However, connection limits do come in handy in some situations:

◆ You want to shut out certain sending SMTP hosts to prevent spamming or other undesirable communications.

◆ Your SMTPVS will contact a smart host to send and receive messages through it.

◆ You need to run a tightly controlled private messaging system over the Internet, and one or more of your SMTP hosts is registered in the public DNS namespace.

To set connection limits, click Connection on the Access property page for your SMTPVS (look back at Figure 13.7). This opens the Connection dialog box. As you can see in Figure 13.8, you can limit access to a specific list of computers or allow access to all computers but those listed.

FIGURE 13.8
Using the Connection dialog box to limit access to an SMTPVS

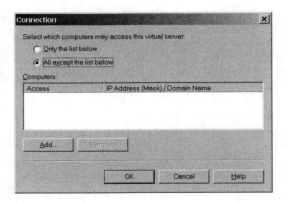

To add a new computer, subnet, or domain, click Add to open the Computer dialog box, shown in Figure 13.9. Here's a brief list of your options and how to use them.

Single computer Enter the computer's IP address, or click DNS Lookup to search for the IP address by inputting the computer's name.

Group of computers Enter the starting IP address of the subnet that you want to reference and the subnet mask for the IP address. This is the easiest way to limit internal user access to the SMPTVS.

Domain Enter the name of the domain that you want to reference.

You can add as many computers, subnets, and domains as you need.

FIGURE 13.9

Using the Computer dialog box to select computers, subnets, and domains to be used in limiting access to an SMTPVS

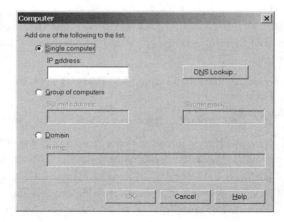

Relay Restrictions   *Relaying* is the process of sending e-mail messages out to the Internet through an SMTP host. Generally, the only computer you want using your SMTPVS's relay service is your SMTPVS itself. You might need to allow relaying by other internal SMTPVSs that aren't directly connected to the Internet or by some of your users who have to use POP3 or IMAP4 clients when out of the office, but you want the packets to stop there. You don't want the Internet's bad citizens to get their hands on your SMTPVS's relay service.

People with malicious intent—spammers, for example—love to use unprotected SMTP host message relaying services to flood the world with junk e-mail. If your SMTPVS isn't properly set up, these cybercowards can use it to send out unsolicited e-mail to their heart's content, while uncaringly overloading your network and server. And, guess who gets blamed for the spamming and snail's-pace system performance? That's right, you. Relay restrictions can stop spammers in their tracks.

To get started protecting your SMTPVS, click the Relay button on the Access property page of the SMTPVS's Properties dialog box (see Figure 13.7, shown earlier). This opens the Relay Restrictions dialog box. This dialog box looks a lot like the Connection dialog box shown back in Figure 13.8. It has one additional field, Allow All Computers Which Successfully Authenticate to Relay, Regardless of the List Above. If this option is checked, computers that provide valid domain authentication credentials (a valid username and password with appropriate permissions) can relay messages. That should be pretty safe.

To control who can use your SMTPVS to relay messages, you need to be sure that the Only the List Below option is selected on the Relay Restrictions dialog box, and you need to add subnets or one or more domains to the Computers list on the dialog box. Click Add on the Relay Restrictions dialog box to open the Computer dialog box. This dialog box looks and functions just like the Computer dialog box, shown earlier in Figure 13.9.

Messages

You use the Messages property page shown in Figure 13.10 to control message traffic and to specify what happens with undeliverable messages. This is an important page because it lets you control both the load on your SMTPVS's CPU and disk drives and the amount of network traffic caused by SMTP host activities. Here's a quick look at the options on the Messages property page.

Limit Message Size To   Sets the maximum size of messages sent out of and into your SMTPVS; the default is 4MB including any attachments. Some SMTP hosts can not receive messages greater than around 3MB, so if users report a lot of rejected messages, you might want to reduce this value to 3MB. If you have enough disk space to store electronic copies of all of the books ever printed, enter a zero in this field to allow unlimited message sizes. That's a joke. Don't ever allow unlimited message sizes. This option is presented on the dialog box in a somewhat misleading fashion. With the option unchecked and grayed out, it looks like no limit has been set. Trust me, the limit is 4096 KB. If you really wanted to set the option to no limit, you would check the box and enter a zero. The same is true of the following option.

Limit Session Size To   Sets the maximum amount of data that can be relayed though the SMTPVS during a session (connection). The default is 10MB. Use this setting to control server load. This setting applies to incoming messages.

Limit Number of Messages Per Connection To   Sets the maximum number of messages delivered by the SMTPVS per connection to other SMTP hosts. Assuming adequate CPU power, a larger number speeds up message delivery by using multiple connections. If you have high message flow to a few remote SMTP hosts, you should up this value significantly. For one client with these sorts of loads, I had to use a setting of 7,500 before mail moved out at a decent rate. You know you have to up this value when messages remain in queues with lots of messages for a long time. I'll talk about queues later in this chapter.

FIGURE 13.10

Using the Messages property page to set limits relating to messages and to specify how undeliverable messages should be handled

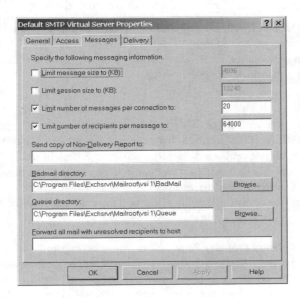

Limit Number of Recipients Per Message To   Sets the maximum number of recipients for any message sent through the SMTVS. The default of 64,000 should be adequate for most environments. Set the value lower to improve message delivery time. If a message is directed to a greater number of recipients than you've set, Exchange opens a new connection to deal with the excess.

Send Copy of Nondelivery Report To   Sets an address to which nondelivery reports (NDRs) are sent. By default, a message is sent only to the originator of an undeliverable message. Enter an address here that will also receive nondelivery reports. In busy environments, this can result in an overwhelming number of nondelivery messages, so use the option with care. I recommend having NDRs sent to the postmaster for your domain. I'll explain how you set up a postmaster in the upcoming section "Setting the Address for the Domain Postmaster."

Badmail Directory   The `Badmail` directory holds undeliverable messages for possible review by Exchange administrative staff. By default, this directory is located in the SMTPVS's `mailroot` directory. For performance reasons, you might want to locate this directory on a different drive from your other Exchange databases—the Information Store, for example. You can change the location of the `badmail` directory here. The directory must be manually emptied periodically.

Queue Directory   The `queue` directory holds SMTP messages that are awaiting delivery. Each message is stored in a file in this directory. You don't manage SMTP message delivery from this directory. Instead, you use the Exchange System Manager's very nice queue-management interface. We'll get to that later in this chapter. As with the `badmail` directory, for disk performance reasons you might want to locate the `queue` directory on a disk drive that doesn't support other Exchange databases. In fact, the `queue` directory is a much better candidate for relocation because it's much more likely to get busy and hog disk resources than the `badmail` directory.

Forward All Mail with Unresolved Recipients to Host   This option forwards undeliverable messages to another SMTP host (SMTPVS or non-SMTPVS) that might be able to resolve unresolved recipient names. Don't set this option on the other host as well, or a game of performance-degrading e-mail ping-pong will ensue.

Delivery

You use the Delivery property page shown in Figure 13.11 to set message retry intervals, specify how long before a sender is first notified that a message has yet to be delivered, and set a period after which a message that has not yet been delivered is returned as undeliverable. You also use this property page to set security options for outbound message delivery, to set limits on connections that your SMTPVS uses to deliver messages, and to set up some pretty neat advanced options. We'll start by examining the fields on the Delivery page itself. Then we'll look at what's behind the three buttons at the bottom of the page.

Fields on the Delivery Property Page   Keep an eye on Figure 13.11 as you track through the options on this property page. Generally, the defaults are fine for continuous connections to the Internet. Based on your experience, you might want to increase some of the settings if your SMTPVS is sending messages over a noncontinuous connection to an SMTP smart host that then delivers the messages to the Internet. More on SMTP smart hosts in just a bit.

Outbound   This section of the Delivery property page applies to messages delivered by your SMTPVS to other SMTP hosts.

First Retry Interval (Minutes)   The number of minutes to wait before trying to send an as-yet undeliverable message.

Second Retry Interval (Minutes)   The number of minutes to wait before making a second attempt to send an as-yet undeliverable message.

Third Retry Interval (Minutes)   You guessed it; I won't say any more.

Subsequent Retry Interval (Minutes)   The number of minutes to wait before each subsequent attempt to send an as-yet undeliverable message.

Delay Notification   Time in minutes, hours, or days before the sender is notified that a message is as yet undeliverable.

Expiration Timeout   Time in minutes, hours, or days after which attempts will no longer be made to deliver the message. The message will be forwarded to another SMTP host, assuming that one was specified on the Messages property page, or a nondelivery message will be issued.

Local   Applies to delivery of messages by the SMTPVS to an internal Exchange mailbox store.

Delay Notification   See "Delay Notification" under "Outbound," earlier in this list.

Expiration Timeout   See "Expiration Timeout" under "Outbound," earlier in this list.

FIGURE 13.11
Using the Delivery property page to set limits regarding messages yet to be delivered

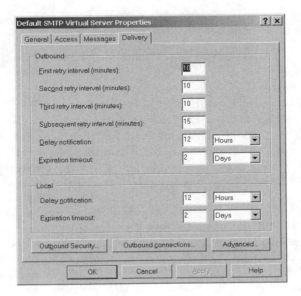

Buttons on the Delivery Property Page There are three buttons on the Delivery property page. These support outbound security, outbound connection settings, and a range of advanced delivery options.

Outbound Security Click Outbound Security on the Delivery property page to bring up the Outbound Security dialog box. As you can see in Figure 13.12, this dialog box is used to configure the security options that your SMTPVS will use when contacting other SMTP hosts. You can pick only one of the three authentication options on the dialog box: Anonymous Access, Basic Authentication, or Integrated Windows Authentication. See the section "Authentication" earlier in this chapter, for more on these three options and on the TLS encryption option.

FIGURE 13.12

Using the Outbound Security dialog box to select the authentication method that an SMTPVS will use when contacting other SMTP hosts

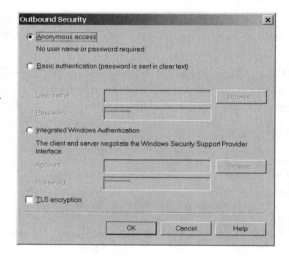

Of course, you must be sure that the SMTP hosts that your SMTPVS will be contacting *all* support the method of authentication and encryption that you choose. You can enter only one username/password (basic authentication) or account/password (integrated Windows authentication) combination, so this severely restricts the SMTP hosts that your SMTPVS can connect to. The nonanonymous access outbound security options are best used for connecting to internal SMTP hosts or to a single SMTP host that will act as a smart host sending and receiving messages for your SMTPVS.

TIP As noted previously, the outgoing authentication option that you set for an SMTPVS applies to all communications initiated by the SMTPVS with other SMTP hosts. If you need authenticated communications with one or a few SMTP hosts and you still need connectivity to the rest of the world's SMTP hosts, try this option. Disable outgoing authentication (select Anonymous Access) for the SMTPVS. Then use an Exchange SMTP connector to set up a specific connection for each SMTP host that requires authentication. As you'll see in the section "Installing and Managing the Exchange SMTP Connector" later in this chapter, one of the ways that SMTP connectors enhance your SMTPVS is by allowing you to send messages to specific domains with specific authentication and connectivity requirements.

Outbound Connections　You learned how to set some parameters for both inbound and outbound connections earlier in this section. Now I'll show you how to set some additional parameters for your SMTPVS's connections to other SMTP hosts.

Click Outbound Connections on the Delivery property page, shown earlier in Figure 13.11, to open the Outbound Connections dialog box (see Figure 13.13). As you can see, you can limit both the total number of outgoing connections and the period in minutes before a connection closes after an SMTP host stops accepting messages. The defaults should be fine. Remember that the real SMTP-based connections-based load on your server is the sum of inbound and outbound connections. Be sure to use Windows 2003's performance monitor to monitor your SMTPVS to ensure that messages are moving with adequate speed and that SMTP message transfer isn't placing undue strain on your Exchange server's CPU or disk drives or your network.

FIGURE 13.13

Using the Outbound Connections dialog box to set limits on connections used by an SMTPVS to deliver messages

The Outbound Connections dialog box adds a new kind of connection limit, a per-domain limit. This enables you to limit the load that you place on any other SMTP host that you connect to. It also assures that you won't use all of your connections for one SMTP host.

You can also change the default TCP port from the standard 25 on the Outbound Connections dialog box. You should never do this if your SMTPVS will be a generic SMTP host sending messages to and receiving messages from any and all Internet-connected SMTP hosts. TCP port 25 is the standard port for SMTP host communications. If you change the port, your SMTP host is dead in the water. If, on the other hand, you're communicating only with other SMTPVSs in your Exchange organization or with other "friendly" SMTP hosts, using another port for SMTP could help enhance security. For more on this option and why you might use it, see the section "General" earlier in this chapter.

Advanced　You can set a variety of options on the Advanced Delivery dialog box of the Delivery property page (see Figure 13.14). Because the options are so diverse, I won't summarize them. Instead, I'll discuss each briefly.

Sometimes it takes several SMTP hosts to relay a message to its final destination. Each time another SMTP host participates in relaying a message is called a *hop*; each SMTP host adds a line to the message, which is how a host knows the current number of hops. To limit Internet traffic, a maximum hop count limit is set. When this limit is reached, the message is treated as nondeliverable by an SMTP host, and a nondelivery message is sent to the originator of the message. When the hop count for a message grows large, it is usually because of an addressing error. A maximum hop count of 15 is reasonable, except in certain networking topologies in which a larger number of hops could legitimately be required to deliver a message.

FIGURE 13.14

Using the Advanced Delivery dialog box to set a range of special options for an SMTPVS

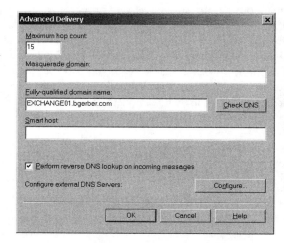

A masquerade domain is an alternate domain to which other SMTP hosts send their nondelivery reports.

The fully-qualified domain name is the full DNS name of the SMTPVS. By default, the fully qualified domain name of my SMTPVS is the name of the server that it's running on—in my case, that was `exchange01.gerber.local`. I changed that to `exchange01.gerber.com` because that is the name published on the Internet in the Host and MX records we discussed earlier in this chapter. You can provide any name here as long as it is registered in the DNS that provides resolution for your Internet-based domain information. Click Check DNS to ensure that the name is indeed resolvable.

When you specify a smart host in the Advanced Delivery dialog box, you're specifying a computer that will receive mail from your SMTPVS and send it out. There is no way with the SMTPVS to also specify that incoming messages received by the smart host for your SMTPVS should be sent to the SMTPVS. To do this, you'll need to set up an SMTP Connector. We'll do that in the section "Installing and Managing the Exchange SMTP Connector," later in this chapter. If you want to use the limited smart host functionality offered here, enter the fully qualified domain name of the smart host.

If you want to know the domain from which each inbound message comes, select Perform Reverse DNS Lookup on Incoming Messages. Then your SMTPVS will use DNS to convert the IP address of the mail originator into a fully-qualified domain name. This can be helpful in troubleshooting or identifying a source of spam messages. Spam messages often show a different domain in the From field than the real domain from which the message has come. Checking this box doesn't cause rejection of the message if the real domain is different from the one in the From line of the message. That is something that must be done by other software—anti-spam software, for example—because you don't necessarily want to reject all messages of this type at the SMTP host level. Also, note that some spamming software sends messages with perfectly legitimate-looking domain information. The reverse lookup option wouldn't be of any use with spam from such programs.

You can set up the addresses of external DNS servers to be used by your SMTPVS when resolving addresses for Internet-bound messages. This allows you to use your internal DNS servers only for resolving internal addresses.

READERS ASK ABOUT INTERNET SECURITY FOR EXCHANGE SERVERS

One question that a number of readers ask involves putting an Exchange server behind a firewall or proxy server. You'll have to wait until Chapter 18 but then I'll tell you everything you need to do to put an Exchange server behind a firewall. I'm not just talking about the easy stuff, the SMTPVS stuff, but about setting up a firewall so that MAPI-based Exchange clients such as the Outlook 200x series can get to Exchange servers.

A proxy server, such as Microsoft's Proxy Server, is designed to protect workstations and servers placed behind it from malicious Internet hackers. When your network is behind a proxy server, there are two ways to make an Exchange server's SMTPVS accessible to e-mail clients and SMTP servers on the Internet. You can put the Exchange server on the same Windows 2003 server as your proxy server, or you can make the proxy server look to the outside world like it's an SMTP host.

Depending on the proxy server product that you use, if you locate your Exchange server with SMTPVS on a proxy server, you must make sure that packet filtering is set correctly, or the SMTPVS will still be invisible. For the details, especially as they apply to Microsoft Proxy Server, see article Q176771, "Using Packet Filters with Exchange Server," in Microsoft's Knowledge Base, accessible at `http://support.microsoft.com`.

If your Exchange server with SMTPVS is behind a proxy server, you need to set parameters to support access by e-mail clients from and to SMTP hosts. Two Knowledge Base articles address this sort of configuration: article Q181847, "How to Configure Microsoft Exchange Server with Proxy Server," and article Q178532, "Configuring Exchange Internet Protocols with Proxy Server."

That's it for the SMTPVS's Properties dialog box and friends. Now, before we tackle the SMTP Connector, I need to show you how to set a passel of other SMTP messaging options.

MANAGING SMTP VIRTUAL SERVER-RELATED FUNCTIONALITY

You can set a variety of SMTPVS-related options outside the SMTPVS Properties dialog box shown earlier in Figure 13.7. These options include setting the address of your domain postmaster and setting a range of Exchange organization—wide formatting and other properties relating to Internet messages. I'll talk about these options and where you set them in this section.

Setting the Address for the Domain Postmaster

At times, both humans and SMTP hosts need a standard address within your Internet messaging domain to communicate with about matters relating to the domain. Here are some key situations in which this address is used.

Your SMTPVS sends nondelivery reports from your domain with `postmaster@[your_domain]` in the From field. Anyone needing to contact a human being about a nondelivery report replies to the postmaster address.

As I noted previously, your SMTPVS will send a copy of each nondelivery report that it sends to the originator of a message to an e-mail address that you enter on the Messages property page of the Properties dialog box for your SMTPVS. This helps you track nondelivery problems. The postmaster address is a good one to use here.

By common agreement, people contact the postmaster address to find the e-mail address of a particular person in an Internet messaging domain. Whether the human behind the postmaster address sends the address or not is a matter of organizational policy, but it's nice to know that the option is there.

Of course, the postmaster is just an e-mail address. It can be any valid SMTP address, so it can be any type of Exchange recipient: a mailbox-enabled user, a mail-enabled user, a distribution group, a contact, or a mail-enabled public folder. (See Chapter 11 and Chapter 12 for more on setting up and using Exchange recipients.) The postmaster address can even be an SMTP address outside your Exchange organization. Most people add the address `postmaster@[your_domain]`—mine is `postmaster@bgerber.com`—to the SMTP addresses for a specific Exchange mailbox. But you can do anything you want, from creating a new Windows 2003 account and Exchange mailbox for a postmaster to sending NDRs to your best friend or, more likely, your worst enemy in Antarctica.

Whatever you do, the key is to monitor this account. It can provide you with rich information on the configuration and performance of your SMTPVS—and it is, after all, a piece of your organization's presence in the outside world.

Setting Global Internet Message Formatting and Other Properties

Up to now, except for the discussion of filters, I've talked exclusively about setting a wide range of properties for a single SMTPVS on a single server in your Exchange organization. By and large, the properties we've talked about so far have related to SMTPVS security and to Internet message delivery and receipt. You can also set Exchange organization–wide parameters that control the format of messages and attachments to them and whether certain automatically generated message content, such as out-of-office responses, is permitted. Settings for most of these parameters can apply to messages sent to all or specific Internet domains, meaning that you can use different message formatting and automatic message content-generation parameters for different Internet domains. Let's look at these properties and how they function in the SMTP messaging environment.

Setting MIME Content Types   Internet-bound messages and attachments to them can not be in 8-bit binary format. They must be encoded into 7-bit ASCII text format. When this happens, all or part of the original look, feel, and behavior of messages and attachments can be lost. To preserve these characteristics, encoding schemes and content type identifiers are used. I'll talk about message encoding later in this section. I'll talk first about content type identifiers.

The Multipurpose Internet Mail Extension (MIME) protocol specifies content types for various kinds of files and documents when those files and documents enter the Internet environment. Content types enable a specific helper application to open when an encoded message attachment is accessed using a MIME-compliant POP3 or IMAP4 e-mail client or a web browser. Content type identifiers provide information that makes it possible for an attachment to be opened in a related helper application.

If you use Windows, you're very likely familiar with the concept of helper applications. When you double-click a Word file in My Computer or Windows Explorer and Word opens, displaying the file, Word is the helper application. You might have had a similar experience when using Microsoft's Internet Explorer: You clicked on a URL for a Word document in your browser, and the document opened either in a separate copy of Word or in Word right inside Internet Explorer. There are also Microsoft and third-party helper applications that let you view but not edit a range of files produced by a specific application. For example, Microsoft makes Internet Explorer view-only plug-ins for such applications as Word and Excel. With these types of view-only helper application, you don't need access to the original application to view a file generated by the application.

A content identifier specifies only the file extension associated with an attachment. It doesn't specify the helper application that should be used for the extension. That information must be present on the computer running the POP3 or IMAP4 e-mail client or the web browser that is accessing the attachment. This is the same information used to open any application associated with a file extension. When they are installed, almost all applications automatically set associations for the file extensions they support. Many applications also let you set associations after installation. You can manage file extension associations in Windows Explorer by choosing View ➤ Options ➤ File Types, or in My Computer by choosing Tools ➤ Folder Options ➤ File Types.

If there is a file extension association for the file extension and the helper application exists on the computer, the attachment opens in the application. If the application doesn't exist, the user sees the same standard error message that would be seen if that user double-clicked to try to open a file in Windows Explorer or My Computer.

Okay, that's enough about MIME content-type identifiers. Now let's see how they're used in Exchange 2003. By default, Exchange Server 2003 adds MIME content-type information when it prepares an attachment for transmission over the Internet through your SMTPVS. That way, assuming that there's a MIME-compatible client on the receiving end, the message recipient can open any attachments and view them as the sender intended.

You can view, add, and remove MIME content types and associated extensions. MIME content types are set for your entire Exchange organization, so you work with them in a subcontainer of the Global Settings container in Exchange System Manager. To access MIME content types, open the Internet Message Formats Properties dialog box by right-clicking Internet Message Formats (see the left side of Figure 13.15) and selecting Properties from the pop-up menu. This opens the Internet Message Formats Properties dialog box, shown on the right side of Figure 13.15.

As you can see in Figure 13.15, Exchange Server 2003 comes with a large number of MIME content types built in. Figure 13.15 shows some of the application-related MIME content types. Other content types include text, audio, and video. These content types use generic extensions that could be associated with any number of applications. For example, one of the text-content types is text/plain, which is associated with the file extension .txt. An attachment with a .txt file extension opens in the application associated with the extension .txt on the user's computer. That application may be Microsoft's Notepad or any other application that can handle ASCII text files.

FIGURE 13.15

Using the General property page of the Internet Message Formats Properties dialog box to view and set MIME content types

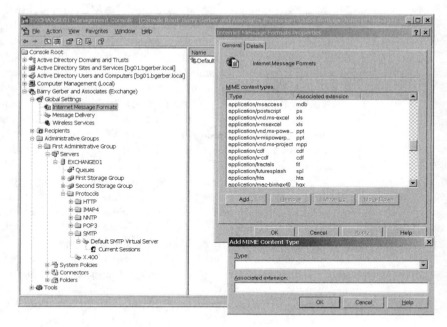

Now let's take a very quick tour of the buttons on the Internet Message Formats Properties dialog box's General property page. You use the Move Up and Move Down buttons to position a content type where you want it. Content types are processed in the order that they appear in the list. To add a content type, click Add on the General property page, and use the Add MIME Content Type dialog box, which is also shown in Figure 13.15. You add a new content type only when both of the following statements are true:

◆ You need to support a new application or other content type, such as text, audio, or video.

◆ Others with whom your Exchange users communicate have messaging clients that can handle the new content type.

Setting Additional Message Format Properties   You can set message format policies. These let you customize the way outgoing SMTP messages are formatted and handled. A policy can apply to all SMTP domains or only to specific domains.

Policies are stored in the Internet Message Formats container, shown on the left side of Figure 13.15, shown earlier. Click the container and then right-click the object labeled Default in the right pane of Exchange System Manager. Then select Properties from the pop-up menu (use Figure 13.16 to orient yourself). This opens the Default Properties dialog box that contains default message format and other property settings for your Exchange organization (see the right side of Figure 13.16). As far as I've been able to determine, Microsoft hasn't given much of a name to this dialog box. Let's call it the

Domain Message Policy Properties dialog box, and let's call things such as the Default object in the Internet Message Formats container *domain message policies.*

FIGURE 13.16

The Properties dialog box for default domain message policies, with its General property page open

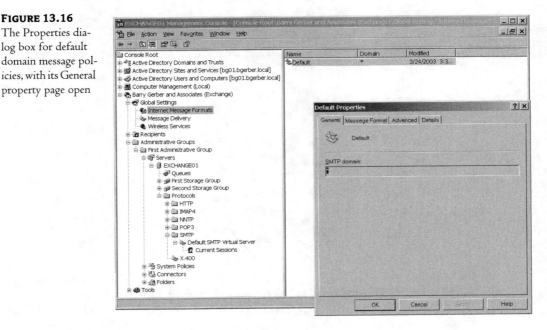

The settings in the Domain Message Policy Properties dialog box labeled Default apply to all SMTP domains in the world. I know that because there's an asterisk in the SMTP Domain field on the General property page, shown in Figure 13.16. This means that whatever a particular dialog box does, it does that for all domains that SMTP messages can be sent to.

Notice that in Figure 13.16 the SMTP Domain field is grayed out. You can't change it. That's because the default policy is designed to apply only to all SMTP domains. To set policies for specific SMTP domains, you have to create new policies. To create a new domain message policy, right-click the Internet Message Formats container and select New ➤ Domain from the pop-up menu. Just be sure to specify the SMTP domain that the message settings apply to on the General property page for each new domain message policy.

WARNING   *You can create different domain message policies that apply to messages going to different external domains. However, all the domain message policies that you create are used by all the SMTP virtual servers in your organization.*

Okay, let's go back to the default Domain Message Policy Properties dialog box. Tab over to the Message Format property page, shown in Figure 13.17. Track along on Figure 13.17 as we move through the rest of this section.

FIGURE 13.17

The Message Format property page of the default Domain Message Policy Properties dialog box

In the last section, I talked about encoding messages so that they can move through the 7-bit ASCII world of the Internet. As you can see in Figure 13.17, you have two options for encoding outbound messages: MIME and UUEncode (Unix-to-Unix encode). You can't have it both ways, so you need to be sure that those who will receive messages from your Exchange client can read messages encoded according to the protocol that you choose. Whichever option you choose, both messages and attachments will be encoded in the format. You can't choose to encode messages in MIME format and attachments in UUEncode format.

You can send MIME-encoded messages as plain text, in HTML format, or both. Plain text is straight 7-bit ASCII text, which is recognizable by any SMTP mail client. HTML encoding is now quite popular for web browsers and e-mail message content. Among other things, HTML supports such things as bold, italic, and colored text as well as different fonts. I'll talk more about HTML encoding in the next chapter. At this point in the history of Internet message formatting, you're pretty safe selecting Both. When Both is selected, the message is always sent in both formats. Then the receiving e-mail client has to sort out what is received and present the appropriately formatted text. Older e-mail clients might display the message in both formats, but the plain-text version will be readable.

UUEncode is an older encoding standard that doesn't support the rich-text capabilities that MIME supports. You should select this option only if you're sure that clients receiving SMTP messages sent from your Exchange server can not handle MIME encoding. This is pretty rare today. Of course, if recipient clients that can't deal with MIME are isolated in identifiable Internet messaging domains, you can create a special domain message policy for them. This is exactly why Exchange lets you create domain-specific message policies.

If you choose UUEncode encoding, you can choose to have attachments sent in BinHex format, which is compatible with the Apple Macintosh computing environment. Be careful here: All messages are sent in BinHex format. Non-Mac users won't be able to open the attachments unless they manually decode them using a BinHex decoder that runs on their particular operating system.

The Apply Content Settings to Non-MAPI Clients option is both interesting and maybe just a bit esoteric. If you check this option, messages from Internet e-mail clients will first be translated from their MIME or UUEncode formats into Exchange's native MAPI format. Then they will be encoded in the format that you chose in the Message Encoding section of the Message Format property page. You'll probably have to read this over a couple times and refer back to Figure 13.17 more than once, but I guarantee that you'll finally figure out what's going on here. You use this option to ensure that all Internet-based messages are stored in a consistent format. If this sort of consistency is important to you, then, by all means, check the box. Do remember, though, that this dual-translation process has a cost in CPU and disk-access cycles, so use it with caution.

You use the Character Sets section to select the character set that's used for outbound Internet messages. There's a drop-down list for MIME and non-MIME. Select carefully: If a receiving client isn't set up to handle the character set, your sent messages will be, at best, difficult to read and, at worst, unreadable. You can use a separate domain message policy to apply different character sets to outbound messages for different Internet messaging domains.

More Text Formatting Options   Now tab over to the Advanced property page of the default Domain Message Policy Properties dialog box (see Figure 13.18). This page contains two more options related to text formatting and options to activate or deactivate different kinds of automatically generated message content. Let's look at each of these in turn.

FIGURE 13.18

The Advanced property page of the default Domain Message Policy Properties dialog box

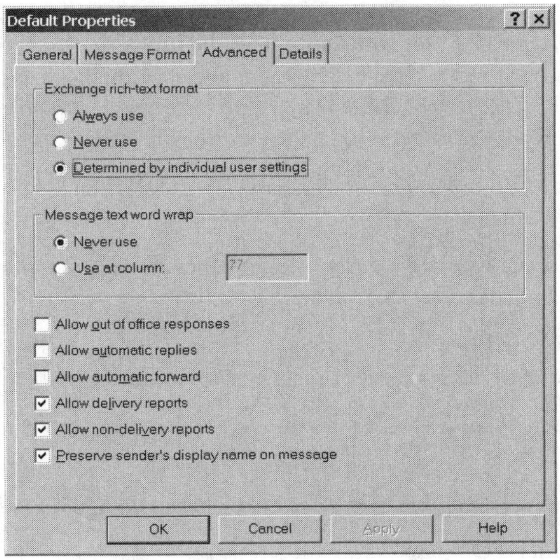

You can send messages in Exchange's native rich-text format. Exchange rich-text format supports such features as bold, italic, and colored text; bulleted and numbered lists; centering; right, center, and left alignment; as well as Exchange-specific attachment encoding. Messages and attachments that are sent out of Exchange in this format are still encoded in MIME or UUEncode and must be decoded by the receiving host. If you choose this option, all message recipient e-mail clients must be able to handle Exchange rich-text messages. Those that can't could have difficulty reading the message, and attachments will show up in an unreadable file called `winmail.dat`.

You can choose to always or never use Exchange rich-text formatting. You can also leave it to individual users to set the option in their Outlook clients. I strongly recommend against allowing users to set this option, however. If they leave the default, Exchange rich-text format, and if you've selected the Determined by Individual User Settings option, then all outbound Internet messages will be sent in Exchange rich-text format. If users change the default to plain text or HTML, then internal Exchange messages lose rich-text formatting.

If Internet recipients need to see messages in Exchange rich-text format, your best bet is to create a separate domain message policy for them, being sure to select Always Use for the Exchange Rich-Text Formatting option. That way, whatever format your users have set in their e-mail clients, outbound messages to those who need Exchange rich-text format are sent using Exchange rich-text formatting.

Unlike messages composed on a typewriter, with computer-generated text, you don't have to press the Enter key at the end of each line. Text is automatically wrapped at whatever the current window size is set to. A few older e-mail clients can't wrap text, leaving you, at best, with text that runs on in one long line until the end of a paragraph is reached. If you expect to be sending messages to domains with these older e-mail clients, select Use At Column. The default, 77, means that an end-of-line marker will be inserted in the text after the space character, which is closest to but not more than 77 characters.

Automatically Generated Message Content   The limits that we're going to deal with here aren't about message length and such. They're about automatically generated message content. These limits are listed in the bottom half of the Advanced property page, shown earlier in Figure 13.18. By default, the last three options are selected. Here's what they're all about:

Allow Out of Office Responses   Enables or disables out-of-office messages set up by users in their Outlook clients.

Allow Automatic Replies   Enables or disables automatic replies to incoming messages set up as rules by users in their Outlook clients.

Allow Automatic Forward   Enables or disables either Outlook client-initiated or administrator-initiated automatic forwarding of messages to another e-mail address.

Allow Delivery Reports   Enables or disables outgoing reports that a message has been received by your SMTPVS.

Allow Nondelivery Reports   Enables or disables sending of nondelivery reports by your SMTPVS.

Preserve Sender's Display Name on Message   Enables or disables user's Windows 2003/Exchange 2003 display name, in addition to their e-mail address, in outbound messages.

Being able to turn off these message content–generating features is a godsend, especially if you're responsible for security or SMTPVS/network performance or the business folks in your organization want to limit the amount of information that is sent to the Internet world, such as the whereabouts of users or their display names. And what's so neat is that, depending on the Internet domain that you need to communicate with, you can create different domain message policies with different rules about which automatic content-generation features are enabled and disabled.

MANAGING SMTP VIRTUAL SERVER-RELATED QUEUES AND SESSIONS

Take a look at Figure 13.4, back at the beginning of this chapter. Notice the Queues subcontainer just below your Exchange server and the Current Sessions subcontainer just below your SMTPVS. You use these containers to manage SMTPVS queues and message transmission sessions.

You can troubleshoot problems with incoming and outgoing SMTP messages in the Queues container. Microsoft moved the Queues container in Exchange 2003. In Exchange 2000 it was just below the SMTPVS Current Sessions container. There were also queues for the X.400 services. In Exchange 2003 both the SMTP and X.400 queues can be found in the Queues container just under the Exchange server. In Figure 13.19, you can see the default queues and one ad hoc queue in the Queues container. Here's a quick rundown on what each is for.

DSN messages pending submission   Holds Delivery Status Notifications that are awaiting delivery. The queue is for nondelivery reports, messages indicating that a specific message could not be delivered to its source. Note that the name of this queue is "*DSN* messages pending submission," not "*DNS* messages pending submission." This queue has nothing to do with the Domain Name System (DNS).

Failed message retry queue   Holds outbound messages when delivery failed, but where another attempt will be made to send a message.

Local delivery   Holds inbound messages to be delivered to a mailbox on the Exchange server.

mail.com   Holds messages destined to a specific e-mail domain. A queue is created ad hoc for each e-mail domain to which an e-mail message has been directed by an Exchange user or a server using an SMTP connector to link Exchange servers. The SMTPVS retains this queue until all messages have been sent from it or have been otherwise dealt with, for example, by being returned to the sender as undeliverable. The queue mail.com was created when I sent a message to joe@mail.com. In Figure 13.19, I managed to capture a screen shot of the queue before the message went out.

Messages awaiting directory lookup   Holds inbound messages with recipients who have not yet been looked up in Active Directory. (This includes messages whose distribution groups haven't been expanded.)

Messages pending submission   Holds messages accepted by the SMTPVS but that are not yet being processed.

Messages queued for deferred delivery   Holds messages queued for delivery at a specific later time. This includes messages sent by Outlook clients for which the Do Not Deliver Before option has been selected.

FIGURE 13.19

Viewing and managing SMTP virtual server queues and sessions with the Exchange 2003 System Manager

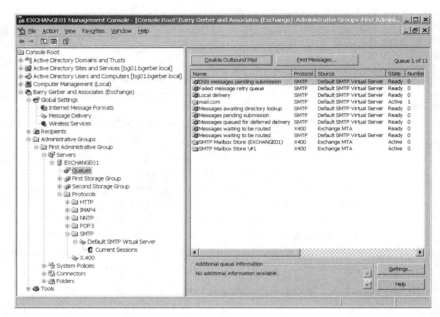

Messages waiting to be routed (X.400)   Holds outbound X.400 messages for which the next destination server has not been determined. (When the next destination server is determined, the message is sent.)

Messages waiting to be routed (SMTP)   Holds outbound SMTP messages for which next destination server has not been determined. (When the next destination server is determined, the message is sent.)

SMTP mailbox store (EXCHANGE01) (X.400)   The X.400 services on your Exchange server are responsible for the movement of messages in and out of Exchange mailboxes. This queue holds messages for the default mailbox store on my Exchange server.

SMTP mailbox store \#1 (X.400)   This queue is for the second mailbox store I created on my Exchange server back in Chapter 12. It serves the same purpose as the queue for the default mailbox store.

Notice that in Figure 13.19 (shown earlier) there's quite a bit of room to horizontally scroll the Queues panel. That's because there are a number of columns of information that can't be displayed in the 1024 × 768 pixel-sized screen I'm using on my Exchange server. Included in this hidden area are Total Message Size, Time Oldest Message Submitted, Time Next Submission Retry, and System. The first three of these columns are very useful when assessing the state of a queue and whether intervention might be required. The last of the columns tells you whether the queue is a system queue. For example, ad hoc queues to send user messages are not system queues.

You can stop a queue from sending messages or start it if it has been stopped. To stop sending, right-click the queue, then select Freeze from the pop-up menu. Frozen queues can receive, but do not send messages. Select Unfreeze to start a frozen queue. You can use the same pop-up menu to force your SMTPVS to connect to the SMTP host for the queue's destination domain. This is useful when you're trying to clear messages from SMTPVS queues or when your SMTPVS or another SMTP host has been down, then comes back up, and you want to flush one or more queues immediately. The pop-up menu also has a Find Messages option. See the paragraph after the next for more on that.

You might need the Disable Outbound Mail button, shown at the top of the right pane back in Figure 13.19, should you need to temporarily stop queues from sending messages. You do this to debug a queue or because a heavily filled queue is placing a burden on your Exchange server or your network. This option disables only ad hoc queues such as mail.com in Figure 13.19. Disabling outbound mail instead of stopping your SMTPVS allows the SMTPVS to continue performing system queue–related functions and receiving incoming mail.

You use the Find Messages button next to the Disable Outbound Mail button to search a specific queue for messages. You might want to look for messages sent by a user who is wondering why a particular message hasn't made it to the outside world yet or you might want to look at messages destined for a particular e-mail domain to see what's going on with them. To see all messages in a queue, leave the Sender and Recipient fields blank. Find Messages is a lot easier to use and offers more functionality than Enumerate 100 Messages in Exchange 2000. Once you find messages, you can sort messages by a variety of criteria—for example, Time Received by Server—and, if necessary, you can delete one or more of the messages you have found. Most of the time, you do this to fix a problem in a queue, for example, a queue that isn't sending out messages because it's stuck trying to send a specific message. As with Exchange 2000, you can delete a message and send or not send a nondelivery report to the sender of the message.

The Settings button at the bottom right of Figure 13.19 has one simple function. You can set the frequency with which the list of queues is refreshed. You can manually refresh information about queues by right-clicking the Queues container and selecting Refresh. However, it's much nicer to have this done automatically.

Now for the Current Sessions container just under your SMTPVS. The Current Sessions container shows the sessions that SMTP hosts including your SMTPVS and user clients have opened on your SMTPVS to send messages. Most of the time, sessions fly by at such breakneck speeds that you aren't able to refresh the Current Sessions container fast enough to see them. However, if a connection gets stuck or seems to be dumping one gigantic message or a very large number of messages, you might want to terminate the connection. You can end all sessions by right-clicking the Current Connections container and selecting Terminate All. Right-click a specific session and select Terminate to end that session.

Okay, now check out the introduction to the next section, which deals with the SMTP connector. If you don't need the functionality of an SMTPC, then you can move on to the "Did It Work?" section to test out your SMTPVS.

INSTALLING AND MANAGING THE EXCHANGE SMTP CONNECTOR

The Exchange Server 2003 SMTP Connector, or *SMTPC*, as I called it earlier in this chapter, is very different from earlier Exchange SMTP-related services. Exchange 5.*x*'s Internet Mail Service (IMS) was a full-blown SMTP host. It could do pretty much anything that Exchange 2003's SMTPVS can do, and more. In Exchange Server 2003, most of the *more* is provided by the SMTPC, allowing the SMTPVS to behave more like a standard SMTP host.

You can use the SMTPC to do the following:

- Control how messages are routed to SMTP hosts or smart hosts through an SMTPVS

- Set additional limits on the types and sizes of messages that can be sent through an SMTPVS

- Prevent Windows 2003 mailbox-enabled or mail-enabled users from sending Internet-bound messages

- Connect Exchange routing groups

In this section, I'll concentrate on the first three items in this list. I'll touch on the fourth use of the SMTPC in Chapter 15, "Installing and Managing Additional Exchange Servers."

NOTE *Those of you who need to send and receive dial-up access to a smart host should pay close attention here. I'll cover about three-quarters of what you need to know to set up dial-up access in this section. For the other quarter, you'll have to wait until the section on demand-dial interfaces.*

You might be wondering how the SMTPC interacts with the SMTPVS. Essentially, the SMTPC sits in front of one of more SMTP virtual servers, providing specialized message-routing functionality. Its most important feature is its support for highly customized connectivity between Exchange SMTP virtual servers and specific external or internal SMTP hosts—including, of course, other SMTP virtual servers. Even though SMTP virtual servers and SMTP connectors work together to move messages, from here on, I'll use the term *SMTPC* if the SMTPC is controlling the action.

If you're having trouble grasping this description of SMTPC/SMTPVS interaction, the best way to clarify matters is to install and configure an SMTPC. So, let's get right to it.

Find and right-click the Connectors container in the Exchange System Manager (see the left side of Figure 13.20). Then select New ➤ SMTP Connector from the pop-up menu. This brings up the SMTPC Properties dialog box, shown in the right side of Figure 13.20.

Right now we need to explore the General, Address Space, Delivery Restrictions, Content Restrictions, Delivery Options, and Advanced property pages. I'll discuss the Connected Routing Groups page in Chapter 15.

General

The General property page is an important one. In it, you name your SMTPC, specify how it will function in transferring SMTP messages, set the SMTPVS that it will function through, and set a parameter relating to how public folder information is handled when the SMTPC is used to connect Exchange routing groups. We'll look at all but the last of these here, saving public folder referrals for Chapter 15.

Name your new SMTPC anything that works for you. It will show up in the Connectors container under this name.

Your SMTPC can use DNS to route messages, or it can forward messages through a smart host. If you choose the DNS method, your SMTPC finds and accesses other computers just like the SMTPVS. If you choose to use a smart host, the SMTPC connects to the smart host and only to the smart host to do its business.

FIGURE 13.20

Creating a new SMTP connector starting with the General property page

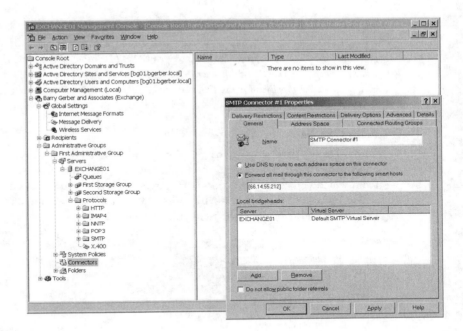

If you choose to use a smart host, the name or IP address that you enter here overrides any entry that you might have made in the Smart Host field on the Advanced Delivery dialog box of the Delivery property page of the Properties dialog box for your SMTPVS. (Whew, that's a mouthful!) Take a look back at Figure 13.14 for a quick visual refresher on the Advanced Delivery dialog box.

The SMTPC lets you do something with your smart host that you can't do with the smart host that you set on the Advanced Delivery dialog box for your SMTPVS: The SMTPC lets you set things up so that the smart host is asked to send messages that it has received for your Exchange Internet domains. If you need full dial-up send and receive smart-host services, this is a key piece of the puzzle. I'll show you how to set up this puzzle piece in just a bit.

You'll notice that I've specified an IP address for the smart host rather than a fully-qualified domain name. You can do this as long as you enclose the IP address in brackets. Do note, however, that if you enter an IP address here, you'll have to change it if the IP address of the smart host changes. Other approaches would be to use a fully-qualified domain name that is maintained in an external DNS or to create an Address record for the smart host in your internal DNS.

You must specify at least one bridgehead server. This is the server that provides the SMTPVS services to make the connection to the DNS or smart host computers that you specified in the Use DNS or Forward All Mail Though fields. Click Add to select a server. You'll notice that I've chosen (actually been forced) to use my one and only Exchange server and SMTPVS. If I had more servers or SMTPVSs, I would have been able to choose from among them.

NOTE   *Connectors live in a routing group inside of an administrative group. You can't see the routing group in Figure 13.20 because we haven't yet turned on the display of routing groups. We'll do that in Chapter 15. Routing groups are not based on a specific Exchange server like SMTP virtual servers. SMTP virtual servers are processes that run on Exchange servers. SMTP connectors refine the functionality of SMTP virtual servers. They aren't processes that run on servers. Rather, they live in Active Directory, and their particular refinements are invoked by associated SMTP virtual servers as the need arises.*

Address Space

The Address Space property page is shown on the left side of Figure 13.21. This is a fairly simple page. You need to add at least one address space: Click Add to do so. This opens a little dialog box from which you can pick the kind of address space that you need. You're offered several options, including SMTP, X.400, and Microsoft Mail. Select SMTP to open the Internet Address Space Properties dialog box (see the right side of Figure 13.21).

FIGURE 13.21

Using the Address Space property page to create a new SMTP address space for an SMTPC

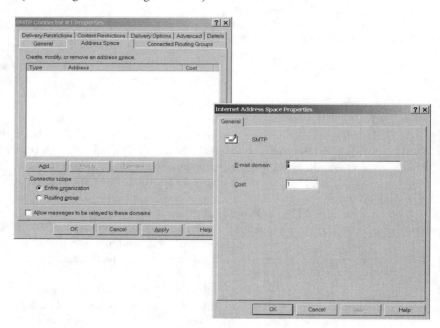

You'll remember the asterisk from our discussion of domain message policies. This means that, with the exception of any parameters set elsewhere on this dialog box, this SMTPC should function for all SMTP domains in the world. If you want this SMTPC to service one or more domains, but not all domains, you can specify a single SMTP domain here. Then you can create additional address space objects to cover the other domains that you want this SMTPC to service.

You use the Cost field to set the relative time or dollar cost of using this connector to process messages for this address space, as opposed to using a different connector to process messages for the same address space. You need this feature only when you set up multiple connectors. You usually set up multiple connectors when you connect two Exchange routing groups to ensure redundant links between the routing groups. When routing, Exchange server always attempts to use the route with the lowest value in the Cost field (which might very well be a higher-cost route in dollars, but also higher speed) before attempting to use a higher-cost route.

The Connector Scope area in the SMTP Connector Properties dialog box on the left side of Figure 13.21 (shown earlier) lets you specify which servers can use your SMTPC. You can allow your entire organization to use the SMTPC, or you can restrict use of the SMTPC only to servers in the routing group where the SMTPC resides. You might use this feature to control security in your organization, but its most important functions are in the area of cost. Say that you've established an inexpensive or high-performance route from the SMTPVS supported by this SMTPC to whatever external computers you plan to connect to. But, say also that this route is inexpensive or fast only for servers in the SMTPC's Exchange routing group, which are servers linked by higher-speed network connections. Other servers in other routing groups in your organization may have their own least-expensive routes and fastest routes to the servers supported by this SMTPC. Limiting use of the SMTPC to servers in the SMTPC's routing group ensures that servers in other routing groups will use their own best routing options, given their location.

The last field in the Address Space property page lets you disable the relaying of messages bound for the address spaces that you've defined. Users and computers that can authenticate using Basic or Integrated Windows authentication can relay messages even if Allow Messages to Be Relayed to These Domains is deselected. If this SMTPC supports a direct connection to the Internet, you probably want to disable this function so that not just anyone with an SMTP client or just any SMTP host can relay messages.

Delivery Restrictions

You use the Delivery Restrictions property page, shown in Figure 13.22, to select the Exchange recipients that can send messages using the SMTPC. If your organization doesn't want everyone to have access to Internet messaging, you use this property page to create a list of users who are not allowed to use this SMTPC to send messages.

As you can see in Figure 13.22, you can simply choose to accept or reject messages from everyone, or you can create lists of Exchange recipients from whom messages may or may not be accepted. You can use only one of the list or both lists. Click the appropriate Add button to add recipients to a list, and then select the recipients from the Select Recipients dialog box that opens.

TIP *To prevent an Exchange recipient from receiving SMTP messages, just remove the SMTP address or addresses on the E-mail Addresses property page of the recipient's Properties dialog box (see Chapters 11 and 12 for more on this property page).*

Content Restrictions

The Content Restrictions property page lets you specify whether messages with certain characteristics may be delivered through the SMTPC (see Figure 13.23). Here's a quick take on the options on this page.

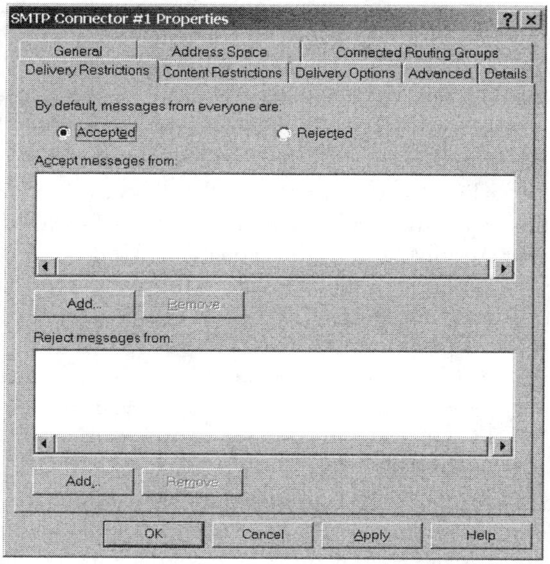

FIGURE 13.22
Using the Delivery
Restrictions prop-
erty page to prevent
Exchange recipients
from sending mes-
sages through an
SMTPC

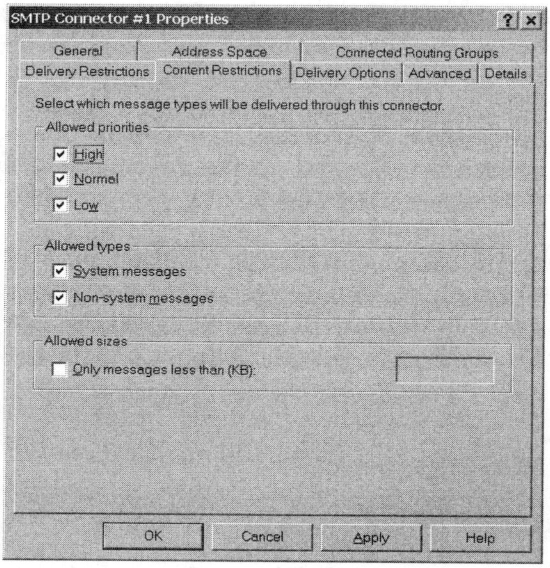

FIGURE 13.23
Using the Content
Restrictions prop-
erty page to specify
the kind of messages
that can be sent
through an SMTPC

Users can specify a priority for each message that they send. Messages with deselected priorities in the Allowed Priorities area are not sent.

Exchange uses system messages for such things as public folder replication. Windows 2003 uses messages to support such things as Active Directory replication. If you deselect System Messages in the Allowed Types area, only standard user-originated messages will be sent. If your SMTPC is going to be used to contact a smart host, deselect System Messages.

You use the Allowed Sizes area to set the maximum size in kilobytes of messages that can be sent through your SMTPC. The default is no size limit. Settings here override settings on the SMTPVC or SMTPVCs with which this SMTPC is associated.

Delivery Options

Okay, now on to the Delivery Options property page, shown on the left side of Figure 13.24. You use this page to specify when and how messages are sent through your SMTPC.

ESMTP, TURN, AND ETRN

Before we jump into the last two property pages on the SMTPC Properties dialog box, I need to clarify some key terms. The next two sections will make a lot more sense if you have a clear understanding of what ESMTP, TURN, and ETRN are all about. All three of these terms identify specific parts of the overall SMTP specification. They are key to message retrieval from an SMTP smart host.

By default, your SMTPC uses the Extended SMTP (ESMTP) command set when contacting other SMTP hosts. This command set includes extensions to the original SMTP protocol's command set. Extensions cover such things as advanced, more secure message interchange, longer To and From fields, and pre-announced message length limits so that an SMTP host doesn't try to send messages that are longer than the receiving SMTP host allows only to fail after megabytes have been sent.

The TURN command essentially reverses or turns around the communication roles between two SMTP hosts. At the start of communications, the contacted SMTP host is expecting the contacting SMTP host to send it messages for domains under the contacted host's control. The TURN command tells the contacted SMTP host that the contacting host wants the contacted host to send messages to it for domains under its control—in other words, "At first you thought that I contacted you to send you messages, but now I want you to send messages to me." TURN is very useful when your SMTPC uses the same smart host to send and receive messages.

The TURN command can be authenticated. The SMTPC will issue the command only if it has a valid username and password to send to authenticate the command. Additionally, the SMTPC will not accept TURN requests from SMTP hosts that can't or won't send a valid username and password.

The ETRN (Extended TURN) specification doesn't allow for password-protected command authentication. However, it does require that the SMTP host issuing the ETRN command also provides the fully-qualified domain name of the SMTP host that supports the domain for which messages need to be picked up. The smart host then initiates a new session with the SMTP host specified in the ETRN command. This can be done on the same link that the original ETRN command was issued on, including an existing dial-up connection. This allows for a fairly secure link between the SMTPC and its smart host.

FIGURE 13.24

Using the Delivery Options property page to specify how and when messages are sent through an SMTPC

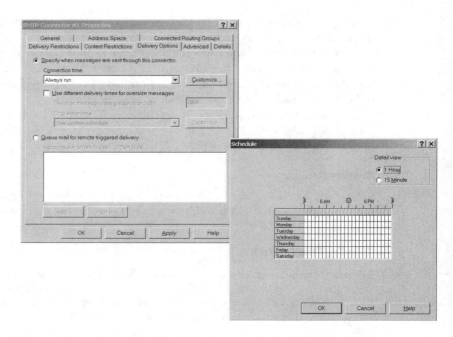

An SMTPC can send messages to an SMTP host, or an SMTP host can contact the SMTPC to pick up outbound messages. An SMTPC can do only one of these things, not both. To implement the first option, select Specify When Messages Are Sent Through This Connector. You can then specify the schedule for connection by selecting from a limited set of choices on the Connection Time drop-down list or by clicking Customize and setting any schedule you want on the Schedule dialog box, shown on the right side of Figure 13.24. You can then go one step further and set another delivery schedule for large messages, for example, to reduce connect costs or conserve server capacity and network bandwidth during busier hours.

This might come as a surprise, but if you need to set up a dial-up send and receive link to a smart host, you should accept the Always Run connection time option. You'll see why when I discuss demand-dial interfaces later in this chapter.

Your second delivery option is Queue Mail for Remote Triggered Delivery. If you select this option, you're telling your SMTPC that another SMTP host will contact it to pick up messages ready for delivery.

To use the remote triggered delivery option, you need another SMTP host whose administrator is willing to initiate a connection to your SMTPC. This isn't impossible, but you're more likely to find that kind of willingness inside rather than outside your organization. For example, few ISPs are likely to agree to initiate communications, especially dial-up connections with your SMTPC to pick up outbound messages. However, most ISPs are willing to let you initiate connections, including dial-up connections, to one of their SMTP hosts so that you can send messages through it in smart host fashion. All this means that you're most likely going to use the first option on the Delivery Options page, Specify When Messages Are Sent Through This Connector (perhaps with ETRN).

Enabling dial-up from another SMTP host would be most useful when two or more Exchange servers in the same organization are set up to connect to each other through a dial-up connection.

Advanced

Up to now, we've spent most of our time moving messages from our SMTPC to other SMTP hosts. Now we're ready to tackle the Advanced property page, shown in Figure 13.25, which lets us reverse the process and get messages from another SMTP host.

FIGURE 13.25

Using the Advanced property page to specify how an SMTPC will retrieve messages for the domains it supports

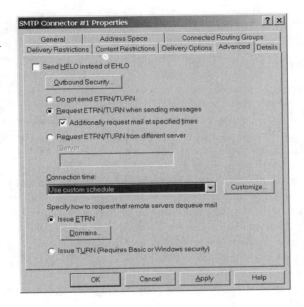

When an SMTP host contacts another SMTP host, it first issues either a HELO or an EHLO command. The HELO command is a request to communicate using standard SMTP commands. The EHLO command tells the other SMTP host that the contacting host wants to use ESMTP commands.

Today, most SMTP hosts can handle ESMTP, so you're pretty safe accepting the default and leaving the Send HELO Instead of EHLO option unselected. Of course, if you've designed this SMTPC specifically to contact an SMTP host that doesn't support EHLO, you can select the option. Note, however, that if you choose to use standard SMTP commands, all the other options on the Advanced property page are grayed out, meaning that standard SMTP commands don't support these options. This means that, among other things, dial-up retrieval of messages from a smart host is not possible. Here's the bottom line: If you need the kinds of capabilities on the Advanced property page, find an ISP that supports ESMTP.

The rest of the Advanced property page is about setting up your SMTPC so that it asks another SMTP host to send it messages. If you need to contact a dial-up send and receive SMTP smart host, pay close attention to this section. If you have no need for this feature, then select Do Not Send ETRN/TURN, and you're done.

Click Outbound Security to open the Outbound Security dialog box if you need to set up an authentication method, username, and password for your SMTPC's connection to its remote host. (Check out Figure 13.12, shown earlier, and related text for more on using the Outbound Security dialog box.) I'll talk a little more about this option at the end of this section.

If you've already set up your SMTPC so that it can send messages through a smart host, and if you want it to ask the smart host for new messages for the domains that your SMTPC supports, then select Request ETRN/TURN When Sending Messages. You specify whether you want to use ETRN or TURN at the end of the Advanced property page. With this option selected, every time your SMTPC contacts its smart host to send messages, it will ask the smart host for new messages. If you also want your SMTPC to ask the smart host for messages on a schedule of some sort, then select Additionally Request Mail at Specified Times. I'll show you how to set the schedule in a moment.

If you want to or must receive incoming messages from a different smart host than the one you contacted to send outgoing messages, select Request ETRN/TURN From a Different Server. Again, you specify whether you want to use ETRN or TURN at the end of the Advanced property page. Be sure to enter either an IP address for the server, in brackets, or the fully-qualified domain name of the server. This option lets you send messages through one smart host and receive them through another. If you pick this option, you can set the schedule for connections to the smart host. Join me in the next paragraph to see how.

You use the Connection Time field to set the schedule for contacts with the smart host that you selected previously. You can pick from a limited number of options from the drop-down list, or you can set a custom schedule. See the right side of Figure 13.24 for the Schedule dialog box.

The last section of the Advanced property page enables you to specify whether the ETRN or TURN command is used to request that an SMTP smart host send messages. You can also set whatever security parameters are available for whichever command you choose. If you need clarification regarding the ETRN and TURN commands, check out the sidebar "ESMTP, TURN, and ETRN" earlier in this chapter.

If you select ETRN, you need to specify the Internet messaging domains that ETRN should be issued for. The SMTPC uses this information to form the fully-qualified domain name that it needs to send with the ETRN command. As Figure 13.26 makes pretty clear, selecting a domain is very easy. Just click Domains in the Advanced property page, then click Add in the Domains dialog box and select the domain from the Add ETRN Domain dialog box.

If you select TURN, of course, you need to enter a username and password using the Outbound Security dialog box. To do this, open the Outbound Security dialog box by clicking Outbound Security near the top of the Advanced property page. Then select either Basic Authentication or Integrated Windows Authentication, and enter a valid username and password.

When you're finished setting parameters for your SMTPC, click OK to close the Properties dialog box for the SMTPC. You'll find your new SMTPC in the Connectors container. It's ready to go to work.

NOTE   *Messages to be sent through an SMTPC to an SMTP smart host all go into one queue on your SMTPVS. This queue is named after your SMTPC. Unlike messages sent directly through an SMTPVS, messages to be sent through an SMTPC do not go into their own separate queues based on the destination e-mail domain of each message. So, you won't see a separate queue in the Queues container for each e-mail domain to which a message is to be sent, as shown back in Figure 13.19.*

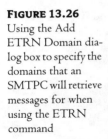

FIGURE 13.26
Using the Add
ETRN Domain dia-
log box to specify the
domains that an
SMTPC will retrieve
messages for when
using the ETRN
command

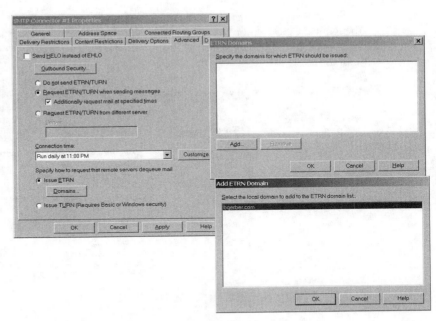

If you've tracked through this section, you probably need a send/receive dial-up link to an SMTP smart host. That's exactly what's covered in the next section. Go there if you need dial-up connectivity. If not, you're ready to test your SMPTC. Skip down to the "Did It Work?" section.

INSTALLING AND MANAGING DEMAND-DIAL INTERFACES

Demand-dial interfaces are a bit magical. In the SMTP messaging world, whenever a connection is needed to a specific IP address and a demand-dial interface exists for that interface, the connection is automatically made through the demand-dial interface to the IP address. If you tracked through all the sections of this chapter and you need a send/receive dial-up connection to an SMTP smart host, you might just have had the following epiphany: "If you set up an SMTP connector to connect to a specific IP address and that IP address is supported by a demand-dial interface, connectivity just happens." That's it! So now all that remains is for us to set up a demand-dial interface.

Demand-dial interfaces are Windows 2003 objects, not Exchange 2003 objects. They're created and managed within the Windows 2003 routing and remote access world.

We'll be setting up a telephone-based interface, so before you do anything else, you need to be sure that a functioning modem is installed in your Exchange server. Let me emphasize that last sentence. If the modem isn't installed, you won't see any options that require a modem when you're following the instructions. Next, you need to enable routing and remote access on your server. We're going to move through setting up routing and remote access at breakneck pace, so hold on to your hat. If you need more information, see Mark Minasi's book, which is referenced in the sidebar "Where to Go for More on TCP/IP, DNS, and SMTP" at the beginning of this chapter.

Select Start ➢ All Programs ➢ Administrative Tools ➢ Routing and Remote Access. This opens the Routing and Remote Access snap-in, shown in Figure 13.27. As an alternative, you can add this snap-in to your Microsoft Management Console. Make sure that your modem is listed in the Ports container.

FIGURE 13.27

The Windows Server 2003 Routing and Remote Access snap-in

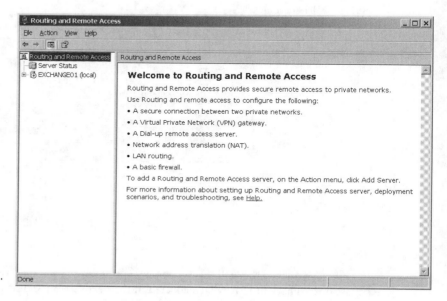

The icon for your Exchange server should have a little down-pointing red arrow, indicating that routing and remote access hasn't been enabled or configured. Right-click your Exchange server in the snap-in and, from the pop-up menu, select Configure and Enable Routing and Remote Access. The Routing and Remote Access Server Setup Wizard opens.

Click Next on the wizard's introductory page to access the Configuration wizard page, and then select Custom Configuration and click Next. On the Custom Configuration page, select Demand-Dial Connection and click Next. Don't worry about the reference to "branch office routing." Click Finish on the final wizard page and accept the wizard's offer to start the Routing and Remote Access Server.

Your Routing and Remote Access window should now look like the one in Figure 13.28. Next you need to add a demand-dial interface. Now, right-click the Network Interfaces container and select New Demand-Dial Interface. This opens the Demand-Dial Interface Wizard shown on the right side of Figure 13.28. We're going to slow down here just a bit because it's very important that you get this part right. Click Next to move on.

Click over to the Interface Name wizard page, shown in Figure 13.29. Enter an intelligible name for your demand-dial interface. I've named mine ISP Smart Host.

FIGURE 13.28
The Windows Server 2003 Routing and Remote Access snap-in with the Demand-Dial Interface Wizard open and ready to go

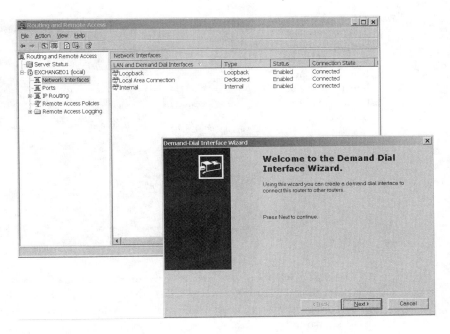

FIGURE 13.29
Naming a demand-dial interface on the Interface Name page of the Demand-Dial Interface Wizard

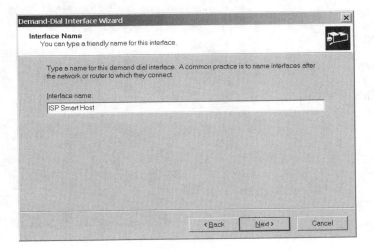

The Connection Type wizard page offers you three connectivity options (see Figure 13.30). Be sure that the Connect Using a Modem, ISDN Adapter, or Other Physical Device option is selected.

FIGURE 13.30
Selecting a connectivity option for a demand-dial interface on the Connection Type page of the Demand-Dial Interface Wizard

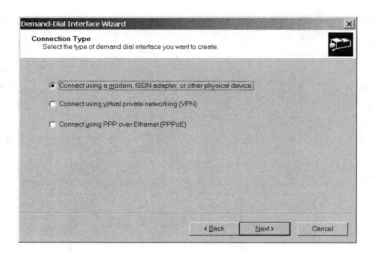

Use the Phone Number wizard page to enter the phone number or numbers of the computer that you want to connect to (see Figure 13.31). Make sure that this number or these numbers are appropriate for reaching the remote SMTP host. Next select a physical device on the Select a Device wizard page, shown in Figure 13.32.

FIGURE 13.31
Entering a phone number for a demand-dial interface on the Phone Number page of the Demand-Dial Interface Wizard

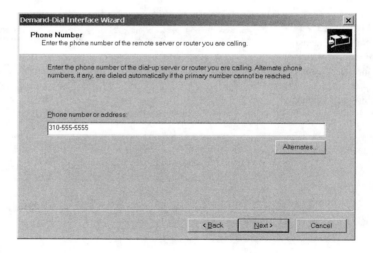

Next you need to ensure that routing and security settings are correct for your demand-dial interface, using the Protocols and Security wizard page, shown in Figure 13.33. Be sure that Route IP Packets on This Interface is selected. Although it should be taken care of in the setup of your SMTPC, also select the option that ensures that a plain-text password will be sent if that is the only way to connect to the dial-up system.

FIGURE 13.32

Selecting a physical device to be used by a demand-dial interface on the Select a Device page of the Demand-Dial Interface Wizard

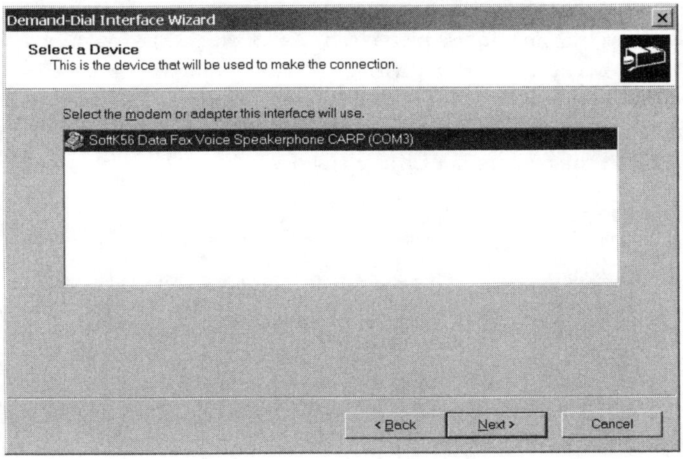

FIGURE 13.33

Selecting networking and security options for a demand-dial interface on the Protocols and Security page of the Demand Dial Interface Wizard

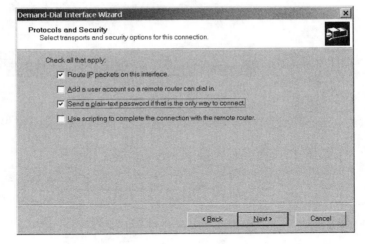

You use the next wizard page, shown in Figure 13.34, to link your demand-dial interface to the IP address of the smart host that you specified when you set up your SMTPC. You need to set up a static route. Click Add on the Static Routes for Remote Networks wizard page to open the Static Route dialog box (see Figure 13.34) and enter the IP address of the network that you want to connect to. This should include the IP address of the smart host that you entered on the General property page of the Properties dialog box for your SMTPC (see Figure 13.20, shown earlier). My smart host has the address 66.14.55.323 (not a real ISP address, by the way). I could have entered a range of addresses or 66.14.55.0 to indicate that I wanted the demand-dial interface to connect to any address in the 66.14.55.*xxx* range. The mask must be appropriate for the address or the address range entered. 255.255.255.255 is appropriate for a single address. 255.255.255.0 is appropriate for an entry covering an address range from *xxx.xxx.xxx.*0 to *xxx.xxx.xxx.*254. You'll have to change the mask if you need to enter a narrower address range. The same rules apply to network masks here as apply to network masks when setting up a Windows 2003 network adapter. For more on this, check out Mark Minasi's book, mentioned in the "Where to Go for More on TCP/IP, DNS, and SMTP" sidebar at the beginning of this chapter.

FIGURE 13.34

Using the Static Route dialog box to set up a static route for a dial-up connection

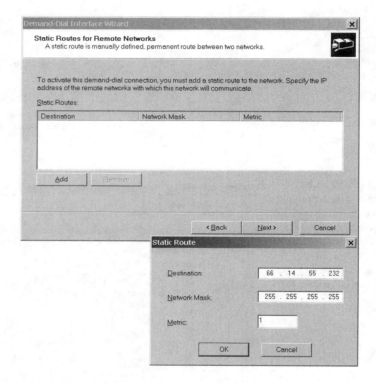

Now, you need to enter the security information expected at the remote site. As per Figure 13.35, you must enter a username and a password in the Dial Out Credentials wizard page. If you're logging in to a Windows network, you might also need to enter the Windows domain name. Leave the metric setting at 1.

You can change the settings that you made in the Demand-Dial Interface Wizard. Find your demand-dial interface in the Network Interfaces container of your Routing and Remote Access window. See Figure 13.36 to orient yourself. Double-click the interface. This opens the Properties dialog box for your demand-dial interface shown on the right side of Figure 13.36. If you need to set up X.25 parameters for an ISDN-based connection, click the X.25 button at the bottom of the Properties dialog box for your demand-dial interface. I'm not going to take you through all the property pages on the demand-dial interface dialog box or talk any more about static routes. For help, take a look at Mark Minasi's book, mentioned in the "Where to Go for More on TCP/IP, DNS, and SMTP" sidebar at the beginning of this chapter.

FIGURE 13.35

Entering security information for a demand-dial interface on the Dial Out Credentials page of the Demand-Dial Interface Wizard

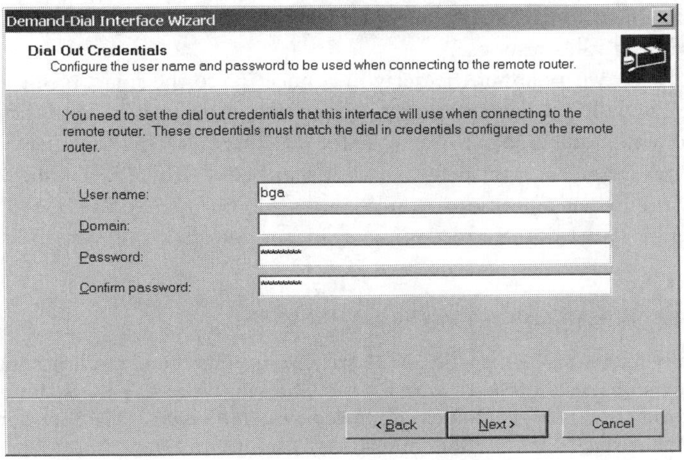

FIGURE 13.36

Using the demand-dial interface Properties dialog box to change settings made in the Demand-Dial Interface Wizard

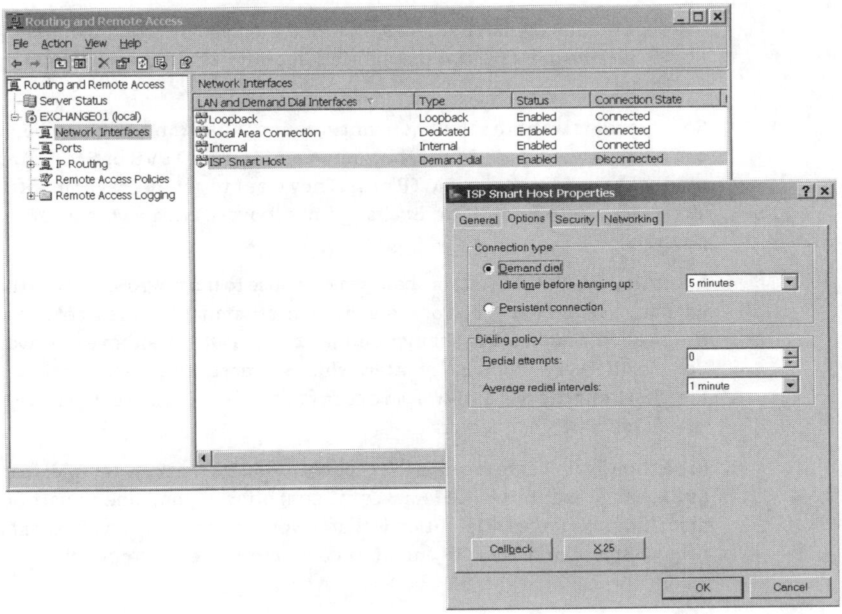

When you've finished configuring your static route, you can test your demand-dial interface. Open a command prompt on your Exchange server and enter the command **ping [IP_address]**. Here, [IP_address] is any IP address in the range that you set for your static route. Your computer will attempt to ping the address and fail, but you should hear it dialing the phone number that you set for the demand-dial interface. After the connection is made, you should be able to reissue the ping command and get a valid response.

Don't worry about the delay in connecting to the smart host's network affecting your SMTPC. The SMTPC will keep trying to connect to its smart host until the dial-up connection is completed. But why should you take my word for it? You're now ready to test your SMTPC, and the next section of this chapter is exactly the place to do so. See you there. Oh yeah, take a look at the following sidebar "More E-mail Questions from Readers" if you want to use SMTP mailboxes, as opposed to an SMTP smart host, to receive messages for your Exchange organization.

MORE E-MAIL QUESTIONS FROM READERS

Many reader problems with SMTP arise from a misunderstanding about the difference between Internet mailboxes and SMTP smart hosts when it comes to noncontinuous SMTP mail connections. An Internet mailbox—a mailbox supported by an ISP's own SMTP host computer—usually holds messages for one user. To access those messages, a user runs a POP3- or IMAP4-compliant Internet e-mail client, connects to the ISP's SMTP host, and reads the messages. On the other hand, an SMTP host is a collection of Internet mailboxes. SMTP hosts connect to each other to send and receive messages; users connect to their Internet mailboxes to access the messages in them.

Internet mailboxes can not receive or send messages on their own. They require the services of an SMTP host to receive messages for them. Internet e-mail clients, not Internet mailboxes, send messages through SMTP hosts.

Some readers want to set up noncontinuous connections, not between their Exchange server's SMTPVS or SMTPC and an SMTP host, but between their SMTPVS or SMTPC and one or more specific Internet mailboxes residing on an SMTP host. They want to get messages in Internet mailboxes residing at an ISP and place them in specific Exchange mailboxes. With two exceptions that I discuss next, this isn't possible.

Exception One: Microsoft, probably in response to messages similar to the ones that I get, devised a way for Exchange Server to use one or more POP3 Internet mailboxes sort of like an SMTP host. However, this solution, called Microsoft Exchange Connector for POP3 Mailboxes, is available only for Microsoft's Small Business Server version 4.5 or later, which supports up to 50 users. For more information on the Connector, check out the website www.microsoft.com/smallbusinessserver/deployadmin. Once at this site, search for "POP3 connector."

Exception Two: There are also third-party products that can get mail from Internet mailboxes and place it in Exchange mailboxes. GFI (www.gfi.com) offers a good one as part of its Mail Essentials package. The nice thing about the GFI solution is that it works on any version of Exchange server, not just the small-business version. For more POP3 mailbox connectors, see the Appendix.

Did It Work?

You have several tools at your command for checking your SMTPVS and SMTPC. These fall into two categories: sending and receiving e-mail like a regular user and sending e-mail like an SMTP host. I discuss both of these below.

Sending and Receiving E-mail Like a Regular User

Assuming that your SMTPVS or SMTPC can connect to the Internet by whatever means you configured, you can now test your setup. First, try sending mail to your Exchange mailbox from outside your Exchange system—for example, from an account that you've set up with an ISP. Use a POP3 or IMAP4 mail client. Next, ask someone on the Internet to send mail to your Exchange mailbox's Internet mail address. For the record, it does no good to send a message from your Exchange mailbox to your Exchange mailbox's Internet address. The address is resolved inside your Exchange server and is delivered directly to your mailbox. The message never gets out to the Internet.

TIP *I have an e-mail account with an ISP. One of the main things that I do with it is test new SMTP virtual servers and SMTP connectors. I use an IMAP4 mail client connected to the ISP's network to send messages to myself on a new SMTPVS or SMTPC and to receive messages that I send through the new SMTPVS or SMTPC from an Exchange client. For more on using IMAP4 clients, see the next chapter.*

If everything works, you're home free. If you have problems, make sure that all your SMTP-based DNS entries are correct. Use the `ping` command to ping key IP address and fully-qualified domain names. Check to be sure that your SMTPVS or SMTPC is connecting to the Internet properly. If all else fails, track back through all the settings that you made for your SMTPVS or SMTPC. If you're working with an SMTP smart host, check with the smart host provider to be sure that all is well on its end. With a little perseverance, everything will fall in place and you'll be movin' mail on the Internet with the best of them.

Sending E-mail Like an SMTP Host

Generally, Exchange administrators have more trouble receiving than sending SMTP mail. That's because, as long as you're connected to the Internet and you've got access to DNS servers that "know" what's where on the Internet, your SMTPVS or SMTPC can figure out where to send messages and do so. Receiving messages requires an appropriate setup in a public DNS server system so that external SMTP hosts can find and connect to your SMTPVS.

You can do a simple test to check the message receive capability of your SMTPVS. It involves the use of Telnet. Telnet is a TCP/IP-based service that lets users open a terminal session on a computer. It is used to remotely administer Unix servers and can be used in a variety of ways on Windows servers. You can do quite a number of interesting things by opening a terminal session to a specific TCP/IP port. Here you want to open a special terminal session to your SMTPVS on port number 25, the standard port that SMTP hosts use to communicate with each other. You will be doing exactly what an SMTP host does when it needs to send a message to your SMTPVS.

Here's what to do:

1. Ensure that your SMTPVS is listening on the IP address you specify. See Figures 13.5 and 13.6 and accompanying text earlier in this chapter.

2. Open a command prompt (All Programs ➢ Command Prompt).

3. Type **telnet** and press the Enter key.

4. Type **set local_echo**.

5. Type **open [*FQDN or IP Address*] 25** and press Enter, where *FDQN* is the fully-qualified domain name of your SMTPVS server as published in a local or public DNS and *IP Address* is the internal or external IP address of your SMTPVS server. Don't forget the *25*.

You'll see something like this: 220 bgerber.com Microsoft ESMTP MAIL Service, Version: 5.0.2195.5329 ready at Mon, 19 May 2003 11:06:24 -0700.

6. Type **ehlo** to invoke the extended SMTP command set.

You should see something like the following code. ehlo is your command; the rest is from your SMTPVS and is a list of extended SMTP commands supported by your SMTPVS. As you can see, I'm working with my internal IP address.

```
ehlo
250-bgerber.com Hello [192.168.0.5]
250-TURN
250-ATRN
250-SIZE
250-ETRN
250-PIPELINING
250-DSN
250-ENHANCEDSTATUSCODES
250-8bitmime
250-BINARYMIME
250-CHUNKING
250-VRFY
250-X-EXPS GSSAPI NTLM LOGIN
250-X-EXPS=LOGIN
250-AUTH GSSAPI NTLM LOGIN
250-AUTH=LOGIN
250-X-LINK2STATE
250-XEXCH50
250 OK
```

7. Type **mail from:[*YOUR_MAILBOX_ALIAS*]**, where *YOUR_MAILBOX_ALIAS* is the Exchange alias for your mailbox; mine is *bgerber* as in bgerber@bgerber.com. Press the Enter key.

Your SMTPVS responds with your SMTP e-mail address and a message indicating that the sender is OK.

8. Enter **rcpt to:[*YOUR_MAILBOX_ALIAS*]** and press the Enter key.

Your SMTPVS responds with your SMTP e-mail address.

9. Type **data** and press the Enter key.

Your SMTPVS will respond with 354 Start mail input; end with <CRLF>.<CRLF>.

10. Type a short test message. If you want to include a subject, the first line you type should be **Subject:**, followed by the subject line and the Enter key. Next enter your message. When you're through, press Enter, type a period, and press Enter again.

Your SMTPVS will respond with a message similar to this: `354 Start mail input; end with <CRLF>.<CRLF>`.

That's it. Type **quit** to exit your telnet session. Then close the command prompt. You should now find the message you sent in your Outlook mailbox.

Summary

TCP/IP, DNS, and SMTP are at the heart of Internet messaging. TCP/IP moves information within LANs and across WANs. IP addresses are at the core of TCP/IP communications. IP addresses identify networked computers so that other computers can connect to them using TCP/IP and other Internet protocols. IP addresses such as 192.168.10.221 are not the stuff of good human communications. DNS allows humans to refer to IP addresses by warm and fuzzy names such as `mycomputer.fuzzyname.com` or `sendmymailherestupid.upodunk.edu`. SMTP hosts are the engines that move inbound and outbound Internet messages between SMTP e-mail clients and SMTP host computers. DNS helps SMTP hosts find the TCP/IP addresses of the SMTP hosts for specific Internet domains.

Internet messaging administrators are responsible for properly setting up TCP/IP, DNS, and SMTP within their Internet domains. This involves configuring IP addresses for computers exposed to the Internet, ensuring that SMTP hosts are correctly registered in DNS and are accessible to the outside world, and setting up internal SMTP host services so that SMTP messages can move smoothly and rapidly between internal and external hosts. When everything is working well, Internet messages flow around the world like the best Vermont maple syrup in the summer.

Exchange Server 2003 implements Internet messaging through SMTP virtual servers. SMTP virtual servers are SMTP hosts. When an SMTPVS is connected directly and continuously to the Internet, SMTP host services pretty much just happen. When continuous connectivity isn't available, an Exchange SMTP connector might be required.

SMTP virtual servers can be configured in a variety of ways, both at the Exchange server and at the Exchange organizational level. At the server level, security can be extensively controlled through a set of authentication, certification, and external domain name-based connection and service access limits. Size limits can be set for inbound and outbound messages. Additionally, limits can be set to control the traffic on both inbound and outbound connections between the SMTP virtual server and its fellow Internet-based servers.

At the Exchange organization level, a number of parameters can be set that affect the operation of SMTP virtual servers. These parameters include a range of options for formatting messages and attachments to them, and determining whether certain types of message content can be generated by SMTP virtual servers in the organization. Exchange 2003 includes a number of organizational level spam-blocking options as well.

The SMTP connector's major strength lies in the way that it adds the capability to connect an SMTP virtual server to specific SMTP hosts in very tightly controlled ways. More than anything else, the connector supports the use of SMTP smart hosts, SMTP hosts that send and receive Internet messages for other SMTP hosts. With a properly configured SMTP connector in place, it is possible for an SMTP virtual server to send its messages out through an SMTP smart host and use the smart host to retrieve messages sent to the smart host in the name of the SMTP virtual server. The SMTP connector can be configured to provide secure interaction between the SMTP virtual server and the smart host.

In addition to this functionality, the SMTP connector can be used to add valuable features to any SMTP virtual server. It can be used to limit access to SMTP services based on Windows 2003 accounts, and to limit the types and sizes of messages that can move though an SMTP virtual server.

Finally, Windows Server 2003 demand-dial interfaces, which are a part of Windows routing and remote access services, can be used to implement dial-up (noncontinuous) links to an SMTP smart host. With a properly set up SMTP connector, dial-up interface, and static route, a dial-up connection with the smart host is initiated whenever the SMTPVS has outbound messages to send or is ready to receive inbound messages.

Well, by now you should have Exchange SMTP host services up and running, or you should at least know how you're going to get them up and running. When everything is working as advertised, why not send me a message celebrating the event? You can find my e-mail address at the end of the Acknowledgments section at the front of this book.

Whew! That was a long chapter, and we still have one Internet-oriented chapter to go. In the next chapter, we continue our focus on Internet messaging as we look at Exchange Server 2003's support for the POP3 and IMAP4 e-mail protocols, as well as Exchange's support for Outlook Web Access, the web browser–based access to Exchange mailboxes. We also devote some time to two other Exchange-relevant Internet protocols: the LDAP directory access protocol and the NNTP network news protocol.

Chapter 14

Managing Exchange 2003 Services for Internet Clients

THIS IS ONE OF the most exciting chapters in this book. Exchange Server 2003 comes with a set of Internet-based client-server protocols that, taken together, raise it from a fairly tightly controlled, proprietary client/server product to an open and flexible electronic messaging system.

Each of the protocols that I discuss in this chapter is a client/server protocol. For each protocol, I'll cover both the server and client aspects of the protocol, in that order. However, before tackling these protocols, I'll spend some time talking about Exchange 2003 virtual servers and what Microsoft calls *front-end/back-end server configurations*.

Featured in this chapter:

- ◆ Virtual servers and front-end/back-end servers
- ◆ Managing Post Office Protocol Version 3 (POP3) messaging
- ◆ Managing Internet Message Access Protocol version 4 (IMAP4) messaging
- ◆ Managing Hypertext Transport Protocol (HTTP) messaging
- ◆ Managing Windows 2003 support for the Lightweight Directory Access Protocol (LDAP)
- ◆ Managing Exchange Server support for the Network News Transfer Protocol (NNTP)

Virtual Servers and Front-End/Back-End Servers

You can't effectively implement the Internet client/server protocols that I discuss in this chapter without understanding two key concepts:

- ◆ Exchange virtual servers
- ◆ Front-end/back-end servers

Virtual servers, upon which SMTP host services are built, also support all of the protocols that we'll be discussing here except Windows 2003's LDAP. Front-end/back-end servers allow users to access the Exchange 2003 environment with POP3, IMAP4, and HTTP (web browser– and Outlook 2003–based) clients without having to reference the specific Exchange server where their mailboxes or public folders are located. They also relieve mailbox servers of authentication loads and can make enhanced firewall-based security easier to implement.

Exchange 2003 Virtual Servers Are Not Just for SMTP

Exchange Server 2003 implements POP3, IMAP4, HTTP, and NNTP protocols using virtual servers that are quite similar to the SMTP virtual servers that we explored in the last chapter. If you haven't read last chapter's section on SMTP virtual servers, "Setting Up and Managing SMTP," I suggest that you do so now.

You deal with Exchange HTTP virtual servers in Windows 2003's web server, Internet Information Server. That makes sense given that all other HTTP services are based in Internet Information Server.

By default and for security reasons, the Exchange POP3 and IMAP4 services and the NNTP service are disabled. If your users need these services to access Exchange messages, you have to enable the services. In Figure 14.1, I'm using the General property page of the Properties dialog box for the Exchange IMAP4 service to enable the service on my Exchange 2003 computer. POP3 and IMAP4 are listed in Services as Microsoft Exchange services. NNTP is simply listed as Network News Transfer Protocol.

FIGURE 14.1
Using the General property page of the Properties dialog box for the Microsoft Exchange IMAP4 service to enable the service

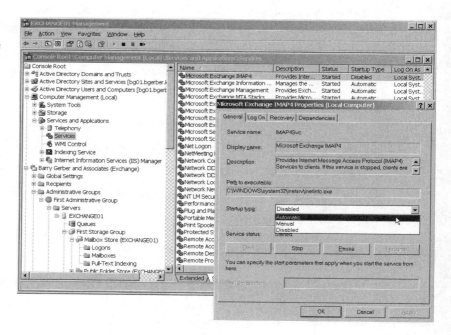

Computer and networking managers are constantly worrying about system uptime, and for good reason. Their jobs depend on reliable, available systems. You can do several things to ensure that your Internet virtual servers remain up and running 24 hours a day. You can manually monitor the services using the monitoring tools that I talked about back in Chapter 12, "Managing the Exchange Server Hierarchy and Core Components," and then do what you can to expediently restart stopped services.

You also can supplement manual monitoring with a server-based self-monitoring system based on features of the Windows Server 2003 operating system. To do this, follow these steps:

1. Find and right-click the service in the `Computer Management\Services and Applications\Services` container. This opens the Properties dialog box for the service (see Figure 14.2).

FIGURE 14.2

Using the Recovery property page of the Properties dialog box for the Microsoft Exchange IMAP4 service to set actions to be taken if the service is no longer running

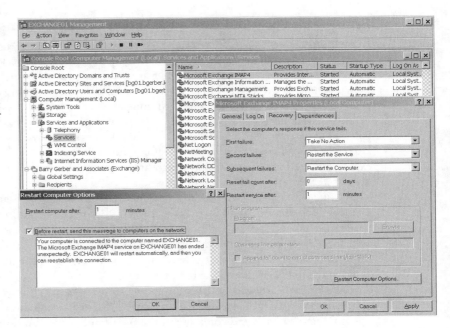

2. Tab over to the Recovery property page of the dialog box. You can use the Recovery page to tell the computer to do anything from attempt to restart the virtual server service to restart itself. As you can see in Figure 14.2, you can specify a different action for each of three successive recovery events. You can also set other parameters, including a message that is sent to users informing them when a restart is about to occur.

WARNING *Be careful about automatic restarts. They can be traumatic not only for users, but also for you. Unless your Exchange server is isolated and difficult to attend to in person, rely on other alternatives, for example, the Exchange server monitors that I discussed in Chapter 12.*

If you don't want to offer one of the Exchange services discussed in this chapter, you either need to leave it disabled or disable it. To disable an enabled service, on the General property page of the Properties dialog box for the service (see Figure 14.1, shown earlier), click Stop to stop the service and then select Disabled from the Startup Type drop-down list. You can reset the Startup Type to Automatic anytime if you decide that you want to offer the service to your users.

NOTE *You can pause, stop, and start a virtual server that supports POP3, IMAP4, HTTP, NNTP, or SMTP services by right-clicking the virtual server in Exchange System Manager and selecting Stop, Pause, or Start. However, this isn't a good way to turn off a service. The service will remain stopped until you restart it, assuming that you didn't set restart parameters for the service on the Recovery property page of the Properties dialog box for the service (see Figure 14.2, shown earlier). However, the service will start right back up when the computer is rebooted.*

Front-End/Back-End Exchange Server Configurations

In multiserver Exchange 5.5 environments, accessing POP3, IMAP4, and HTTP services could be a royal pain. Generally, users had to point their e-mail and web browser clients to the Exchange server that contained their mailboxes, so there was no way to provide a single fully-qualified e-mail server domain name or web server URL that worked for everyone in an organization. Instead, you had to give each user the specific fully-qualified domain name or URL for the Exchange server where their mailboxes were stored. And, if you added or removed a server or moved a mailbox to a different server, you had to give the user a new e-mail server domain name and web server URL. Additionally, in Exchange 5.5, all communications took place between the client and server. All servers had to be exposed to the Internet. And, if a client wanted Secure Sockets Layer (SSL) encryption and decryption, the Exchange server had to do it.

Starting with Exchange 2000, all that changed. You can configure an Exchange 2003 server to act as a front-end server that all users contact for POP3, IMAP4, and HTTP services. The front-end server then acts as a proxy (intermediary) server for requests from the user's client to the back-end Exchange server that contains the user's mailbox. The front-end server also acts as the intermediary for information returned from the back-end server to the user's client. There is no direct interaction between the user's client and the back-end server.

Users are authenticated on the front-end server using Basic (clear text) Authentication. This is the default, and you can't change it. That way, any POP3 or IMAP4 clients and web browsers will work. For front-end-to-back-end communications, you can use Basic Authentication or Integrated Windows Authentication. I talked quite a bit about these authentication alternatives in Chapter 13, "Managing Exchange 2003 Internet Services."

Exchange Server 2003 front-end/back-end topologies have two other advantages. A back-end server placed behind a firewall offers another level of security for Exchange servers. Additionally, front-end servers can offload SSL encryption and decryption from back-end servers. You can optionally use SSL encryption/decryption with all of the Exchange Internet services that I discuss in this chapter. When a client requests SSL encryption/decryption, your front-end server performs these tasks for back-end servers, letting back-end servers focus their energies on Information Store access. I will discuss SSL security and its implementation in Chapter 18, "Exchange Server System Security."

The front-end server's Information Store can remain, but Internet clients do not access it. For better performance, Microsoft recommends eliminating unnecessary components such as storage groups and routing groups, and disabling unnecessary services on front-end servers such as the Information Store service.

Of course, front-end servers make sense only in multiserver Exchange environments with sufficient resources to dedicate a computer to front-end services. If you have but one Exchange server, you don't need to worry about front-end services, unless you want to reduce SSL message encryption/decryption loads on the server.

Enabling a front-end server is easy. Find and right-click the server in Exchange System Manager, and select This Is a Front-End Server from the pop-up menu. (This option is available only when there are at least two Exchange servers in your Exchange organization.) Next restart the server. After it is up and running, remove all private and public stores.

At this point, we've installed only one Exchange server in our organization, so we can't implement a front-end/back-end server system right now. Just keep this very nice and most user/administrator-friendly Exchange 2003 enhancement in mind as you read through this section. In the next chapter, "Installing and Managing Additional Exchange Servers," we'll get into implementing a front-end/back-end system.

Managing Post Office Protocol Version 3 (POP3) Messaging

Exchange Server includes full support for POP3. POP3 is a simple but effective way for a client to pull mail from an e-mail server. There's no fancy support for access to folders other than your Inbox or all the fine bells and whistles that you find in the Outlook 200x clients. However, if you're looking for a simple lightweight client that can function readily over the Internet, POP3 isn't a bad choice.

NOTE *IMAP4 is implemented in Exchange Server 2003 in much the same way as POP3. I'll cover IMAP4 in the next section. I strongly suggest that you read this section even if you're not planning to implement POP3, though, because in the section on IMAP4, I'm going to discuss only the areas where POP3 and IMAP4 differ.*

POP3 Setup: The Exchange Server Side

When you install Exchange Server, a default POP3 virtual server is installed. After installation (and assuming that you want to support POP3 e-mail client access to your Exchange information store), your job is to decide whether you need to change a set of default parameters to customize your POP3 environment to the needs of your organization and users.

You customize POP3 default parameters at the server level. You can override some POP3 defaults at the individual mailbox level.

SETTING UP POP3 AT THE SERVER LEVEL

The first step in setting up POP3 for your server is to find the Protocols container for your server (see Figure 14.3). The Protocols container includes six protocol containers. Five of these are Internet protocols. We worked with SMTP in the last chapter. Exchange Server uses the X.400 protocol for some internal communications and it can be used to connect to external X.400-oriented e-mail systems. We'll cover the other protocols in this chapter. In addition, we'll talk about the Lightweight Directory Access Protocol, which is no longer an Exchange server component—it's part of Windows Server 2003, but it is such a key piece of the electronic messaging puzzle that it deserves coverage in a book on Exchange server.

FIGURE 14.3

The server Protocols container and its six protocol subcontainers with the HTTP, IMAP4, NNTP, POP3, and SMTP default virtual servers shown

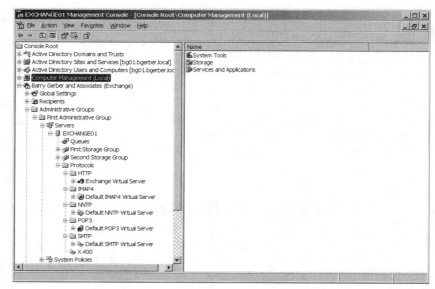

NOTE *I'm not going to extensively discuss the Default POP3 Virtual Server Properties dialog box, and I'm going to include screen shots of dialog box property pages only when required for clarity. Why? Well, as I noted previously, Microsoft used the SMTP virtual server model to implement POP3 services. I already discussed SMTP virtual servers in Chapter 13. So, I just want to talk here about what's unique in relation to POP3 virtual servers. I'll discuss the POP3 virtual server property pages and call your attention to the appropriate explanatory text and figures in the section "Setting Up and Managing SMTP" in Chapter 13.*

Right-click Default POP3 Virtual Server, and select Properties to open the Properties dialog box for the default POP3 virtual server (see Figure 14.4). Except for the absence of the Message and Delivery property pages and the presence of the Message Format and Calendaring property pages, the Properties dialog box for POP3 virtual servers looks a lot like the Properties dialog box for SMTP virtual servers (see Figure 13.4, back in Chapter 13). Let's look at each property page in turn.

General

This page looks much like the General page for an SMTPVS, as shown in Figure 13.4 in Chapter 13. You can link the POP3 virtual server to all unassigned IP addresses or to a specific IP address. You can also set advanced properties for your connection using the Advanced dialog box (see Figure 13.5 and related text in Chapter 13). On the POP3 Advanced dialog box, the SSL Port field replaces the Filter Enabled field. The SSL port supports the encrypted transfer of logon information and messages between your Exchange server's POP3 virtual server and its clients. The SSL port is set automatically. SSL requires the use of security certificates on your Exchange. I discussed certificates in Chapter 13 and will discuss them further in Chapter 18.

As with SMTP virtual servers, you can also limit the number of connections to your POP3 virtual server and set the number of minutes after which an inactive POP3 client connection times out and is disconnected. I suggest that you leave the default number of connections, which is no limit. Monitor POP3 activity with Windows Server 2003's performance tool (Start ➤ All Programs ➤ Administrative Tools ➤ Performance). If you see heavy POP3 activity, start by limiting the number of connections to some number less than that shown by the Performance tool. The default timeout setting of 10 minutes is really about as low as you should go. Idle clients really don't require much of your server's resources. Don't depend on timeouts to help you much with load problems.

TIP   *You can manage connections to POP3 virtual servers using the Current Sessions subcontainer of the POP3 virtual server container. Within this subcontainer, you can view and terminate connections. As you know from Chapter 13, this feature is also available for SMTP services. It is also available for IMAP4 and NNTP services.*

Access

The Access property page is the spitting image of the SMTP virtual server Access property page, shown in Figure 13.7 in Chapter 13, except that it doesn't include the Relay button because message relaying is a unique feature of SMTP hosts. The Authentication dialog box, also shown back in Figure 13.7, doesn't include the anonymous authentication option because we're talking here about somebody's private mailbox, not a public SMTP host. What is called "Integrated Windows Authentication" for SMTPVSs (see Figure 13.8 in Chapter 13) is called "Simple Authentication and Security Layer" for POP3. It's pretty much the same thing. The Authentication dialog box also lacks the TLS (advanced SSL) encryption option. You set up SSL for POP3 on the server side by installing a key certificate using the Certificate button in the Secure Communication area of the Access property page. You don't have to mark any of the check boxes.

You manage SSL in exactly the same way for IMAP4 and NNTP clients as you do for POP3 clients.

Message Format

You use the Message Format property page to set default message-encoding parameters and the type of character set to be used in messages, and to tell Exchange Server whether to send messages in Exchange's rich-text format. Except for two differences, the POP3 Message Format property page looks just like the one for SMTP virtual servers shown in Figure 13.17 in Chapter 13. The Apply Content Settings to Non-MAPI Clients field and the MIME and non-MIME character-set fields, neither of which makes sense for a POP3 server, are absent on the POP3 Message Format property page. As you'll see in the next section, "Customizing POP3 Support for a Mailbox," you can change the defaults that you set here on a mailbox-by-mailbox basis.

Calendaring

The Calendaring property page, shown in Figure 14.4, is new to Exchange Server 2003. It allows you to set up parameters for dealing with Outlook meeting request messages. Outlook users can invite others to meetings. Meeting requests are special e-mail messages. When users view them in Outlook, they can accept or decline meetings. Appointments for accepted meetings can be automatically scheduled in a user's Outlook calendar. Standard POP3 clients don't have the features required to make all of this work.

FIGURE 14.4

The Calendaring property page of the Default POP3 Virtual Server Properties dialog box

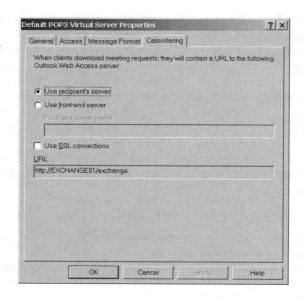

You use the Calendaring page to set up parameters that enable POP3 user meeting-request functionality. Basically, this functionality is enabled using Outlook Web Access (web access to Exchange mailboxes). When a meeting notice is viewed in a POP3 client, the message includes an attachment. When you open the attachment, you see a form that looks like an Outlook meeting-acceptance message. Users can perform most meeting request response functions with this interface, including clicking an Accept or Decline button. As you can see in Figure 14.4, you can specify whether users should be directed to the URL for their own Exchange server or to the URL for a front-end server that directs them to their own Exchange server. If you choose to set a front-end server, you enter its URL in the Front-End Server Name field. You can choose to use Secure Sockets Layer security for the OWA connection. The URL field contains the URL that will be used. It is formed based on the choices that you made earlier in the Calendaring page.

NOTE   *For POP3-based meeting setup to work, users must set their POP3 clients to leave a copy of messages on the server. This is necessary so that the messages can be accessed later when an OWA client is used to respond to a meeting notice. I'll show you how to leave a copy of a message on a server in a bit.*

NOTE   *POP3 clients (and IMAP4 clients, for that matter) pull incoming messages from POP3 (IMAP4) servers. However, POP3 and IMAP4 servers do not provide outgoing messaging services for their clients. SMTP hosts provide this service. In the last chapter, I talked about how Exchange 2003 SMTP virtual servers can provide outgoing SMTP host services (relay services) to Internet e-mail clients such as POP3 and IMAP4.*

CUSTOMIZING POP3 SUPPORT FOR A MAILBOX

To customize POP3 support for a specific mailbox, follow these steps:

1. Find and right-click the user in `Active Directory Users and Computers\Users`, and then select Properties from the pop-up menu. This opens the Properties dialog box for the user.

2. Tab over to the Exchange Features property page (see the left side of Figure 14.5). You can enable or disable POP3 for the mailbox by clicking the Enable and Disable buttons. The protocol is enabled by default.

3. To set different parameters for this mailbox, click POP3 and then click Properties to open the Exchange Features dialog box, shown on the right side of Figure 14.5. In this figure, I changed the default Provide Message Body as HTML to Both. Now messages sent from the mailbox will be in both plain text and HTML format.

FIGURE 14.5

Using the POP3 Exchange Features dialog box to manage POP3 properties for a mailbox

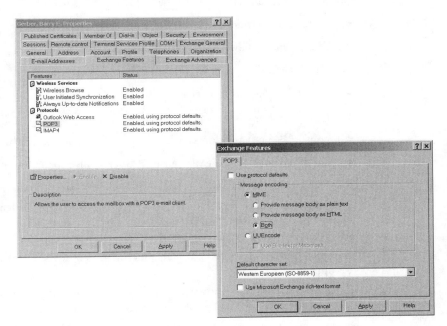

You've seen all the options on the POP3 Exchange Features dialog box, and you should be clear on what they are and when you might want to change them. So, that's all for managing POP3 at the mailbox level.

POP3 Setup: The Client Side

I've always thought of POP3 clients as one of life's little miracles. You set some basic parameters and tell the client to check for mail on your POP3 server, and your mail shows up. I'm sure that building sophisticated POP3 servers and clients is quite a task, but using them is a snap. Let's get a client configured so that you can experience the miracle.

START WITH MICROSOFT'S OUTLOOK EXPRESS CLIENT

Although you can use any POP3-compliant Internet mail client to access your Exchange Server's POP3 server, you'll find that Microsoft's Outlook Express client is not only one of the best, but it's also enabled to support all the Internet protocols that I cover in this chapter. I strongly suggest that you use the Outlook Express client for the exercises in this book, even if you plan to use another one later.

The Outlook Express client comes with Microsoft Internet Explorer version 4 and above. You install IE with Windows. You can download the latest version of IE from Microsoft's website, www.microsoft.com.

GETTING CONNECTED TO AN EXCHANGE SERVER–BASED POP3 SERVER

First you need to set up your POP3 client to connect to an Exchange Server–based POP3 server. Before you start, you need to gather the following information:

- Name of the sender to be displayed in the From field of POP3 messages

- Your Windows 2003 account logon user name

- The password for your Windows 2003 account

- Your Exchange mailbox alias name

- Your Windows 2003 or pre–Windows 2000 domain name

- Your POP3 e-mail address, which is your Exchange Server Internet mail (SMTP) address

- The IP address or name of your POP3 server (for incoming messages)

- The IP address or name of your SMTP server (for outgoing messages)

Let's take a look at how each of these is used to set up a POP3 client. As we move along, note the other options on the various wizard pages you see. Your users might need an alternative to the ones we use here, for example, a dial-up modem connection.

1. Open Outlook Express 6, which comes with Windows 2003. The New Connection Wizard opens.

2. On the second wizard page, select Connect to the Internet. The next page, shown in Figure 14.6, offers a number of options for connecting.

3. For this chapter, we'll connect directly over our LAN. So, select Connect Using a Broadband Connection That Is Always On. The next wizard page warns you that your broadband connection should be configured and ready to use.

4. Click Finish to bring up the Internet Connection Wizard.

As you can see in Figure 14.7, the first thing you need to do on the Internet Connection Wizard is to enter the name of the sender that will be displayed in the From field of each message that you send. I've cleverly chosen Barry Gerber. Click Next, and you're asked to enter your Internet e-mail address (see Figure 14.8). This is the Internet address for your Exchange server mailbox. Mine is bgerber@bgerber.com.

FIGURE 14.6

Selecting the manner in which the Outlook Express POP3 client will connect to the Internet

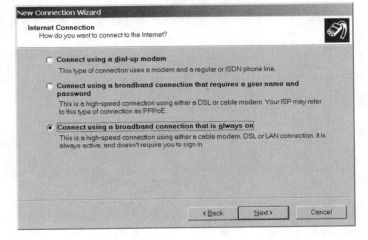

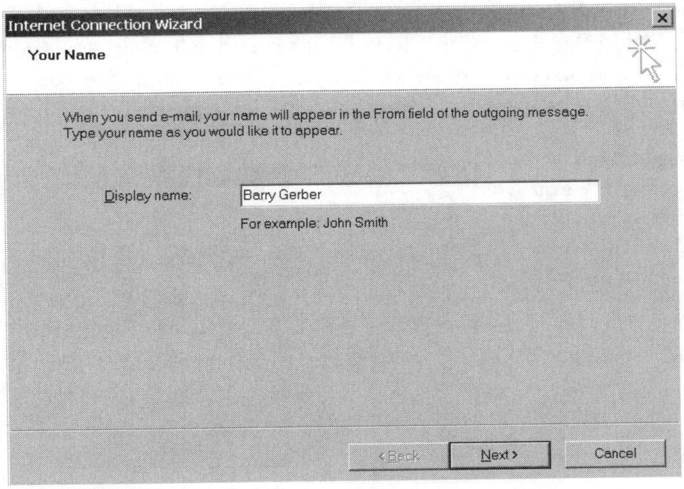

FIGURE 14.7

Entering a name to be displayed in each sent message as the message's sender

FIGURE 14.8
Entering the SMTP e-mail address for an Exchange mailbox

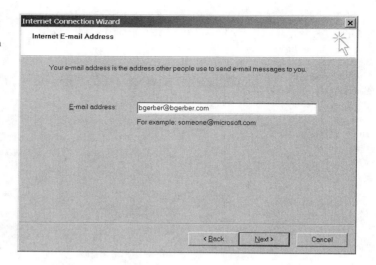

Click Next to select the kind of incoming mail server that you're setting up an account for (POP3 or IMAP4) and to enter the names of the servers that will handle incoming and outgoing mail for your client (see Figure 14.9). Your incoming mail server name is the IP address or Internet domain name of the Exchange server where your mailbox resides. POP3 server services must be running on this server. Your outgoing mail server name is the IP address or Internet domain name of a server running SMTP mail services, a server that can and will relay (send) your mail out to the Internet for you. Although you could use any SMTP mail server that allows you to relay outgoing messages through it, your best bet for this chapter is your Exchange server.

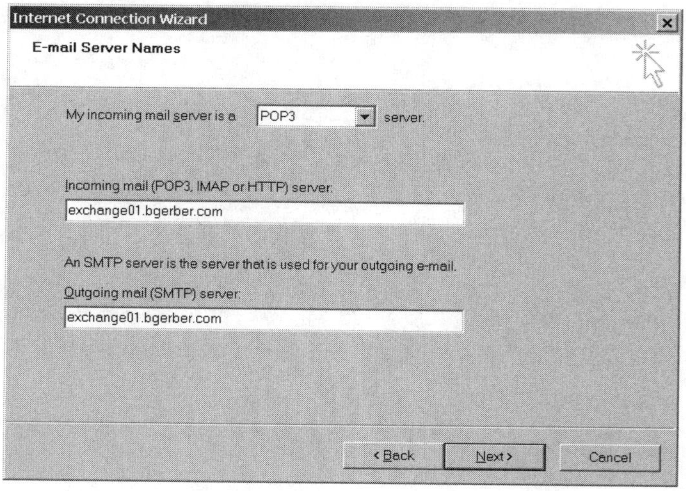

FIGURE 14.9
Selecting an e-mail server type (POP3 or IMAP4) and entering e-mail server names

Note in Figure 14.9 that I've entered the fully-qualified domain name for the Exchange server `exchange01.bgerber.com` that runs both POP3 services and Windows 2003 SMTP virtual services. You can use a different name for the SMTP server side of things, for example, I could have used `mail.bgerber.com`. Just be sure to register the name with whoever provides your public DNS services.

In Figure 14.10, I've moved on to the next Internet Connection Wizard page, where I entered my POP account name and password, which are my Windows 2003 logon username and password. It's this simple if you've accepted the default when mailbox-enabling your Windows 2003 account and allowed your mailbox alias to be set to the same value as your logon username. If your Windows 2003 logon username is different from your mailbox alias, you need to enter your POP3 username in the following format: ***Windows_2003_user_account_name\mailbox_alias_name***. You can find your logon account name on the Account property page of the Properties dialog box for your Windows account, which is in the `Active Directory Users and Computers\Users` container. Your mailbox alias is on the Exchange General property page of the same dialog box.

FIGURE 14.10

Entering information to log on to a POP3 mailbox

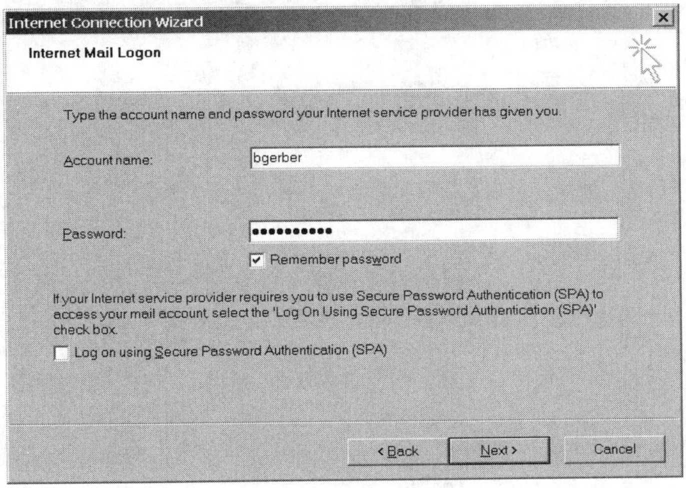

Secure Password Authentication (SPA) refers to a set of authentication protocols, any one of which can add a level of security to clear-text passwords. SPA is not the same as SSL. You don't need it to access your Exchange server's POP3 server, but you can use it to enhance security.

Click Finish on the last wizard page. Notice that your new account is now listed on the Mail page of the Internet Accounts dialog box (Figure 14.11). Leave the dialog box open; we'll get back to it in a minute.

TIP *You might need to set up another type of connection, for example, a modem link. To do so, choose Tools ➢ Options, select the Connection tab, and click Change in the Internet Connection Settings area. This brings up the New Connection Wizard, a page from which was shown earlier in Figure 14.6. Use the wizard to set up another type of connection.*

HOW EXCHANGE SERVER 2003 POP3 AUTHENTICATION WORKS

You're authenticated to access your Exchange mailbox with a POP3 client in a number of ways. First, Exchange Server attempts to authenticate your use of your mailbox just as it would if you were using a standard Messaging Application Programming Interface (MAPI) Outlook client. That is, it attempts to authenticate you through the Windows 2003 security system. It needs to find your Windows 2003 domain and account name, and to validate that you've entered the correct password for that account. To speed up the authentication process if your Windows 2003 system includes a large number of domains, you can add the name of the domain where your Windows 2003 account resides in the following format: *Windows_ 2003_domain_name\POP3_account_name* (for example, bgerber.com\ bgerber). Next Exchange Server needs to check to be sure that your Windows 2003 account is authorized to access the mailbox. Finally, it must verify that your mailbox is enabled for POP3 services.

FIGURE 14.11
A newly created e-mail account is displayed in the Mail page of the Internet Accounts dialog box.

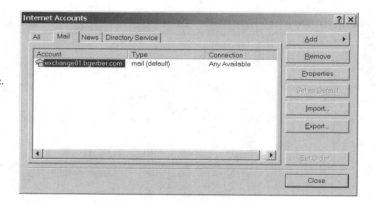

OTHER POP3 CLIENT SETTINGS

Various POP3 clients enable you to set a range of other parameters. One of the most important involves whether you leave copies of your messages on the POP3 server. To better understand this option, you need to understand that POP3 clients download each message that is on the server. If you don't leave copies of messages on the POP3 server, they aren't available when you access them with a different client on the same or a different computer.

Your POP3 server is also your Exchange server. If you don't choose to leave a copy of all messages downloaded by your POP3 client on the server, you won't be able to access them with another POP3 client or a MAPI Outlook client such as Outlook 2003. Whether you leave copies depends on how you work. If you're going to work from one place with the POP3 client, you can suck all your messages down into that client and deal with them there. If you're going to use a POP3 client when you're away from the office and an Outlook client when in the office, you'll want to be sure to leave a copy on the server. Also, remember that you need to leave copies of messages on your Exchange server if you are going to use the calendaring (meeting request) function of Outlook/Exchange.

To leave a copy of messages on your Exchange server, you need to turn back to the Internet Accounts dialog box that you left open a bit ago (see Figure 14.11, shown earlier).

Highlight the name of your account—mine is `exchange01.bgerber.com`—and click Properties to bring up the (POP3) Properties dialog box, shown in Figure 14.12.

FIGURE 14.12

The (POP3) Properties dialog box, with the Advanced property page displayed

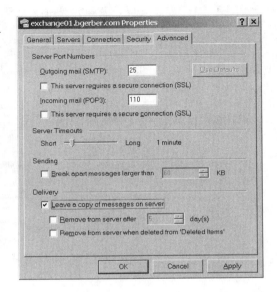

The first three pages of the dialog box contain information that you entered with the Internet Connection Wizard. You use the Security page to install certificates for digitally signing messages and for encrypting them. The Outlook Express docs do a pretty good job of explaining certificates or directing you to web sources for more information. If you've enabled SSL for POP3 on your Exchange server, you tell the POP3 client to use SSL in the Advanced property page of the POP3 virtual server Properties dialog box shown in Figure 14.12. Selecting the option This Server Requires a Secure Connection (SSL) changes the POP3 port from 110 to the secure port 995.

In Figure 14.12, down in the Delivery area, I've told Outlook Express to leave a copy of my messages on my Exchange server when it downloads messages to my POP3 client. Because I want to control what happens to my messages with my regular Outlook client when I'm connected in the office, I didn't check either of the Remove options in the Delivery area.

*TIP   While the POP3 Properties dialog box, shown earlier in Figure 14.12, is open, tab over to the General property page. Use the first field on this page, Type the Name by Which You Would Like to Refer to These Servers, to set a name you like. The name you enter here is displayed in the Internet Accounts dialog box shown earlier in Figure 14.11. As you add accounts, a unique name will help you find the one you need. For example, I renamed my POP3 account **exchange01.bgerber.com POP3** and I will name my IMAP4 account **exchange01.bgerber.com IMAP4** when I create it in the next section.*

I'll leave it to you to explore these and other client settings offered by Outlook Express or your favorite POP3 client.

DID IT WORK?

Figure 14.13 shows the rewards of all the server- and client-side configuring that we've been through. As you can see, we're looking at a message sent to me by Barry Gerber and Associates money maven, Jane Dough. It was sent from her Outlook 2003 client and includes a couple of fonts that I can see in my Outlook Express client because, in this case, my Exchange server's POP3 server is configured to send me messages in HTML format, and my Outlook Express client is configured to show me messages in HTML format (in the Outlook Express main window, choose Tools ➢ Options, tab over to the Read page, and deselect Read All Messages in Plain Text). Very nice.

FIGURE 14.13
Viewing an HTML-formatted message with Microsoft Outlook Express

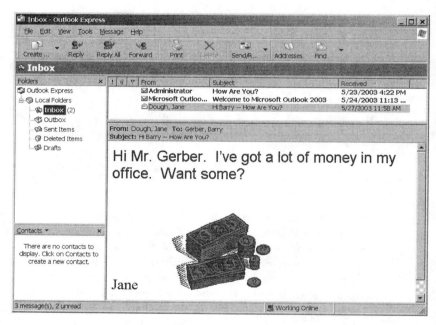

WARNING *Don't confuse the POP3 Sent and Deleted Items folders with the folders of the same name on your Exchange server. The POP3 versions of these folders contain only messages that you've sent and received with your Outlook Express POP3 client. Because POP3 lets you access only your Exchange server–based Inbox, messages sent with or deleted from your standard Outlook client don't show up in your POP3 client's Sent and Deleted Items folders. Additionally, messages sent or deleted from your POP3 client don't show up in your standard Outlook's Sent and Deleted Items folders. If you want that kind of fancy stuff, then consider IMAP4.*

I'm going to leave it to you to figure out how to send and retrieve messages with your POP3 client. It's easy and, hey, what's life without new things to learn?

TROUBLESHOOTING POP3 PROBLEMS

Generally, I've found POP3 to be one of the easiest and least vexing protocols of all to use. If you do have trouble, ensure that your network connection is working. If you can't ping the fully-qualified domain name of your Exchange server, try using the server's IP address; if that doesn't fix things, retrace your steps through the process outlined previously. If you still can't get POP3 to work, there are three major troubleshooting tools for POP3 connections: protocol logging, event logging, and counters for Windows's Performance Monitor. See the Exchange Server documentation for help using these.

Managing Internet Message Access Protocol Version 4 (IMAP4) Messaging

Exchange Server 2003 includes support for the Internet Message Access Protocol version 4 (IMAP4). The major difference between IMAP4 and POP3 is that IMAP4 lets you access messages in folders in your Exchange mailbox and in Exchange public folders by subscribing to specific folders. With both protocols, you can permanently download messages to your local computer and view them. IMAP4 also lets you view messages without permanently downloading them, much like the standard MAPI Outlook client. In fact, the main attraction of IMAP4 lies in its capability to provide users with access to messages in folders in a manner very much like the standard Outlook client. The IMAP4 client isn't an answer to all standard Outlook client users' dreams. For example, it doesn't give users formatted access to their Outlook calendars or journals. For that, you'll have to turn to the HTTP-based Outlook Web Access client discussed in the upcoming section "Managing Hypertext Transport Protocol (HTTP) Web Browser–Based Messaging."

IMAP4 setup is very much like POP3 setup on the server and client sides, so I'll just call your attention to the differences between the two protocols as I discuss IMAP4.

IMAP4 Setup: The Exchange Server Side

As with POP3, we'll look at your IMAP4 configuration options at the server and individual mailbox levels. As I promised earlier, I'll discuss only differences between POP3 and IMAP4 setup.

SETTING UP IMAP4 AT THE SERVER LEVEL

In Exchange System Manager, find the default IMAP4 virtual server in your Exchange server's Protocols container, and double-click it. Select Properties to open the Properties dialog box for the virtual server (see Figure 14.14). Only two of the property pages on the dialog box are significantly different from the POP3 pages. Let's take a quick look at these two pages, the General and Message Format property pages.

General

Just like the POP3 General property page, the IMAP4 General page, shown in Figure 14.14, lets you specify IP addresses, advanced settings, connection limits, and a timeout value for inactive connections for your virtual server. Because of the nature of IMAP4, however, the IMAP General page has two additional options.

FIGURE 14.14

The General property page of the Default IMAP4 Virtual Server Properties dialog box, one of two pages that differ from the pages for POP3 setup

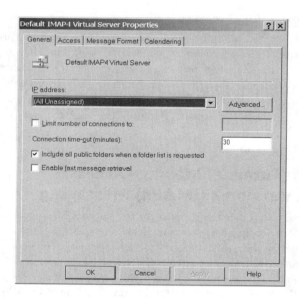

Because they can access all the folders on an IMAP4-compatible server that a user has rights to, IMAP clients need information about available folders. To get this information, the clients make requests for lists of folders. Some IMAP4 clients suffer from performance problems when receiving lists with large numbers of public folders. If you're using such a client, to access your Exchange server, deselect Include All Public Folders When a Folder List Is Requested to eliminate public folders from folder lists sent by the IMAP4 server to the client.

An IMAP4 server also sends information about messages in folders to its clients. To speed up this process, Exchange Server's IMAP4 server can estimate message size. Some clients require exact message size information. If your IMAP4 client is one of these, ensure that Enable Fast Message Retrieval is deselected so that the IMAP4 server sends exact message sizes to its clients.

Message Format

IMAP4 supports only MIME encoding. Unlike POP3, it doesn't support the older UUencode standard. That explains the absence of the UUencode option in the IMAP4 Message Format property page (see Figure 14.15).

CUSTOMIZING IMAP4 SUPPORT FOR A MAILBOX

I've already discussed the IMAP4 options that you can set for mailboxes. So, let me close this section on server-side IMAP4 setup by noting that you can adjust at the mailbox level for some of the differences in IMAP4 clients that I mentioned earlier. For example, if specific users are running a client that demands precise message size information, you can deselect the Fast Message Retrieval option on the mailboxes of those users.

FIGURE 14.15

The Message Format property page of the IMAP4 (Mail) Virtual Server Properties dialog box

IMAP4 Setup: The Client Side

Once you've installed your first Outlook Express 6 e-mail account, you add accounts in a different way. Follow these steps to add POP3 or IMAP4 accounts using the Internet Connection Wizard:

1. Open Outlook Express's Tools menu, and select Accounts.

2. In the resultant Internet Accounts dialog box, tab over to the Mail page and click Add.

3. Select Mail from the little menu that opens. This brings up the Internet Connection Wizard, which takes you through the steps for adding a POP3 or IMAP4 Internet mail account.

With the exception of choosing IMAP4 in the drop-down list on the E-mail Server Names page of the Outlook Express Internet Connection Wizard (see Figure 14.9, earlier), the initial setup of an IMAP4 account is no different from the setup of a POP3 account.

The only difference in the account Properties dialog box is on the IMAP4 property page. As you can see in Figure 14.16, you can do the following:

◆ Set a root folder path for the folders that you access with your IMAP4 client.

◆ Choose whether your IMAP4 client should ask its IMAP4 server to check all folders for new messages.

◆ Specify whether two special folders, Sent Items and Drafts, and their contents are to be stored on your IMAP4 server.

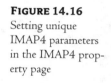

FIGURE 14.16

Setting unique IMAP4 parameters in the IMAP4 property page

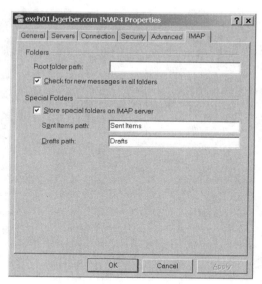

An IMAP4 client can tell an IMAP4 server where in your folder hierarchy it should begin accessing folders. For example, if I entered {**exchange01.bgerber.com**}INBOX in the Root Folder Path field shown in Figure 14.16, Outlook Express would display only my Exchange Server Inbox, and I wouldn't even see any of the other folders on the server. If you want to see all those folders, leave this field blank.

A new message is any message that shows up in a folder, whether it was received there as a new e-mail message or you dragged it to the folder. To be sure that you see new messages in all folders, ensure that the option Check for New Messages in All Folders is selected.

You want to see the same items in your Sent Items and Drafts folders whether you are using your IMAP4 or your MAPI Outlook client. To keep these in sync, be sure to select the option Store Special Folders on IMAP4 Server.

WARNING *A limitation in IMAP4 prevents you from accessing folders with forward slashes (/) in their names. The only fix is to rename any folders with the "offending" character.*

When you're finished setting up your new IMAP4 client, click Finish on the wizard and close the Internet Accounts dialog box. Next you're asked whether you want to download a list of folders on your IMAP4 server. Responding in the affirmative initiates a connection to your IMAP4 server and a download of available mailbox and public folders.

When the download is finished, you'll see a dialog box like the one in Figure 14.17. You use this dialog box to view the folders to which you've subscribed. By default, you have subscriptions to only your Inbox and the Sent Items and Drafts folders. That's why these folders have a little icon in front of them in Figure 14.17. You can always tab over to the page labeled Visible to see the folders to which you have subscribed. To subscribe to a folder, select it, as I've selected Public Folders in Figure 14.17, and click Show. You must click each folder that you want to subscribe to and then click Show. Clicking the folder

Public Folders and then clicking Show subscribes to only the folder Public Folders, not to any of its subfolders. Click OK when you're done, and Outlook Express opens with your IMAP4 connection in place (see Figure 14.18).

FIGURE 14.17
Using the Show/ Hide IMAP Folders dialog box to subscribe to specific Exchange server folders

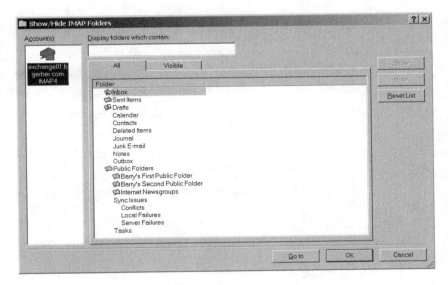

FIGURE 14.18
Outlook Express includes features that make it easy for users to manage their IMAP4 clients.

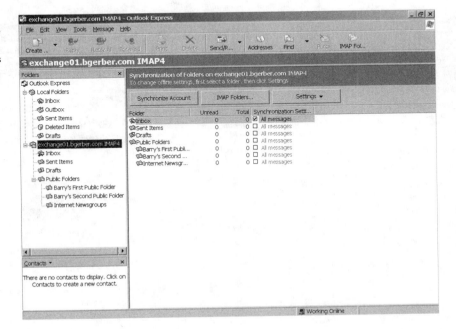

DID IT WORK?

Notice in Figure 14.18 that both my POP3 and IMAP4 client connections are available, with POP3 in the top half of the left pane and IMAP4 in the bottom half of the left pane. If you set up your POP3 and IMAP4 clients in the same copy of Outlook Express, your Outlook Client should look a lot like the one back in Figure 14.18.

Also take a long look at those nice buttons and the drop-down list at the top of the right pane in Figure 14.18. The buttons allow you to do the following:

Synchronize   Initiate a synchronization of folders on your IMAP4 client with folders on your Exchange server (based on parameters set using the Settings drop-down list two buttons to the right).

IMAP Folders   Subscribe to folders on your Exchange server (opens the dialog box shown previously in Figure 14.17).

Settings   Select a synchronization option for each folder (Don't Synchronize, All Messages, New Messages Only, Headers Only).

In Figure 14.19, you can see my favorite message from Jane Dough in all its HTML-enhanced glory.

Now, go ahead and play around in your IMAP4 folders. Note that all the folders are a direct reflection of the folders on your Exchange server. If you have any problems with IMAP4, take a look at the troubleshooting discussion at the end of the section "POP3 Setup: The Client Side," earlier in this chapter.

That's it for IMAP4. I leave the rest to you, your brain, your eyes, and your fingers. Have fun.

FIGURE 14.19

Using IMAP4 client support included in Outlook Express to view a message stored in an Exchange Server Inbox

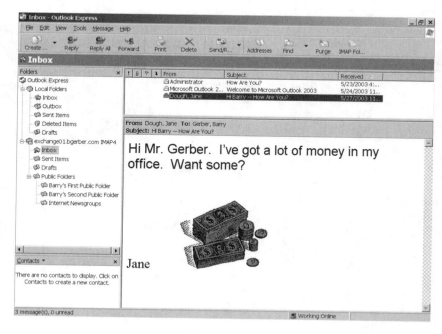

Managing Hypertext Transport Protocol (HTTP) Messaging

Exchange Server 2003's web browser–based technology for accessing mailboxes and other folders is very different from the technology used in Exchange 5.*x* server. This is so even though both the 5.*x* and 2003 versions of the technology answer to the name *Outlook Web Access* (OWA). The good news is that Exchange 2003's new technology is more stable and reliable, and capable of handling larger numbers of users. It also provides a look and feel that is reminiscent of the Outlook 2003 MAPI e-mail client. So far, there doesn't appear to be any bad news.

Exchange 5.5 was cobbled together using Microsoft's HTML-oriented Active Server Pages (ASP) for communications between a client and an Exchange server's Internet Information Server (IIS). Exchange 5.5's OWA used MAPI and Collaboration Data Objects (CDO) to communicate with the Exchange server's information store. In essence, OWA was a part of IIS. MAPI-based access was slow, and it limited the number of users who could use the service at the same time.

Exchange 2003's OWA implementation takes a very different approach. Clients still use HTTP and the much improved ASP.NET service for Active Server Pages functionality to communicate with an IIS. However, the IIS accesses Exchange information stores directly, without help from MAPI or CDO. If the store is on the same server as the IIS, access is direct and fast. If the store is on a back-end computer and the IIS computer is serving as the front-end computer, communications are still quite fast and use HTTP.

OWA 2003 allows users to access their mailboxes and public folders using an Internet browser that is compliant with the HTML 3.2 and JavaScript standards. Both Microsoft Internet Explorer 4 (IE 4) and later and Netscape 4 and later meet this specification. IE 5 and later supports Dynamic HTML and Extensible Markup Language (XML), which allows for faster client-side performance and such very cool features as expandable folder hierarchies, drag-and-drop capabilities, HTML composition, right-click menu options, toolbar tips, and Kerberos authentication. Kerberos authentication is available only when IE 5 or later runs on Windows 2000 or later or on Windows XP.

The newest OWA client doesn't support a number of features included in the standard Outlook client. For example, it doesn't include support for offline use, all of the Outlook journal, moving or copying between private and public folders, and auto-dialing of contact phone numbers. Still, OWA does provide enough functionality to make web browser–based e-mail access both easy and fun. You could do worse than to standardize on OWA as your users' one and only remote e-mail access client. If you can live with its limits, you might even go one step further and make it your local standard as well.

Support for OWA is installed when you install Exchange Server 2003. As with support for other Internet services, OWA is one of the basic Exchange Server 2003 messaging services. Unlike with Exchange 5.5 Server, OWA is installed automatically, and you can't choose not to install it or to install it later.

OWA 2003 USER CONNECTIVITY IS A DREAM

If everything I've said so far about Exchange Server 2003's OWA has failed to excite you, I know that this will. Based on my experience to date, the security and related mailbox access problems that plagued OWA 5.5 have been eliminated in OWA 2003. From a connectivity perspective, OWA 2003 works as advertised right out of the box. For example, there is no need for users to have rights to log on locally for the Exchange server where their mailboxes are located.

Outlook Web Access Management: The Server Side

Outlook Web Access just works. There's nothing you have to do to set it up, although you do have some configuration options at the server and mailbox levels. Unlike the other Exchange virtual servers, you can perform most OWA setup functions with either Exchange System Manager or the IIS administrator. Though this section is officially about managing OWA, you'll find that, unless you need to implement specialized applications based on OWA, you really won't have to do anything other than assuring that Exchange server and IIS server are up and running with all of the required, preinstalled software that comes with Exchange.

SETTING UP OWA AT THE EXCHANGE SERVER 2003 LEVEL

The default HTTP or OWA virtual server is different from other Exchange virtual servers. Look at Figure 14.20 for a graphic indicator of this difference. First, notice that the default HTTP virtual server is labeled Exchange Virtual Server and sports a different icon from the other virtual servers. That's just the cosmetics. You have to administer most of OWA functionality using IIS. The only thing you can administer directly on the Exchange HTTP virtual server is forms-based authentication. Right-click the HTTP server's icon and select Properties from the pop-up menu. On the dialog box that opens, select the Settings page. With forms-based authentication, a special form is sent to the user's web browser that stores authentication information (username and password) in a memory-based local cookie. When an OWA session ends, the cookie is destroyed. Cookies even time out after a certain interval of non-use. Without forms-based authentication, authentication is stored in the browser and remains there as long as the browser is open, meaning that anyone accessing the open browser can access an open OWA session or reopen an old session. So, forms-based authentication provides better security for OWA sessions. When forms-based authentication is set, you can also set a compression level for web pages sent to the browser. Options include None, Low (compress only static pages), and High (compress static and dynamically created pages).

"Huh?" I can hear you saying, "Why can't I manage much of the HTTP virtual server at the server itself?" There is a method to Microsoft's apparent madness, but it will take a while to explain.

FIGURE 14.20

The HTTP virtual server (Exchange Virtual Server) with the General property page of the server's Exchange virtual directory open

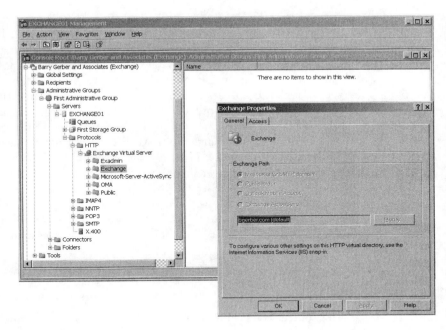

The default HTTP virtual server supports web browser access to mailboxes, public folders, and certain administrative functions as well as remote mobile access on your Exchange server. Take a look at the virtual server's virtual directories in Figure 14.20. They're labeled Exadmin, Exchange, Microsoft-Server-ActiveSync, OMA, and Public. The Exadmin, Exchange, and Public virtual directories represent the three basic types of web browser access that you have to your Exchange server. The other two directories support some neat new remote access features.

Exadmin   Used by Exchange System Manager itself to access mailboxes and public folders (can also be used by custom applications).

Exchange   Provides access to mailboxes.

Microsoft-Server-ActiveSync   Provides support for wireless synchronization of Windows PocketPC-based personal digital assistants (see Chapter 19).

OMA (Outlook Mobile Access)   Similar to OWA, but specifically designed for wireless devices with smaller screens such as PDAs and cellular telephones (see Chapter 19).

Public   Provides access to public folders.

The five virtual directories are not Exchange Server 2003 virtual directories; they are web server virtual directories that are part of the IIS environment. Web server virtual directories map physical directories, shares on other computers, or URLs on a server in such a way that web browser users can include virtual directory names in URLs. For example, to get to an Exchange server mailbox, you use the URL `http://SERVER_NAME/Exchange/MAILBOX_NAME`, as in `http://exchange01.bgerber.com/`

Exchange/bgerber. *Exchange* refers to the virtual directory Exchange. By the way, you can use uppercase or lowercase, so *exchange* is as good as *Exchange*. I'll show you how virtual directories work in the section "Managing OWA at the Internet Information Server Level" later in this chapter.

Although you must manage the default HTTP virtual server using the IIS administrator, you can perform some management tasks on the default server's virtual directories (right-click on a virtual directory and select Properties). At first glance, it might not seem that you can do all that much. As you can see on the right side of Figure 14.20, there's nothing that you can change on the General property page for the virtual directory labeled Exchange. The Exchange Path field was set and locked down on installation of Exchange Server 2003. The Exchange virtual directory is for mailbox access, so the path is set for mailboxes in my domain, bgerber.com. The Exadmin and Public virtual directories are similarly locked down and point to paths that support their functionality. I'll talk more about these paths in the later section "Managing OWA at the Internet Information Server Level."

Tab over to the Access property page of the Exchange virtual directory Properties dialog box (see Figure 14.21). Okay, you control freaks, here's something to control. The Access Control area on the property page lets you select rights that enable or disable what can be done within the virtual directory. Rights include these:

Read   Users can read or download files or directories and their properties.

Write   Users can upload files and their properties, or change content in write-enabled files.

Script source access   Users can access the source code for scripts (read or write permissions must be selected).

Directory browsing   Users can see a list of files and subdirectories, but they must name the file or subdirectory because they do not get full browsing rights to the virtual directory and all its subdirectories.

FIGURE 14.21
The Access property page of the HTTP virtual server's Exchange virtual directory

All access rights shown in Figure 14.21 are granted as they are required for OWA to function properly. Don't mess with them unless you know what you're doing. If you have trouble using OWA, this is not the place to go and start mucking around. See my OWA troubleshooting recommendations later in this section.

The Execute Permissions area determines what a user can do with executable files. Here's a quick look at the Execute Permissions options:

None   Users can access only HTML or image files.

Scripts   Users can access JavaScript, ASP, and other types of scripts.

Scripts and Executables   Users can access scripts and standard executable files (such as `DestroyMyComputer.exe`).

OWA requires only access on the user's part to HTML and image files, so the option None is selected. Most of the work of OWA is done at the server level. Only the usernames under which the server level applications are run need execute permissions greater than None. These permissions are granted on installation of OWA. You don't need to change them.

By default, the Authentication methods for access to virtual directories are basic clear text and integrated Windows authentication. You can enable anonymous authentication—although, as with other OWA parameters, you should do so only if you really know what you're doing—by clicking Authentication and selecting the option from the Authentication Methods dialog box. For more on anonymous authentication and the anonymous account, see the section "NNTP Setup: The Server Side" later in this chapter.

You can change access, execute permissions, and authentication settings in the Public virtual directory's dialog box. However, while you can modify access and execute settings on the dialog box for the Exadmin virtual directory, you can not change authentication settings. Administrative access to mailboxes and public folders is something to be tightly guarded, so no authentication changes are allowed, although, as you'll see in a bit, you can change these settings on the IIS side.

GENERAL RULE: DON'T MESS WITH DEFAULT HTTP VIRTUAL SERVER VIRTUAL DIRECTORY PROPERTIES

I decided to discuss virtual directory properties in this section not because I want you to dash off and change them, but for three other reasons. First, I want to show you what is available in Exchange for accessing and managing HTTP virtual servers and their virtual directories. Second, I want to prepare you for what you're going to see in a minute or so as we move into the IIS side of OWA. And, third, I want you to know something about managing virtual directories in Exchange in the unlikely event that you need to create additional HTTP virtual servers.

Notice that nowhere here do I say anything about changing default HTTP virtual server properties. Unless you know Exchange Server 2003 and IIS like you know the back of your hand, you can only mess things up. For example, granting anonymous access to the Exchange virtual directory moves you pretty close to enabling anyone to access any mailbox on your Exchange server.

CUSTOMIZING OWA SUPPORT FOR A MAILBOX

You have only one configuration option at the individual mailbox level. You can disable OWA for a mailbox. By default, OWA is enabled.

MANAGING OWA AT THE INTERNET INFORMATION SERVER LEVEL

Now let's look at HTTP virtual server management through the IIS manager. If you're working on your Exchange server, you can find the IIS administrator snap-in in the container `Computer Management (Local)\Services and Applications\Internet Information Services (IIS) Manager.` You can also find the snap-in by choosing Start ➢ All Programs ➢ Adminstrative Tools ➢ Internet Information Services Manager. If you want to manage your Exchange server's IIS from another computer that is running IIS, you can add the Internet Information Service snap-in to your MMC and then connect to your Exchange server's IIS. To do this, right-click Internet Information Service and select Connect from the pop-up menu. Then enter the name of your Exchange server in the resultant Connect to Computer dialog box. And, of course, you can add a Computer Management snap-in to your MMC for your Exchange server.

Figure 14.22 shows a basic view of my IIS administrator. Notice the five virtual directories Public, Exchange, Exadmin, OMA, and Microsoft-Server-ActiveSync. These are the same virtual directories that you saw in Exchange System Manager under the default HTTP server.

The right pane in Figure 14.22 shows the mailboxes that have been created on my Exchange server either by the system or by me. If the right pane for your Exchange virtual directory is blank, that's because you didn't map a drive letter to the Installable File System share. I showed you how to do that in Chapter 12. If you didn't map a drive letter, don't worry about it at this point. My goal here is to show you how IIS and Exchange OWA are interlinked. You don't need the drive mapping to see that.

FIGURE 14.22

An Exchange HTTP virtual server's virtual directories, as seen in the Internet Information Services plug-in

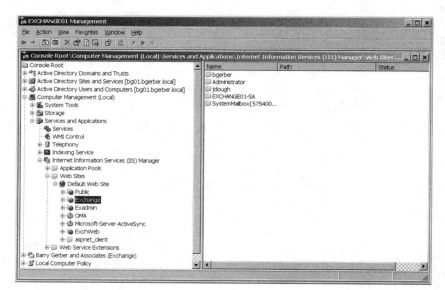

In Figure 14.23, you can see an expanded view of two of the OWA virtual directories, the Public and Exchange directories. Notice all the stuff that's in those directories. It's everything you'd see if you looked in the Information Store on your server using Exchange System Manager. That shouldn't come as too much of a surprise, given that these virtual directories are designed to provide web browser access to the Information Store.

FIGURE 14.23

An expanded view of an Exchange HTTP virtual server's virtual directories

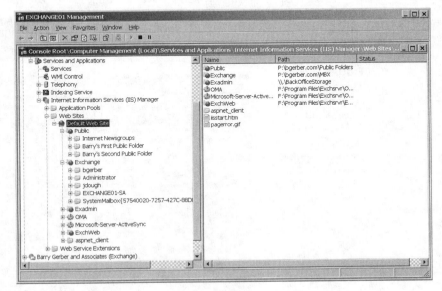

Figure 14.23 makes it easier to see why `http://exchange01.bgerber.com/exchange/bgerber` takes me to my mailbox via my web browser. In a similar vein, `http://exchange01.bgerber.com/public/barry's first public folder` lets me access my first achievement in public folder creation.

NOTE   Notice the virtual directory labeled ExchWeb in Figures 14.22 and 14.23. That's where key OWA support files reside. You don't have to worry about it; I just want you to know what it's for because its name implies that it has something to do with Exchange Server.

Okay, now let's look at the properties for these virtual directories. I'm going to move pretty quickly through these properties because there's a lot more here than an Exchange administrator needs to worry about and because Windows 2003 IIS management is the stuff of long and winding books. If you want to get into IIS management, you'll find just what you're looking for in *Mastering Windows Server 2003*, by Mark Minasi, Christa Anderson, Michele Beveridge, C.A. Callahan, and Lisa Justice (Sybex, 2003).

Let's open the Properties dialog box for the Exchange virtual directory. Right-click the virtual directory labeled Exchange, and select Properties. In Figure 14.24, you can see how, on the Virtual Directory property page, the virtual directory name is tied to a physical directory on an Exchange server. If you mapped a drive to the virtual directory, you should see that the local path points to the physical directory on your Exchange server. In my case it is `P:\bgerber.com\MBX`. See the Local Path field in Figure 14.24. If you didn't map a drive, then you should see something like `\.\BackOfficeStorage\<Your_Domain>\MBX`, where `Your Domain` is the name of your Windows 2003 domain. Though the names differ a bit, the drive mapping and the BackOfficeStorage mapping point to the same physical place on your Exchange server's hard disk.

FIGURE 14.24
The Properties dia-
log box for the Ex-
change virtual
directory, with its
Virtual Directory
property page open,
as seen in the Inter-
net Information Ser-
vices snap-in

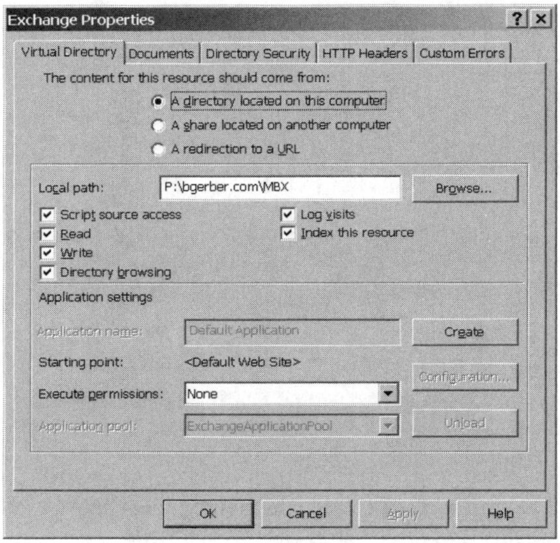

It should come as no surprise that the virtual directory Public ties to the physical directory `P:\<Your Domain>\Public Folders` or to `\.\BackOfficeStorage\<Your_Domain>\Public Folders`. The virtual directory Exadmin ties to `\.\BackOfficeStorage`, or, if you have a drive mapping, to `P:\bgerber.com`, the root of my Exchange server's mailbox and public folder store.

Except for a few fields, the rest of the Virtual Directory property page should look familiar to you. It includes the access control and execute permissions that you saw on the dialog box for this virtual directory in Exchange System Manager (see Figure 14.21, shown earlier). Yep, you can set these properties here or in Exchange System Manager. Authentication settings aren't on this page; they're over on the Directory Security property page. That's also where you enable SSL encryption.

Each virtual directory and subdirectory that you see in the Internet Information Services snap-in has a Properties dialog box just like the one back in Figure 14.24. Just for fun, you might want to roam around the IIS snap-in and check out the permissions that are granted and the directory map-pings for some of the virtual directories.

Outlook Web Access (HTTP) Setup: The Client Side

Client-side setup is a breeze. Just fire up your web browser and specify that you want to connect to the IIS or front-end server that supports your Exchange server plus/exchange. I use the URL `http://exchange01.bgerber.com/exchange` to connect.

When you run IE 6 on Windows 2003 and you're logged in to the Windows 2003 domain/account that has access to your Exchange mailbox, you're automatically authenticated for access to your Exchange Server 2003. The Exchange user interface opens right up. If this is not true, you'll see the Enter Network Password dialog box, shown in Figure 14.25; I've entered my user logon name and my Windows 2003 domain separated by @ (`bgerber@bgerber.com`). I've also entered my password. As long as my logon name is the same as that of my mailbox, entering the previous URL works fine. If the two were not the same, then I would need to add a forward slash and the name of my mailbox to the URL, such as `http://exchange01.bgerber.com/exchange/gerber`, if my mailbox alias name was gerber, but my logon name was bgerber.

FIGURE 14.25

Logging in to an
Exchange mailbox
using the Enter
Network Password
dialog box

In Figure 14.26, I'm using the Microsoft Internet Explorer web browser to look at my favorite message from Jane Dough, complete with HTML text formatting. Notice the Options button on the left side of Figure 14.26. You can use it to set up an out-of-office message; set messaging options such as playing a sound when mail arrives and inserting a signature at the end of each message; set spell-checking options; set e-mail security using S/MIME; filter SPAM messages; set time and date formats; set calendar and contacts options; and recover deleted items. And, that Rules button lets you set rules for handling incoming messages just as with MAPI versions of Outlook.

The Calendar and Contacts folders and buttons, shown in Figure 14.27, let you work with your Exchange server–based calendar and contacts almost as if you were using a standard MAPI Outlook client. Figures 14.27 and 14.28 offer graphic proof that OWA really supports these two key Outlook/Exchange Server features. You can even check the availability of those you want to include in a meeting just as you can with the standard Outlook client.

Just to be sure you're clear on what's happening, check out Figure 14.29, which shows the contact that I just created using OWA in the standard Outlook 2003 client. Fantastic!

FIGURE 14.26
Viewing an Exchange message with a web browser

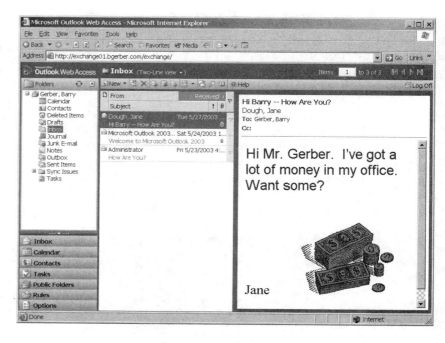

FIGURE 14.27
Creating a new calendar appointment with a web browser

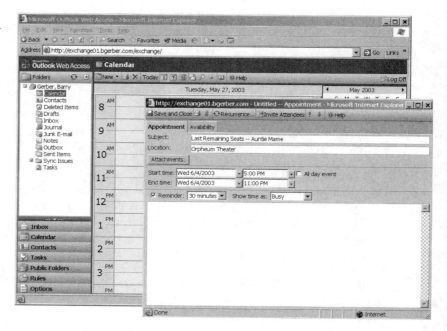

FIGURE 14.28
Creating a new contact with a web browser

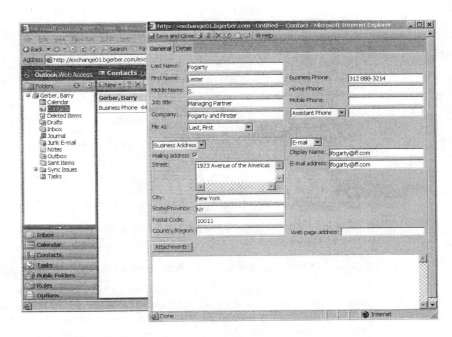

FIGURE 14.29
Viewing a contact created in a web browser using the standard Outlook client

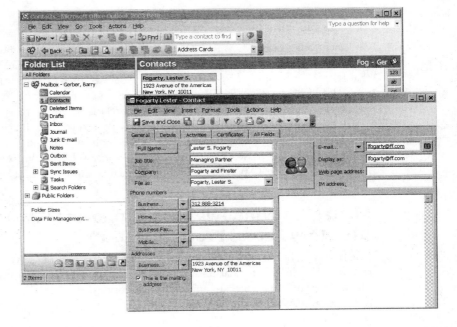

SOME INTERESTING OWA URLS

You can access a number of items on an Exchange server using a set of special URLs. Here are just three of them:

To access the calendar in a user's mailbox `/EXCHANGE_SERVER_NAME/exchange/MAILBOX_NAME/calendar`

Example: `/exchange01.bgerber.com/exchange/bgerber/calendar`

To start composing a new message in a user's mailbox `/EXCHANGE_SERVER_NAME/exchange/MAILBOX_NAME/?Cmd=new`

Example: `/exchange01.bgerber.com/exchange/bgerber/?Cmd=new`

To open a public folder `/EXCHANGE_SERVER_NAME/public/PUBLIC_FOLDER_NAME`

Example: /exchange01.bgerber.com/public/barry's first public folder

---

A NEW ERA FOR EXCHANGE-ORIENTED WEB APPLICATION DEVELOPERS

Although it's beyond the scope of this book, I must say something about the fantastic new programming options enabled by Microsoft's exposing Exchange Server 2003's Information Store through the Windows 2003 file system and the Web. Using a variety of built-in and custom file system, HTML, and other commands, it's possible to program sophisticated custom applications with third-party products and proprietary products ranging from Microsoft Word to Visual Basic and C++.

TROUBLESHOOTING OUTLOOK WEB ACCESS

As I mentioned earlier, OWA 2003 is a stable, reliable, and pretty much maintenance-free product. I encountered only one problem when attempting to use OWA on a Windows 2003 server. I found that IE 6 is, by design and by default, a tightly locked-down piece of software. I was able to get OWA to work fine by dropping both Internet and Intranet security settings from High to Medium, depending on whether I was accessing my Exchange server from the Internet or on an intranet.

One other piece of advice: If you can't seem to get to your Exchange server, the problem might be with DNS name resolution. Try pinging your server by its fully-qualified domain name at a command prompt. If that doesn't work, try the server's IP address. Until you fix any DNS problems you might have, you can access OWA by using a URL such as this one: `http://192.168.1.123/exchange`.

Managing Windows 2003 Support for the Lightweight Directory Access Protocol (LDAP)

The Lightweight Directory Access Protocol (LDAP) is a client/server protocol that lets you browse, read, and search for information stored in an electronic directory. It was developed at the University of Michigan to allow access to an X.500 directory using TCP/IP without the overhead required by the original X.500 Directory Access Protocol.

Microsoft's first implementation of LDAP was in Exchange Server 5. LDAP services were implemented to provide access to the Exchange directory, which, of course, served as the model for Windows 2000's and then Windows 2003's Active Directory. So, it should come as no surprise that today LDAP services are central to Windows Server 2003 and Active Directory. As I pointed out in Chapter 3, "Two Key Architectural Components of Windows Server 2003," LDAP is one of the four naming conventions used in Windows 2003. Key tools for access to Active Directory by administrators and developers rely on LDAP services and protocols. LDAP support is installed when you install Windows 2003.

From a messaging standpoint, LDAP plays a key role. The Exchange 2003 Active Directory Connector, used to migrate from Exchange 5.5 to Exchange 2003, communicates extensively using LDAP. An LDAP interface is used to select filtering rules that define Exchange recipient policies. LDAP is also important in migrations from other messaging systems to Exchange Server.

From an electronic messaging perspective, LDAP clients and Windows 2003's LDAP server work together to give users access to e-mail addresses and other information independently of the standard MAPI Outlook client. This allows POP3, IMAP4, and OWA clients to look up e-mail addresses almost as easily as if they were using the standard Outlook client, no matter where on the Internet or an intranet they happen to be.

Windows Server 2003's LDAP server accesses Active Directory, which, as I'm sure you're aware by now, contains, among other things, user-related data attributes such as recipient display names, phone numbers, and e-mail addresses. Upon request, the LDAP server returns directory data to LDAP-compatible clients. Server-to-client data transmissions are limited by the user authentication rules and directory attribute permissions that are in place for the LDAP server on your Windows Server 2003.

LDAP Setup: The Server Side

You can set up LDAP at the server level in three different areas:

- Set limitations.
- Hide Active Directory attributes from users.
- Create and modify users, distribution groups, and contacts.

I'll discuss each of these in turn.

SETTING LIMITATIONS

LDAP is chock full of limitations. As with POP3, IMAP4, and OWA, these limits help you control computer and network resource usage. You can set limits on such things as connections to the LDAP server, the number of active queries at any given time against the server, how long a query can take, and the maximum size of a returned results set.

Server-side support for POP3, IMAP4, and OWA is a piece of cake when compared with the same thing for LDAP. At this writing, the tools for accessing and managing LDAP security and other settings are, to put it mildly, cryptic.

You don't manage LDAP limits and other attributes in Exchange System Manager. Instead, because LDAP is a Windows 2003 service that accesses Windows 2003's Active Directory, you have to manage it in Windows 2003. There is no simple MCC snap-in that you can use to view and change LDAP server properties. You have to edit Active Directory entries directly, using a program such as Active Directory Service Interface (ADSI), which I discussed in the "Setting the Default Format for Display Names" section in Chapter 11, "Managing Exchange Users, Distribution Groups, and Contacts."

Figure 14.30 shows just how deeply you have to dig into Active Directory with ADSI to find and modify LDAP's administrative limits. How do you modify a specific limit? Why, it's simple: Just delete the old one and add a new one. Yuk!

Because of these complexities and the dangers of editing the Active Directory schema without a complete understanding of what you're doing, and because LDAP is a Windows 2003 component, I'm going to forgo discussing LDAP limits setup here. Instead, I'm going to direct you to a very helpful book on Active Directory and LDAP: Microsoft Consulting Services's *Building Enterprise Active Directory Services, Notes from the Field* (Microsoft Press, 2000). This book, which is out of print but available used from vendors such as Amazon, rings true because it's based on real-world experiences. Chapter 5, "Designing a New Exchange 2000 System," should prove especially helpful for those responsible for LDAP configuration. Don't worry that the book isn't about Windows 2003's active directory. You should gain enough of an understanding about Active Directory and its modification from the book to handle any differences in Windows 2003's Active Directory. Of course, you should always test Active Directory modifications in a safe test environment before moving on to a production Windows 2003 environment.

FIGURE 14.30

Using the Active Directory Service Interface (ADSI) to view LDAP administrative limits

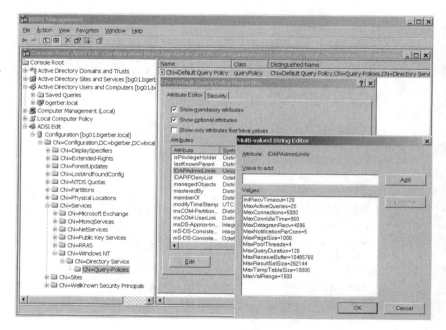

HIDING ACTIVE DIRECTORY ATTRIBUTES FROM USERS

Hiding Active Directory object attributes, such as the telephone numbers of all Windows 2003 users, is even more challenging than messing with LDAP limitations. In fact, it's so challenging that I'm going to punt and defer to someone far more knowledgeable about Active Directory security than I am: Alistair Lowe-Norris. He has written a book with Robbie Allen on Active Directory that picks up where most others leave off, *Active Directory, 2nd Edition* (O'Reilly and Associates, 2003). His Chapter 10, "Active Directory Security: Permissions and Auditing," brings together theory, concept, and practice in a masterful way. You're in good hands with Alistair.

TIP   In relation to this and the previous section, keep your eyes open for better Active Directory management and editing tools from Microsoft and third-party vendors. It shouldn't be too long before we see them.

CREATING AND MODIFYING USERS, DISTRIBUTION GROUPS, AND CONTACTS

This one's easy. As you already know, you create and modify mailbox-enabled users, mail-enabled users, distribution groups, and contacts using the Active Directory Users and Computers snap-in. You should be an old hand at using this snap-in by now because you've been using it since way back when you installed Windows 2003. For a refresher, you can check out Chapter 11.

In Figure 14.31, I'm adding some information to my own user object. You'll see some of it again when we look at information about me in Active Directory using an LDAP client.

FIGURE 14.31

Adding information about a user in Active Directory Users and Computers

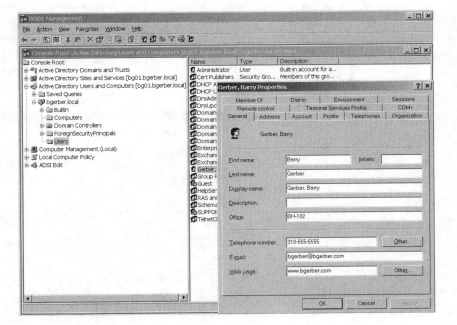

WINDOWS 2003'S LDAP SERVER IS NOT THE RIGHT CHOICE FOR A PUBLIC LDAP SERVER

By default, Windows 2003's LDAP server does not allow anonymous access. That makes good sense because we're talking here about the crown jewels of the Windows 2003 operating system. You certainly could manipulate Active Directory permissions to make anonymous access less of a threat, but it would be a significant challenge. If you're thinking about operating a public, anonymous access LDAP server, Windows 2003 is not the way to go. There are other LDAP servers out there, including the one that comes with Microsoft's Commerce Server (www.microsoft.com/commerceserver), that are more appropriately designed for public LDAP access.

LDAP Setup: The Client Side

In this section, I'll show you how to set up and test LDAP functionality in Microsoft Outlook Express.

SETTING UP AN ACCOUNT FOR AN LDAP DIRECTORY SERVICE

We need to set up an account to access Windows 2003's Active Directory using LDAP. So, select Accounts from Outlook Express's Tools menu. When the Internet Accounts dialog box opens, tab over to the Directory Service page. As you'll notice, Microsoft has already set up a bunch of LDAP servers for you to play around with. If you installed Internet Explorer and Outlook Express on a computer that is a member of your Windows 2003 domain and if you are logged in to your domain, you should see a directory service called Active Directory. You can use this service immediately. It points directly to the Global Catalog for your Windows 2003 Active Directory, using a special non-SSL-TCP port number of 3268 instead of the standard port 389 for non-SSL access or 636 for SSL access.

Now let's install our new directory service client, one that connects to our LDAP server using standard port numbers. On the Internet Accounts dialog box, click Add and select Directory Service from the menu that pops up. This starts our old friend, the Internet Connection Wizard, shown in Figure 14.32.

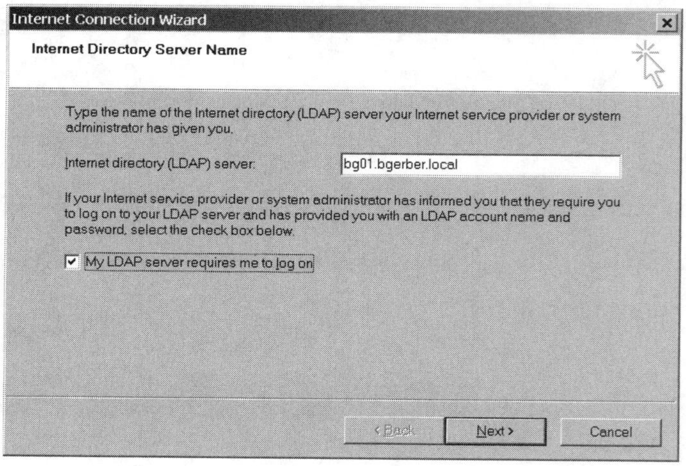

FIGURE 14.32

Adding a new directory service with the Internet Connection Wizard

Fill in the IP address or domain name of your LDAP server (domain controller), and check the box labeled My LDAP Server Requires Me to Log On. Remember, whatever name you use for your LDAP server must be registered in the DNSs you use to resolve the server's name. I used `bg01.bgerber.local` here. I could also have used `bg01.bgerber.com`, if that name was registered in an appropriate set of DNSs.

The next wizard page lets you enter an LDAP account name and password and indicate that you need to log on to your LDAP server using Secure Password Authentication (see Figure 14.33). Enter your Windows 2003 user logon name and password, and check the secure password authentication box. By default, Windows LDAP service requires secure logons. If you don't check the box, you won't be able to connect to your LDAP server.

On the next wizard page, be sure that Yes is checked in the field Do You Want to Check Addresses Using This Directory. Outlook Express will now check your LDAP server to find e-mail addresses associated with partial names typed into the To or Cc fields of a new message. You'll see how that works in just a bit. When you're done with this page, click Next and then click Finish to complete configuration of your new directory service.

As with POP3 and IMAP4 accounts, you manage your LDAP account by opening the Properties dialog box for the account. You need to open the Properties dialog box to set at least one additional parameter for your LDAP client. To do so, in Outlook Express, select Tools ➢ Accounts, and then find and double-click your new directory service. You don't need to change anything on the General property page, so tab over to the Advanced page, shown in Figure 14.34.

As you can see, you need to enter some information in the Search Base field at the bottom of the property page. The search base is the location in the directory where a search begins. We want to start at the top of the directory at the domain level. So, first you need to break your Windows 2003 domain name into separate components at every dot (period). My domain name is `bgerber.local`, so I wind up with two components, `bgerber` and `local`. Then, starting with the leftmost component in your domain name, enter **DC=** followed by the name of a component. Separate components by commas. As Figure 14.34 shows, `DC=bgerber,DC=local` is my Search base entry.

FIGURE 14.33

Entering information required for logging on to a directory server

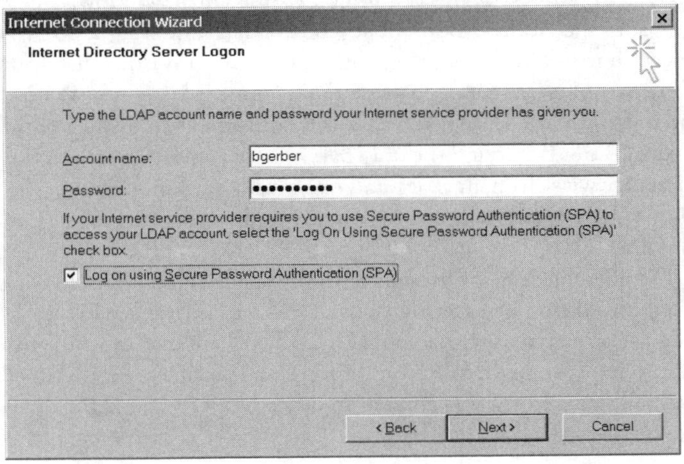

FIGURE 14.34
The Advanced property page of the Properties dialog box for a newly created directory service

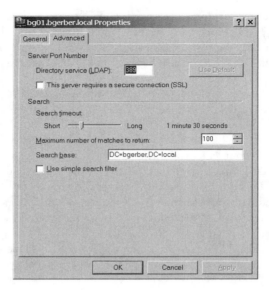

This is important: You must enter Active Directory names here. If I enter **com** after the second **DC** and my domain is **bgerber.local** in Active Directory, directory searches will fail. This would be so, even if I had registered **bgerber.com** in an appropriate set of DNSs. DNS entries help find the LDAP directory server. They don't override settings in Active Directory for the Windows 2003 domain to be searched at the request of an LDAP client.

DID IT WORK?

First, let's try to find a name in Active Directory using Outlook Express's basic Find function; track along in Figure 14.35. In the Outlook Express main window, click Address Book on the toolbar. This brings up the Address Book dialog box. Click Find People to bring up the Find People dialog box. Select your LDAP account from the Look In drop-down list at the top of the dialog box, and type all or part of a name in the Name field. You can type in just your first name here. Click Find Now, and in a flash, the LDAP service returns information on all matching entries in Active Directory. In Figure 14.35, I've found the only Barry in my Active Directory. If there were five people in my Active Directory with the name Barry, all five would have shown up in the results box. The search works for all unhidden users, distribution groups, and contacts in the Active Directory Users and Computers container.

Double-click one of the entries in the results box. I double-clicked Gerber, Barry. This opens the Properties dialog box for my Active Directory entry (see Figure 14.36). Notice the information on the first property page. As you'll remember, I entered most of it back in the section "Creating and Modifying Users, Distribution Groups, and Contacts" earlier in this chapter. Some of the information in Figure 14.36 was entered in other property pages for my Active Directory user object.

FIGURE 14.35
A list showing the
one user who meets
the criteria for an
LDAP search using
the Outlook Express
client's Address
Book

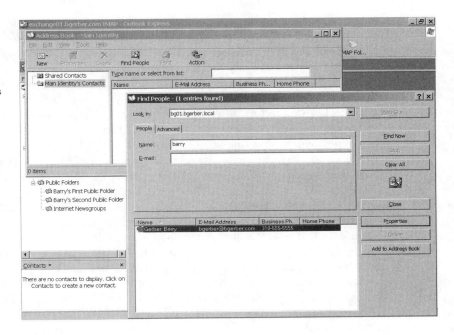

FIGURE 14.36
Use the Properties
dialog box for a re-
turned directory
entry to view other
information about
the Active Directory
object.

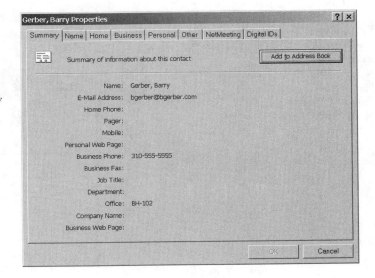

All those tabs on the dialog box open worlds of possibilities. If information is available on an LDAP server, it will be displayed in the appropriate fields in each of the six pages of the dialog box. The Home and Business pages have room for lots of contact information, including business and personal website URLs. The Other page provides space for general notes and information about group memberships. The NetMeeting page is for information used in initiating network-based conferences, and the Digital IDs page contains information about such IDs associated with this person.

This LDAP directory searching stuff is a lot of fun, especially on a cold winter night. If you're connected to the Internet, try some of the directory services that Microsoft provides with Outlook Express. See if you can find an old acquaintance, friend, or enemy.

Okay, now let's try composing a new message and using LDAP to find the e-mail addresses of the folks we want to send it to. Click Compose Message on the Outlook Express toolbar. This opens a new message window (see Figure 14.37). Type all or part of the name of one of your Exchange Server recipients into the To or Cc field, and click the Check [Names] icon on the message's toolbar. Assuming correct spelling and such, the name that you typed in should be resolved into an e-mail address by your LDAP client and server. You know that an address has been resolved when the name is underlined in the To, Cc, or Bcc field, as it is in Figure 14.37. If you want to know more about this recipient, double-click the resolved address to open a Properties dialog box similar to the one shown back in Figure 14.36.

Go ahead and send your message. If it got through to the recipients that you intended, all is well in the world, and you can take a break or move on to the next section on the Network News Transfer Protocol and the newsgroups that it supports. If nothing has worked, make sure that your network connection is working, ensure that your network security settings are in sync on your LDAP client and server, and, if that doesn't help, go back over the previous steps. If things are still not working, take a look at the troubleshooting section in the discussion of POP3.

FIGURE 14.37

A new message with an e-mail address that has been resolved using LDAP against Windows 2003's Active Directory

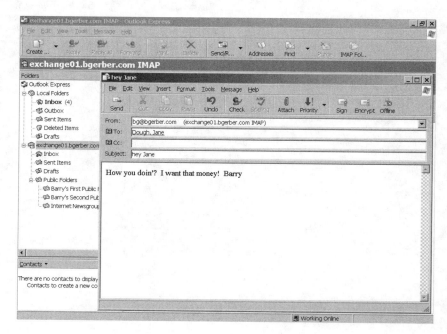

NOTE *If you don't need to send or receive messages and just want to browse Active Directory with an LDAP client, the Address Book is available in on Windows 2003 computers as a separate application. To run it, select Start ➢ Programs ➢ Accessories ➢ Address Book. The stand-alone Address Book application uses the same settings as the Outlook Express Address Book, so you don't have to set up LDAP server access twice.*

Managing Exchange Server Support for the Network News Transfer Protocol (NNTP)

Aren't these advanced Internet protocols fantastic? Well, we're not finished with these wonders yet. We've got one more to go, the Network News Transfer Protocol (NNTP). Many people think of NNTP as the protocol that supports those wild, woolly, and sometimes useful public Internet newsgroups that are home to everything from the infamous and sometimes offensive .alt groupings to the fairly staid German-language .zer groupings. However, my goal in this section is to show you how to implement newsgroups internally. I'll spend a little time talking about linking up to external groups and making all or some of them available to your Exchange users, but I really want to show you how you can use newsgroups and the threaded conversations that they enable to improve productivity in your organization.

Like SMTP, NNTP is a Windows 2003 service based in IIS. Unlike SMTP, you must consciously choose to install NNTP when or after you install Windows 2003. When you installed the Windows Server 2003 that was to become your Exchange server back in Chapter 7, "Installing Windows Server 2003 as a Domain Controller," you might remember that I asked you to be sure that NNTP was selected for installation.

As with SMTP services, when you installed Exchange, it sort of hijacked NNTP and brought it under its control. In this case, in addition to adding the NNTP virtual server to its Exchange System Manager Protocols container, Exchange installed a public folder called Internet Newsgroups, which is the default home for NNTP newsgroups on your default NNTP virtual server. The neat thing about this is that users can view newsgroups with MAPI clients such as the standard Outlook client and or with an IMAP4 or NNTP client.

Exchange public folders aren't the only place you can store newsgroups. Newsgroups can also be stored in the Windows 2003 file system. When newsgroups are stored in the file system, of course, they're not visible as public folders.

When setup is done, your Exchange server's NNTP virtual server acts just like any other NNTP server. Anyone who can get to the Internet Newsgroups public folder by use of the standard Outlook client, the Outlook Express IMAP4 client, or the OWA client can get to the newsgroups on your Exchange server. In addition, your NNTP server fully supports standard newsreader clients such as FreeAgent, WINVN, or the news client built into Outlook Express.

By whatever means users get to your Exchange NNTP server, if they have the rights to do so, they can post new or reply messages to any newsgroup, or they can respond directly to the original sender of a news message by e-mail. Your server sees to it that those messages and postings are available not only locally but also, if you want, to users of the newsgroup outside your Exchange site or organization.

If all this isn't enough, your NNTP server can also feed its newsgroups to other NNTP servers. Couple all this good stuff with the kind of user-friendly interface that you've come to expect from Exchange Server, and you've got it all NNTP-wise. Let's get right to NNTP setup.

NNTP Setup: The Server Side

Unlike most of the other virtual servers that we've looked at, the default NNTP virtual server is chock full of subcontainers whose functions are not obvious from the names of the containers. So, before we look at these containers in more detail, let's start with a quick overview of each. As you read this list, follow along on the left side of Figure 14.38.

Default NNTP Virtual Server Holds subcontainers; supports configuration on Properties dialog box.

Newsgroups Holds some default newsgroups and all the newsgroups that you create for this virtual server.

Feeds Holds links to other NNTP servers that either send newsgroup articles to or receive newsgroup articles from your virtual server.

Expiration Policies Holds policies specifying when articles stored in the file system (not in Exchange public folders) should be deleted from newsgroups managed by your virtual server.

Virtual Directories Holds specifications for other locations (Exchange stores, file system directories, or shares) where newsgroups managed by your virtual server can be stored.

Current Sessions Shows connections to your virtual server and allows for termination of selected or all connections.

FIGURE 14.38
The default NNTP virtual server with its subcontainers and Properties dialog box open

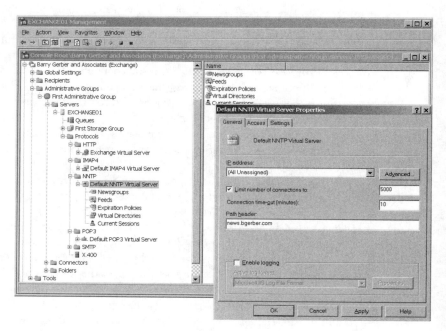

NNTP VIRTUAL SERVER PROPERTIES

As with the other Internet protocols, you can set a range of properties for your default NNTP virtual server. These include general properties, access properties, and a number of other settings. Let's take a closer look at these properties.

General

Open the Properties dialog box for your server by right-clicking it and selecting Properties from the pop-up menu. You can see the dialog box and its General property page on the right side of Figure 14.38.

The only field that you haven't seen elsewhere in this chapter is the Path Header field. You need to enter into this field the fully-qualified domain name of the Windows 2003/Exchange 2003 server that is supporting this virtual server. I entered `news.bgerber.com`, which is associated in an appropriate set of DNS servers with the IP address of my Exchange server using a host record. The path header is included in newsgroup articles from your NNTP server. It's used to prevent the sending of multiple copies of a message (looping) when an NNTP server is connected to other NNTP servers through multiple Internet providers.

Access

As you do with most of the other Internet protocols that we've looked at in this chapter, you use the Access property page of the Default NNTP Virtual Server Properties dialog box to control who can access your server and how they can access it. Figure 14.39 shows the Access page; nothing here should be foreign to you. However, the Authentication Methods dialog box, which you open by clicking Authentication on the Access property page, is a little different. Figure 14.40 shows the Authentication Methods dialog box. First, note that anonymous access is supported for your NNTP server. Most public newsgroup servers allow anonymous access at least to users with IP addresses serviced by the operator of the server. If this is to be an internal newsgroup server, you might want to enable anonymous access. If this is to be an internal server that is connected to the Internet, you'll very likely want to ensure that anonymous access is disabled. As you'll see in a bit, you can control access to newsgroups on the Exchange server side, so enabling anonymous access isn't absolutely necessary. It's just a good idea, at least until you've been able to get more specific newsgroup access controls in place.

The Anonymous button in the Authentication Methods dialog box lets you select the Windows 2003 account that is used to connect to your NNTP virtual server when a user connects anonymously. Clicking the button opens the Anonymous Account dialog box. You use this dialog box to set the name of the account and its password.

As you can see in Figure 14.40, you can set SSL client authentication in the Authentication Methods dialog box. Note that this only covers SSL for client authentication, not encryption of data. As noted earlier in this chapter, I'll talk about all aspects of SSL in Chapter 18.

WARNING *Remember that when you've secured your NNTP virtual server from NNTP clients, you've completed only half the job. If your NNTP newsgroups are stored in Exchange public folders, you also have to secure those folders from users who can access them with standard Outlook clients or IMAP4 or OWA clients. For more on public folder security, see the section "Managing Public Folders" in Chapter 12.*

FIGURE 14.39

The Access property page of the Default NNTP Virtual Server Properties dialog box

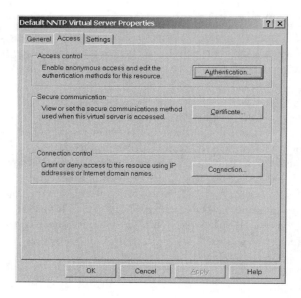

FIGURE 14.40

The Authentication Methods dialog box

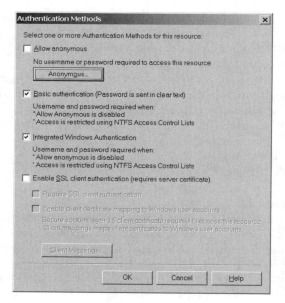

Settings

The Settings property page is heavily laden with property fields, as you can see in Figure 14.41. However, most of the fields on the page are pretty easy to understand and manage. Let's take a quick tour of the Settings property page.

FIGURE 14.41

The Settings property page of the Default NNTP Virtual Server Properties dialog box

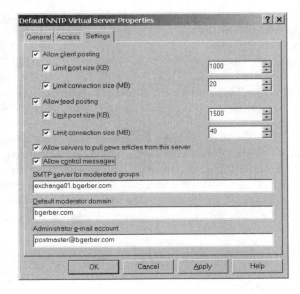

When you allow users to post messages to your NNTP server, you need to set some limits on the largest single article that users can post and on the total size of all articles posted during one session (connection). The defaults of 1MB and 20MB, respectively, are a bit large for my tastes, but I'll leave it to you to determine whether you have adequate bandwidth and disk storage to handle such settings.

Other NNTP servers can be allowed to connect to your NNTP server and feed it news articles. As with user posting, if you select this option, then you can limit the maximum size of any single article that can be posted and the total size of all articles posted during one session.

If you want other servers to connect to your NNTP server and get news articles from it, be sure to check the option Allow Servers to Pull News Articles from This Server. Don't worry that NNTP servers will just start connecting to your server; you still have to create a feed for any pull NNTP server. We'll talk about feeds in the section "Setting Up Feeds to or from Other NNTP Servers" later in this chapter.

Before I explain the Allow Control Messages field, let's talk a little about what control messages are. There are three types of control messages:

Cancel Request from an NNTP client to delete a specific news article

Newsgroup Request, usually from an NNTP server, to create a newsgroup

Rmgroup Request, usually from an NNTP server, to delete (remove) an existing newsgroup

On your NNTP server, there is a newsgroup for each type of control message. Someone must process each control message. If Allow Control Messages is selected, your NNTP server queues control messages and treats them in a way that makes processing easy. If this option is not selected, control messages show up in their respective newsgroups as nothing more than standard news articles. I'll talk a bit more about control messages in the next section, "Managing Newsgroups."

Sometimes you don't want a new article to show up in a newsgroup before someone, a moderator, reviews and approves the articles. You can designate any newsgroup as a moderated newsgroup, and you can specify a different moderator or the same moderator for any moderated newsgroup. New articles are sent to the moderator by e-mail, so you need to set an SMTP server that your NNTP server will use to send articles to the moderator. Back in Figure 14.41, I entered the fully-qualified domain name of my old reliable Exchange server, **exchange01.bgerber.com**.

You can also set a default moderator domain for your NNTP server. This one's a little tricky. When you specify that a particular newsgroup should be moderated, you can specify the e-mail address of the moderator. If you've entered a default moderator domain, as I have in Figure 14.41, and you choose to use the default address, the address is constructed from the default moderator domain that you enter here and the name of the newsgroup. Say there was a newsgroup called Stuff, and I chose the default, the moderator address would be **stuff@bgerber.com**. Of course, I would also have to create a mailbox on my Exchange server with an SMTP address of **stuff@bgerber.com**.

Now that we've got our NNTP virtual server configured, we're ready to tackle newsgroups.

MANAGING NEWSGROUPS

Newsgroup management includes the following:

- Maintaining, creating, and deleting newsgroups
- Creating and using virtual directories
- Setting expiration parameters for news articles
- Administering NNTP server connections
- Setting up feeds to or from other NNTP servers

I discuss each of these tasks in the sections that follow.

Maintaining, Creating, and Deleting Newsgroups

You create, maintain, and delete newsgroups in the Newsgroups container of your NNTP server. You can see the Newsgroups container for my default NNTP virtual server in Figure 14.42. Notice the three special newsgroups for control messages in the right pane. They're created automatically on installation of your NNTP virtual server.

Before I do anything else, let me tell you about the Find Newsgroups dialog box, on the right side of Figure 14.42. You open it by right-clicking your Newsgroups container and selecting Limit Groups Enumeration from the pop-up menu. You use this dialog box to limit the newsgroups displayed in the right pane. Right now, with only three newsgroups, who needs limits? The asterisk in the Newsgroups field of the dialog box ensures that I'll see all newsgroups. But, imagine that I had thousands of newsgroups to manage. Seeing all of them in my Newsgroups container could make it very difficult to find and work with a specific newsgroup. So, I can use the Find Newsgroups dialog box to specify search criteria that show me only certain newsgroups or a maximum number of news-groups. For example, if I entered **control.c*** in the Newsgroups field and clicked OK, I'd see only the newsgroup control.cancel.

FIGURE 14.42

The Find News-groups dialog box

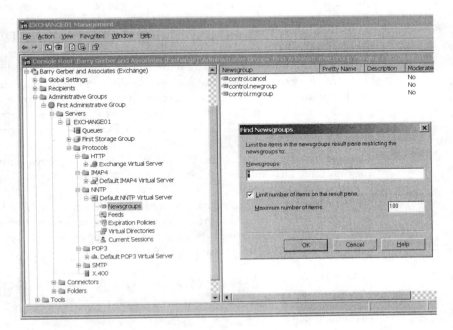

We'll create a new newsgroup in just a bit, but first we need to secure our control message news-groups. We don't want just anyone going into the control message newsgroups and accepting the cre-ation or deletion of groups or the deletion of messages. There are three ways to secure your control message newsgroups:

◆ Set each of the three control message newsgroups as moderated.

◆ Limit access to the newsgroup server where you administer newsgroups.

◆ Set permissions on the directories for the message control newsgroups so that only newsgroup administrators can access the newsgroups.

You can implement any one or all three of these options. I'm partial to the third option because, as you'll see in a bit, it hides the control message newsgroups from the NNTP clients of all but those who need to access the newsgroups. Here's a quick take on each of the three options for restricting access to message control newsgroups.

If the control message newsgroups are set as moderated, messages are e-mailed to each message control newsgroup's moderator for action before they're displayed in the newsgroup. When the mod-erator acts on the messages, the messages disappear from the newsgroup, so there's no way anyone will see them. You can set any newsgroup as moderated by right-clicking it and selecting Properties from the pop-up menu. On the resultant dialog box, select Moderated and set the e-mail address of the moderator.

Controlling access to your newsgroup server works best when anyone who might see the control messages can be trusted to ignore them. Take a look at the earlier section "Access" for your options on access control.

As with the HTTP virtual server, virtual directories on the NNTP server point to physical directories somewhere. The message control newsgroups are stored in a virtual directory named Control. This virtual directory points to a subdirectory of the IIS's Inetpub directory, specifically \Inetpub

Here's how to change permissions on the directory named Control. In Figure 14.43, I opened the Properties dialog box for the directory named Control by right-clicking the directory and selecting Properties from the pop-up menu. Next I gave full permissions on the directory named Control to the Windows 2003 security group, Domain Admins. I clicked Advanced on the dialog box and deselected Allow Inheritable Permissions from Parent to Propagate to This Object. That removed the default permissions that the Windows 2003 groups Anonymous and Everyone had on the directory. That's all there is to it. You don't have to set permissions on the subdirectories of the directory named Control.

Just for the record, I could have created a new Windows 2003 security group just for NNTP administrators and given that group full permissions on the directory named Control. Then I could allow users to administer the NNTP server by adding them to the group. If I did this, I'd still grant full permissions to Domain Admins, just so that they could retain control of the directory.

FIGURE 14.43
Limiting access to the physical directory mapped to the virtual directory for message control newsgroups

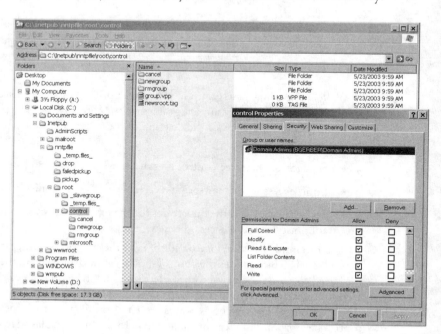

You have one more task to complete before your permissions settings will work. You have to tell your NNTP server that you want to restrict the visibility of the virtual directory named Control. To do this, find and right-click the virtual directory named Control in your NNTP server's Virtual Directory container. Then select Properties from the pop-up menu. The Properties dialog box for the virtual directory opens. Select Restrict Newsgroup Visibility, and click OK.

Okay, we're ready to create a newsgroup. This really is simple. First, right-click on your Newsgroups container and select New ➤ Newsgroup from the pop-up menu. This opens the New Newsgroup Wizard, shown in Figure 14.44. Enter the name you want to use for the newsgroup. Newsgroups are structured hierarchically, from highest to lowest component. Components are separated by periods. In Figure 14.44, I'm creating a newsgroup to hold articles containing discussions about proposals that Barry Gerber and Associates has submitted for funding. As you can see, the newsgroup is named BGA.Discussion.Proposals.Pending.

FIGURE 14.44

Entering a name for a new newsgroup using the New Newsgroup Wizard

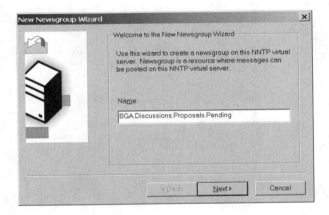

On the next wizard page (see Figure 14.45), you enter a description of your new newsgroup and a pretty name. What's a pretty name? It's the name that's displayed whenever possible for us mere mortals.

FIGURE 14.45

Entering a description and a pretty name for a new newsgroup using the New Newsgroup Wizard

When you're done, click Finish on the last wizard page and take a look at your Exchange System Manager, which should look something like the one in Figure 14.46. Not only should your new newsgroup appear in the right pane of System Manager along with your message control newsgroups, but you should also see a new public folder under Internet Newsgroups (see the lower-left corner of Figure 14.46). If you don't see the new public folder, right-click Internet Newsgroups and select Refresh. That should bring the new folder into view. Notice that while the new public folder has the pretty name you entered for your newsgroup, the newsgroup itself has the ugly name.

FIGURE 14.46

The default NNTP virtual server, with a newly created newsgroup and its supporting public folders displayed

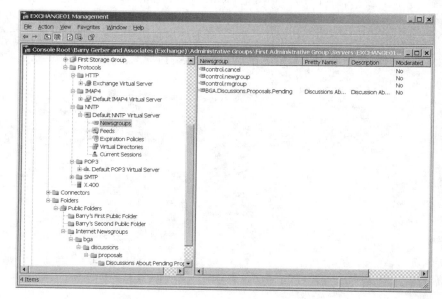

Now I want to make sure that you understand what's going on here. Not only have you created a newsgroup that users can access with NNTP clients, but you've also created a public folder that any user with the right permissions can access as a public folder with a standard Outlook client or any IMAP4 or OWA client. That is very cool.

Just for fun, I added some more newsgroups to the newsgroup hierarchy BGA.Discussion. You can see them in Figure 14.47, along with the public folders created to support the newsgroups. To create each of these newsgroups, I just entered the full newsgroup name that you see in the figure into the Name field on the New Newsgroup Wizard. My NNTP server, with help from Exchange, created the public folder hierarchy.

Deleting newsgroups is very easy. Just right-click the newsgroup and select Delete from the pop-up menu. Although a newsgroup's parallel public folder is created automatically, you must delete the parallel public folder manually. You delete the public folder in the same way as you delete the newsgroup.

FIGURE 14.47

The default NNTP
virtual server, with
several newly created
newsgroups and
their supporting
Exchange public
folders displayed

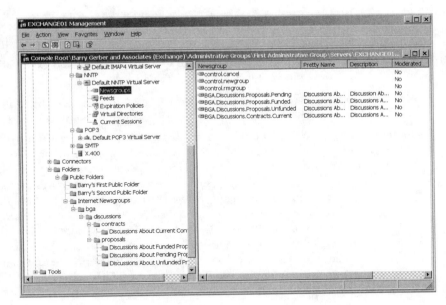

Creating and Using Virtual Directories

Newsgroups and the articles that they contain are stored on virtual directories. Virtual directories can map to an Exchange public folder, a file system directory local to your NNTP server, or a network file share. Double-click the virtual directory named Default in the Virtual Directory container of your default NNTP virtual server. Then click Contents in the directory's Properties dialog box. Notice that the virtual directory named Default is mapped to the Exchange public folder Internet Newsgroups. By default, all newly created newsgroups are stored in that public folder.

Aside from functioning as repositories for the default newsgroup store on an NNTP virtual server, virtual directories enable you to place selected newsgroups on storage media other than the media that contains the server's default public folder store. For example, you can store some newsgroups in the Internet Newsgroups public folder and other newsgroups in directories on one or more disk drives.

There are several advantages and some disadvantages to storing newsgroups outside your Exchange public folder system. On the positive side are these:

- You can offload newsgroups with large numbers of large news articles to disk drives and tape or disk backup units external to your Exchange system.

- NNTP client users see all the newsgroups, whether they're stored in Exchange or on the file system.

- You can still manage your NNTP servers from inside Exchange.

Negatives include these:

◆ You have to back up and restore Exchange-based and file system–based newsgroups separately.

◆ Exchange users with standard Outlook, IMAP4, and OWA clients can see only newsgroups stored inside Exchange public folders.

◆ You have to manage the files that support file system–based newsgroups separately from the public store that supports Exchange-based newsgroups.

Here's how to set up file system–based newsgroup storage using NNTP virtual directories. First, open Windows Explorer. Then create a directory on one of the disk drives on your Exchange server. You can name your directory anything you want and nest it as deeply as you want. In naming your directory, let clarity rule. The subject matter of the newsgroups that will be created in the directory should be clear from the name that you give to your directory. Also, for clarity's sake, I strongly suggest that you name the root of the directory \Newsgroups. I've chosen to name my directory \Newsgroups\BGA\SWDev because I'll be storing newsgroups in this directory that are related to software developed by my consulting group, Barry Gerber and Associates.

Okay, now we're ready to create that virtual directory. Find and right-click the Virtual Directories container for your default NNTP virtual server. Then select New ➢ Virtual Directory from the pop-up menu. This opens the New NNTP Virtual Directory Wizard, shown in Figure 14.48.

FIGURE 14.48

Entering a newsgroup subtree using the New NNTP Virtual Directory Wizard

You enter a name for the root-level of the newsgroup tree that you want to create. You're not going to store anything in a newsgroup with the name that you enter here. You're going to create newsgroups by appending newsgroup names to this root level. I'll show you how in just a minute. As you can see in Figure 14.48, I've entered **BGA.Software** as my root-level newsgroup tree name. Don't forget: no spaces, just periods. You can't enter anything here that would duplicate the newsgroup structure that you already created in the Internet Newsgroups public folder. So, I couldn't enter **BGA.Discussions.Clients** here because I already have a BGA\Discussions tree in my Internet Newsgroups public folder. Getting root levels right is a little tricky. As with almost everything else, practice is the best teacher.

When you're done entering the name of your root-level newsgroup tree, click Next. On the next wizard page (see Figure 14.49), select the File System option. Then on the next page, browse to and select the lowest level of the disk directory that you created above (see Figure 14.50). Click OK and then Finish on the wizard, and you're done creating your virtual directory. Figure 14.51 shows my NNTP virtual server with its new virtual directory, BGA.Software, in place.

FIGURE 14.49

Selecting a path where newsgroup content should be stored using the New NNTP Virtual Directory Wizard

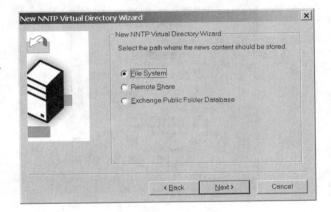

FIGURE 14.50

Selecting the disk directory to which a new virtual directory should be mapped

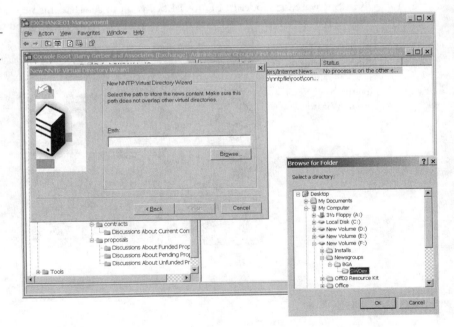

FIGURE 14.51
An NNTP virtual
server with a newly
created virtual direc-
tory

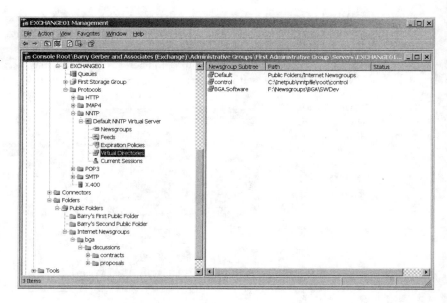

Now you need to create your new newsgroup. In Figure 14.52, I'm creating a newsgroup named
BGA.Software.GS.Code. In Figure 14.53, you can see that this newsgroup will hold discussions
among BGA staff about software that we are developing for a hospital named Good Samaritan.

FIGURE 14.52
Entering a name for a
new newsgroup us-
ing the New News-
group Wizard

FIGURE 14.53
Entering a description and pretty name for a new newsgroup using the New Newsgroup Wizard

FIGURE 14.53
Entering a description and pretty name for a new newsgroup using the New Newsgroup Wizard

Now go back to My Computer, and take a look at the disk directory that you created a bit ago. Notice that it's now got subdirectories for the new newsgroup that you created. My directory is shown in Figure 14.54, with its two new subdirectories, gs and code, which parallel the last two components of the name of the newsgroup that I just created, BGA.Software.GS.Code. The BGA.Software part of the newsgroup name is already taken care of as the newsgroup subtree name associated with the virtual directory.

FIGURE 14.54
Viewing new disk directories created by an NNTP virtual server to support a new file system—based newsgroup

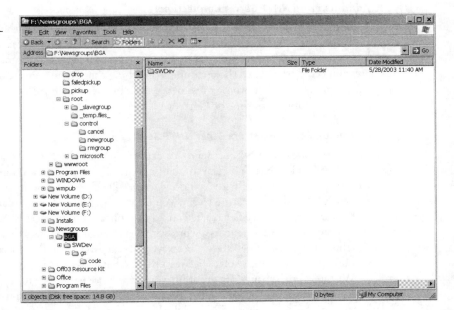

Now click Refresh and look at your Internet Newsgroups public folder. You shouldn't see any subfolders in the folder for the new newsgroup that you just created. That's because this newsgroup's news articles will be stored on the file system, not in your Exchange server's public store.

That's about it for virtual directories. Remember that you can create new NNTP virtual servers and plop their newsgroups anywhere you like in new Exchange public stores, Windows 2003 file systems, or Windows 2003 file shares. You can mix and match these three storage options. The possibilities are endless, although I'm sure your time isn't.

Setting Expiration Parameters for News Articles

If you expect users to add lots of articles to all or some of your newsgroups, you'll want to be sure to set rules for automatic deletion of articles after the passage of a certain amount of time. You set rules for newsgroups stored in public folders differently than for newsgroups stored in the file system.

For newsgroups stored in the Internet Newsgroups public folder, you set the number of days that a news article may remain in a public folder before it's deleted. This is no different from the way you handle autodeletion in any other public folder. For more on public folder item expiration, see the section "Creating and Managing Public Folders," in Chapter 12.

If you're working with newsgroups stored on the file system, you set an expiration policy. You do this in the NNTP virtual server's Expiration Policy container. Just right-click the container and select New ➤ Expiration Policy. Then use the New NNTP Expiration Policy Wizard that opens to set expiration periods for one or more of your newsgroups.

Administering NNTP Server Connections

As with most of the other Internet protocols that I've discussed in this chapter, you manage connections to your NNTP virtual server in the server's Current Users container. You can review and see how many connections there are anytime. You can also terminate connections in this container. Users are connected only when they're doing something that downloads or uploads data. So, if you've got a lot of users who do nothing most of the time but keep their NNTP clients open all day, you won't see tons of connections in the Current Users container.

Setting Up Feeds to or from Other NNTP Servers

Newsfeeds allow one NNTP server to export some or all of its newsgroups and their contents to another NNTP server. You can think of newsfeeds as a newsgroup replication process. The NNTP virtual server that comes with Windows Server 2003 is not newsfeed-enabled. Installing Exchange Server 2003 adds this feature to the Windows 2003 NNTP virtual server.

Historically, newsfeeds have been used to replicate public Usenet newsgroups between news servers around the world. Usenet is a worldwide network of computers that supports sharing of news articles through the use of newsfeeds. However, that doesn't mean that there's no place for newsfeeds that synchronize newsgroups solely between the Exchange servers in your Exchange organization.

Within your Exchange organization, you can not use newsfeeds to replicate newsgroups stored in the Internet Newsgroups public folder. That's because such a replication would have to create another instance of the newsgroup folder, inside the Internet Newsgroups folder, with exactly the same name as the newsgroup that you're trying to replicate. This would violate basic principles of both Active Directory naming and logic, so it can't be done. However, you can use newsfeeds to replicate newsgroups that are stored in virtual directories other than the Internet Newsgroups folder. We created such a newsgroup earlier, and we'll soon use newsfeeds to replicate it on another Exchange server in our organization.

TIP   Although you can't use newsfeeds to replicate newsgroups stored in the Internet Newsgroups folder to other Exchange servers in your organization, you can replicate any newsgroup in the Internet Newsgroups folder as you would any other public folder. For more on public folder replication, see the section "Managing Public Folders" in the next chapter.

Key to setting up a newsfeed is an arrangement with the manager of the NNTP server that has the newsgroups that you want to replicate. You must arrange to either send newsgroup information to or retrieve it from the other server. When that agreement is in place, you can exchange newsgroup information with the other NNTP server within the limits that you and the manager of that server set. We'll explore those limits later in this section.

Newsfeeds are set up between two NNTP servers. A feed must be set up on each server. Exchange Server 2003 supports three different kinds of newsfeeds:

◆   Master

◆   Subordinate

◆   Peer

Master/subordinate newsfeed configurations enable you to distribute the load on a group of NNTP servers. Depending on your needs, you can set up one or more subordinate servers. The master NNTP server can send news articles to or receive news articles from its subordinate servers. The master NNTP server assigns a unique ID to each news article that moves between it and its subordinate servers. The master uses these IDs to keep track of the news articles on each subordinate server. Using information in its news article ID database, the master sends only new news articles to its subordinate servers. Master/subordinate server configurations are generally used inside an organization.

Peer newsfeed configurations usually are used to support the exchange of news articles between two Usenet NNTP servers. IDs are not attached to news articles transmitted between peers. As news articles are received, the peer server adds IDs to them. Armed with its ID database, a peer NNTP server can interact with subordinate servers just like a master server.

The same NNTP virtual server can be a master server or a peer server, but not both. Either a master or a peer server can support subordinate servers. In either case, the effect is the same. Peer and master servers interact with their subordinate servers in exactly the same way, and you set up master/subordinate server relationships in exactly the same way.

I could spend a good deal of time going over the range of possible newsfeed configuration permutations and combinations. Instead, I'm going to focus on a simple scenario and then let you take it from there, setting up whatever peer and additional master/subordinate server configurations you need.

Rather than work with Usenet newsgroup feeds, I'm going to concentrate on setting up a master/subordinate server newsfeed internal to your Exchange organization. This should give you enough exposure to newsfeeds that you can set up a Usenet feed if and when you need one. I'm going to set up newsfeeds to support the master/subordinate server replication of a newsgroup that we created in a new NNTP virtual directory back in the section "Creating and Using Virtual Directories." This isn't a hollow and meaningless exercise. Newsgroup replication using newsfeeds is the only way that you can create a replica of a newsgroup stored in an NNTP virtual directory other than the one where the Internet Newsgroups public folder is stored.

Before we go any further, I have a little secret to tell you: While you weren't looking, I set up another Exchange server, EXCHANGE02. Well, actually, I set it up in the next chapter. Talk about time warps! Anyway, I'm going to use EXCHANGE02 as the subordinate server in my master/subordinate server newsfeed configuration. Don't let your lack of a second Exchange server stop you cold. I suggest that you read through the rest of this section, while newsgroups are fresh in your mind. Then, after you've set up at least one more Exchange server in the next chapter, you can come back and complete the master/subordinate server feed exercise that follows.

Before we start creating newsfeeds, you need to create a new NNTP virtual directory exactly as you did in the earlier section "Creating and Using Virtual Directories." You must create this virtual directory on the server where you want to replicate your newsgroup. For me, that's EXCHANGE02. *This is important: You must create the directory, but you must not create the newsgroup that you're going to replicate.* Your newsfeeds will take care of creating the newsgroup and populating it with news items.

Okay, assuming that you've created your new NNTP virtual directory, we're ready to go. First we need to create a feed to our subordinate server on the server that will function as our master NNTP server. This is the server on which you created your first NNTP virtual directory. For me, that's EXCHANGE01.

To set up a newsfeed, right-click the Feeds subcontainer of your NNTP virtual server and select New ➤ Feed. Then use the resultant New NNTP Feed Wizard, shown in Figure 14.55, to create your newsfeed.

FIGURE 14.55

Entering the name of the remote newsfeed server on the first page of the New NNTP Feed Wizard

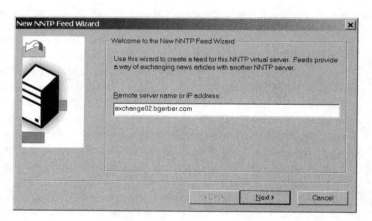

Enter the fully-qualified domain name or IP address of the newsgroup server in the first page of the wizard (see Figure 14.55). You want to enter the name or IP address of the server that will become the NNTP subordinate server for this newsfeed. For me, that's `exchange02.bgerber.com`. Ideally, at this time, your master server should be capable of making a network connection to the slave server. If it can't, when you click Next, you'll see a dialog box telling you so and asking if you want to use the domain name or IP address anyway. If you know that the connection will be in place when you activate your master/subordinate server configuration, click Yes. If not, then your master/slave configuration won't work, but at least you can get some experience setting up a master/slave news-feed configuration. When you're done, move on to the next wizard page.

On this page, you specify the role that the remote server will play (see Figure 14.56). You're creating a newsfeed from what will be your master NNTP server to your NNTP subordinate server. The remote server will be a subordinate server. Select the Subordinate Server option.

FIGURE 14.56

Specifying the role that the remote newsfeed server will play on the second page of the New NNTP Feed Wizard

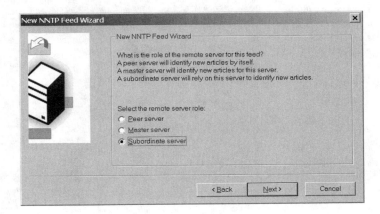

Now you must set the direction of this newsfeed. You do this on the next wizard page. You want your master NNTP server to send news articles to your NNTP subordinate server; this is the master side of the configuration, so you should select Outbound Feed, as I have in Figure 14.57.

FIGURE 14.57

Specifying whether the newsfeed master server will receive (Inbound Feed) or send (Outbound Feed) news articles to its newsfeed slave on the third page of the New NNTP Feed Wizard

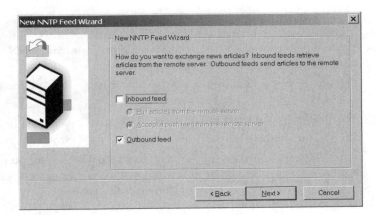

Finally, you must specify the newsgroup(s) to be sent to your slave NNTP server. When you first see the wizard page, shown in Figure 14.58, there's an asterisk in the Newsgroups field. You should delete that entry by selecting it and clicking Remove. Now you need to add an entry for the newsgroup that you want to replicate. In my case, this is the newsgroup `bga.software.gs.code`. Click Add to open the Add Newsgroup dialog box. Enter the newsgroup's name and click OK to go back to the wizard page. Click Finish on the wizard page, and you should see your new newsfeed in the newsfeeds container on the server that is to be the master NNTP server for the newsfeed.

FIGURE 14.58
Specifying which newsgroups will be included in the newsfeed on the fourth page of the New NNTP Feed Wizard

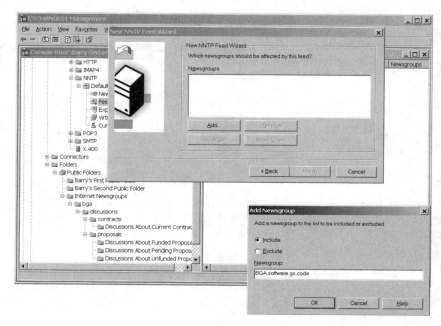

Now you need to create a newsfeed on what will be your NNTP subordinate server. Follow the directions that you used to set up the newsfeed for your master NNTP server, making only the following changes:

1. On the first wizard page, enter the domain name or IP address of your master NNTP server. (Mine is exchange01.bgerber.com.)

2. On the second wizard page, select Master.

3. On the third wizard page, select Inbound.

On the fourth wizard page, do exactly as you did when setting up the same page for your NNTP subordinate server. It should be clear why you filled in the master newsfeed wizard as you did. If not, review the explanatory text at the beginning of this section.

Master servers replicate only when a new news article shows up in a newsgroup, so until you post a news article in a newsgroup, nothing will happen. The master doesn't even send information about the newsgroup itself until a new item appears in the newsgroup, so you won't see the newsgroup on your subordinate server until you post a new article to the group on your master server. I'll show you how to post news articles in the next section, "NNTP Setup: The Client Side."

Now we need to look at the dialog box that you use to manage newsfeeds. Find the newsfeed for your NNTP subordinate server. Remember, it's on your master server, not on your subordinate server. Double-click the newsfeed to open its Properties dialog box. The General property page of the dialog box is shown in Figure 14.59. On the General page, you can see what kind of feed you're working with, enable or disable the newsfeed, modify the name of the subordinate server, and change the TCP port used to link the master and subordinate servers for this newsfeed. Both servers must use the same TCP port.

FIGURE 14.59

The General property page of the subordinate newsfeed, as created on the NNTP master server for the newsfeed

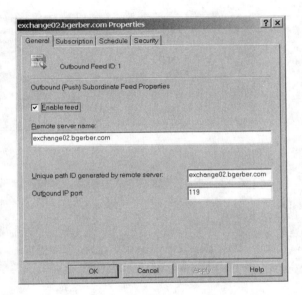

You use the Subscription property page to add and remove newsgroups from a newsfeed. As you can see in Figure 14.60, the page looks pretty much like the New NNTP Feed Wizard page, shown earlier in Figure 14.58. You use this page in exactly the same way to change the newsgroups that will be sent to your subordinate server.

The Schedule property page in Figure 14.61 is a bit deceiving. As I noted earlier in this section, master NNTP servers send new newsgroup information when a new news article appears in a newsgroup, so this schedule isn't for initiating the sending of new news articles. Rather, it's for setting a retry interval and the maximum number of retries allowed, and for indicating when (if ever) the master should stop trying to connect to the subordinate to send queued newsgroup information. The defaults are okay for reliable network connections. For less reliable network connections, however, you should experiment to find a good combination of run interval and maximum number of attempts.

FIGURE 14.60
The Subscription
property page of the
slave newsfeed, as
created on the
NNTP master server
for the newsfeed

FIGURE 14.61
The Schedule prop-
erty page of the slave
newsfeed, as created
on the NNTP mas-
ter server for the
newsfeed

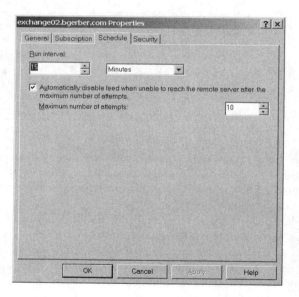

Except for the fact that it's for a subordinate server newsfeed, the dialog box for a subordinate server newsfeed looks pretty much the same as the dialog box for a master server feed. The only major difference is that the Schedule property page is grayed out, which makes sense because the subordinate server isn't doing any sending in the newsgroup configuration that we've set up. Of course, you can set up subordinate server configurations in which the subordinate server sends outbound newsgroup information to a master, such as to provide the master with newsgroup postings made by users to the NNTP subordinate server. As you might expect, the Schedule property page for a subordinate server so configured is not grayed out, meaning that you can set retry interval, maximum retries, and other properties.

That's about all the time we have for newsfeed management. For more information, check out the Exchange 2003 documentation and the book *Managing Usenet,* by Henry Spencer and David Lawrence (O'Reilly and Associates, 1998).

NNTP Setup: The Client Side

If you use the standard Outlook client or a web browser to access newsgroup folders, you don't have to do a thing. You access newsgroup folders just as you'd access any other public folder.

If you use a standard NNTP client such as FreeAgent, WinVN, or Outlook Express, you'll have to do a bit of configuring. You need to enter the Internet domain name or IP address of the Exchange server that supports your NNTP server. You also have to enter the appropriate security information, if required.

Each NNTP client has its own unique user interface, and all of these are pretty straightforward. So, unless you're using Outlook Express, I'll leave it to you to figure out how to set up and use your favorite client.

Here's how to set up a news account in Outlook Express:

1. Select Tools ➤ Accounts. On the Internet Accounts dialog page, click Add and select News from the pop-up menu.

2. When the Internet Connection Wizard opens, enter your name.

3. In the next wizard page, enter your e-mail address.

4. Use the next wizard page to enter the fully-qualified domain name or IP address of your news server; my server is `news.bgerber.com`.

5. If you've not turned on anonymous access to your news server, select My News Server Requires Me to Log On, and click Next.

6. If you don't need to log on to your NNTP server, you're done. If you need to log on, enter your logon name and password on the next wizard page, and select Secure Password Authentication. Secure Password Authentication is required by default. Close the wizard and the Internet Accounts dialog box and you're done.

Next you are asked if you want to view a list of available newsgroups. Answer in the affirmative. Outlook Express's news client then downloads a list of newsgroups, and the Newsgroup Subscriptions dialog box, shown in Figure 14.62, opens. Select the accounts that you want to subscribe to, and click Subscribe. When you're done, click OK and take a look at Outlook Express. Your new news account and the newsgroups that you subscribed to should now show up in the left pane of Outlook Express (see Figure 14.63). Notice in Figure 14.63 how I'm also viewing my Exchange public folder–based newsgroups using my IMAP4 account. Finally, notice that the one newsgroup that isn't stored in my public folders, BGA.Software.GS.Code, shows up in my news account, but not among the public folders in my IMAP4 account. Yahoo! Everything works as advertised.

FIGURE 14.62
Subscribing to news-
groups using the
Newsgroup Sub-
scriptions dialog box

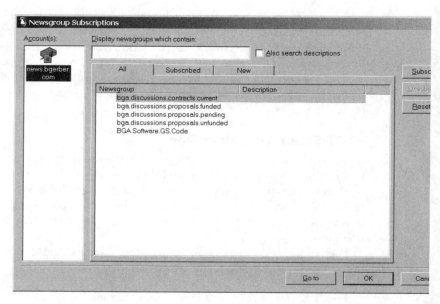

FIGURE 14.63
Viewing news-
groups in Outlook
Express and compos-
ing a news article

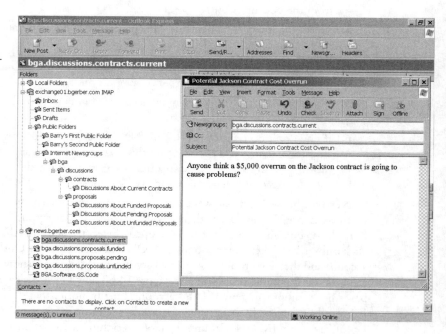

In Figure 14.63, I'm composing a news article that I want to post to the BGA.Discussions.Contracts.Current newsgroup. I just selected the newsgroup and clicked New Post in the top-left corner of Outlook Express. That opened the window that I'm using to compose a message about a cost over-run on a BGA contract. Actually, I'm asking a question that I hope others will respond to. To post the message, I click Send. The message goes into my Outlook Express outbox. To send it, I click Send/Receive on the Outlook toolbar. Actually, all you can see in Figure 14.63 is Send/R.

To view the news article that I sent, I need to synchronize my newsgroups. As Figure 14.64 shows, Outlook Express newsgroup accounts have an account management bar in the right pane that is much like the one for IMAP4 accounts. After clicking the Synchronization Settings check box for each newsgroup, I simply clicked Synchronize to download from my NNTP virtual server all available articles in the newsgroups to which I subscribed. Notice that there's one unread news article in the BGA.Discussions.Contracts.Current newsgroup. That's the one that I posted back in the last paragraph. I can also read the article in the public folder Discussions About Current Contracts. I had to synchronize my IMAP4 folders to receive the message I posted in the last paragraph.

FIGURE 14.64

Synchronizing newsgroups using the Outlook Express news account management bar

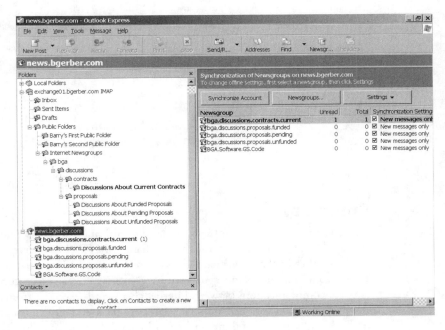

Okay, it's a little later now, and as Figure 14.65 shows, Jane Dough and I have been carrying on a conversation about the Jackson cost overrun. Notice that the conversation is displayed in threaded format. Each response is linked to the specific news article to which the response was made. In this case, Jane responded to me, and I responded to her response. Conversation threading is very nice. You can also view news articles in threaded format using the standard Outlook client by selecting By Conversation Topic from the drop-down list on the Advanced toolbar on the Outlook 2003 main menu. This is not some special feature for newsgroups. You can view the contents of any Outlook folder in threaded format. By the way, in IMAP4 clients, threaded views aren't available for Exchange public folders or any other folders, for that matter. You can verify this for yourself by checking out your public folders in the IMAP4 client.

FIGURE 14.65
Viewing a threaded newsgroup discussion in Outlook Express

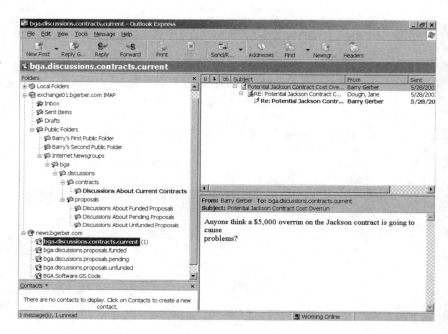

Summary

Virtual servers and front-end servers play a significant role in the delivery of Exchange Server 2003 Internet services. In the same way that Exchange SMTP virtual servers enable Internet mail transport services, other Exchange virtual servers enable additional Internet mail services as well as news services. Front-end servers in league with back-end servers provide security and load-leveling functionality for communications between Internet clients and servers. A front-end server, whether behind an Internet firewall or not, enhances the security of back-end servers. Front-end servers also lighten loads on back-end servers by taking on encryption and decryption tasks that back-end servers would otherwise have to perform.

This chapter focused on configuring and using five advanced Internet client/server protocols: the Post Office Protocol version 3 (POP3), the Internet Message Access Protocol version 4 (IMAP4), the Hypertext Transfer Protocol (HTTP), the Lightweight Directory Access Protocol (LDAP), and the Network News Transfer Protocol (NNTP). POP3, IMAP4, and NNTP can be configured and managed entirely through Exchange Server 2003. HTTP requires occasional forays into the world of

Internet Information Server. LDAP is based in Windows Server 2003, which is at the heart of that operating system's Active Directory and must be managed entirely on the Windows 2003 side.

POP3, IMAP4, and HTTP (Outlook Web Access, or OWA) let users access all or part of the folders in their Exchange mailboxes with something other than a MAPI client, such as the standard Outlook client. IMAP4 and OWA also allow users to access Exchange public folders. POP3 and IMAP4 clients are available in a number of flavors for a wide range of computing platforms, from the smallest of personal digital assistants to Windows, Macintosh, and Unix computers. OWA enables access to Exchange mailboxes and public folders with a web browser.

POP3 offers the least sophisticated but also one of the easiest routes to Exchange mailbox access on both the client and server ends. Users can download only the messages that are in their Inboxes. They can see neither the other folders in their mailboxes nor Exchange public folders. IMAP4 adds access to all available folders, both private and public. However, server and especially client setup and management are considerably more complex. OWA is the easiest way to gain non-MAPI access to Exchange mailboxes and the folders in them, as well as to public folders.

LDAP adds e-mail address and other Active Directory attribute lookup functionality to POP3, IMAP4, and OWA message access. The Windows 2003 LDAP server interacts with Active Directory to find and return information based on queries from LDAP clients. LDAP server management is the least user-friendly of all. Only those well schooled in the intricacies of Active Directory should attempt to alter its settings. By default, the LDAP server is tightly secured to protect the rich and highly sensitive data that is maintained in Active Directory. Generally, it is very good practice to leave security as it is.

Exchange NNTP support brings Internet newsgroups to Exchange public folders while preserving newsgroup access from standard NNTP clients. This functionality enables threaded discussions that are accessible through standard MAPI and NNTP clients. Although NNTP services are generally associated with public news servers operated by Internet service providers, organizations should also seriously consider using NNTP to support intranet communications.

As with the SMTP service, virtual servers support POP3, IMAP4, HTTP, and NNTP services. Multiple virtual servers can be created for any of the four protocols. This allows for the dedication of different servers to different organizational or user needs.

Implementing each of these protocols involves setting limits that protect computers and networks against overloading. These limits revolve around such things as the total number of connections to the protocol server, and the amount of data moved in one operation or during a single connection.

Additionally, each protocol allows for tight or loose security, at both the user authentication and the packet encryption levels. Security is enough of an issue when Internet protocol communications take place on an intranet. It is critical when sensitive data must travel the Internet. Strong security is available from Microsoft for these protocols. These include security based on Windows 2003 account-based authentication and Secure Sockets Layer (SSL) encryption. Some POP3 and IMAP4 clients support client-side digital signatures and other types of encryption for additional user authentication. Internet client security will be discussed in more detail in Chapter 18.

POP3 and IMAP4 also support different kinds of message formatting. This includes plain-text and MIME formatting, as well as choices of character sets.

None of the Internet protocols supported by Windows Server 2003/Exchange Server 2003 offers the rich set of features available with the standard Outlook MAPI client. However, in certain circumstances, such as for home and on-the-road use, a simpler, easier-to-install, and lighter-weight client could very well be the right choice.

In the next chapter, we'll add another Exchange server to our domain and another server to a new administrative group in our domain. Then we'll add a new domain and an Exchange server in that domain. This will give us a chance to explore a range of Exchange server features, from front-end/back-end server configurations to folder replication.

Chapter 15

Installing and Managing Additional Exchange Servers

OKAY, WE'RE READY TO add new Exchange servers to our Windows 2003 domain and to a new domain in our Windows 2003 forest. We'll start by adding a new server to our first domain and its default administrative group. Generally, you add new servers in an administrative group to handle the load created by additional users or to provide LAN connectivity for a group of users with slower wide-area links to other Exchange servers in the group. We'll be moving pretty fast in this chapter, so fasten your seat belts.

Featured in this chapter:

◆ Adding an Exchange server to a domain's default administrative group

◆ Managing multiple servers in a domain's default administrative group

◆ Adding an Exchange server to a new administrative group in a domain

◆ Managing multiple administrative groups in a domain

◆ Installing an Exchange server in a new domain in the same Windows 2003 forest

◆ Managing Servers in multidomain environments

Adding an Exchange Server to a Domain's Default Administrative Group

You've already installed one Exchange server in your administrative group. Installing another is a pretty basic task. You'll need a second Windows 2003 server on which to install Exchange Server. Instead of going through the second installation in detail, I'll just call your attention to any differences that you'll encounter when installing another server in your domain. You'll find full details on installing Windows Server 2003 in Chapter 7, "Installing Windows Server 2003 as a Domain Controller," and on installing Exchange Server 2003 in Chapter 8, "Installing Exchange Server 2003."

Installing an Additional Windows 2003 Server

For our purposes here, you should install your new server in your existing Windows 2003 domain, the one that you used for your first installation. (For me, that's my `bgerber.local` domain.) Like your first Exchange server, it's better that your second Exchange server not be a domain controller. Don't forget to name the server according to the naming conventions that you've set up. (Mine will be called EXCHANGE02.) When you're done and your new Windows Server 2003 is up and running, ensure that you can see it from your first server. Try pinging the server by name: `ping exchange02.bgerber.local`, for example. This will work just fine if you follow the directions in Chapter 7 for installing a Windows 2003 server that is to become an Exchange server.

Installing an Additional Exchange 2003 Server

Installing another Exchange server in a domain is about the easiest thing you'll ever do. Because there can be only one Exchange organization in a domain or forest, the installation program uses a good deal of existing information about your Exchange organization to install your second Exchange server. For starters, insert the Exchange Server CD-ROM into the CD-ROM drive of your new Windows Server 2003. When the setup program starts, select Exchange Deployment Tools and then select the option to install Exchange on additional servers. You'll next see that great interactive checklist that I discussed in detail in Chapter 6, "Upgrading to Windows Server 2003 and Exchange Server 2003," and Chapter 8. Refer to those chapters for more on the checklist and how to use it to install Exchange Server 2003.

When the installation program is finished, to prove that all is working properly, open the Exchange System Manager program on your first server. You should now see two servers under your administrative group (see Figure 15.1). Now go over to your new server and set up a Microsoft Management Console with Exchange System Manager and other relevant snap-ins. You should see the same two servers in exactly the same format as on your first server (see Figure 15.2). In fact, things look so much the same that I opened the Properties dialog box for each computer's Computer Management (Local) container—which you can see just above Exchange System Manager (Barry Gerber and Associates (Exchange) in Figures 15.1 and 15.2—just to prove that two different Exchange servers are involved here.

TIP   *Both Active Directory and Exchange servers take a little while to properly replicate and display information. After installing your new server, wait 15 to 30 minutes for everything to settle down before moving through this chapter. Additionally, if you make a change in Exchange System Manager on Server A and don't see the change on Server B, you can try right-clicking the container on Server B where the change should be visible, and selecting Refresh. You should then see the change on Server B. When you create new Exchange recipients, you can speed up the assignment of e-mail addresses to them by right-clicking Recipients ➤ Recipient Update Services ➤ Recipient Update Service (`<your_domain>`) and clicking Update Now.*

WARNING   *Sometimes you will experience problems because one or more of what are called "system folders" are not synchronized from one server to another. For example, Outlook e-mail clients might issue messages about free busy information being unavailable. Later in this chapter, I'll discuss system folders and their synchronization. See the sidebar "Replicating System Folders" in the section "Public Folder Replication."*

FIGURE 15.1

A newly installed Exchange server, viewed through the Exchange System Manager, running on a previously installed Exchange server

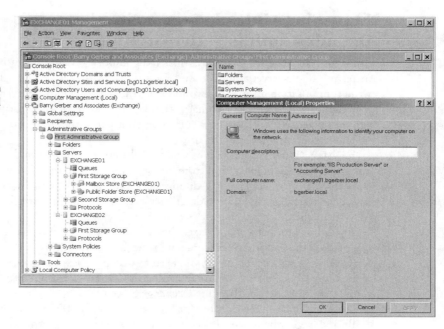

FIGURE 15.2

A newly installed Exchange server, viewed through the Exchange System Manager, running on the new server

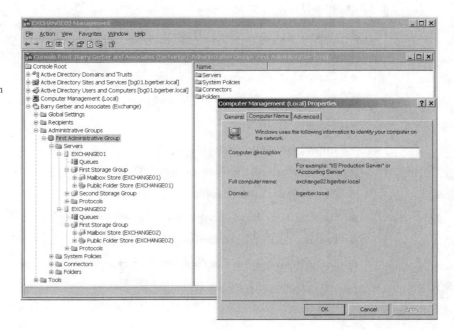

Managing Multiple Servers in a Domain's Default Administrative Group

For most Exchange server features, managing multiserver administrative groups is no different than managing single-server administrative groups. Exchange servers in an administrative group read and write configuration information to and from the same Windows Server 2003 Active Directory. They communicate automatically so that such tasks as cross-server monitoring or public-folder replication can take place without any intervention on your part, other than setting up a particular monitoring or public-folder replication scenario.

Exchange System Manager is central to multiserver management. It was designed to let you manage a whole Exchange organization from one server or workstation. It works far more transparently and smoothly than Exchange 5.5's Administrator program. You usually don't have to manually connect to a server to manage it, and you don't have to do anything to switch focus from one server to another, other than clicking on that server or one of its containers.

In addition to managing an Exchange server locally or from another Exchange 2003 server, you can manage Exchange servers from a non–Exchange Windows 2003 server or a Windows XP Professional workstation. To do so, you need to install the Exchange management tools on the server or workstation. For information on installing the Exchange management tools under these circumstances, see the sidebar "Running Exchange System Manager Remotely" in the section "Setting Up Microsoft Management Console for Exchange Server 2003" in Chapter 8.

By and large, when managing one Exchange server from another computer running Exchange System Manager, you can pretty much follow the directions in Chapter 11, "Managing Exchange Users, Distribution Groups, and Contacts," and Chapter 12, "Managing the Exchange Server Hierarchy and Core Components." However, multiserver administrative groups do offer some opportunities and challenges that are not present in single-server groups. I'll focus on these in this section. In multiserver administrative group environments, opportunities and challenges arise in the following areas:

- Creating mailbox-enabled Windows 2003 users

- Enhancing Exchange server monitoring

- Using system policies

- Implementing full-text indexing

- Creating Information Store databases

- Working with public folders

- Moving a mailbox from one Exchange server to another

- Backing up Exchange databases

- Implementing front-end/back-end server topologies

Let's look at each of these in more detail.

Creating Mailbox-Enabled Windows 2003 Users

The only difference between creating a new mailbox-enabled user when you have multiple Exchange servers and when you have a single Exchange server is that you have the opportunity to create the mailbox on a mailbox store on any of your Exchange servers. You already know how to create new users, so I'll walk you through this scenario quickly. If you need a refresher on new user creation, see the section "Managing Exchange Users" in Chapter 11.

In Figure 15.3, I'm creating a new user. I'm setting a password for the new user in Figure 15.4, and in Figure 15.5, I'm choosing to create the new mailbox on my second Exchange server, EXCHANGE02. As soon as I make this choice, Exchange automatically selects the default mailbox store on the server that I've selected. That is, First Storage Group/Mailbox Store (EXCHANGE01) automatically changes to First Storage Group/Mailbox Store (EXCHANGE02) as soon as I select Barry Gerber and Associates/First Administrative Group/EXCHANGE02.

Now check out Figure 15.6. Notice that Bob Freeman's new mailbox is indeed on the default mailbox store on my new server, EXCHANGE02.

A new mailbox doesn't show up on an Exchange server until it has been accessed at least once. To make a mailbox visible, send a message to the mailbox, or open the mailbox with an Outlook client or Internet e-mail client. If you're logged on to your domain as a user other than the one who owns a mailbox, to open the mailbox with Outlook Web Access, use the following URL: *<your_server>*/exchange/*<new_mailbox_name>*. To get to Bob Freeman's mailbox in OWA, I'd enter the following URL in my web browser: exchange02/exchange/bfreeman. When using the recommended URL, the username under which you are logged on must have Full Mailbox Access rights to the mailbox you're trying to open. Set or check these on the Exchange Advanced page of the user's Properties dialog box (click Mailbox Rights).

FIGURE 15.3

Creating a new Windows 2003 user

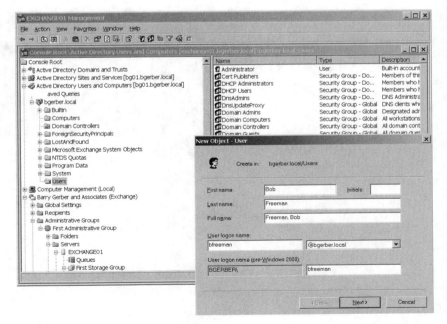

FIGURE 15.4
Entering a password for a new Windows 2003 user

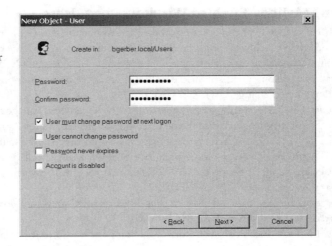

FIGURE 15.5
Choosing to create a new Exchange mailbox on a second Exchange server

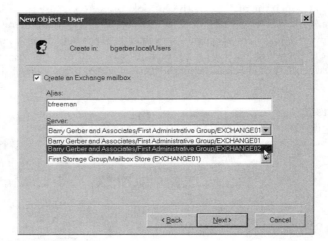

FIGURE 15.6
A new mailbox is stored on a second Exchange server.

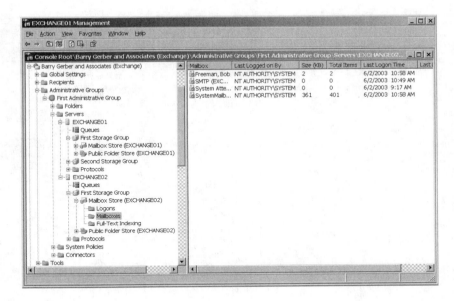

Enhancing Exchange Server Monitoring

Back in Chapter 12, I discussed server monitoring in the section "Monitoring." As you'll remember, you can monitor any service on an Exchange computer. You can also monitor such things as available virtual memory, CPU utilization, free disk space, and SMTP queue growth. When monitors are in place, you can set up your Exchange server so that e-mail or scripted notifications are sent when a monitored resource reaches a particular state. Scripted notifications allow you to send a message to a pager, for example.

In single Exchange server environments, it's possible for services or other resources on the server to deteriorate to such a level that the server can no longer send a notification. In multiple-server environments, one server can monitor another server, increasing the possibility that a notification will be successful.

In Figure 15.7, I'm setting up an e-mail notification in which EXCHANGE01 monitors EXCHANGE02. I'm setting up the notification on EXCHANGE01. I opened the Custom List of Servers dialog box by clicking Customize in the Properties dialog box for the e-mail notification. Note that the notification will be sent to my mailbox, which is on the monitoring server. It doesn't make a lot of sense to send a notification to a mailbox on the monitored server because that server could enter a state in which it would be incapable of receiving messages.

I also need a notification for EXCHANGE01. I'm setting up that notification in Figure 15.8. Notice that notification will be sent to `bfreeman@bgerber.com`, the mailbox that we created on EXCHANGE02 in the last section.

Setting up an e-mail notification in which one server, EXCHANGE01, monitors another, EXCHANGE02

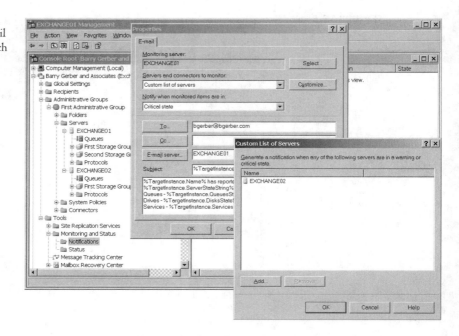

Setting up an e-mail notification in which one server, EXCHANGE02, monitors another, EXCHANGE01

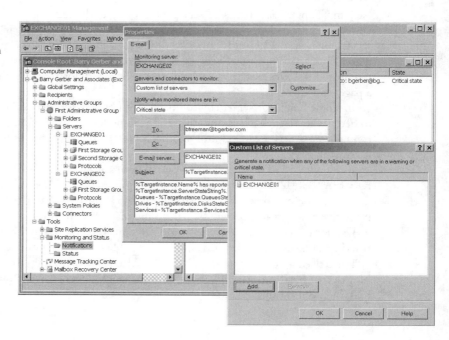

You should also run notifications for the server being monitored on the server being monitored. For example, I should run notifications for EXCHANGE01 on EXCHANGE01 and notifications for EXCHANGE02 on EXCHANGE02. This protects against a situation in which network failures prevent one Exchange server from seeing another, but in which the server with problems can still be reached by an e-mail client or access resources required to send a scripted notification.

Using System Policies

System policies enable you to create a template that specifies how certain properties will be set for servers, mailboxes, and public stores in an administrative group. Figure 15.9 shows the system policy that we created back in Chapter 12 in the section "Creating and Managing Server Policies." Remember that server policies cover only a server's General property page. When I created my server policy in Chapter 12, I added EXCHANGE01 to the policy and then applied the policy. After installing EXCHANGE02, I added that server by right-clicking the policy, selecting Add Server, and then selecting the server from the resultant dialog box Select Items to Place Under the Control of This Policy. Then I responded Yes in the dialog box that asked Are You Sure You Want to Add the Item(s) to This Policy?

FIGURE 15.9

A server policy for the servers in an administrative group

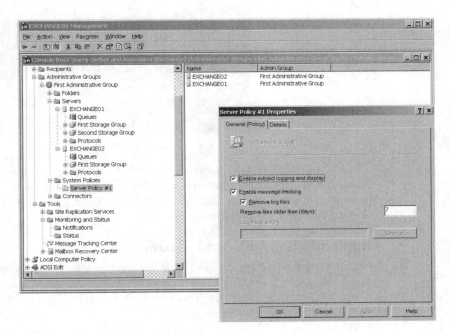

In Figure 15.10, you can see the General property page of the Properties dialog box for each of my Exchange servers. You can tell that the policy is in effect on each server because the properties designated in the policy in Figure 15.9 are grayed out and therefore unchangeable on each server's respective Properties dialog box.

FIGURE 15.10

A server policy applied to both servers in an administrative group

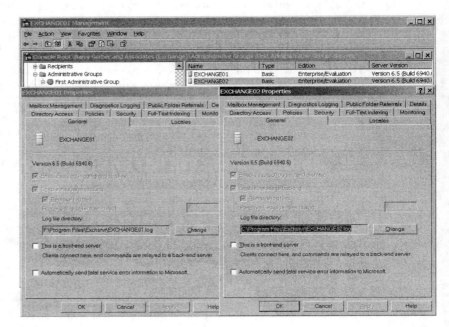

This little exercise should make it clearer how helpful system policies can be when you need to install and manage multiple servers in an administrative group. First, you don't have to set key properties for the servers or their Information Stores. Second, you can lock down certain settings so that they can't be changed inadvertently.

Implementing Full-Text Indexing

Exchange Server 2003 supports full-text indexing of items stored in mailbox and public stores. This significantly speeds searches for specific content in stored items. I discussed full-text indexing in Chapter 12, in the sections "Implementing Full-Text Indexing on a Mailbox Store" and "Use of Public Store Management Containers."

As in Figure 15.11, you can see and manage mailbox stores and information stores on any Exchange server in an administrative group from any computer running Exchange Systems Manager. When you create full-text indexing using an instance of Exchange System Manager that is running on a computer other than the one on which you want to create indexing, you will run into one easily resolved problem.

FIGURE 15.11

Full-text indexing can be managed from any computer running Exchange System Manager, but indexes should be created with care when the manager isn't running on the target Exchange server.

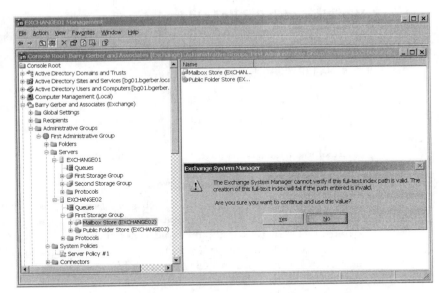

The catalog for a full-text index is stored on a local drive on the Exchange server where indexing runs. When you try to turn on full-text indexing from another computer, Exchange System Manager selects a local path on the Exchange server where you want to run indexing on which to place the catalog. If you accept the path or change it, Exchange System Manager then tells you that it can't be sure that the local path is valid (see Figure 15.11). This happens because Exchange System Manager isn't running on the target Exchange server. If you're satisfied that the path is correct, you can respond Yes and the index will be created.

As an alternative, you can run Exchange System Manager on the server where you want to create full-text indexing. You can still take advantage of cross-computer management of full-text indexing after the index is created.

That's all I need to tell you about full-text indexing in multiserver administrative groups.

Creating Information Store Databases

When you use Exchange System Manager on one computer to create a new mailbox or public store on another Exchange server, you'll run into the same issue as you do with full-text indexes. Exchange System Manager won't be able to verify that the database and log paths that it has chosen for the store's database are valid.

As with full-text indexing, if you're sure about the path, or if you've changed it to one that you know is correct, click Yes, and the database is created. As an alternative, you can create new mailbox and public stores by running Exchange System Manager on the Exchange server where they will reside.

See the sections "Creating a Mailbox Store" and "Creating a Public Store" in Chapter 12 for more information.

Working with Public Folders

In this section, we'll talk about three issues relating to public folders in multiserver administrative group Exchange Server environments:

◆ Public folder hierarchy replication

◆ Public folder replication

◆ How to access segments of the default (organizational) public folders tree stored on different Exchange servers

Let's look at each of these in a bit more detail.

PUBLIC FOLDER HIERARCHY REPLICATION

You can create public folders on any Exchange server that has a default public store (called Public Folder Store). Public folders can contain items in the form of messages, forms, files, and so on. A public folder hierarchy is a list of public folders and their subfolders that are stored in the default public folder stores on the Exchange servers in an Exchange organization. The hierarchy also includes the name of the server on which a copy of each folder resides. The hierarchy does not contain the actual items in the folders. There is one organization-wide public folder hierarchy.

In a single Exchange server environment, the hierarchy exists and is stored on the Exchange server. In multiserver administrative groups, each Exchange server has a copy of the public folder hierarchy. Exchange servers work together to ensure that each Exchange server in an administrative group has an up-to-date copy of the public folder hierarchy. This process, called *public folder hierarchy replication*, is automatic.

Exchange System Manager uses the public folder hierarchy to appropriately display public folder objects in various containers and to retrieve information about public folders, whether that information is stored in the hierarchy or on the server where the public folder physically resides. E-mail clients use the hierarchy to display a list of public folders available on all servers in the organization and to access items in a specific folder. Security limits associated with a given public folder, of course, limit actual access by Exchange System Manager and e-mail clients.

NOTE *The public folder hierarchy also includes what are called "system folders" such as the Schedule + Free Busy Folder. I mentioned this folder earlier in this chapter and I'll talk about it and the other system folders later in this chapter.*

PUBLIC FOLDER REPLICATION

By default, Outlook and Outlook Web Access clients look first for a public folder on the user's public folder store, which might or might not be the same Exchange server where the user's mailbox is located. The default public store is configured on the General property page of the Properties dialog box for a mailbox store. If a specific public folder doesn't exist in the default public folder store, the client is directed to a server where the public folder resides. As you can imagine, when many public folders are accessed over a lower-bandwidth network, server and network loads can get pretty heavy as users access public folders on one or a limited number of Exchange servers. So, if you need to, you can replicate folders on one Exchange server to other Exchange servers in an administrative group. This is most useful in two situations:

◆ When you need to balance public folder access loads on your Exchange servers

♦ When an Exchange server or group of Exchange servers is separated from other servers by lower-bandwidth links

There are two other reasons why you might need to replicate public folders. First, IMAP4 clients see folders only on the Exchange server to which they connect. This includes public folders. If you want an IMAP4 client to see public folders on other Exchange servers, you must replicate the folders to the IMAP4 client's Exchange server. Second, public folder replication is essential when you're planning to remove an Exchange server from your organization. If the server you're removing is the only physical home for a set of public folders and you don't want to lose those folders, you must replicate them to another server. This can be another existing Exchange server in your organization or an Exchange server you plan to install to replace the server you're removing.

Having whetted your appetite regarding public folder replication, I'm going to ask that you wait a bit before we tackle the subject. We'll get into replication later in this chapter in the section "Managing Public Folders."

ACCESSING SEGMENTS OF THE DEFAULT (ORGANIZATIONAL) PUBLIC FOLDERS TREE STORED ON DIFFERENT EXCHANGE SERVERS

You'll remember from the section "Creating and Managing Public Folders" in Chapter 12, that you can create and manage public folders in Exchange System Manager. For the most part, public folder management is straightforward in multiserver Exchange Server environments. There is one gotcha, which I'll get to in a bit. First, let's look at the straightforward side.

Figure 15.12 shows the public folders on my server EXCHANGE01. Most of those folders should look quite familiar. We created them at various points in our passionate pursuit of that occasionally elusive little animal, Exchange Server. You can double-click any of these folders and see its Properties dialog box. Refer back to Figure 12.21 in Chapter 12 for a view of that dialog box.

FIGURE 15.12

Public folders stored on the Exchange server EXCHANGE01

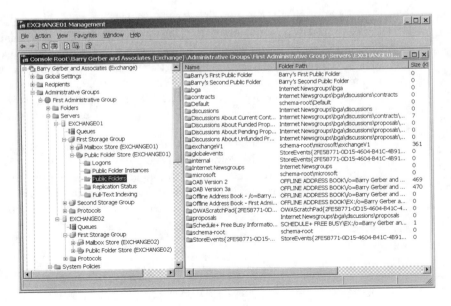

Now look at Figure 15.13. It shows the public folders on EXCHANGE02. First, notice that none of the public folders that I created on EXCHANGE01 exist on EXCHANGE02. Refer to Figure 15.12 to substantiate this claim. Also note that EXCHANGE02 has a public folder that I created on EXCHANGE02 that is called Folder on EXCHANGE02. This folder doesn't exist on EXCHANGE01. All of this should demonstrate that by default the Public Folders container in each Exchange server's Public Folder store contains only folders created on the server itself.

FIGURE 15.13

Public folders stored on the Exchange server EXCHANGE02

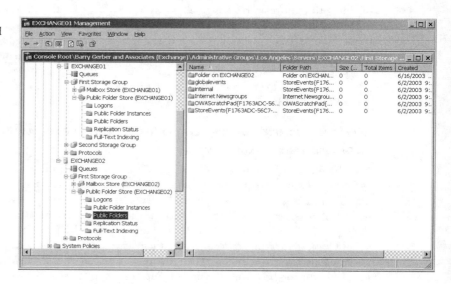

Now we're ready for the gotcha. Let's say that I want to create a new public folder on EXCHANGE02. First, I need to locate the Public Folders container that holds the default public folder tree for my organization. I've selected that container in Figure 15.14. To ensure that I'm working in the public folder store on EXCHANGE02, I need to right-click the Public Folders container and select Connect To from the pop-up menu. Then I need to select EXCHANGE02\Public Folder Store (EXCHANGE02) from the Select a Public Store dialog box, and click OK (see Figure 15.14). Now I know that I'm working on the correct public folder store, and I can manage and create public folders on EXCHANGE02 to my heart's content.

Note that you can't be sure that you're connected to the correct public folder store by the folders that are displayed in the Public Folders container. This display is based on the organization-wide public folder hierarchy. So, you see all public folders in your organization, regardless of whatever server they are stored on in the Public Folders container. In Figure 15.14, I'm connected to EXCHANGE01, but I still see the folder named Folder on EXCHANGE02.

FIGURE 15.14
Selecting the public folder store on EXCHANGE02 so that a new public folder can be created on that server

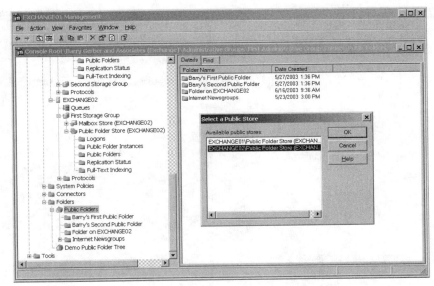

Moving a Mailbox from One Exchange Server to Another

You might need to move an Exchange mailbox to another server for a couple of reasons:

◆ A user moves to a new physical location where a different Exchange server is used to hold user mailboxes

◆ You need to balance the load on the processors or disks of your Exchange servers, or the load on your networks, by changing the distribution of mailboxes across your Exchange servers

Mailbox moves are quite easy. Find and right-click the user in the Users subcontainer in the Active Directory Users and Computers container. Then select Exchange tasks from the pop-up menu. This opens the Exchange Task Wizard. Click over to the Available Tasks page, and select Move Mailbox (see Figure 15.15). Click Next, and select the new location for the mailbox, as I have done in Figure 15.16. Click Next, and the wizard initiates the mailbox move. When the move is complete, close the wizard by clicking Finish. The mailbox should now show up in the mailbox store on the server to which the mailbox was moved.

TIP You move mailboxes between servers in different administrative groups in the same way as you move them between servers in the same administrative group. You can also use the Exchange Task Wizard to move mailboxes between mailbox stores on the same Exchange server. You'd do this, for example, if you were having disk capacity or performance problems and had created a new mailbox store on a different disk drive.

FIGURE 15.15
Using the Exchange Task Wizard to move a mailbox to a different server

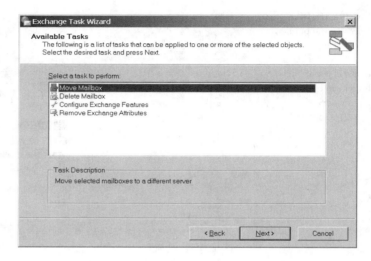

FIGURE 15.16
Using the Exchange Task Wizard to specify the server and mailbox store to which a mailbox should be moved

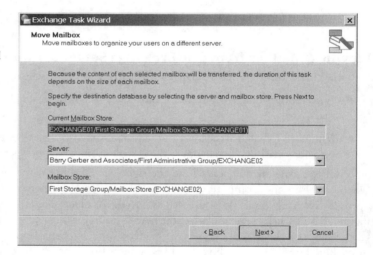

Backing Up Exchange Databases

Any backup product worth its salt will let you back up and restore Exchange Information Store databases, regardless of the server they reside on. As Figure 15.17 indicates, the Windows 2003 backup program once enhanced by installation of Exchange Server can indeed back up mailbox and public stores, regardless of their home server.

FIGURE 15.17

Preparing to back up Information Store databases on different Exchange servers using the Windows 2003 backup program, as enhanced by installation of Exchange Server 2003

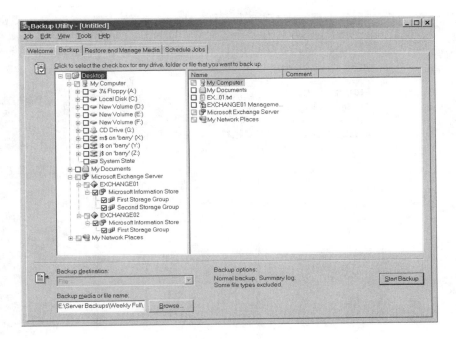

Third-party backup products from a variety of vendors also support multiserver Exchange database backup. For more on third-party options in specific and Exchange Server backup in general, see the section "Backing Up Exchange Server 2003" in Chapter 8 and Chapter 17, "Exchange Server Reliability and Availability."

WARNING *Windows Server 2003's backup program can not back up either registry or system state information on remote servers. Third-party backup products are usually capable of backing up these two vital Windows 2003 components.*

Implementing Front-End/Back-End Server Topologies

I introduced you to the notion of front-end/back-end servers in Chapter 14, "Managing Exchange 2003 Services for Internet Clients," in the section "Front-End/Back-End Exchange Server Configurations." Basically, when using a POP3, IMAP4, or HTTP (Outlook Web Access or OWA client), a user contacts a front-end server. The front-end server then relays or proxies, bi-directional communications between the user's client and the back-end server that contains the user's mailbox and public folder hierarchy information. The front-end server makes an LDAP query to determine the user's Exchange server. The front-end server also handles Secure Sockets Layer (SSL) data encryption tasks.

Setting up a front-end/back-end configuration is very easy. Select the server that is to function as your front-end server, and open the server's Properties dialog box by right-clicking the server and selecting Properties from the pop-up menu. I've decided to make EXCHANGE02 my front-end server. In Figure 15.18, I've done the one and only thing that I need to do to accomplish this end: I selected This Is a Front-End Server. Then all I had to do was stop and restart all of the default POP3, IMAP4, and HTTP virtual servers and all of the Exchange services on EXCHANGE02, and my new server is up and running.

FIGURE 15.18

Turning an Exchange server into a front-end server

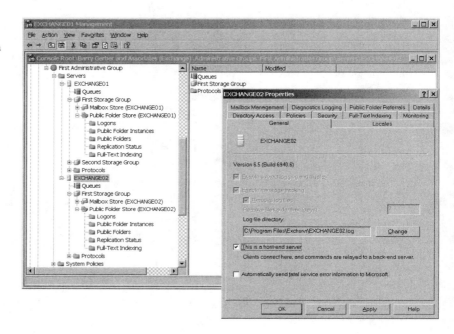

To make things easier, I added some host records to my DNS. As you can see in Figure 15.19, I added records for POPMAIL, IMAPMAIL, OWAMAIL, and SMTPMAIL. All but the last record points to EXCHANGE02, my front-end server. SMTPMAIL points to my other Exchange server, EXCHANGE01. Now when users need to enter a URL, or a POP3 or IMAP4 server name, or an OWA URL, they can just enter the appropriate name based on these host records. Now let's see how this all works.

In Figure 15.20, you can see the login dialog box that opens when I enter the URL http:// owamail.bgerber.com/exchange in my web browser. I'm trying to access my mailbox, which resides on EXCHANGE01. I don't need to point to EXCHANGE01; my front-end server, EXCHANGE02, takes care of communications between my web browser and EXCHANGE01, where my mailbox and public folder hierarchy information reside. In Figure 15.21, I'm reading a "very informative" news article about a new contract.

FIGURE 15.19
New DNS host records make it easy for users to take advantage of a front-end server.

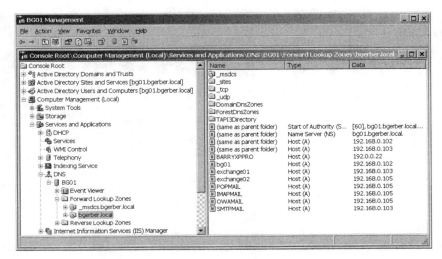

FIGURE 15.20
Logging on to an Exchange server through a front-end server to use Outlook Web Access

Finally, take a look at Figure 15.22, where I'm setting up my Outlook Express IMAP4 client to access my IMAP4 and SMTP servers using the new host records that I created. Again, even though my mailbox and public folder hierarchy information are located on EXCHANGE01, my front-end server, EXCHANGE02, will handle communications between my IMAP4 client and EXCHANGE01 in a way that's totally transparent to me.

I really like front-end/back-end server topologies. They make it easier for users to access key Exchange Internet access protocols on back-end servers, and they significantly reduce the security-related load on back-end servers.

FIGURE 15.21
Accessing an Exchange mailbox and public folders through a front-end server using Outlook Web Access

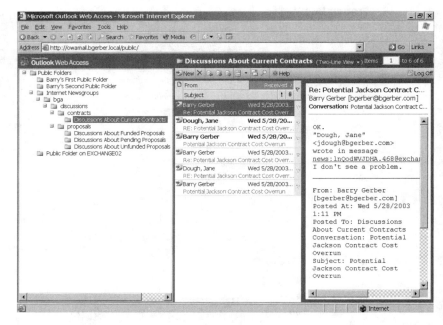

FIGURE 15.22
Setting up an IMAP4 client to access an Exchange server through a front-end server

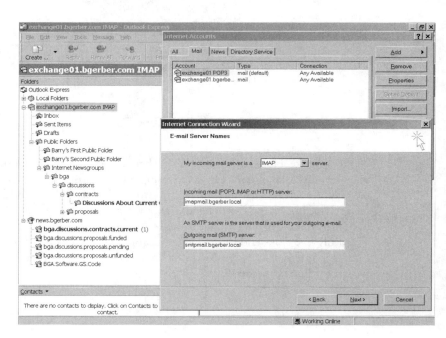

Adding an Exchange Server to a New Administrative Group in a Domain

I introduced you to administrative groups in Chapter 12, in the section "Managing Administrative Groups." I talked about how you use administrative groups to distribute management of an Exchange organization based on such criteria as geography or organizational hierarchy. In this chapter, I'll extend that discussion to multi-administrative group Exchange organizations. In this section, I'll cover these topics:

◆ Handling administrative groups, routing groups, and Exchange 5.5 Server sites

◆ Adding a new administrative group to an Exchange organization

◆ Installing an Exchange server in a new administrative group

Let's get right to these three very interesting topics.

Administrative Groups, Routing Groups, and Exchange Server 5.5 Sites

In Exchange Server 5.5, you created a new site by installing the first Exchange server in the site. As you installed a new server, you designated either that it would join an existing site or that a new site should be created when the server was installed. Servers could not be moved between sites.

Exchange 5.5 sites served two major purposes. First, they served as a means of controlling management of a specific set of servers. You could give management rights for different sites to different Windows NT groups or users. Sites also served as a place to corral a set of servers linked by reliable, higher-bandwidth networks and as the management locus for intersite message routing. By setting up connectors between sites, you enabled the routing of e-mail and Exchange server administrative messages between sites, and you specified the network services to be used for routing. To enhance reliability, you could also set up multiple redundant routing links between any pair of sites.

In Exchange 5.5, administrative and routing functions were co-terminous with the site. Administrative control was granted over the entire site. All servers in the site were linked to other sites and the servers in those sites by the same set of connectors.

With Exchange Server 2003, administrative and routing functions are separated. Administrative groups work like Exchange 5.5 sites in that you can delegate control over an entire administrative group to Windows 2003 groups or users.

Routing is handled differently in Exchange 2003 than it was in Exchange 5.5. It's done through routing groups, which reside inside Routing Groups containers within administrative groups. Visualize it this way: \Exchange Organization\Administrative Group\Routing Groups Container\Routing Groups. A Routing Groups container can hold many routing groups. A routing group holds information on both the Exchange servers that belong to the routing group and the connections that are used to connect the routing group to other routing groups in an Exchange organization.

Administrative and routing groups work differently, depending on whether an Exchange organization is operating in Mixed or Native mode. You'll remember from Chapter 12 (in the section "The Exchange Server Hierarchy") that, upon installation, Exchange servers run in Mixed mode. This means that they can connect to and communicate with Exchange 5.5 servers using Active Directory

Connector. To retain compatibility with Exchange 5.5 sites, Exchange 2003 administrative groups and routing groups are co-terminous in Mixed mode. A Routing Groups container is installed when the first Exchange server is installed in an administrative group. The servers in an administrative group must all reside in one of the routing groups in the administrative group's Routing Groups container. They can not reside in routing groups in other administrative groups. Additionally, Exchange 2003 servers can not be moved between Administrative groups in Mixed mode.

When an Exchange organization is switched to Native mode, Exchange servers can be moved to any administrative or routing group container in an Exchange organization. This enables you to delegate control of message routing for a set of Exchange servers to a group of managers other than the managers who handle other administrative tasks for those servers (for example, management of system policies or public folders).

WARNING   *Before you even think about switching to Native mode, please read the warning note in Chapter 12, in the section "The Exchange Server Hierarchy." Key point: You can't return to Mixed mode after changing to Native mode.*

Adding a New Administrative Group to an Exchange Organization

Unlike in Exchange 5.5, in which a new site is created when the first Exchange server is installed in it, in Exchange 2003, you have to create a new administrative group before you install your new server. I love simple tasks, and this is one of the simplest. To add a new administrative group to your Exchange organization, right-click the Administrative Groups container in your Exchange organization and select New ➢ Administrative Group. Use the resultant Properties dialog box, shown in Figure 15.23, to give your administrative group a name. You can name the group anything you want, and you can change the name anytime, so don't be too concerned about what you name it right now. When you're done, click OK. You should see your new administrative group in the Administrative Groups container (see Figure 15.24).

Note in Figure 15.24 that both of my administrative groups now show their routing groups containers. To display the routing groups containers, I had to open the Properties dialog box for my Exchange organization, Barry Gerber and Associates (Exchange), and select Display Routing Groups from General property page. Go ahead and set this parameter for your Exchange organization. If you're not seeing administrative groups, you can make them visible on the same property page.

Also note in Figure 15.24 that the First Routing Group container in the routing groups container in my first administrative group includes Connectors and Members subcontainers. Once I specified that routing groups should be displayed, the Connectors container, which originally lived in the First Administrative Group container (see Figure 15.14), moved to the routing groups container. The Members subcontainer holds the Exchange servers that belong to the routing group. It is displayed when Display Routing Groups is selected as per the previous paragraph. By default, the second and succeeding administrative groups you create have no routing groups in them. You have to create them by right-clicking the Routing Groups container and selecting New ➢ Routing Group, or you have to allow them to be created automatically during the installation of a new Exchange server in an Administrative group.

Now let's move onward and install a new Exchange server in our new administrative group.

FIGURE 15.23
Using the new administrative group Properties dialog box to create a new administrative group

FIGURE 15.24
A new administrative group displayed in Exchange System Manager

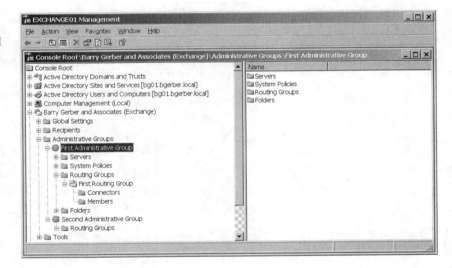

TIP *Add administrative groups only when you need to distribute management responsibilities. That statement might seem a bit redundant, given the discussion of administrative groups in this chapter and in Chapter 12. However, I want to make it clear that Exchange 2003 organizations of significant size can exist quite happily with only one administrative group. Because you can create as many routing groups as you need in an administrative group, you can handle a wide range of server location/networking topology issues within a single administrative group. If you determine that one administrative group is enough, you'll still find the following discussion useful as it deals with cross-routing group communications.*

Installing a New Exchange Server in a New Administrative Group

This is another very simple task. Follow the directions in the earlier sections of this chapter, "Installing an Additional Windows 2003 Server" and "Installing an Additional Exchange 2003 Server." The only difference is that the Exchange Installation Wizard now shows you a drop-down list from which you can pick the administrative group in which you want to install your new Exchange server (see Figure 15.25). Select your new administrative group, and your new server will be installed in the group. Figure 15.26 shows my new server, EXCHANGE03, installed in my new administrative group. Yessssssss! You can also see my other Exchange servers in Figure 15.26. Notice the Members container for First Routing Group in First Administrative Group. As advertised earlier in this section, it holds EXCHANGE01 and EXCHANGE02. I'll talk more about the Members container later in this chapter.

FIGURE 15.25

Selecting the administrative group into which a new Exchange server will be installed

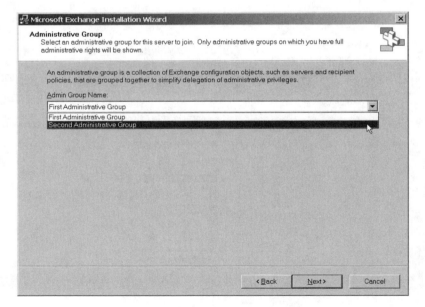

FIGURE 15.26

A new Exchange server after it has been installed in a new administrative group

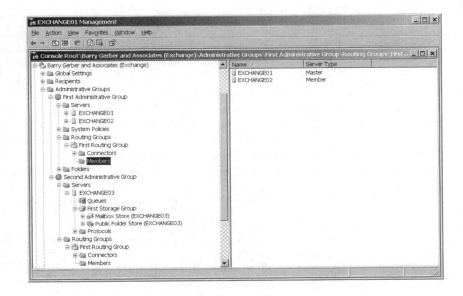

Upon installation of the first Exchange server in your organization, your first administrative group was populated with three subcontainers: Servers, Folders, and Routing Groups. The Routing Groups container doesn't show up in Exchange System Manager until you tell Exchange System Manager to display routing groups, as we did earlier in this chapter. As you have seen, when you create a new administrative group in Mixed mode, the group has only a Routing Groups container. When you install the first Exchange server in the new administrative group, the new administrative group is populated with a Servers subcontainer and its Routing Groups subcontainer is populated with a First Routing Group container, which in turn is populated with Connectors and Members subcontainers. The server is placed in the Servers group. It is also represented in the `Routing Groups\Members` container of the new administrative group. Compare Figures 15.24 and 15.26 for visual confirmation of these events.

For some of the exercises we'll be doing from here on, you need to switch your Exchange organization to Native mode. Before you make the final move to Native mode, let me remind you once again that this is bridge-burning time. After you've switched to Native mode, you can't go back without reinstalling your entire Exchange organization. So, think before you leap. If you can't switch to Native mode, you can still track through the remaining sections of this chapter. I'll point out those tasks that require Native mode. Furthermore, if it's possible to do a particular task in some form in Mixed mode, I'll tell you how.

To switch your Exchange organization to Native mode, right-click your organization (at the top of Exchange System Manager) and select Properties. On the General property page of the resultant Properties dialog box for your organization, select Change Mode and then click Yes to confirm your choice. That's it: Your bridges are burned.

Before we leave this section, I'm going to rename my two administrative groups. You can change the name of an administrative group *only* when your Exchange organization is running in Native mode. I'm going to call the first administrative group Los Angeles and the second group New York. This will add a little realism to some of the tasks that we're going to do in the next section and will make it easier for you to see what's going on than if we used the original names: First Administrative Group and Second Administrative Group.

To rename an administrative group, right-click it and select Rename from the pop-up menu; then change the group's name. Figure 15.27 shows my newly named administrative groups. You can also change an administrative group name by clicking it, waiting a second or two, and clicking it again. When you do this, the old name is highlighted and you can then type in the new name just as you can with directory and file names in the Windows Explorer directory and file browser.

FIGURE 15.27

Two Exchange Server administrative groups after they have been renamed

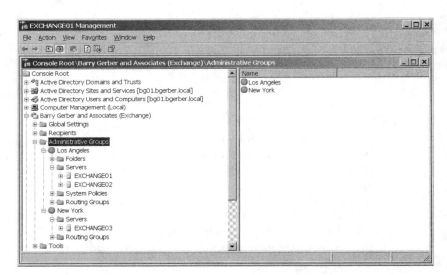

Managing Multiple Administrative Groups in a Domain

Now that you've installed a new Exchange server in a new administrative group, you have to manage that server and its relationship to other Exchange servers. We'll talk about a number of management tasks in this section:

♦ Delegating control of an administrative group

♦ Adding subcontainers to administrative groups

♦ Using routing groups and connectors

♦ Managing public folders

The first three of these tasks relate directly to the management of administrative groups and routing groups. You'll most likely need to perform the last management task in this list in multirouting group environments, whether one or more administrative groups are involved. I've chosen not to go into specifics on single-administrative group/multiple-routing group environments (see my earlier tip "Add Administrative Groups Only When You Need to Distribute Management Responsibilities"). So, it turns out that this section is the best place to discuss public folder management. I'll also point you back here when I discuss management of Exchange servers that you install in new Windows 2003 domains.

Delegating Control of an Administrative Group

In Chapter 8, in the section "Granting Permission for the Exchange Administration Group to Manage Exchange Server," I showed you how to delegate control of your Exchange organization to the Windows 2003 group Exchange Admins. That delegation gave anyone in the Exchange Admins group permission to fully manage your Exchange organization.

Now let's say that you want to give a different Windows 2003 security group permission to manage each of your administrative groups, which are subcontainers of your Exchange organization. Except for the fact that your administrative group names will have the standard names in Mixed mode, you delegate control over administrative groups *in exactly the same way*, whether your Exchange organization is operating in Mixed or Native mode.

First, you need to create your security groups. I need two security groups: one for each of my administrative groups, Los Angeles and New York. As you'll remember, you create users and groups using the Active Directory Users and Computers snap-in. Find and right-click the Users container, and select New ➤ Group from the pop-up menu. Enter the name of the group on the New Object - Group wizard, shown in Figure 15.28, and ensure that Global and Security are selected. On the next wizard page, accept the default (do not create an Exchange e-mail address). Then click Next and Finish on the last wizard page. Now follow these same instructions to create a group to manage your other administrative group.

FIGURE 15.28
Creating a Windows 2003 security group to which control of an administrative group will be granted

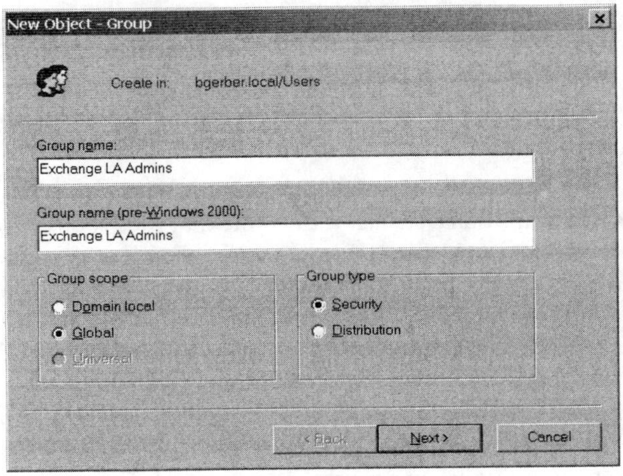

To delegate control of an administrative group to a security group, right-click the administrative group and select Delegate Control from the pop-up menu. In Figure 15.29, I'm delegating control of my Los Angeles administrative group to the security group that I created in the last paragraph, Exchange LA Admins. I clicked Add on the Users or Groups page of the Exchange Administration Delegation Wizard. This opened the Delegate Control dialog box. I selected Exchange Full Administrator in the dialog box and then clicked Browse so that I could select the group Exchange LA Admins in the Select Users, Computers, or Groups dialog box, shown in the bottom-right corner of Figure 15.29. For more on the role options in the Delegate Control dialog box, check out the section "Granting Permission for the Exchange Administration Group to Manage Exchange Server" in Chapter 12. After selecting the appropriate security group, I selected OK until I was out of the two dialog boxes, then clicked Next on the wizard, and then clicked Finish.

FIGURE 15.29

Delegating control of an administrative group to a Windows 2003 security group

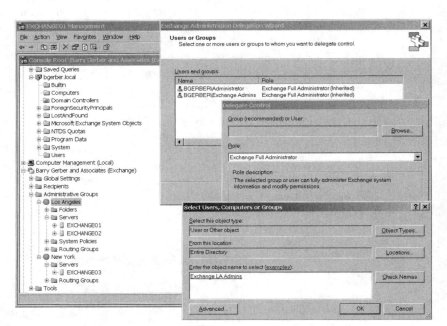

Exchange System Manager then warned me that the group or user to which I had just delegated control of my administrative group Los Angeles needed to belong to the local Administrator group on each Exchange computer to be managed. I happily clicked OK and immediately did as Exchange System Manager asked.

Note in Figure 15.29 that on the Users or Groups page of the Exchange Administration Delegation Wizard, the security group Exchange Admins has Exchange Full Administrator permissions on the administrative group by virtue of inheritance. Exchange Admins has permissions on my entire Exchange organization, and these permissions pass down to subcontainers in the organization. The only way to remove this group's control over this administrative group is to remove its control at the

Exchange organization level. You can do this if it makes sense, but do leave your domain administrator in control of your organization, or there will be no way to manage organization-wide Exchange functionality. Additionally, if you don't leave your domain administrator in control, only the group(s) delegated control over your administrative groups will be able to delegate (add or remove) control for those groups.

Be sure to delegate control over your other administrative group to your other security group. Then add the appropriate users to each security group using the Members property page in each group's Properties dialog box.

Adding Subcontainers to Administrative Groups

As you know, administrative groups can have subcontainers that hold a variety of useful objects. Four types of subcontainers exist:

Servers   Created when the first server is installed in an administrative group. Servers are added to the subcontainer upon installation into the administrative group. You can not add new servers containers.

Folders   Holds public folders (public folder trees). Created when the first server is installed in the first administrative group. A subcontainer must be manually created in other administrative groups. You can add one new folders container to an administrative group that doesn't already have one.

Routing Groups   Holds routing groups. Created when the first server is installed in the first administrative group. A subcontainer must be manually created in other administrative groups. You can add new routing groups containers in Exchange Native mode.

System Policies   Holds system policies. Subcontainer must be manually created in an administrative group when needed. You can add system policy containers in Exchange Mixed or Native mode.

In either Mixed or Native mode, you add subcontainers to an administrative group by right-clicking the group and selecting New ➤ *SUBCONTAINER*, where *SUBCONTAINER* is the kind of subcontainer that you want to add. In the next section, we'll add a routing groups container to our new administrative group.

You've already worked with the servers, system policies, and folders subcontainers. In the next section, you'll get a chance to experiment with routing groups; in the section "Default Public Folder Tree Management," you'll use the folders subcontainer to control management access to the organization-wide public folders tree.

Using Routing Groups and Connectors

Routing groups containers hold routing groups. Routing groups contain connectors and members. Connectors support network links between the Exchange servers in a routing group and Exchange servers in other routing groups. Members are the Exchange servers that are included in a routing group. An Exchange server can exist in the Members container of one and only routing group at any given time. Figure 15.30 shows the contents of the Members subcontainers of the routing groups in both my Los Angeles (inset) and New York administrative groups.

FIGURE 15.30

A server can exist in
one and only one
routing group's
Members
subcontainers

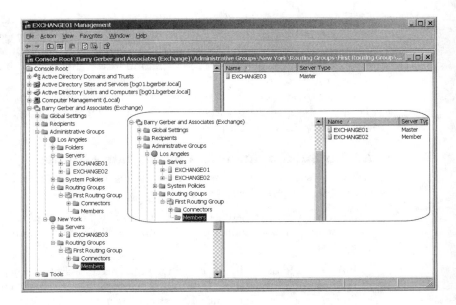

NOTE   *Notice in Figure 15.30 that EXCHANGE03 is a master in its routing group and that EXCHANGE01 is the master in its routing group while EXCHANGE02 is a member. There can be only one master server in a routing group. This server keeps up-to-date information on the status of all connectors in the routing group. It receives link state information directly from various sources, including member servers. The master then propagates this information to member servers. Knowing the latest link state information limits the number of tries by servers in a routing group because only currently unavailable routes are used.*

You can use routing groups and connectors in a variety of ways. Here are two examples, each of which I'll expand upon in this section.

If you have two or more administrative groups, each with its own routing group and set of Exchange servers, you can set up routing between the two groups with one or more connectors. If you like, you can delegate control over your administrative groups to different Windows 2003 security groups, thus restricting management of routing in each routing group to a specific group of individuals.

If your Exchange server is running in Native mode, you can create one or more administrative groups that contain no servers and then create a Routing Groups container and routing groups in your new administrative group(s). Then you can drag appropriately connected servers from their original routing group(s) to your new routing groups and create connectors between these routing groups. Then by delegating control of the new administrative group(s), you can place control of message routing in the hands of a security group(s) entirely different from the group(s) that manage other functionality on your Exchange servers.

CONNECTING EXCHANGE SERVERS IN TWO ADMINISTRATIVE GROUPS, EACH OF WHICH HAS ITS OWN ROUTING GROUP

To connect the Exchange servers in two administrative groups, you need to do two things:

1. Ensure that each of your Exchange servers is in the appropriate routing group.
2. Create connectors between your routing groups.

Each of these tasks is relatively simple. Let's tackle them in order.

Ensuring That Each Exchange Server Is in the Appropriate Routing Group

An Exchange server should be a member of a routing group if it is linked to other Exchange servers on a continuous, high-bandwidth, highly reliable network (a quality network) and/or if its administrative group or routing functionality must be managed by different personnel than who manage administrative-group or routing functionality for other Exchange servers. My Los Angeles servers are on a quality 100Mbps Ethernet network and I want one Windows 2003 security group to manage them. My New York server is also on a quality 100Mbps Ethernet network and I want it to be managed by another Windows 2003 security group. Conclusion: My Exchange servers are in the appropriate routing groups.

NOTE *Think creatively about routing group connectors. The example we're working with here is straightforward and pretty simple. Using serverless administrative groups to hold routing groups opens numerous possibilities for both organizing routing and delegating routing group management to appropriate personnel, especially in a large organization.*

Connecting Routing Groups

Now that I've got servers appropriately placed in routing groups in each of my two administrative groups, I can link them with a connector. I have three options:

- Routing group connector
  - Is the simplest of the three connectors to set up.
  - Has the fewest parameters to set.
  - If security permits, you can automatically connect two routing groups by configuring properties for one of the two routing groups.
  - Uses an SMTP connection.
  - Requires a continuous connection.
- SMTP connector
  - Is similar to a routing group connector, but more parameters must be set.
  - Involves manually setting up a connector for each routing group to connect two routing groups.
  - Also supports Internet SMTP mail services in conformance with RFC 821.

- ◆ Works with a continuous or noncontinuous (TCP/IP) connection (for example, a PPP dial-up connection).

- ◆ Allows for custom authentication and encryption, remote triggering of e-mail delivery, and message size limits.

◆ X.400 connector

- ◆ Requires understanding of X.400 services.

- ◆ Involves manually setting up a connector for each routing group to connect two routing groups.

- ◆ Also supports X.400 messaging services in conformance with 1984 and 1988 CCITT X.400 standards.

- ◆ Works with a continuous (TCP/IP) or noncontinuous connection (for example, an X.25 connection).

You can create one or multiple connectors to link a pair of routing groups. You create multiple connectors to support redundant links between the routing groups. If you want to set up redundant connections, be sure that each link uses a different physical connection. For example, don't set up a routing group connector and an SMTP connector that both use the same physical network connection. Instead, use different connections, such as a wide-area T1 on a frame relay connection for your routing group connector, and a dial-up link for an SMTP connector.

Because I have a quality T1 network link between my Los Angeles and New York locations and because of its simplicity, I'm going to use a routing group connector here. You would use an SMTP connector here for the same reasons that you would use one for Internet messaging, mainly to control dial-up links between Exchange routing groups. For more on the SMTP connector, see the section "Installing and Managing the Exchange SMTP Connector" in Chapter 13, "Managing Exchange Internet Services." The X.400 connector is most useful in organizations in which X.400 is already known and used for messaging connectivity. For example, although it has been replaced by SMTP in many venues, X.400 still has a presence in Europe, especially in the world of electronic document interchange.

To set up an Exchange routing group connector, right-click the Connectors container in one of your two administrative groups, and select New ➤ Routing Group Connector. In Figure 15.31, I'm going to create a routing group connector in the first routing group in my Los Angeles administrative group.

Figure 15.32 shows the Properties dialog box for my new routing group connector. Let's look more closely at the property pages in the dialog box.

General   Because this connector will link my servers in Los Angeles and New York, I've named the connector Los Angeles To New York on the General property page. The drop-down list presents me with the only choice that I have right now for the routing group to which I want to connect, First Routing Group (New York). This is very nice because I don't have to type in anything. If I had set up a number of routing groups in my Exchange organization, the drop-down list would allow me to choose from among them.

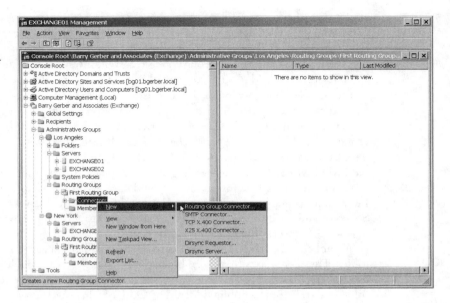

FIGURE 15.31

Preparing to create a routing group connector in an administrative group

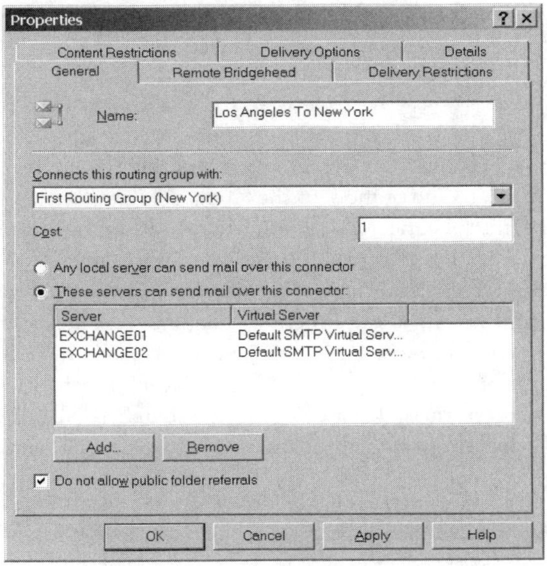

FIGURE 15.32

The Properties dialog box for a new routing group connector, with its General property page open

The Cost setting is useful for establishing usage priorities for multiple connectors between the same two routing groups. For example, if I had both a routing group connector and a dial-up SMTP connector, I would give the routing group connector a cost of 1 and the dial-up SMTP connector a cost of, say, 10. That way, the routing group connector would always be used unless its link became unavailable. Then the dial-up SMTP connector would be used. Costs are also used to determine the closest server when multiple copies of a public folder exist on different servers. Costs can range from 1 to 100.

You can choose whether all or only selected servers in the routing group can send mail over the connector. In Figure 15.32, shown earlier, I've chosen to include both of the servers in the routing group. I could have accomplished the same end by selecting Any Local Server Can Send Mail over This Connector. I made the choice I did because I wanted to hammer home the point that those good old SMTP virtual servers are sending those messages. If I had more than the default SMTP virtual server on one or both of my servers, I would have been offered an opportunity to pick the one that I wanted to handle this traffic. Remember that different virtual servers can serve different IP addresses. So, you could use different virtual servers connected to different networks to provide redundant routing group connector links. That's pretty spiffy.

A public folder referral tells an Outlook client which Exchange servers have a copy of a public folder. The client looks first on its home public folders server, which might or might not be its mailbox server. If the public folder isn't on that server, the home public folder server provides public folder referrals for the public folder. The Outlook client uses these referrals to search other servers for the public folder. If you plan to replicate public folders that exist in other routing groups to at least one Exchange server in the target routing group, then you probably don't want to allow public folder referrals. If you forward referrals, an Outlook client could try to find a public folder on a distant Exchange server before looking on a local server.

Remote Bridgehead   A *bridgehead server* is an Exchange server in a routing group that communicates with bridgehead servers in other routing groups. Bridgehead servers receive messages for themselves and other servers in a routing group. They process their own messages and route messages for other servers to those servers. One or more of the Exchange servers in a routing group can be set as a bridgehead server. For fault tolerance, it's a good idea to set up multiple bridgehead servers, if you have them. In Figure 15.33, I've designated the only server in my New York administrative group as the remote bridgehead server. You can choose which SMTP virtual server on an Exchange bridgehead server will perform the bridgehead function. That grayed-out stuff about Exchange 5.*x* credentials is used when you're connecting to an Exchange 5.*x* server. By default, Exchange 2003 cross-routing group communications use Windows Server 2003–based authentication. When you're connecting to an Exchange 5.*x* server, the fields aren't grayed out, and you can override this default by entering a Windows NT 4 domain name and account to be used to authenticate this connector.

NOTE   *Only routing group connectors allow multiple bridgehead routers. SMTP and X.400 connectors can communicate with only one bridgehead router. So, to create multiple Exchange server–based fault-tolerant connections with SMTP and X.400 connectors, you have to set up multiple connectors.*

TIP   *You don't have to use the default SMTP virtual server on each Exchange server. You can create new virtual servers and use them to handle bridgehead serving. In fact, if you have a number of connectors in a routing group, using only the default virtual servers, you might run out of SMTP virtual servers.*

Delivery Restrictions   You can limit message transmission through your connector based on the sender. As you can see in Figure 15.34, you can tell the connector which Exchange recipients to accept messages from and which recipients to reject messages from. When you click either of the two Add buttons, you're offered a list of recipients from which to choose. This page should be somewhat familiar from earlier chapters, so I'll let you take it from here.

FIGURE 15.33

The Remote Bridgehead property page of the Properties dialog box for a new routing group connector

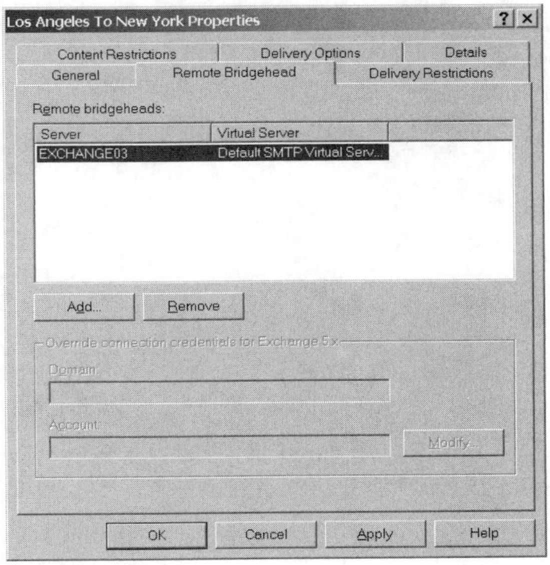

FIGURE 15.34

The Delivery Restrictions property page of the Properties dialog box for a new routing group connector

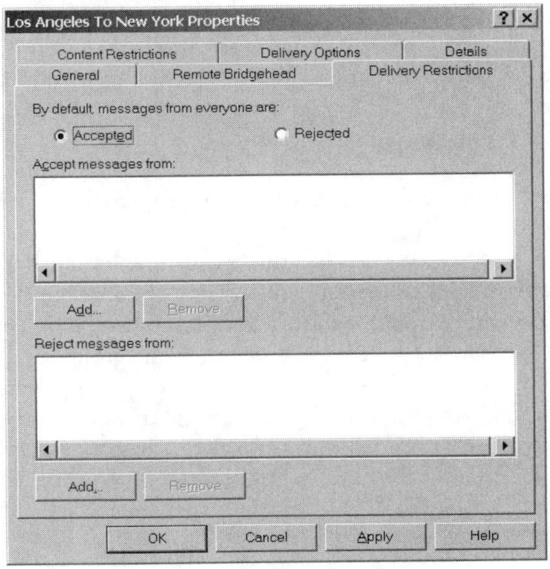

Content Restrictions   Figure 15.35 shows the Content Restrictions property page. You can allow or disallow transmission of messages based on the priorities set by their senders. The default is to allow messages of all priority levels through the connector.

FIGURE 15.35

The Content Restrictions property page of the Properties dialog box for a new routing group connector

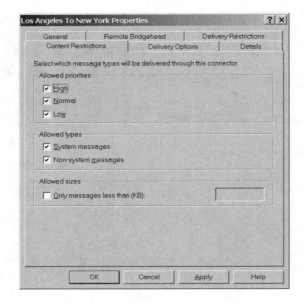

Everything that travels between Exchange servers by way of a connector moves as SMTP messages. Nonsystem messages are the e-mail messages that users, contacts, and distribution groups send. System messages are messages from the Exchange or Windows 2003 system. These include public folder replication messages, delivery and nondelivery reports, and Exchange monitoring tool messages. You can dedicate a connector to system or nonsystem messages, or to both.

You can also limit the size of messages sent through your connector. The default is no limit. You might want to do this if the routing group connector you're setting up rides atop a slower network link than another routing group connector.

Delivery Options   You use the Delivery Options property page (see Figure 15.36) to specify when your connector should run and whether larger messages should be delivered on a different schedule than smaller messages. You've seen pages like this one before, so I'll leave it to you to work out the details.

When you've finished with the Properties dialog box for your new connector, click OK. You're immediately offered the option to create the routing group connector for your other routing group (see Figure 15.37). This is that wonderful feature of routing group connectors that's not available with SMTP or X.400 connectors. Based on the information that you entered for your routing group connector, after it creates your local connector, Exchange creates a connector for your other routing group. Click OK to accept Exchange's most gracious offer, and your second connector is created in a flash.

FIGURE 15.36
The Delivery Options property page of the Properties dialog box for a new routing group connector

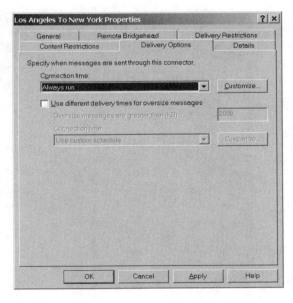

FIGURE 15.37
Exchange offers to automatically create the routing group connector for the second of two connected routing groups.

WARNING *You must have Exchange Full Administrator permissions for an administrative group to create a new connector in the administrative group. Automatic creation of a remote routing group connector works only if you have such permissions for both administrative groups. If you don't have Exchange Full Administrator permissions for the remote administrative group, someone with such permissions can manually set up the connector for the remote routing group.*

In Figure 15.38, you can see the two connectors that support two-way communication between my two routing groups. Exchange automatically created the connector in my New York administrative group. The connector received the same name as my Los Angeles connector. I renamed it to reflect the fact that it is a connector from New York to Los Angeles. Figures 15.39 and 15.40 show the General and Remote Bridgehead property pages of the dialog box for my New York routing group connector as they were configured automatically by Exchange. That's not bad for a Microsoft product, he said tongue-in-cheek.

FIGURE 15.38
Two newly created routing group connectors link two routing groups in two different Exchange administrative groups.

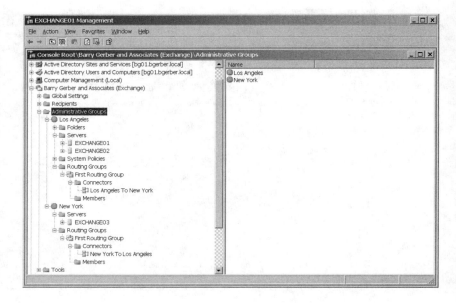

FIGURE 15.39
The General property page of the Properties dialog box for an automatically created routing group connector

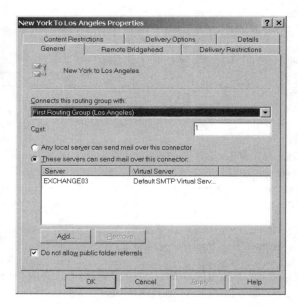

Figure 15.41 shows the status of the Exchange servers and routing group connectors in my Exchange organization. In Figure 15.42, I'm creating a new e-mail notification that will inform me when there is a problem with the connectors in EXCHANGE01's routing group. For more on notifications, see the section "Setting Up Notifications" in Chapter 12.

FIGURE 15.40

The Remote Bridgehead property page of the Properties dialog box for an automatically created routing group connector

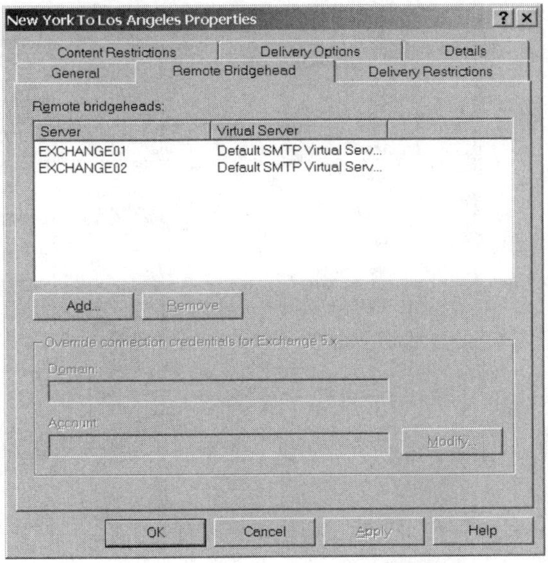

FIGURE 15.41

Two new routing group connectors are up and running.

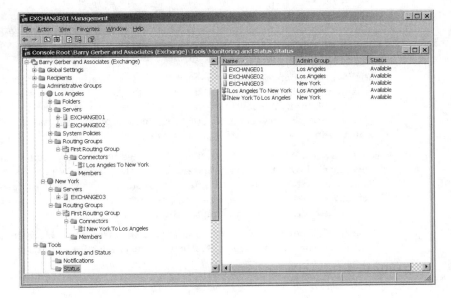

FIGURE 15.42

Creating an e-mail notification for the routing group connectors in a routing group

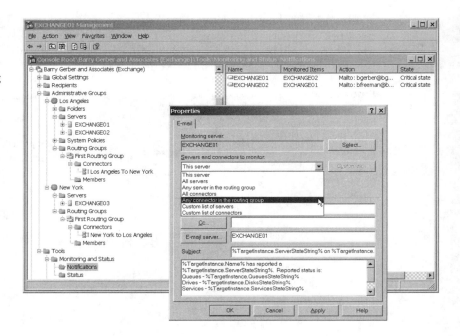

USING PARALLEL WINDOWS 2003 ORGANIZATIONAL UNITS AND SITES

When you've decided to delegate control of Exchange tasks to multiple administrative groups, it might also make sense to similarly delegate control of Windows management tasks. This requires the use of Windows 2003 organizational units (OUs), which work a lot like administrative groups. OUs are created in the container \Active Directory Users and Computers*DOMAIN_NAME*, where *DOMAIN_NAME* is the Windows 2003 domain name; mine is bgerber.local.

Right-click the domain name and select New ➢ Organizational Unit from the pop-up menu. Give the OU a name and click OK; your new OU shows up in the *DOMAIN_NAME* container. You can then delegate control over the OU to any Windows 2003 security group or user or combination thereof. When the OU is in place, you can then add a new Computer, User, or other subcontainer to the OU, and drag objects from other similar containers and drop them in the new subcontainer.

There is also a Windows 2003 parallel to Exchange 2003 routing groups. They're called *sites*. Sites group together well-connected servers and are the locus for intersite Windows 2003 message routing. You create sites in the Active Directory Sites and Services container. You can delegate control for different sites to different Windows 2003 users and groups. Sites are somewhat more complicated than OUs, so I'll leave it to you to further understand and implement them.

You can find out more about OUs and sites in *Mastering Windows Server 2003*, by Mark Minasi, Christa Anderson, Michele Beveridge, C.A. Callahan, and Lisa Justice (Sybex, 2003).

CONNECTING EXCHANGE SERVERS USING ROUTING GROUPS IN ADMINISTRATIVE GROUPS THAT HAVE NO EXCHANGE SERVERS

I'm not going to take too much of your time here. Basically, to set up routing groups in administrative groups without Exchange servers, you do the following:

1. Ensure that your Exchange organization is running in Native mode.
2. Create one or more administrative group(s).
3. Delegate control to your new administrative group(s).
4. Create a Routing Groups container in your new administrative group(s).
5. Create one or more routing groups in your new Routing Groups container(s).
6. Add (drag and drop) each of the Exchange servers for which you want to manage routing to the appropriate newly created routing group.
7. Install connectors between your routing groups.
8. Establish appropriate notifications.
9. As appropriate, delegate control over the administrative group to the appropriate Windows 2003 user or group.

Based on your experience in this chapter, you should be able to take it from here and create a very sophisticated routing group setup. Go to it and have fun.

Managing Public Folders

All of what I said about public folders in single administrative group environments in an earlier section of this chapter ("Working with Public Folders") applies to public folders in multi-administrative group environments. Look to that section for more conceptual discussions of public folder hierarchy replication and public folder replication, as well as accessing the organizational public folder tree from different Exchange servers using Exchange System Manager.

Public folder management gets to be more complex as additional administrative groups are created and connected by routing groups. Two issues come immediately to mind.

First, an Exchange organization's one and only MAPI-based default public folder tree can remain in the first administrative group where it was originally created or it can be moved to another administrative group. In either case, when the default public folder tree has been moved to a new administrative group, control of its management can be delegated to a specially constituted Windows 2003 group. Thus, from a security perspective, folders containers and the default public folder hierarchy are somewhat analogous to routing groups containers and routing groups.

Second, as Exchange organizations grow in size and complexity, nothing becomes more important on the public folders side than the location of public folders and replicas of public folders. You can significantly reduce network traffic and decrease folder access times by replicating heavily accessed public folders to Exchange servers in different routing groups with relatively low-bandwidth links to the Exchange servers where the public folders currently reside.

Let's take a closer look at public folder tree management and public folder replication.

DEFAULT PUBLIC FOLDER TREE MANAGEMENT

As I noted in the introduction to this section, you can control management access to the default pub-lic folder tree by moving that tree to an administrative group other than the one in which the tree was originally created. To do this, you must create a new Folders container in an administrative group, and then drag and drop the default public folder tree into the new Folders container.

In Figure 15.43, I'm dragging my default public folders tree from its default location to a new administrative group and Folders container created just for public folder management. Managers of that administrative group can both view and change the properties of all public folders in the tree and create new folders in the tree. I've delegated control over my administrative group Public Folders Management to a Windows 2003 security group that includes only those users whom I want to be able to manage the public folders in my organization. Now, the managers of my Los Angeles and New York administrative groups who are not members of the new security group have limited control only over the public folders in their administrative groups through the public folder stores on the Exchange servers in their administrative groups. Check out Figure 15.44 for an illustration. Managers of my Los Angeles and New York administrative groups who aren't included in the security group delegated control over my public folders administrative group can no longer create new public fold-ers. That's because administrative creation of public folders can be done only on the default public folders tree to which they no longer have access.

Just for the record, if I needed to do so for security reasons, I could also have created the Folders container in my New York administrative group and dragged the default public folders tree to that container. This would give the managers of my New York administrative group control over my organization-wide public folder hierarchy.

For more information on managing public folders using the default public folders tree, see the sec-tion "Accessing Segments of the Default (Organizational) Public Folders Tree Stored on Different Exchange Servers" earlier in this chapter.

FIGURE 15.43

Dragging the default public folders tree from its default loca-tion to a newly creat-ed Folders container in a newly created administrative group

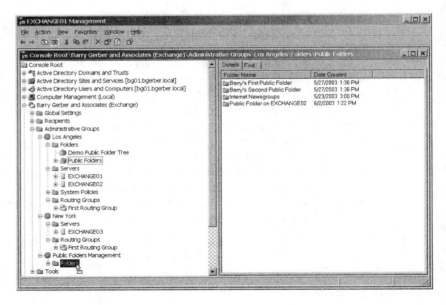

FIGURE 15.44

Public folder management options are limited to the default public folder store in other administrative groups after the default public folders tree for an organization is moved to its own administrative group.

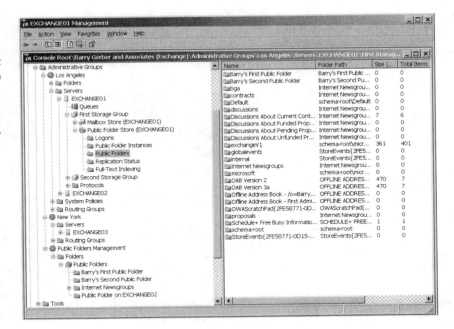

> *TIP* *You can limit all administrative access to public folders in administrative groups that contain Exchange servers (Los Angeles and New York, in my case). You do this by creating an administrative group and installing Exchange servers that support only public stores into the new administrative group. Then you delegate control over the new administrative group to a Windows 2003 security group that includes only those Windows 2003 users whom you want to be able to manage public folders.*

PUBLIC FOLDER REPLICATION

Technically, all copies of a public folder, including the one on the Exchange server where the folder was originally created, are called *replicas*. There's good reason for this. After a folder has been replicated, users will place items into it via the replica on their own default public folders server or on the nearest server as calculated using connector costs. So, no replica of the folder can be considered a master copy. The replicas of a folder update each other on a regular basis, reinforcing the idea that there is no master copy.

You can set up replication of a public folder on either the server that will provide the folder or the server that will hold the new replica of the public folder. To replicate a folder, follow these steps:

1. Right-click the folder in either the Public Folders subcontainer of the Public Folders Store or the default public folders tree. Then select Properties from the pop-up menu. This opens the Properties dialog box for the public folder.

2. Tab over to the folder's Replication property page. In Figure 15.45, I'm setting up a replication of Barry's First Public Folder from EXCHANGE01 (in my Los Angeles administrative group) to EXCHANGE03 (in my New York administrative group). I clicked Add on the Replication property page to open the Select Public Store dialog box.

FIGURE 15.45
Setting up replication of a public folder from one server to another

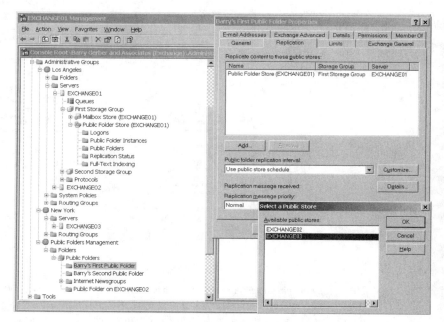

3. Clicking OK in the Select a Public Store dialog box adds EXCHANGE03 to the list of public stores to which the folder's contents will be replicated.

Let's look quickly at some of the other properties that you can set on the Replication property page. The public folder replication interval is based on a schedule that you can set. Depending on the importance of the contents of the folder and available network bandwidth, you can accept the default Always Run, select other options from the drop-down list, or create your own custom schedule for replication of this folder.

When replication has started, the Replication Message Received field shows the latest replication status message when you click the Details button. We'll look at this field later, after replication has occurred. You can give replication messages for a folder more or less transmission priority. Options include Not Urgent, Normal, and Urgent. Select Normal or Urgent for folders with contents of some importance to your organization; select Not Urgent for messages of lesser importance.

When replication has taken place, you should see the folder in the Public Folders container of the public folders store on the server on which the new replica was created. Figure 15.46 shows the replica on the original server, EXCHANGE01. In Figure 15.47, you can see that a replica of the folder Barry's First Public Folder does not exist on EXCHANGE02, as it shouldn't. Finally, the replica that I just created does indeed show up on EXCHANGE03 (see Figure 15.48).

FIGURE 15.46
The original replica
of a public folder on
EXCHANGE01

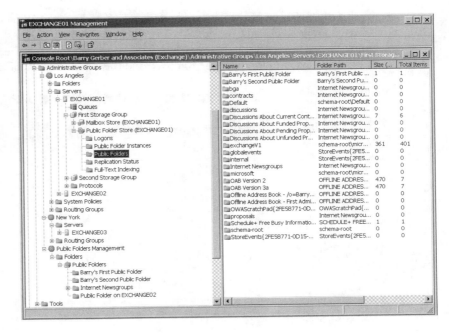

FIGURE 15.46
The original replica
of a public folder on
EXCHANGE01

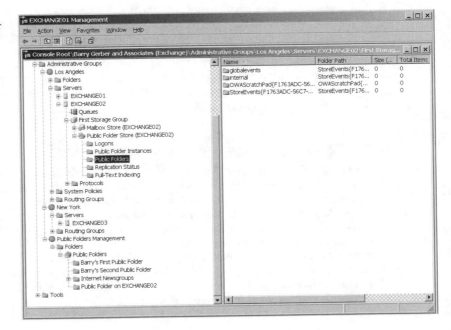

FIGURE 15.47
There is no replica of
the public folder on
EXCHANGE02.

Finally, as Figure 15.49 shows, the synchronization between the two replicas of the public folder is current. I right-clicked the public folder in the `Folders\Public Folders` subcontainer (see Figure 15.49) and selected properties. In the resultant dialog box, also shown earlier in Figure 15.45, I clicked Details for Replication Message Received and this opened the Replication Status dialog box.

FIGURE 15.48

The new replica of the public folder on EXCHANGE03

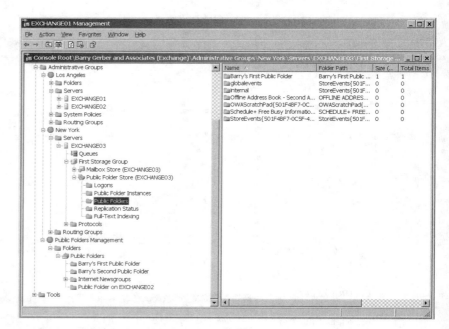

That's really all there is to public folder replication. Monitoring replication is a matter of attending to the dialog box shown in Figure 15.49 and, of course, ensuring that the connectors between your routing groups are up and running.

REPLICATING SYSTEM FOLDERS

The Exchange system uses a series of a special type of public folder to hold information used by Exchange servers and their clients. However, they are normally invisible. To see them, right-click Public Folders in the Folders container and select View System Folders. Some of these folders must be replicated to assure smooth functioning of your Exchange system. One of these is the Schedule + Free Busy folder. This folder holds information for the calendars in every mailbox in your Exchange organization. If the folder isn't replicated, users will not be able to schedule meetings while looking at the free busy times for people they want to invite. The folder's absence on a given Exchange server can also cause some Outlook clients to issue regular and very annoying warnings about not being able to find free busy information. Ensure that at least the free busy folder is replicated. Be careful about most of the other system folders. Unless you know what you're doing, let the system replicate them.

FIGURE 15.49
FIGURE 15.49
The Replication Status dialog box shows that all replicas of the folder are synchronized.

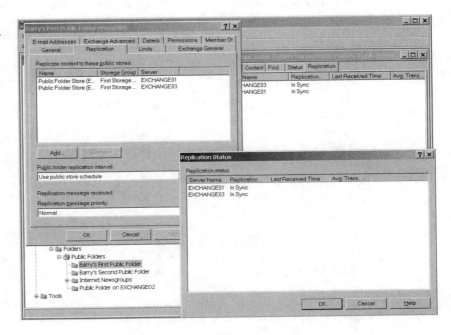

Sometimes replication doesn't seem to be happening, even though the dialog box shown in Figure 15.49 says all is well. You can push replication along in two ways. First, make sure that there is at least one item in the public folder you're replicating. Second, in the Folders\Public Folders subcontainer, shown on the left in Figure 15.49, right-click the folder you're interested in and select All Tasks ➤ Send Contents. Use the Send Contents dialog box that pops up to select the server or servers you want to synchronize and the number of days into the past that you want to resend the contents.

TIP   Don't forget that newsgroups are public folders that you can replicate like any other public folder. Everything works as it does with other public folders.

Installing an Exchange Server in a New Domain in the Same Windows 2003 Forest

In this section, we need to start by setting up a new domain. That means we have to install a new Windows Server 2003 domain controller for the new domain. Then we need to install Exchange Server 2003. As with our previous installations, it's best if the domain controller and Exchange aren't installed on the same computer. However, if you're running out of computers, feel free to put both Windows and Exchange on the same machine to complete this section.

Installing a Domain Controller for a New Windows 2003 Domain

A Windows 2003 forest is the boundary of an Active Directory namespace. Two types of domains can be set up in the same Windows 2003 forest:

◆ A child domain of an existing root domain tree

◆ A new root tree

As you read on, you might find it useful to refer to the section "Namespaces" in Chapter 3, "Two Key Architectural Components of Windows Server 2003."

I might add a new child domain to my bgerber.local root domain tree for one of the subdivisions of Barry Gerber and Associates, for example, my consulting department. I'd likely name the child domain consulting.bgerber.local. The domain consulting.bgerber.local sits below the parent domain, bgerber.local. As you might remember, this sort of domain structure is called a *single contiguous namespace.* From a security perspective, all domains in a single contiguous namespace trust each other. A user who logs on to a subdomain can, depending on security settings, have access to all resources in the single contiguous namespace.

When you install Windows Server 2003 in any child domain in a single contiguous namespace, you don't have to do anything special to create a basic security link between the parent and child domains. An irrevocable two-way trust is set up between the parent and the child domain, meaning that users in either domain can access resources in the other domain as long as they have the appropriate security permissions. The trust is transitive, meaning that if domain A trusts domain B, and domain A trusts domain C, then domain B trusts domain C, and vice versa.

In multiroot tree or noncontiguous namespaces, you add a new root domain that is parallel to other root domains in your Windows 2003 forest. I might add a new root domain to support a new venture by my consulting group, such as selling frozen vanilla yogurt. Hey, that's not so far-fetched. I've certainly spent some time in recent years thinking about such a business (well, actually, any business other than consulting). I'll call this new root domain bgyogurt.com.

As with child domains, when you install an Exchange server in a new root domain, you don't have to worry about a basic security link. Irrevocable two-way trusts are created between the root domains.

In this section, we're going install an Exchange server in a new root domain. When you've done this, you shouldn't have any problems installing an Exchange server in a child domain. As we go through the Windows 2003 and Exchange 2003 installation processes, it should be clear how you'd do an installation in a child domain.

By creating a new root tree, we're violating the rule that you should try to build single-domain tree forests with as many child networks as needed, but with no parallel root trees. However, I think from a business perspective that my new frozen yogurt enterprise merits its own root tree. More importantly, we get to work with the more challenging of the two intraforest domain creation scenarios.

You install Windows Server 2003 just as you have in the past. I'll leave it to you to perform that task. For help, check out the references in the first paragraph of the section "Adding an Exchange Server to a Domain's Default Administrative Group," earlier in this chapter.

While installing Windows 2003, or immediately thereafter, be sure to set DNS server addresses for your new server to the IP addresses of your existing Windows 2003 DNS servers. Promoting your new server to a domain controller for a new root domain in an existing Windows 2003 forest requires that your new server contact a domain controller in the forest to authenticate its right to join the forest.

The DNS entries are essential to that the server finding a domain controller. You could rely on simple NetBIOS if there are no routers between your new server and at least one of your Windows 2003 domain controllers. If there are routers, you must rely on WINS. However, DNS feels so right and is, after all, the name resolution tool of choice for Windows 2003 networks.

After you've installed Windows Server 2003, you're ready to promote the server to domain controller status. There are a few tricky steps in this process, so I'm going to walk you through the installation process.

1. Select Start ➤ All Programs ➤ Run, type **dcpromo**, and click OK. You'll soon see the Active Directory Installation Wizard. Click Next.

2. In the Domain Controller Type wizard page, select Domain Controller for a New Domain, as I have done in Figure 15.50. Don't worry; you'll get a chance later to tell the wizard that you want your new domain to live in an existing forest.

FIGURE 15.50

Using the Active Directory Installation Wizard to create a domain controller for a new domain

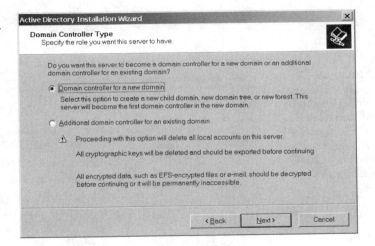

3. In the next wizard page, select Domain Tree in an Existing Forest (see Figure 15.51). You don't want to create a domain in a new forest or a child in an existing domain tree, so the third option is the correct one.

4. You enter a Windows 2003 username, password, and domain name in the Network Credentials wizard page (see Figure 15.52). You need to enter a username from your existing domain that can be used to authenticate the creation of a new domain in the forest. The administrator account will work fine unless you've altered its permissions.

Notice that I've entered the domain name bgerber.local. I can do that because of the steps I took relating to DNS servers a few paragraphs back. If I were relying on NetBIOS or WINS, I'd enter the pre–Windows 2003 or NetBIOS name of my domain, BGERBER.

FIGURE 15.51
Using the Active Directory Installation Wizard to create a new domain tree in an existing forest

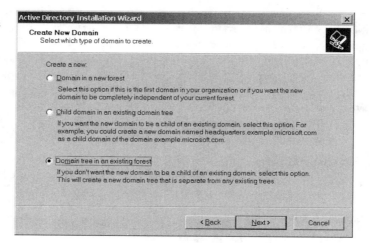

FIGURE 15.52
Using the Active Directory Installation Wizard to enter information required to authenticate creation of a new domain in a forest

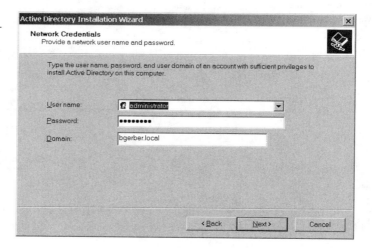

WARNING   *Don't skip this one! If you're using DNS, you must enter the full name of your domain, bgerber.local in my case. If you enter just the NetBIOS name, BGERBER in my case, installation of Windows 2003 will fail.*

5. You enter the full DNS name of your new root domain tree in the next wizard page. As you can see in Figure 15.53, I've entered the name bgyogurt.local.

6. You enter the pre–Windows 2003 NetBIOS name of your domain in the next wizard page (see Figure 15.54). My new domain's NetBIOS name is BGYOGURT.

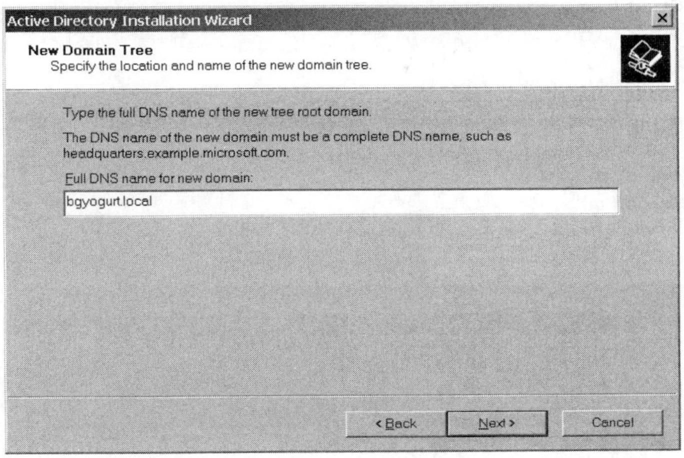

FIGURE 15.53
Using the Active Directory Installation Wizard to enter the name of a new root domain tree

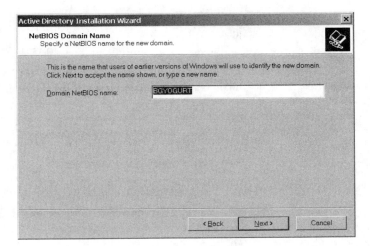

FIGURE 15.54
Using the Active Directory Installation Wizard to enter the pre–Windows 2000 NetBIOS name of a new root domain

7. Use the next two wizard pages to specify where on your new domain controller the Active Directory database and log files and shared system files should be located.

Next, the wizard displays a kind of scary message (see Figure 15.55). All it is telling you is that there is no DNS for your new domain. This is the first controller for the domain, and you didn't set up a zone for the new domain in your first domain's controllers. So, it's a reasonable thing to tell you that you need to do so. I just wish the dialog box was a little less threatening. Anyway, select Install and Configure the DNS Server on This Computer and click Next.

FIGURE 15.55
Using the Active Directory Installation Wizard to specify that a DNS server should be set up while Window 2003 is being installed

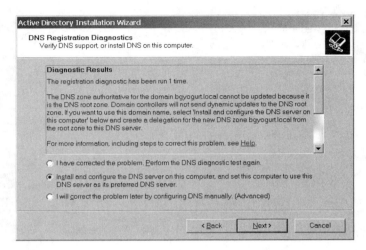

8. In the next wizard page, you're asked whether you want permission on your new domain controller to be compatible with pre–Windows Server 2003. This choice you make depends on where you are in the process of converting existing NT servers to Windows 2003, and whether you want your new domain to be a pure Windows 2003 domain.

9. Click Next and, in the next wizard page, enter and confirm a password to be used when you start your new domain controller in Directory Services Restore mode.

10. The last wizard page shows you the options that you've chosen. When you click Next in this page, domain controller promotion begins. (see Figure 15.56). When promotion is finished, reboot your computer, and your new domain is up and running.

WARNING   *Don't skip this paragraph and the two lists following it or you might not be able to complete the tests that follow or install Exchange Server 2003 in your new domain.*

Now you need to be sure that the DNS servers for both of your domains are set up properly. Basically, you need to ensure that the DNS set up for each of your two domains includes a forward lookup zone for the other domain. Here's how to do that.

First, you have to check to see if both of your domains are represented in the DNS servers for each of your domains:

1. Go to a DNS server for one of your Windows 2003 domains. My domains are named bgerber .local and bgyogurt.local. By way of example, I'll work on the DNS server for my domain bgerber.local. If you followed the instructions I gave you in this and earlier chapters, your DNS server(s) should be on the controller(s) for each of your two domains. Open the DNS manager for the domain you've chosen by selecting Start ➢ All Programs ➢ Administrative Tools ➢ DNS.

FIGURE 15.56

The final Active Directory Installation Wizard page (top left) and the installation progress dialog box (lower right)

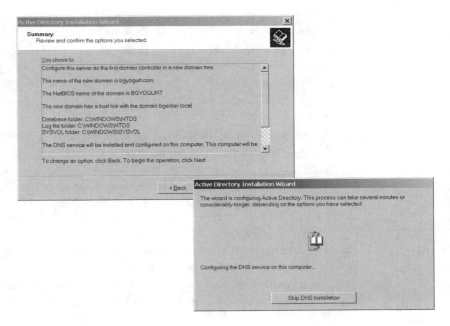

2. Expand the DNS tree until you can see the tree under Forward Lookup Zones. Note whether you see forward lookup zones for both of your domains (mine would be bgerber.local and bgyogurt.local). If you see an _msdcs zone for one of the two zones, that's okay too. For example, I might see bgyogurt.local and _msdcs.bgerber.local in the DNS for my domain bgyogurt.local.

3. Repeat steps 1 and 2 for a DNS server for your other domain.

The following steps apply only to DNS servers where you don't see both of your domains:

1. Go to a DNS server that supports the domain that you didn't see in your other DNS. Let's say that I couldn't see the domain bgyogurt.local in a DNS server for my domain bgerber.local. I'd go to the DNS server for bgyogurt.local. Still working in the DNS manager, right-click the zone for the domain in which your DNS server resides (for me, that would be bgyogurt.local) and select Properties.

2. In the Properties dialog box that pops up for the zone, select the Zone Transfers property page. In this page, click Allow Zone Transfers, then select the Only to Servers Listed on the Name Servers tab.

3. Now you have to add the DNS server(s) for your other domain to the Name Servers page. Select the Name Servers page and add an entry for the DNS server or servers for your other domain. You can just enter the IP address of the server(s) or the fully-qualified domain name (for me, that would be 192.168.0.3 or bg01.bgerber.local).

By performing the last two steps, you've made it possible for the DNS server you are on to send information about itself to the DNS server or servers for your other domain.

4. Now go to a DNS server for your other domain (for me, that would be the DNS server for bgerber.local). Open the DNS manager. Expand the DNS so you can see the Forward Lookup Zones folder, right-click the folder, and select New Zone from the pop-up menu.

5. Use the New Zone Wizard to create a new zone. In the Zone Type wizard page, select Secondary Zone and click Next.

6. Enter a zone name in the next wizard page. You should enter the exact name of your other domain (mine would be bgyogurt.local).

7. In the next wizard page, enter the IP address of the DNS server in your other zone (mine would be the IP address of my new domain controller for bgyogurt.local, which is also the DNS server for bgyogurt.local: 192.168.0.112). Click Next and then click Finish to create the zone. Your new secondary zone should immediately be populated with information from the other domain's DNS server.

8. If you did not see both of your domains in the Forward Lookup Zones folder on the DNS(s) for your other domain, repeat steps 1 through 7.

You'll notice that I am a bit vague about how to deal with domains with multiple DNS servers. You can just set up secondary zones on each DNS server, set up one DNS server with a secondary zone, and point the other DNS servers in the domain to that server in their network settings, or you can do other neat tricks. These options are beyond the scope of this book. For more information, check out *Mastering Windows Server 2003* (Sybex, 2003).

Before moving on, we need to check to be sure not only that our new domain is functioning properly, but also that it is communicating with its sibling domain. You can conduct many tests of interdomain communications, but the most useful is to verify the trust relationships between the two domains.

You use the Active Directory Domains and Trusts snap-in to perform the verification. Here's how you do it (follow along in Figure 15.57):

1. While logged in to your first domain (mine is bgerber.local), find that domain in Active Directory Domains and Trusts.

2. Right-click the domain and select Properties from the pop-up menu to open the Properties dialog box for the domain.

3. Select the Trusts property page. Then select your new domain in the field Domains Trusted by This Domain (mine is bgyogurt.local). Then click Properties.

4. The dialog box for the trust relationship opens (see the upper-right corner of Figure 15.57). Click Validate in the newly opened dialog box, and, if asked, enter the authentication information that you're asked for.

5. Go ahead and choose to validate the incoming trust when asked, and enter the required authentication information.

6. Next, you should see the Active Directory dialog box, shown in the lower-right corner of Figure 15.57.

7. Repeat this test while logged in to your new domain.

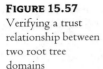

FIGURE 15.57
Verifying a trust
relationship between
two root tree
domains

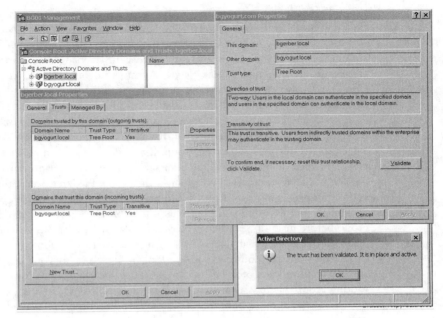

If all is well, you're ready to install Exchange 2003.

NOTE   *While you're playing around with trusts, you should try another experiment. Click on either of the trust rela-*
tionships in the Trusts property page. Notice that the Remove button remains grayed out. That's because, as I mentioned
earlier in this section, these trusts are irrevocable. A basic security pipeline is in place between your two domains, and there's
no valve to close the pipeline. You must rely on delegation of control and security settings for individual objects to expose
and protect cross-domain resource access.

Installing Exchange Server 2003

Okay, let's get right to installing Exchange in our new domain. Be sure that you're logged in to the
Administrator account for your new domain or its equivalent (any account that is a member of the
Domain Admins security group). As always seems to be true, you must do a couple things before actu-
ally installing Exchange.

First, you need to delegate Exchange full administrator permissions to your Exchange organization
to whatever account you're going to use to install Exchange in your new domain. I suggest that you
use the Administrator account for your new domain. Here's how to set up those permissions. On an
Exchange server in your first domain, right-click your Exchange organization and select Delegate
Control. Then use the Exchange Administration Delegation Wizard to assign the administrator for
your new domain Exchange full administrator permissions. You could also include the Administrator
account for your new domain in the Exchange Admins group you created back in Chapter 8. This
group, like all Active Directory groups, is available Windows forest–wide. So, assuming that you followed my instructions for creating and delegating control to Exchange Admins, members of the

group have full administrator permissions for installing and managing all Exchange servers in your Exchange organization, no matter which Windows domain they reside in or will reside in.

Second, unless you want to put your new Exchange server in an existing administrative group, you should create a new administrative group in your Exchange organization. Right-click the Administrative Groups container, select New ➤ Administrative Group, enter a name for the group, and click OK. I called my new administrative group Yogurt Business. Now wait for five minutes or so to be sure that the changes you've just made have been fully established in Active Directory.

If you want, you can also create a Routing Group container in your new administrative group and a new routing group in the container. If you do, you'll be offered the opportunity to have your new server placed in the new routing group. If you don't do this now, after installing Exchange, you can create the routing group and drag your server from whatever other routing group it was placed into when installed to your newly created routing group. I will need a routing group because, although my yogurt business is in Los Angeles, it's located some distance from my consulting business and is linked by a relatively low-speed and somewhat unreliable DSL connection. I decided to create a new routing group before installing Exchange Server. I called it Yogurt Business–Los Angeles.

With the new Exchange 2003 server interactive installation checklist to guide you, installation should be a breeze. You need to run DomainPrep to ready your new domain for Exchange. The checklist reminds you of this. You also need to select the administrative group and, if you created one, routing group where your new server is to be installed (see Figures 15.58 and 15.59).

As soon as your new Exchange server is up and running, you're ready to begin managing it and your new Windows 2003 server. Join me in the next section, where we'll take on these tasks.

FIGURE 15.58

Selecting the administrative group into which a new Exchange server will be installed

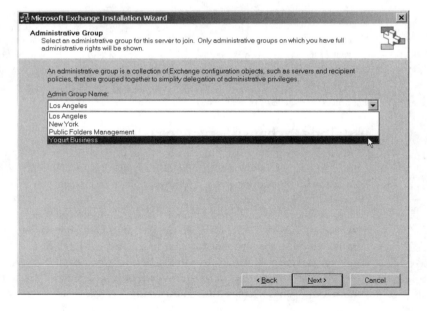

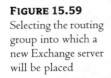

FIGURE 15.59
Selecting the routing group into which a new Exchange server will be placed

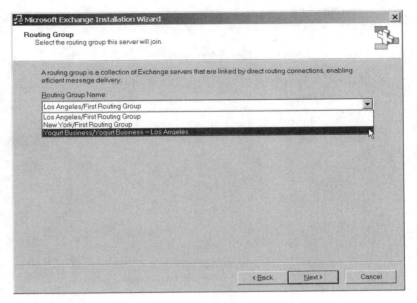

Managing Servers in Multidomain Environments

Windows Server 2003 includes an impressive array of cross-domain management functionality. With the appropriate permissions, you can manage Active Directory and individual Windows 2003 servers from any server in any domain in a forest. Exchange Server works very much the same way, again with appropriate permissions, enabling you to manage your Exchange organization from any workstation or server in a forest on which at least the Exchange management tools are installed.

Interestingly, managing both Windows 2003 and Exchange 2003 servers in multidomain environments is pretty much like managing these servers in a single-domain, multi-administrative group environment. So, in this section, I'm going to talk a little about cross-domain permissions that you might need to put in place and about some of the Windows 2003 and Exchange 2003 tasks that you might undertake in a cross-domain environment. Let's start with Windows Server 2003.

Cross-Domain Management of Windows 2003 Servers

With the right permissions, you can manage anything in Active Directory from any computer on which the Windows 2003 management tools have been installed. It doesn't matter in which domain in the forest the computer resides. In Figure 15.60, I'm logged in to the Administrator account on my first domain, bgerber.local. Without changing the permissions in place after my new Windows 2003 domain, bgyogurt.local, was created, I am able to manage Active Directory components in my second domain from my first domain as though I were logged in to my second domain.

FIGURE 15.60

Managing a new Windows 2003 domain using a new instance of Active Directory Users and Computers while logged in to the first Windows 2003 domain created in a forest

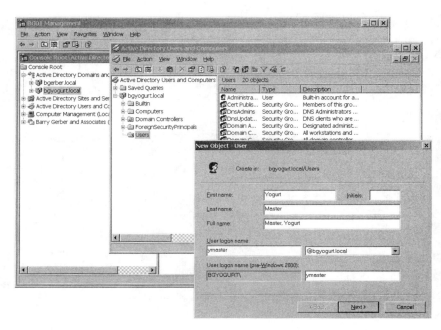

Here's what's going on in Figure 15.60. First, in Active Directory Domains and Trusts, I right-clicked my new domain and selected Manage from the pop-up menu. That opened a separate instance of Active Directory Users and Computers for my new domain. In Figure 15.60, I'm adding a new mailbox-enabled user to my new domain, bgyogurt.local. And I'm doing all of this while logged in to my first domain, bgerber.local.

You can also manage another domain by right-clicking Active Directory Users and Computers and selecting Connect to Domain. Next, select Browse from the resultant Connect to Domain dialog box, and then select the domain to which you want to connect in the Browse for Domain dialog box (see Figure 15.61). Click OK to exit the various dialog boxes, and your Active Directory Users and Computers snap-in should look something like the one in Figure 15.62 where I'm creating a new user in my domain bgyogurt.local from the domain controller for my domain bgerber.local.

If you try to do what you just did from your new domain, you'll be able to see objects and, depending on permissions, even edit Exchange Server objects, but you won't be able to modify or create Windows 2003 objects. Specifically, you won't be able to create a new user in your first domain from your new domain. That's because the Domain Admins security group in the first domain created in a forest always has full control over objects subsequently created in the forest, including new domains and the objects that they contain. The Administrator account for a domain is a member of the Domain Admins security group in the first domain, so it has full control over all domains.

FIGURE 15.61
Connecting to a Windows 2003 domain that will be managed using the existing Active Directory Users and Computers snap-in

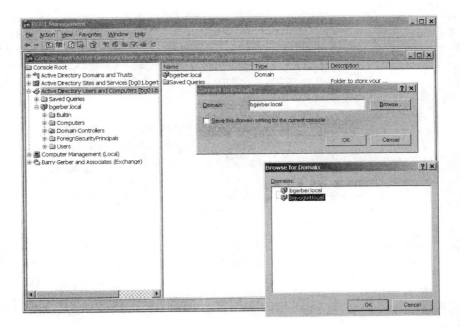

FIGURE 15.62
Creating a new user for the second Windows 2003 domain while logged on to the domain controller for the first domain, using the Active Directory Users and Computers snap-in, which is connected to the second domain

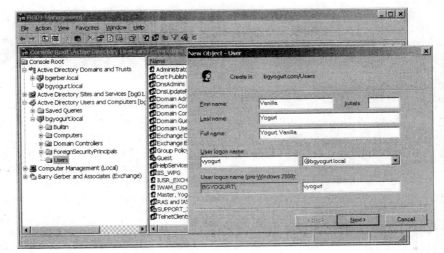

The reverse, however, is not true. Users or groups in other domains must be delegated full or partial control over the first domain. You do this while logged in to your first domain using an account that is a member of the domain's Domain Admins group. Right-click your domain in the Active Directory Users and Computers container, and select Delegate Control. This opens the Delegation of Control Wizard. In Figure 15.63, I'm about to delegate control to the Domain Admins security group in bgyogurt.com.

FIGURE 15.63

Delegating control over users and other objects in the first Windows 2003 domain created in a forest to a group in the second domain

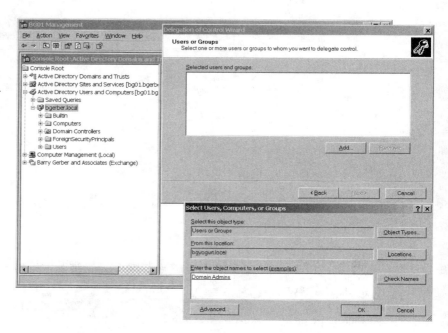

Move to the Tasks to Delegate wizard page, select Create a Custom Task to Delegate, and click Next. In the next wizard page, select This Folder, Existing Objects in This Folder, and Creation of New Objects in This Folder, and then move to the next wizard page. The Permissions page offers many options. If you know exactly which permissions you want to delegate, select them. If not, select Full Control, but be aware that you're giving away the keys to the kingdom to members of the Domain Admins group in your new domain. When you're done with the Permissions page, click Next and then Finish in the final wizard page. The permissions that you've selected are then applied to your first domain.

Now, while logged in to your new domain, open an existing user or create a new user in your first domain. All should work fine.

I want to tell you about one other cross-domain (really cross-server) management tool. You can add a Computer Management snap-in to the Microsoft Management Console for any Windows Server 2003 for which you have management permissions. Use the Add/Remove Snap-ins dialog box to add a Computer Management snap-in. Select Another Computer in the Computer Management dialog box, and then browse to select the remote computer that you want to manage. When you finish using the Add/Remove Snap-ins dialog box, you'll find a new snap-in for the computer that you selected in your Microsoft Management Console.

In Figure 15.64, I'm looking at the application log for my new Exchange server, EXCHANGE04, which resides in my new domain, bgyogurt.local. I'm doing this from the domain controller for my domain bgerber.local while logged in to that domain. Sure, you could do this with NT 4's Server Manager, but could you get to almost everything on an NT server with Server Manager or the other remote management tools such as DHCP Manager? No way! And, there were lots of things that you couldn't do remotely in NT 4, such as disk management. Life is definitely better for systems administrators with Windows 2003.

FIGURE 15.64

Viewing the application event log on a remote Exchange server

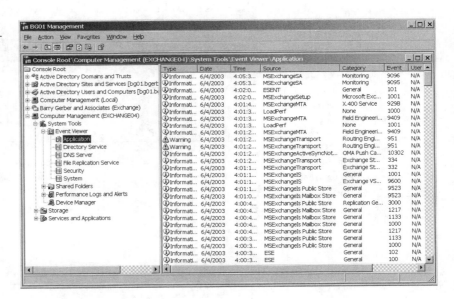

As you work with a remote Computer Management snap-in, you'll discover that you can view and manage some of the objects on the computer and that you can't do a thing with others. This is a permissions problem. Usually you'll be told what needs to be changed to open access to you. For example, if you try to manage a DNS server on a remote computer and you don't have adequate permissions to do so, you'll see a message specifying the permissions that you need.

I'll leave it to you to explore the rest of the wonders of multidomain Windows 2003 management.

Managing Exchange 2003 Servers in Multidomain Environments

One of the first things that you might want to do on the Exchange side is to add users or security groups in your new domain to the Exchange Admins security group that you created when you set up your first Exchange server. If you did as I suggested in Chapter 8 and granted Exchange full administrator permissions to Exchange Admins, then users or security groups from your new domain that are added to this group are able to fully manage your Exchange organization. If you need a refresher on the Exchange Admins group, see the section "Component Management Security" in Chapter 8.

As an alternative, you might want to limit Exchange management for users and security groups in your new domain only to the new Exchange administrative group into which your new Exchange server was installed. To do that, you delegate control at the administrative group level.

You might be wondering how that new mailbox-enabled user, Yogurt Master, that I created in the last section came out. Figure 15.65 shows the E-mail Addresses property page for my friend Yogurt Master. Notice that her address suffixes are the same as everyone else's in my Exchange organization. For example, her SMTP address is `ymaster@bgerber.com`, not `ymaster@bgyogurt.com`. That's because there is only one Exchange recipient policy and that policy causes new SMTP addresses to be created with the suffix `@bgerber.com`. And thank goodness for that, because the outside world currently has no idea what to do with a message addressed to someone at `bgyogurt.com`.

FIGURE 15.65

Without special intervention, mailbox-enabled users in a new Windows 2003 domain receive e-mail addresses with the same suffixes as Exchange users in other Windows 2003 domains.

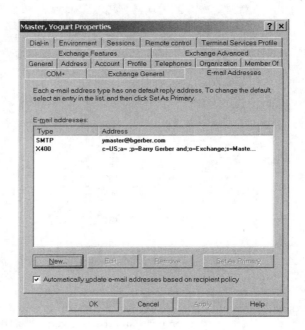

To give Ms. Yogurt a `bgyogurt.com` e-mail address, I would have to publicly register the domain name `bgyogurt.com` and ensure that the correct host and MX records were set up in my DNS or another public DNS, if my DNS wasn't exposed to the Internet. Then I'd have to add a new SMTP address for her in the E-mail Addresses property page shown in Figure 15.65. If I wanted all e-mail addresses for all new and existing users who reside in the domain bgyogurt.local to be automatically set using the `@bgyogurt.com` suffix, I would have to create and apply a recipient policy for that domain. I'll talk about how you can do this in Chapter 16, "Advanced Exchange Server Administration and Management."

As I mentioned earlier, managing Exchange servers in multidomain environments isn't all that different from managing them in single-domain environments. You use the same tools in the same way, and, with the appropriate permissions in place, cross-domain management is transparent. Want an example? Take a look at Figure 15.66. I set up the new message routes between my new routing group Yogurt Business—Los Angeles and the routing groups in my Los Angeles and New York administrative groups in exactly the same way as I would set them up in a single-domain environment. I didn't have to use any new tools or use existing tools in any different way. And, I could have set up routing from any Exchange server in my Exchange organization.

Having read this and the previous chapters, you should now have a number of Exchange Server 2003 building blocks at your disposal. Now it's your turn. Go ahead, mix and match these building blocks to create a customized cross-domain Exchange organization that meets your needs.

WHAT'S POSSIBLE ACROSS EXCHANGE ORGANIZATIONS?

Because this section is about multidomain Exchange systems, you might be wondering about Exchange 2003 organizations that live in other Windows 2003 forests. You can't directly incorporate such organizations into your current Exchange system, and you can't manage them from your current system.

Of course, users in different Exchange organizations can send SMTP- or X.400-based messages to each other, just as they'd send such messages to users on any other SMTP- or X.400-enabled mail server in the world.

You can share Free Busy information (for scheduling meetings with Outlook) between your Exchange organization and other Exchange organizations. You can also share public folders. See Exchange Server 2003 help for more on interorganizational replication. Search for "interorg."

Microsoft Metadirectory Services 2003 (MMS) can be used to synchronize global address lists across Exchange organizations (Windows 2003 forests). MMS is not specifically an Exchange 2003 product. It's tied to Windows 2003. MMS can synchronize what is called "identity information" (usernames, passwords, address lists, and so on) across a range of "identity repositories." Identity repositories can be Windows Active Directories or be foreign to Windows and Active Directory. MMS includes a feature specifically for synchronizing Exchange 2000/2003 global address lists between Exchange organizations. MMS comes in two flavors: Standard and Enterprise. MMS Standard Edition is a part of Windows 2003, though it shipped separately after Windows 2003 shipped. MMS Enterprise Edition is sold separately. Standard Edition supports only Active Directory synchronization and only up to five forests. Enterprise Edition offers all of the features I mentioned above. For more on MMS, check out www.microsoft.com/mms or search for "Microsoft Metadirectory Services" on the Windows Server 2003 site (www.microsoft.com/windows).

If you need to move user information between Exchange organizations (Windows 2003 forests), Microsoft has a nice tool for you: Exchange 2003 Migration Wizard. You can use it to move Exchange server–based mailboxes, local mailboxes (.OST), mailbox rules and delegates, and even Outlook profiles from one Exchange organization to another. Migration Wizard is far superior to the older EXMERGE.EXE, which moved only mailboxes. Migration Wizard is part of Exchange Server 2003. It is installed when you install the product. Use Migration Wizard help to guide you through its use.

FIGURE 15.66

Viewing a new set of multidomain Exchange Server message routes in Exchange System Manager

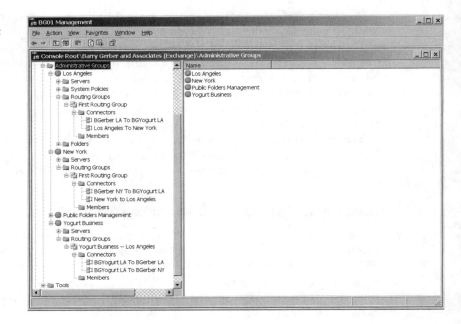

Summary

An understanding of Exchange Server 2003 administrative groups is central to the installation of additional Exchange servers in an Exchange organization. Not only are administrative groups for the servers in an Exchange organization, but they also contain system policies, routing groups, and public folders. In addition, administrative groups are central to distributed management in Exchange 2003 organizations. Administrative access can be delegated to specific Windows 2003 users or security groups on an administrative-group-by-administrative-group basis.

Routing groups support the movement of system messages and user e-mail messages between the Exchange servers in an organization. Routing groups enable connectivity between groups of Exchange servers linked by higher-speed, more reliable networks. Routing groups can be connected using SMTP- or X.400-based protocols. Multiple connections can be set up between a pair of routing groups for reliability enhancing redundancy.

Administrative groups and routing groups are tightly coupled in Exchange Server 2003 Mixed-mode environments. This allows Exchange Server 2003 to integrate with Exchange 5.5 Server sites. To an Exchange 5.5 server, an Exchange 2003 administrative group and the routing groups that it contains appear to be an Exchange 5.5 site. Exchange 2003 servers see an Exchange 5.5 site as a contiguous administrative group/routing group.

In Exchange Server 2003, Native-mode administrative groups and routing groups can be decoupled. An Exchange 2003 server can be placed in any administrative or routing group in an Exchange organization. However, it can be placed in any routing group in any administrative group in an Exchange organization.

Special administrative groups that contain only routing groups can be created. This allows for the decentralization or consolidation of message routing administration. Administrative groups also allow for similar handling of public folder and system policy management.

Additional Exchange servers can be installed in an Exchange organization that exists in a single-root tree Windows 2003 domain. Exchange servers also can be installed in child domains in single-root tree domains. Finally, Exchange servers can be installed in Windows 2003 forests with multiple-root domains. All such installations are relatively easy to do because the installation process is guided by good pre-installation tools and graphical user interfaces.

Managing multiple Windows 2003 or Exchange 2003 servers, whatever the Windows 2003 domain topology used, is also quite simple when the correct permissions are in place. The same tools are used in the same way, whether two or hundreds of computers are being managed.

Part 6

Exchange and Outlook: The Next Level

Chapter 16

Advanced Exchange Server Administration and Management

As you've probably realized, Exchange Server is loaded with fancy and fantastic features. Although we've covered a lot of these already, a number of Exchange Server and Exchange-related Windows Server 2003 advanced features remain to be explored. We'll tackle many of these features in this chapter and other features in the remaining chapters in this book. I think you'll be pleased to see that most of these features are quite easy to use.

Featured in this chapter:

◆ Tracking messages

◆ Adding proxy addresses to a mailbox

◆ Managing organization-wide settings

◆ Monitoring Exchange connectors

◆ Active Directory imports and exports

◆ Troubleshooting Exchange Server

◆ Supporting remote and roving clients

◆ Migrating foreign messaging system users to Exchange

Tracking Messages

One of the biggest pains in the management of electronic messaging systems comes from lost (or *allegedly* lost) messages. With Exchange Server's message-tracking capability, you can get information on the status of messages in your Exchange system. This includes those between Exchange users and those generated by Exchange system components. You can track an outgoing Internet message up to the point at which the message is handed to an SMTP virtual server. Beyond that, you have to use the message-logging features of the SMTP virtual server. For incoming SMTP messages, message tracking begins where an SMTP virtual server hands the message to Exchange.

You'll remember that in earlier chapters, I always suggested that you turn on message tracking for whatever Exchange server or other messaging component we were working with. This is because Exchange Server's message-tracking system relies on logs created when tracking is turned on. So, if you haven't already done so, I suggest that you go back and turn tracking on. You enable mailbox and public store message tracking for each Exchange server on the General properties page for the server, using Exchange System Manager.

As I noted earlier, you can track both user messages and system messages. Let's begin with user messages.

Tracking User Messages

Start up Exchange's Message Tracking Center (or, as we'll call it here most of the time, the *tracker*). To do so, find and click the Messaging Tracking Center subcontainer in the Tools container in Exchange System Manager. This opens the Message Tracking Center dialog box, shown on the right side of Figure 16.1.

FIGURE 16.1

The Message Tracking Center dialog box

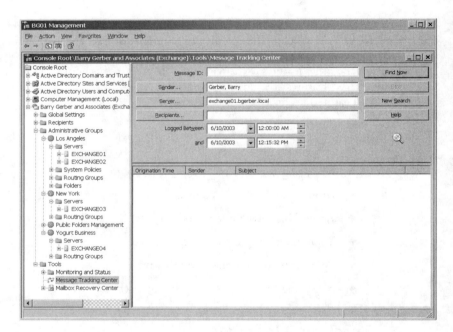

In Figure 16.1, I'm preparing to find messages that I sent to others. I clicked the Sender button to the left of the Sender field and used the Select the Sender of Message to Locate dialog box to find and select my mailbox. You can leave the Sender field blank, in which case you're asking the tracker to find messages from all senders including system-based senders. (We're not using the Recipients field, but if you want to narrow your search for messages, you can select one or more specific recipients using this field.) After filling in the Sender field, I browsed in the Server field for the server where my mailbox resides and selected EXCHANGE01. You can select one or more Exchange servers in the Server field. Instead of browsing for servers, you can also type in the names of servers. When you do this, separate multiple server names with semicolons. Next I used the Logged Between fields to select a date and time range to apply to my search. Finally, I clicked Find Now to display the results, shown in Figure 16.2.

FIGURE 16.2

Viewing messages sent by a user over a specific time period

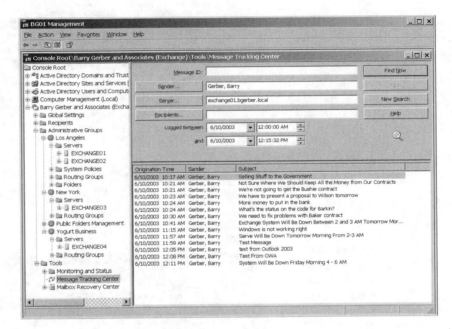

As you can see in Figure 16.2, the tracker found 14 messages sent by me on June 10, 2003. To find out more about a message, double-click it. I double-clicked the last message in Figure 16.2. This brings up the Message History dialog box (see Figure 16.3). Notice the recipients in the To field. Between them, these recipients have mailboxes on all four of my Exchange servers. Figure 16.3 gives you a very nice view of the process by which a message enters into and moves through the Exchange environment. The Message History dialog box graphically shows how important SMTP is to the internal movement of messages. It's not just for Internet mail. You can see that my message was delivered to Jane Dough, whose mailbox resides on EXCHANGE01, but what about the other recipients?

Note in Figure 16.3 that that last thing that happens is the transfer of messages to the Exchange servers of other recipients. In Figure 16.4, you can see what happened to messages for recipients on EXCHANGE04, my yogurt business server. Again, you can see the message move into EXCHANGE04 and finally to the mailboxes of the three recipients that reside on that server. The tracker finds information for delivery of a message to a specific Exchange server in the tracking log files for that server.

FIGURE 16.3
Viewing message-tracking results for selected e-mail messages from a specific Exchange server

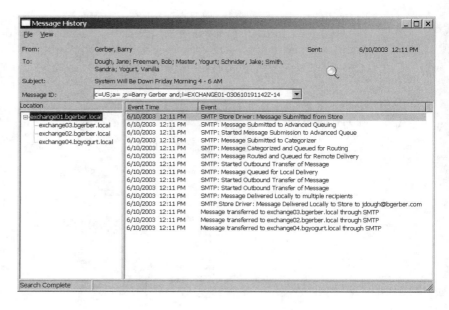

FIGURE 16.4
Viewing the detailed history of a message's trip through an Exchange server after being transferred to that server

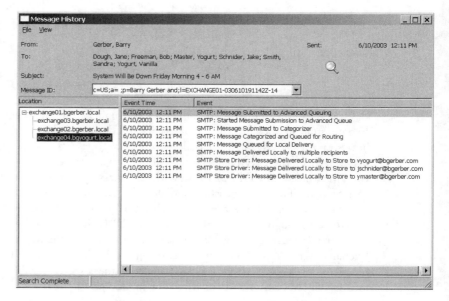

If you need a permanent record, you can save the tracking history for a message to a text file. To do so, while focused on the Message History dialog box, press Ctrl+S or select File ➢ Save and choose the file where you want to store the history.

Setting up another search is easy. Click New Search in the Message Tracking Center dialog box (see Figure 16.1 or 16.2). This clears the tracking dialog box, making it ready for you to enter your new search criteria.

TIP   Message-tracking logs are text files. A separate log file is created for each day that message tracking is enabled on a server. The logs for an Exchange server are located on the server in the directory `\PROGRAM FILES\EXCHSRVR\` `SERVER_NAME`.`LOG`, *where* `SERVER_NAME` *is the name of the Exchange server being logged. For easy identification and sorting, the logs are named using the convention* `YYYYMMDD`.`LOG`. *You can process log files in your own programs, extracting information about message flow, quantity, and so on from them. See the Exchange online documentation for information about the structure of log files.*

Before we leave user message tracking, take a look at the Message ID field near the top of the Message Tracking Center dialog box. You use this field to find a message by its ID. Every Exchange message has a unique identifier that includes the address of the originating organization, the name of the originating Exchange server, the date, and a series of digits. Here's an example of an Exchange message ID:

```
c=US;a= ;p=Barry Gerber and;1=EXCHANGE04-030610172926Z-1
```

Can you pick out the date and time (06/10/03, 5:29 PM) in the digits just after the server name and the dash? The date is in reverse order. The time is based on a 24-hour clock.

The ID is one of the properties of a message; you can use it to track a message using the Message Tracking Center. But how do you find the ID? First, you must find a copy of the message. If you're trying to figure out why a message never arrived at its intended location—which is generally why you'd use the tracker—you'll want the copy of the message stored in the Sent Items folder for the originating mailbox.

Using an Exchange client, find and open the message. Then select Properties from the message's File menu. Tab over to the Message ID property page in the resultant message Properties dialog box for the message. There, in all its lengthy glory, is the message ID (see Figure 16.5). In fact, the message ID is so long that you can't even see all of it in the Message ID field. When you have the message ID, you can enter it in the Message Tracking Center's Message ID field. Be sure to enter a server or set of servers to search, and a date/time range that covers the date and time when your message was sent. Click Find Now, and you'll see any information on the message that is available in your messaging tracking logs.

THAT MESSAGE ID IS AWFULLY LONG!

Worried about accurately typing in that long message ID? Relax. If you're running an Outlook client and Exchange System Manager on the same machine, you can use Ctrl+C to copy the ID from the Message ID property page, and then use Ctrl+V to paste it into the Message ID field. If you're running the client and the Exchange System Manager on different servers, you can paste the ID into a message and send it to yourself. Or you can drag the original message into a new message and send it to yourself as an attachment to the new message. When you open the attachment in the new message, you can look at all the properties, including the ID, just as if it were the original message. If you need to track the message for a user, this last approach is especially useful. Users don't have to know anything about message IDs—all they need to do is send you the message that needs to be tracked.

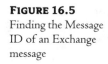

FIGURE 16.5

Finding the Message ID of an Exchange message

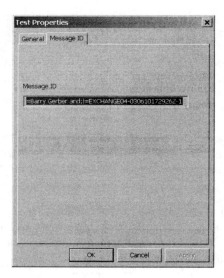

Tracking System Messages

If you're interested in messages generated by key Exchange Server components such as information stores or the System Attendant, don't enter anything in the Sender field on the tracker. You must still enter one or more servers and ensure that an appropriate date/time range is set. Leaving the Sender field blank tells the tracker to find all messages that moved through the selected Exchange server or servers. You can't pick the system components that send messages from the Select Recipients list that pops up when you click the Recipients field's Browse button. And, unlike with Exchange 5.5, you can't choose to see system messages. The only way to see system messages is to leave the Sender field blank. Unfortunately, you'll also see ordinary user e-mail messages.

Figure 16.6 shows the results of a search against EXCHANGE01 with a blank Recipients field. The highlighted line on the bottom right side of the figure is for a message from EXCHANGE01 to all other servers requesting that they send information on the current status of their public folder stores. In Figure 16.7, you can see the progress of the message inside of EXCHANGE01. If you click any of the other servers on the left side of the figure, you'll see the movement of the message inside that server.

FIGURE 16.6

Viewing message-tracking results for selected e-mail and Exchange system messages

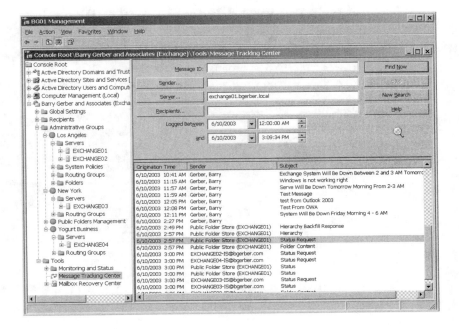

FIGURE 16.7

Viewing message-tracking results for a request from an Exchange server to other Exchange servers for public folder store status information

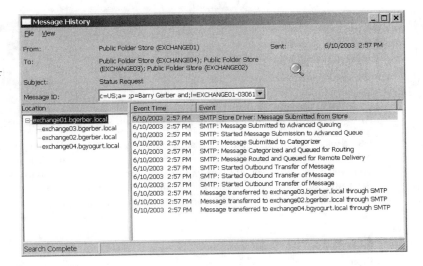

Adding Proxy Addresses to a Mailbox

Back in Chapter 11, "Managing Exchange Users, Distribution Groups, and Contacts," in the section "E-Mail Addresses," we looked briefly at the E-Mail Addresses property page of the mailbox dialog box (see Figure 16.8). I promised then to talk more about how you can add new addresses for a mailbox. Well, you're now ready for all the gory details, so here we go.

FIGURE 16.8

The E-Mail Addresses property page of the user Properties dialog box for a mailbox

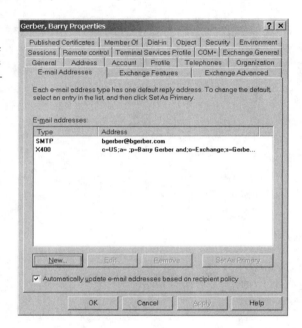

Creating Proxy Addresses

First, why would you want to add a new address for a mailbox? Well, maybe your default Internet address is jjones@giganto.com. Now, that's okay, if you don't mind getting lost among the millions of employees at good old Giganto Corp. Let's say that you're in Sales at Giganto Corp., and you'd at least like to have that recognized in your e-mail address: jjones@sales.giganto.com. The first step is to add what's called a proxy address to your mailbox.

Open the dialog box for your user account in \Active Directory Users and Computers\Users, tab over to the E-Mail Addresses property page, and click New. This brings up the New E-Mail Address dialog box, shown in Figure 16.9. As you can see, you can create secondary proxies for all the address types supported by Exchange Server. Select SMTP Address and click OK. The new Internet Address Properties dialog box pops up (see Figure 16.10). Type in the new address and click OK. As you can see in Figure 16.11, the new address is created.

FIGURE 16.9

Selecting the type of proxy address to create

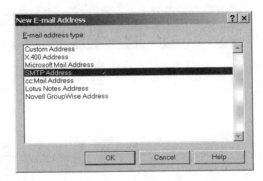

FIGURE 16.10

Entering the new proxy address

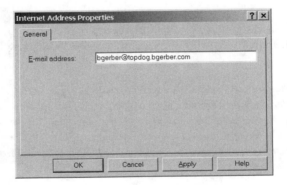

Notice in Figure 16.11 that "smtp" in the new address is in lowercase and that the address is not bolded. That tells you immediately that this address is a secondary proxy address. You can make it the primary address by clicking it and then clicking the Set As Primary button. After you click Set As Primary, SMTP is displayed in lowercase for what was the primary proxy address (bgerber@bgerber.com, in my case), indicating that it has become a secondary proxy address for the mailbox. The primary address is the one that shows as your return address on messages that you send.

New proxy addresses aren't limited to Exchange Server mailboxes. You can add a new proxy to any of the other Exchange recipient types: contacts, distribution groups, and public folders. Secondary proxy addresses can be very useful in a lot of places. Let your imagination roam. When you get the basics down, you can both help your organization and have great fun with secondary proxies.

FIGURE 16.11
The new proxy address is a secondary proxy address.

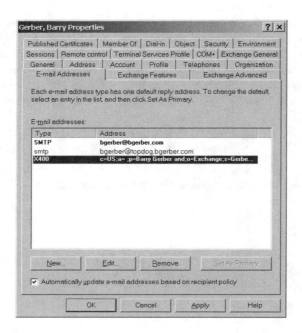

If you have to add secondary proxy addresses to a bunch of mailboxes, you can use a recipient policy to do so. I'll show you how to do this in the section "Managing Organization-Wide Settings," later in this chapter.

TIP   *One of my favorite uses for secondary proxies is to provide simpler SMTP addresses for a user. For example, my primary SMTP address is* bgerber@bgerber.com. *My secondary proxy address is* bg@bgerber.com. *The secondary address is quicker to write and somewhat easier to remember. Internet messages sent to either address come to my Exchange mailbox. Don't believe it? Send messages to both addresses. The really nice thing about this kind of proxy is that you don't have to enter any new information in your public DNS because the Internet domain name (*bgerber.com, *in my case) is already registered.*

Telling DNS about New Proxy Addresses

When you've created a proxy address, Exchange Server is ready to receive mail addressed to it. However, before the mail can be received, you might have to make some changes in your Internet-connected Domain Name Service. For example, if a new Internet secondary proxy uses a new Internet domain name such as the one in my example (bgerber@topdog.bgerber.com), you'll have to add host and MX records to your public Domain Name Service, telling the world that you're now handling messages addressed to the new proxy. See the section "Setting Up and Managing DNS," in Chapter 13, "Managing Exchange 2003 Internet Services," for a refresher on DNS.

Managing Organization-Wide Settings

Using Exchange global settings, you can do a number of quite interesting tasks. These include managing the following:

◆ Recipient policies

◆ Address lists

◆ Details and address templates

Let's take a look at each of these in turn.

Managing Recipient Policies

You use recipient policies to specify how e-mail addresses will be set for a group of Exchange users. In this section, I'll show you how to play some neat tricks with recipient policies and how to manage the recipient update service that ensures that recipient policies are applied as you set them. We'll cover two topics.

◆ Setting different default e-mail addresses for different recipients

◆ Managing the recipient update service

SETTING DIFFERENT DEFAULT E-MAIL ADDRESSES FOR DIFFERENT RECIPIENTS

In the section "Setting the Default Format for Organizational E-Mail Addresses" in Chapter 11, I showed you how to change the default e-mail addresses for an organization using the default recipient policy for the organization. In Chapter 15, "Installing and Managing Additional Exchange Servers," in the section "Managing Servers in Multidomain Environments," I noted that you could change default e-mail addresses for select groups of users. In that chapter, the focus was on recipients in a different Windows 2003 domain. I promised in that chapter to show you how to do this. In a previous section of this chapter, "Adding Proxy Addresses to a Mailbox," I also promised to show you how to set a secondary proxy address for specific users. Let's get to it!

In Chapter 15, I created a second Windows 2003 domain for my nascent frozen yogurt business. I called the new domain bgyogurt.local and added it to my Exchange organization by installing an Exchange server, EXCHANGE04, in the domain. You'll remember that, by default, SMTP addresses for my bgyogurt.local domain are automatically formed using the default e-mail suffix for my bgerber.local domain, @bgerber.com. Now, I want to use @bgyogurt.com as the e-mail suffix for my new company. In other words, I want to ensure that the default e-mail address for every user in the domain bgyogurt.local is set to $EMAIL\_ALIAS$@bgyogurt.com, where $EMAIL\_ALIAS$ is the user's Exchange e-mail alias. Here's how you do that.

First, find the Recipient Policies container for your Exchange organization. Refer to the left side of Figure 16.12 for help in locating the container. Right-click the container and select New ➤ Recipient Policy from the pop-up menu. If you didn't implement mailbox management back in Chapter 12, "Managing the Exchange Server Hierarchy and Core Components," the Properties dialog box in Figure 16.12 will open immediately. If you implemented mailbox management in Chapter 12, you will next see the New Policy dialog box. Select E-Mail Addresses and click OK. This opens the Properties dialog box for your new policy.

FIGURE 16.12

The dialog box for a new recipient policy, and the Find Exchange Recipients dialog box used to modify filter rules for a recipient policy

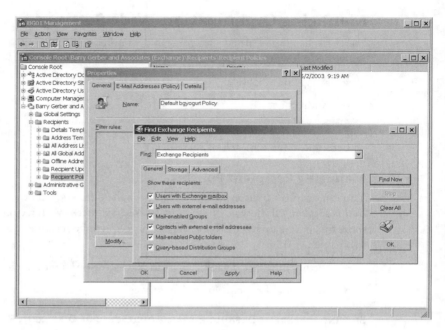

Give your policy a name. I called mine "Default bgyogurt Policy." Now you have to add filters to ensure that the policy applies only to the recipients that you want. Click Modify in the Properties dialog box to open the Find Exchange Recipients dialog box (see the right side of the figure). Here you select the recipients to which you want to apply your new policy.

You use the General property page of the Find Exchange Recipients dialog box to select the types of Exchange recipients for this policy. In the case of my domain bgyogurt.com, I want to apply my new policy to all recipients, so I'll leave all of them checked.

In Figure 16.13, I selected the Storage page of the Find Exchange Recipients dialog box and I'm specifying that my new recipient policy should apply to all mailboxes on the server EXCHANGE04. This is the only Exchange server in the domain bgyogurt.com, and I want the policy to apply to all recipients in the domain. So, selecting EXCHANGE04 is all I have to do to ensure that my new recipient policy will do what I want. You can select only one specific Exchange server per policy. So, if I were to add a new Exchange server to bgyogurt.com, I would have to add a recipient policy for it.

After selecting an Exchange server and clicking OK on the Select Exchange Server dialog box, click OK on the Find Exchange Recipients dialog box. A warning dialog box opens (see Figure 16.14), telling you that the policy you're creating won't apply until you take the necessary action to apply it. You need to do one more thing before you're finished, so don't worry about applying the policy yet. Click OK to clear the warning dialog box.

FIGURE 16.13
Specifying the Exchange servers to which a new recipient policy should apply

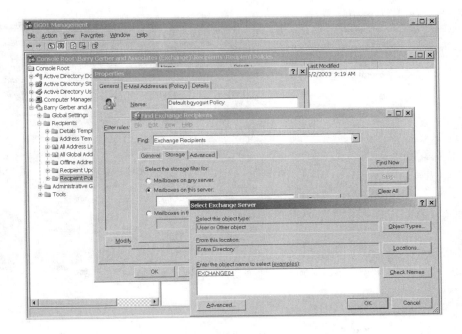

FIGURE 16.14
A dialog box warns that a recipient policy must be applied when its filter changes.

Figure 16.15 shows the script that is used to select the Exchange recipients to which your new policy will apply. The script was generated from the choices that you made earlier. As you can see in the figure, the script is pretty easy to read.

Next you must set the e-mail defaults that you want to use for this recipient policy. You do that in the E-Mail Addresses property page of the Properties dialog box for your new recipient policy. In Figure 16.16, I'm changing the default SMTP address format from @bgerber.com to @bgyogurt.com. Now all recipients on the server EXCHANGE04 will receive an SMTP e-mail address EMAIL_ALIAS@bgyogurt.com instead of the organization-wide EMAIL_ALIAS@bgerber.com.

FIGURE 16.15
The filter that is used to select the recipients to which a recipient policy applies

FIGURE 16.16
Setting default e-mail address formats for a recipient policy

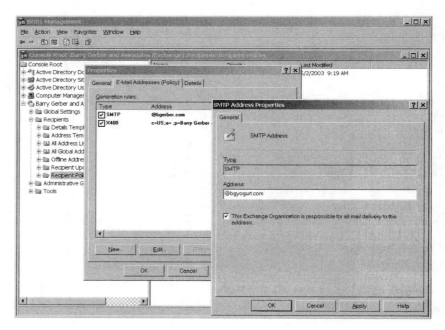

When you close the Properties dialog box for your new recipient policy, you'll see the dialog box shown in Figure 16.17. Click Yes, and all existing e-mail addresses that meet the criteria of the filter that you created are updated to the e-mail addresses that you set in your new recipient policy. You should now see a new recipient policy in the Recipient Policies container (see Figure 16.18).

FIGURE 16.17

A dialog box that initiates updates of all e-mail address affected by a recipient policy

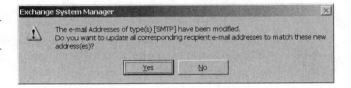

FIGURE 16.18

A new recipient policy in the Recipient Policies container

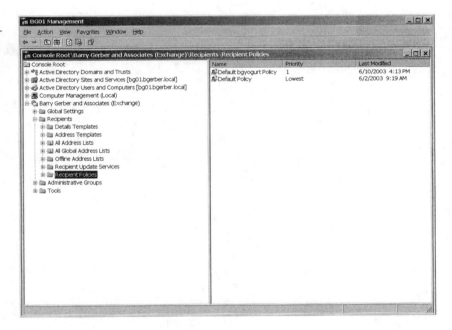

To apply your new policy as you were instructed to do in the warning dialog box, right-click the policy and select Apply This Policy Now. Anytime you change a recipient policy, be sure to reapply it. Okay, the policy now affects existing and newly created recipients to whom it applies.

Notice in Figure 16.18 that the organization-wide default recipient policy (Default Policy) has a priority of Lowest. This means the default policy will apply only when no other policy exists for a user. Notice also that my new policy (Default bgyogurt Policy) has a priority of 1, meaning that it supersedes the organization-wide default policy. Newly-created recipient policies are assigned a priority number that is one higher than the highest existing priority. A priority of 1 is the highest priority. If you have multiple policies that might apply to a user or set of users, set priorities to ensure that the correct policy applies.

Policies are listed in descending priority order in the Recipient Policies container. To change a policy's priority, right-click it and select All Tasks ➤ Move Up, or All Tasks ➤ Move Down from the pop-up menu. You can't change the priority of the default recipient policy, although you can delete it. Before deleting the default policy, ensure that other policies you've created cover your organization.

Figure 16.19 shows the new address for Vanilla Yogurt, a user whose mailbox resides on the bgyogurt.local server. Vanilla now has a primary SMTP address of **vyogurt@bgyogurt.com**. Notice that Vanilla's original address, **vyogurt@bgerber.com** is still there. That's because it was created before the new recipient policy was created. If, after creating a new recipient policy, you create a new user to whom the new policy applies, the user will get only the e-mail address specified in the new policy. You can delete the old e-mail address if you want.

FIGURE 16.19

A recipient to whom a new recipient policy applies gets an e-mail address as specified in the new policy

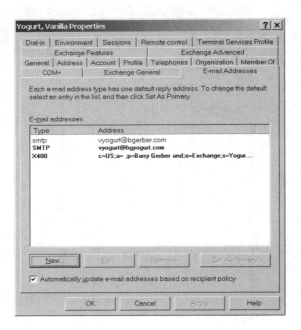

Okay, now let's set up a policy to give certain users a secondary SMTP proxy address. I'm going to set up a policy to give Barry Gerber and Associates executives an SMTP address format of **@topdog.bgerber.com**. Because you've been through this process once, I'm going to move quickly here. Open the dialog box for a new recipient policy. Select the recipient types to which you want the policy to apply in the General property page. I want this policy to apply only to users with an Exchange mailbox, so I'll pick that option.

Next tab over to the Advanced property page. In Figure 16.20, I've selected the Department field and specified that a user must have a value of Executive Management in the field for the filter to apply to the user. You can select from among a number of operators, including Starts With, Ends With, Is Not, Present, and Not Present. You can set multiple filter criteria for the same or different recipient types. Click Add to add the filter to the list of filters.

FIGURE 16.20
Using the Advanced property page of the Find Exchange Recipients dialog box to set a recipient policy filter based on the department to which a user belongs

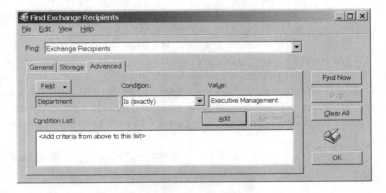

Next, on the E-Mail Addresses property page in the Properties dialog box for my new recipient policy, I added a secondary SMTP proxy address @topdog.bgerber.com. Finally, I applied my new recipient policy. Now every existing and newly created mailbox-enabled user whose department is set to Executive Management will receive an SMTP primary e-mail address formatted as *EMAIL_ALIAS@bgerber.com* and a secondary SMTP address formatted as *EMAIL_ALIAS@topdog.bgerber.com*.

MANAGING THE RECIPIENT UPDATE SERVICE

Among other things, the recipient update service is responsible for applying recipient policies to Exchange recipients. When a recipient or recipient policy is created or altered, the service creates or modifies recipient e-mail addresses based on recipient policies. The recipient update service doesn't always do its thing immediately. Try this: Right after you create a new mailbox-enabled user, tab over to the user's E-Mail Addresses property page. I'll bet that the addresses aren't there yet. Close the user's Properties dialog box, wait 30 seconds or so, and then right-click the `Active Directory\Users` container and select Refresh. Open the user's properties dialog box and tab over to the E-Mail Addresses property page. The addresses should now be there.

The recipient update service runs on Exchange servers. The recipient update service updates information in Active Directory, which, of course, exists on Windows 2003 domain controllers. An Exchange server running the recipient update service can update one and only one domain controller. A domain controller can be updated by one and only one Exchange server. So, you can have multiple recipient-update services in a domain only if you have multiple domain controllers.

For redundancy, you should have at least two domain controllers in a domain. That means that you can also have redundant Exchange servers running the recipient update service. If portions of your network are linked by slower, less reliable connections, you should place Exchange servers that run the recipient update service on both sides of such links.

Two types of recipient update service servers exist. One of these updates the Active Directory for a Windows 2003 domain. The other updates Active Directory for an entire Windows 2003 forest of Exchange servers.

Most of the time, you don't have to worry a bit about the recipient update service. However, if you add a domain controller, or if an existing recipient update service server goes down, you're very likely to find yourself messing with recipient update services.

Here's a quick overview of recipient update service management.

The Recipient Update Services container appears on the left side of Figure 16.21. The Properties dialog box for the recipient update service in my Windows 2003 domain bgerber.local is on the right side of the figure. As you can see, it currently runs on EXCHANGE01. I can change the server any time by clicking the Browse button to the right of the Exchange Server field. I can also use this dialog box to change the domain controller being serviced by the recipient update service and the update interval.

FIGURE 16.21

The Recipient Update Service container and the dialog box for an instance of the recipient update service that runs on a specific Exchange server

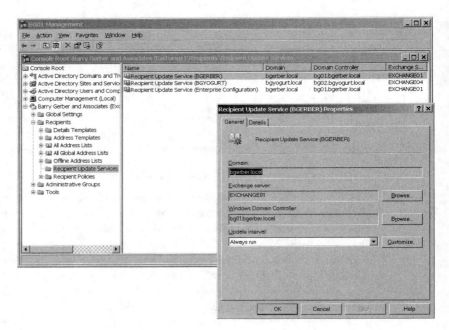

To force an update of recipients by a service, right-click the service in the left pane of Exchange System Manager and select Update Now. To force a service to re-create all e-mail addresses under its control, right-click the service and select Rebuild. A rebuild can take several hours in a domain with a large number of recipients. Exchange System Manager kindly warns you of this possibility and asks whether you want to continue.

TIP   If you have multiple domain controllers, you can create a new recipient update service to parallel the ones that already exist. To do so, right-click the Recipient Update Services container and select New ➤ Recipient Update Service. Use the resultant dialog box to create the new service.

Managing Address Lists

Exchange 2003 supports a range of address lists. These include both global and narrower address lists. You can see these lists on the left side of Figure 16.22. You can create your own address lists in either the All Address Lists or the All Global Address Lists container. In the figure, I'm creating a new list for employees of Barry Gerber and Associates who work in the Los Angeles office. I right-clicked the All Address Lists container and selected New ➤ Address List from the pop-up menu. In the Properties dialog box for the list, I named it BGA Los Angeles and clicked Filter Rules to open the same Find Exchange Recipients dialog box that we used in the section "Setting Different Default E-Mail Addresses for Different Recipients," earlier in this chapter. First, I selected Only Users with Exchange Mailbox in the General property page of this dialog box. This ensures that other recipient types won't appear in the list. In Figure 16.22, in the Advanced property page, I'm specifying that recipients should be included in this list if the field City equals Los Angeles.

FIGURE 16.22

Creating a new address list using the Create Exchange Address list dialog box

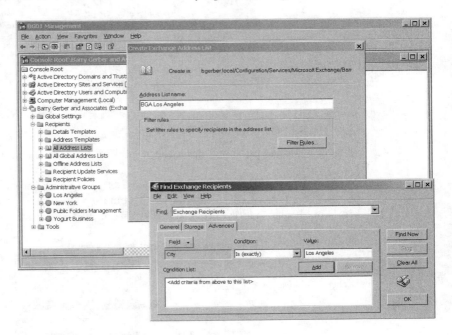

That's it. After I click OK to exit the two dialog boxes, my list is created. Figure 16.23 shows the membership of the list. To view a list's membership, find and right-click the list object, and select Properties from the pop-up menu. Then click Preview in the resultant Properties dialog box for the list. In the figure, the Preview button is hidden by the Address List Preview dialog box. Notice that any user with Los Angeles as their city appears in the new list, including the LA folks who work in my yogurt business.

FIGURE 16.23
Previewing the members of a newly created address list

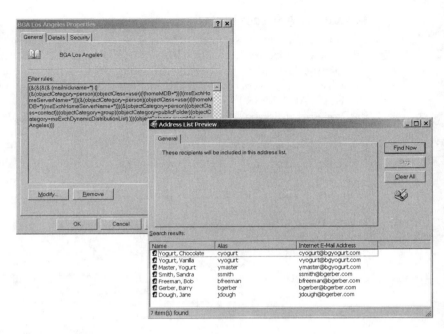

The new address list shows up in an Outlook client's address book. You can see this in Figure 16.24.

You can create address lists within address lists. In this way, you can create hierarchies of lists. For example, I could create a BGA Los Angeles list but then set its filters so that it never has any addresses. Then I could create address lists inside that list for different departments.

FIGURE 16.24
Viewing a new address list in an Outlook client's address book

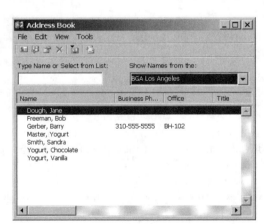

How are address lists kept current? You might have guessed it by now. The recipient update service keeps address lists, including address lists that you create, up to date.

THE OFFLINE ADDRESS LIST

The offline address list is copied to a computer, usually a mobile computer, so that a user can address and compose e-mail messages while disconnected from the Exchange Server environment. You manage the offline address list in the Offline Address Lists container (see the left side of Figure 16.22). There is a default offline address list. You can create additional offline address lists (right-click the Offline Address Lists Container, and select New ➤ Offline Address List). The default offline address list draws its recipients from the default global address list. You can change this option by adding or removing address lists using the address list's Properties dialog box (right-click the list and select Properties). Offline address lists are not kept up-to-date by the recipient update service. A specific Exchange server is assigned responsibility for keeping each offline address list current.

Managing Details and Address Templates

The only subcontainers in the Recipients container that I haven't covered are the Details Templates and Address Templates subcontainers. There's little that you can or have to do with these objects, but it does help to understand them a bit.

Outlook clients use details templates to display the properties of a recipient or to perform other Outlook client functions, such as a search for a specific recipient. Address templates are used when an Outlook client user creates a one-off address for a foreign messaging system. Templates exist for a wide range of languages. You can add to or modify these templates. See the Exchange Server documents for more information about template management.

Managing Organization-Wide Mailbox Message Defaults

You can set global maximum inbound and outbound message size limits, as well as limits on the number of recipients that a message may contain. These limits apply to user mailboxes. Message size limits apply to messages entering or leaving a mailbox. Recipients per message limits apply to messages sent from a mailbox. If a message exceeds any of these limits, it is returned to its sender. The default for all three of these limits is No Limit.

You can set inbound and outbound message size limits on a mailbox-by-mailbox basis (see the section "Delivery Restrictions" in Chapter 11). The default for a mailbox is No Limit. If a mailbox has no limit and if you've set global limits, the global limits apply. You can't set maximum recipients per message limits on a mailbox-by-mailbox basis. The only way that you can set mailbox-based limits of this kind is by establishing global limits.

You set global message size and recipients limits using the Message Delivery Properties dialog box, shown in Figure 16.25. Open the dialog box by right-clicking the Message Delivery container, selecting Properties from the pop-up menu, and tabbing over to the Defaults property page. In the figure, I've changed the limits for maximum sending and receiving message size.

FIGURE 16.25

Using the Message Delivery Properties dialog box to set maximum size and recipient limits for mailboxes in an Exchange organization

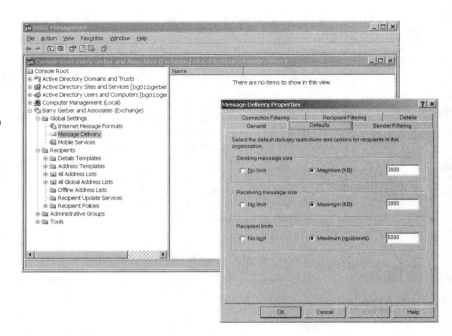

In Chapter 13, in the section "Messages," I discussed setting incoming and outgoing message size and per-message recipient limits for an SMTP virtual server. You might be wondering how these limits relate to the global limits discussed in this section. SMTP virtual server limits apply to messages passing through that server. Global limits apply to messages entering and leaving a mailbox. If a user tries to send a message that meets mailbox limits but that doesn't comply with SMTP virtual server limits, the message is returned by the SMTP virtual server. If the SMTP virtual server attempts to pass an incoming message that doesn't meet global limits to a mailbox store, the mailbox store rejects the message. The virtual server then sends a nondelivery report to the sender of the message.

Looking at Figure 16.25, you might be wondering about the Filtering property pages in the Message Delivery Properties dialog box. I mentioned this page in Chapter 13, in the section "Managing SMTP Virtual Servers." In a few words, filters let you screen out SMTP messages from specific e-mail addresses, enabling such things as spam e-mail control. I will discuss these filters in more detail in Chapter 18, "Exchange Server System Security."

Monitoring Exchange Connectors

I discussed Exchange server monitoring in some detail in Chapter 12, in the section "Monitoring," and in Chapter 15, in the section "Enhancing Exchange Server Monitoring." You can also monitor Exchange connectors. You'll remember that we installed some Exchange routing group connectors in the last chapter. Now we're ready to look at connector monitoring.

As Figure 16.26 shows, you monitor connectors in the same place that you monitor servers, in the `\Tools\Monitoring and Status\Status` container. On the right side of the figure, you can see that there is a problem with the routing group connector between my Los Angeles–based consulting organization (BGerber LA) and my yogurt business (BGYogurt LA), which is also in Los Angeles, but at another physical location. The routing group connector icon on the Los Angeles side of the route has a little red *X* on it and it's shown as unavailable. The server in the routing group in the Administrative group BGYogurt, EXCHANGE04, has its own little red *X* and shows a status of unreachable.

FIGURE 16.26
Using the Status container to monitor servers and connections

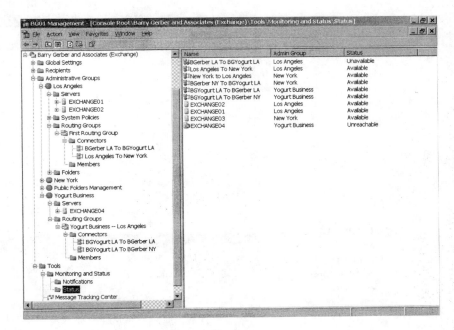

How did this catastrophe occur? Simple, I unplugged the network cable for EXCHANGE04.

"But why," you might be asking, "is the route from BGYogurt LA to BGerber LA not also shown as unavailable?" After all, I did pull the plug on EXCHANGE04. Here's why. In the last chapter, I pointed out that one Exchange server in a routing group is the routing master. Other servers are member servers. If the routing group master is unavailable to report connector problems in its routing group, you won't see problems with those connectors. EXCHANGE04 is down and I know it. However, EXCHANGE04 can't tell my other Exchange servers that its own connector is down.

The problem with my routing group connectors is confirmed in Figure 16.27, which shows an e-mail notification sent to me noting that my connector from BGerber LA to BGYogurt LA is down. To set up the notification, I right-clicked the Notifications container, shown earlier in Figure 16.26, and selected New ➤ E-Mail Notification from the pop-up menu. I then filled in the resultant Properties dialog box, as shown in Figure 16.28. You can set up a notification for one, many, or all connectors in a routing group, or for all connectors in an Exchange organization. In Figure 16.28, I'm choosing to set up a notification for all the connectors in my Exchange organization. You set up connector notifications in the same way that you set up server notifications. For more information, check out the section "Setting Up Notifications" in Chapter 12.

FIGURE 16.27
An e-mail notification that a connection is down

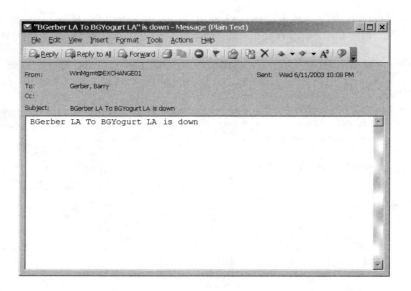

FIGURE 16.28
Settings for an e-mail notification for a routing group connector

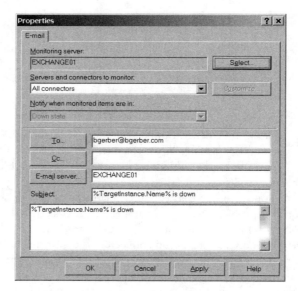

Active Directory Imports and Exports

Wouldn't it be nice if you could move information into and out of Active Directory? For example, then you wouldn't have to worry about manually creating users and their mailboxes. The good news is that you can import information into and export it from Active Directory. The bad news is that this is not a task for someone who lacks a sophisticated understanding of Active Directory.

In this section, I'm going to point you to a Windows Server 2003 tool for doing Active Directory imports and exports. I'll show you how to use it to do a basic export so that you can see how Active Directory exports and imports are structured. Then I'll point you to some books that you can use to gain the understanding that you need to become competent at Active Directory importing and exporting.

The tool is LDIFDE.EXE. It comes with Windows Server 2003. LDIF stands for *LDAP Data Interchange Format*, which is an Internet standard for a file format that can be used to move data into and out of a database compliant with Lightweight Directory Access Protocol (LDAP). Active Directory is LDAP-compliant. DE in LDIFDE.EXE stands for *data exchange*.

To run LDIFDE.EXE, open a command prompt (Start ➤ Command Prompt). Type **LDIFDE -?** for a list of command-line switches. To export Active Directory information on users, type the following: **ldifde -f** *OUTPUT_FILE_NAME* **-s** *DOMAIN_CONTROLLER_NAME* **-d "dc=***DOMAIN_NAME_1-x*"** -p subtree -r objectclass=user**. Here, *OUTPUT_FILE_NAME* is the name of the file to which output from LDIFDE.EXE should be sent, *DOMAIN_CONTROLLER_NAME* is the name of the Windows 2003 domain controller with the Active Directory from which you want to export, and *DOMAIN_NAME_1-x* is a portion of your Windows 2003 domain name, starting with the lowest level (for example "dc=bgerber,dc=local").

Figure 16.29 shows the LDIFDE command line that I entered to export user information from the Active Directory on my domain controller, bg01.bgerber.local. In Figure 16.30, you can see some of the information about my user account and mailbox that was exported.

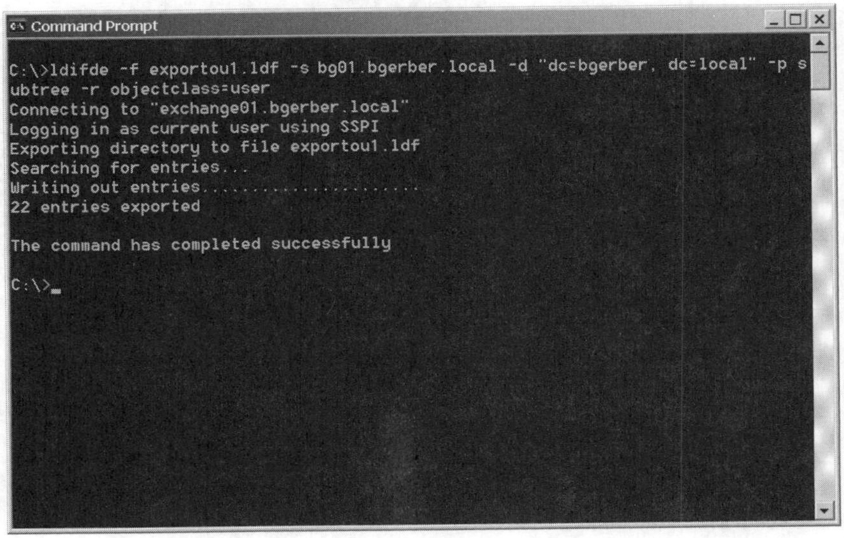

FIGURE 16.29

Running LDIFDE.EXE

```
C:\>ldifde -f exportou1.ldf -s bg01.bgerber.local -d "dc=bgerber, dc=local" -p s
ubtree -r objectclass=user
Connecting to "exchange01.bgerber.local"
Logging in as current user using SSPI
Exporting directory to file exportou1.ldf
Searching for entries...
Writing out entries.....................
22 entries exported

The command has completed successfully

C:\>_
```

I hope that Figure 16.30 instills in you just enough awe to prevent you from going much further without boning up on Active Directory. These references should help:

◆ Microsoft Knowledge Base article 237677, "Using LDIFDE to Import/Export Directory Objects to the Active Directory" (available at www.microsoft.com)

◆ *Active Directory,* Second Edition, by Robbie Allen and Alistair G. Lowe-Norris (O'Reilly and Associates, 2003)

◆ *Active Directory for Microsoft Windows Server 2003,* by Stan Reimer and Mike Mulcare (Microsoft Press, 2003)

TIP   Another program that comes with Windows Server 2003, CSVDE.EXE, also performs exports and imports from Active Directory. It formats exports and expects imports in comma-delimited format. The output is difficult to read. However, because you can specify what Active Directory objects you want to export and import, you can produce fairly readable files.

FIGURE 16.30
A small portion of the output from running LDIFDE.EXE in Figure 16.29

```
exportou1.ldf - Notepad
File  Edit  Format  View  Help
cn: Gerber, Barry
sn: Gerber
l: Los Angeles
physicalDeliveryOfficeName: BH-102
telephoneNumber: 310-555-5555
givenName: Barry
distinguishedName: CN=Gerber\, Barry,CN=Users,DC=bgerber,DC=local
instanceType: 4
whenCreated: 20030523231736.0Z
whenChanged: 20030611005126.0Z
displayName: Gerber, Barry
uSNCreated: 20699
uSNChanged: 52979
homeMTA:
 CN=Microsoft MTA,CN=EXCHANGE01,CN=Servers,CN=Los Angeles,CN=Administrative Gro
 ups,CN=Barry Gerber and Associates,CN=Microsoft Exchange,CN=Services,CN=Config
 uration,DC=bgerber,DC=local
proxyAddresses: smtp:bgerber@topdog.bgerber.com
proxyAddresses: X400:c=US;a= ;p=Barry Gerber and;o=Exchange;s=Gerber;g=Barry;
proxyAddresses: SMTP:bgerber@bgerber.com
homeMDB:
 CN=Mailbox Store (EXCHANGE01),CN=First Storage Group,CN=InformationStore,CN=EX
 CHANGE01,CN=Servers,CN=Los Angeles,CN=Administrative Groups,CN=Barry Gerber an
 d Associates,CN=Microsoft Exchange,CN=Services,CN=Configuration,DC=bgerber,DC=
 local
mDBUseDefaults: TRUE
mailNickname: bgerber
wWWHomePage: www.bgerber.com
name: Gerber, Barry
objectGUID:: Y3AnLnTwAUGLSGL1K7P4Sg==
userAccountControl: 512
badPwdCount: 0
codePage: 0
countryCode: 0
badPasswordTime: 126997666755468750
lastLogon: 126998308540781250
pwdLastSet: 126982054567644144
primaryGroupID: 513
objectSid:: AQUAAAAAAUVAAAA/hize1Z77wFftARmYwQAAA==
accountExpires: 9223372036854775807
```

Troubleshooting Exchange Server

Advanced Exchange server troubleshooting is beyond the scope of this book. Additionally, no one can answer every question about your Exchange server environment that might come up any time in the future. So, I'm going to describe a number of troubleshooting resources in this section. If you use them wisely and logically, I guarantee you'll be able to resolve any Exchange problem you encounter.

Later in 2003, Sybex, the publisher of this book, will release an update to what was already a great book, *Exchange 2000 Server 24seven* (2001). The book's author, Jim McBee, is an Exchange professional with lots of experience fixing broken Exchange servers and clients. So, my first tip on troubleshooting Exchange Server is that you buy Jim's book, *Exchange Server 2003 24seven* (Sybex, forthcoming). Even the Exchange 2000 version will help you with a lot of Exchange 2003 troubleshooting. And, while we're at it, you can't go wrong with Mark Minasi's collection of books on Windows Server 2003 and Windows XP. Mark is another hands-on type who gives you lots of good troubleshooting advice. Also, you might want to subscribe to Mark's e-mail newsletter (`www.minasi.com`).

My second tip is that you make Microsoft's Internet-based Knowledge Base your home away from home. In a world paced by the clock of Internet immediacy, things change very fast. Microsoft's Knowledge Base does a respectable job of keeping up with the frenzied pace of the company's development teams. You will most often be driven to the Knowledge Base by something you find in the event logs on an Exchange or a Windows server. So, you should consider the event logs as integral to your use of the Knowledge Base.

As of this writing, you can get to the Knowledge Base through the URL `www.microsoft.com`. On the site's home page, select the Knowledge Base option from the Support menu. Figure 16.31 shows the Knowledge Base search page. Select Exchange Server 2003 from the Select a Microsoft Product drop-down list. Then select from the available options and type in your search terms in the Search For field. Click Go and sift through the answers presented to you. If the Using option Any of the Words Entered gets you too many irrelevant articles, try changing the option to All of the Words Entered.

There's an art to posing Knowledge Base questions. Basically, you should keep your questions simple. If you are trying to solve a problem about an error message, search for all or part of the error message and be sure to select All of the Words Entered from the Using drop-down list. If the error message includes an Event ID, enter that. If your question is really about another Microsoft product, select that product from the drop-down menu. Be sure to follow any promising links to other Knowledge Base articles. Finally, make sure that you look for the latest information on any subject that you're concerned about.

The Microsoft Knowledge Base is a great tool, but without the event logs on your Exchange server, you're unlikely to have much use for it. Whenever something happens that you're not sure about, check the event logs. They provide not only messages about almost anything that happens on your server, but they also include an error code (Event ID) you can search for in the Knowledge Base. Assuming Microsoft has cataloged an Event ID in the Knowledge Base, Event ID searches tend to be very fast and accurate.

FIGURE 16.31

Accessing Microsoft's Internet-based Knowledge Base

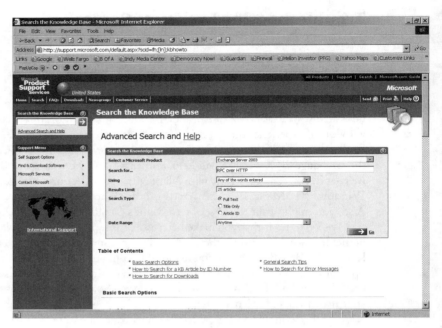

The quickest way to the logs is through Start ➤ All Programs ➤ Administrative Tools ➤ Event Viewer. Event logs always include System, Security, and Application logs. Other logs, such as a DNS log, are included if specific functionality is turned on. System logs are a great place to go for things such as hardware problems, failed driver loads, or the failure of Exchange services to start. Application logs are chock full of events about Exchange and other applications. Once a system is running smoothly, you'll find that most even log entries are informational. You can usually ignore these when troubleshooting a problem and concentrate on warning and error events.

My third tip is that you get, test, and install all service packs for Exchange Server and Outlook and other clients. Many of the problems that you'll experience with Exchange Server are recognized in Knowledge Base articles and, if they're deemed significant enough, are fixed in service pack releases.

My fourth tip is that you stay in touch with the Exchange community. Microsoft supports a set of newsgroups at `www.microsoft.com/exchange/community/newsgroups/default.asp`. *Windows and .NET Magazine* offers a set of Exchange newsgroup-like forums as well as many other useful resources at `www.winntmag.com`. The print edition of *Windows and .NET Magazine* offers excellent articles on Exchange Server. Check their website for subscription information. You should also subscribe to the Exchange and Windows e-mail newsletters offered by the magazine. The publisher of *Windows and .NET Magazine* also offers a high-powered, no-nonsense, no-advertising monthly publication called *Exchange and Outlook Administrator*. Again, check out the magazine's website for more information. Another good website is `www.slipstick.com`.

Tip number five? Consider paid support from Microsoft and others. It can be pricey, and the best support services cost the most. However, this is often the best way to get your problems solved fast. Check out `http://support.microsoft.com/directory/` for Microsoft's options. The Microsoft consulting operation can put you in touch with Microsoft staff or independent consultants who can help. I really like their phone support. Currently, for $245, you get the ear of an experienced, well-schooled, trained consultant who will spend as much time with you as it takes to solve a problem. I recently spent 13 hours over three days on the phone with one such consultant who helped me through a problem with a failed effort to remove Active Directory Connector before installing a second Exchange server in a domain. It was a complex mess and he stuck with me until every problem was resolved.

Armed with Jim McBee's book, access to Microsoft's Knowledge Base and other information sources, the latest Exchange Server and client service packs, and a modicum of paid support, your life as an Exchange administrator will be, if not a vacation in Maui, at least far less harried than it would be without these useful troubleshooting aids.

Supporting Remote and Roving Clients

In Chapter 14, "Managing Exchange 2003 Services for Internet Clients," I discussed three ways to access Exchange server mailboxes from off-site Internet-based locations: POP3, IMAP4, and HTTP or Outlook Web Access (OWA). Even though IMAP4 and OWA provide very good mailbox-access capabilities, some organizations or users might want to use the standard MAPI Outlook client such as Outlook 2002 or 2003. You can use these clients remotely over the Internet. Traditionally, such connections employed the same protocol that is used for local MAPI client/server connects, Remote Procedure Call (RPC) using TCP/IP packets (ROTI). Though ROTI works in many situations, it is a cumbersome combination of protocols that some ISPs are now blocking. RPC blocking makes MAPI-based client/server connections over the Internet impossible.

Exchange 2003 and Outlook 2003 bring to the table a new approach to MAPI client/server communications, RPC over HTTP (ROH). In this section, I'll discuss both this new approach and the more traditional approach using ROTI. When I talk about both of these options, I assume that remote users have access to the Internet through an ISP.

In some organizations, users tend to roam from one workstation to another. To do this conveniently, you need a setup that automatically establishes Outlook profile settings such as mailbox name when a user logs in to a different workstation. I'll cover roaming Outlook profiles at the end of this section.

RPC Over HTTP

Outlook 2003, together with Exchange Server 2003, Windows Server 2003, and Windows XP Professional, offers a new approach to MAPI-based client/server connectivity, RPC over HTTP (ROH). Put simply, RPC communications are wrapped up in standard web protocol packets at the client, sent across the Internet, and then unwrapped by Windows 2003/Exchange2003 once inside the local network where Exchange servers reside. The reverse is also true for packets sent from the server environment to the client.

ROH is implemented in a very specific set of operating system and application software. Workstations *must* run Windows XP (any edition). You'll need XP Service Pack 1 or later, plus a special patch for Service Pack 1. To find it, search for "Outlook 2003 HTTP RPC" in the Microsoft Knowledge Base. (Microsoft expects the patch to be integrated into Windows XP Service Pack 2 and later.) Additionally, Windows XP workstations also *must* be running Outlook 2003. On the server side, you need Windows Server 2003 and Exchange Server 2003.

Before I show you how to set up ROH, here's a little bit of background on this whole process. First, while both Outlook 2003 and Exchange 2003 have built-in capability to handle ROH, it is the Windows XP and 2003 operating systems that actually support the process. Microsoft has said that it probably won't be porting ROH to earlier operating systems, because the capability is deeply embedded in the newer operating systems and would be very difficult to implement in, say, Windows 2000 Server and Professional.

A basic ROH set up is pretty simple. First, you assure that all of the operating system/application software mentioned previously is in place. Then you set up Exchange server to deal with ROH packets. Finally, you set up an Outlook 2003 profile that uses ROH; point the client to the correct Exchange 2003 server and you're up and running.

An ROH Outlook 2003 client can communicate with an Exchange Server 2003 environment in a couple of ways. The client can talk directly to the Exchange server on which the user's mailbox resides or the client can access the user's Exchange server through an ROH front-end Exchange server. Exchange ROH front-end servers receive HTTP packets from Outlook 2003 clients, strip out the RPC information, and pass it along to the user's back-end server. They also receive RPC information from back-end servers, package it in HTTP packets, and pass it on to Outlook 2003 clients. Additionally, ROH front-end servers handle security.

It's important to note that ROH servers are conceptually similar to, but not the same as, the Exchange Internet protocol (POP3, IMAP4, and OWA) front-end servers that I discussed in Chapters 14 and 15. Both types of servers off-load back-end servers and networks at the security and traffic levels. However, Internet protocol front-end servers don't have to deencapsulate and encapsulate protocol traffic. So, given equal amounts of traffic, ROH front-end servers tend to require greater server hardware capacity than Internet front-end servers. For the record, Exchange ROH and Internet front-end servers can reside on the same hardware.

Okay, let's set up an ROH client/server environment. I'm going to set up the second Exchange server I installed, EXCHANGE02, as my ROH front-end server. I will access my mailbox, which resides on EXCHANGE01.

Here are some basic requirements:

◆ Windows 2003 server must be running on any Exchange 2003 server that will be accessed using ROH.

◆ If you use an Exchange 2003 ROH front-end server, it too must run Windows 2003.

◆ The Windows global catalog server used by Outlook 2003 clients and Exchange ROH servers must be running Windows 2003.

◆ All domain controllers that communicate with Outlook 2003 ROH clients and Exchange ROH servers must be configured to use ROH.

Server and client setup for ROH includes the following steps:

1. Configuring one or more Exchange 2003 servers to use ROH

2. Configuring Windows XP to use ROH

3. Configuring an Outlook 2003 client to use ROH

I'll discuss each of these steps in the following sections.

WARNING   At the time of this writing, some parts of RPC over HTTP were still in beta testing. This is especially true for Outlook 2003. Some of the procedures that I discuss here and some of the user interface details might be different in the release version of Outlook 2003. I've provided enough information in this section so that you shouldn't have difficulty finding the right option even if the user interface is slightly different.

CONFIGURING EXCHANGE 2003 SERVERS FOR RPC OVER HTTP

Any Exchange server that Outlook 2003 clients contact directly must be configured to use ROH. If you use an Exchange 2003 ROH front-end server, the preferred approach, you need to configure only that server. If you want Outlook 2003 clients to directly contact the Exchange server where the user's mailbox resides, then you need to configure each Exchange server where this might happen to support ROH.

The actual configuration process involves two steps. In the first step, you install the Windows 2003 RPC over HTTP Proxy networking component. Then you need to configure the RPC virtual directory in Internet Information Services. Here's how to complete each of these steps.

NOTE   Let me reiterate a key point here. You can set up one or more Exchange 2003 servers to act as ROH servers, or you can set up an ROH front-end server and have it communicate with all or some of your other (back-end) Exchange 2003 servers. In the first case, you perform the two steps that I discuss next on the Exchange server or servers to support ROH. In the second case, you perform the two steps only on the front-end server.

Installing the RPC Over HTTP Networking Component

Follow along on Figure 16.32 to install the Windows 2003 RPC over HTTP Proxy networking component.

1. On each Exchange 2003 server where you need to install the networking component, open Add or Remove Programs (Start ➤ Control Panel ➤ Add or Remove Programs).

FIGURE 16.32

Installing the RCP over HTTP proxy on an Exchange 2003 server

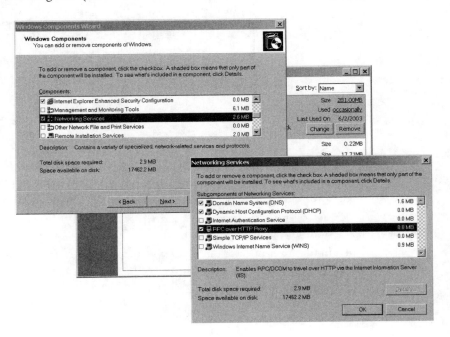

2. In Add or Remove Programs, click Add/Remove Windows Components.

3. In the Windows Components page of the Windows Components Wizard, find and choose Networking Services and then click Details.

4. In the Networking Services page, select RCP over HTTP Proxy, click OK, and then click Next. This will install the component. If you're asked, insert the Windows CD-ROM.

Configuring the RPC Virtual Directory in Internet Information Services

On each Exchange 2003 server where you installed the ROH networking component, you need to configure a new Internet Information Services virtual directory. To do so, follow these steps:

1. Select Start ➢ All Programs ➢ Administrative Tools ➢ Internet Information Services (IIS) Manager. (In Figure 16.33, I opened IIS Manager from my MMC.)

FIGURE 16.33

Setting IIS virtual directory security parameters for an Exchange 2003 RCP over HTTP server

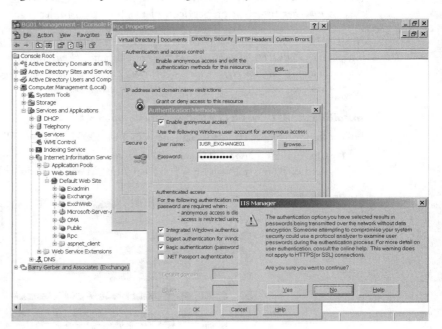

2. In the IIS Manager tree, expand the server you want, expand Web Sites and expand Default Web Site. Right-click the RPC virtual directory and select Properties.

3. Tab over to the Directory Security page in the RPC Properties dialog box and in the Authentication and Access Control area, click Edit.

4. In the Authenticated Access area of the Authentication Methods dialog box, select Basic Authentication (Password Is Sent in Clear Text) and click OK. This ensures that Internet-based access will work. Even if Anonymous Access on this page is selected, ROH will not allow such access.

NOTE *Once you've performed the two steps discussed here, Exchange 2003 servers are set to run as ROH servers. You need do nothing more to your Exchange 2003 or Windows 2003 servers to make ROH work. Under these circumstances, at the ROH level, Exchange servers communicate with each other and with Windows 2003 servers using a wide range of ports. If you wish, you can configure your ROH setup to use a very narrow range of specific communications ports. Configuring specific ports simplifies the process of managing and monitoring ROH network communications. It can also be useful in certain complex network access control situations involving multiple firewalls. Setting up specific ports involves registry editing on Exchange ROH front-end and back-end servers as well as on Windows domain controllers and the global catalog server. For more about this, search Microsoft's Knowledge Base under Exchange 2003 by typing* **configuring the rpc proxy server to use specified ports***.*

CONFIGURING WINDOWS XP TO USE RPC OVER HTTP

If you're using Windows XP with Service Pack 1, you need to download a post-SP1 patch. At the time of this writing, the patch is available at `http://go.microsoft.com/fwlink/?LinkId=16687`. If you can't find it there, search the Microsoft Knowledge Base under Windows XP by typing **rpc updates for Exchange 2003**. Once you've downloaded the patch, install it by double-clicking it in Windows XP's My Computer.

CONFIGURING AN OUTLOOK 2003 CLIENT TO USE RCP OVER HTTP

To set up an Outlook 2003 client to use ROH, you need to create a profile that includes ROH as your preferred method of communication with your Exchange 2003 server environment. Here's how you do this.

Right-click the Outlook 2003 icon in your Windows XP Start menu and select Properties, or double-click the Control Panel Mail icon (Start ➤ Control Panel). This opens the Mail Setup–Outlook dialog box. Click Show Profiles to bring up the Mail dialog box shown in Figure 16.34. As you can see, I already have an Outlook profile. This one uses standard RPC calls to communicate with Exchange server. To add a profile, click Add. Type a name for your profile in the New Profile dialog box and click OK (see Figure 16.35).

FIGURE 16.34

Using the Outlook 2003 Mail profiles dialog box to add a new profile

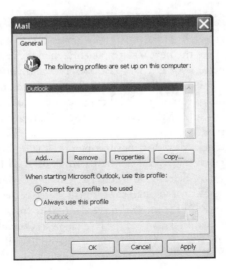

FIGURE 16.35

Entering a name for a new Outlook 2003 profile

This opens the E-Mail Accounts Wizard, shown in Figure 16.36. Ensure that Add a New E-Mail Account is selected and click Next. In the Server Type wizard page, select Microsoft Exchange Server and click Next, as I have done in Figure 16.37.

FIGURE 16.36

Using the E-Mail Accounts Wizard to create a new mail account for a new Outlook 2003 profile

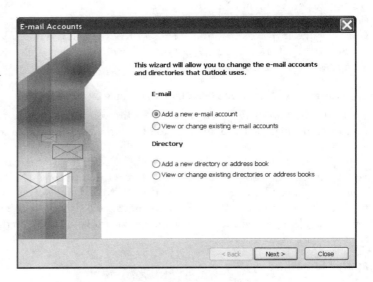

In Figure 16.38, you can see the next wizard page, Exchange Server Settings. Here you enter the fully-qualified domain name of your Exchange 2003 server and your Windows 2003 username. Make sure that Use Local Copy of Mailbox is checked. Because you'll be using a less reliable Internet connection, you want to be sure you have a local copy of your mailbox both to speed access to items already saved to the local copy and so that you can work in Outlook 2003 even when your computer isn't connected to the Internet.

Don't click Next. First, click More Settings to open the dialog box shown in Figure 16.39. Tab over to the Connection property page. This is where you set up ROH. Don't worry about the offline stuff at the top of this dialog box. Select Connect to My Exchange Mailbox Using HTTP. Then click the Exchange Proxy Settings button to open the Exchange Proxy Settings dialog box, shown in Figure 16.40. If you're using an ROH front-end server, enter the fully-qualified domain name of the server; if not, enter the fully-qualified name of the Exchange server your mailbox resides on. I'm using EXCHANGE02 as my ROH front-end server, so I've entered its fully-qualified domain name. Next, select Mutually Authenticate the Session When Connecting With SSL to assure the highest level of security. Then, in the Principal Name for Proxy Server field, enter the name of your ROH front-end server or the server that contains your mailbox if you're not using a front-end server. Be sure to prefix the server name with **msstd:**, as in Figure 16.40. I'm using the internal Windows 2003 domain names of my ROH front-end server, because I'm doing this test not on the Internet but within my local area network.

FIGURE 16.37
Specifying that a new e-mail account should be for an Exchange server mailbox

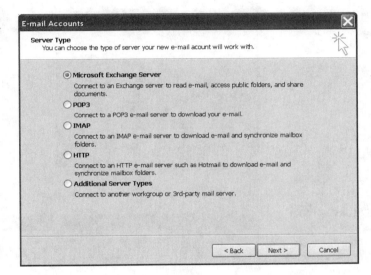

FIGURE 16.38
Entering information required to locate an Exchange server–based mailbox

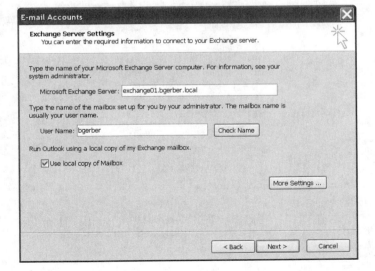

FIGURE 16.39
Setting Outlook 2003 to connect to Exchange server using ROH

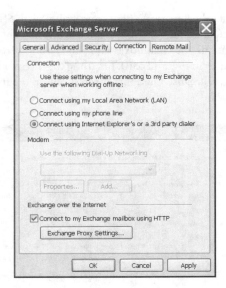

FIGURE 16.40
Setting parameters required to connect Outlook 2003 to Exchange server using ROH

Next, select Connect Using HTTP First, Then Connect Using My Local Area Network (LAN). This ensures that your Outlook 2003 client always tries to connect using HTTP. If an attempt to connect using HTTP fails, the client reverts to a RPC over TCP/IP–based connection. Finally, select Basic Authentication in the Proxy Authentication Settings area of the Exchange Proxy Settings dialog box. OK your way out of the two dialog boxes you opened.

You should now be back in the Exchange Server Settings wizard page shown earlier in Figure 16.38. Click Next and a dialog box opens, asking for your username and password. The wizard uses these to connect to your Windows/Exchange environment and to check the Exchange server and mailbox information you provided. If all goes well, you'll find yourself back in the mail profiles dialog box, shown in Figure 16.41. I have two profiles. I've selected Prompt for a Profile to Be Used so that when I start up Outlook, I have a choice of using one or the other of my two profiles. If you have only one profile, checking this box is unnecessary.

FIGURE 16.41

A newly created ROH-based Outlook 2003 profile is in place.

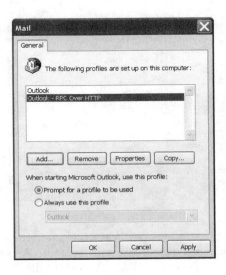

In Figure 16.42, I've started Outlook. I'm offered a choice of profiles. I'm choosing the one that supports RCP over HTTP. Figure 16.43 shows my Outlook 2003 client as it opens using ROH. Because Outlook can fall back to RPC over TCP/IP mode if it can't connect to your Exchange server using ROH, there's no way in looking at the Outlook client to know for sure that ROH is in use. There are a couple of ways to check the protocol. If your Outlook client is on the Internet and your internal network is protected by a firewall that allows external access using only the HTTP protocol and you can open your Exchange mailbox, you have to be using HTTP. Another way to check the protocol your Outlook 2003 client is using to communicate with your Exchange 2003 servers is with a packet sniffer. Packet sniffers can show you the ports being used by a particular network node to communicate with another network node.

FIGURE 16.42

Choosing to use an ROH-based profile when opening Outlook 2003

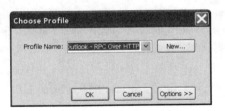

FIGURE 16.43
Outlook 2003 opened using an ROH profile

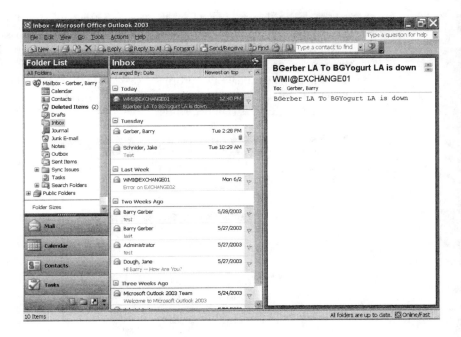

In Figure 16.44, I'm using CommView (www.tamos.com), a very nice and inexpensive software-based packet sniffer, to monitor communications between my Windows XP workstation set up for ROH Outlook 2003–to–Exchange 2003 connectivity, BARRYXPPRO (IP address: 192.168.0.247), and my Exchange ROH front-end server, EXCHANGE02 (IP address 192.168.0.105). CommView is running on EXCHANGE02. Notice in the second line in Figure 16.44 that communication between the two computers uses only port 443. That proves ROH is being used. "What!" you might be exclaiming, "I thought HTTP used port 80." It does, but secure HTTP communications, such as those that use https:// instead of http://, use port 443. Secure HTTP is supported by the Secure Sockets Layer (SSL) protocol, which you'll notice is an unchangeable default on the dialog box shown earlier in Figure 16.40.

When I use CommView to look at communications between EXCHANGE02 and my mailbox server, EXCHANGE01, a variety of ports are used, but not port 443. This demonstrates that Exchange ROH front-end servers talk to back-end servers using standard Exchange server–to–Exchange server communications ports.

TIP   One quick and dirty, though not always as reliable, alternative to a packet sniffer such as CommView is the netstat *command built into Windows. Open a command prompt, type* **netstat***, and press Enter. It might take as much as a minute to complete, but you'll soon see a list of the other computers your computer or server is connected to and the ports being used for the connection. Some ports will be listed numerically, others will be listed by the name of the service they support, such as LDAP.*

That does it for RPC over HTTP. Now let's look a bit at RPC over TCP/IP.

FIGURE 16.44

FIGURE 16.44

A software-based packet sniffer shows that an ROH-based Outlook 2003 client and an Exchange ROH server are communicating using the secure HTTP port, 443.

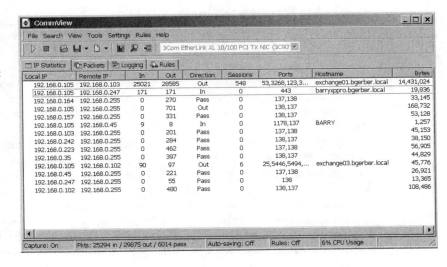

RCP Over TCP/IP

Aside from ensuring that remote users install and set up their Outlook client properly, you don't have to do much else to support ROTI remote users on the server side. Users will have to create an entry for the server in the HOSTS file on the computer on which they are running Outlook. Except for Outlook 2003, the entry must be for the Exchange server name only, not the fully-qualified domain name of the server—that is, EXCHANGE01, not EXCHANGE01.BGERBER.COM. Outlook 2003 accepts fully-qualified domain names as well as server names. For more on the HOSTS file, see *Mastering Windows Server 2003* (Sybex, 2003).

The remote procedure calls that support Exchange client/server communications must be capable of passing through the ISP-based link between your client and server. Technically, this requires that certain TCP/IP ports be enabled on all firewalls and routers between the client and the server. I'll talk more about using ROTI with firewalls in Chapter 18.

To connect Outlook to the server, you need to get to the MS Exchange Settings Properties dialog box. To do this for Outlook 2000 and earlier, right-click the Microsoft Outlook icon on your desktop, and select Properties. Double-click Microsoft Exchange Server in the MS Exchange Setting Properties dialog box. Enter the name of your Exchange server as named in your HOSTS file. Then type in your mailbox's display name or alias, and click Check Name. You'll know that all is well if the display name for your mailbox shows up underlined. Click OK to exit the various dialog boxes and open your mailbox. It takes a while the first time, but when your client is capable of talking to the server directly over the Internet, you will be able to do virtually anything that you can do locally. If you're using Outlook 2002 or 2003, follow the instructions in the previous section for entering and checking a connection to an Exchange mailbox, ignoring all the stuff about ROH.

Supporting Roving Users

Some users sit at the same desk all day, every day. Others move around all the time, often not even having a computer of their own. These users are often referred to as *roving users*. Basically, you want all roving users to have a directory on a server where they can pick up their Exchange and other settings every time they log in to the network, whatever workstation they use to log in.

The Exchange settings that you're interested in are those for home server and mailbox name. You want a roving user to get the same server and mailbox name, no matter what workstation he or she chooses to log in on.

Supporting a roving Exchange user is no different from supporting a roving user who is working with any other software, such as Microsoft Word. With Exchange, you want to present the same server and mailbox name. With Word, your goal is for the user to get the same default template, window-size settings, and so on. The specific procedures that you must follow to support roving users depend on the workstation (and sometimes network) operating system that you're using.

Fortunately, Microsoft has a tool for simplifying the job of setting up correct profiles for roving Exchange users. This tool, PROFGEN.EXE, can be found in the Exchange Resource Kit. You can also download the program for free from Microsoft's Exchange website.

A third-party product, Profile Maker, is easier to use and more comprehensive in scope than PROFGEN.EXE. Check it out at the site of its manufacturer, AutoProf.com (`www.autoprof.com`).

Migrating Foreign Messaging System Users to Exchange

You can move users from foreign messaging systems to your Exchange system. In some cases, Microsoft provides specific migration tools, while in others it provides more generic tools. Remember that your primary goal is to import data from your legacy messaging system into Windows 2003's Active Directory and Exchange's information stores.

Migration is a complex process. Rather than describe it here in detail, I just want to make sure that you know it's available. Most of the documentation for migration is provided only online and on the Exchange Server CD-ROM, in the Migrate directory. Let's take a quick look at your options.

Exchange Server ships with comprehensive migration tools for the following foreign messaging systems:

◆ Other Exchange Server organizations

◆ Microsoft Mail for PC Networks

◆ Lotus cc:Mail

◆ Lotus Notes versions

◆ Novell GroupWise

Migrations for all the systems listed are done entirely using the Microsoft Exchange Server Migration Wizard, which is installed along with Exchange Server. To start the wizard, select Start ➢ All Programs ➢ Microsoft Exchange ➢ Deployment ➢ Migration Wizard. Migrations move most available directory and message data to the Exchange 2003/Windows 2003 environment, and both also assume a live network link between your Exchange system and the foreign messaging system. If everything is running properly, these migrations are a piece of cake.

You can also migrate from the following foreign messaging systems by extracting data from the old system into a file using a Microsoft-supplied source extractor and then importing it into Exchange using the Migration Wizard:

◆ Microsoft Mail for AppleTalk networks

◆ IBM PROFS

◆ NetSys (formerly Verimation MEMO)

If that's not enough, Microsoft provides information on building your own migration source extractor to produce data that can be imported into Active Directory using the Migration Wizard.

Finally, and this is very neat, using the Migration Wizard, you can migrate directory information from any LDAP-compliant directory. And, if your legacy messaging system supports IMAP4, you can move mailbox data from it to Exchange mailbox stores using the Migration Wizard.

NOTE *Whichever route you take, be sure that someone on your migration team fully understands both the foreign electronic messaging system that you're working with and the computer operating system that it runs on top of. Without this expertise, you can get into some very hot water. If no one in your organization qualifies for this distinction, consider getting help from the vendors of your electronic messaging system and operating system, or think about hiring a knowledgeable consultant or two.*

Summary

This chapter covered a number of advanced features of Exchange Server 2003 and Exchange-related features of Windows Server 2003. These features enable Exchange administrators to do everything from tracking Exchange Server–based messages to modifying e-mail address formats to migrating foreign messaging system users to Exchange.

The Exchange Message Tracking Center is used to follow a message through an Exchange organization. Messages can be tracked as they move across Exchange servers and connectors, right up to the point that they leave an Exchange organization. Both e-mail and system messages can be tracked. Message tracking is useful both to prove to users that a message did indeed reach its destination and for troubleshooting Exchange system problems or apparent problems.

Exchange managers can modify the default e-mail address formats used to create e-mail addresses for Exchange recipients. One of the most interesting and often-used modifications involves the creation of secondary SMTP proxy addresses for a user. Secondary proxies enable a user to have multiple Internet addresses. When secondary proxies are created that involve domains not already registered in an Internet-connected DNS server, MX and host records for the domain must be created in the DNS, or other SMTP hosts won't be capable of sending messages to the new secondary proxy address.

Several Exchange features are implemented at the global or Exchange organization-wide level. Using recipient policies, Exchange managers can set up differently formatted default e-mail addresses for different Exchange recipients. A variety of selection criteria is available for specifying the recipients covered by a recipient policy. Exchange managers can also set up address lists using similar filters. Address lists are visible to users in their Outlook address books. The Exchange recipient update service, running on an Exchange server, keeps recipient e-mail addresses and address lists current as selection criteria change and new recipients are added to recipient policies and address lists. Multilingual details and address templates, respectively, support Outlook client features and one-off address creation in Outlook. Exchange administrators can set Exchange organization–wide message size and recipients per message limits for Exchange mailboxes.

Manual creation of Windows 2003 users and Exchange 2003 mailboxes and other recipients can be very labor-intensive. It is possible to import information into Windows 2003 Active Directory and export it from Active Directory. The programs LDIFDE.EXE and CSVDE.EXE can be used for Active Directory imports and exports. The programs are run at a command prompt and are not very easy to use. Exchange administrators must possess a good deal of knowledge regarding Active Directory and the format of LDIFDE.EXE and CSVDE.EXE import files, as well as the format of individual entries in LDIFDE.EXE and CSVDE.EXE import files, before they can safely undertake Active Directory imports.

Exchange server troubleshooting is a constantly moving target. The best tools are an advanced Exchange server management book; use of online support from Microsoft and others, ensuring that the latest Windows 2003 and Exchange 2003 service packs are installed on servers; and, if all else fails, use of paid Microsoft or other consulting support.

Connectors that link Exchange routing groups can be monitored to assure that they are available. The status of each connector is automatically displayed in the `Monitoring and Status\Status` container in Exchange System Manager. You can also set things up so that you are notified when a connector is down.

Supporting both remote and roving Outlook clients is quite easy with Exchange. Remote clients can be supported over the Internet connection using either a traditional RPC over TCP/IP connection or an RPC over HTTP link. Roving users are most easily supported using a product such as Microsoft's PROFGEN.EXE.

Exchange Server 2003 comes with a variety of tools for migrating users from foreign messaging systems to Exchange. The Exchange Migration Wizard simplifies migration from a number of messaging systems, supporting live links to these systems during migration. For other foreign messaging systems, Microsoft provides source extractors to pull data from the systems and place it into files. The files can then be imported using the wizard.

Chapter 17

Exchange Server Reliability and Availability

ONE OF THE BIGGEST issues for my clients is Exchange server disaster recovery. The first time a client brings up the subject, I tell them that disaster recovery is the last thing they should worry about. After they get up off the floor, I tell them that they should focus first on Exchange server reliability and availability, of which disaster recovery is but the last part. I go on to tell them that if they worry about the whole reliability and availability spectrum, they'll not only prepare themselves for serious nondisaster recovery scenarios, but they also might be able to avoid many of the disasters that haunt their nightly dreams.

If you want to achieve optimal Exchange server reliability and availability, you have to focus on three major areas:

- ◆ System redundancy

- ◆ Standard backup and recovery

- ◆ Disaster recovery

In this chapter, I'll focus on each of these in detail. When you're done, you'll know what you need to protect your Exchange server system and to assure both yourself and your users that their Exchange environment is as well protected as possible given available resources.

Featured in this chapter:

- ◆ Redundant systems

- ◆ Standard backup and recovery vs. disaster recovery

- ◆ Standard backup and recovery

- ◆ Disaster recovery

Redundant Systems

Redundant computing and networking systems can be an easy, though not always inexpensive, route to Exchange server reliability and availability. Automatic failover from a nonfunctional to a functional component is best. However, even if you have to bring your system down for a short time to replace a component with no or minimal data loss, you'll be a hero to your users. In addition to eliminating or sharply reducing downtime, redundant systems can help you avoid the pain of standard or disaster-based Exchange server recovery.

Systems redundancy is a complex matter. It's mostly about hardware, though a good deal of software, especially operating system software, can be involved. I'm going to deal here with two areas that are essential to redundant systems: server redundancy and network redundancy.

Server Redundancy

There are two basic kinds of server redundancy:

◆ Intraserver redundancy

◆ Interserver redundancy

Intraserver redundancy is all about how redundant components are installed in a single server. Interserver redundancy involves multiple servers that, in some form or other, mirror each other. The goal with either kind of redundancy is for good components or servers to replace bad ones as quickly as possible. Automatic replacement is highly desirable.

Okay, let's look at redundant components and servers in more detail.

INTRASERVER REDUNDANCY

When you think redundancy in a server, you think about storage, power, cooling, and CPUs. Redundant disk storage and power components are the most readily available in today's servers. Tape storage has lagged behind disk storage in the area of redundancy, but it is available. Redundant cooling fans have been around for some time. Historically, Intel has not offered good support for redundant CPUs. However, the company now provides hardware for this purpose, and that hardware is finding its way into production servers.

Let's look at each aspect of server redundancy in more detail.

Redundant Storage

Redundant disk storage relies on a collection of disks to which data is written in such a way that all data continues to be available even if one of the disk drives fails. The popular acronym for this sort of set up is RAID, which stands for Redundant Array of Independent Disks.

There are several levels of RAID, one of which is not redundant. Here's a quick look at each:

RAID 0 Part of each byte of data is written (striped) to each drive in the array. RAID 0 is not redundant, but it provides the highest performance, because each byte of data is written in parallel, not sequential, fashion. RAID 0 is included here because RAID 0 strategies are used in another RAID design that I discuss later.

RAID 1   All data on a drive is mirrored to a second drive. This provides the highest reliability. Write performance is fairly slow, because data must be written to both drives. Read performance can be enhanced if both drives are used when data is accessed. Mirroring requires lots of disk storage compared to RAID 5 (see below).

RAID 0+1   As with RAID 0, data is striped across each drive in the array. However, the array is mirrored to one or more parallel arrays. This provides the highest reliability and performance, but has the same high disk storage requirements as RAID 1.

RAID 5   Part of each byte of data is striped to each drive in the array. However, writes include parity information that allows any data to be recovered from the remaining drives if a drive fails. RAID 5 is reliable, though performance is slower. With RAID 5, you lose the equivalent of one disk in total GB of storage. For example, a RAID 5 array of three 36GB drives gives you 72GB, not 108GB of storage. This is more efficient than RAID 1 or 0+1, which require a disk for each drive mirrored, but write performance is about one-third of RAID 0+1, and read performance is about one-half of RAID 0+1.

So, which RAID level is right for you? RAID 0+1 is nice, but I reserve it for clients with really demanding performance requirements. You compromise some with RAID 5, but it's the best price-performance-reliability option.

It should be clear how RAID works from a general redundancy/reliability perspective. Now you're probably wondering how it works to assure high availability. The answer is pretty simple. With a properly set up RAID 1, 0+1, or 5 system, you simply replace a failed drive and the system automatically rebuilds itself. If the system is properly configured, you can actually replace the drive while your server keeps running and supporting users. If your RAID system is really highly neat, you set up hot spares that are automatically used should a disk drive fail.

So, how do you know a RAID disk failed, and what do you do about it other than inserting a good drive? Most systems make entries in the Windows system event log. Many also let you know by talking to you. I'll never forget the first time a RAID 5 disk failed in one of my client's Dell servers. I got a call about a high-pitched whistling sound. They reported that they were "going nuts from the sound." So I had to figure out what was up as quickly as possible. I contacted Dell premium support and within five minutes, I knew it was a failed RAID drive. I used the administrative terminal server option in Windows 2000 to get to the computer over the Internet, using a virtual private network connection for security. Using Dell's support software for its RAID arrays, I was quickly able to shut off that horrible sound and set the server to the tasks of checking the failed drive and attempting to reinsert it into the array. Meanwhile, users were happily working away on their Exchange-based e-mail, knowing nothing about the failure. The drive recovered without a problem.

If the failed drive was not recoverable, I would have asked my clients to remove the failed drive and insert a ready-to-go standby drive into the server. The server has three active RAID drives and three empty slots all on a hot-swap backplane. So, drive removal and insertion can be done without interrupting user access to the server. I could have also installed a fourth drive and set it up to act as a standby drive. The initial failure would then have triggered a rebuild of the array onto the standby drive. Then, at my leisure, I could come by and check the failed drive to see if it was still serviceable.

If RAID sounds like a good idea, but you're worrying about costs, consider this. On my recommendation, one of my clients recently (June 2003) bought a Dell PowerEdge 1600SC server with

72GB of usable RAID 5 storage, hot-swappable drives and power supplies, a hot-spare drive, a 2.4GHz Intel Xeon processor, and 1GB of memory for around $3,000. Figure out what you'd pay for a quality server without all these features and I think you'll conclude that the peace of mind that comes with redundant server hardware is worth the extra cost.

WARNING *As you'll remember from Chapter 12, "Managing the Exchange Server Hierarchy and Core Components," Exchange Server quickly writes data to simple transaction logs and then later commits the data to the information store when time is available. This assures that data are on disk and will not be lost should system memory fail. If you're using RAID 5 for your information stores, you should place your log files on RAID 1 or 0+1 mirrored drives. Disk mirroring is faster than RAID 5's parity bit-based striping.*

TIP *For the best performance, be sure to use a RAID solution that is implemented in hardware on a RAID adapter. Limited software-based RAID is available in Windows Server 2003, but you're not going to be happy with the speed of such an implementation.*

RAID solutions don't necessarily have to be implemented inside a server. There is one very viable, if expensive, RAID solution that connects to your server or servers via a very high-throughput link. The technology is called a *Storage Area Network* (SAN). SAN devices connect to servers using fiber optic cable. You can connect multiple servers to a SAN. Each server is connected to the SAN through one or more very high-speed switches. This provides excellent throughput between the SAN and each server. Backups also benefit from SAN's high levels of performance. Tape units are available that connect directly to SAN fiber switches.

SANs include fairly complex storage and management software. Support is not a trivial matter, though support requirements are reduced somewhat because data can be consolidated onto one device. Minimal SAN implementations are measured in terabytes (TB) of storage. Five TB is not unusual for such an implementation. At this writing, because of their costs and complexity, SANs are being promoted by vendors for really high-end storage capacity and performance requirements. Microsoft takes the same position regarding running Exchange on SANs.

Generally, if you're going to implement a SAN solution, you'll do it in a clustered server environment. For more on server clustering, see the following section, "Interserver Redundancy."

If SANs are too rich for your blood, take comfort: There are alternatives. You can buy lower throughput, lower capacity, external RAID boxes that attach to your server or servers using sufficiently high-speed links to support an Exchange environment. Vendors such as Compaq (www.hp.com) and Dell (www.dell.com) offer this hardware.

WARNING *If you've been tempted by Network Attached Storage (NAS) solutions, forget it. Exchange databases must reside on a disk that is directly attached to the server. Through their switches, SANs are attached to the servers they support. NAS devices are not. It is no different than if you tried to install an Exchange information store on a disk residing on another server on your network. It doesn't work.*

Devices are available based on Redundant Array of Independent Tapes (RAIT) technology. Like RAID disk units, RAIT tape backup systems either mirror tapes one to one or stripe data across multiple tapes. As with disk, multi-tape striping can improve backup and restore performance as well as provide protection against the loss of a tape. Obviously, RAIT technology includes multiple tape drives. It is almost always implemented with tape library hardware so that tapes can be changed automatically, based on the requirements of backup software.

Redundant Power

Redundant power supplies are fairly standard in higher-end servers. You'll remember that a set of redundant power supplies was included in the $3,000 Dell server that I asked a client to purchase. That Dell had two power supplies. Each power supply has its own power cord and runs all of the time. In fact, both power supplies provide power to the server at all times. Because either power supply is high enough in wattage to support the entire computer, if one power supply fails, the other is fully capable of running the computer. As with storage, system monitoring software lets you know when a power supply component has failed.

Many higher-end servers offer more than two redundant power supplies. These are designed for higher levels of system availability. They add relatively little to the cost of a server and are worth it.

Ideally, each power supply should be plugged into a different circuit. That way, the other circuit or circuits will still be there if the breaker trips on one circuit. I urge my hospital clients go a step further and ensure that one of the power supplies is plugged into an emergency circuit that is backed up by the hospital's gasoline-powered standby electricity-generating system. And, of course, each circuit should be plugged into an uninterruptible power supply (UPS).

Compaq, now a part of Hewlett Packard, offers another form of power redundancy, redundant voltage regulator modules (VRMs). In some environments, it's fine to have multiple power supplies, but if the power to your server isn't properly regulated because the computer's VRM has totally or partially failed, you'd be better off if the power had just failed. I expect that redundant VRMs will quickly become standard on higher-end servers from other manufacturers.

Redundant Cooling

Modern CPUs, RAM, and power supplies produce a lot of heat. Internal cooling fans are supposed to pull this heat out of a computer's innards and into the surrounding atmosphere. If a fan fails, components can heat to a point where they stop working or permanently fail. Redundant cooling fans help prevent this nightmare scenario. In most systems, there is an extra fan that is always running. Monitoring software lets you know when a fan fails. The system is set up so that the remaining fans can support the server until you are able to replace the failed fan.

One-for-one redundant fans are becoming more and more available. With these, each fan in a system is shadowed by an always-running matching fan. When a fan fails, monitoring software lets you know so you can replace the fan.

Redundant CPUs

As I mentioned in the introduction to this section, redundancy has not been a strong point of Intel CPUs. Mainframe and specialty mini-computer manufacturers have offered such redundancy for years. Pushed by customers and large companies such as Microsoft, Intel now has a standard for implementation of redundant CPUs.

Each CPU lives on its own plug-in board. Each CPU has its own mirror CPU. Mirroring happens at extremely high speed. When one CPU board detects problems in the other CPU, it shuts down the

CPU and takes over the task of running the server. Intel claims that these transitions are transparent to users.

System monitoring software lets you know that a CPU has been shut down. You can use management software to assess the downed CPU to see if the crash was soft (CPU is still okay and can be brought back online) or hard (time to replace the CPU board). If the board needs replacing, you can do it while the computer is running. This is another victory for hot-swappable components and high system reliability and availability.

Intel is marketing this technology for extremely high-reliability devices such as telecommunications networking. However, I expect that it will quickly find its way into higher-end corporate server systems.

NOTE *While they don't fall into the category of redundancy because they don't use backup hardware, error-correcting code (ECC) memory and registered memory deserve brief mention here. ECC memory includes parity information that allows it to correct a single bit error in an 8-bit byte of memory. It can also detect, but not correct, an error in two bits per byte. Higher-end servers use special algorithms to correct full 8-bit errors. Registered memory includes registers where data are held for one clock cycle before being moved onto the motherboard. This very brief delay allows for more reliable high-speed data access.*

INTERSERVER REDUNDANCY

Interserver redundancy is all about synchronizing a set of servers so that server failures result in no or little downtime. There are a number of third-party solutions that provide some synchronizing services, but Microsoft's Windows clustering does the most sophisticated and comprehensive job of cross-server synchronization. I'm going to focus here on this product. I'll also spend a bit of time on redundant SMTP hosts using a simple DNS trick.

Windows Server Clusters

The Enterprise and Datacenter editions of Windows Server 2003 include clustering capabilities. Interserver redundancy clustering is supported by the Microsoft Cluster Service (MSCS). MSCS supports clusters using up to eight servers or nodes. The servers present themselves to clients as a single server. A server in a cluster uses ultra-high-speed internode connections and very fast, hardware-based algorithms to determine if a fellow server has failed. If a server fails, another server in the cluster can take over for it with minimal interruption in user access. It takes between one and two minutes for a high-capacity Exchange server cluster with a heavy load (around 5,000 users) to recover from a failure. With resilient e-mail clients such as Outlook 2003, client-server reconnections are transparent to users.

Clusters share disk storage, ideally SAN disk storage. More basic, stand-alone, sharable RAID boxes work fine too, as long as they can be connected on high-bandwidth links to multiple servers. It's important to note that clusters alone do not provide any protection for data stored on disks. Such protection comes from the redundancy built into disk storage components.

In addition to providing a level of redundancy, clusters can also be used to implement network load-balancing (NLB) strategies. NLB requires the installation of supporting Microsoft software. NLB is especially useful in Exchange environments with lots of incoming POP3, IMAP4, OWA, RPC over HTTP, and LDAP traffic.

Implementing MSCS clusters is beyond the scope of this book. For more information on planning and deploying MSCS clusters, check out *Mastering Windows Server 2003* (Sybex, 2003) and Microsoft's Windows Server 2003 website.

Redundant SMTP Servers

Back in Chapter 13, "Managing Exchange 2003 Internet Services," I talked about DNS MX records and how they are used to tell SMTP hosts how to find a particular e-mail domain, for example, `bgerber.com`.

Here's the sample MX record that I showed you in Chapter 13:

```
bgerber.com. IN MX 10 exchange01.bgerber.com.
```

That number 10 in the MX record is called a priority value. If I were to add another MX record for `bgerber.com` that pointed to a different server, say `exchange02.bgerber.com`, and if I were to give that record a priority value of 20, guess what would happen: SMTP servers would continue to deliver messages to `exchange01.bgerber.com`. However, if an SMTP server had trouble contacting EXCHANGE01, it would then look for other MX records for `bgerber.com`. If EXCHANGE02 were available, it would send to that server.

You can have as many MX records for a mail server as you want. Just be sure each points to a different server and has a different priority value.

Network Redundancy

As you'll remember from Chapter 15, "Installing and Managing Additional Exchange Servers," Exchange Server 2003 connectors support redundant networks. Connector cost settings provide priority settings for the order in which a connector is to be used. This section supplements the discussion in Chapter 15, focusing on intranetwork- and internetwork-device hardware redundancy.

The same redundancy concepts that apply to servers also apply to network redundancy. There are network adapters, switches, bridges, and routers that support intradevice redundancy. Of course, as we learned with Exchange connectors, redundancy doesn't mean much if redundant devices are connected to the same physical network.

You can achieve network interface card (NIC) redundancy by using what is called *NIC teaming*. With teaming, two or more NICs are treated by your server and the outside world as a single adapter with a single IP address. For fault-tolerance, you connect each NIC to a separate layer 2 MAC address–based switch. All switches must be able to physically communicate with each other, that is, they must be in the same layer 2 domain and they must support NIC teaming. All the network cards work together to send and receive data. If one NIC fails, the others keep on chugging away doing their job and you are notified of the failure. You need Windows 2003–based software from your NIC vendor to pull this off. Compaq and Dell, among others, offer this software and compatible NICs.

Beyond the switch, you can use routers with redundant components. Cisco Systems (`www.cisco.com`) makes a number of these. Cisco also offers some nice interdevice redundancy routing options. These can get expensive so if you want redundant physical connections to the Internet or other remote corporate sites, you need to factor in the cost of these.

If you use an ISP, you should pick one with more sophisticated networking capabilities. Maybe you can't afford multiple redundant links to the Internet, but your ISP should. Look for ISPs that use the kinds of routers discussed in the previous paragraph.

Standard Backup and Recovery vs. Disaster Recovery

In life, as in IT, one person's everyday occurrence can be another person's disaster. If your systems support staff is small or you are the systems support staff, and if you haven't had the time to keep up to date on or test the latest backup and restore techniques, the loss of a single Exchange information store can seem like a disaster that ranks right up there with a major earthquake. On the other hand, to a very large systems staff that has extensively prepared for and tested Exchange server backup and recovery, only that earthquake and its consequences might qualify as a real disaster.

All of the above is well and good, but it doesn't help us make distinctions that are important when it comes to the allocation of resources to deal with standard backup and recovery and disaster recovery. For the sake of this book, I'll assume the following definitions:

- I'll treat standard backup and recovery as involving the rebuilding of a server, including restoration of Windows 2003 and/or Exchange 2003.

- I'll treat disaster recovery as a situation in which there are major systems losses including multiple servers and networks.

I've had a lot of experience with standard backup and recovery and some experience with actual disaster recovery scenarios. I can tell you without question that I could do standard backup and recovery all day without my blood pressure rising above normal. But, hand me a disaster, and I'm ready for blood pressure medication and a nice long sleep when I've finished.

I think the main reason for the difference is that I've done a lot of the standard stuff and have an approach that seems to get me through the process fairly smoothly. On the disaster side, I'm usually called in after the disaster and asked to get things up and running again. I have to learn the client's system, often without much, if any, documentation, and figure out the best and most cost-effective way to get them back up and running. It's grueling. Given my experience, you've probably guessed that you're going to hear a lot in the following two sections about planning, documentation, and testing.

Before we move on to standard backup and recovery and disaster recovery, I need to remind you about the role of intraserver and interserver redundancy. Think of redundancy as protection against having to do a recovery, at least from a passive offline device such as backup tape or disk. Consider redundancy as the first line of defense in your war against downtime caused by unreliable hardware. Recovery is a fallback position that you turn to only when everything else has failed.

PREVENTING RECOVERY WITH GOOD VIRUS-CONTROL SOFTWARE

I will discuss virus-control software in the next chapter, "Exchange Server System Security." However, I want to take a moment to encourage you to look at server and e-mail anti-virus software as an additional tool in your battle for reliability and availability. I've been in a situation where a virus attack literally destroyed every one of a client's servers. By my definition, fixing a problem such as this is disaster recovery, not standard backup and restore. Believe me, my blood pressure told me in a minute that I was into disaster recovery, not a standard restore—and the bill I sent my client reinforced that reality.

Standard Backup and Recovery

To plan for standard backup and recovery, you need to come up with strategies for backing up and recovering your servers. These strategies should specify what you'll back up or restore and how you'll do it. Strategies should focus on both Windows and Exchange. Once your strategies are in place, you need to think about the backup hardware and software that you'll use.

Windows Server 2003 Backup

Windows Server 2003 backup is a complex matter that is by and large beyond the scope of this book. However, I want to take a little time to talk more generally about Windows backup options and a couple of options that rely on little or no actual backup. These include

◆ Automatic System Recovery (ASR) backups

◆ Volume Shadow Copy Service (VSCS) backups

◆ Backup of all system files on a Windows server, including the System State

◆ A spare server with Windows and possibly Exchange already installed

◆ A fresh installation of Windows on a server, followed by restoration of System State files

The new ASR backup feature of Windows 2003 makes it much easier to correctly back up and recover the system components of a Windows server. This feature is available in the built-in Windows 2003 backup program, and ASR-like features are included in third-party backup software for Windows 2003. For more on ASR and Windows Server 2003 backup in general, see *Mastering Windows Server 2003* (Sybex, 2003).

It's important to remember that ASR doesn't back up the nonsystem data on your computer. For example, it doesn't back up the Exchange server application itself or Exchange information stores.

Another really exciting option for Windows backup is Windows 2003's new VSCS. VSCS lets you make a consistent copy of a disk volume at any given point in time. You can restore that copy and be almost 100 percent sure that the restored volume will function just as it did when the shadow copy was made. Because VSCS has much to offer Exchange Server 2003 administrators, I'll discuss VSCS in more detail in the section "How to Back Up," later in this chapter.

Another Windows backup strategy involves backing up everything on a Windows server, including System State data on all servers and Active Directory data on domain controllers. Recovering a server so backed up isn't as easy as if you use ASR or VSCS, but it works.

There are two other options for recovering from a Windows server crash. First, you can put together a spare Windows/Exchange server and use it when it comes time to do a Windows and/or Exchange recovery. This server should be a member of your Exchange organization, but not actively networked with the servers in your Exchange organization. Second, after a server crash, you can literally do a fresh installation of Windows and Exchange on the same or a different piece of server hardware. In any of these cases, you still need to recover your Exchange information store databases once Windows is in place.

Throughout the rest of this chapter, I assume that you or someone responsible for Windows Server 2003 is dealing with Windows backup and recovery. This includes all the niceties connected with backing up and recovering Active Directory on domain controllers. You'll remember that Active

Directory includes a ton of Exchange objects. If you've followed my recommendations and you have not installed Exchange Server 2003 on a Windows 2003 domain controller, and your Exchange server goes south, your only worry about Active Directory will be assuring that your recovered Exchange server is properly registered in Active Directory and properly installed in your Exchange organization.

I also assume in the rest of this chapter that Windows Server 2003 is already on an Exchange server that you need to recover. This might be because only Exchange Server failed on that server, or you recovered Windows to that server, or you are using a freshly installed copy of Windows on that or another server.

Exchange Backup Strategies

A backup strategy should include decisions about the following:

- What to back up
- How to back up
- When to back up
- Protecting and retaining backups

Let's look at each of these in a bit more detail.

WHAT TO BACK UP

For Exchange Server 2003, you should always do a full backup of your Exchange information store(s). In my experience, restoring from incremental or differential (transaction logs only) backups of an Exchange information store adds complexities that you don't need when you're under pressure to get back up and running quickly. Full information store backups might take more tape or disk space, but that stuff is cheap compared with the tension and user ire generated by longer recovery times.

If you've set up things correctly, simply backing up an Exchange information store with Exchange-aware software forces unprocessed transaction log data into the information store and deletes processed transaction logs. (See the section "Enable Circular Logging" in Chapter 12. For the record, the answer is to disable circular logging, not to enable it.) An information store backup with Exchange-aware software also backs up any logs created during the backup itself. Logs are created during a backup because Exchange continues running and performing its messaging functions.

TIP   You can separately back up each information store in a storage group. However, it's more efficient to back up entire storage groups. For example, when you back up individual information stores, all transaction log files are backed up for each store. This not only extends backup times, but it also results in less efficient use of disk or tape backup space.

You should also back up what is called the *metabase*. The metabase is an Internet Information Server entity that includes a good deal of Exchange information, such as Internet protocol and routing information. Metabase backup is a manual process. You use the Internet Information Services manager in the Computer Management snap-in or by choosing Start ➤ All Programs ➤ Administrative Tools ➤ Internet Services Manager. Right-click on your server in Internet Services Manager and select Backup/Restore Configuration. Use the resultant dialog box to set up a backup. When you close the dialog box, the backup is done. To protect the metabase backup, copy it to tape. The backup is stored in the file `\WINNT\SYSTEM32\INETSRV\metabase.bin`.

You need to back up the metabase only when you make changes in Exchange. You need to restore the metabase only when it is necessary to recover Windows Server 2003 on an Exchange server. Because the metabase is not backed up automatically, you must be sure to go through this manual backup and recovery operation.

NOTE *Some people like to back up the Exchange files in* `\PROGRAM FILES\EXCHSRVR` *and its subdirectories. This was more or less necessary with earlier versions of Exchange. Newer Exchange recovery methods make such a backup unnecessary.*

HOW TO BACK UP

I showed you how to do a basic backup of Exchange information stores in Chapter 8, "Installing Exchange Server 2003," in the section "Backing Up Exchange Server 2003." Examples there were based on the backup program built into Windows 2003. In Figure 17.1, I'm using another product, Veritas Backup Exec for Windows Servers (`www.veritas.com`), to back up the information store database files on EXCHANGE01. You can't see it, because the option is set elsewhere but, as I advised earlier, I'm doing a full backup of the information store, not an incremental or differential backup.

FIGURE 17.1

Backing up an Exchange 2003 server's information store using Veritas Backup Exec

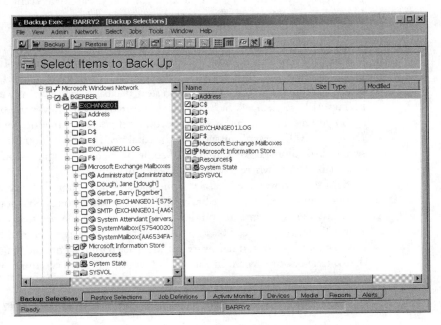

Notice in Figure 17.1 that you can back up Exchange mailboxes and, I should note, any item or items they contain. This is a nice feature, because it lets you restore a mailbox or a few items from a mailbox. However, you should use mailbox backup with caution. In my experience, mailbox backups are very slow. Backing up as few as 100 moderately sized mailboxes can take a number of hours. Mailbox backup is not supported in the Windows Server 2003 built-in backup program even after you install Exchange. It's available only in third-party backup products.

WARNING *Individual mailbox backup is not a substitute for backing up an information store. Mailbox backup is designed to let you restore a mailbox or some of the items in it to an existing information store. Don't even think about recovering individually backed up mailboxes to a newly created information store.*

I've saved the best for last. Windows Server 2003, in league with Exchange Server 2003, can do some really neat things using VSCS, which I briefly introduced earlier in this chapter. With VSCS, the backup of a volume reflects the state of the volume at the beginning of the backup. Changes that take place during the backup are not reflected in the backup. This has its downside in that your backup doesn't include anything that happened after the backup started. The upside is that there are no inconsistencies in your volume backup. You can restore an entire disk volume with every expectation that the volume will function perfectly.

You can get around VSCS's lack of change history by doing more frequent backups. If you're correctly doing a regular nightly backup using older technology, your data might be up to date when you do the backup, but by the time you do your next backup, it's 24 hours old. With VSCS and fast backup devices such as high-speed RAID disk storage units, you should be able to do hourly backups. Even if you overwrite your last backup, you'll always have a recent backup from which to recover. Good practice, of course, dictates that you retain at least a sample of several weeks of regular VSCS backups. For example, you might choose to commit your midnight VSCS backup to tape each night.

VSCS backup of the Windows Server 2003 portion of a volume is built into the Windows 2003 backup program. This includes the nondatabase aspects of Exchange—Exchange program files, for example. Exchange Server 2003 adds a set of application programming interface (API) hooks that support VSCS backup of Exchange information store databases. However, as with Exchange individual mailbox backup APIs, Exchange VSCS APIs are supported only by third-party backup software vendors.

So you need to buy a third-party product if you want the full benefits of VSCS backup of an Exchange 2003 server. But think of the total neatness here. You can back up an entire Exchange server, disk volume by disk volume. If something goes wrong, you can reliably restore whole volumes in a snap. VSCS, where have you been all my life?

Be sure to coordinate VSCS volume backups. For example, if Windows Server 2003 is installed on one volume and Exchange Server 2003 on another, you should start the backup of both volumes at exactly the same time. If you don't do this, you run the risk that your two volumes will be out of sync. Of course, you need backup software and devices that can handle multiple simultaneous backups to make this work. If hardware performance requirements and realities permit, you can get around the volume backup synchronization problem by putting everything on the same disk volume.

CAN VSCS BACKUP REPLACE TRADITIONAL BACKUP APPROACHES?

If I were you, I wouldn't run off and implement VSCS as the only backup approach in my backup strategy right now. First, I'd want to be sure that VSCS works and supports all of the recovery scenarios I can think of. Second, I'd want to retain the ability to recover an Exchange database from an information store backup. Let's say I wanted to recover a few items from a single Exchange mailbox. A full VSCS recovery not only seems like overkill, but it wouldn't provide as easy a path to recovery as an information store restore or restoration from an individually backed-up mailbox.

However you choose to back up your Exchange environment, you need to set up your backups so that you can rotate backup copies off site without impairing your ability to quickly restore data in an emergency. Ideally, I like to make initial backups to disk, copy the backups to tape, and move the tapes off site. If you can't afford this approach, then you should design a backup plan that at least allows you to take yesterday's backup off site.

WHEN TO BACK UP

I already touched on the matter of backup timing in previous sections. Here's a bit more on the subject. At a minimum, you should back up your Exchange information stores on a daily basis. For most organizations, it's best to do this backup in the late evening (after 10 P.M.) or early morning (before 3 A.M.).

PROTECTING AND RETAINING BACKUPS

Having implemented a backup strategy that lets you rotate tapes off site, you should be sure the rotation happens. Also, you should buy a fireproof, magnetic-media storage safe and keep all other backups on site in that safe. A fireproof safe for paper does not protect magnetic media. Temperature and humidity control requirements for magnetic media are higher than for paper.

As I've implied throughout this chapter, you can make an initial backup to tape or disk. If you choose to do initial backups to disk, here are a few precautions you might want to consider. First, don't back up to the disk that contains what you're backing up. You can't recover the disk if the backup is blown away when the disk is blown away. Second, immediately back up to tape whatever you backed up to disk. Even if your backup is on a different disk, it will do you no good if that disk fails. Third, rotate and store these tapes just as you would initial backups to tape. You can no more afford to lose these tapes than your initial backups to tape.

Tape retention policies are, unfortunately, only partly related to technical issues. For legal reasons, some organizations must retain data, including e-mail data, for extended periods. Other organizations, to avoid the legal hassles associated with the subpoenaing of data, choose to dump their backups almost as quickly as they are created. For you, there is only one issue. Your users need to understand the implications for data recovery of whatever retention schedule is implemented. If legal niceties aren't an issue in your organization, I recommend that you retain daily backups for the last five weeks, and one weekly full backup for three months to a year, depending on your level of comfort.

Exchange Recovery Strategies

You need to recover all or part of your Exchange system. How do you do it? That depends on what you backed up and how, what failed, and what you need to recover. You might need to recover

- Items to a mailbox
- A mailbox to an information store
- All or part of an information store to a server
- An entire Exchange server

Let's look at each of these recovery requirements and see how you might do a recovery depending on what and how you backed up.

RECOVERING MAILBOX ITEMS

Imagine that John Bumblefingers manages to delete three key messages from his Inbox. He then empties his Deleted Items folder and doesn't discover his deed until the retention time for recovering deleted items has expired. How do you get John's three precious items back?

There are two ways to recover mailbox items. You can restore the items from an individual mailbox backup, or you can restore the information store containing the mailbox and copy the items from the restored mailbox to the real mailbox.

If you backed up John's individual mailbox using a third-party backup product, and that backup is available, recovery is easy. You just run the backup software, go into Restore mode, find the items you want to restore in the product's GUI, and start the restore. The backup program places the items in the mailbox in the correct folder, and you're done.

If you didn't back up John's mailbox, you've got a fair amount of work ahead of you. Here's how to recover those deleted items:

1. Recover the Exchange information store that contains John's entire mailbox to an Exchange server that is physically separate from your Exchange organization. (See the section "Restore a Mailbox from Backup to a Recovery Server" in Microsoft Knowledge Base Article 813337.)

2. Connect to the newly recovered mailbox using Outlook.

3. Create a personal folder in Outlook.

4. Drag the items you need to recover from John's newly recovered mailbox to the personal folder.

5. Connect to John's real mailbox.

6. Add the personal folder to John's real mailbox.

7. Drag the recovered items from the personal folder to John's real mailbox.

If you need to do a lot of mailbox item restores, I strongly suggest that you spring for a third-party backup product that supports individual mailbox backup and individual item restores. Then, of course, you have to back up mailboxes individually and deal with the relative slowness of such backups. An alternative is to set up a reasonable deleted-item retention period, say, 30 days, and then to set a policy that you do not do mailbox item restores.

RECOVERING A MAILBOX TO AN INFORMATION STORE

As with individual mailbox items, if you've made a backup of a mailbox with third-party backup software, you can simply restore it directly to its home information store. If you haven't made such a backup, but you have backed up the information store that contains the mailbox, then things still aren't too bad, thanks to a new Exchange Server 2003 feature, recovery storage groups (RSGs).

In one sense, RSGs are just like mailbox or public folder storage groups. However, you can restore only Exchange mailbox stores to RSGs. You can't restore public folders, and users can't access mailboxes in an RSG. Put simply, RSGs are for recovering mailbox data. More specifically, they are for recovering mailboxes and, in a more gross way than individual mailbox backups, they are for recovering items from mailboxes. Except for certain kinds of recovery (see the previous section for an example), RSGs eliminate the need to set up a special Exchange recovery server when you need to recover a mailbox or its content.

An Exchange 2003 server can have one and only one RSG. By default, the RSG does not exist. You must create it. To do so, right-click the appropriate Exchange server in Exchange System Manager and select New ➢ Recovery Storage Group. This opens the Recovery Storage Group Properties dialog box, shown on the right side of Figure 17.2. You can change the names and location of the RSG's files if you wish. Click OK in the dialog box, and your RSG is created. As you can see in Figure 17.3, your new RSG exists on the same level as mailbox and public folder storage groups.

FIGURE 17.2

Setting parameters for a new Exchange Server 2003 recovery storage group

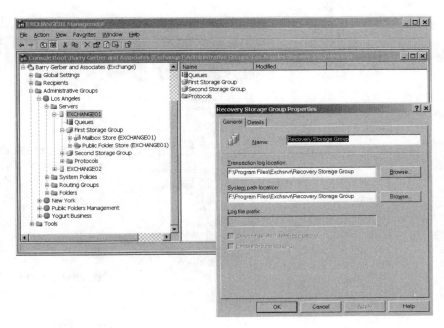

FIGURE 17.3

A new recovery storage group exists on the same level as mailbox and public folders.

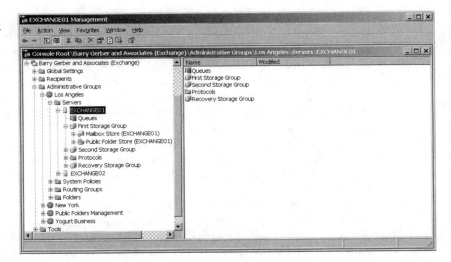

You must specify mailbox stores that are to be restored to the RSG. Right-click the RSG and select Add Database to Recover. Next use the Select Database to Recover dialog box, shown on the right side of Figure 17.4, to pick the database on your server that you want to recover. In the figure, I'm selecting the mailbox store in the first storage group on the server EXCHANGE01. Click OK to finish.

FIGURE 17.4

Specifying the Exchange database to be recovered to a recovery storage group

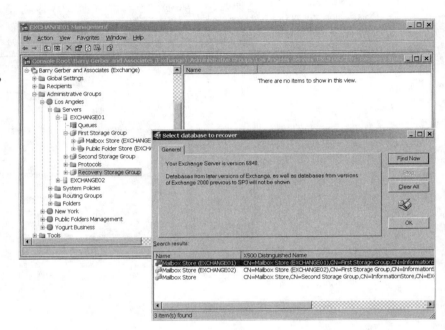

This opens a Properties dialog box for the mailbox store you have selected (see Figure 17.5). Note that the default public folder store and offline address list are specified, but can not be altered. The same is true of other store information in the General property page. This is current information for the mailbox store you've selected. You can't change it because you want existing settings for the store you're going to recover to rule here. You can use the Database page of the Properties dialog box to change the location of the files that will hold the recovered mailbox store.

When you're finished with the Mailbox Store Properties dialog box, click OK. As you can see in Figure 17.6, the mailbox store you selected is added to the RSG.

You can select as many mailbox stores to recover as you want as long as the stores reside in the same storage group. I have only one mailbox store in my first storage group, so if I were to select Add Database to Recover again, an error dialog box would open, telling me that there are no more databases to select.

At this point, if I restore the mailbox store in my first storage group, the restoration places the mailbox store backup into the RSG I created. The backup is not placed into my real first storage group, overwriting my existing production mailbox store. If the latter happened, I'd curse Microsoft until my dying day. Why, it would be a catastrophe of major proportions!

FIGURE 17.5

The General property page of the dialog box that opens when a database is selected for inclusion in a recovery storage group

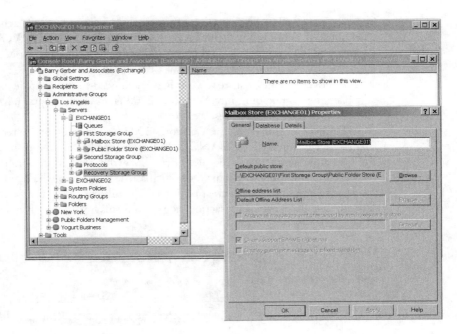

FIGURE 17.6

A new mailbox store in its recovery storage group

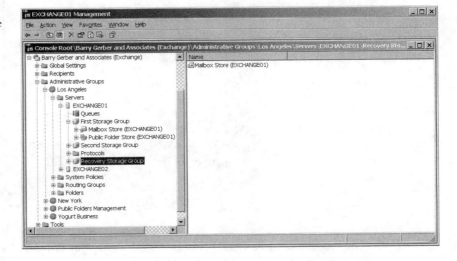

If you ever need to recover a mailbox store to its original storage group, just delete your RSG or at least the parallel mailbox store in the RSG. If you want to retain your RSG configuration, you can modify the registry on your Exchange server to override recovery to the RSG on the server. Be careful when editing the registry. Choose Start ➢ Run, type **REGEDIT** in the Open field, and click OK. Find the registry key HKEY_LOCAL_MACHINE\SYSTEM\CurrentControlSet\Services\MSExchangeIS\ParametersSystem. Click the key, right-click REGEDIT's right pane, and select New ➢ DWORD. Name the new value **Recovery SG Override**, then double-click the object and enter **1** in the Value Data field. Whenever you need to recover to the RSG, set the value of Recovery SG Override to zero.

To recover a mailbox store to your RSG, you need to do a restore using an RSG-aware program. The backup program built into Windows 2003 is one such program. Most third-party products can also perform RSG mailbox restores.

In Figure 17.7, I'm using the Windows 2003 backup program to recover the mailbox store in the first storage group on EXCHANGE01. Notice that I've chosen to restore both the mailbox store database and its transaction log files. If you knew that the transaction log files contained actions that you didn't want applied to a mailbox, such as the deletion of the mailbox, you wouldn't want to recover the logs and have them applied to the mailbox store. I discuss this in more detail in the next section, in the sidebar "Transaction Logs: To Replay or Not to Replay." After specifying what to recover, click Start Restore.

FIGURE 17.7

Restoring a mailbox store and its transaction logs to a recovery storage group

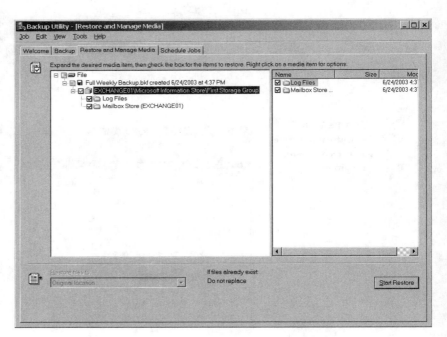

At this point, the Restoring Database Store dialog box pops up. You're offered the opportunity to specify the Exchange server to restore to. Unless you're running your restore on a different server from the one with the RSG, leave the Restore To field as is. You do need to enter a directory to hold temporary log and patch files. I use a directory called \EXTMP for this purpose. Enter the name of your directory, and don't forget the disk drive letter if you use disk drive designations. If this is the last backup to be restored to the database, select Last Restore Set so that the log files are replayed into the database. If you wish, you can also select Mount Database After Restore. Finally, click OK to start recovery. In more or less time, depending on the size of the mailbox store you're recovering, the database is recovered to the RSG and, if you specified their recovery, the transaction log files are played into the database.

WARNING   *If your backup includes a public folder store, don't select it for recovery to an RSG. Remember, RSGs are only for mailbox recovery. If you include a public folder store in a recovery to an RSG, the restore will fail.*

Figure 17.8 shows the RSG with the mailbox store database recovered. Those little Xs next to the mailboxes indicate that the mailboxes are not active and you can't activate them. All you can do is merge their contents with existing mailboxes. To do this, you use the Exchange Mailbox Merge Wizard. The wizard merges data in the RSG version of the mailbox with data in the real version of the mailbox. As of this writing, the wizard is available at the following website: `www.microsoft.com/exchange/2003/updates`. The Mailbox Merge Wizard is well documented and pretty easy to use. I'll leave it to you to apply it to your recovery needs.

FIGURE 17.8

A recovery storage group with a restored mailbox store

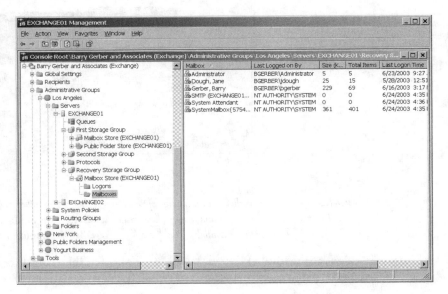

NOTE   *Technically you can use the Exchange Mailbox Merge Wizard to recover items deleted from a user's mailbox. The problem is that with a merge, you can't see what items are being recovered. Depending on the age of the backup, you could wind up restoring tons of unwanted items. If you need to restore specific items to a mailbox, it's better to use the two techniques I discussed earlier in this chapter, in the section "Recovering Mailbox Items."*

RECOVERING ALL OR PART OF AN INFORMATION STORE TO AN EXCHANGE SERVER

If you have a problem accessing a mailbox or public folder store, your first recovery strategy should be to attempt to fix it. The program ESEUTIL.EXE is the tool you use to fix Exchange databases. You run ESEUTIL from a command prompt. Before you can run ESEUTIL on a mailbox or public folder store database, you should check to see if the database is mounted. Sometimes problem stores can't be mounted, but if the store is mounted, you have to dismount it to run ESEUTIL on its database. If you need to dismount a store, find the store in Exchange System Manager, right-click it, and select Dismount Store from the pop-up menu (see Figure 17.9).

FIGURE 17.9

Dismounting an Exchange mailbox store prior to running ES-EUTIL against it

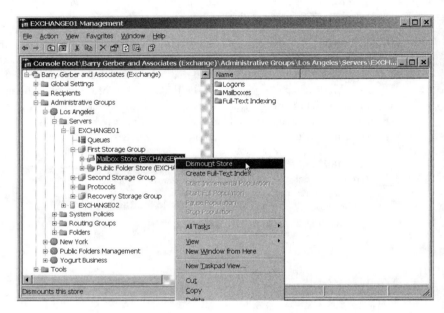

WARNING   *ESEUTIL includes a number of options, and there are a number of precautions you should take before using it. I strongly urge you to read and make sure you understand everything in Microsoft Knowledge Base article number 317014. If the article isn't available, search the Knowledge Base for* **eseutil command line switches**.

You can use ESEUTIL to do a variety of tasks. The following three tasks are the most useful when you're trying to recover a mailbox or public folder store database.

◆ Checking the integrity (consistency) of a store [command line switch /g]

◆ Recovering a store that is "dirty" due to an unplanned shutdown; plays transaction log files into the store database [command line switch /r, plus the three-character log file base name. For example, E00; check \PROGRAM FILES\EXCHSRVR\MDBDATA for the base name of the log files you want to use]

◆ Repairing a damaged or corrupt store [command line switch /p]

An integrity check doesn't fix anything, but it gives you a sense of where you stand at any given time. Figure 17.10 shows a sample integrity check; note especially the command-line syntax used.

You should run an integrity check before you run either of the other two ESEUTIL options. After running an integrity check, you should run ESEUTIL in Recovery mode. Then run an integrity check and, if the database passes the check, try to mount and access it. If you still can't access the database, dismount it again, run ESEUTIL in Repair mode, do an integrity check, and mount and try to access the database. If you still can't access the database, it's time to do a recovery from tape or disk.

FIGURE 17.10

Results of a database integrity check using ESEUTIL

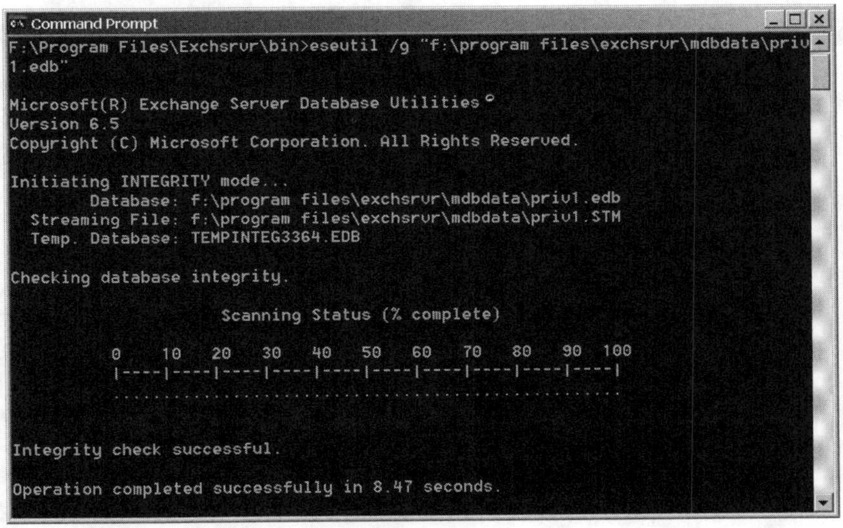

```
F:\Program Files\Exchsrvr\bin>eseutil /g "f:\program files\exchsrvr\mdbdata\priv
1.edb"

Microsoft(R) Exchange Server Database Utilities
Version 6.5
Copyright (C) Microsoft Corporation. All Rights Reserved.

Initiating INTEGRITY mode...
        Database: f:\program files\exchsrvr\mdbdata\priv1.edb
  Streaming File: f:\program files\exchsrvr\mdbdata\priv1.STM
  Temp. Database: TEMPINTEG3364.EDB

Checking database integrity.

                  Scanning Status (% complete)

        0    10   20   30   40   50   60   70   80   90   100
        |----|----|----|----|----|----|----|----|----|----|
        ...................................................

Integrity check successful.

Operation completed successfully in 8.47 seconds.
```

If you have a tape or disk backup of a mailbox or public folder store in the information store, you can recover it to a storage group on an Exchange server. The storage group and mailbox or public folder store must have the same name as the original store, which means you can recover the store to the original Exchange server or to a clone of the original server. Exchange-aware backup programs make information store recovery very easy. You can recover an entire information store or specific mailbox or public stores within an information store. Be sure that the database you need to recover isn't mounted before starting a recovery.

TRANSACTION LOGS: TO REPLAY OR NOT TO REPLAY

When you recover an information store database, the content of available unprocessed transaction log files is written to the recovered database. This is called *replaying transaction logs*. If the logs contain stuff that's messing up your database in one way or another, you don't want them to be replayed. In many instances, you can prevent the replaying of logs during an information store database recovery. Check out Microsoft Knowledge Base article number 298901 for help. Also, watch for options to not replay logs in Exchange-aware backup programs. This option is included in the Windows Server 2003 built-in backup program as augmented by the installation of Exchange Server 2003.

RECOVERING AN ENTIRE EXCHANGE SERVER

If you lose an entire Exchange server, how you recover it depends on how you backed up or didn't back up the original server. Your main goal is to get Windows and then Exchange up and running on the old server or a new one.

If you have a VSCS backup of your Windows/Exchange server, restore it, and you should be good to go. If you don't have a VSCS backup, you need to get Windows up and running on your server. There are a few ways to do this.

◆ Restore Windows 2003 from an ASR backup.

◆ Use a spare server with Windows and possibly Exchange 2003 already installed on it.

◆ Reinstall Windows 2003 from scratch and recover System State and, if appropriate, Active Directory data.

Once Windows is installed on your server, and assuming you didn't use the spare server option with Exchange already installed, you need to install Exchange 2003 on your server. When you install Exchange, you don't want to mess up Active Directory and such by doing a full, standard installation of the product. You want to nudge Exchange back to life as though it never died. You can do this by running the Exchange installation program with a special switch.

Finally, with the Exchange system back on your server, you need to restore the server's Exchange databases from information store backups. Let's look at each of these activities in more detail.

Restoring Windows 2003 and Exchange 2003 from a VSCS Backup

After only a little time with VSCS backups, I'm a dedicated fan. VSCS makes it so easy to recover Exchange servers. A restore slaps Windows 2003 and Exchange 2003 onto the old or a new server in a pretty much ready-to-go state. You might have problems with drivers if you are using hardware that is different from the hardware on the server you backed up. Such problems are usually easily solved and your server can be up and running in record time, and you're done with this section. Well, almost done. Check out the following warning before moving on to the next section.

DON'T FORGET THAT METABASE BACKUP YOU MADE

Before we move on, I need to talk about restoration of the metabase. I showed you how to back up the metabase earlier in this chapter, in the section "What to Back Up." You should restore the metabase no matter which method you use to recover Windows 2003. If you don't restore the metabase, Exchange won't function properly. It is not enough that there is a metabase file in the correct directory. The file created when you backed up the metabase is the one that you need to restore. To perform the restore, copy the metabase backup file, `metabase.bin`, to the directory `\WINNT\SYSTEM32\INETSRV\metabase.bin`. Then, open `Backup/Restore Configuration` in `Internet Services Manager`, click the database, and choose Restore.

Restoring Windows 2003 from an ASR Backup

If you used ASR to back up your Windows 2003 system, you need to restore that backup. All you have to do is insert the ASR disk you made when doing your backup and turn on your server. It will boot up, and if all is well, ASR will access any attached disk or tape drives and begin recovery. You just have to be sure that the correct drivers are available for your backup device, if they're not included in Windows Server 2003's large library of drivers.

Using a Spare Server with Windows 2003 and Possibly Exchange 2003 Installed

If your ready-to-go spare server includes only Windows, then you need to install Exchange. For more on installing Exchange, see the upcoming section, "Installing Exchange Server 2003." If Exchange is already installed, then you just need to recover your Exchange mailbox and public folder stores. See the upcoming section "Recovering Exchange Mailbox and Public Folder Stores" for more information.

Reinstalling Windows 2003 on a Server

You need to reinstall Windows. Then you have to restore System State and Active Directory (domain controllers only) data from backups. When you are finished with these tasks, you can move on to the next section, "Installing Exchange Server 2003."

Installing Exchange Server 2003

Once Windows is available and running, you need to focus on Exchange server. You can do a special installation of Exchange that sets things up pretty much as they were before your server crashed. Insert the Exchange CD, find the program SETUP.EXE. Select Start ➤ Run, type **D:\SETUP.EXE /DisasterRecovery** (where **D:** is the drive letter and path) and click OK. With the **DisasterRecovery** switch, Exchange is installed without any modifications to Active Directory settings. Existing AD settings are used. The installation also sets the correct Exchange registry entries on your new server and builds the Exchange directory (folder) structure, including the BIN directory that contains the Exchange executables.

When the installation is finished, open Exchange System Manager. You should see your rebuilt server in the tree for your organization, and you should be able to open it and mess around a bit with its objects. Don't get too smug. You're not finished yet. You have to recover your Exchange stores. Move on to the next section.

Recovering Exchange Mailbox and Public Folder Stores

I discussed the recovery of Exchange stores earlier and I'm sure not going to repeat that discussion here. ☺ So, if you will, please refer to the earlier section, "Recovering All or Part of an Information Store to an Exchange Server."

Testing Backups

Everyone who writes about backups always warns you to test your backups. Don't let the monotony of repetition lead you to ignore this warning. As many have said, a backup is useless if you can't restore from it. I test my backups when I first set them up, and then again whenever I change anything from server software and hardware to backup hardware software. I restore to hardware that is as much like the hardware on my real server as possible, though I sometimes like to restore to really different hardware just to be sure I can handle some diversity.

A number of systems managers tell me that they just don't have the time to test backups. Actually, they usually use the past tense, as in "I just didn't have time to test my backups." And this is usually in response to calls from clients who have drifted far up the Exchange creek (crashed server) and now find themselves without a paddle (backup).

What can I say? If you really don't have time to test backups, tell your boss and ask for more resources or work with the boss to prioritize the tasks you have. While you're talking with bossy, be sure to add that without backup tests, you can't guarantee you'll be able to bring e-mail back up in case of a hardware or software failure. You can also use this argument when requesting the kinds of redundant hardware that I discussed at the start of this chapter. If nothing else comes of these discussions, you will have at least set your boss's expectations at a more realistic level should all or part of all hell break loose.

Disaster Recovery

From a hardware and software perspective, I have already talked about at least 90 percent of the disaster recovery puzzle. If you're an Exchange system manager and you've protected your servers with redundant hardware, especially interserver redundant hardware, or you can restore any crashed Exchange server under your management, you've pretty much got it made. If you also have to worry about Windows 2003 and you can bring a domain controller or stand-alone server back from the dead with VSCS or ASR backups or even clunky, more traditional backups, you're in a good place too.

Disaster recovery adds another dimension to the reliability and availability picture. You have to deal with simultaneous multisystem unavailability, up to and including the sudden disappearance of all or a major part of your server, storage, workstation, and networking systems. The cause of such a disaster can be anything from a terrorist attack to an earthquake to a building fire to a major power outage to a lightning strike.

Disaster recovery isn't usually fun to think about. There are so many variables, including the potential for astronomical costs, that it's easy to either go bonkers or avoid even thinking about the whole thing. The best way to calm yourself and your boss when disaster recovery rears its ugly head is by building and living by a set of best-possible, cost-realistic strategies that specify what you'll do to avoid disasters and the actions you'll take if disaster strikes.

In this section, I'll talk about

- Disaster recovery strategies
- The Tao of disaster recovery

Disaster Recovery Strategies

I buy my cars on the Internet now and I don't put up with any infamous dealer games such as those $1,500 sprayed-on paint-protection rip-offs. When I bought at the dealership, it always bugged me when the salesperson urged me not to worry about price and just test-drive the car I really wanted. I mean, my time is limited, and I can't see myself spending hours literally driving down dead-end roads when there's no way I could ever afford my ideal car.

Well, developing disaster recovery strategies can be like buying a car at a dealership. You call in a company that traffics in disaster recovery and before you know it, you've got a proposal for a multimillion-dollar solution. The solution, by the way, is usually quite impressive. If only you could afford it.

The first thing you need to consider when developing a disaster recovery strategy is what your organization does and how a disaster might affect what it does. If e-mail and related Exchange services are central to your organization's operation and bottom line, then you need a very aggressive disaster recovery strategy. If your organization could do without e-mail for a few days, then a less aggressive strategy should be acceptable.

In building your disaster recovery strategy, don't be driven by unrealistic assessments of the importance of e-mail. And don't take a seat on the curb in discussions about the role of e-mail in your organization. You live with Exchange. You know what users are doing with e-mail, and you hear user complaints when your Exchange system isn't available. Your goal must be to drive e-mail disaster recovery deliberation toward a solution that you are comfortable with—the checkbooks, egos, or misperceptions of your bosses notwithstanding. As strategies are considered, you need to make sure your management clearly understands the limits of each. This is not just to protect yourself, but to set realistic management expectations from the get-go.

PIGGYBACKING ON NON-E-MAIL DISASTER RECOVERY STRATEGIES

Unless e-mail is all your organization does, it should have a disaster recovery strategy for other IT functionality. Adding e-mail to an existing strategy can be a relatively inexpensive option. But don't piggyback if you know the non-e-mail strategy won't work for e-mail. I've been in situations where e-mail was both more and less important than other IT functions. Management loved it when I told them that e-mail required a less aggressive disaster recovery strategy. They hated it when I pressed for a more aggressive (more expensive) strategy for e-mail.

I'm going to discuss five disaster recovery strategies, from the fanciest and most costly to the more mundane and reasonably priced. Remember that most of these strategies can be implemented in house or by a third party. Don't write off outsourcing for disaster recovery. For some organizations, it is a good, cost-effective option.

Here are the disaster recovery strategies that I'll cover in this section:

◆ Offsite replication of an entire system

◆ Offsite replication of servers, workstations, disk storage, backup hardware, software, and data

◆ Onsite replication of an entire system

◆ Onsite replication of servers, disk storage, backup hardware, software, and data

◆ Onsite presence of spare server, disk storage, and backup hardware

For many organizations, a combination of these strategies makes the most sense. Disasters come in all flavors and intensities. Sometimes they require the aggressive solutions of offsite full-system replication. Sometimes a less aggressive strategy is all that's required. The key is to understand the various disaster recovery strategies and pick the ones that best serve your organization.

WARNING *Keep in mind as you read through the discussion of disaster recovery strategies that a strategy is not a plan. Once you've selected the strategy or strategies that work for your organization, you should develop a written plan that provides specifics. You need to specify your strategy in detail and provide step-by-step up-to-date instructions for recovering after a disaster. You also need clear and up-to-date documentation for your hardware systems and the software running on them. And, once you've completed your disaster recovery plan, make sure paper and electronic copies are available off site. The best-laid plans have no value if you can't find a copy when you need it.*

OFFSITE REPLICATION OF AN ENTIRE SYSTEM

I live in Los Angeles. Any disaster recovery strategy I develop for my LaLaLand clients has to take into account the possibility of earthquake-related collapsing buildings and fractured WAN infrastructure. For those clients who need to operate without missing a beat and who can afford it, offsite replication of their entire system, including up-to-the-minute replication of data, is the right answer.

The idea is that the minute a production system takes a major hit, the offsite system becomes the production system. Appropriate IT and other staff go to the offsite location and begin doing their thing. While the transition is never going to be totally transparent, with networking switchovers and the loss of last-minute data to deal with, a total offsite strategy can get an organization up and running quickly.

One addendum to this strategy is to actually use the disaster site to conduct the organization's business. Staff at each site performs a portion of all or some of the IT and other business tasks of the organization. When disaster strikes, required personnel are already at the disaster recovery site and able to keep the organization running until reinforcements arrive.

As you can imagine, this sort of disaster recovery strategy is very, very expensive. It's for banks and other financial institutions, really big hospitals, and other corporate giants who both need this sort of quick recovery capability and can afford to put it in place.

None of my clients has placed their system in one of those bunkers built into a mountain in Colorado that you might have read about or seen in the movies. However, they have implemented less aggressive strategies where a replicated system is set up in a nearby structure and data is kept up to date, though not up to the minute, using tape backups. Often the offsite location is in a single-story building, which is less likely to be seriously damaged in an earthquake. They still have to worry about potential damage and loss of WAN infrastructure, but it's quite okay if these folks come back up within a day or so and not within minutes or hours of a disaster. So this strategy is fine for them.

OFFSITE REPLICATION OF SERVERS, WORKSTATIONS, DISK STORAGE, BACKUP HARDWARE, NETWORKS, RELATED SOFTWARE, AND DATA

The major difference between this strategy and the previous one is that you don't replicate your entire production system off site. You replicate just enough of the system to get your organization back up and running in a reasonable time. In this disaster recovery scenario, you replicate hardware and operating system and applications software as required. However, you don't necessarily replicate data, being happy to recover data from backups shortly after a disaster strikes. You also don't necessarily replicate WAN links.

If you need to replicate data or even your entire disk storage system, consider the SAN systems that I discussed earlier in this chapter. Using capabilities built into SAN systems or the Windows Server 2003 cluster service, you can replicate the data on one SAN to another SAN. Such replication is fairly quick and well suited to disaster recovery strategies where data needs to be readily available after a disaster strikes.

This disaster recovery strategy works if your organization can stand up to a few days of downtime. You and other IT staff need to be ready to scramble to get things running, but you don't have to stand the staff expense and other costs associated with trying to build a full mirror of your production system.

ONSITE REPLICATION OF AN ENTIRE SYSTEM

This strategy is the same as the first one I discussed, except your replicated disaster recovery system exists in close physical proximity to your production system. This is a pretty fancy strategy, especially if you also have an offsite replication of your entire system. However, if you need to get up and running after a major system failure, onsite full-system replication might be the only answer.

Windows Server 2003 cluster services can play a major role here and in the next two strategies. Because your system is on site, you can use the very high-speed, server-to-server, server-to-storage, and server-to network links that make clustering such a great server and storage replication solution. It won't solve all of your replication problems, but it takes care of major components in the replication equation.

ONSITE REPLICATION OF SERVERS, DISK STORAGE, BACKUP HARDWARE, NETWORKS, RELATED SOFTWARE, AND DATA

As I'm sure you've gathered, this strategy is an onsite version of the second disaster recovery strategy I discussed previously. It can provide the tools you need to meet the operating requirements of your organization. As I noted in the last section, Windows Server 2003 cluster services can make this strategy much easier to implement.

ONSITE PRESENCE OF SPARE SERVER, DISK STORAGE, BACKUP AND NETWORK HARDWARE, SOFTWARE, AND DATA

Under this strategy, you have spares at hand, but they're not kept up to date by replication. Rather, you activate spares when a disaster requires.

Like so much of my discussion of disaster recovery strategies, this one brings to mind my earlier discussions of server recovery in nondisaster situations. I hope, as I come to the end of my relatively brief treatment of disaster recovery strategies, that you begin to synthesize the content of this chapter into a coherent view of the Exchange Server 2003 reliability and availability continuum.

The Tao of Disaster Recovery

A detailed discussion of actual disaster recovery operations is beyond the scope of this book. This whole chapter and the specific disaster recovery strategies that I've discussed provide detail and hints as to the how of disaster recovery. Your disaster recovery plan will provide the specific operational steps to be taken when a disaster occurs.

What I really need to talk about here is what might be called the Tao of disaster recovery. Taoism is a way of life that associates every aspect of existence with a kind of overarching spirituality. It mixes the right and left sides of the brain, and in so doing, can bring calm and understanding to even the most stressful experience.

I participated in disaster recovery operations after the September 11, 2001 tragedy in New York City. I wasn't on site and I didn't work for the biggies in the World Trade Center, but I was involved in a number of phone conversations with IT types in two buildings damaged but not destroyed by the airplane crashes. Most of what I talked about involved Exchange server recovery.

I'm a hands-on visual type, so I was especially nervous as I tried to provide help in a voice-only situation. I'm not a Taoist, but I've had enough exposure to the philosophy to know that going bonkers wasn't going to help. So I slapped myself in the face and began breathing in a consciously slow and regular manner before taking the first phone call.

It helped. I was relatively calm until I began talking to a bunch of people who had hours before seen two massive buildings collapse and kill thousands and who were worried about their own personal safety. Understandably, these folks were in a much worse state than I. My first suggestion to them was that they take a few minutes or even a few hours to relax—after, of course, clearing it with their bosses.

My clients agreed to try and called me back in 15 minutes to tell me that they had the go-ahead to wait for an hour. I strongly urged them to do anything but IT work during that hour. Given the mess that portion of New York was in, there wasn't a lot they could do. So they decided to see if they could help others in that hour.

Almost two hours later, my clients called back. It turned out that venturing out to help others made it very clear to them how lucky they were to be alive and still able to do their jobs. In spite of what they'd seen, my clients seemed calm and relaxed about the task ahead of us.

We took the recovery process in steps. After they got their power generator going, we started up their Exchange server, which had been pelted by a major portion of the ceiling and a bunch of heavy chairs from the floor above. Fortunately, they were able to shut off power to the server before its UPS had run out of battery power. Unfortunately, the server did not come back. Not only was their Exchange server dead, so were their two Windows 2000 domain controllers.

Not being major players in trade and finance, these folks didn't have any offsite disaster-recovery setup. They also had no real onsite setup. Fortunately, they had backups that were stored both on site and off site. And, they had two standby servers in a closet that more or less survived the disaster. The servers both worked, but didn't have current software on them.

So we set up a replacement Windows 2000 domain controller and recovered a backup of Active Directory to it. Then we set up a Windows 2000 server to support the Exchange server. At this point, I suggested we stop for 20 minutes and just talk about what was going on. I actually had a better view of things from Los Angeles by TV than they had in the still-smoky and dusty environment where they were working. This brief respite helped all of us relax, and we were able to recover the Exchange server fairly quickly.

The next day, employees were able to get some work done using internal e-mail. It took more than a week to get some sort of Internet connection running. It wasn't until several weeks later that they had their 1.5Mbps Internet connection back in place.

It took about four hours, including relaxation breaks, to get the job done. If we had pushed ourselves, I estimate it would have taken maybe 10 hours with all the mistakes we'd have made and had to correct. While these folks had a written plan for the recovery, they didn't have an easy-to-use checklist, which would have made things easier. They have one now.

The moral of this story is quite simple: Disasters are stressful. Don't try to recover from one when you're at your most stressed. And you can often make your job easier by involving someone who doesn't have the same emotional and job-related connection to your organization as you do. Don't call me. I'm disaster-recoveried out. However, you should try to get someone else involved in your recovery efforts, whether it's other Windows/Exchange system managers in your area or Microsoft or third-party consultants.

Now that you have some tools to increase the reliability and availability of your Exchange system, you're ready to tackle Exchange system security. As I noted earlier in this chapter, system security can affect reliability and security. So, after we both pause to take a few slow and regular breaths, I'll see you in the next chapter.

Summary

Providing users with reliable and available Exchange server services is a complex task. You have to combine redundant hardware with a whole range of backup and recovery strategies and, if the unusual should happen, disaster recovery strategies.

You have to pay attention to both intraserver and interserver hardware redundancy. RAID storage systems, including fiber-attached Storage Area Network (SAN) devices, should be used in any intraserver solution where redundant hardware is a requirement. Redundant server power supplies and fans are readily available and are relatively inexpensive. Redundant CPUs are also an option, though they are fairly new to the Windows server world. Error-correcting registered memory, though technically not fully redundant, can help ensure system reliability and availability.

Microsoft's own Windows server platform, with its cluster services, leads the market in providing Windows interserver redundancy. Clustered servers share standard RAID or SAN devices. They can benefit greatly from all forms of intraserver redundancy.

Backing up and restoring Windows Server 2003 and Exchange Server 2003 is easier than it was with earlier versions of the two products. An Automatic System Recovery (ASR) backup of a Windows 2003 server captures everything you need to reconstruct a stand-alone server or domain controller. A backup using Windows 2003's Volume Shadow Copy Service (VSCS) enhanced by Exchange 2003 APIs can provide a very easy to restore, internally consistent snapshot of a server. Older Windows and Exchange backup/restore methods work with the 2003 versions of the products, but they tend to require considerably more work than ASR or VSCS backups and restores.

A VSCS copy of an Exchange server could be used to restore a user mailbox or items in a user mailbox. However, there are better ways to accomplish this end. You can back up and restore individual mailboxes, but such a backup takes much longer than a backup of an Exchange storage group or mailbox store. You can back up and restore whole Exchange storage groups or the mailbox or public folder stores they contain. With Exchange 2003's new recovery storage groups, you can easily recover a mailbox from a restored mailbox store.

Hardware redundancy and mastery of backup and recovery strategies takes you a long way down the path to high server reliability and availability. It also gives you a leg up as you enter the complex world of disaster recovery. Disaster recovery strategies depend significantly on hardware redundancy and Windows and Exchange server backup and recovery strategies.

Good disaster recovery strategies and plans are based on a careful balance between organizational needs and the resources required to meet those needs. E-mail disaster recovery needs might or might not be met by an organization's non-e-mail disaster recovery strategies. When disaster recovery strategies are considered, it's most important that bosses and managers understand the benefits and disadvantages of each strategy. Whatever strategy or set of strategies is chosen, bosses and managers must have a clear set of expectations regarding what can be recovered in what time frame.

Disaster recovery strategies can range from complex and costly offsite replications of entire systems to the onsite presence of spare pieces of hardware. The mechanics of a recovery after a disaster are the easiest things to specify and carry out. Maintaining the presence of mind required to pull off a disaster recovery is not so easy, but just as important.

Chapter 18

Exchange Server System Security

THERE WAS A TIME when I didn't take e-mail server security all that seriously. My e-mail career started long before the emergence of the mass of weirdoes who attempt to earn their special place in hell by making their fellow humans miserable. I'll never forget the first server I lost to a worm virus that was deposited on the server over the Internet and slowly ate away at whatever rationality the then-current Windows operating system possessed. That was my wakeup call. Since then, I have been a zealous adherent to the practices of computing and networking system security.

In this chapter, I'll tackle some key security threats and talk about ways to deal with them. This includes

- ◆ Sabotage of computer and networking hardware
- ◆ Unauthorized access to data on servers, workstations, and networks
- ◆ Attacks designed to limit access to computers and networks
- ◆ Viruses
- ◆ Spam

That's a pretty scary list. The good news is that security threat control is a thriving industry with lots of solutions. You have to pick your way carefully through a minefield of products and services, but the answers are there. To help you through that minefield, this chapter provides some grounding in security, especially as it relates to Exchange Server 2003. Additionally, I'll mention some security products that I like, and you'll find more in the Appendix, "Cool Third-Party Applications for Exchange Server and Outlook Clients." Let's get started.

Featured in this chapter:

- ◆ So much security and so little time to implement it
- ◆ Physically protecting computing and networking hardware
- ◆ Putting Exchange servers behind firewalls

- Keeping current with Microsoft security updates

- Adhering to Windows and Exchange Server security best practices

- Securing Exchange messages

- Logging and monitoring Windows and Exchange Server activities

- Securing Windows/Exchange networks

- Dealing with viruses and spam

So Much Security and So Little Time to Implement It

"Help," I can hear you saying, "there's already enough to do and you want me to deal with all that security stuff too?" I wish that I could tell you that some of the security threats listed earlier are more serious than others, but I can't. All of the threats are of equal import and any of them could put your organization temporarily out of business. If your organization doesn't have the wherewithal to deal with all of these security threats, then you'll have to draw up a priority list based on your assessment of each threat.

I suggest that you first harden the physical space where your servers and networking hardware are located. More on that in the next section. Then put your Exchange system behind a firewall, get some sort of anti-virus software running and assure that your servers are kept up to date with the latest Microsoft security updates. When you have the time and other resources to tackle the remaining security threats, get to them, but don't wait too long. There's too much at stake.

I know you don't want to hear this, because it means you have to expend more resources, but before you implement any security measures, you should take the time to develop a written security plan. The plan should at least list the security steps you are going to take, give some estimated dates of arrival for implementation, and include cost estimates. Your management should agree on the plan and understand what you want to do, why, and the implications of the implementation schedule you've developed. As you go along, you can add to your plan. Don't let the need to plan become an excuse for not implementing security solutions. And, don't wait until your entire plan is completed in great detail before beginning. By then, it could be too late.

The Internet is the biggest enemy in your war on security violations. One way to assure a modicum of security before you are able to implement your plan is to not connect to or to disconnect from the Internet. This might put a big dent in the ability of some organizations to do business, but it emphasizes the security threats and the need to do something about them.

Physically Protecting Computing and Networking Hardware

It should be very difficult for unauthorized persons to access your servers; workstations; and network cabling, routers, switches, and hubs. You can best physically secure hardware by placing it behind strong, locked doors and fixing it to racks, shelves, and tables that have been attached to walls and floors. Disk drives and other data-bearing devices should also be protected. Finally, storing data on servers, rather than workstations, can enhance hardware security.

Locking It Up and Locking It Down

Your servers and networking hardware—hubs, switches, routers—should be in locked rooms. Keys or combinations to the locks should be hard to come by. Only staff who really need to access hardware should have them.

For some organizations, exposed network cabling can be a big, big problem. A disgruntled employee or outside saboteur might snip one or many cables or an interloper might tap into a cable and steal precious information. I'll talk later about making data on your network cables secure, but if the stuff on your network is sensitive, do all you can to install cabling in hardened conduit.

While you're physically securing your hardware, don't forget to lock it down. If you're using rack-mounted servers, make sure that the rack is connected to walls with security screws and that the servers are securely mounted in the racks. If you're using free-standing servers, use computer lockdown devices to hold the servers securely to whatever furniture the computers rest upon. And, make sure that furniture is secured. I remember one instance several years ago when a client had these wonderful lockdown devices for its computers, but the computers sat on a lightweight folding table and the servers were in a locked room to which it seemed half the world had keys. A couple of thieves just folded the legs and carried the whole assembly out of the client's "secure" server room.

Don't forget user workstations. They should be locked down too. First, you don't want to lose the hardware itself. Second, if there's sensitive information on local workstations (not a good idea, by the way), theft could expose your organization to a number of risks.

While you're securing stuff, don't forget server components. Buy servers with locks and intrusion-detection firmware. You not only don't want someone opening a server and yanking out disk drives or other components, you also want to know when the yanking happened, if it does.

Also, don't leave disk drive slots exposed. You might still need such drives for automated recovery of server volumes, but you don't want someone to walk off with sensitive data that they have written to a disk. And, don't order servers with read/write CD drives or, if you do, don't leave the drives in place all the time. It would take quite a number of disks, but many fewer CDs to steal a major database. If you need a read/write CD drive, consider a removable USB-2 or firewire unit.

Tape backup devices are another invitation to data theft. If you can, keep them in a locked cabinet and, of course, secure all of your onsite and offsite tapes.

Where appropriate, you should also apply the above security principles to workstations. I urge my clients to buy computers without read/write CD drives no matter how attractively priced they are today. And I insist on disk-slot locks. They use disks to start network installs of drive images on new and refurbished computers, but their users don't need the drives to "borrow" data or infect their computers with viruses. You should also outlaw the use of USB memory sticks and other portable memory cards. My clients transfer data by e-mail, where anti-virus software ensures that it is disease free.

Storing Data on Servers, Not Workstations

No matter what you do to secure a workstation, it's not going to be all that secure. Almost by definition, workstations need to be where lots of people circulate. Data on them is never as secure as you want it to be.

By storing data on your secure servers, you remove one source of unauthorized access. Though I understand the value of local copies of Outlook mailboxes, especially with Outlook 2003, I still try to avoid implementing such mailboxes in situations where e-mail data is considered sensitive. I give my clients a choice, but make sure they understand that e-mail on a local workstation is never as secure as it is on a server.

Additionally, workstations are hard to back up. If a user works offline on their local mailbox copy and you don't back it up and something happens to the mailbox copy, their work is lost.

Putting Exchange Servers Behind Firewalls

Firewalls are great. I started using them early on to protect Internet-exposed servers from such things as denial-of-service attacks, downloaded password-breaking software and viruses, and unauthorized attempts to log on and access files. However, I was almost frightened to place Exchange servers behind firewalls. Some of it was rational. I didn't quite know what I needed to do to correctly expose Exchange so as to give standard Outlook clients access to Exchange mailboxes. Some of my reluctance to firewall Exchange servers was totally irrational. Put simply, I didn't want to break anything.

For the last several years, however, I've been happily hiding Exchange servers behind firewalls, and now I'm ready to tell you how to do it. Before I begin, however, I suggest you review the "Supporting Remote and Roving Clients" section in Chapter 16, "Advanced Exchange Server Administration and Management." Pay special attention to the difference between Outlook client access to Exchange using RPC over TCP/IP (ROTI) and RPC over HTTP (ROH). In the rest of this section, I assume that you understand the difference.

If you plan to place an Exchange 2003 server behind a firewall, you need to answer five basic questions:

- What is a firewall?

- What kind of firewall should I use?

- What protocols should I use?

- What ports do I need to open on my firewall?

- How do I test firewall settings?

Join me in the next section for a discussion of each of these.

What Is A Firewall?

Basically, a firewall manages packets of data that move in and out of a network, usually between LAN and WAN connections. The packets are built and transmitted using specific standard protocols, such as TPC/IP or UDP. Packets hold data organized according to other standard protocols, such as HTTP, FTP, POP3, IMAP4, RPC, and PING. Packets are addressed to specific software ports. Operating system software supports these ports on such devices as computers, switches, and routers.

Many protocols include both nonsecure and secure ports. For example, nonsecure HTTP packets use the TCP protocol and are targeted to port 80. Secure HTTP packets also use the TCP protocol, but are targeted to port 443. I talk more about this sort of security later in my discussion of the Secure Sockets Layer protocol.

By opening only the ports to the outside world that you need, you can protect your network against a number of security threats. Port 139, for example, supports NetBIOS access to Windows servers. Blocking it helps stop evildoers from accessing resources on your Internet-exposed servers.

Firewalls usually start with everything blocked. It's then your job to open the ports you want.

In addition to blocking ports, firewalls include logic to detect and control certain kinds of illegitimate activities carried out using ports you've opened. These include such network deceivers and destroyers as IP address spoofing (an Internet packet appears to have come from the intranet) and smurf attacks (your server is made to flood Internet servers with huge amounts of traffic).

The simplest firewalls have two hardware ports: one for a LAN connection and one for a WAN link (see Figure 18.1). Generally, these are Ethernet ports with throughput ranging from 10Mbps to 1Gbps. You plug a hub, switch, or router into the LAN side of a firewall. Depending on a firewall's computing power, anything from a few to many workstations and other devices can be located behind the LAN-side port. The WAN hardware port on a firewall is used to connect to a WAN modem, hub, switch, or router. Each of the two ports has an IP address that reflects the addressing used on the device that connects to it. I'll talk more about firewall port addresses in a bit.

FIGURE 18.1

A simple firewall with one LAN and one WAN port

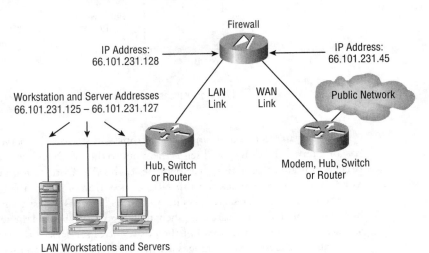

In the simplest firewall configuration (shown in Figure 18.1), servers and possibly workstations with external IP addresses sit behind the LAN port. The firewall is configured to allow only packets for these addresses to pass through, but it blocks any packet types that have been disallowed. The firewall has external IP addresses on both its LAN and WAN ports.

Most firewalls support Network Address Translation (NAT). NAT allows you to give all or selected workstations and servers on your LAN access to an external public network such as the Internet. Each workstation or server receives an internal IP address. This is an address that is not legal on the Internet. See the Internet Request for Comment (RFC) 1918. An example of an internal address range is 192.168.0.1 to 192.168.0.254. In addition to configuring a workstation's or server's IP address, you also give it a gateway router address. This is the address of your firewall's LAN port. Check out Figure 18.2 for an example of this type of configuration.

FIGURE 18.2
A simple firewall
with one LAN and
one WAN port and
NAT capability

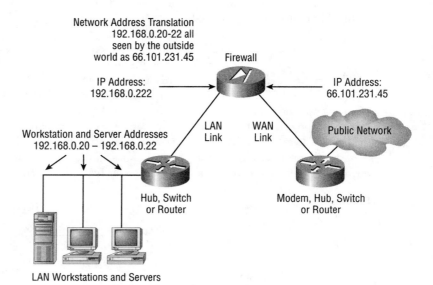

The firewall receives outgoing packets from workstations and servers through its LAN port, which has an external IP address, and sends them out to the WAN using its own external IP address. WAN packets contain information that identifies each LAN workstation or server using NAT addressing. When a packet comes back for a specific workstation or server, the firewall routes it on to the LAN and the workstation or server gets it. All of this happens in less than the blink of an eye so the user has no idea of all the IP addressing shenanigans going on behind the scenes. NAT-based workstations and servers can benefit from all of the port control services of the firewall.

Because different address ranges are involved, it's difficult to mix protection of computers with internal and external addresses on the same firewall LAN port. This problem is resolved through the implementation of a demilitarized zone (DMZ) on a firewall. A DMZ adds a third hardware port to a firewall. Servers connected to a DMZ port are available to both NAT-based LAN workstations and servers and to servers and workstations on external WAN networks. Firewall packet management protects servers and workstations on the DMZ and on the LAN. Figure 18.3 shows a firewall configured as the one in Figure 18.2, but with a DMZ.

What Kind of Firewall Should I Use?

For most of my clients, firewalls with DMZ ports work best. Though they cost more a bit more, such firewalls make it very easy to control both workstation and server access.

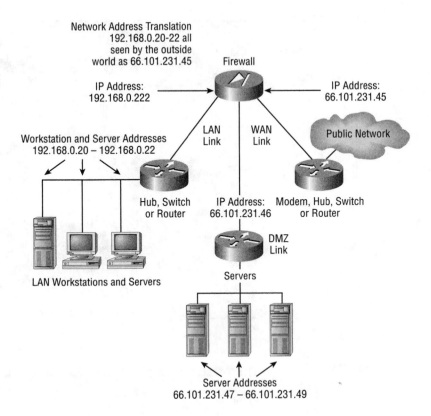

FIGURE 18.3

A firewall with one LAN, one WAN port, NAT capability, and a DMZ port

I am responsible for a number of networks. On the smaller ones, I like to use firewall products from SonicWall (`www.sonicwall.com`). In Figure 18.4, you can see how easy it is to allow or disallow blocking of specific types of packets entering the DMZ or exiting the LAN. In this case, LAN-based computers can send out any kind of packet, as indicated by the check mark in the Default box. Incoming WAN packets are limited to the ones checked. Notice that pinging from the Internet to the DMZ is specifically disallowed.

Figure 18.5 shows some of the rules that control the passage of packets between the WAN and the DMZ and between the LAN and both the DMZ and the WAN. An asterisk in the Destination column tells you that LAN packets can go to the DMZ or the WAN. Many of these rules are built into the firewall. I created others, for example, the rules labeled Exchange Port 1 through Exchange Port 3. These ports are central to TCP/IP-RPC-based Outlook client access to Exchange server. I'll discuss them later in this chapter, in the section "What Ports Do I Need to Open on My Firewall?"

Is a firewall with a DMZ right for you? You'll have to decide based on your needs.

FIGURE 18.4
Setting packet types that will be allowed through and blocked on a firewall

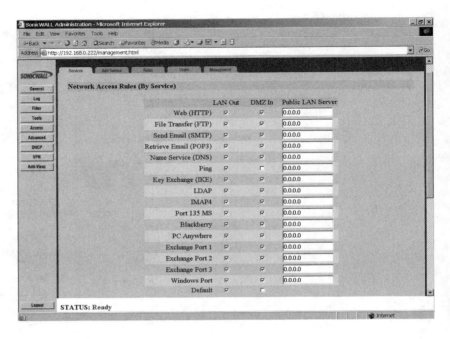

FIGURE 18.5
Some of the rules that control the passage of packets through a firewall

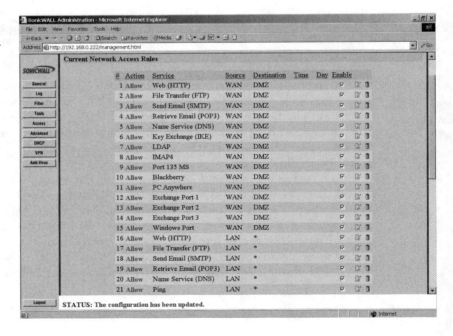

NOTE   Microsoft makes an interesting software firewall product called Internet Security and Acceleration Server (ISA). The product has some neat features such as more or less automatic configuration for Exchange servers placed behind ISA and the ability to control LAN-to-WAN access down to the URL level by Windows username or security group. It provides a standard two-port (LAN-WAN) firewall. If you opt for ISA, be sure to install it on a powerful enough server to support the user loads you expect and the ISA functionality you plan to implement.

What Protocols Should I Use?

Though you could use firewalls to protect non-Internet-based public network connections, I'm going to assume here that you need safe Internet connections. Once your Exchange server is behind a firewall, you have to decide which protocols you want to expose to the Internet. First, unless you're not running an Exchange SMTP server, you need to support the SMTP protocol. Next, for standard MAPI-based Outlook clients, you have two protocol choices: ROH and ROTI.

ROH is much easier to implement behind a firewall and, because it simply uses the standard web browser ports 80 and 443, your embedded RPC packets are going to have a happy ride over the Internet. Unfortunately, as I pointed out in Chapter 16, ROH is an option only with Outlook 2003 and the Windows XP operating system. If your remote users are blessed with these two pieces of software, I strongly urge you to use ROH. If resources are available, I also strongly urge you to upgrade remote users to Outlook 2003 and Windows XP. If that can't happen, you're stuck with ROTI.

Most networking gurus hate ROTI. They argue that ROTI was designed for LANs where tight, continuous communications between a client and server are possible. The Internet, they contend, is far too busy to support such a protocol. I have used ROTI with good success, but I understand the concerns of others and am quite happy that Microsoft has implemented a redesigned WAN-based RPC solution in ROH.

Once you've chosen the protocols you're going to use, it's time to move on to the actual ports that you need to open to allow the outside world to communicate with your Exchange server environment.

What Ports Do I Need to Open on My Firewall?

The first answers here are easy. For SMTP, open port 25. For ROH, open port 80 and 443. ROTI isn't so simple. It requires an extended discussion. If you want to use the other e-mail protocols—OWA, IMAP4 or POP3—you need to open some ports. I'll discuss these after I deal with ROTI.

Setting Up a Firewall for ROTI

ROTI requires changes on Exchange servers. Also, you need to make changes on the domain controllers that are *global catalog servers* (GCSs) if they're exposed to the Internet. Depending on the networks that support your user's RPC-based Outlook clients, you might also need to make changes on the client side. Let's start with servers.

First we'll deal with the easy part. Open up port 135 on your firewall so that Outlook clients can use it to access your Exchange server and any domain controllers that are also GCSs and connected to the Internet. Port 135 is used to obtain basic directory information from GCSs. If your GCSs aren't connected to the Internet, Exchange will, by proxy, query the GCSs on port 135. This works, but it somewhat slows down access to Exchange mailboxes. Putting your GCSs on the Internet exposes them to security risks. So, if you can live with slower access, keep your GCSs off the Internet.

Port 135 communications aside, by default, Exchange servers and RPC-based Outlook clients communicate over a very wide range of ports. The server-based changes we're going to make allow us to reduce the number of ports on the incoming packet side to just four, allowing us to open only four ports on our firewall.

Okay, get ready to say "Oh no!" To set up your Exchange and domain controller servers to use a limited set of ports, you have to edit the registry on each server. Meet me in the next paragraph after you've said "Oh no!"

Actually registry editing isn't all that bad. You just have to be very careful to do exactly what you're told.

To start, you need to come up with three port numbers in the range 1024–5000 for your Exchange server(s). You also have to settle on one port number in the same range for your GCS(s) that are connected to the Internet. You use the same port numbers on all of your servers. So you need only four numbers in all, no matter how many actual Exchange and GCSs you need to expose to the Internet through a firewall.

To ensure that you don't pick ports that are already in use, you can use the `netstat` command to find free ports. Open a command prompt, type `netstat -an`, and press Enter. I issued the command on my server EXCHANGE01. Figure 18.6 shows some of the output from the command. Both sides of each connection are shown, the local side first, followed by the foreign side. Both 127.0.0.1 and 192.168.0.103 are the IP addresses of EXCHANGE01. So, what you're looking at in Figure 18.6 are intra–EXCHANGE01 server communications. Port numbers are shown after the colon for both local and foreign addresses. Run `netstat` on your Exchange servers and GCSs that will be exposed to the Internet.

Though things might change over time, you can fairly safely use any four unused ports in the range 1024–5000. For the sake of this example, let's select ports 3875–3878.

FIGURE 18.6

Using the `netstat` command to determine four port numbers that can be used in exposing Exchange and Windows catalog servers to the Internet through a firewall

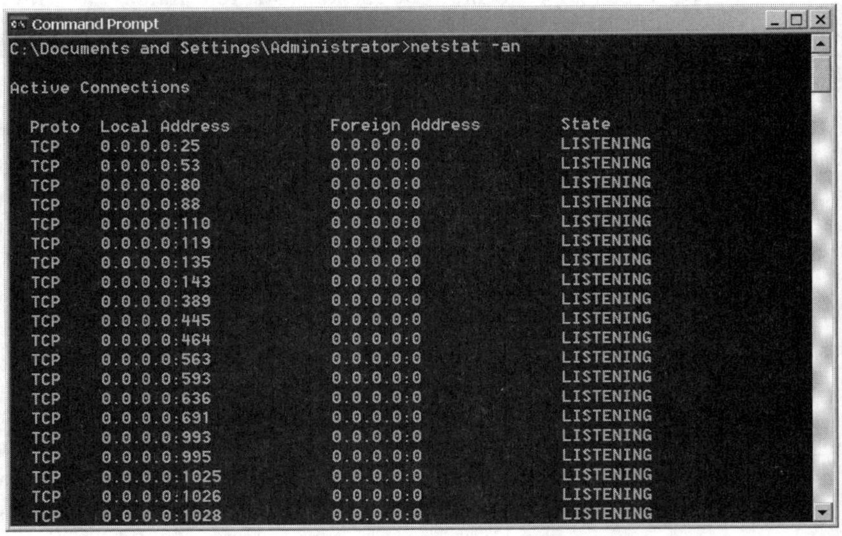

You need to make the following changes on each of the Exchange servers you want to be accessible through your firewall. These instructions are for the Windows 2003 registry editor. For clarity, I'll give you full instructions for each registry entry.

1. Start the Registry Editor (choose Start ➢ Run; then enter `REGEDT32.EXE` in the Open field).

2. Select Options ➢ Auto Refresh to turn off auto refresh and make it easier to locate items in the registry tree.

3. Find and click the registry key named `HKEY_LOCAL_MACHINE\System\CurrentControlSet\Services\MSExchangeSA\Parameters`.

   ◆ Right-click the right pane and choose New ➢ DWORD Value.

   ◆ Name: TCP/IP Port (type over "New Value #1"). Double-click the new value.

   ◆ Value Data: Click Decimal and enter one of the four port numbers you selected, for example, **3875**.

   ◆ Click OK to save your new value.

4. Find and click the registry key named `HKEY_LOCAL_MACHINE\System\CurrentControlSet\Services\MSExchangeSA\Parameters` (this is the same registry key you used in step 3).

   ◆ Right-click the right pane and select New ➢ DWORD Value.

   ◆ Name: TCP/IP NSPI Port (type over "New Value #1"). Double-click the new value.

   ◆ Value Data: Click Decimal and enter one of the remaining port numbers you selected, for example, **3876**.

   ◆ Click OK to save your new value.

5. Find and click the registry key named `HKEY_LOCAL_MACHINE\System\CurrentControlSet\Services\MSExchangeIS\ParametersSystem` (this is a different registry key from the one you used in steps 3 and 4).

   ◆ Right-click the right pane and choose New ➢ DWORD Value.

   ◆ Name: TCP/IP Port (type over "New Value #1"). Double-click the new value.

   ◆ Value Data: Click Decimal and enter one of the remaining port numbers you selected, for example, **3877**.

   ◆ Click OK to save your new value. Reboot the server to activate your registry changes.

That wasn't too bad, was it? Now here's the change you need to make on any domain controllers that are also GCSs and exposed to the Internet.

6. Find and click the registry key named HKEY_LOCAL_MACHINE\SYSTEM\CurrentControlSet\ Services\NTDS\Parameters (this is a different registry key from the one that you used in steps 3, 4, and 5).

- ◆ Right-click the right pane and select New ➢ DWORD Value.

- ◆ Name: TCP/IP Port (type over "New Value #1"). Double-click the new value.

- ◆ Value Data: Click Decimal and enter the remaining port number you selected, for example, **3878**.

- ◆ Click OK to save your new value. Reboot the server to activate your registry changes.

WARNING *Don't forget to make the registry changes discussed here on any Exchange servers that support only public folder stores. If there is only one instance of a public folder and it is on such a server and a user wants to get to it and the registry changes haven't been made on that server, all the user will see when attempting to access the folder is a nasty "folder not available" message.*

Aside from opening up the four ports you selected on the firewall, that's all you need to do to make your Exchange servers available to Internet-based Outlook clients. You don't have to do anything on the clients themselves. Servers will let clients know that they need to use the ports you've selected.

There's one more issue I need to discuss, however. When Exchange notifies an Outlook MAPI client that new mail is available, the packets it sends out can be targeted at any UDP port on the client in the range 1000–6500. To reduce this range as you just did with Exchange server, you have to make registry changes in Outlook clients. I'd stay away from this little can of worms. Why? First you have to change every client out there. Second, changes aren't the same for different versions of Outlook. Third, any information I've been able to get from Microsoft on required changes is both limited and often confusing.

Why is this so? With the advent of Outlook 2003 and ROH, Microsoft is no longer interested in supporting ROTI through firewalls. I guess we should consider ourselves lucky that we have the information required to modify our Exchange and Windows servers so they can reside safely behind firewalls and still provide ROTI-based services to Outlook MAPI clients. Getting a better handle on the client side is not currently in the cards. The bottom line: Start saving for Windows XP and Outlook 2003 so you can use ROH to connect Outlook to Exchange without worrying about registry edits and spewing UDP packets at Outlook clients in the netherworld of the Internet.

SETTING UP A FIREWALL FOR OWA, IMAP4, AND POP3

You can avoid the hassles of Internet-based RPC entirely by using the other Internet-based e-mail clients supported by Exchange server. As you know from Chapter 14, "Managing Exchange 2003 Services for Internet Clients," you have three options for remote access to Exchange mailboxes in addition to RPC-based Outlook clients: OWA, IMAP4, and POP3. If users who need to access their mail over the Internet can live with one of these client protocols, you're out of the remote RPC business. In addition to the ports for OWA, IMAP4, and POP3, you have to open the LDAP port or ports. LDAP is used by Microsoft IMAP4 and POP3 clients to resolve e-mail addresses on your Exchange server(s) when users are composing messages.

Here are the ports you need to open on your firewall:

- OWA (TCP port 80, secure TCP port 443)
- IMAP4 (TCP port 143, secure TCP port 993)
- POP3 (TCP port 110, secure TCP port 995)
- LDAP (TCP port 389, secure TCP port 636)

If you decide on secure communications, there are some things you have to do on your Exchange server and clients to enable security. On Exchange servers, you need a Secure Sockets Layer (SSL) security certificate. (For more on security certificates, see "Securing Exchange Messages," later in this chapter.) On Exchange clients, you need to turn on SSL communications. (For more on SSL and clients, see Chapter 14.)

It's important to note that SSL is a generic secure *transport* protocol. It secures communications between clients and servers. It authenticates clients and servers and scrambles and unscrambles data as it passes over networks. SSL does not authenticate e-mail senders and it does not specifically scramble and unscramble data in e-mail messages. For that, other protocols are needed. See "Securing Exchange Messages" later in this chapter for more on these protocols.

How Do I Test Firewall Settings?

Testing firewall settings is straightforward, if not always easy. Every time I put an Exchange server behind a firewall, I position myself outside the firewall, start up whatever client needs to get through the firewall, and try to connect to a mailbox. You can do this without leaving the building by connecting the WAN port to a hub or switch and then connecting a workstation to the hub or switch.

What if you can't connect? Make sure you can get to the server. Try to ping the server. This, of course, assumes that your firewall hasn't been closed to pinging. Try to telnet to your Exchange server's SMTP server and send an e-mail message. For instructions, see the "Sending SMTP E-Mail Like an SMTP Host" section in Chapter 13, "Managing Exchange 2003 Internet Services." Make sure that the correct ports are open. If they are, go back and ensure that everything is set up properly on the server side. If you're trying to connect through a firewall with a ROTI-based MAPI client, check your registry settings. Registry editing is a pain—even with my peerless instructions.

Don't forget the packets that aren't supposed to be getting through the firewall. As I noted earlier, most firewalls start with everything blocked. You have to open the ports you want. However, it's always worth a quick test to be sure that this is the case. Here's my favorite test: By default, I don't turn on pinging. It's a quick way for Internet miscreants to discover you're there. So I try to ping a machine behind the firewall. If I get a reply, I know I've got a problem and need to check out the firewall's defaults. If I don't get a reply, I know the firewall is working as expected. So I open the ping port and try to ping. A response confirms that the firewall is operating fine. I close the port and move on. In the highly unlikely event that I still get no response, I need to be sure that the firewall is properly connected to the WAN and LAN networks and that my target computer is pingable from inside the LAN.

Keeping Current with Microsoft Security Updates

For as long as I can remember, Windows has required frequent software patches to fix newly discovered bugs, including a slew of security-based bugs. If you're a Windows person, you're probably aware of the nice automated update capabilities built into current Windows products. These can be helpful, but they won't solve all of your Windows software currency issues.

In the old days, manually keeping Windows servers up to date provided full-time work for a lot of people. Tasks included keeping current on bugs and patches, finding patches on disk or on the Internet, testing patches, documenting patch installation, and installing the patches in production environments.

In the new days, automated updates make keeping current on and finding patches easier. However, the other tasks still have to be done. Furthermore, not all fixes are covered in auto-updates. You'll often find problems in the Windows event logs for which no immediate answer is available, even if you click the URL that is now included in many event log entries. You or a consultant still have to track these down in the Microsoft Knowledge Base and other places and you still have to manually find, test, document, and install patches.

Whether it's easy or not, you have to keep up to date with Windows security fixes. When you set up Windows Update, don't select the fully automatic installation of updates. You need to read about each update and be sure that you really need it. For example, it makes little sense to update most servers to the latest and greatest version of Microsoft's DirectX graphical support software.

Historically, Exchange Server updates have focused on program bug fixes and product enhancements. Key Exchange updates are usually delivered in service packs. However, in an emergency Microsoft will issue interim hot-fixes for both program and security bugs. You need to know about these and apply them, but if and only if they apply to your circumstances. Hot-fixes are often not tested as thoroughly as service packs, so you don't want to apply them if you don't need them. If you choose to apply them, be sure to test them.

To stay up to date on Windows and Exchange fixes, keep close tabs on Microsoft's TechNet site (`www.microsoft.com/technet`). You can search for and download Windows and Exchange updates, set yourself up to receive security fix notifications by e-mail, join relevant newsgroups, and more. With auto-updates, event logs, and the Microsoft Knowledge Base and TechNet, you should be able to keep one step ahead of the security-breach monster.

Oh yes, don't forget about onsite and offsite workstations. They are also vulnerable to security threats. You can use all of the tools that I discussed earlier on modern Windows workstations. Updates, automatic or not, are more complicated on workstations because there are usually so many of them relative to the number of servers that you have to worry about and you have the option of letting users run updates. If you're comfortable with the fully automatic updates provided by Windows Update functionality, go for it. You will have to give users full administrative rights to their workstations or run the auto-update yourself logged in as the workstation or domain administrator. If you're not comfortable with auto-updates, then you're going to have to apply workstation updates manually or use an automatic update technology that you are comfortable with.

TIP   *Microsoft offers a free tool that you can run on a local or networked server or workstation to check for needed security updates. It's called Microsoft Baseline Security Analyzer. As of this writing, you can download it at* `www.microsoft.com/technet/treeview/default.asp?url=/technet/security/tools/Tools/` `MBSAhome.asp`*.*

FIREWALLS AND SECURITY UPDATES

The good news regarding Windows security updates is that, in certain circumstances, firewalls reduce the urgency of updating or the need to update at all. Some server and workstation security problems arise because the computer is exposed directly to the Internet. With a firewall in place and the appropriate ports secured, these threats are no longer significant. That doesn't mean, of course, that you can just forget security updates if you've got a firewall. In fact, I strongly urge you to install all security updates unless you really know your firewall and the specific security threat and you're able to fully assess the implications of not installing an update.

Adhering to Windows and Exchange Server Security Best Practices

Though they are essential, security best practices are often a can of worms. With Windows and Exchange Server 2003, Microsoft has implemented a set of security best practices right inside the products. Both Windows and Exchange 2003 start out very secure; some would say too secure. You can modify these default security settings, but you should be sure that you know what you're doing and what the consequences of any changes might be. Here are my thoughts on all of this.

Windows Security Best Practices

Windows security is a very complex topic. It ranges from enabling logging for and monitoring a wide range of events that can occur on a Windows server to ensuring that Windows users and security groups have just the resource access privileges they need and no more. Good logging tells you who is doing what where, including who is attempting to or succeeding at changing resource access privileges. Careful attention to user and group privileges can prevent innocent or malicious changes that can undermine the security of the computers that support your Exchange system.

I'll talk a little about some Windows security issues as they relate to Exchange server later in this chapter. However, with one exception (Windows passwords, grrrr), an extended discussion of Windows security best practices is beyond the scope of this book. If you need help understanding and implementing Windows security, I suggest you start with *Mastering Windows Server 2003* (Sybex, 2003).

Now for a little rant on Windows passwords. As I'm sure you know, Windows passwords control access to Windows resources, including Exchange server mailboxes and public folders. They play a very important role in overall Exchange system security. When establishing best practices for passwords, you have to walk a fine line between the absurdly simple and the absurdly complex. Windows Server 2003 makes it very easy to see that fine line and the simple-to-complex continuum on either side of it.

Microsoft has graciously built a vision of password best practices into Windows Server 2003 but, when you first encounter these best practices, unless you're ready for them, I don't think "graciously" is the first word that'll come to mind. When I created my first Windows 2003 user, it was all I could do to avoid swearing in a variety of languages. The password had to be three miles long, with numbers and uppercase and lowercase letters, and it expired almost before I created it. Now, I have nothing against password security, but these password policies have "put it on a Post-It and stick it on the computer monitor" written all over them.

If you agree with me, you can make Windows 2003 password policies less absurdly complex. However, if you do so, don't revert to the almost-no-security-at-all default policies of pre–Windows 2003 operating systems.

Password policy modification requires the kind of extensive discussion that is beyond the scope of this book. You can find more on this subject and related issues in *Mastering Windows Server 2003*.

There is one exception to Windows 2003's long and winding password requirements. When you install a new server and create a local Administrator account, you can have a password of any length and complexity you want. You can even use a blank password. Simple recommendation: Follow the same reasonable rules for password length, complexity, and expiration for Administrator passwords as for all your other Windows accounts.

Exchange Server Security Best Practices

Out of the box, Exchange server is quite secure. I'm quite satisfied with access control on the server. In my experience, Exchange administrators tend to expand their and others' privileges to deal with one or another specific situation and then forget to revoke those privileges when they're no longer needed. These administrators soon find themselves managing Exchange systems that are as full of holes as a piece of Swiss cheese. Insecure Exchange systems can be a great source of embarrassment for their administrators, as you'll see in a bit when I tell you a sad real-world story.

Before story time, however, let me offer some general cautions. Try very hard to avoid granting sweeping Exchange privileges when lesser privileges can work. Grant privileges at the most granular level. Windows security groups are great because they let you give rights to multiple users with a few mouse moves and clicks. This capability also makes security groups dangerous, because people who neither need nor should have certain privileges wind up having them. If a few people in a security group need a privilege, create a group just for them or grant each person the privilege. Don't grant the privilege to the entire group. Document the privileges you grant at both the individual and group level. And, be sure to review the privileges that you've granted on a very regular basis to see which rights are still required.

Back in Chapter 8, "Installing Exchange Server 2003," I showed you how to create a group called "Exchange Admins" and delegate Exchange full administrator control to that group at the Exchange organization level. Full administrator privileges: wow. It sounds as if you hold the life and death of your Exchange system in your hands. Not true, as you'll see in a bit. But, does everyone who works on your Exchange system need full administrator privileges? As I showed you in Chapter 8 and in Chapter 15, "Installing and Managing Additional Exchange Servers," you can grant less than full control and you can delegate control at a lower level in the Exchange hierarchy, the administrative group. Think through your Exchange administrative needs and ensure that you delegate the least amount of control commensurate with getting the job done.

EXCHANGE ADMINISTRATOR ETHICS

Before telling the sad real-world story, I want to talk about Exchange administrator ethics. I thought long and hard about including the story. A fair number of Exchange administrators don't know how to do what I talk about in the story and I wondered if I should be the one to tell them. I decided that I would, but only after a brief lecture on the ethics of Exchange administration. Before the lecture, I need to lay out a few facts that you might not know.

With the right Exchange security settings, anyone can look at the contents of anyone else's mailbox. There are simple tools in Outlook that allow a user to easily grant other users access to all or part of their mailbox. This is a useful feature because there are a number of perfectly legitimate reasons why someone might need to let others into all or part of their mailbox. At the administrative level, by fiddling with default Exchange security settings, Exchange administrators can give themselves access to any mailbox on their Exchange system. There might be valid reasons for an Exchange administrator to access a single mailbox every now and then, but I can't think of any justification for an administrator to have access to all mailboxes.

Okay, here comes the lecture: Being an Exchange system administrator is a kind of sacred trust. You should never look at anyone else's e-mail unless they give you permission to do so. Period! If you break this trust, you not only open yourself up to ethical criticism, you also open yourself up to being fired should you be discovered, and you hurt every other Exchange administrator while damaging the reputation of e-mail in general and Exchange server specifically. Of course, the ethical issues are different if someone with the proper authority needs to see another person's e-mail. End of lecture and on to the story.

A SAD REAL-WORLD STORY

One day I received an e-mail from an old friend who is responsible for a large IT department's networking infrastructure. She was concerned that she had a serious security problem on her hands. There were two symptoms. First, a laptop belonging to the head systems administrator for her network appeared to be attempting to log on to workstations on the network. Second, an Outlook meeting request notice was apparently sent to others by the head of the IT department, my friend's boss. I say "apparently," because the department head claimed he hadn't sent the message.

My task, should I be foolish enough to accept it, would be to find out what really went on and to determine if the systems administrator was guilty of real or attempted security violations. In a fit of foolishness and attracted by the dollars being waved in my face, I accepted the task. Here's what I found out, after a week and a half of onsite and offsite research.

The laptop ran Windows XP Home edition. Though no one believed me at first, including Microsoft, I was able to replicate the attempted logons by just connecting an XP Home computer to a Windows 2000 network and leaving it there. It was clear that the logon attempts were totally innocuous. Furthermore, the systems administrator had administrator-level access to the network and could see virtually anything he wanted without being discovered. These facts and a few others exonerated the administrator of any security breaching with the laptop.

Believe it or not, the laptop issue was harder to resolve than the Outlook meeting notice issue. My friend and her boss feared that the system administrator might be logging in to the boss's workstation and that was how he sent the meeting notice in the boss's name. In a short time, the system administrator admitted to innocently setting up the meeting. Here's how he said he did it.

A number of IT staff members were able to open the calendars of others. Why? Certain IT staff liked to call in and have someone check their appointments while they were out of the office. The system administrator said that he was setting up a meeting involving a number of IT staff including my friend and her boss.

My friend acknowledged that the systems administrator indeed was to set up such a meeting. However, instead of using the free-busy information available for each invitee when you set a meeting using an Exchange-connected Outlook client, the system administrator had opened each invitee's calendar while his mailbox was open in Outlook. (In Outlook, he chose File ➤ Open ➤ Other User's Folder.) The system administrator claimed that he had set up the meeting while focused on the window that held the calendar of the head of IT. Kablooie! The meeting notice message was sent out and looked just as if it had been sent by the IT head, or so the systems administrator argued.

There are at least two ways I know of for A to get access to B's calendar: B can grant that access in Outlook or A can be given access in Exchange. But access to B's calendar wouldn't have been enough here. The system administrator needed to have Send As permissions for the IT head's mailbox in order to send the meeting request as the head of IT. Because the system administrator was on administrative leave while I conducted my investigation, I couldn't ask him how all this might have happened. No one else on the system administration team knew. So, I had to dig into my client's Windows/Exchange security system.

I quickly discovered that the group Exchange Admins had been made a member of the Windows security group Domain Admins and had been granted the privilege Full Control at the Exchange server level in the Exchange hierarchy. Why was Exchange Admins even present at the Exchange server level? That's because the group was granted some rights at the server level when Exchange Full Administrator control was delegated to it at the Exchange organization level. That delegation gave it permissions at various levels in the Exchange hierarchy, including at the Exchange server level. One click in the Full Control box on the Security page of the properties dialog box for the Exchange server was all it took, not only to grant permissions to access every mailbox on the server but to also send as the owner of each of those mailboxes.

The previous paragraph is chock-full of juicy information. To help you better appreciate that information, here's a graphically illustrated restatement. Figure 18.7 shows the permissions the group Exchange Admins has on my server EXCHANGE01 after the group has been delegated Exchange Full Administrator control at the Exchange organization level. Notice that the permission Full Control is not granted. Also notice that the permissions granted to the group are grayed out. This means the permissions are inherited. In this case, the permissions were initially granted at the Exchange organizational level when Exchange Full Administrator control was delegated to Exchange Admins.

In Figure 18.8, I've scrolled down so that you can see that Exchange Admins does not have permission to Send As. I've granted Full Control permissions to Exchange Admins in Figure 18.9. Notice how all of the white boxes are checked. In Figure 18.10, you can see that, along with all other permissions, Exchange Admins now has Send As permissions. At this point, any member of Exchange Admins could open all or part of any user's mailbox and send messages as the user.

A little more fishing revealed that full control had been granted to Exchange Admins at the server level so that some members of the group could help users with various problems. There appeared to be no malevolent intent behind this act. It was just easier to get things done this way. And, a nice side benefit of what had been done was the ability to open people's calendars and help them when they were out of the office.

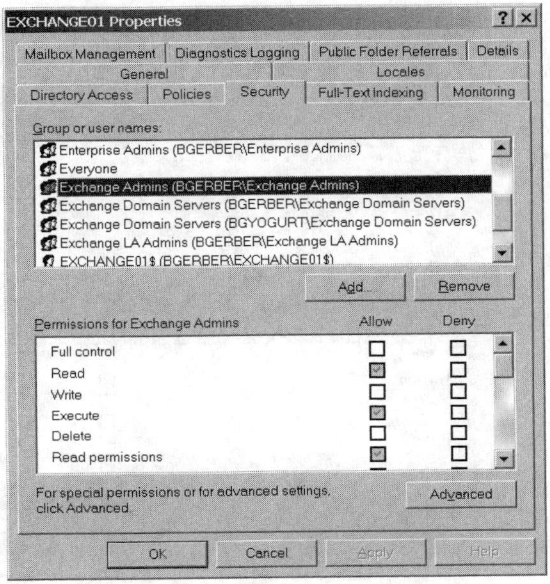

FIGURE 18.7
The group Exchange Admins has limited control on an Exchange server after it has been delegated Full Exchange Administrator control at the Exchange organization level.

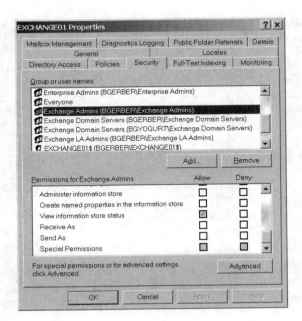

FIGURE 18.8
The group Exchange Admins does not have Send As permissions on an Exchange server after it has been delegated Full Exchange Administrator control at the Exchange organization level.

FIGURE 18.9
Full Control at the Exchange server level has been granted to the group Exchange Admins.

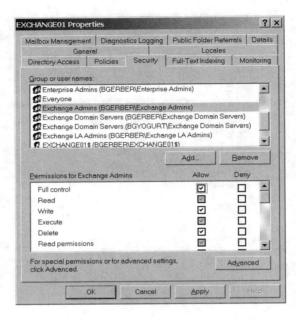

FIGURE 18.10
Once Full Control is granted at the Exchange server level, the group Exchange Admins has Send As permissions on the server.

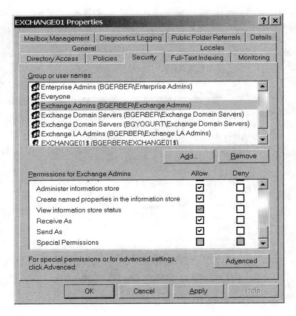

These folks could have achieved their goals with much less drastic security modifications. People who wanted others to open their calendars could have granted others permission to open their calendars. When a system administrator needed to have full access to a user's mailbox, such access (Full Mailbox Access) could have been temporarily granted by using the Mailbox Rights button on the Exchange Advanced tab in a user's properties dialog box (go to \`Active Directory Users and Computers\Users` and double-click the user). That's a long sentence. Figure 18.11 will help you digest it.

FIGURE 18.11

Granting Full Mailbox Access permissions on a user's mailbox

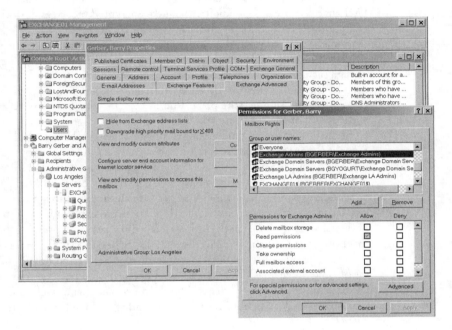

You might have noticed that I didn't once mention Windows security logs. Those logs can contain juicy tidbits of information that can help explain when, how, and by whom security might have been compromised. Well, I didn't mention the security logs because there weren't any that could help me. Security logging was turned on, but logs grew so quickly that, in most cases, they were retained for only a day on disk. Only a week's worth of tape-based log backups were kept. By the time I came on the scene, there were no logs that I could use in my investigations. Luckily I was able to get the job done without the logs. My friend is now not only retaining logs for longer periods, but she also has, at my suggestion, implemented a security log monitoring product that provides daily reports on key log entries.

The system administrator and my friend survived the Exchange security violations wars. However, they and I learned quite a bit from our experience.

Securing Exchange Messages

You can protect Exchange messages as they traverse your internal network or the Internet and as they are stored on your Exchange servers. Your goal is to ensure (1) the name that appears in the Send field of a message identifies the true sender of the message and (2) a message is unreadable by anyone but its sender and receiver. The first goal is achieved with digital signatures, the second by encrypting (scrambling) and decrypting (unscrambling) messages.

It's important to note that message security is a client, not a server, responsibility. While an Exchange server can store digitally signed, encrypted messages, it does not do the actual signing and encrypting. This is done by the user's e-mail client.

For an e-mail client to digitally sign and encrypt messages, a security certificate is required. A security certificate allows for the creation of public and private security keys that can be used in a variety of data security tasks including digitally signing and encryption of e-mail messages. Private keys are used by the e-mail client to do encryption and signing. Private keys never leave the computer where encryption and signing take place. Public keys are used by the recipient computer to assure the authenticity of the signature and to decrypt the message.

Security certificates can be obtained from an external or internal certificate authority (CA). VeriSign (www.verisign.com) is a well-known external CA. A Windows 2003 server can be enabled as a CA. CA Server is a Windows 2003 component similar to an SMTP or Internet Information Server. A Windows CA Server should have its own security certificate to assure others of its authenticity.

Installing and managing a CA Server is fairly simple, though the recovery of lost certificates can be a bit tricky. However, CA Server installation and explanations of the somewhat esoteric principles of digital signing and encryption as well as public key encryption schemes are all beyond the scope of this book. See *Mastering Windows Server 2003* (Sybex, 2003) for more on this stuff.

Again, because this is a book about Exchange Server and not about e-mail clients, I can't spend a lot of time on client-side certification and security. I'll point you in the right directions and let you take it from there. There are good books on e-mail clients such as Outlook, Outlook Express, and Outlook Web Access, but I find I can generally get along fine using the documentation built into the clients.

Outlook MAPI clients can obtain a security certificate from an internal or external CA. Newer Outlook MAPI clients include built-in interfaces for obtaining certificates. You can import a certificate from a file or obtain one online. In Figure 18.12, I opened the Outlook 2003 Security page on the Options dialog box (Tools ➤ Options). Then I clicked Get a Digital ID to open a web page that presents a number of organizations that provide security certificates. I can click the URL for any one of them and get my certificate. Most external authorities charge for certificates. The web page includes a free certificate site operated by Thawte Certification.

Outlook MAPI clients use the Secure Multipurpose Internet Message Extensions (S/MIME) protocol to sign and encrypt messages. As you know from Chapter 13, MIME is a protocol for encoding a range of 8-bit content so that it can travel in the 7-bit world of the Internet. Such content includes graphic images, sound, video, and formatted text. S/MIME adds a method for scrambling messages to make them unreadable except by those who have the appropriate public key.

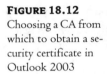

FIGURE 18.12
Choosing a CA from which to obtain a security certificate in Outlook 2003

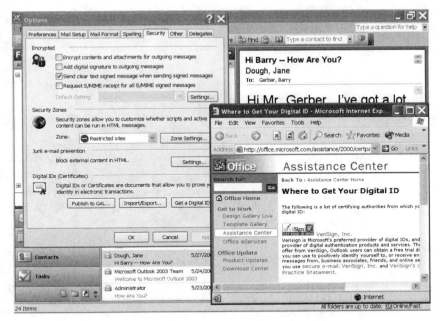

RPC over HTTP offers three levels of security:

◆ Standard Outlook MAPI client S/MIME digital signatures and encryption (See the previous paragraph.)

◆ SSL security between the client and server (at the HTTP level)

◆ RPC packet encryption

You can use any combination of these three security levels.

To turn on SSL for RPC over HTML in Outlook 2003 and later, select Tools ➤ E-Mail Accounts ➤ View or Change Existing E-mail Accounts ➤ Change ➤ More Settings ➤ Connection Tab ➤Exchange Proxy Settings ➤ Connect Using SSL Only.

To turn on RPC encryption in Outlook 2003 and later, select Tools ➤ E-Mail Accounts ➤ View or Change Existing E-mail Accounts ➤ Change ➤ More Settings ➤ Security Tab ➤ Encrypt Information.

As I noted in the section "Setting Up a Firewall for OWA, IMAP4, and POP3"earlier in this chapter, you can enhance the security of OWA, POP3 and IMAP4 client-server communications using the SSL protocol. Take a look at Chapter 14 for more on where you set up SSL for POP3 and IMAP4. To turn on SSL for OWA, you need to obtain a certificate for your Internet Information Server. The easiest way to do this is with the IIS Certificate Wizard. To start the Wizard, follow these steps:

1. Open IIS Manager on your Exchange server.

2. Find and right-click Default Web Site. Tab to the Directory Security page and click Server Certificate.

3. Follow along on the Wizard to obtain your certificate. When you have the certificate, install it.

4. Go back to the Directory Security page and click Server Certificate. The Wizard starts up again, but it now assumes you want to install the certificate. Use the wizard to install the certificate.

5. When you're done, click Edit in the Secure Communications area on the Directory Security page. Select Require Secure Channel (SSL).

WARNING   There's an option in the General properties page of Exchange 2003 mailbox stores called Clients Support S/MIME Signatures. By default, this option is selected. It has nothing to do with the ability of e-mail clients that use the store to create digitally signed messages. Rather it's about the ability of clients of the store to read digitally signed messages. If you deselect this option, S/MIME messages in the store are converted by Exchange to MIME messages. You deselect this option only if you have a mailbox store that was specifically set up for clients that can't deal with digitally signed messages. Modern Outlook MAPI and Outlook Express clients (post-1998) can handle digitally signed messages. So, don't deselect the option if the store supports these client types.

WHAT HAPPENED TO THE KEY MANAGEMENT SERVICE (KMS)

Up through Exchange 2000, the KMS was responsible for the creation and management of the security certificates required when Outlook MAPI clients signed and encrypted messages. With Exchange 2003, that has changed. KMS is gone. Certificate creation and management is now supported by standard CAs. You can maintain more control over the entire process by using a Windows 2003 CA rather than an external CA. If you're an old Exchange hand, you might find this change awkward. But once you realize that pre–Exchange 2003 Outlook MAPI client certificate services management was a glaring exception to a very long-established standard rule, the changes in 2003 should make good sense to you. Also, if certificate management is handled by another group in your organization, you no longer have to worry about it.

Logging and Monitoring Windows and Exchange Server Activities

The occurrence of many security threats can be discovered in Windows and Exchange server logs. Ensuring that logging is turned on for specific Windows and Exchange processes means you're capturing the data you need to discover, repair, and affix blame for security threats. Logs can easily grow to the point where it's impossible to monitor them manually. Fortunately, a number of applications are available that can take the raw content of logs and convert it into useful summary reports not just about security issues, but about anything in the logs, from potential hardware problems to a problem on your Exchange server's SMTP virtual server.

Logging Exchange Virtual Server Activity

Logs for Exchange SMTP, HTTP, IMAP4, POP3, and NNTP virtual servers can help you track down security problems. I suggest you turn on logging for at least your SMTP and HTTP virtual servers.

Except for the HTTP virtual server, you enable logging in the General properties page of the virtual server. To do so, find and right-click the appropriate virtual server in Exchange System Manager, then select Properties. The General properties page is visible when the virtual server's properties dialog box opens. To enable logging on the HTTP virtual server, open the IIS Manager, find and right-click Default Web Site, and select Properties. On the Web Site page, ensure that Enable Logging is turned on.

The default Active Log Format, W3C Extended Log File Format, should work just fine for all virtual servers. You can read W3C files using Windows' Notepad application.

Be sure to click Advanced on the page where you set log file format. Behind the Advanced button, you'll find a veritable three-ring circus of options for the frequency at which a new log file is generated and for customizing logging to allow for the recording of such information as port used, time taken to complete the logged event, and username under which an authenticated login occurred.

On Windows 2003 servers, logs are stored in the directory `\WINDOWS\SYSTEM32\LOGFILES\ <VIRTUAL_SERVER_NAME>`, where `<VIRTUAL_SERVER_NAME>` is—surprise—the name of the virtual server for which logging has been turned on. The directory for the default SMTP virtual server's log files is SMTPVC1.

Using Security Scanners and Log Monitors

Security scanners look at your network from a variety of perspectives and tell you where the security holes are. There are all kinds of security scanners on the market.

Security log monitoring software plows through Windows event and other logs looking for the occurrence of specific events based on built-in or user-created criteria. These criteria focus on a variety of issues ranging from hardware and software problems to potential security violations. Monitors issue reports that neatly summarize the data they collect.

Security scanner and log monitor prices range from quite low to very high. I'll leave it to you to find one to your liking. You can find vendors by searching the Web using the terms *security monitor* and *security scanner*. Also see the Appendix for some products that I like.

Securing Windows/Exchange Networks

Aside from physically protecting your network cable and hardware, you can use a couple of software-based tools to secure your networks: virtual private networks and secure IP. Both of these provide security by reliably and effectively wrapping standard network packets in a secure shell that lets them cross private and public networks while keeping their content inaccessible to network peeping Toms.

Using Virtual Private Networks

Unless you secure Exchange messages (see "Securing Exchange Messages," earlier in this chapter), they are fairly easy to read as they pass through a public network such as the Internet. If your users need to communicate over a public network and you're not using secure Exchange messaging, consider a virtual private network (VPN). VPNs encrypt data so it can sail the dangerous waters of public networks safe from curious or evil eyes. To switch analogies, think of a VPN as a private tunnel through a public network.

VPNs aren't necessarily just for public networks. Some organizations use VPN technology on their internal networks to protect against internal data snoopers.

Secure Sockets Layer (SSL) communications are like a VPN. SSL supports a private connection between the client and server using a special handshake algorithm. It also allows the client to authenticate the server, ensuring that the server is really who it says it is. Packets that pass over an SSL link are encrypted. Additionally, their reliability is ensured because data integrity checking information is included with the data transmitted. The server must have a security certificate and you must turn on SSL on the client and server. As you'll remember from the earlier sections, "Setting Up a Firewall for OWA, IMAP4, and POP3" and "Securing Exchange Messages," and from Chapter 14, SSL is available for HTTP, POP3, IMAP4, and LDAP clients. See Chapter 14 for more on enabling SSL on the client and server side.

Many books have been written on VPNs. Get a hold of one of them or browse the Internet, which contains more information on VPNs than anyone could possibly read in a lifetime.

Using Secure IP (IPsec)

VPN technologies aren't always standards-based. IPsec, on the other hand, is fully standards-based, making it a very good choice to support internal and external secure packet transmission.

IPsec combines a number of standard protocols to produce very secure packets. These protocols assure that

◆ A packet was sent from the IP address specified and was not sent by an impersonator.

◆ A packet was not modified in transmission.

◆ A packet is very securely encrypted.

◆ Encryption keys can be shared across organizations.

IPsec is available now. It is implemented at the operating system level. It must be available on both clients and servers. Windows 2000, 2003, and XP all support IPsec.

As with VPNs, I encourage you to check out the many books and websites that deal with IPsec. It's a great idea that can add much needed security protection to a network, if, of course, encryption keys are kept secure.

WARNING   *Don't turn IPsec on unless you fully understand how it works, or you're very likely to wind up with a bunch of client and server machines that can no longer communicate.*

Dealing with Viruses and Spam

I'll close this little tour of steps you can take to better secure your Windows/Exchange system with one of my favorite subjects: virus and spam control. There is almost nothing more professionally satisfying than to know that you've done all you can to stop potentially system-destroying viruses and productivity- and disk-storage-draining spam messages.

Controlling Viruses

Nothing strikes terror in the heart of network administrators like computer viruses. Viruses are bad enough when carried from computer to computer on disks. But, store files containing them on a network file system for all to access, or send them to one and all by e-mail, and computer viruses become true threats to mission-critical systems. I've done quite a bit of work in public health, and I can tell you that there's more than a little similarity between computer viruses and those that cause influenza and other menaces to actual human health.

There are two ways to deal with e-mail-borne viruses. You can catch them while the files that contain them are still inside your e-mail system, or you can catch them when users try to run the files containing them. You really have to do both, because e-mail server–based anti-virus programs can't catch non-e-mail-based viruses, for example, viruses that come in a Word document carried to the office on a disk or on a memory card.

A number of third-party, Exchange Server–based virus control products are on the market. The Appendix lists several worthy products. My current favorite is GFI's Mail Security for Microsoft Exchange (`www.gfi.com`).

GFI implements a very nice multi-vendor virus scanning engine option. The idea is that if your e-mail messages are scanned by multiple virus pattern files, you're more likely to catch a virus, especially a new virus for which the pattern files of all vendors might not have been updated. I also like Mail Security's Microsoft Management Console (MMC) integrated user interface (see Figure 18.13). Another personal favorite is the GFI product's automatic Internet-based virus updates with e-mail notification to managers that updates have taken place. A great e-mail-based feature relates to messages with viruses. They can be placed in quarantine and managers can be notified by an e-mail message that the message is in quarantine. The notification message also contains an interface that allows a manager to approve the message, delete it, or delete it and send the recipient a message indicating the message was deleted.

FIGURE 18.13

GFI's Mail Security includes a very nice MMC-based user interface.

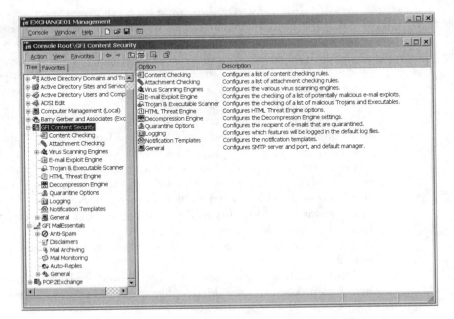

To help prevent the loss of intellectual property, Mail Security also includes functionality to check for and control outgoing messages with specific content. Additionally, it can look for vulnerabilities that come in e-mail but aren't necessarily viruses. The latter includes the ability to squash a set of HTML-based script components that can be embedded in a message and create security holes on a workstation when the message is opened. As a brief aside, you can also see the user interface for another GFI product, MailEssentials, in Figure 18.13. MailEssentials lets you do such things as set up automatic disclaimer messages that are appended to all outgoing e-mail messages, do spam control, and grab e-mail messages from ISP-based POP3 mailboxes and bring them right into an Exchange mailbox.

WARNING   *Be sure your virus software (virus engine, and so on) and virus pattern files are up-to-date. If you don't, having such virus software in place is like taking a flu shot using an old vaccine.*

Controlling Spam

I hate spam! I also hate some of the ways folks have come up with to "control" spam. Join me in a brief review of spam and some of the methods that have been developed to allegedly control it.

Exchange Server 2003 includes anti-spam functionality. It's not all that much, but it might serve the needs of some organizations. In this section, I'll talk about anti-spam programs in general and Exchange 2003's anti-spam features in specific.

WHAT ANTI-SPAM PROGRAMS DO AND HOW THEY DO IT

Spam is any unauthorized and unwanted message. I know, you think of most of the messages from your boss as spam. However, those are at least authorized. Spam is a security threat because it breaks into one of the prime communications systems in an organization: e-mail. Spam can clog an e-mail server with junk, filling its disks and backups with gigabytes of trash messages. Spam is a great source of viruses. It can at least be a time-waster for employees.

The problem with spam is that one person's spam can be another person's most desired message. Most spam solutions don't take this reality into consideration. So that you can better understand why this is so, let me discuss the different approaches to spam control.

Spam programs focus on catching and blocking spam messages. Basically you can catch spam based on the content or the source of a message. Content-based spam catchers focus in one way or another on what's in a message. Some simply look for keywords such as *breast* or obscenities while others use complex algorithms to discover what they believe to be spam. Source-based spam programs focus on who sent the message. This includes a specific e-mail address, an e-mail domain, or the IP address of the SMTP server sending the messages. Source-based anti-spam programs usually use black or white lists. Black lists are lists of SMTP server IP addresses that allegedly send spam. White lists include only SMTP servers that supposedly don't send spam. Some black and white lists are downloaded and installed on an e-mail server; others are accessed directly at the list provider's website.

Neither content- nor source-based spam "killers" are 100% effective. Worse, they often identify non-spam messages as spam. Here's why.

Many spam programs fail to deal with individual user needs. Identifying a message as spam because it has the word "breast" in it might catch a sexually-oriented message. However, it might also label a message about breast cancer or chicken breasts as spam.

Most black and white lists are a joke. They are operated by dictators who purport to be the ultimate arbiters of what is and isn't spam. My innocent little SMTP server and those of some of my clients were identified as spammers by one blacklist service. My server was so identified because the blacklister lumped my server with that of some guy in Santa Monica, California, whose first name is also Barry. I have no idea who this Barry person is and, I must report, the IP address of my server is nowhere in the range of the IP addresses of servers operated by the other Barry. There is no way to communicate with this particular blacklister to attempt to get him to drop my server from his list. Meanwhile, my wife can't send messages to people in her quilt-making guild. Grrrr!

There are server- and workstation-based anti-spam programs. The server-based ones are nice for their centralized management functionality. However, they are the least flexible when it comes to adapting to the needs of users. Good workstation-based anti-spam programs allow a user to mark as spam messages with specific content or from specific sources. They also let a user identify safe sources. In other words, good workstation-based spam catchers let users set the parameters for spam content and set their own black and white lists. They don't force a one-size-fits-all view of spam on users. This is very different from server-based programs. Mostly because of the complexities of integrating workstation front-ends with server-based anti-spam backends, individual user preferences are not generally taken into account in server-based spam programs. This will change as anti-spam technology becomes more sophisticated. It can't happen soon enough for me.

NOTE   *At this writing, one product, iHateSpam Server Edition from Sunbelt Software (`www.ihatespam.org`), is beginning to integrate a modicum of user input into a server-based anti-spam product. While it doesn't take input directly from users, it does allow administrators to individualize spam filtering for users and to quarantine spam in a quarantine folder at the user level.*

ANTI-SPAM FEATURES IN EXCHANGE SERVER 2003

Anti-spam features in Exchange Server 2003 are based on the message source. You can block messages from specific senders or e-mail domains and you can use black and white lists. Back in Chapter 13, I asked that you wait until this chapter for a discussion of Exchange 2003 spam blocking (filtering). Well, now's the time to take it on.

To create filters, find and right-click the Message Delivery container in the Global Settings container in Exchange System Manager. Select Properties from the pop-up menu to open the Message Delivery Properties dialog box shown on the right side of Figure 18.14. The two filters for spam blocking are the Sender Filter (also included in Exchange 2000) and the Connection Filter (new to Exchange 2003).

The Recipient Filter is not a spam control filter, though it has security implications. It prevents the sending of messages from Exchange server users and other objects with e-mail addresses to specific external addresses that are not included in Active Directory Contacts. It's designed to prevent e-mail to competitors and to undesirable recipients. This includes frivolous communications with recipients who might have originally gotten to a user through spam messages.

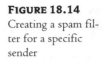

FIGURE 18.14

Creating a spam filter for a specific sender

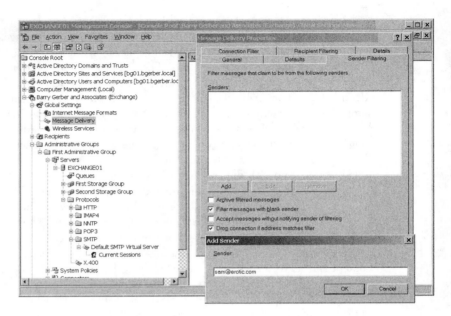

To add a filter for a sender, follow these steps:

1. Tab over to the Sender Filtering page and click Add (see Figure 18.14).

2. Enter the SMTP address of an Internet-based sender that you want the SMTPVS to reject messages from, and click OK.

   You can also enter just the suffix for an e-mail domain prefixed by *@, *@bgerber.com for example. Then all messages from that e-mail domain will be rejected.

Here's a quick look at other options on the Sender Filtering page. With the Archive Filtered Messages option, archived messages go into a file. The file can get large, so archive with care.

You'll notice in Figure 18.14 that I've asked that messages with a blank sender (From) field be filtered. That's a nice way to cut back on your daily intake of spam messages.

Sending a message to a sender whose messages are being filtered might lead the sender to stop sending messages, thereby lightening the load on your Exchange server. However, most spammers don't monitor return messages, so don't get your hopes up too high.

I've also asked that connections meeting the criteria of sender filters be dropped. This not only gets spammers off your SMTPVS's back as quickly as possible. It also means that the spamming SMTP host has to re-establish a connection with your SMTPVS if it has more messages for your Exchange recipients. That slows down the spamming host and gives your SMTPVS a little breathing room.

With Exchange 2003, Microsoft added a new kind of filter: the connection filter (see Figure 18.15). Connection filters let you use block lists (blacklists) provided by others (just choose the Add button). These filters support accessing block lists at the list provider's website. You can use multiple block lists. Additionally, you can specify on a block-list-by-block-list basis how connection filters should handle error messages and status codes returned by a block list provider. To offset at least a bit of the kind of bogus listings I talked about earlier, you can add SMTP server addresses that should be allowed to send messages even if the address is on a block list (choose the Exception button). If this isn't enough, you can also configure your own white (Accept button) or black (Deny button) lists.

FIGURE 18.15

Creating a spam filter that uses a connection-based block list

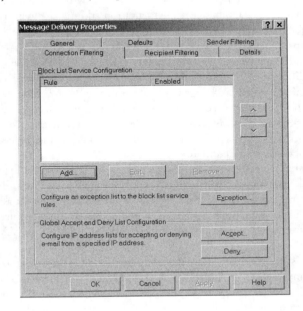

Connection filters always cut things off before a connection is made with the foreign SMTP server. This can significantly reduce server load because most spammers will likely be sending messages to more than one user in your Exchange organization.

I will leave it to you to play with connection filters and set them up to meet your needs.

TIP *One good source of information on spam in general and block list providers specifically is* www.thecrystal-cave.net. *On the Crystal Cave home page, find and click Block Lists.*

As you might remember from Chapter 13, creating a spam filter doesn't automatically implement it. You must turn on filtering. You turn on filters at the SMTP virtual server level. Right-click the SMTP virtual server you want to turn filtering on for and select Properties. In the General property page, click Advanced and then click Edit (or Add) and select the filter or filters you want to apply. If you need a graphical orientation, see Figure 13.6 in Chapter 13.

As you work with filters, you'll notice that you can't create filters or apply them with much granularity. After all, filters live at the global settings level, meaning that they apply across all Exchange administrative groups and servers. All filters of a given type either apply or don't apply to a given SMTP virtual server. This makes sense if your goal is spam filtering and you want to get rid of all spam, regardless of the SMTP virtual server it comes through.

Summary

Protecting an Exchange server environment requires the expenditure of time and money. This can result in a situation where Exchange security takes a back seat to the basics of implementing and managing Exchange servers. Operating Exchange systems with no or little security is risky business and it is essential to balance Exchange implementation and management requirements against an organization's unique messaging security needs.

Locking up and locking down Exchange server and networking hardware can be a simple first step in securing an Exchange server environment. When Exchange servers and networks and user workstations are difficult to get to and into, Exchange systems are more secure.

While local storage of Exchange mailboxes can help with Exchange performance, it can also open new security holes. Data stored on Exchange servers can be secured much more readily than data stored on workstations. Additionally, because workstation data is usually not backed up, work done offline on workstation-based Exchange mailboxes could be lost before it is synchronized with the user's Exchange server–based mailbox.

Placing an Exchange server behind a firewall can offer significant protection from external and even internal attackers for a relatively limited amount of resources. Firewalls with demilitarized zones are the easiest to implement in situations where firewall-based network address translations services are also required in the same unit. Successful Exchange firewalling requires good knowledge of the firewall ports that need to be opened for SMTP services, as well as OWA, POP3, IMAP4, ROTI, and ROH client access.

Microsoft issues security updates for Windows and Exchange Server. Windows updates are issued individually and regularly. Current Exchange Server updates are almost always included in less frequently issued service packs for the product. Using Microsoft's automated Windows update service and security status reporting software helps make staying up to date easier.

By default, both Windows Server 2003 and Exchange Server 2003 implement strong security best practices. Default Windows security is so tight that it can sometimes be frustrating. Windows security can be modified, but it should not be modified to the point where a Windows network becomes as highly transparent as older Windows networks were by default. Exchange security best practices dictate that administrators remember the ethical requirements that go with managing e-mail. Full rights to another's mailbox and Send As permissions should be granted only in rare circumstances when Exchange system maintenance is required and should be revoked when the need has passed. Generally with both Windows and Exchange, administrators should be granted only the rights they need to do their jobs and no more.

Digital signatures and message encryption help to secure e-mail messages. Signing and encryption are workstation tasks that require the presence of a workstation-based security certificate. Security certificates are obtained from a certificate authority. CAs can be internal to Windows networks or they can be accessed through the Internet. Messages are stored in the secure format on Exchange servers, enhancing message security.

Logging should be turned on for Exchange virtual servers, especially for virtual servers exposed to the outside world. Logs can provide useful information about attempted security breaches.

Security scanners can be an effective tool for finding security holes on servers, workstations, and networks. Scanners search for a range of proprietary and generic security problems and provide reports that make it easy to see and understand these problems. Log monitors regularly plow through

Windows and other logs summarizing massive amounts of data. Like scanners, monitors make it easier to deal with security issues, especially those related to Windows' own security system.

Data on LANs and WANs should be protected using some form of source and destination authentication and encryption. Virtual private networks can provide this sort of protection. VPNs aren't always based on standards. Secure IP is a standard that can be used to fashion effective VPNs.

Computer viruses borne by e-mail can be controlled on an Exchange server or after the user opens an attachment with a virus. Ideally, both Exchange Server–based and user workstation–based anti-virus software should be in place. Both anti-virus software and virus pattern files should be kept up to date.

Spam control is a relatively new endeavor. Spam catching can be based on message content or source. There are server- and workstation-based anti-spam applications. Solutions that allow users some say in what is considered spam tend to work better. Server-based applications are less likely to allow for user input. Spam black lists can inappropriately list an SMTP server as a source of spam and it can be very difficult to get an inappropriately listed server off the list.

Now let's look at something completely different, wireless access to Exchange Server. This is one of my favorite subjects, and I can't wait to get to it.

Chapter 19

Wireless Access to Exchange Server 2003

WIRELESS NETWORKING IS ONE of the most exciting and often one of the most disappointing areas in the e-mail constellation. E-mail is central to the operation of most organizations. It is a given that people who spend hours out of the office need to access their e-mail remotely. What better way to do this than wirelessly? But it's still far from easy.

While server and client options for wireless networking have progressed quite far, the networks themselves have lagged behind. Wireless data WANs, whether based on voice (telephone) or data technologies, have traditionally been slow, with spotty coverage. Higher-bandwidth wireless WAN technologies are in the offing, but they have been slow in coming to market and they are likely to continue the technology's tradition of limited geographic availability for some time. The only bright spots in all of this have been a WAN product, Blackberry, and the promising rise and wider availability of higher-speed wireless LANs.

Exchange Server 2003 adds considerably to server-side wireless networking. Exchange ActiveSync (EAS) wirelessly synchronizes e-mail, calendar, and contact items between Outlook MAPI clients and Pocket PC Outlook clients. Exchange 2003's Outlook Mobile Access (OMA) brings the benefits of Outlook Web Access (OWA) to devices with smaller screens such as PDAs and cell phones.

Client devices are available that can take advantage of both EAS and OMA. The Pocket PC 2002 operating system supports most of EAS on PDAs. Windows Mobile 2003, Microsoft's new name for the Pocket PC operating system, fully supports EAS. Both the 2002 and 2003 operating systems for Pocket PCs support OMA. Many wireless phones have been enhanced to wirelessly support OMA.

I love wireless e-mail. For all its current limitations, I still can't live without it. Nothing can beat opening, reading, and responding to a newly arrived message in an elevator, at the doctor's office, at the movies, or even in the car while waiting for a stoplight to change. Do I really need such immediate access to e-mail? I'll answer that with another question. Do you really need your cell phone? And I'll take that one step farther. My cell phone sits in a drawer in my office. I hardly ever use it. But take my wireless e-mail away, and I'd shrivel up and die. I'm really going to enjoy talking to you about wireless messaging.

Featured in this chapter:

◆   Wireless networking technologies

◆   Wireless networking servers

◆   Wireless networking clients

Wireless Networking Technologies

Wireless networking technologies come in two basic flavors: wide-area network (WAN) and local-area network (LAN). The idea of moving data across wide and narrow geographic spaces is not new. The telephone, telegraph, radio, fax machine, and television can all be considered WAN-based data transmission technologies. Some of these are wireless from end to end. Others employ wireless somewhere in the data-transmission process. However, with the exception of the telephone, none of these has been extensively used to move the kinds of data required by computing devices. And, until relatively recently, most phone-based data transmission was wired, not wireless.

Over the past several years, WAN- and LAN-based wireless networking technologies have become more sophisticated, delivering or promising to deliver higher reliability and significantly increased throughput. Wireless WAN services, especially the newer ones, are still difficult to find in many geographic locations. However, this is a matter of inadequate implementation financing and not a technological flaw.

Let's look at WAN and LAN wireless technologies in greater detail. Once you understand these, you'll be ready to look at specific options for the Exchange server environment.

NOTE   *Throughout this chapter, when I talk about wireless networks, I mean networks that can carry TCP/IP packets. I don't care how the packets are encapsulated to allow them to travel across the ether. However, for a wireless network to work with the client-server technologies I discuss here, TCP/IP packets must retain their integrity and present themselves in all their glory to clients and servers once they've completed their wireless journey.*

Wireless WAN Technologies

With the advent of the wireless voice-oriented telephone, people began moving data wirelessly. Early phone-based wireless data transmission involved connecting a standard analog modem to a cell phone, dialing up the number of an ISP or other contact point that had its own modem, and using the same two-way data exchange system that millions use today to connect to the Internet on wired phones. Some "modern" wireless phones have built-in modems, but the process and effect is the same.

If you've worked with a wired or wireless, analog, dial-up modem, then you've experienced the two most significant weaknesses of traditional phone-based data interchange: slow initial connections and slow data transmission. Traditional phones use circuit switching. Circuit-switching networks are not always on from the perspective of the user. You have to identify the entity you want to connect to, for example, by using a phone number. Then a pathway for the connection has to be set up. This is done by closing a number of switches between the source and target phone. Once the pathway is in place, your phone and its modem and the target phone and its modem can begin exchanging data. Establishing a pathway can take 5 to 15 seconds. That's not a long time compared with the age of the earth, but when you're anxious to check your e-mail or send responses to e-mail that you've received, it seems like a year.

And as if this weren't enough, because of the quality of traditional phone signals, data throughput with analog modems is slower than a turtle in molasses. The best wired modems run at 56kbps, if you're lucky. The best wireless modems come in somewhere between 9 and 19kbps. That's slow.

But wait, there's more. Wireless phone services are notorious for the spotty availability of their signals. Say you're talking to a business contact and you move into a no-signal zone. Suddenly you're talking into air. Then, when the signal returns, you have to go through the all-too-familiar dance of attempting to reconnect, with both you and the other person getting a busy signal because you're each trying to dial up the other. All this is bad enough if you're talking to someone and suddenly lose your connection. If you're in the middle of downloading even a short e-mail message, after cursing the gods of technology and once the signal is back, you have to initiate a reconnect, which takes another 5 to 15 seconds, and blah, blah, blah. Wireless switched circuit modems are not ready for prime-time, interactive, e-mail-based business applications and, from my perspective, they never will be.

The good news is that there are alternative wireless technologies that avoid most of the pitfalls of circuit-switched modems. These provide continuously available connections based on radio signals and direct connections to public or private data networks. Traditional cell phones use radio technology too, but only to connect your phone to the nearest circuit-switching facility. After that, you're dependent on a mostly wired, switched network and its connection to a public or private network for data transmission.

Newer radio-based wireless WAN systems offer higher bandwidth, up to 2.2 mbps. However, like older wireless phone technologies, their signals are far, far from ubiquitously available. In fact, because of their newness and the high cost of implementing these new systems, there are currently many more no-signal areas with radio than with older wireless WAN systems.

New wireless WAN options come in a variety of packages. Some are built into telephones, with the phone turning into a mini-PDA, often using one or another variant of the Wireless Application Protocol (WAP) to squeeze lots of data onto smaller screens. Modern wireless WAN options also come built into devices, such as Blackberry, Palm, and Pocket PC PDAs, as well as PCMCIA, Compact Flash (CF), and Secure Digital (SD) cards that plug into laptops and PDAs.

There are many non-circuit-switched, always-on wireless systems. I'm going to spend a little time talking about some of the leaders in this area. These include Mobitex, GPRS, CDMA2000, UTMS, and EDGE. As we look at each of these, keep in mind that I have tried to cut through the marketing hype surrounding these networking services and bring you a realistic, balanced view of each technology.

TIP   As you read the following sections, remember that bandwidth citations don't reflect the actual throughput you can expect. For example, current GPRS networks are cited as having a bandwidth of 170kbps. In practice, under ideal conditions, GPRS throughput is more like 50kbps. If you work with Ethernet LANs, this shouldn't surprise you. A 100mbps Ethernet connection between two nodes on an isolated LAN typically provides from 50 to 75mbps of throughput.

MOBITEX

Mobitex has been around for quite some time. Along with a number of other systems, Mobitex is the low-end wireless network for the popular Blackberry wireless PDA. Mobitex's throughput is low, around 9kbps. Blackberry optimizes its use of the Mobitex network by automatically downloading small portions (800 bytes) of each new e-mail message and then letting you download more of a message on demand. It is able to do this because it has full control over the Blackberry operating system and the e-mail and other applications in the Blackberry.

My experience with other wireless providers that use Mobitex has not been all that good. I've tried using it with standard IMAP4 clients. Because the amount of data that moves between an IMAP4 client and server is controlled by the user, not by a special application as with the Blackberry, you quickly begin to see the effects of Mobitex's bandwidth limitations and its good, but far from universal, coverage. The user experience is one of slow message transfer and the need to restart transmission when the signal is lost.

GPRS

GPRS (General Packet Radio Service) was designed to run on GSM (Global System for Mobile communication) and PCS (Personal Communication System) phone networks. GPRS bandwidth ranges from 9kbps to around 170kbps. Bandwidth up to 384kbps is promised for the future.

From my hands-on experience in the Western United States, GPRS often delivers throughput in the 9–19kbps range. That's due to the slow spread of radio equipment able to handle the higher bandwidths GPRS is designed to support. As with Mobitex, and again in my experience, this is too slow to support interactive messaging applications. Interestingly, GPRS is now an option for Blackberry.

A GREAT NEW PDA AND BETTER GPRS SERVICES

News on the GPRS front is getting better. Very recently, I began using a SideKick mobile device from Danger, Inc. The SideKick is a very cool wireless phone-PDA device with its own color screen and a very good keyboard. You can see it at www.tmobile.com. T-Mobile is one of the communications companies that sell and support the SideKick. In Los Angeles, GPRS signal availability is great and I'm getting data transfer rates well above 19 kbps. I've combined the SideKick with Pumatech's Loud PC which gives me web browser access to my Exchange e-mail and all of the other folders in my mailbox. Check out Loud PC at www.loudpc.com. Microsoft and its Pocket PC partners are going to have to run a bit to catch up with the SideKick on GPRS.

CDMA2000

CDMA stands for Code Division Multiple Access. It is an older wireless voice technology. CDMA2000 is an upgrade to CDMA that offers higher bandwidth for voice and data. CDMA2000 1x can move data at up to 144kbps. CDMA2000 1xEV-DO is optimized for data and can deliver throughput up to 307kbps. CDMA2000 1xEV-DV provides data throughput rates up to 1mbps. That's pretty good bandwidth, and this is a real product, not a bunch of promises like so many high-speed wireless products. We'll see how fast it becomes widely available.

UTMS

UMTS (Universal Mobile Telecommunication System) is based on wideband CDMA (WCDMA), which is a different technology from CDMA2000. UMTS provides WAN data rates up to 384kbps. UTMS is the only standard of the five I'm discussing that includes a LAN data service. This service offers a fast 2mbps. However, because it is likely to be based on per-byte charges, I don't think that this service is going to compete well with the other wireless LAN technologies that have no per-byte costs. I'll discuss these other technologies later in this chapter.

EDGE

Like its competitors, EDGE (Enhanced Data rates for GSM Evolution) provides bandwidth up to 384kbps. This technology was designed to raise throughput for GSM phone devices. GSM currently uses GPRS for data. Unfortunately, today's GSM systems can not provide a good enough signal to support EDGE. So EDGE is a technology in waiting.

WIRELESS WAN RECOMMENDATIONS

At the time of this writing, the best available wireless option is GPRS. It is available from a fairly wide range of telecommunications carriers, both built into telephones and PDAs and in PCMCIA and CF form factors. If you want to consider other, higher-bandwidth options, be sure to look at true throughput and signal availability in areas where your users are likely to find themselves.

Wireless LAN Technologies

Wireless LANs (WLANs) have taken off in the last few years. Based on a trio of relatively short range 802.11 wireless standards, WLANs first found their way into home and office environments and are now popping up in coffee shops, malls, and other public locations. WLANs make it possible to place networked computers in places where the installation of network wiring would be difficult or impossible. WLANs allow users to roam within the confines of a building or even beyond.

WLAN clients communicate wirelessly with access points, which are wired directly to the LAN. Access points can handle a number of simultaneously connected WLAN devices and transfer packets between the devices and the LAN. When a WLAN device moves out of the range of its current access point, it can switch to a new in-range access point. So, by slightly overlapping access points, you can extend the range of a WLAN beyond that of a single access point.

On the client side, WLAN technology is available in PCMCIA, CF, and SD form factors. It also comes built into a number of devices including laptops, PDAs, and even phones. Modern laptop and PDA operating systems can identify a WLAN device, immediately enable it, and obtain IP addressing information from a DHCP server.

On the security side, WLAN systems support simple access point passwords and encrypted data transfer. If access point security is set low enough, it's possible for a WLAN device to connect to and use an access point without any intervention on the part of the user. While such low security access is far from desirable in business environments, it is seen as desirable in some public WLANs, where ease of use is highly valued.

The growth of public WLANs is due mostly to frustration with slow and spottily available wireless WAN solutions. WAN wireless solutions become less necessary for some, when they can step into almost any Starbucks coffee shop in the United States and check their e-mail or browse the Web on their WLAN laptops, PDAs, or phones. Before you turn your users loose in the wide, wide world of WLANs, be sure they are operating under a level of security appropriate to the data that they will be accessing on their WLAN devices.

NOTE   *The term* WiFi *is often used to identify 802.11 devices. I like* WLAN *better.* WiFi *has the ring of marketing hype and says nothing about the purpose of or the technologies behind 802.11 topologies.*

802.11 WIRELESS TOPOLOGIES

There are three WLAN topologies: 802.11a, 802.11b, and 802.11g. They are all part of the IEEE 802.11 wireless LAN specification. I'm going to cover the three topologies fairly quickly. Check out `http://grouper.ieee.org/groups/802/11` for more on each. You can download various documents relating to the standard. Unfortunately, the site uses frames and I can't give you any better URL, so you'll have to hunt around the site a bit.

I've organized my discussion of 802.11 topologies in order of their availability.

802.11b

As of this writing, 802.11b is the most widely used WLAN topology. It offers a maximum data bandwidth of 11mbps. 802.11b uses a 2.4GHz radio signal to carry data. It has a maximum range of 300 feet. As with WAN wireless topologies, all the 802.11 technologies deliver lower throughput than advertised maximums. Maximum ranges are also generally lower than specs, especially inside buildings with thick, metal-framed walls.

One of the biggest problems with 802.11b is its wireless transmission frequency. 2.4GHz is also used by a number of wireless phone systems. Another problem relates to the number of transmission channels on 802.11b access points. Radio signal bandwidth is used in such a manner that only three channels are available. Each access point uses a channel. So you can have only three overlapping access points, which limits the size of your WLAN.

802.11a

802.11a provides a maximum data bandwidth of 54mbps. It uses a 5GHz radio signal, which is more than twice that of 802.11b and doesn't interfere with devices in the 2.4GHz range. Maximum 802.11a range is significantly shorter, about 80 feet. So you need more access points for continuous service. The good news is that 802.11a supports up to 12 radio signal channels. So you can build 802.11a WLANs equivalent in size to 802.11b WLANs.

802.11a and 802.11b are not interoperable. So you need different access points for each technology. Vendors are working on chips that support both standards. So we are likely to see both client devices and access points that can handle both topologies.

802.11g

Like 802.11a, 802.11g supports maximum data throughput of 54mbps. Like 802.11b, it uses 2.4GHz radio signals. Its range is shorter than 802.11b's 80 feet. The good news is that it's compatible with 802.11b. So 802.11b and g devices can communicate with each other's access points.

Unfortunately, 802.11g supports only three radio channels, meaning you can have only three overlapping access points and are limited to very small WLANs, given the short range of 802.11g.

NOTE   *For security, current 802.11 devices use Wireless Equivalent Privacy (WEP). WEP's 40- and 128-bit encryption keys are pretty weak. So it's fairly easy to break WEP security. There is another, much stronger wireless security standard: 802.11z. It requires that the wireless client encrypt data using a certificate from the server. Pocket PC operating systems don't yet support 802.11z.*

WIRELESS LAN RECOMMENDATIONS

The basic rules are: more users, more data bandwidth and more space to be covered, more access-point channels. 802.11a is the best compromise because it delivers high data bandwidth and features a larger number of channels. However, 802.11a's lack of compatibility with the large installed base of 802.11b access points makes it a less desirable choice for those environments where 802.11b is in use. This includes not only office WLANs, but also public WLANs, which as of this writing mostly use 802.11b.

The arrival of 802.11a and b–compatible WLAN client devices and access points would, of course, make 802.11a a no-brainer. Until that happens, you can implement 802.11a in the office and give your public WLAN users an 802.11b device to plug in when they're on the road.

Wireless Networking Servers

There are two servers that support wireless access to Exchange servers that are worth talking about. The first, of course, is Exchange Server 2003 itself with its great new features that support wireless access. The second server is Blackberry Enterprise Server, which is software that runs on an Exchange server. Each of these has strengths and weaknesses that will emerge as we examine each.

In this section, I'll talk about the two server products from a more conceptual perspective. Then I'll discuss the implementation of each product. In the next section, "Wireless Networking Clients," I'll show you how to implement some wireless networking clients.

Exchange Server 2003

Exchange Server 2003 supports wireless clients with two new services: Exchange ActiveSync (EAS) and Outlook Mobile Access (OMA). EAS brings wireless synchronization to Windows-based PDAs and telephones. OMA is Outlook Web Access for devices with small screens, such as PDAs and telephones.

EXCHANGE ACTIVESYNC

Historically, you kept the Outlook-based applications on your Microsoft Windows PDA up to date with a desktop application called ActiveSync. You placed the PDA in a cradle attached to the computer running Outlook and let ActiveSync synchronize your e-mail, calendar, contacts, tasks, and other folders. Exchange was involved, but only because Outlook was connected to Exchange, not because your PDA and Exchange talked to each other. Microsoft changed all of this with Exchange 2000 when it implemented a separate product, Mobile Information Server (MIS), to support synchronization directly between Exchange server and Windows PDAs and other devices. MIS worked with standard cradle-attached ActiveSync links or with wireless links.

Some shops implemented MIS, but Microsoft quickly learned that most customers didn't want to worry about yet another server. So MIS was integrated into Exchange Server 2003, where it's called

Exchange ActiveSync (EAS). EAS synchronizes e-mail, calendar items, and contacts between Exchange server and built-in e-mail, calendar, and contacts applications in Windows PDAs and other devices. Like MIS, EAS works with cradle- or wirelessly-connected devices.

EAS is integrated with the desktop version of ActiveSync. Synchronization settings can be entered on the desktop or on the PDA. EAS supports replies and forwarding with full copies of the original message and its attachments even if full messages and attachments were not downloaded to the PDA. Such replies and forwards are constructed on the server from messages and attachments stored on the server.

EAS supports three wireless synchronization modes: Manual, Scheduled, and Automatic. You can initiate a manual synchronization session from your PDA. You can schedule synchronization sessions at specific time intervals, for example, every 5 minutes. Finally, Exchange ActiveSync can send out what are called *up-to-date notifications* when new e-mail, calendar, or contacts items are available. When a PDA receives a notification, it automatically initiates a synchronization session. Devices that support notifications were not available at this writing, but Microsoft said they would be available sometime in 2003.

So, how does EAS work at the wireless network level? As should be fairly obvious from the previous paragraph, all synchronization is initiated on the wireless device. The device connects to the Exchange server using TCP/IP and logs in, and synchronization begins. Up-to-date notifications are sent to the wireless device by EAS. Notifications are SMTP messages. They are sent through SMTP carriers.

In addition to Windows-based PDAs, EAS works with Windows-based telephones. These include versions of PDA e-mail, calendar, and contacts applications nicely fitted to the smaller graphics screens on most phones.

Implementing EAS

You manage EAS settings using the Mobile Services Properties dialog box. Follow along in Figure 19.1 as I discuss EAS configuration. In Exchange System Manager, find and right-click the Mobile Services container and select Properties from the pop-up menu. You can modify three settings in the Mobile Services Properties dialog box. If you deselect Enable User Initiated Synchronization, you disable EAS for all users. The other two EAS choices on the dialog box let you enable up-to-date notifications and permit users to specify the SMTP carrier to be used to send up-to-date notifications to their wireless devices. All synchronization modes are essentially user initiated. So, it makes no sense to disable user-initiated synchronization while the other two options are enabled. Users' PDAs will receive notifications, but they won't be able to initiate synchronization.

You can set up one or more SMTP carriers for EAS. Like the carriers users can specify, these are used to send up-to-date notifications to wireless devices. Think of these as your official carriers. If you do not permit users to specify their own SMTP carriers, they will be limited to your list of official carriers. To add a carrier, right-click the right pane of the Mobile Services container and select New ➤ Mobile Carrier. As Figure 19.2 shows, you enter an identifying name for the carrier and the SMTP domain name the carrier uses for messages sent to its wireless devices.

In MIS, both administrators and users could set mobile carrier and wireless device e-mail addresses. EAS supports only user setting of this information. The only limit on what a user can set is the list of official carriers you can set up.

FIGURE 19.1
Configuring Exchange ActiveSync using the Mobile Services Properties dialog box

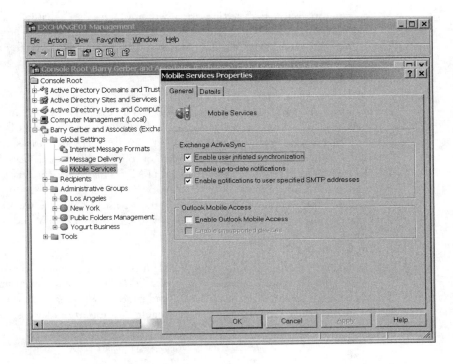

FIGURE 19.2
Creating a new mobile SMTP carrier for Exchange ActiveSync

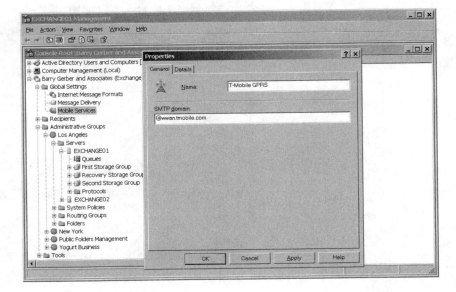

You can disable EAS settings for any user. Open a user's dialog box in `\Active Directory Users and Computers\Users`. In Figure 19.3, I've opened my user dialog box and tabbed over to the Exchange Features page. To disable a particular feature, click the feature, then click Disable.

OUTLOOK MOBILE ACCESS

OMA presents a simple text interface for accessing Exchange server–based e-mail, calendars, contacts, and tasks. As you'll see in the next section, "Wireless Networking Clients," the text on OMA screens includes URLs to make navigating around your Exchange mailbox fairly easy.

OMA was designed for telephones with small screens and at least basic web browser capabilities. OMA can generate differently formatted output for different devices. It can provide screens formatted in WML, HTML, xHTML, and cHTML. This allows for very simple-looking screens or very fancy ones. Some phone vendors have worked with Microsoft to set up special page formats for their devices. However, any device that supports at least HTML can use OMA to access Exchange mailboxes. In the next section, I'll also show you OMA on a Dell Windows-based PDA.

Implementing OMA

By default, OMA is disabled. You enable it on the same dialog box that you use to configure EAS (see Figure 19.1, shown earlier). To make OMA available to your users, select Enable Outlook Mobile Access. If you want OMA to send pages to web-enabled devices that haven't been specially set up to receive OMA output, select Enable Unsupported Devices.

FIGURE 19.3
Configuring Exchange ActiveSync at the user level using the Exchange Features page of a user's dialog box

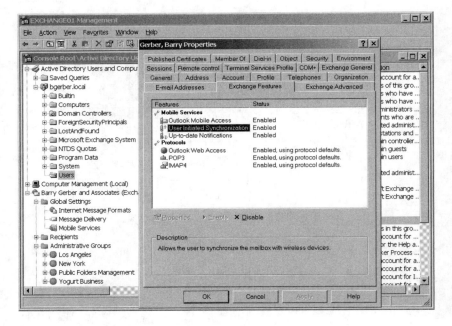

As with other Exchange HTTP-based services—OWA and RCP over HTTP—OMA clients can access a mailbox's home server through front-end servers. They can use the same front-end servers as the other two services.

You turn on OMA SSL security the same way you turn on OWA SSL security. See Chapter 18, "Exchange Server System Security" for more information.

Blackberry Enterprise Server

The Blackberry Enterprise Server (BES) has gained great popularity for three reasons:

◆ It handles all aspects of wireless networking.

◆ It takes a sensible approach to network bandwidth.

◆ It has been doing everything that MIS and EAS do for about as long.

When you send a message from your Blackberry wireless device, it travels over the Mobitex or GPRS network to BES. BES then sends the message from your Exchange server, even putting a copy of the sent message into your Sent Items folder if you so requested in Outlook. Once the message is sent, it travels the Internet just as any other Exchange message. BES picks up incoming messages and sends them to your Blackberry via the Internet through a Blackberry-supported SMTP server. Mobitex or GPRS provides the final link between the Blackberry SMTP server and your Blackberry wireless device.

Setting up your Blackberry PDA to use a wireless network is a total no-brainer, because the network provider does the setup. Basically you turn on your device and off you go.

The Blackberry SMTP server treats 9 to 19kbps networks like the tiny pipes that they are. It doesn't try to send your Blackberry a 25KB message with a 50KB attachment all in one gulp. It sends 800 bytes. If you want to see more, you can ask for more. And you don't have to sit there watching your Blackberry device to make sure it doesn't lose contact with the outside world. The device recovers from network problems without forgetting what it was doing before its connection failed.

About the time of the release of MIS, BES came out. Over the next couple of years, BES became more and more sophisticated. As of this writing, BES synchronizes Exchange server e-mail, calendars, and contacts in both directions. This is the same functionality provided by EAS.

So why should you consider BES? First, it's a known product. Second, though it's a bear to install, once installed, it works flawlessly. Third, EAS is new to Exchange server. I expect it'll work just fine, but if you need a certifiably reliable wireless e-mail solution, you could do worse than to go with BES.

Check out `www.blackberry.com` for more on BES.

NOTE *There is a desktop version of the Blackberry system for Outlook/Exchange. It works much like the desktop version of ActiveSync when you're connecting through Outlook and not directly to your Exchange server. I used this version before moving to BES. This version is not BES, though BES integrates with the desktop version beautifully once BES has been installed.*

IMPLEMENTING BES

I'm not going to walk you through all of the steps involved in implementing BES. Rather I'll talk a bit about a few quirks in product installation and give you some tips regarding various BES management tools.

Once you've set up a user and given rights to the user and various Windows security groups, installing BES is very easy. The BES rights-granting process is truly grueling. This is partly because you have to grant rights to the same group to do different tasks (run BES as a service, monitor BES activities, manage a BES server).

Some tasks require fewer privileges than others. Instead of creating a list indicating the most rights that you need to grant if your group will perform a particular set of tasks, the BES documentation lists the rights required task by task. As you work your way through the documentation, you could find yourself removing rights that you assigned to a group earlier.

The result of all this is that BES won't work at all or it works but can't initiate certain functionality. The best advice I can give you when installing BES: Print out the documentation and follow it line by line using a ruler to keep your place.

Actually installing BES is very straightforward. You can install it on an Exchange server or on another server. Be sure Outlook isn't installed on the server where you plan to install BES. Also, be sure that the correct version of CDO.DLL is installed on the BES server before you do the installation. The BES documentation is very specific on these two requirements, both of which relate to CDO.DLL, the DLL that supports Exchange calendar access and, as such, is essential to BES calendar synchronization.

Once BES is installed, managing it is very easy. Figure 19.4 shows the interface for managing a specific BES server. You're looking at the BESAlert page, where you can set up e-mail alerts to notify managers of problems on the server.

FIGURE 19.4

Setting parameters for a range of BES functions using the Blackberry Server Properties dialog box

You set up the equivalent of product ID and outgoing server contact information on the General page. Users can set up their own filters for which messages get sent to their Blackberry devices (only if I'm in the To field; if the message has this subject; and so on). You use the Global Filters page to set filters on the BES server that override any user filter settings.

The E-Mail Options page lets you set a disclaimer message that is appended to each message sent through the BES server; send a copy of all messages sent from Blackberry handhelds to a specific address; support S/MIME encryption on the BES server; and allow a handheld to force e-mail reconciliation with the server. Finally, you use the Logging page to set up activity and error logging on the BES server.

Monitoring user activity on a BES server is pretty simple. Figure 19.5 shows the Statistics dialog box for my Exchange mailbox. This is my real Blackberry setup. I've been using my Blackberry for almost three years. As you can see, a lot of messages—37,290—have been sent out to the PDA. The dialog box shows that all is well with my connection: Status, (EXCH011) Running and Pending to Handheld, 0.

FIGURE 19.5

Using the Blackberry User Statistics dialog box to check the status of a BES server's activities on behalf of a user

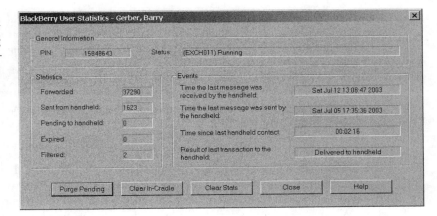

There are other BES management interfaces that support such tasks as adding and removing users, sending test or informational messages to all users, checking server status, and disabling redirection of messages to a specific user's Blackberry handheld.

Wireless Networking Clients

I'm going to focus here on wireless clients supported directly by Exchange Server 2003 over TCP/IP connections. These include

◆ Pocket Outlook with EAS

◆ POP3 and IMAP4

◆ OMA and OWA

I'm going to show you some of these clients in action and talk about what you need to do to make them work with Exchange Server 2003.

Pocket Outlook with EAS

Pocket Outlook runs on Pocket PC PDAs and Windows-enabled telephones. It includes Inbox, Calendar, Contacts, Tasks, and Notes from the MAPI Outlook/Exchange mailbox. Full synchronization with all of Pocket Outlook's folders is supported only by the desktop version of ActiveSync. As I noted earlier in this chapter, EAS supports only Inbox, Calendar, and Contacts.

You can use ActiveSync to set up Pocket Outlook for EAS on your PC or PDA. Let's do it on a PDA, specifically, my Dell AXIM X5 with Pocket PC 2002 and a Symbol Wireless Networker 802.11b Compact Flash WLAN card installed.

Open ActiveSync on your PDA (Start ➤ ActiveSync). When ActiveSync opens, select Tools ➤ Options and tab over to the Server page (see Figure 19.6). In this page, you can choose the folders you want to synchronize. Remember only the Inbox, Calendar, and Contacts can be synced. Click Settings to enter specific synchronization parameters for each of the folders. The server name should be a fully-qualified domain name registered in a public DNS if you're going to access EAS from the Internet.

NOTE *The PDA screens you see here are from my AXIM X5. They were displayed on my PC monitor using Microsoft's Remote Display Control v2.03 (*`www.microsoft.com/windowsmobile/resources/downloads/pocketpc/powertoys.mspx`*). The screens were then captured using my regular screen-capturing software, Jasc Software's PaintShop Pro v8 (*`www.jasc.com`*).*

Next, click Advanced. You use the Connection page of the Advanced Connection Options dialog box, shown in Figure 19.7, to enter logon information for your Exchange server and set logging detail options. When you're done with the Server page, tab over to the Rules page. It's safest to leave the replacement rule set as it is in Figure 19.8.

Click OK to close the Advanced Connection Options dialog box and return to the main ActiveSync tools dialog box. Tab to the Schedule page (see Figure 19.9). This is where you set intervals for regular synchronization and specify whether you want your device to disconnect when synchronizing with your PC. The last option is not relevant for server-based synchronization.

When you're done with the Schedule page, click OK to return to the main ActiveSync window, shown in Figure 19.10. Any time you want to manually synchronize with your Exchange server, just open ActiveSync on your PDA and click the Sync icon. I can't show you how to set up EAS notifications that would trigger automatic PDA–Exchange 2003 synchronization, because that requires Windows Mobile 2003, which was not available at the time of this writing.

FIGURE 19.6

Setting folder and server name parameters for EAS synchronization

FIGURE 19.7
Setting Exchange server logon information and selecting a level of logging for EAS synchronization

FIGURE 19.8
Selecting a rule to be applied when there is a conflict between an Exchange server and Pocket Outlook during EAS synchronization

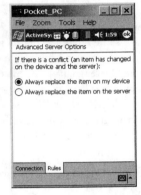

FIGURE 19.9
Setting synchronization schedules

FIGURE 19.10
The main Active-Sync page from which EAS synchronization is initiated

POP3 and IMAP4

If you have a POP3 and/or IMAP4 client on your PDA and a TCP/IP connection, you can access Exchange servers just as you would with the same clients available in such products as Outlook Express. When I'm on the road or even roaming around the office or the house, I use Pocket PC's IMAP4 client to stay in touch with e-mail. It's faster than ActiveSync because it syncs only e-mail and I can keep track of e-mail folders other than my Inbox as easily as with ActiveSync. Figure 19.11 shows my IMAP4 Inbox folder. I set up my IMAP on my PDA so that I can see other folders in my Exchange mailbox. To look in one of these folders, I simply click the Inbox icon with the little down-pointing arrow on it and pick the folder from a drop-down list.

FIGURE 19.11
A Pocket PC IMAP4 mailbox wirelessly connected to an Exchange server

I showed you how to set up POP3 and IMAP4 clients in Chapter 14, "Managing Exchange 2003 Services for Internet Clients." You should have no trouble applying that information to the Pocket PC versions of these two clients.

One of the nice things about POP3 and IMAP4 is that their availability is not limited to Pocket PC devices. If you have a Palm PDA and a POP3 or IMAP4 client for it, you can do anything that a Pocket PC owner with the same clients can do.

OMA and OWA

In Figure 19.12, I've connected to my Exchange server mailbox using OMA. Dell hasn't created special support specs and web pages for my Dell AXIM PDA, so OMA starts up telling me that. However, because I set up OMA to handle unsupported devices, it will work just fine. So I'll just click OK.

FIGURE 19.12

The OMA warning screen appears when support for a particular client has not been set up by the client's manufacturer.

And lo and behold, doesn't the home page in Figure 19.13 look just perfect for a telephone with a tiny graphics screen? Truth be told, it doesn't look so bad on my Dell PDA, even with its small graphics screen.

FIGURE 19.13

The home page for an Exchange mailbox as displayed by OMA

Let's look at my mail. After I tap Inbox on the home page, I'm transported to a view of my messages. In Figure 19.14, I've scrolled down because I want to open the message from Jane Dough. Before I do, notice the four URLs at the bottom of the screen. In this case, they let me do such tasks as move to the top of the list of my messages, compose a new message, see my other folders, and go back to the home page. OMA makes very good use of in-context action URLs.

FIGURE 19.14
The contents of an
Exchange Inbox as
displayed by OMA

Okay, to open the message, I tap it with my stylus. And there it is in Figure 19.15. This is the message from Jane Dough with the graphical stack of currency that you might remember from Chapter 14 (Figure 14.19). No money, but the message is easy to read—and notice the in-context action URLs at the bottom of the message.

FIGURE 19.15
Reading a message
with OMA

That should give you an idea how OMA works. Now let's move on to OWA.

Exchange 2000 Server didn't support OWA on Pocket PCs at all. Exchange 2003 does. However, at least with the version of Internet Explorer that comes with Pocket PC 2002, managing the OWA screen is a bit of an unwieldy task. But all is not lost. At least OWA is capable of showing Jane Dough's graphical pile of money (see Figures 19.16 through 19.19). Windows Mobile 2003's Internet Explorer is supposed to handle larger screens better. Unfortunately, it was not available for testing at this writing.

FIGURE 19.16
An Exchange mailbox as initially displayed by OWA on Pocket PC 2002's Internet Explorer

FIGURE 19.17
A view of an Exchange mailbox displayed by OWA on Pocket PC 2002's Internet Explorer with the right pane horizontally scrolled to show the From column

FIGURE 19.18
A view of an Exchange mailbox displayed by OWA on Pocket PC 2002's Internet Explorer with the right pane horizontally scrolled to show the message Subject colum

FIGURE 19.19
Part of a message displayed by OWA in Pocket PC 2002's Internet Explorer

Summary

Wireless access to Exchange Server 2003 begins with an appropriate TCP/IP-based wireless network. There are many wireless WAN and LAN options that meet this criterion. Many newer, higher-bandwidth wireless WAN options are in the early stages of implementation. Thus their geographic coverage is often severely restricted and their throughput can be far lower than advertised maximums. Of currently available wireless WAN options, GPRS is the best choice. However, in most circumstances even GPRS currently delivers throughput well below its promised 170mbps in many implementations.

Wireless LAN networks are another story entirely. They provide solid performance up to a high fraction of their 54mbps bandwidth. Their range is short, as would be expected of LAN networking products, but it is fine for the office and public hot-spot applications currently running on them.

There are two server products that support Exchange Server 2003 worth talking about. One is Exchange 2003 itself with its new Exchange ActiveSync and Outlook Mobile Access options. The other server option is Blackberry Enterprise Server with its proprietary client devices. Both options synchronize Outlook/Exchange Inbox, Calendar, and Contacts folders. Blackberry Enterprise Server offers no alternative to Outlook Mobile Access, which can best be typified as Outlook Web Access for devices with small graphical screens. Blackberry Enterprise Server is a strong contender and will continue to be so until Exchange ActiveSync has proven itself in production environments.

On the clientside and aside from the Blackberry client/server solution, there are a number of options. Modern Pocket PCs and Windows-based phones come with Pocket Outlook built in. As noted earlier, Exchange ActiveSync supports wireless synchronization of the Pocket Outlook Inbox, Calendar, and Contacts folders with the same folders on Exchange Server 2003.

PDAs with POP3 or IMAP4 clients can also be used to access Exchange 2003 servers. This includes both Pocket PC and other devices such as Palm PDAs.

Outlook Mobile Access provides a nice HTML-based interface to Exchange 2003 mailboxes for devices with small screens. Some vendors have created customized specifications and web pages for their devices. Others have chosen not to provide special support for their devices. Surprisingly, Outlook Mobile Access works nicely on unsupported devices, as tests with a Dell AXIM PDA demonstrate.

Outlook Web Access didn't work with Pocket PCs on Exchange 2000 Server. It does work on Exchange 2003. However, at least with the version of Internet Explorer included in the Pocket PC 2002 operating system, Outlook Web Access is nearly unusable. Because Outlook Mobile Access does work so well with PDAs, this is less of a problem. However, it is expected that Windows Mobile 2003's Internet Explorer will better handle Outlook Web Access pages.

Chapter 20

Building, Using, and Managing Outlook Forms Designer Applications

NOBODY LIKES FILLING IN forms, right? Well, the answer probably seems obvious—until you consider the alternative: a blank piece of paper. Imagine doing your taxes without all those wonderful IRS and state forms. Imagine trying to process tax reports formatted every which way but clearly. Done right, forms—especially electronic forms—make it easier for users to get through complex or repetitive data-entry tasks with minimal pain. In addition, these forms help their creators collect data in a uniform manner and process it easily.

You create forms for use in Exchange 2000 and 2003 server environments with Microsoft Outlook Forms Designer (OFD). OFD is available in Outlook 32-bit clients. It is a nice forms-development environment. It lets you use ActiveX and OLE controls to enhance your forms. You can't build very interesting applications without some form of Visual Basic scripting, which OFD supports.

When you start working with OFD, you might even find yourself waking up at night with fantastic ideas for forms. Here are some examples:

Request forms   Used to ask for something:

- Purchase orders
- Computer program modifications
- Computer hardware maintenance
- Travel requests
- Vacation or sick-day requests

Data collection forms   Used to gather information:

- Data for line-of-business applications such as patient management or product/services purchasing
- Employee feedback on health insurance plans

           edback on products or services

           Employee participation in company picnics

Report forms   Used to provide required information:

- Employee status reports to supervisors

- Employee travel and mileage reports

- Department budget reports

Other forms   Used for a variety of purposes:

- Standardized communications forms (for example, telephone notes, while-you-were-out memos)

- Forms for playing multiuser tic-tac-toe, chess, and other games

The decision to create a form should be informed by a clear understanding of the process that you're automating and the people involved in that process. If this is the case, you'll be a winner, reducing paper shuffling and increasing the productivity and satisfaction of everyone involved. On the other hand, if you don't study processes and people carefully, you'll frustrate your bosses and users alike to the point that your forms will hinder rather than help the workflow that you're trying to automate.

Featured in this chapter:

- The Outlook/Exchange application design environment

- Outlook Forms Designer basics

- Building the picnic form

- Publishing a new OFD form

- Creating the message form used to send the picnic form

- Using forms

- Don't stop here!

The Outlook/Exchange Application Design Environment

As I indicated way back in the first chapter of this book, OFD isn't the only way to design applications. The Exchange application design environment includes the following:

Forms design tools   The Outlook tools used to make your own forms.

Folder design tools   The Outlook tools used to create, organize, and set actions to take place within folders.

OLE-based applications   A word-processing document, a spreadsheet, or another element from an OLE-capable application such as Microsoft Word or Excel is pasted or inserted as an object into an Exchange message. The message becomes the application.

Exchange Application Programming Interfaces (APIs)   APIs are used to develop custom-coded applications using Visual Basic, C++, J++, or any other compatible programming language.

Exchange Server 2003 file- and web-based data access   Use file- and web-based access to Exchange private and public stores to create applications using end-user applications such as Word or programming languages like Visual Basic, C++, or J++.

The Outlook client folder design tools are quite easy to use. Creating OLE apps is just a matter of pasting or inserting the appropriate application object into an Exchange message. You don't need my help with those two. To do justice to API-based and Exchange 2003 file- and web-based application design, I'd need to write another book at least the size of this one. That's why I'm focusing this chapter on form design—and even then, as you'll see, we only touch the surface of this fascinating topic.

So that leaves OFD. Although OFD is fairly easy to use, it is a full-featured application, and I can't possibly teach you everything that you need to know about using it. My goal here is to show you how easy forms design can be and to get you started doing a simple form with OFD. For more details, you need to look at the OFD documentation and, if you want to get into serious programming, a good book on Visual Basic, such as *Mastering Visual Basic .NET* by Evangelos Petroutsos (Sybex, 2002).

OFD is part of the Outlook 98, 2000, and 2003 client. The Outlook Visual Basic help files and Microsoft Script Debugger are part of the Outlook Development Tools package. Install these when you install Outlook on your computer, or add them with the Add/Remove option in the Control Panel.

We'll start with a firm grounding in OFD basics. Then we'll actually build a form. Don't run too far ahead, or you just might build a form that doesn't work very well, if at all.

Outlook Forms Designer Basics

Begin by opening the OFD environment. In your Outlook client, from the Tools menu, select Forms ➤ Design a Form. The Design Form dialog box opens (see Figure 20.1). I've clicked the Advanced button near the bottom right of the dialog box. This extends the dialog box and shows information about a highlighted form type.

As you can see in the figure, you can create a form using a variety of Outlook message types from appointments to tasks. You use the drop-down menu at the top of the form to select the container or location from which to choose forms. The Design Form dialog box opens with the Standard Forms Library selected. Forms can be stored in a personal forms library unique to each user, in any Outlook private or public folder, and in other special storage locations. Take a look at the drop-down menu for all the options.

Outlook Message Forms

We're going to design a message form, so double-click Message in the Standard Forms Library in the Design Form dialog box. This opens the Forms Designer environment, as shown in Figure 20.2. For all intents and purposes, the Forms Designer environment is nothing more than an Outlook object— in this case, a message. You can work on it, save it to disk, and come back and work on it some more at any time.

Before we actually start developing a form, let's take a quick tour of the Outlook Forms Designer environment. Keep your eyes on Figure 20.2.

FIGURE 20.1

The Outlook Forms Designer Design Form dialog box

FIGURE 20.2

Editing a compose page in the Outlook Forms Designer environment

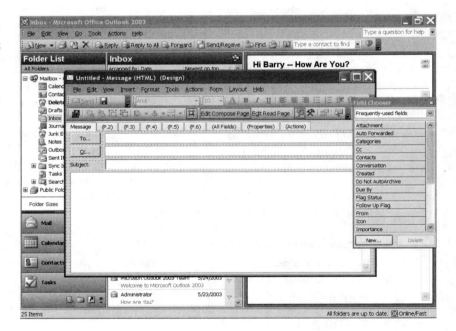

Notice the tabs on the form. They're labeled Message, (P.2) through (P.6), (All Fields), (Properties), and (Actions). These delineate specific property pages on the form. When a form's tab label is in parentheses, the property page is hidden when the end user opens the form. Generally, you hide unused property pages and pages where you don't want users to know what's going on. For example, if you don't want an end user to know where a reply to a form is being sent or to be able to change the subject of the reply, you hide the property page with the To and Subject fields on it.

Messages have two basic kinds of pages: compose pages and read pages. Note the two buttons just above the property page tabs labeled Edit Compose Page and Edit Read Page. You use compose page to create new Outlook items, such as messages. You use read pages to view composed items that have been processed by Outlook or Exchange Server. Outlook e-mail messages offer a good example of these two types of pages. When you click the New Message button in Outlook, a compose form opens. You enter addressing information, a subject line, and a message using the compose form. After you send the message, you can view it with a read form by double-clicking it in your Sent Items folder.

Any customizable page on a form can have compose and read pages. This option is enabled by default in the Message page. You must enable the option on all other pages by selecting Form ➤ Separate Read Layout when in the page. You can also choose Form ➤ Separate Read Layout to disable the compose/read page option in the Message page. When a message form page has no separate read page, users see data in the same format whether composing or reading a message. If a field is editable, it can be edited whether the message is being read or composed.

WARNING *Create message pages without read pages with care. You could be courting disaster if you let readers edit the content of messages that they receive. Be sure that recipients of filled-in forms without read pages are trustworthy and have no reason to alter the data in messages.*

By default, you start out editing the compose page of the Message page (see Figure 20.2, shown earlier). Click Edit Read Page to see what a read page looks like (see Figure 20.3). Default read pages have From, To, and Cc fields that are read-only. Users can't enter data into these fields. The Subject and Message fields on a read page are editable.

The Field Chooser and Control Toolbox

You use two key dialog boxes when you design forms: the Field Chooser and the Control Toolbox. The Field Chooser is visible in Figures 20.2 and 20.3. You can drag and drop any Exchange Server field, including fields that you design yourself, from the Chooser to your form. For example, if you wanted to include the size of your message on your form, you drag a message size field onto the form. You use the drop-down menu at the top of the Chooser to select the kinds of fields to be displayed. By default, you see the most frequently used fields. Among others, you can also see only address fields, only date/time fields, only the fields that you created, or only the fields in other forms. Open the drop-down list to see all your options.

We're done with the Field Chooser for now, so click the Field Chooser button (shown in Figure 20.4) to close the Chooser. Next, click Edit Compose Page on your new message form, and then click the Control Toolbox button (also shown in Figure 20.4) to open the toolbox.

FIGURE 20.3
The Outlook Forms Designer environment editing a read page

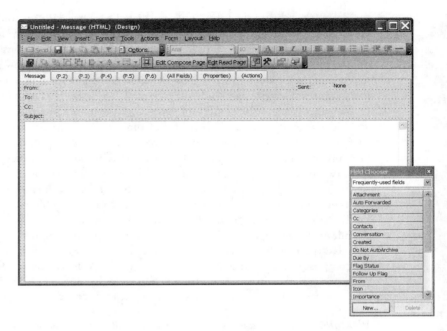

FIGURE 20.4
The Outlook Forms Designer ready for action

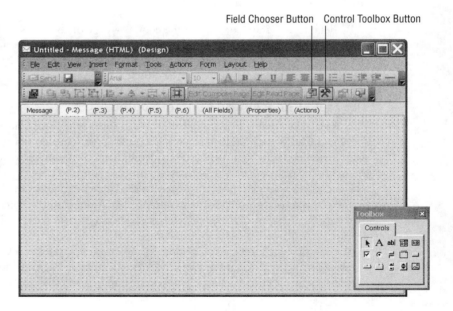

Figure 20.5 shows the Control Toolbox. With the exception of the button with an arrow on it, each of the buttons in the toolbox creates a different control for your form. You drag and drop controls onto your form.

FIGURE 20.5
The Outlook Forms Designer Control Toolbox

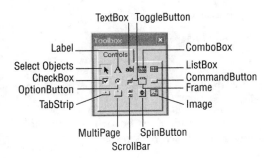

Controls define data input and viewing fields or provide additional means for managing activity on the form. Figure 20.5 includes the names of each of the controls.

Figure 20.6 shows the key OFD controls as they appear in a real Outlook message. Here's what each is for.

TextBox   A place to enter one or more lines of text.

CheckBox   For options that can be toggled on or off.

FIGURE 20.6
Key controls that can be used on an OFD form

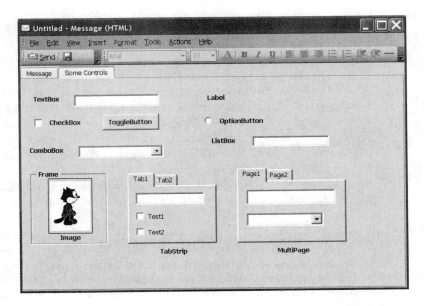

ToggleButton Similar to CheckBox, but the button is either pushed in (on) or not (off).

ComboBox A drop-down or drop-list box where users can type responses or select from a choice of optional responses.

Frame Frames or groups together other fields.

Image Display a graphic image.

Label Text labels.

OptionButton Enter multiple-choice options; users can not select multiple option buttons in the same frame field.

ListBox A drop-down or standard list box where users can select from a choice of optional responses but not type in their own responses.

TabStrip A multipage control where you add additional controls; the controls on each page are the same.

MultiPage A multipage control where you add additional controls; each page is a separate form with its own unique controls.

Other controls, such as the CommandButton, ScrollBar, and SpinButton controls, are used to manage activities on the form. For example, to build a data input field in which the user can move through a set of numbers and select a specific number, you use a SpinButton. We'll work with a SpinButton later in this chapter.

Form and Control Properties

Forms and controls have properties. To look at the properties of a form or a control that you have dragged onto your form, right-click anywhere on the form or control (the gray dotted area of a form or control) and select Properties or Advanced Properties.

Take a look at the Properties and Advanced Properties of the To control on the Message page of your form. You can change the properties of a To control to make it read-only or read/write. To do so, open the control's Advanced Properties dialog box, as indicated previously. Then find the Read Only property in the Properties dialog box and click it to change the property from False to True, or vice versa. If a control doesn't have a read-only property, it is a fixed read/write control. The Subject control is a fixed read/write control.

By the way, the colors of a control have nothing to do with whether it is editable. Control colors are simply properties of the control. You change them as you do any other property.

THE DIFFERENCE BETWEEN CONTROLS AND FIELDS

What's the difference between controls and fields? You use most OFD controls to build fields for entering and viewing data. You can refer to a specific control on a form as a field when it has been bound to a data field in an Exchange Server database. Until then, it's only a control. We'll talk more about data binding in a bit.

Building the Picnic Form

Okay, we're ready to begin building our first form. This form is to collect information from Barry Gerber and Associates (BGA) employees about an upcoming picnic, so we'll call it the Picnic Form. Be sure that the OFD environment is open and ready for you to create a message form. If you've closed the environment, refer back to the beginning of this chapter for details on opening it.

Among other things, you can customize the To and Subject fields for your message on the Message page. We're not ready for that yet, though. We need to start on one of the blank form-building pages, so tab over to page two (P.2) on your form.

Working with Properties

First, let's change the form's background color. Right-click your form and select Advanced Properties from the pop-up menu. This opens the Advanced Properties dialog box for the form page (see Figure 20.7). You can use this dialog box to set all kinds of attributes for the window itself; I'll leave it to you to explore all its great features. To change the background color, double-click the first item in the Properties dialog box, BackColor. Use the Color dialog box to select a new background color for your form page. In Figure 20.7, I'm choosing white.

Adding Controls

Now we're ready to add controls. As we move along, I'll show you how to do lots of neat stuff. Virtually everything you learn when adding one type of control can be used when you create other types. I'll tell you how to do a particular task as we set up a particular control; after that, I'll assume that you know how and when to use what you've already learned in creating other controls. As we go along, refer back to Figure 20.5 if you need to look for the location of buttons on OFD's Control toolbar.

FIGURE 20.7

Changing a form's background color

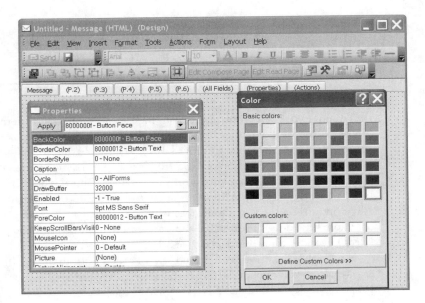

Let's start by adding a label that will serve as the title of our form. Click the label button on the Control toolbox with your left mouse button. The label button is the one with the letter *A* on it. Continuing to hold down your left mouse button, drag your mouse pointer over to the general location where you want the label to appear—I'm putting mine at the top of the message. Let go of the left mouse button. This brings up a little rectangular box with the word Label1 inside.

Click inside the box until it's surrounded by a dark rectangle with eight small white boxes around it. You use the small boxes to change the size of the label control. Just put the pointer on one of the small white boxes, hold down the left mouse button, and drag the box to make the control larger or smaller. Resize your label control until it's about the size of the one in Figure 20.8.

FIGURE 20.8

Creating a title label for a form

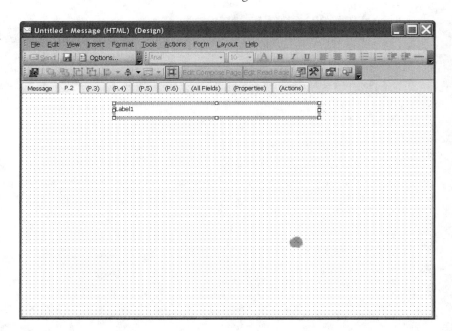

To move your label control, put your mouse cursor anywhere on the control, hold down the left mouse button, and drag the control to the desired location on the form. By default, controls are snapped to a grid when they are moved. If you'd rather have very fine-grained control over where your control is placed, select Snap to Grid from the form's Layout menu. This toggles Snap to Grid off. Select Snap to Grid again to turn it on. Fine-grained control is great in some circumstances, but it can be a pain when you want to line up your controls in an aesthetically pleasing manner. You can use the Align options on the Layout menu to help tame unruly non–Snap to Grid controls.

Those little dots on your form show the grid that things are being snapped to. If they bother you, select Layout ➤ Show Grid to toggle off grid visibility.

Next, right-click the label field and select Properties from the pop-up menu to bring up the Properties dialog box for your label (see Figure 20.9). Type the text for your label in the Caption field in the Properties dialog box. My label is "The BGA Picnic Is Coming Soon." Next, change the font size to 10 and make it bold. Then click OK. If the field is too small for the text that you've added, resize it and drag the label field around the form until it's attractively placed (see Figure 20.10). To make the rectangular box with the little resizing boxes disappear, simply click the form anywhere outside the field.

FIGURE 20.9
Changing the text of a title label for a form

FIGURE 20.10
A label field resized to become the title of a form

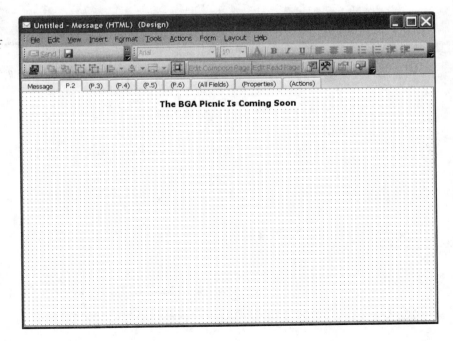

We took a lot of time fiddling around with sizing and placement on that first field. From here on, I'll leave it to you to do that kind of stuff on your own. Let's add another field.

WARNING *Be sure to save your form to disk on a regular basis. As with any other Windows application, use the File ➢ Save As and the File ➢ Save options. I like to save forms that I'm working on to my desktop. To reopen your form to work on it at a later date, you have to choose Tools ➢ Forms ➢ Design a Form in the Outlook main window. Then select User Templates in File System in the Design Form dialog box that pops up, and browse to the location of your form.*

For planning purposes, we need to find out what people want to drink at the picnic. Let's create a set of multiple-choice options and a control for people to enter other preferences.

Because people should be able to select more than one drink option, we'll use CheckBox fields grouped in a frame field to represent the options. (If we used OptionButton fields grouped on a frame, people would be able to select only one option in the group.) First, drag and drop a frame control from OFD's Control toolbar; check out Figure 20.5 if you need a refresher on the Control toolbar buttons.

We'll be offering four picnic drink options—coffee, tea, milk, and beer—so we need four Check-Box controls. Drag and drop four CheckBox controls onto the frame that you just created. Place the four CheckBox fields in a vertical line (see Figure 20.11).

NOTE *When you place fields on a frame field and then drag the frame, its associated fields stay in place and move with it. This makes it easy to properly locate a frame field and its associated fields.*

FIGURE 20.11

Creating a set of drink options for a company picnic

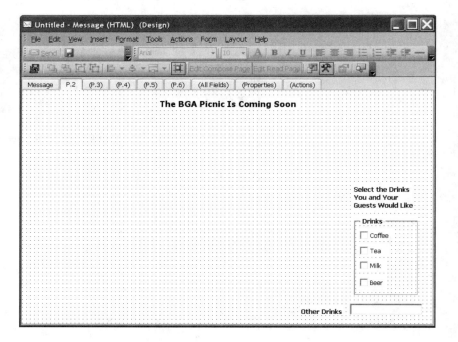

Next you need to set the captions for each of the four controls. The captions on the four controls in the figure are Coffee, Tea, Milk, and Beer. You set these captions just as you did for the title label that you created. Right-click the first control and select Properties from the pop-up menu. The Properties dialog box opens in the Value property page (I'll explain why later). For now, tab over to the Display property page and type **Coffee** in the Caption field. Click OK, and your first control now has the label Coffee. If you don't see the label, resize the control. Go ahead and do the other three controls; then we'll move on.

Okay, let's continue developing our Picnic form. I'm going to move much more quickly now that you have the basics of forms design under your belt.

Change the name of the frame to Drinks. Add a label above the frame for your Drinks CheckBox fields. "Select the Drinks You and Your Guests Would Like" seems to be a good choice for my form.

Now we need to add a control so that people can type in other drink choices. Add a TextBox and label, as shown in the lower-right corner of Figure 20.11.

Binding Controls to Exchange Server Data Fields

Now we're going to do something that is absolutely vital to the working of Outlook forms. We're going to bind each of the four CheckBox controls to a field in the Exchange Server database. If you don't do this, data entered into a form won't be available for viewing or manipulation after the form has been filled in and sent back to you. Think of it this way: Controls aren't data. They don't store data. They're just a way to enter data, but if they aren't bound to Exchange Server database fields, the data entered in them dies when a message containing an Outlook form is sent to someone or posted in a folder.

Remember the sidebar in the section "Form and Control Properties," earlier in this chapter, where I discussed the difference between controls and fields? Well, this is where a control earns the right to be called a field.

You can bind controls to standard Exchange fields, or you can create new fields and then bind controls to them. We'll be binding our controls to new Exchange fields.

Here's how to bind the Coffee CheckBox control to an Exchange database field. Open the Properties dialog box for the control. The dialog box opens by default in the Value property page, just as it did when you entered captions for the four drink controls. This is the cyberworld equivalent of a nagging spouse. Microsoft doesn't want you to forget to bind each control to an Exchange Server database field. Until you do, the Properties dialog box always opens in the Value page.

Click New in the Value page. This opens the New Field dialog box. Type in a name for the new Exchange Server database field. I like to use a combination of the form name and a meaningful name for the field. In Figure 20.12, I'm using the name PicnicCoffee.

Before you close the Properties dialog box, you need to change the Type field to Yes/No. CheckBoxes and ToggleButtons must be set to type Yes/No. If you don't do this, when people select a CheckBox or depress a ToggleButton, values that they check will not be in the form when they send it back to you. When you set the Type to Yes/No, notice that the Format changes to *Icon*. This means that the actual graphic image of the button, checked or not checked, is saved. Set the format to Yes/No or True/False. That way, data from this field will be saved in the Exchange Server database in a format that's easy to manipulate.

FIGURE 20.12
Binding an Outlook
form control to a
new Exchange data-
base field

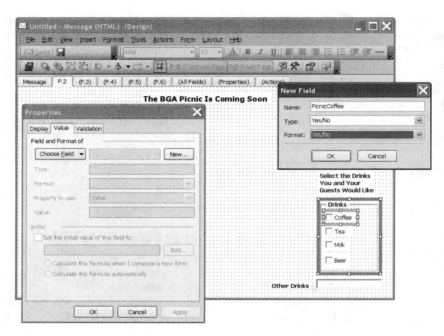

While you're at it, take a look at the other Type options that are available. The lineup is very rich, including (in addition to text) number, percent, currency, date/time, and formula. Each field includes formats appropriate to its content. For example, the Date/Time field includes a number of ways of displaying the day of the week (such as Monday, Tuesday, and so on), the month, the day of the month (such as 1st, 20th, and so on), year, and time.

Now back to the task immediately before us. Click OK, and you've created your new field and bound your control to it. Next bind each of your other controls that will contain data to a new field. Don't forget to bind each data control that you create from here on to a new field.

TIP *You're very likely to create a number of bogus fields while experimenting with Outlook forms. It's easy to get rid of unwanted fields—maybe too easy. To remove a field, open the Field Chooser, click the field that you want to remove, and click Delete at the bottom of the Chooser. Then you need to delete the field from the current form. Tab over to the All Fields page on the form and delete the field. This probably goes without saying, but I'll say it anyway: Be careful not to delete valid fields, especially after lots of forms have been filled out and their fields are snugly stored in your Exchange Server database.*

Setting Initial Values for Controls

Before we continue building our form, I want to show you how to set initial values for a control. Figure 20.13 shows the Properties dialog box for the Coffee ComboBox. Notice the frame with the caption Initial at the bottom of the dialog box. This is where you set the value that a user will see when they first open the form. You don't need to set any initial values for a CheckBox. However, you might want to set a specific initial value for other fields. For example, you could set the initial value of a ComboBox to one of the possible values for the ComboBox. More about ComboBoxes, possible values, and such in a bit.

FIGURE 20.13

Use the Properties dialog box to set the initial value of a field.

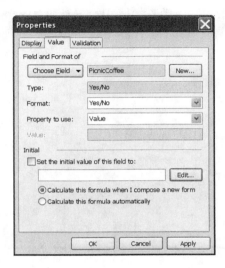

Testing an Outlook Form

You can run a form at any time while you're creating it. Just select Form ➤ Run This Form on the form itself. In the case of a message form, a standard Outlook message is displayed that looks just like your form (see Figure 20.14). You can just look at the form to admire your work, or you can fill in the form and send it to yourself to see how it works.

The capability to run a form at any time is a fantastic feature of OFD. As you can see, it makes format checking and debugging extremely easy.

Adding More Controls to the Picnic Form

Next we'll add a set of CheckBox fields so that people can pick the main dishes that they want. We'll also provide an entry field to indicate a preference for other main-dish options.

Well, we're certainly not about to go through all the steps that we just went through to create this new set of fields; we'll just copy and paste:

1. Put your mouse pointer an inch or so to the left and above the Select the Drinks You and Your Guests Would Like label. Hold down the left mouse button and drag your mouse pointer until the select rectangle includes everything up to and including the Other Drinks control (see Figure 20.15).

FIGURE 20.14
Testing an incomplete Outlook form

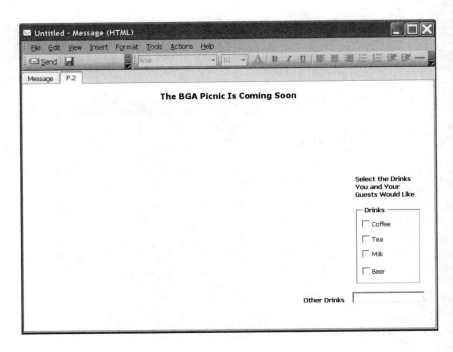

FIGURE 20.15
Selecting a set of controls that will be copied and pasted elsewhere in a form

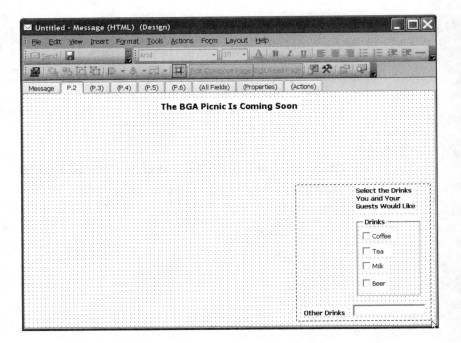

2. Release the left mouse button. All the controls within the rectangle should be highlighted.

3. Select Copy from the form's Edit menu (or use the keyboard shortcut, Ctrl+C).

4. Then choose Paste from the Edit menu (or press Ctrl+V).

If you don't see the new frame, its associated CheckBox, and the text box and labels fields, they've probably been pasted right on top of the old frame, CheckBox, and text box and labels fields. In that case, just move the top frame and related objects with your mouse and you'll see the original frame and related objects underneath. You now have two identical frames, CheckBox buttons, text boxes, and labels. Move the copy to the left of the original.

Now edit the leftmost Drinks frame and its associated CheckBox fields. Change the Coffee, Tea, Milk, and Beer captions to Hamburger, Turkey Burger, Veggie Burger, and Hot Dogs. Next add new database fields for the four new controls, and set their types to Yes/No and their formats to Yes/No or True/False. Then edit the Drinks label, frame label, and the Other Drinks entry field and label so that they are appropriate for a main dish. When you're done, your form should look something like the one in Figure 20.16.

We need to know how many guests each person plans to bring and what kinds of games people will want to play. So, we need to add a TextBox for the number of guests, plus a label and two Combo-Boxes for favorite games (see Figure 20.17).

We're going to set up a fancy TextBox for entering the number of guests. Follow these steps:

1. Create the TextBox control and bind it to a new field, setting the type for the Number of Guests TextBox to Number. Don't worry about the format.

FIGURE 20.16

The picnic form with main-dish fields in place

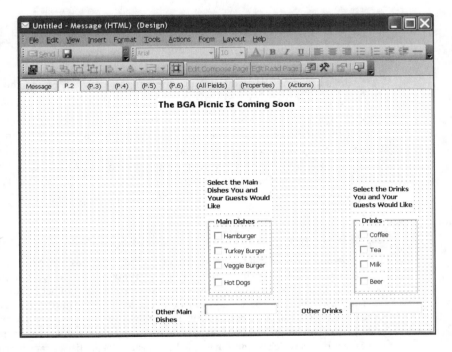

2. Next, drag and drop a SpinButton onto the right edge of your TextBox, just as you see in Figure 20.17.

FIGURE 20.17

The picnic form now collects information on the number of guests and favorite games.

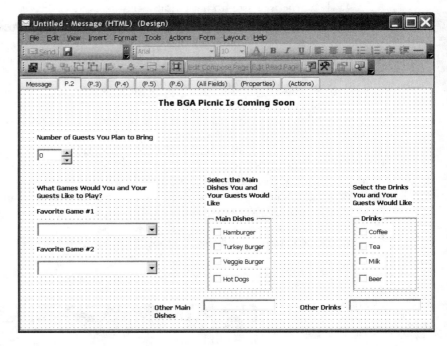

3. Then bind the SpinButton to the same field as you bound the TextBox.

Run your form, and you'll see that you can use the spin button to pick whatever numeric value you want. The problem is that you can spin up to some pretty grand numbers of guests or down to negative numbers of guests. We don't want to bankrupt my little company, so let's set the minimum and maximum values that you can spin to. Right-click the SpinButton and open the Advanced Properties dialog box. Find the Max and Min properties, and set Min to 0 and Max to 8.

Now run your form. The initial value is 0, even though you didn't set an initial value. That's because you set Min to 0 for the SpinButton. And you can spin only up to 8. Pretty nifty, huh?

VALIDATION

You've probably noticed the Validation tab in the Properties dialog box. You use this tab to require that users enter data into a field or to ensure that data entered by users meets a specific set of criteria. For example, we could have required that the value entered into our Number of Guests field should be greater than -1 and less than 9. We could even have put in a message that would be shown to users if they entered a number outside the range of acceptable values. In this case, the SpinButton works much more elegantly than any set of validation checks. So validation isn't needed here, but I'm sure that you can imagine a number of scenarios in which validation would help ensure the quality of data entered into a form.

Now, go ahead and create the two ComboBoxes for favorite games. The ComboBoxes start out blank. At this point, if form users opened the drop-down list, they'd find nothing to select from. To add some options, right-click the first games ComboBox and select Properties from the pop-up menu. Then enter some games in the Possible Values field. If you want one of the values to show in the ComboBox when the form is first opened, type that value into the field named Set the Initial Value of This Field To. Check out Figure 20.18 for the details.

FIGURE 20.18

Adding values to a ComboBox

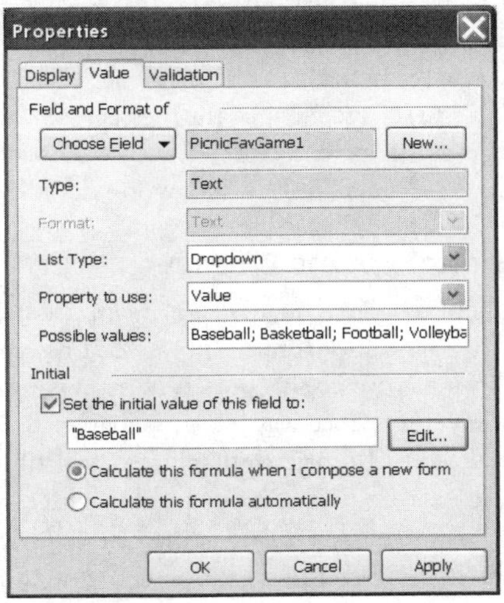

Notice in the figure that I set the initial value for the ComboBox to Baseball. That way, the field shows the value Baseball when the form is initially opened. Finish up the games section of the form. Don't forget to bind the data controls you created to new fields.

We need to do two more things before we finish. First, we need to rename the second page on our form from P.2 to something else, such as Please Fill In Survey Here. Click the tab for P.2 and select Form ➤ Rename Page. Enter a new name in the Rename Page dialog box, and click OK.

Second, we need to set a subject for our message. That way, all messages sent to us will have a standard subject line. The initial value of my subject field is Survey for BGA Picnic. Tab over to the Message property page of your form, right-click the form's Subject field, and select Properties. When the Properties dialog box for the field opens, tab over to the Value property page and type in an initial value.

That's it. We've finished creating our form. Be sure to save it.

Now we need to publish our form.

Publishing a New OFD Form

You can publish an OFD form in a number of locations:

◆ An Exchange Server organizational forms library

◆ Your own personal forms library

◆ Your own Outlook folders

◆ Exchange Server public folders

Exchange Server organizational forms libraries reside on an Exchange server and are available to all users by default. Forms in your personal forms library are available only to you when you're logged in to your Exchange Server mailbox, as are forms in your own Outlook folders. Exchange Server public folders are available to any user who is granted permissions to use them.

As you'll see in a bit, the form that we just created is invoked when a user replies to a message. The user receives a message, opens it, and replies to it. The reply is the form. When the user is finished filling in the form, they send the reply back to the original sender.

The form needs to be available to the recipient of the message, so we can't publish it in a personal forms library or private folders. To accomplish the end outlined above, the form must be published in an Exchange Server organizational forms library. Even a public folder won't do. I'll show you why in a short while.

Creating an Organizational Forms Library

So you're probably asking, "Where's this Exchange Server organizational forms library thingie?" Right now, it's nowhere. You must create an organizational forms library on one of your Exchange Servers. That means that you have to shift gears, go over to your Exchange Server, open your MMC, and go to the Exchange System Manager, your constant companion since way back in Chapter 8, "Installing Exchange Server 2003."

To create an organizational forms library, right-click your Public Folders container and select View System Folders from the pop-up menu. Your public folders will disappear, and in their place, you'll see your system folders. Right-click the one named EFORMS REGISTRY and select New ➤ Organizational Form from the pop-up menu. This opens the organizational forms library Properties dialog box, shown in Figure 20.19. Fill in the form, being sure to select the correct language so that accents and other characteristics of the language are supported. You can create multiple organizational forms libraries. The only requirement is that there can be only one library per language.

FIGURE 20.19

Using the organizational forms library Properties dialog box to create a new organizational forms library

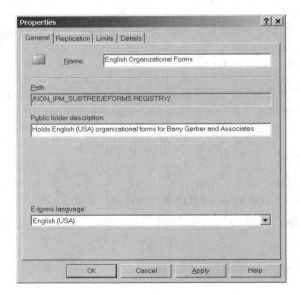

When you're done with the dialog box, click OK, and your new organizational forms library shows up in the EFORMS REGISTRY system folder (see Figure 20.20). Double-click the new library in the left pane of your MMC to open its full Properties dialog box. Notice that this folder has all the property pages that any other public folder has. You can assign access permissions and replicate a forms library just as you would with any other public folder. Just a reminder on replication: don't forget to replicate your new forms library to other Exchange servers with users who might need access to forms in the library. For more on public folder management, take a look at Chapter 12, "Managing the Exchange Server Hierarchy and Core Components."

FIGURE 20.20

A newly created organizational forms library in the EFORMS REGISTRY system folder

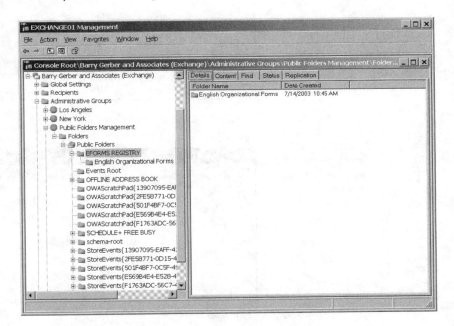

To perform the following steps, you must have domain Administrator privileges. To publish your form, on the form itself, select Tools ➤ Forms ➤ Publish Form or choose Tools ➤ Forms ➤ Publish Form As. Then select the location where you want to store your form from the drop-down list in the Publish Form or Publish Form As dialog box (see Figure 20.21).

In Figure 20.22, I'm publishing my picnic form in the organizational forms library. I've chosen to name the form BGA Picnic Form.

WARNING   *Any time you're asked if you want to save the form definition with the form (item), unless you really know what you're doing, save the definition. Sometimes OFD seems to be offering a very logical reason not to save the definition, but, trust me, save the definition. You might need it later.*

When the form is saved, we're ready to move on to the next step. Yes, there is a next step.

FIGURE 20.21
Selecting the forms
library where the
form will be stored

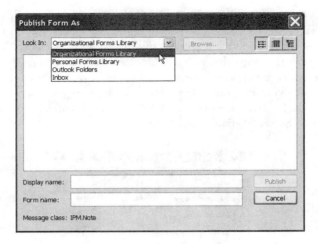

FIGURE 20.22
Storing a form in the
organization forms
library

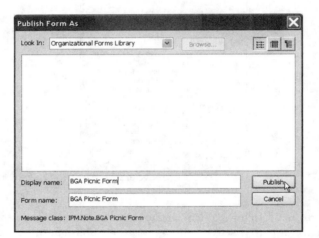

Creating the Message Form Used to Send the Picnic Form

I'll bet you thought we were done. Nope. The form that we just created is, for all intents and purposes, a reply form, not a send form. If you run the form, you get a Message tab to address the message and show its subject, and you get the Picnic Survey tab. If you send this form to someone and that person clicks the Reply button on the message, all that person will get is a standard reply message. The Survey tab won't be there.

You can provide users with a reply version of the form in two ways.

◆ Attach your saved form to a message. In the message, tell users to double-click the attachment to open it and then to fill in the survey and send it back. In this case, you might want to make your mailbox alias or display name the initial value in the To field of the message. Then users won't have to enter your e-mail address to send back the form.

◆ Create a message with a reply that is itself your form.

Although the first option is easier for you to pull off, it requires a lot more work for the user than the second option. There's also more room for error with the first option. So we're going to take the more elegant approach of option two.

Our second message is very simple. You've already done everything required to create it. Here's what to do:

1. Choose Forms ➤ Design a Form from Outlook's Tools menu.

2. Select Message from the Design a Form dialog box.

3. Add the same subject line that you created for the original message; you'll remember that mine is "Survey for BGA Picnic."

4. On the Properties page of the form, click the CheckBox labeled Send Form Definition with Item.

5. On the Actions page of the form, double-click the row with the action name Reply.

6. In the Form Action Properties dialog box, on the frame labeled This Action Creates a Form of the Following Type, use the drop-down list to change the form name from Message to the name of the form that you just published in your organizational forms library (BGA Picnic Form, in my case).

7. Repeat steps 5 and 6 for Reply to All.

8. Save your form, and publish it in your personal forms library under a name such as Message with BGA Picnic Form as a Reply.

Okay, that's it. Now, we're ready to put our forms to use.

NOTE   *When you selected the form BGA Picnic Form in step 6, you were offered only three containers from which to select the form: Standard Forms Library, Organizational Forms Library, and Personal Forms Library. Those are all the choices there are. Now do you see why a public folder wouldn't do here? Public folders are not a choice because they might not have been replicated across an entire Exchange organization. Organization forms libraries are cross-organization by definition, meaning that they are replicated to all Exchange servers in an Exchange organization.*

TIP   *Like fields, you just might wind up with a bunch of useless forms in a library or folder. You delete forms from folders just like any other item in a folder. To delete forms from libraries, from the Outlook main menu, select Tools ➤ Options ➤ Other. Next, click Advanced Options, and in the Advanced Options dialog box, click Custom Forms, then click Manage Forms. Use the resultant Forms Manager dialog box to delete and otherwise manage your forms.*

Using Forms

To use the form we just created, select New ➢ Choose Form from the File menu of Outlook's main window. Use the Choose Form dialog box to find your personal forms library and double-click the form that you created in the previous section (Message with BGA Picnic Form as a Reply, in my case).

In Figure 20.23, I'm sending a message off to an Outlook distribution list that includes all BGA staff. Note that there is no sign of the form at this point. In Figure 20.24, a member of BGA's staff (me again) has clicked Reply on the original message and has just finished completing the picnic survey form that opened as part of the reply message. When I click Send, the message with the form is sent to the original sender (me, yet again).

THE DIFFERENCE BETWEEN SAVE, SAVE AS, PUBLISH, AND PUBLISH AS

Outlook Forms Designer is full of ways to save and publish your work. As you're building a form, it's a good idea to save or republish it frequently; just be sure that you know where things go when you use all the save and publish options that OFD provides.

Save and Save As don't work like they do in other applications such as Microsoft Word. Save saves your form to your Outlook client's Drafts folder. Save As is more traditional and saves your work to a disk file of your choice. If you want to save or resave your form to a file, use Save As.

Publish As lets you choose the forms library or folder where you want to publish your form. Publish republishes your form in the forms library or folder where you opened the form or anywhere you chose with Publish As.

FIGURE 20.23

Sending a form to an Exchange recipient

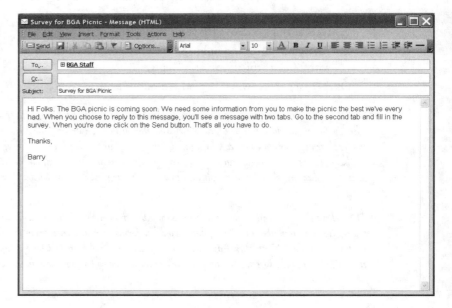

FIGURE 20.24

The data in a completed form ready to be returned to the form's sender

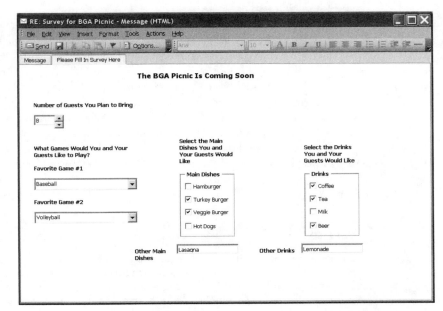

To be fancy, I could show you the form as it looks to the original sender when the reply is received. However, it would be anticlimactic because the form looks just like it does in Figure 20.24.

TIP   Do you find the two-tab reply message annoying? I mean, why should someone have to tab over to the survey tab to fill it in? This little aesthetic nightmare is easy to fix. All you have to do is cut the To and Cc fields from the Message page and paste them on the survey page. Then hide the Message page. Now your reply form is a beautiful single page. If you do make this change, be sure to save and republish your results.

Just one thing before we conclude this section: All those fields that you created are available in the Outlook client. You can open the Field Chooser in the client and drag and drop any of these fields onto the field bar in your Inbox. The field bar is the one near top of an Outlook folder (for example, the Inbox) with From, Subject, Received, and so on, on it. To open the Field Chooser, on the main Outlook window, right-click the field bar and select Field Chooser. To find the fields in a form in the Field Chooser, select Forms from the drop-down list near the top of the Chooser and use the resultant dialog box to find the form that you're interested in. Select the form and you'll see its fields in the Field Chooser. Select the picnic form field Number of Guests from the Field Chooser and drag it to the field bar. Now for every picnic form that is returned, you can see not only who sent it and when, but you can also see how many guests each sender plans to bring to the picnic.

Don't Stop Here!

Unfortunately, we have to stop our exploration of OFD here, but don't let that stop you from exploring it further on your own. You can do so many great things with OFD, such as creating forms for posting in public folders, setting group meetings, or collecting key line-of-business information.

Also look into Visual Basic scripting. You'd be amazed at what you can do when you combine Outlook forms and VB scripting. You can do simple tasks, such as collating responses from Outlook forms, all the way up to complex applications that help your organization sell its products or services, maintain its inventory, or manage its customers, clients, or patients.

OFD has a very good user interface. Combine that with its fine online help, and you can usually have a project based on newly discovered OFD features up and running in minutes. As with any piece of technology—Outlook and Exchange Server included—your OFD watchwords should be *plan, do, test,* and *have fun.*

WHERE TO GET SAMPLE FORMS AND HELP WITH FORMS DEVELOPMENT

Exchange Server comes with a number of sample forms-based applications, and you can download more at Microsoft's website. These apps support such functions as customer tracking and help desks. They're worth looking at both because they might help you understand how to build multiform applications and because they use Exchange's public folders to organize apps as well as deliver them to users throughout an Exchange organization.

Check the shelves of your favorite bookstore for weighty (5 pounds at least) tomes on OFD. And take a look at Microsoft's website, which has some fairly good stuff. You can also find useful OFD and Visual Basic programming information and even Exchange Server information at www.slipstick.com.

If you expect to get into forms programming, get a hold of one of the books out there on Visual Basic scripting for Microsoft Office. You might even want to buy Microsoft's Visual Basic.NET Standard Edition. It sells for less than $100 and is a good way to get started on VB as a language rather than just VB scripting.

Summary

There are a number of ways to develop applications in the Exchange Server 2003 environment. This includes using electronic forms, customized Exchange folders, OLE-based applications, Exchange API-based applications, and Exchange 2003 file- and web-based applications. Electronic forms are a fairly easy way to create quite sophisticated applications that elicit information from Exchange users. They can be used to fulfill a wide variety of corporate tasks, from issuing purchase orders to submitting monthly expense information.

Outlook Forms Designer is one of the best form-design interfaces around. You create forms in a logical, intuitive, object-oriented visual environment. You can add controls to a form that support everything from labels and text to check boxes, radio buttons, and drop-down lists. You can modify the properties of forms and of the controls that you place on them to alter the function and look of both. And, you can create send and reply forms, combining the two into seamless messages in which the reply form with all its controls pops up when the recipient clicks Reply.

You bind controls to fields stored on your Exchange server. So, data from each recipient of a message is stored in Exchange and is available for analysis using a range of tools, including Visual Basic or C++ programs.

You can store Outlook Forms Designer forms in a variety of places, including private and public folders. However, for ease of access within an Exchange organization, organizational forms libraries make the most sense. Organizational forms libraries are public folders with all the characteristics and capabilities of public folders, including the capability for replication and easy management of user access.

Well, folks, this is the last chapter of *Mastering Exchange Server 2003*. For me, researching and writing the book has been a lot of fun and relatively painless. I hope that your experiences with Exchange Server are as positive and rewarding.

Appendix

Cool Third-Party Applications for Exchange Server and Outlook Clients

I never appreciated the meaning of *cool* until I started playing with Exchange Server and its clients and some of the fantastic applications that third-party vendors have created to extend the reach of an already-great set of products. Here I'll tell you about some of my favorite products at the time of this writing.

Products are listed by category, along with information on how you can contact the vendors. Some vendors provide live demos or even trial versions of their products that you can download over the Internet.

Most of the vendors listed here either have begun shipping or are committed to shipping Exchange 2003 versions of their products. Contact the vendor for more information.

WARNING *Remember, I can't take responsibility for the workability of these products in your Exchange Server and organizational environments. That's up to you.*

Administration and Management

Exchange administration and management covers a wide variety of topics. The products listed here do the same. Some monitor Exchange servers and connectors, reporting on such things as e-mail loads and network availability. Other products assist in migrating mailboxes and other Exchange objects within an Exchange organization or between Exchange organizations. Still other products help you automate the resource-draining creation of Outlook profiles for Exchange server. And one product in this section is a substitute for Windows clustered servers.

AppAnalyzer for Exchange   AppAnalyzer for Exchange lets you monitor the health and performance of an entire distributed Exchange system. It can tell you such things as the time it takes to deliver e-mail, where Internet e-mail is being sent, what is making some mailboxes as large as they are, and where offensive e-mail resides on your server. Contact: NetIQ (www.netiq.com)

Argent Exchange Monitor Argent Exchange Monitor is for small to very large Exchange environments (up to 2,000 Exchange servers). Monitoring includes response-time tracking, SMTP connectivity, top senders and receivers of messages, and mailboxes over storage limits. Contact: Argent Software (`www.argent.com`)

Control Suite for Exchange Control Suite for Exchange is a monitoring, alerting, and reporting tool for Exchange. It includes two products: Insight for Exchange (usage reporting with histories) and ExRay for Exchange (monitoring, alerting, and reporting). Contact: Intellireach Corp. (`www.intellireach.com`)

Co-StandbyServer AAdvanced for Microsoft Exchange Co-StandbyServer AAdvanced for Microsoft Exchange creates a mirror image of an Exchange server on another server. If the main Exchange server fails, the standby server takes over automatically. This is similar to the functionality provided in Microsoft cluster server technology. Contact: Legato Systems, Inc. (`www.legato.com`)

Exchange Administrator Exchange Administrator is a nice front-end for managing the Active Directory side of Exchange server. It supports the automation of administrative tasks such as mailbox creation. The product is an add-on to NetIQ's Directory and Resource Administrator. Contact: NetIQ (`www.netiq.com`)

Exchange Migrator Another product from NetIQ, Exchange Migrator simplifies the migration of Exchange objects from one Exchange organization to another. Contact: NetIQ (`www.netiq.com`)

ExMS Exchange Mailbox Manager ExMS Exchange Mailbox Manager moves mailboxes between servers in an organization. Moves can be scheduled and full mailbox permissions can be retained in the move. Mailbox selection can be based on a variety of filters. Contact: Discus Data Solutions (`www.discusdata.com`)

ExMS Exchange Migration Manager ExMS Exchange Migration Manager is the industrial-strength version of ExMS Exchange Mailbox Manager. It's designed for very large migrations and it supports moving Exchange objects between and within Exchange organizations. Contact: Discus Data Solutions (`www.discusdata.com`)

Exchange POP Exchange POP is a gateway that downloads messages from non-Exchange POP3 and IMAP4 mailboxes to Exchange mailboxes. This product is useful for users who receive all or some of their e-mail outside of Exchange, for example, at an ISP. Exchange POP includes anti-virus and anti-spam screening. See also "Mail Essentials for Exchange/SMTP" in the section "Virus, Spam, and Content Control" later in this appendix. Contact: Kinesphere Corporation (`www.exchangepop3.com`)

Message Manager Message Manager can scan e-mail databases for specific content to find information leaks, track specific messages and investigate e-mail related to specific employees or subjects. Contact: Intellireach Corp. (`www.intellireach.com`)

POPMaster/ex POPMaster/ex is a POP gateway similar to Exchange POP. At this writing, the product is scheduled for third-quarter 2003 release. Contact: OmniTrend Software, Inc. (`www.omnitrend.com`)

Profile Maker   Profile Maker helps Exchange managers build and support common Outlook/Exchange Server profiles. It allows for configuration of local file paths, message retention settings, addressing, delivery, and folder options. If a user changes their profile, that profile is replaced with their Profile Maker profile the next time they log in to the network. Contact: AutoProf.com (`www.autoprof.com`)

Heroix eQ   Heroix eQ (formerly RoboMon) monitors Exchange Server environments, including everything from CPU usage to end-to-end connectivity. This utility provides extensive reports. Contact: Heroix (`www.heroix.com`)

Backup and Archiving Software

The key here is support for Exchange Server. Windows Server 2003's own backup program backs up the Exchange mailbox and public information stores while they're open and in use. That's really nice, but Windows Server 2003's Backup isn't the most full-featured backup product around. For example, it doesn't back up individual Exchange mailboxes and its disaster recovery capabilities aren't all that sophisticated. Still, the Windows 2003 backup program can work well for small networks, especially if each server is backed up locally. For more features, turn to third-party backup solutions that include such features as Windows Server 2003's ability to do volume shadow copy backups of Exchange databases.

Organizational requirements, governmental regulations, or just plain diminishing disk-storage resources might require that e-mail be archived. Whether it's to protect employee pension or other rights, or to meet the financial requirements of agencies such as the Securities Exchange Commission, or to free up space on Exchange server disks, e-mail archiving is becoming an important function in IT shops. You can do some archiving with tools built into Exchange Server and Outlook, but third-party add-ons make archiving much easier.

Brightstore ARCserve Backup   ARCserve has been around for a long time and is a good package. Under the enterprise-oriented hand of Computer Associates, the Brightstore ARCserve Backup suite has become a very strong contender in large system backup. Contact: Computer Associates (`www.cai.com`)

Backup Exec   Like ARCserve, Backup Exec has been around for eons and is a good backup product with nice backup-scheduling capabilities. Also check out Veritas's Remote Storage for Exchange, which archives message attachments to a secondary storage device such as tape and then seamlessly returns the attachment when a user tries to access it. Contact: Veritas (`www.veritas.com`)

Exchange Archive Solution   Exchange Archive Solution archives Exchange messages so that they can be managed and retrieved as needed. This is a high-powered product that allows for centralized backup while leaving room for local control and end-user recovery of archived messages. Contact: EDUCOM TS, Inc. (`www.educomts.com`)

Galaxy Backup and Recovery for Microsoft Exchange   Galaxy Backup and Recovery for Microsoft Exchange is a very nice product. It has a fine user interface and it allows individual recovery of messages and other Exchange items. Contact: CommVault Systems (`www.commvault.com`)

Legato EmailXtender   This is an e-mail archiving application. It runs on a separate server and can archive mail in a variety of server environments including Exchange, Lotus Notes, and Unix Sendmail. Data is stored in Microsoft SQL Server. Administration includes the ability to set retention parameters and policies for categorization of messages. Contact: Legato Systems, Inc. (www.legato.com)

Legato NetWorker   Well known for the excellence of its Unix backup products, Legato also supports the Windows NT 4 and Windows 200x Server environments with its NetWorker backup product. An optional module for Exchange Server extends support to Exchange Server. Contact: Legato Systems, Inc. (www.legato.com)

NetBackup   NetBackup is the industrial-strength enterprise backup product from Veritas, makers of Backup Exec. The product provides centralized control of the backup process and comes in three flavors for different-sized organizations and backup needs. Contact: Veritas (www.veritas.com)

UltraBac   UltraBac Software's backup entry sports very nice backup setup and scheduling interfaces. An optional Exchange information store backup module is available. Contact: UltraBac Software (www.ultrabac.com)

Fax Servers

Generally, fax servers enable users to send and receive faxes through a central server instead of their own workstations or traditional fax machines. Fax servers that integrate with Exchange Server add a new address type for faxing. To send a message to an e-mail user, select the user's e-mail address from an Exchange address book. To send a message to a fax user, select the fax address from an Exchange address book.

FACSys Fax Connector 2000   FACSys Fax Connector 2000 operates pretty much like any other connector on an Exchange server, but it sends faxes. The product is managed right inside Exchange System Manager. Contact: FACSys (www.facsys.com)

Faxcom for Exchange   Faxcom for Exchange runs as a Windows service. Faxcom for Exchange integrates Exchange recipient information so users can send faxes using their Outlook contacts. Contact: Biscom, Inc. (www.biscom.com)

Faxination Server for Microsoft Exchange   Faxination Server for Microsoft Exchange provides full Exchange Server integration and supports a range of languages. It allows for off-hours scheduling and least-cost routing. Contact: Fenestrae, Inc. (www.fenestrae.com)

FAXmaker for Exchange   FAXmaker for Exchange runs as a Windows service and allows faxes and GSM phone service SMS messages to be sent from an Outlook client with seamless Exchange Server integration. It includes call cost accounting. Contact: GFI (www.gfi.com)

DM Fax Server   DM Fax Server installs and works as a Windows service. It can function as a high-traffic fax server and it can support a range of e-document distribution functions, such as automated faxback. Contact: IMECOM Group (www.imecominc.com)

Genifax   Genifax is a sophisticated fax server that works with a wide range of high-end messaging platforms including Lotus Notes and Exchange Server. Omtool, the product's manufacturer, specializes in the legal and healthcare industries. Genifax can be expanded to include e-document distribution functionality. Contact: Omtool (`www.omtool.com`)

MsXfax XP for Exchange   MsXfax XP for Exchange can be installed on an Exchange or Windows server. It integrates with Active Directory without modifying the schema. Contact: BSN Group (`www.bnsgroup.com.au`)

RightFax   RightFax is an enterprise-level product focusing on e-document delivery. The product is tightly coupled with application solutions from SAP AG. Contact: Captaris, Inc. (`www.captaris.com/rightfax`)

Network Security Monitors, Scanners, and Intrusion Detectors

I talked about network security monitors and scanners in Chapter 18, "Exchange Server System Security." Scanner products plow through network nodes on an IP-by-IP basis looking for such things as missing service packs and hot fixes; open ports; weak passwords; potentially dangerous assignments of security privileges; and services, applications, and registry key entries that might threaten security. Security monitors examine system logs for potential security holes and breaches.

Intrusion detectors are sort of intelligent firewalls for networks, servers, and workstations. They can find and thwart internal and external attempts to access resources far beyond the port and protocol level.

LANGuard Security Event Log Monitor   LANGuard Monitor combs Windows event logs looking for evidence of internal and external security violations. It provides real-time notifications and reports to systems managers. LANGuard also supports system-wide log management, including automated archiving and clearing of event logs. Contact: GFI Software (`www.gfi.com`)

LANGuard Network Security Scanner   LANGuard Scanner looks at network nodes for known security problems. It's fast and I have found it to be quite accurate. It produces very nice reports in HTTP format. LANGuard can remotely install service packs and hot fixes. Contact: GFI (`www.gfi.com`)

Monitor Magic   Monitor Magic stores its findings in Microsoft SQL Server or Access databases. It comes with a range of very useful preconfigured security and other reports. A web interface is also included. Contact: Advanced Toolware (`www.advtoolware.com`)

Network Monitoring Suite   Network Monitoring Suite includes features similar to LANGuard Monitor. The product also includes performance monitoring based on Windows performance logs and Windows service monitoring with auto restarts if necessary. Contact: LANWare, Inc. (`www.lanware.net`)

RealSecure Network Protection Components   The RealSecure Network Protection Components suite includes modules for networks, gateways, servers, and workstations. The modules detect attempted internal and external intrusions and stop them in real time. Contact: Internet Security Systems (`www.iss.net`)

RealSecure Vulnerability Assessment   The RealSecure Vulnerability Assessment suite includes components for the Internet, servers, databases, and 802.11b wireless networks. These components scan their targets, looking for a range of security threats. This product offers the most comprehensive approach to system security. Contact: Internet Security Systems (`www.iss.net`)

RETINA Network Security Scanner   Like LANGuard, RETINA scans network nodes for known security problems. The program includes an interesting if not easy to validate artificial intelligence component that tries to get into a network as a hacker might. In my experience, RETINA is fast and quite accurate. Contact: eEye Digital Security (`www.eeye.com`)

SecureIIS   SecureIIS is designed to protect Microsoft's Internet Information Server from external and internal attacks. The product examines traffic coming into IIS and stops packets that pose a threat. It can protect IIS servers with security problems for which Microsoft has not yet issued fixes. Contact: eEye Digital Security (`www.eeye.com`)

Unified Messaging

Unified messaging, the linking of a variety of messaging tools from pagers to telephones to e-mail clients to fax, has long been a dream of forward-looking communications types. As these products indicate, the tools for accomplishing unified messaging have emerged.

Mitel Networks 6510 Unified Messaging   Mitel Networks 6510 Unified Messaging brings together voice, incoming fax, and e-mail messaging. It also supports text-to-speech conversion and is scheduled to support speech-to-text in the near future. Wireless PDAs are supported. Contact: Mitel Networks Corporation (`www.mitel.com`)

PageMaster/ex   PageMaster/ex allows Exchange server users to send pages and text messages to pagers. Page recipients appear on Exchange and can be selected from global or personal address lists. Messages can be sent in pager alphanumeric or GMS SMS format. Contact: OmniTrend Software, Inc. (`www.omnitrend.com`)

Unified Messenger   Unified Messenger is a high-end product that integrates with Exchange Server. It stores voicemail messages inside users' Exchange mailboxes. You can reply to voicemail with e-mail and vice versa. More real coolness! Contact: Avaya, Inc. (`www.avaya.com`)

Virus, Spam, and Content Control

What scares users more than the boss? Viruses, junk mail, and outgoing messages containing confidential information! These products let you catch mail-borne viruses, spam messages, and messages with sensitive content in their natural habitat: your Exchange server. They automatically download and install virus updates. Most also scan for viruses in real time as messages pass through your Exchange server and can perform scheduled and on-demand scans of information stores for viruses.

Antigen for Exchange Server   Antigen for Exchange Server does real-time virus scans and repairs of inbound and outbound messages. It also does scheduled scans and fixes. Antigen supports third-party virus-scan engines for better virus coverage, especially with new viruses. Contact: Sybari Software (`www.sybari.com`)

iHateSpam Server Edition   iHateSpam is server-based anti-spam software. It allows for extensive customization according to individual user needs. This overcomes one of the real weaknesses of server-based anti-spam solutions. There is a desktop version of iHateSpam that is not integrated with the server version. Contact: Sunbelt Software (www.sunbelt-software.com)

Mail Essentials for Exchange/SMTP   Mail Essentials for Exchange/SMTP is a multi-featured package that does spam control with keyword and black-and-white lists, addition of disclaimers to outgoing messages, mail archiving, mail monitoring, and automatic replies. It also can download mail from POP3 mailboxes into Exchange mailboxes. Contact: GFI (www.gfi.com)

Mail Security for Exchange/SMTP   Mail Security for Exchange/SMTP is comprehensive virus-control package that supports multiple virus-scanning engines. It also does content checking and HTML script checking and blocking. Contact: GFI (www.gfi.com)

Mail Security for Microsoft Exchange   Mail Security for Microsoft Exchange provides full-service virus scanning and cleaning. It also includes spam control features. Contact: Symantec Corporation (www.symantec.com)

MailWise   MailWise isn't a product that's installed on servers or workstations. Rather, it's a third-party service set up to receive mail destined for an SMTP server and quarantine it if it contains viruses or spam. Administrators can then either delete quarantined mail or send it along to its recipient. Contact: MailWise (www.mailwise.com)

MessageScreen   MessageScreen supports virus and spam control as well as detection and prevention of information leaks. Contact: Intellireach Corp. (www.intellireach.com)

Panda Anti-Virus for Exchange Server   Panda Anti-Virus for Exchange Server does most of the Exchange Server–based virus scanning and cleaning tricks performed by its competitors. Contact: Panda Software (www.pandasoftware.com)

Power Tools for Exchange   Power Tools monitor messages and attachments for violations of corporate policy, offensive language, viruses, and spam content. The product also adds signatures to outgoing Internet messages, enabling the insertion of corporate disclaimers in all messages. Contact: NEMX Software (www.nemx.com)

Praetor for Microsoft Exchange Server   Praetor for Microsoft Exchange Server includes both anti-virus and anti-spam functions. The product includes proprietary technology developed through the analysis of techniques used by spammers. Contact: Computer Mail Services, Inc. (www.cmsconnect.com)

ScanMail   ScanMail looks for viruses on an Exchange server, even in encoded and compressed items. The product also does limited spam control. Contact: Trend Micro Inc. (www.antivirus.com)

SecurExchange Anti-Virus   SecurExchange Anti-Virus, like most of its competitors, scans e-mail and attachments, including zipped files on an Exchange server for viruses. Contact: Nemx Software (www.nemx.com)

SurfControl E-Mail Filter for SMTP   SurfControl E-Mail Filter for SMTP is a comprehensive package that includes multi-engine virus scanning, high-powered anti-spam control, and very sophisticated content-checking functionality. SurfControl is the only product at the time of this writing that can check graphic images for textual and other indicators of spam. Contact: Surf-Control (`www.surfcontrol.com`)

Workflow

The great promise of electronic messaging systems such as Exchange Server lies in their capability to help manage the flow of documents to complete a specific task among the various persons who need to be involved in the task. The products listed here add to Exchange Server's already wide-ranging capabilities in the workflow arena.

80-20 Document Manager   80-20 Document Manager works with Exchange, IBM DB2, and Microsoft SQL Server databases. It enables users to share files with full document-level security, version control, check-in/check-out, and full-text indexing. This product enables serious Exchange-based groupware applications. Contact: 80-20 Software (`www.80-20.com`)

KnowledgeMail   KnowledgeMail scans corporate e-mail looking for topic areas and connections based on senders and recipients. It seeks to find sources of organizational expertise and activity. Users can then access the KnowledgeMail database when embarking on new projects or to enhance ongoing projects. Contact: Tacit Knowledge Systems, Inc. (`www.tacit.com`)

Transform Response   Transform Response is a tool for developing group inbox applications. The product can be used to support such applications as a customer service center for a website, an e-mail extension to a call center, or a corporate or customer help desk. Contact: Transform Research (`www.transres.com`)

Index

Note to the Reader: Throughout this index boldfaced page numbers indicate primary discussions of a topic. Italicized page numbers indicate illustrations.

E

O

S

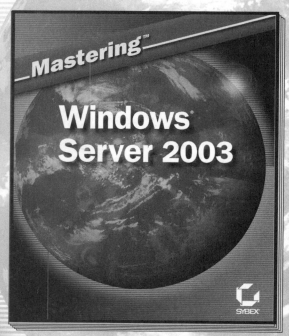

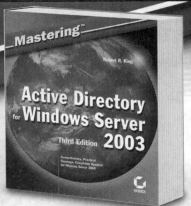

TELL US WHAT YOU THINK!

Your feedback is critical to our efforts to provide you with the best books and software on the market. Tell us what you think about the products you've purchased. It's simple:

1. Go to the Sybex website.
2. Find your book by typing the ISBN or title into the Search field.
3. Click on the book title when it appears.
4. Click **Submit a Review.**
5. Fill out the questionnaire and comments.
6. Click **Submit.**

With your feedback, we can continue to publish the highest quality computer books and software products that today's busy IT professionals deserve.

www.sybex.com

SYBEX Inc. • 1151 Marina Village Parkway; Alameda, CA 94501 • 510-523-8233